D0667280

The Major International
Treaties of the Twentieth Century

The Major International Treaties of the Twentieth Century surveys the history of treaty-making throughout the twentieth century. It accessibly provides the texts of all the major treaties that either continue in force today, or are of historical importance. These treaties are essential for an understanding of recent history and for analysis of current international relations.

The Major International Treaties of the Twentieth Century is truly global in scope and covers treaties of all aspects from political and economic agreements to environmental and human rights pacts. From the great many treaties set out and discussed, examples include:

- the Treaty of Versailles, 1919
- the Pact of Steel, 1939
- the Charter of the United Nations, 1945
- the North Atlantic Treaty, 1949
- the Treaty between the Federal Republic of Germany and the German Democratic Republic, 1990
- the Belfast Agreement, 1998
- the Charter of the Organization of African Unity, 1963
- the Universal Declaration of Human Rights, 1948

Drawing on the previous volumes of their books on *The Major International Treaties*, the authors bring the picture up to date in this definitive work with the events of the 1980s and 1990s, many of which have rendered earlier treaties redundant. This is an invaluable resource for all those interested in modern history, politics and international relations.

J.A.S. Grenville is Professor Emeritus of History at the University of Birmingham and his books include *A History of the World in the Twentieth Century* (Harvard U. P., 1994). **Bernard Wasserstein** is Professor of History at the University of Glasgow and his publications include *Vanishing Diaspora* (Harvard U. P., 1996).

The Major International Treaties of the Twentieth Century

A History and Guide with Texts

Edited by J.A.S. Grenville and Bernard Wasserstein

Volume One

London and New York

First published 2001
by Routledge
11 New Fetter Lane, London EC4P 4EE

Simultaneously published in the USA and Canada
by Routledge
29 West 35th Street, New York, NY 10001

Routledge is an imprint of the Taylor & Francis Group

© 2001 Edited by J.A.S. Grenville and Bernard Wasserstein

Typeset in Baskerville by RefineCatch Limited, Bungay, Suffolk
Printed and bound in Great Britain by
TJ International Ltd., Padstow, England

British Library Cataloguing in Publication Data
A catalogue record for this book is available from the British Library

Library of Congress Cataloging in Publication Data
Grenville, J. A. S. (John Ashley Soames), 1928–
    The major international treaties or the twentieth century / edited by John Grenville and
Bernard Wasserstein.
        p. cm.
    Revision of 2 works issued in 1987: The major international treaties, 1914–1945 and
The major international treaties since 1945.
    Includes bibliographical references and index.
    ISBN 0–415–23798–X (v.1)—ISBN 0–415–23799–8 (v.2)
        1. Treaties—Collections. I. Grenville, J. A. S. (John Ashley Soames), 1928–II.
Wasserstein, Bernard. III. Grenville, J. A. S. (John Ashley Soames), 1928– Major
international treaties, 1914–1945. IV. Grenville. J. A. S. (John Ashley Soames), 1928–
Major international treaties since 1945. V. Title.

KZ64 .G74 2000
341'.026—dc21
                                                                00–032833

ISBN 0–415–14125–7 (Set)
ISBN 0–415–23798–X (Volume 1)
ISBN 0–415–23799–8 (Volume 2)

Contents

Preface

The purpose of this book is to provide a history of international treaty-making in the twentieth century together with the texts of the major treaties. The treaties in this volume are of two kinds: those that are of historical importance, for example, the Nazi–Soviet Pact of 1939, and those that continue in force today. The age of a treaty is by itself no indication whether it is only of historical significance or continues to play a role in contemporary international relationships. Treaties not so long ago regarded as of fundamental importance in east–west relations, such as the various agreements concerning Berlin, have been made redundant by German reunification. Much of the post-1945 Soviet treaty system also became defunct in the 1990s. Not so the United States security treaties originating in the late 1940s and 1950s which retain their validity in Europe and Asia, though adapted to new conditions. Thus the treaties discussed in this volume form an essential basis both for the study of history and for analysis of current international relations. This is not meant to be a diplomatic history. The commentary sections have accordingly been limited to the minimum necessary to render the treaty texts and their context intelligible to the reader.

The first edition of this book, *The Major International Treaties 1914–1973*, edited by J.A.S. Grenville, appeared in 1974. The second edition was published in 1987 in two volumes: Volume One, *The Major International Treaties 1914–1945*, edited by J.A.S. Grenville, and Volume Two, *The Major International Treaties since 1945*, edited by J.A.S. Grenville and Bernard Wasserstein. That updated the original edition to 1986. This third edition not only updates further until 1999 but also includes an expanded introduction and several new chapters. The entire text has been checked, revised, and where necessary rewritten, particularly to take account of new developments, notably the end of the cold war, and advances in historical knowledge.

The most authoritative sources for treaty texts are the *League of Nations Treaty*

Series in 205 volumes covering the period 1920 to 1945 and the *United Nations Treaty Series*, covering the period since 1946. By 1999 more than 1,900 volumes had appeared in the UN series. Unfortunately this suffers from some drawbacks. Article 102 of the *UN Charter* (p. 309) requires that 'every treaty and every international agreement entered into by any Member of the United Nations after the present Charter comes into force shall as soon as possible be registered with the Secretariat and published by it.' Most treaties are so registered but not all: secret treaties, of course, are neither registered nor published; and many states delay before registering treaties. Non-membership of some states in the UN has further limited registration of treaties. Not all treaties that are registered are necessarily published in the series: in 1978 the UN Secretariat was authorized to exclude treaties judged of 'limited interest' from publication. Even in the case of treaties that are both registered and published, a further long delay often ensues before publication. For example, the most recent volume, number 1,969, dated 1997 (it actually appeared only in 1999) contained treaties that had been concluded in 1954, 1971, 1978 and 1979. By 1999 the UN series contained more than 30,000 treaties and about sixty new volumes were being published each year. Yet in spite of the prodigious scale of the enterprise, the series faces a Sisyphean task as modern diplomacy churns out ever larger numbers of treaties both bilateral and multilateral. For all these reasons, the UN series, although the best starting point for the collection of treaty texts, is incomplete – and virtually useless for the most recent treaties.

Treaty texts in this book have generally been drawn from one of these two series or (in the case of more recent treaties which have not yet been reached by the United Nations series) from the facsimile reproductions in the periodical, *International Legal Materials*. Many treaties are printed in full. But others are so long that they have had to be edited. In all cases where excisions have been made these have been indicated by an ellipse mark (. . .). In general, the parts omitted have been the more technical sections of treaties or those containing purely formal material. To have included the entire texts of treaties discussed or mentioned in this book would have required at least a hundred volumes and would have defeated our purpose which is to highlight the significant and to bring the operative sections of the major treaties within one manageable volume.

The choice of treaties has been difficult and inevitably subjective. It is estimated that over a 100,000 treaties have been signed in the twentieth century. Some of these, for example, the *Convention on the Law of the Sea, 1982* (p. 881), fill thousands of pages and many volumes. In this book, even with excisions, we have room for the texts of not much more than a hundred treaties. Clearly, therefore, we have had to be highly selective. Our basic criterion has been the long-term political and diplomatic importance of treaties. We have thus excluded those dealing with purely technical, legal, military, or financial matters. In addition to providing the texts of many of the most important treaties, however, we have discussed a large number of other treaties. Specialists in particular areas will no doubt wish to consult more narrowly defined collections. But for the reader who seeks a general grasp of the diplomacy of the twentieth century, we hope that this volume will provide the necessary documentary basis.

Certain internet sites now contain extensive collections of background material and texts of treaties. Among those we have found most useful are:

Avalon Project, Yale University	http://www.yale.edu/lawweb/avalon/
Chemical Weapons Convention	http://www.opcw.nl/
NATO	http://www.nato.int/
Organization of American States	http://www.oas.org/
Tufts Multilaterals Project	http://www.tufts.edu/fletcher/ multilaterals.html/
UN High Commission for Refugees	http://www.unhcr.ch/refworld/legal/ instruments/
UN Human Rights Website	http://www.unhchr.ch/
UN Treaty Collection	http://www.un.org/Depts/Treaty/
US Arms Control and Disarmament Agency	http://www.acda.gov/
US State Department	http://www.state.gov/
World Trade Organization	http://www.wto.org/
World War I Document Archive	http://www.lib.byu.edu/~rdh/wwi/ treaties.html

Many of the treaties printed here deal with sensitive territorial issues. In general we have used geographical designations most familiar to English-speaking readers (thus Persian rather than Arabian Gulf, Falkland Islands rather than Malvinas and so on); needless to say, such usages should not be taken to imply any particular political view. In their original forms treaties dealing with territorial issues often include large-scale maps; it is not practicable to include these here.

We are grateful to Professor Celia Fassberg for reading and commenting on part of the manuscript and Dr Elisabeth Albanis for help with proof-reading. We also wish to thank the staffs of the various libraries and archives in which we have worked, as well as our editors at Routledge, Heather McCallum and Victoria Peters, and our agent, Bruce Hunter of David Higham Associates.

John A. S. Grenville
Bernard Wasserstein

July 2000

Introduction: International treaties

The role of treaties

Pacta sunt servanda ('agreements must be kept') – this precept of Roman law has been recognized as the fundamental principle of modern international law. The Latin tag heads article 26 of the *Vienna Convention on the Law of Treaties, 23 May 1969* (p. 18), which provides: 'Every treaty in force is binding upon the parties to it and must be performed by them in good faith.' Yet international treaties have frequently turned out to be no stronger than the paper on which they are written.

How then does one explain the fact that during the five decades after the end of the Second World War more treaties were signed than during the whole of the previous four centuries? The inflation in the sheer number of the treaties has been accompanied in the twentieth century by an expansion in their length and complexity. Some post-war treaties, such as the *Treaty of Rome, 1957*, establishing the European Economic Community, run to hundreds of articles and fill a single volume; others occupy several volumes; and still others, with accompanying amendments, for example, the *General Agreement on Tariffs and Trade*, signed at Geneva in 1947, fill several shelves.

There are some obvious explanations for the increase in the number and length of treaties. There exist now more sovereign nations than ever before; there has also been a spectacular growth of international organizations which sign treaties in the same way as single states; treaties since 1919 have moreover been increasingly concerned with economic and social questions. The one explanation that cannot be seriously advanced is that mutual faith in the honourable behaviour of countries party to a treaty has been noticeably strengthened over the years. The solemn undertakings and promises, the general intentions of friendship and cooperation embedded in the language of the treaties, do not by themselves carry more conviction now than they did in times past; they are no guarantee of observance. Nor has there developed any fully effective way of bringing to justice a treaty violator by an international tribunal backed by effective international sanction, especially when the offending nation is a powerful one. That morality as the basis of international dealings has not been strengthened in the twentieth century even the least cynical observer has to admit.

International lawyers have not had an easy time attempting to reconcile the realities of policy with the notion of the rule of law in international affairs. Ultimately there has to be some moral foundation to law and this is difficult to demonstrate as a fundamental consideration in the formation of national policies the world over. There has indeed been an interesting shift in the way in which international lawyers and diplomats have looked upon treaties during this century. A standard work on diplomatic practice was compiled by Sir Ernest Satow in 1917 (*A Guide to Diplomatic Practice*, 2 vols, London, 1917). The chapters dealing with treaties in the edition of 1922 were based on the principle of the absolute sanctity of treaties once signed; they could not be altered or abandoned by one party to them without the agreement of the others, national necessities notwithstanding. This Satow was able to assume. By the time a new 1957 edition was prepared by Sir Nevile Bland, who had served in the Treaty Department of the British Foreign Office, the whole question of whether or not treaties could be unilaterally terminated without violating the normal practice of international law required lengthy discussion. The world meantime had witnessed the disregard of treaty obligations by Hitler, Stalin, Mussolini and the Japanese in the 1930s. Certain questions now had to be posed even if they could not be answered satisfactorily. Is a country bound by the provisions of a treaty even when the conditions prevailing when the treaty was made have greatly changed? Can there ever be permanent treaties in a rapidly changing world? One distinguished international lawyer replied a little obscurely with a double negative: 'There is nothing juridically impossible in the existence of a treaty creating obligations which are incapable of termination except by agreement of all parties . . . [there is thus a] general presumption against unilateral termination.' Another authority on international law concluded that a commercial treaty could 'always be dissolved after notice, although such notice be not expressly provided for', and he extended this possibility to alliance treaties. There is in fact no agreement among international lawyers. The late Professor Hersch Lauterpacht, one of the most distinguished lawyers, used to ask his students whether international law was law properly so called. International law is 'incomplete' and in a 'state of transition', he concluded. Although a body of customary international law is developing, the rule of law among nations in our own time remains far removed from the rule of law as generally recognized and practised by civilized communities within their own borders.

There are international judicial institutions such as the International Court of Justice of the United Nations, the successor of the Permanent Court of International Justice set up after the First World War. All members of the United

Nations (and also some non-members, such as Switzerland) are parties to the *Statute of the International Court of Justice, 1945* (see chapter XIV of the *United Nations Charter*, p. 322). Under article 36 of the Statute, states 'may at any time declare that they recognize as compulsory . . . the jurisdiction of the Court'. But by July 1996 only fifty-nine states had accepted compulsory jurisdiction. Moreover, most states accepting compulsory jurisdiction did so only with reservations or conditions. Some states that had earlier accepted compulsory jurisdiction later withdrew their acceptance when confronted with decisions or the prospect of decisions that they disliked. For example, Israel gave notice on 19 November 1985 of termination of her acceptance of such jurisdiction effective 21 November 1986; and the United States gave similar notice on 7 October 1985, effective 7 April 1986. In these circumstances the power of the International Court or of international arbitration tribunals to reach enforceable decisions in serious political disputes is obviously limited. The possibility of international sanctions based on a legal judgment is thus unlikely to prove a serious deterrent to the prospective treaty-breaker.

Nor is time on the side of treaty observance. The longer a treaty is intended to last the more chance there is that it will cease to correspond to national interests and international conditions. On this the most diverse of men who have guided national policies in the twentieth century are agreed. This was one of Lord Salisbury's objections to the proposal to conclude an Anglo-German alliance at the turn of the century: 'the British Government cannot undertake to declare war, for any purpose, unless it is a purpose of which the electors of this country would approve . . . I do not see how, in conscious honesty, we could invite other nations to rely upon our aids in a struggle, which must be formidable and probably supreme, when we have no means whatsoever of knowing what may be the humour of our people in circumstances which cannot be foreseen.' He concluded that national honour as well as good principles of policy required that future decisions should not be mortgaged by treaty obligations. By way of contrast, Hitler regarded morality, good faith and principles of international law as decadent democratic weaknesses. He wrote in *Mein Kampf:* 'No consideration of foreign policy can proceed from any other criterion than this: Does it benefit our nationality now or in the future, or will it be injurious to it? . . . Partisan, religious, humanitarian and all other criteria in general are completely irrelevant.' The conclusion and violation of treaties were decisions of policy, and other states could be, and were, misled by Hitler's repeatedly proclaimed readiness to conclude and abide by the agreements he signed for he broke them without the slightest scruple.

During the inter-war period apologists for treaty-breakers sometimes invoked the Roman law principle under which every contract carried with it the implication *rebus sic stantibus* (provided the situation remains the same). National Socialist

Germany invoked this doctrine, that an international agreement is binding only so long as the state of affairs present at the time of its signature continues to exist, in order to justify its remilitarization of the Rhineland in 1936. Meanwhile in the Soviet Union, the doctrine was reformulated to signify that every international agreement was the expression of the established social order and must be observed only so long as that order endured. The 1969 *Vienna Convention on the Law of Treaties* expressly excluded (in article 62) the *rebus sic stantibus* doctrine as a basis for unilateral termination of treaties, declaring: 'A fundamental change of circumstances may not be invoked as a ground for terminating or withdrawing from a treaty.' (Only very limited exceptions were allowed.) Nevertheless it is still sometimes argued (for example, by Athanassios Vamvoukos, *The Termination of Treaties in International Law*, Oxford, 1985, p. 216) that 'the rule of *rebus sic stantibus* is neither an exception to, nor in conflict with, the rule of *pacta sunt servanda*'.

After the Second World War, Dean Acheson, the American Secretary of State, grappled with the dilemma of whether treaty obligations could be relied on when the passage of time had changed international circumstances. When negotiating the North Atlantic Treaty Organization Acheson asked himself, 'What was this sovereign – the United States of America – and how could it insure faith in promised future conduct?' Acheson recognized, as Salisbury had done half a century earlier, that the fundamental problem did not affect only a government dependent on representative institutions. 'In reality,' wrote Acheson, 'the problem was general and insoluble, lying in inescapable change of circumstances and of national leadership and in the weakness of words to bind, especially when the juice of continued purpose is squeezed out of them and their husks analyzed to a drily logical extreme.'

Important treaties have been and still are signed with much ceremony, with film and television cameras ensuring some public involvement. The handshake between Yasser Arafat and Yitzhak Rabin at the signing, in front of a large audience, of the joint Declaration of Principles by Israel and the Palestine Liberation Organization on 13 September 1993 seemed an indispensable part of the ritual. Such displays of cooperation may make a temporary impression on public opinion but are discounted by the professional diplomat. The trappings are eventually forgotten; the text of the treaty endures.

With the archives of the Foreign Office in London, of the Ministry of Foreign Affairs in Moscow, of the State Department in Washington and every other capital full of broken treaties, how can treaties be viewed other than in a cynical and negative way? If the behaviour of the policy-makers is rational – even if, according to the opinion of historians, sometimes misguided – why are scores of new treaties negotiated and signed every year?

In the first place, notwithstanding the many well-publicized instances of broken treaties, the fact remains that most treaties (particularly the large number dealing with financial or technical matters) are in fact observed – just as most debts are paid. Nobody would expect a banker to put up his shutters merely because of the existence of a minority of bad debtors; the prudent banker will instead make adequate provision for bad debts. Similarly the prudent diplomat makes provision (as adequate as the circumstances may allow) for the faithless treaty-maker – or for the change in circumstances which might lead to the breaking of a treaty obligation. One example of such 'provision' is the device of the 'treaty of guarantee' whereby one or more powers pledge to ensure that treaty obligations will be honoured. The *Cyprus Guarantee Treaty, 16 August 1960* (p. 753) is an instance of such a treaty – although subsequent history also demonstrated the limited effectiveness of such arrangements. Another device is the additional side-arrangement whereby a major treaty (for example, the *Israel–Egypt Peace Treaty, 26 March 1979*, p. 734) is accompanied by one or more subsidiary agreements, sometimes with third parties (in the case of the Israel–Egypt Peace Treaty there were several such agreements involving the United States, some trilateral, some bilateral), designed to secure the better observance of the main treaty.

Even when there is no expectation that a country will remain faithful to its treaty obligations in perpetuity, calculations of national self-interest may make it probable that treaty provisions will be kept for a foreseeable future period of time. At least one of the parties has to believe that, whatever the secret plans of the other, or no agreement would be reached. Should there be a presumption that treaty obligations might be broken then there still has to be the possibility in the mind of one of the signatories that they will not be. The claim has been made for Chamberlain's foreign policy that he signed the *Munich Agreement* with Hitler on *29 September 1938* (p. 220) to test Hitler's good faith; but even so, Chamberlain must have thought that there was a worthwhile chance that Hitler would keep the undertakings of Munich. An open breach of treaty, such as Hitler's violation of this settlement, can (and did) still serve one important purpose in helping to rally public opinion and reluctant allies.

Not many treaties are as cynically or immediately broken as the Munich Agreement. An international treaty can be viewed as a bargain or contract. There are three inducements for keeping treaty provisions which are generally more important than any other: first, the positive one that a treaty contains a balance of advantages and the country which violates a treaty must expect to lose its advantages. At the simplest level, for example, when one country expels a foreign diplomat a reciprocal expulsion often follows. More important is the fact that a serious violation of a treaty may end it. Sometimes a violation is not easy to establish. Treaties on arms limitations are for this reason especially difficult to negotiate; control of armaments has not proved easy to reconcile with national sovereignty. The second inducement for keeping a treaty is the deterrent element

it may contain. Before acting, political leaders have to decide whether the violation of a treaty is worth the risk of the possible counter-measures taken by the
aggrieved state or states. A third inducement is that a government has to consider
its international credibility; failure to fulfil a treaty may well weaken the defaulting
country's international position as other states calculate whether treaties still in
force with it will be honoured, and whether new agreements can any longer
usefully be concluded.

Treaties are landmarks which guide nations in their relations with each other.
They express intentions, promises and normally appear to contain reciprocal
advantages. Treaties represent attempts to reduce the measure of uncertainty
inherent in the conduct of international affairs. In a world of growing interdependence, economic, political and strategic, where relations have become
exceedingly complex and where no nation can prosper and feel secure in complete isolation from all its neighbours, the endeavour to reach agreements is an
attempt to safeguard at least some vital interests.

Treaties concluded many decades ago are less likely to have remained in force
than more recently concluded treaties. Yet this is not necessarily the case. Treaties
signed long ago may evolve to meet the changed conditions of later times. There
are many examples of such agreements: NATO, the European Union, the US
commitments to defend South Korea and Taiwan, for instance. There are also
treaties in force in their evolved forms that were first concluded in the nineteenth
or early twentieth centuries, such as those covering the International Red Cross,
the International Postal Union and the Geneva Conventions. Then we have the
cases of agencies of the League of Nations, for example, the International Labour
Organization, that have been incorporated into the United Nations. There are
also many treaties that are now defunct: the pre-1914 alliances, the agreements
concerning western access to post-1945 Berlin, the Warsaw Pact, and so on. Thus
The Major International Treaties of the Twentieth Century encompasses treaties essential
for the understanding both of the *history* of diplomacy and of *contemporary* international relations.

It must be remembered that the signing of the actual treaty is only the starting
point of the relationship it purports to establish. Cooperation and further detailed
agreements based on the principles of the original treaty, as for instance was the
case with the development of the European Union, may strengthen it. On the
other hand, a treaty may be drained of its effectiveness by disuse or mutual
suspicions long before it is actually broken or abandoned. An example of this is
the *SEATO Treaty* (p. 371). Despite appearances the treaty does not 'freeze' relationships; they remain fluid, and the treaty may become more meaningful or just a
form of words. No one would judge the strength of a marriage by the form of
vows exchanged at a ceremony. So it is with treaties; they may prosper and
encompass an increasingly wide range of agreements as time passes or they may

end in disillusionment. The contents of the treaty may indeed be less important than the relationship that is established as the result of agreement.

Some political scientists have spoken of the 'treaty trap' – the false hope of basing foreign policy on the expectation that the legal requirements of a treaty will be fulfilled. When measured against historical evidence this reliance is seen to be a 'trap'. Such a trap exists, however, only for those who divorce the signing of a treaty from the necessary continuous vigilance over the relations that develop after its signature. Careful assessment has to be made of how 'national interests' are viewed by the leaders of other countries, the personalities of the leaders and future leaders, and all the likely influences including public opinion which can affect their policies, because it is against this 'total' policy background that the continuing strength of a treaty, once signed, has to be judged. When this is neglected, or when serious miscalculations are made, then one party may be taken by surprise by the other's breach of a treaty, as was Stalin when, in spite of the *Nazi–Soviet Pact of 1939* (p. 229), Hitler invaded the Soviet Union in 1941. No practising diplomat can sensibly view a treaty merely from a juridical point of view, in a kind of legal vacuum separated from all those influences which actually shape the conduct of foreign policies. The treaty may be one of the very important influences on that policy; it can never be the sole consideration.

The alternative to imperfect agreements is either anarchy or complete uncertainty. Treaties do not by themselves assure peace and security, but far more often than not they have contributed to stability for a measurable and worthwhile period of years. The spectacular instances where they have become instruments of aggression should therefore not blind us to the utility of treaties in general.

A fundamental rule of international conduct is that of non-interference by one state or a group of states in the internal affairs of another. In the early nineteenth century Metternich had claimed the right to put down revolution abroad. Castlereagh, in response, set out the 'doctrine of non-intervention' as the norm of relations between states. Article 15 of the League of Nations Covenant excluded the right to recommend settlement in a dispute which arose 'out of a matter which by international law is solely within the domestic jurisdiction of that party'. This was reaffirmed in 1945 by article 2:7 of the Charter of the United Nations but with the significant proviso that 'this principle shall not prejudice the application of enforcement measures under Chapter VII', that is, action with respect to threats to peace. Also article 34 empowered the Security Council to 'investigate any dispute likely to endanger the maintenance of international peace and security'. Nevertheless, the potential implications for state sovereignty have restrained such interventions. Pol Pot's Khmer Rouge forces committed genocide in Cambodia in the 1970s with impunity and Vietnam was condemned for intervening to oust his regime. Only in the 1990s were there some signs of change as jurists and concerned humanitarian bodies asserted a *droit d'ingérence*, a right of interference.

Humanitarian intervention was given international authority in December 1988 by resolution 43/131 of the UN General Assembly, permitting 'access to victims' of natural disasters. The UN then went a step further, authorizing the establishment of corridors through war zones to provide food and essential supplies to victims. The conflicts in southern Sudan and former Yugoslavia in the 1990s reinforced the new trend in thinking. Interventions in Somalia in 1992–93 and the protection of the Kurds of northern Iraq from the regime of Saddam Hussein were further evidence that the prohibition against intervention in internal affairs had weakened when overwhelming humanitarian considerations applied. The *droit d'ingérence* is an area of evolving international law still controversial but of increasing importance.

The form and structure of treaties

The most significant generally agreed formulation of the law of treaties is to be found in the *Vienna Convention on the Law of Treaties, 22 May 1969* (p. 18). This agreement was to enter into force (under its penultimate article, number 84) when thirty-five states had deposited instruments of accession or ratification. Although thirty-two states signed immediately, not all of these ratified it. The United States, for example, signed in 1970, but never ratified the convention. More than a decade passed before the convention finally entered into force on 27 January 1980, following the accession of Togo. By 1986, 47 states were parties. The USSR acceded, with reservations, in that year and Russia, as legal successor to the Soviet Union, remained a party to the Convention, and in 1995 enacted a Federal Law on International Treaties, that gave effect in the country's internal legislation to its commitment to the Convention. Of the major powers, France and China still were not parties but China acceded in 1997. By 1999 the number of parties to the Vienna Convention had risen to ninety – still under half the membership of the United Nations. Although the United States did not ratify the Convention, the US State Department nevertheless declared that the convention was 'generally recognized as the authoritative guide to current treaty law and practice'. It therefore carries considerable international authority in spite of the fact that only a minority of states are parties to it.

The convention was preceded and succeeded by other international agreements that have a bearing on its contents. The most important of these were the *Vienna Convention on Diplomatic Relations, 18 April 1961,* the *Vienna Convention on Consular Relations, 24 April 1963,* and the *Vienna Convention on the Law of Treaties between States and International Organizations or between International Organizations, 21 March 1986.*

Definition

A treaty is defined by the Vienna Convention as 'an international agreement concluded between States in written form and governed by international law, whether embodied in a single instrument or in two or more related instruments and whatever its particular designation'.

International treaties are generally concluded between sovereign states and pre-suppose their existence. There have been a few exceptions to this simple working definition: states under the suzerainty of another state have sometimes concluded international treaties; the degree of a state's sovereignty may be in dispute, as for instance in the case of the two Boer Republics, the Transvaal and the Orange Free State, which in 1899 went to war with Britain to assert their complete independence. There are other exceptions, but the overwhelming number of treaties are concluded between sovereign states; in the twentieth century they are also concluded between an organization of states such as the European Union and another state. Here the organization of states acts in a collective capacity as one party to a treaty.

Until the late nineteenth century most treaties were bilateral rather than multi-lateral. The main exceptions were treaties ending wars (such as the *Treaty of Paris*, ending the Napoleonic wars, signed on *30 May 1814* by Britain, Austria, France, Portugal, Prussia, Russia, Spain and Sweden), treaties of alliance (such as the *Holy Alliance treaty* signed by Austria, Prussia and Russia on *14–26 September 1815* – and later by other states) or treaties of guarantee (such as the *treaty guaranteeing Belgian independence and neutrality* signed by Britain, Austria, France, Prussia and Russia – as well as Belgium – on *19 April 1839*). In the late nineteenth century, however, multilateral treaties, dealing with both political and other subjects, became more common. The twentieth century brought a further increase and the post-war period witnessed a veritable explosion of such treaties. In the period 1946–56 alone, more than 576 multilateral treaties were recorded by the United Nations. Some of the most important of such post-war multilateral treaties, such as the *United Nations Charter* (p. 309), are printed in this volume.

The major treaties discussed and printed in this book are those that are intended to create legal rights and obligations between the countries that are party to them. Whether there can be 'treaties' properly so called which do not create such rights and obligations depends on definition. The *Atlantic Charter of 14 August 1941* was a 'Joint Declaration' by Roosevelt and Churchill setting out certain agreed principles of policy; no legal obligations were incurred by Britain and the United States, though Churchill's signature as prime minister had been approved by the War Cabinet. Was it a genuine treaty or a press communiqué? The point need not be laboured. Not all diplomatic agreements of importance need be 'treaties' in the conventional sense: it has been established in international law that even oral undertakings may be enforceable as international agreements – even where such validity is contested by one of the parties.

In the nineteenth century and earlier, treaties were always concluded between the heads of state, whether monarchs or presidents. This still remains true for many treaties. But equally important treaties may be concluded between governments rather than heads of state, as was the *North Atlantic Treaty of 4 April 1949* (p. 359) and the Peace Treaty with Italy of 10 February 1947 (p. 285).

It is generally accepted that unless there are contrary provisions laid down by the signatories of a treaty not inconsistent with overriding principles of international law, all questions concerning the interpretation and execution of treaties, their validity and how they may be ended, are governed by international custom and where appropriate by general principles of law recognized by civilized nations.

FORM

What a treaty is called may be a matter of chance or design but it is not significant in itself. The obligations and rights have to be studied in each case with equal care: for example, an 'alliance' may not create the relationship and obligations which the common meaning of the word would lead one to expect. The *Alliance for Progress of 1961* (p. 351) was not, in fact, an 'alliance' in the conventional meaning of the word. On the other hand, not all alliance treaties are so named. It is therefore not possible to distinguish treaties, or the rights or obligations arising from them, or their relative importance, by their particular form or heading. One has to work from the other end and disentangle from the contents of the treaty the precise obligations and rights. This is a point of great importance in the understanding of international relations. The historian, for instance, will be especially concerned to discover whether a treaty contains commitments to go to war, or merely promises support in more general terms avoiding any automatic commitment to go to war in conditions specified by the treaty. Whether the treaty is called an 'Alliance Treaty' or a 'Declaration' makes no difference. Treaties have been called by many other names and each type of treaty is usually cast in its own conventional form. Some of the more common types of treaties are headed Convention, *Acte Final*, Pact, Agreement, Protocol, Exchange of Notes, *Modus Vivendi*, or Understanding, as well as Treaty, with some prefix such as alliance, boundary, etc.; and this list is not comprehensive. It also has to be noted that until the actual contents of a document are examined it cannot be assumed that any legal rights or obligations arise, and so the document may not be a treaty at all despite appearances. The historian thus has to exercise extreme caution in distinguishing between the 'content' and the 'form' or 'packaging' of diplomatic agreements.

LANGUAGE

The language of treaties varies. Until the seventeenth century most treaties (at any rate, most treaties involving European states) were in Latin. Thereafter French became the major language of diplomacy and of treaties. Hence the frequency of Latin and French expressions in the vocabulary even of current diplomacy and treaty-making. In the twentieth century English has emerged as the dominant language in treaty-making. Nationalistic considerations have often, particularly since 1945, dictated the use of a particular language as the 'authentic' text of a treaty. The Vienna Convention specifies that 'when a treaty has been authenticated in two or more languages, the text is equally authoritative in each language, unless the treaty provides or the parties agree that, in case of divergence, a particular text shall prevail'. A case in point of such agreement was the Israel–Egypt Peace Treaty of 1979 which was written 'in triplicate in the English, Arabic, and Hebrew languages, each text being equally authentic' – with the added proviso that 'in case of any divergence of interpretation, the English text shall prevail'. All the treaties in this book are, of course, printed in English. It should therefore be borne in mind by the reader that, in cases where the 'authentic' text is not English, the version given here in a technical sense is not legally binding – even where it is an 'official' translation.

THE VALIDITY OF TREATIES AND THEIR RATIFICATION

It is not necessary that states have diplomatic relations with each other in order to conclude treaties (although it helps). This book contains a number of agreements concluded between states which had no diplomatic relations at the time of signature. The *Cuba–United States agreement on hijacking of 15 February 1973* (p. 786) is a case in point. An interesting example of such an agreement was the arrangement between Iran and the United States for settlement of the hostage crisis in January 1981 (p. 763). Here relations between the two parties were so strained that the agreement took the form of a declaration by a third party (Algeria). It was none the less regarded as legally binding on the USA and Iran.

There is a wide range of choice as to the means by which a country may assume treaty obligations. There is no one answer to the question of what needs to be done before a treaty becomes binding and precisely when this moment occurs. If the treaty is in the form of an exchange of notes it usually comes into force as soon as the documents have been signed, and only rarely is additional ratification provided for. The number of treaty agreements under this heading has become large. Such treaties are not necessarily confined to questions of a technical nature or of minor importance. Exchanges of notes may deal with questions of major importance or with delicate issues which the parties may prefer not to magnify by the conclusion of a 'treaty'. An example of the latter was the *Anglo–Argentine agreement on the Falklands in 1971* (p. 798).

Most treaties do not come into force immediately upon signature but require ratification. In some cases, normally emergency situations, however, treaties may be concluded which expressly stipulate that they come into force at the moment of signature and require no ratification. This can sometimes be the case even in states whose normal constitutional practices require ratification by a legislative body.

In practice, a government has to choose how it will assume treaty obligations. Even where a country has a written constitution which requires the submission and consent of a representative assembly to a treaty, as is the case in the United States where Senate is required to approve treaties by a two-thirds majority, means may be found to circumvent the powers of such assemblies. Senator William Fulbright, the former Chairman of the Senate Foreign Relations Committee, once observed that since 1940, 'the beginning of this age of crisis . . . the Senate's constitutional powers of advice and consent have atrophied into what is widely regarded as, though never asserted to be, a duty to give prompt consent with a minimum of advice'. Presidents have resorted to 'executive agreements' at times when the consent of Senate to a treaty appeared doubtful. The important *Anglo–American destroyers/bases agreement, 2 September 1940* (p. 231) was concluded in this form.

A treaty is concluded when signed, but where ratification is necessary becomes binding only when ratified. Traditionally, ratification signified the consent of the sovereign to a treaty negotiated by the sovereign's plenipotentiary, who might have no means of consulting the sovereign when negotiating in distant countries. In modern times speed of communication has made it possible to submit the actual text of a treaty to the government before it is signed. The practical importance of ratification now lies in the need to secure the consent of a parliament or other elected assembly before the government is ready to advise ratification of a treaty. In Britain, though treaty-making powers are vested in the sovereign, the real decision lies with the government and, where legislation is required to adapt British law to bring it into line with that required by the treaty, also with parliament, for the necessary enabling legislation must first be passed by parliament before the treaty can be ratified 'by the sovereign' on the advice of the government. The legislative and treaty-making process of Britain's adhesion to the European Economic Community provides a good example. It is the practice in Britain for the texts of all treaties requiring ratification to lie on the table of the House of Commons for twenty-one days before ratification by the sovereign. In France, the 1946 constitution, though vesting treaty-making power in the president, required that a wide range of treaties did not become valid unless embodied in a law passed by the French parliament. The precise powers of representative assemblies differ widely, and the constitution and practice of each country have to be considered separately.

Non-ratification need not necessarily destroy the political effectiveness of a treaty (although it prevents it from having any legal enforceability). The *SALT II Agreement, 18 June 1979* (p. 836) was never ratified by the US Senate, but the United States nevertheless undertook voluntarily until 1986 to comply with its provisions. The ratification process may, on the other hand, introduce significant modifications into treaties (though these are not binding on other parties except by agreement). The reservations attached by the US Senate to its acceptance of the *Panama Canal Treaties of 1977* (p. 777) are a case in point.

Ratification is therefore not always a formality; important treaties may have to be submitted to the approval of elected assemblies before the government of the state concerned is able to give its consent to the treaty becoming binding. This may be due to constitutional custom or constitutional requirement, or to a government's desire to retain the support of a majority of the elected representatives in order to continue in power.

The drafting of treaties

By this stage it will have become clear that there are no rules as to how a treaty has to be drawn up. This is a question on which the participants have free choice. But it is possible to speak of some widely adopted conventions which tend to give treaties certain common forms. Many diplomats in the world's various foreign ministries are employed in treaty drafting: their task is to put the intentions of the parties to a treaty in acceptable professional legal phraseology, which can at times strike the reader as rather stylized and even archaic. By way of example, a common form of treaty is here considered.

Such a treaty commences with a *descriptive title*, as for instance the 'Treaty of Mutual Cooperation and Security between the United States of America and Japan'. Then follows the *preamble*, beginning with the names or description of the High Contracting Parties as 'The United States of America and Japan'; next the general purpose is set out, 'Desiring to strengthen the bonds of peace and friendship traditionally existing between them etc . . . Having resolved to conclude a treaty of mutual cooperation and security, therefore agree as follows. . . . ' The preamble often includes also, though not in the particular treaty here cited, the names and designation of the plenipotentiaries who have produced their full powers, which have been found in good order, and have agreed as follows. . . . Next follow the *substantive articles* each with a numeral, I, II, III, etc. which constitute the objectives, the obligations and the rights of the signatories; these articles are frequently arranged beginning with the more general and leading to the more specific. Where appropriate, an article follows which sets out the provisions for other states which may wish to accede to the treaty. Next follows an article (or articles) concerning *ratification* where this is provided for, the *duration* of the treaty and provisions for its *renewal*. Finally a clause is added stating 'in witness whereof' the undersigned plenipotentiaries have signed this treaty; the *place* where the treaty is signed is given, together with a statement as to the *authentic languages* of the treaty texts; and last the *date* is written in, followed by the *seals* and the *signatures* of the plenipotentiaries. *Conventions, Protocols* and other types of treaties each have their own customary form.

The vocabulary of treaties

Some terms used in treaty-making – a few of them in French and Latin – have special meanings.

Accession or adhesion: these terms are used interchangeably to describe the practice where a state which is not a party to a treaty later on joins such a treaty. No state has a right to accede to a treaty; the possibility and method of accession are often contained in a clause of the treaty as signed by the original parties to it.

Aggression: the common meaning of the term is an unjustified attack, and efforts have been made to define aggression by means of treaties. For example, a convention was signed in July 1933 by Russia, Afghanistan, Estonia, Latvia, Persia, Poland, Rumania and Turkey which defined aggression as having been committed by the state which first (*a*) declares war on another state, or (*b*) invades another state with its armed forces, or (*c*) attacks with its armed forces the territory, naval vessels or aircraft of another state, or (*d*) initiates a naval blockade of coasts or ports of another state; or (*e*), most interestingly of all, renders 'aid to armed bands formed on the territory of a state and invading the territory of another state, or refuses, despite demands on the part of the state subjected to attack, to take all possible measures on its own territory to deprive said bands of any aid and protection'. On 14 December 1974 the UN General Assembly adopted a resolution which defined aggression as 'the use of armed force by a state against the sovereignty, territorial integrity or political independence of another State, or in any other manner inconsistent with the Charter of the United Nations'. The definition went on to specify invasion, bombardment, blockade, or the sending into another state of 'armed bands, groups, irregulars or mercenaries' as examples of aggression. But it specified that the list was not exhaustive and that 'the Security Council may determine that other acts constitute aggression under the provisions of the Charter'. Despite the existence of such declarations, however, in the last resort each state or international tribunal has to judge on the merits of the facts before it decides whether particular actions constitute aggression or not.

Bilateral treaties are those between two states; *multilateral* treaties are concluded between three or more states.

Casus foederis is literally the case contemplated by the treaty, usually one of alliance; it is the event which when it occurs imposes the duty on one or more of the allies to render the assistance promised in the treaty to the other; *casus belli* has a different meaning frequently confused with *casus foederis; casus belli* is the provocative action by one state which in the opinion of the injured state justifies it in declaring war.

Compromis in diplomacy has a meaning different from the everyday modern meaning of 'compromise'. Deriving from the Latin word *compromissum*, meaning 'mutual promise', a *compromis* in diplomacy is an agreement to abide by an arbitrator's award.

Convention is often used as a synonym for treaty. But in recent years it has tended to be used for multilateral rather than bilateral treaties, as in *Genocide Convention* (p. 865), *Convention on the Law of the Sea* (p. 18), etc.

Charter, in the context of treaty-making, is generally used of a treaty that is also a constitutive document, as in *Charter of the United Nations* (p. 309).

A treaty may also take the form of a *Declaration*, as in the *Israel–PLO Declaration of Principles, 13 September 1993* (p. 742). It may be bilateral as in that case or multilateral as in the case of the *Universal Declaration of Human Rights* (p. 847). A *declaration* may also be a statement made by a signatory in order to clarify (but not modify) its position in relation to the treaty.

Delimitation and *demarcation* of boundaries: boundaries of state territories are the lines drawn to divide the sovereignties of adjoining states. They form the frontiers of each country. Concern for frontiers is the basis of the majority of political treaties, and the cause of many conflicts and wars. When a boundary can be drawn on a map and is accepted by the states which are divided by it, even though the boundary has not been physically marked out on the ground by frontier posts, then it is said to have been *delimited*. The frontier is also *demarcated* when it has been physically set out on the ground and not just marked on a map. The distinction between delimitation and demarcation is an important one. European frontiers have all been both delimited and demarcated. The same is not true of all boundary lines in the world, especially in difficult and unpopulated regions. There are no settled principles of demarcation, though there are certain common practices, such as to draw boundary lines through the middle of land-locked seas and rivers where they lie between two states. Estuaries and mountain ranges, however, cause more difficulty. In the absence of specific agreements the demarcation of an actual frontier based on a general boundary treaty signed much earlier – quite possibly when the state of geographical knowledge was imperfect – can become a matter of serious dispute. To avoid such disputes countries sometimes sign treaties setting out how a boundary is to be demarcated; an example is the boundary treaty between Great Britain and the United States of 11 April 1908 respecting the demarcation of the boundary between Canada and the United States. In other cases of dispute the two nations may resort to arbitration by a third party; or a commission of two states or an international commission may have the power to demarcate boundaries. There are still boundaries which have been neither delimited nor demarcated; instead there is a *de facto* line. This is true of many stretches of boundaries in Asia. Sometimes boundaries have been arbitrarily drawn by cartographers over country so difficult that it has not been surveyed and mapped with complete accuracy.

Demilitarization is an agreement between two or more states by treaty not to fortify or station troops in a particular zone of territory; such zones are known as *demilitarized zones*.

Denunciation is the giving of notice by a state of its intention to terminate a treaty. Some treaties provide for termination by one of the parties on giving of a certain period of notice. Others contain no such provision but are nevertheless denounced. Denunciation of treaties is a common occurrence after revolutionary changes in government, where the incoming régime adopts a different diplomatic stance from its predecessor. But international law recognizes no automatic right to such unilateral denunciation.

Internationalization refers to the placing under multilateral control of land or sea areas. Rivers (such as the Danube) have also often been the subject of such agreements.

L.S. = *loco sigilli*, '[in] place of the seal', formula sometimes used by signatories of formal agreements.

Modus vivendi usually refers to a temporary or provisional agreement which it is intended shall later be replaced by a more permanent and detailed treaty.

Most-favoured-nation clause: many commercial treaties between countries contain this clause, the effect of which is that any commercial advantages either state has granted in the past to other nations, or may grant in the future, have to be granted also to the signatories of a treaty which contains a most-favoured-nation clause. The intent is therefore that the commercial advantages of two states which have signed a treaty with this provision shall never be less than those of any third state which is not a signatory. The United States has not recognized quite so unconditional an operation of this clause.

Procès-verbal is the official record or minutes of the daily proceedings of a conference and of any conclusions arrived at, and is frequently signed by the participants; a *Protocol* is sometimes used in the same sense but more accurately is a document which constitutes an international agreement.

Ratification is the act whereby a state indicates its consent to be bound by a treaty. Often the internal laws or constitutions of a state prescribe the particular form or procedure for ratification.

Registration is required under article 102 of the Charter of the United Nations for all treaties entered into by UN members. The non-registration of a treaty does not affect its validity – although non-registered treaties may not be invoked before any organ of the UN.

Reservation is defined in the Vienna Convention as meaning 'a unilateral statement, however phrased or named, made by a state, when signing, ratifying, accepting, approving or acceding to a treaty, whereby it purports to exclude or to modify the legal effect of certain provisions of the treaty in their application to that State'. The International Court of Justice, in an advisory opinion in 1951 concerning reservations to the Genocide Convention (see p. 865), declared that 'no reservation was valid unless it was accepted by all the contracting parties'. The Vienna Convention does provide for reservations, and lays down rules (articles 19–23) concerning their formulation, acceptance, legal effects, withdrawal, and procedure.

Revision of treaties (save where the treaty itself specifically provides for subsequent changes) is generally permissible only by agreement of the parties.

Where a negotiator signs a treaty *ad referendum*, this means that his signature is conditional upon confirmation by his government.

Sine qua non describes a condition or conditions that have to be accepted by another party to a proposed agreement; it implies that without such acceptance the agreement cannot be proceeded with.

Status quo: the common meaning is the state of affairs existing, but an agreement can refer specifically to a previous state of affairs as for instance in the phrase *status quo ante bellum* which means the state existing before the war began, for example, as relating to frontiers.

Succession has been the subject of a further *Vienna Convention* on the *Succession of States in Respect of Treaties*, which was opened for signature on *23 August 1978*. This states that ' "succession of states" means the replacement of one State by another in the responsibility for the international relations of territory'.

Vienna Convention on the Law of Treaties, 23 May 1969

The States Parties to the present Convention

Considering the fundamental role of treaties in the history of international relations,

Recognizing the ever-increasing importance of treaties as a source of international law and as a means of developing peaceful co-operation among nations, whatever their constitutional and social systems,

Noting that the principles of free consent and of good faith and the *pacta sunt servanda* rule are universally recognized,

Affirming that disputes concerning treaties, like other international disputes, should be settled by peaceful means and in conformity with the principles of justice and international law,

Recalling the determination of the peoples of the United Nations to establish conditions under which justice and respect for the obligations arising from treaties can be maintained,

Having in mind the principles of international law embodied in the Charter of the United Nations, such as the principles of the equal rights and self-determination of peoples, of the sovereign equality and independence of all States, of noninterference in the domestic affairs of States, of the prohibition of the threat or use of force and of universal respect for, and observance of, human rights and fundamental freedoms for all,

Believing that the codification and progressive development of the law of treaties achieved in the present Convention will promote the purposes of the United Nations set forth in the Charter, namely, the maintenance of international peace and security, the development of friendly relations and the achievement of co-operation among nations,

Affirming that the rules of customary international law will continue to govern questions not regulated by the provisions of the present Convention,

Have agreed as follows:

Part I · Introduction

Article 1. Scope of the present Convention. The present Convention applies to treaties between States.

Article 2. Use of terms. 1. For the purposes of the present Convention:

(a) 'treaty' means an international agreement concluded between States in written form and governed by international law, whether embodied in a single instrument or in two or more related instruments and whatever its particular designation;

(b) 'ratification', 'acceptance', 'approval' and 'accession' mean in each case the international act so named whereby a State establishes on the international plane its consent to be bound by a treaty;

(c) 'full powers' means a document emanating from the competent authority of a State designating a person or persons to represent the State for negotiating, adopting or authenticating the text of a treaty, for expressing the consent of the State to be bound by a treaty, or for accomplishing any other act with respect to a treaty;

(d) 'reservation' means a unilateral statement, however phrased or named, made by a State, when signing, ratifying, accepting, approving or acceding to a treaty, whereby it purports to exclude or to modify the legal effect of certain provisions of the treaty in their application to that State;

(e) 'negotiating State' means a State which took part in the drawing up and adoption of the text of the treaty;

(f) 'contracting State' means a State which has consented to be bound by the treaty, whether or not the treaty has entered into force;

(g) 'party' means a State which has consented to be bound by the treaty and for which the treaty is in force;

(h) 'third State' means a State not a party to the treaty;

(i) 'international organization' means an intergovernmental organization.

2. The provisions of paragraph 1 regarding the use of terms in the present

Convention are without prejudice to the use of those terms or to the meanings which may be given to them in the internal law of any State.

Article 3. International agreements not within the scope of the present Convention. The fact that the present Convention does not apply to international agreements concluded between States and other subjects of international law or between such other subjects of international law, or to international agreements not in written form, shall not affect:

(a) the legal force of such agreements;

(b) the application to them of any of the rules set forth in the present Convention to which they would be subject under international law independently of the Convention;

(c) the application of the Convention to the relations of States as between themselves under international agreements to which other subjects of international law are also parties.

Article 4. Non-retroactivity of the present Convention. Without prejudice to the application of any rules set forth in the present Convention to which treaties would be subject under international law independently of the Convention, the Convention applies only to treaties which are concluded by States after the entry into force of the present Convention with regard to such States.

Article 5. Treaties constituting international organizations and treaties adopted within an international organization. The present Convention applies to any treaty which is the constituent instrument of an international organization and to any treaty adopted within an international organization without prejudice to any relevant rules of the organization.

Part II · Conclusion and entry into force of treaties

SECTION 1 · CONCLUSION OF TREATIES

Article 6. Capacity of states to conclude treaties. Every State possesses capacity to conclude treaties.

Article 7. Full powers. 1. A person is con-sidered as representing a State for the purpose of adopting or authenticating the text of a treaty or for the purpose of expressing the consent of the State to be bound by a treaty if:

(a) he produces appropriate full powers; or

(b) it appears from the practice of the States concerned or from other circumstances that their intention was to consider that person as representing the State for such purposes and to dispense with full powers.

2. In virtue of their functions and without having to produce full powers, the following are considered as representing their State:

(a) Heads of State, Heads of Government and Ministers for Foreign Affairs, for the purpose of performing all acts relating to the conclusion of a treaty;

(b) heads of diplomatic missions, for the purpose of adopting the text of a treaty between the accrediting State and the State to which they are accredited;

(c) representatives accredited by States to an international conference or to an international organization or one of its organs, for the purpose of adopting the text of a treaty in that conference, organization or organ.

Article 8. Subsequent confirmation of an act performed without authorization. An act relating to the conclusion of a treaty performed by a person who cannot be considered under article 7 as authorized to represent a State for that purpose is without legal effect unless afterwards confirmed by that State.

Article 9. Adoption of the text. 1. The adoption of the text of a treaty takes place by the consent of all the States participating in its drawing up except as provided in paragraph 2.

2. The adoption of the text of a treaty at an international conference takes place by the vote of two-thirds of the States present and voting, unless by the same majority they shall decide to apply a different rule.

Article 10. Authentication of the text. The text

of a treaty is established as authentic and definitive:

(a) by such procedure as may be provided for in the text or agreed upon by the States participating in its drawing up; or

(b) failing such procedure, by the signature, signature *ad referendum* or initialling by the representatives of those States of the text of the treaty or of the Final Act of a conference incorporating the text.

Article 11. Means of expressing consent to be bound by a treaty. The consent of a State to be bound by a treaty may be expressed by signature, exchange of instruments constituting a treaty, ratification, acceptance, approval or accession, or by any other means if so agreed.

Article 12. Consent to be bound by a treaty expressed by signature. 1. The consent of a State to be bound by a treaty is expressed by the signature of its representative when:

(a) the treaty provides that signature shall have that effect;

(b) it is otherwise established that the negotiating States were agreed that signature should have that effect; or

(c) the intention of the State to give that effect to the signature appears from the full powers of its representative or was expressed during the negotiation.

2. For the purposes of paragraph 1:

(a) the initialling of a text constitutes a signature of the treaty when it is established that the negotiating States so agreed;

(b) the signature *ad referendum* of a treaty by a representative, if confirmed by his State, constitutes a full signature of the treaty.

Article 13. Consent to be bound by a treaty expressed by an exchange of instruments constituting a treaty. The consent of States to be bound by a treaty constituted by instruments exchanged between them is expressed by that exchange when:

(a) the instruments provide that their exchange shall have that effect; or

(b) it is otherwise established that those States were agreed that the exchange of instruments should have that effect.

Article 14. Consent to be bound by a treaty expressed by ratification, acceptance or approval. 1. The consent of a State to be bound by a treaty is expressed by ratification when:

(a) the treaty provides for such consent to be expressed by means of ratification;

(b) it is otherwise established that the negotiating States were agreed that ratification should be required;

(c) the representative of the State has signed the treaty subject to ratification; or

(d) the intention of the State to sign the treaty subject to ratification appears from the full powers of its representative or was expressed during the negotiation.

2. The consent of a State to be bound by a treaty is expressed by acceptance or approval under conditions similar to those which apply to ratification.

Article 15. Consent to be bound by a treaty expressed by accession. The consent of a State to be bound by a treaty is expressed by accession when:

(a) the treaty provides that such consent may be expressed by that State by means of accession;

(b) it is otherwise established that the negotiating States were agreed that such consent may be expressed by that State by means of accession; or

(c) all the parties have subsequently agreed that such consent may be expressed by that State by means of accession.

Article 16. Exchange or deposit of instruments of ratification, acceptance, approval or accession. Unless the treaty otherwise provides, instruments of ratification, acceptance, approval or accession establish the consent of a State to be bound by a treaty upon:

(a) their exchange between the contracting States;

(b) their deposit with the depositary; or

(c) their notification to the contracting States or to the depositary, if so agreed.

Article 17. Consent to be bound by part of a treaty and choice of differing provisions. 1. Without prejudice to articles 19 to 23, the consent of a State to be bound by part of a treaty is effective only if the treaty so permits or the other contracting States so agree.

2. The consent of a State to be bound by a treaty which permits a choice between differing provisions is effective only if it is

made clear to which of the provisions the consent relates.

Article 18. Obligation not to defeat the object and purpose of a treaty prior to its entry into force. A State is obliged to refrain from acts which would defeat the object and purpose of a treaty when:

(a) it has signed the treaty or has exchanged instruments constituting the treaty subject to ratification, acceptance or approval, until it shall have made its intention clear not to become a party to the treaty; or

(b) it has expressed its consent to be bound by the treaty, pending the entry into force of the treaty and provided that such entry into force is not unduly delayed.

SECTION 2 · RESERVATIONS

Article 19. Formulation of reservations. A State may, when signing, ratifying, accepting, approving or acceding to a treaty, formulate a reservation unless:

(a) the reservation is prohibited by the treaty;

(b) the treaty provides that only specified reservations, which do not include the reservation in question, may be made; or

(c) in cases not falling under sub-paragraphs (a) and (b), the reservation is incompatible with the object and purpose of the treaty.

Article 20. Acceptance of and objection to reservations. 1. A reservation expressly authorized by a treaty does not require any subsequent acceptance by the other contracting States unless the treaty so provides.

2. When it appears from the limited number of the negotiating States and the object and purpose of a treaty that the application of the treaty in its entirety between all the parties is an essential condition of the consent of each one to be bound by the treaty, a reservation requires acceptance by all the parties.

3. When a treaty is a constituent instrument of an international organization and unless it otherwise provides, a reservation requires the acceptance of the competent organ of that organization.

4. In cases not falling under the preced-ing paragraphs and unless the treaty otherwise provides:

(a) acceptance by another contracting State of a reservation constitutes the reserving State a party to the treaty in relation to that other State if or when the treaty is in force for those States;

(b) an objection by another contracting State to a reservation does not preclude the entry into force of the treaty as between the objecting and reserving States unless a contrary intention is definitely expressed by the objecting State;

(c) an act expressing a State's consent to be bound by the treaty and containing a reservation is effective as soon as at least one other contracting State has accepted the reservation.

5. For the purposes of paragraphs 2 and 4 and unless the treaty otherwise provides, a reservation is considered to have been accepted by a State if it shall have raised no objection to the reservation by the end of a period of twelve months after it was notified of the reservation or by the date on which it expressed its consent to be bound by the treaty, whichever is later.

Article 21. Legal effects of reservations and of objections to reservations. 1. A reservation established with regard to another party in accordance with articles 19, 20 and 23:

(a) modifies for the reserving State in its relations with that other party the provisions of the treaty to which the reservation relates to the extent of the reservation; and

(b) modifies those provisions to the same extent for that other party in its relations with the reserving State.

2. The reservation does not modify the provisions of the treaty for the other parties to the treaty *inter se*.

3. When a State objecting to a reservation has not opposed the entry into force of the treaty between itself and the reserving State, the provisions to which the reservation relates do not apply as between the two States to the extent of the reservation.

Article 22. Withdrawal of reservations and of objections to reservations. 1. Unless the treaty otherwise provides, a reservation may be withdrawn at any time and the consent of a

State which has accepted the reservation is not required for its withdrawal.

2. Unless the treaty otherwise provides, an objection to a reservation may be withdrawn at any time.

3. Unless the treaty otherwise provides, or it is otherwise agreed:

(a) the withdrawal of a reservation becomes operative in relation to another contracting State only when notice of it has been received by that State;

(b) the withdrawal of an objection to a reservation becomes operative only when notice of it has been received by the State which formulated the reservation.

Article 23. Procedure regarding reservations. 1. A reservation, an express acceptance of a reservation and an objection to a reservation must be formulated in writing and communicated to the contracting States and other States entitled to become parties to the treaty.

2. If formulated when signing the treaty subject to ratification, acceptance or approval, a reservation must be formally confirmed by the reserving State when expressing its consent to be bound by the treaty. In such a case the reservation shall be considered as having been made on the date of its confirmation.

3. An express acceptance of, or an objection to, a reservation made previously to confirmation of the reservation does not itself require confirmation.

4. The withdrawal of a reservation or of an objection to a reservation must be formulated in writing.

SECTION 3 · ENTRY INTO FORCE AND PROVISIONAL APPLICATION OF TREATIES

Article 24. Entry into force. 1. A treaty enters into force in such manner and upon such date as it may provide or as the negotiating States may agree.

2. Failing any such provision or agreement, a treaty enters into force as soon as consent to be bound by the treaty has been established for all the negotiating States.

3. When the consent of a State to be bound by a treaty is established on a date after the treaty has come into force, the treaty enters into force for that State on that date, unless the treaty otherwise provides.

4. The provisions of a treaty regulating the authentication of its text, the establishment of the consent of States to be bound by the treaty, the manner or date of its entry into force, reservations, the functions of the depositary and other matters arising necessarily before the entry into force of the treaty apply from the time of the adoption of its text.

Article 25. Provisional application. 1. A treaty or a part of a treaty is applied provisionally pending its entry into force if:

(a) the treaty itself so provides; or

(b) the negotiating States have in some other manner so agreed.

2. Unless the treaty otherwise provides or the negotiating States have otherwise agreed, the provisional application of a treaty or a part of a treaty with respect to a State shall be terminated if that State notifies the other States between which the treaty is being applied provisionally of its intention not to become a party to the treaty.

Part III · Observance, application and interpretation of treaties

SECTION 1 · OBSERVANCE OF TREATIES

Article 26. Pacta sunt servanda. Every treaty in force is binding upon the parties to it and must be performed by them in good faith.

Article 27. Internal law and observance of treaties. A party may not invoke the provisions of its internal law as justification for its failure to perform a treaty. This rule is without prejudice to article 46.

SECTION 2 · APPLICATION OF TREATIES

Article 28. Non-retroactivity of treaties. Unless a different intention appears from the treaty or is otherwise established, its provisions do not bind a party in relation to any act or fact which took place or any situation which ceased to exist before the date of the entry into force of the treaty with respect to that party.

Article 29. Territorial scope of treaties. Unless a different intention appears from the treaty or is otherwise established, a treaty is binding upon each party in respect of its entire territory.

Article 30. Application of successive treaties relating to the same subject-matter. 1. Subject to article 103 of the Charter of the United Nations, the rights and obligations of States parties to successive treaties relating to the same subject-matter shall be determined in accordance with the following paragraphs.

2. When a treaty specifies that it is subject to, or that it is not to be considered as incompatible with, an earlier or later treaty, the provisions of that other treaty prevail.

3. When all the parties to the earlier treaty are parties also to the later treaty but the earlier treaty is not terminated or suspended in operation under article 59, the earlier treaty applies only to the extent that its provisions are compatible with those of the later treaty.

4. When the parties to the later treaty do not include all the parties to the earlier one:

(a) as between States parties to both treaties the same rule applies as in paragraph 3;

(b) as between a State party to both treaties and a State party to only one of the treaties, the treaty to which both States are parties governs their mutual rights and obligations.

5. Paragraph 4 is without prejudice to article 41, or to any question of the termination or suspension of the operation of a treaty under article 60 or to any question of responsibility which may arise for a State from the conclusion or application of a treaty, the provisions of which are incompatible with its obligations towards another State under another treaty.

SECTION 3 · INTERPRETATION OF TREATIES

Article 31. General rule of interpretation. 1. A treaty shall be interpreted in good faith in accordance with the ordinary meaning to be given to the terms of the treaty in their context and in the light of its object and purpose.

2. The context for the purpose of the interpretation of a treaty shall comprise, in addition to the text, including its preamble and annexes:

(a) any agreement relating to the treaty which was made between all the parties in connexion with the conclusion of the treaty;

(b) any instrument which was made by one or more parties in connexion with the conclusion of the treaty and accepted by the other parties as an instrument related to the treaty.

3. There shall be taken into account, together with the context:

(a) any subsequent agreement between the parties regarding the interpretation of the treaty or the application of its provisions;

(b) any subsequent practice in the application of the treaty which establishes the agreement of the parties regarding its interpretation;

(c) any relevant rules of international law applicable in the relations between the parties.

4. A special meaning shall be given to a term if it is established that the parties so intended.

Article 32. Supplementary means of interpretation. Recourse may be had to supplementary means of interpretation, including the preparatory work of the treaty and the circumstances of its conclusion, in order to confirm the meaning resulting from the application of article 31, or to determine the meaning when the interpretation according to article 31:

(a) leaves the meaning ambiguous or obscure; or

(b) leads to a result which is manifestly absurd or unreasonable.

Article 33. Interpretation of treaties authenticated in two or more languages. 1. When a treaty has been authenticated in two or more languages, the text is equally authoritative in each language, unless the treaty provides or the parties agree that, in case of divergence, a particular text shall prevail.

2. A version of the treaty in a language other than one of those in which the text was authenticated shall be considered an authentic text only if the treaty so provides or the parties so agree.

3. The terms of the treaty are presumed to have the same meaning in each authentic text.

4. Except where a particular text prevails in accordance with paragraph 1, when a comparison of the authentic texts discloses a difference of meaning which the application of articles 31 and 32 does not remove, the meaning which best reconciles the texts, having regard to the object and purpose of the treaty, shall be adopted.

SECTION 4 · TREATIES AND THIRD STATES

Article 34. General rule regarding third States. A treaty does not create either obligations or rights for a third State without its consent.

Article 35. Treaties providing for obligations for third States. An obligation arises for a third State from a provision of a treaty if the parties to the treaty intend the provision to be the means of establishing the obligation and the third State expressly accepts that obligation in writing.

Article 36. Treaties providing for rights for third States. 1. A right arises for a third State from a provision of a treaty if the parties to the treaty intend the provision to accord that right either to the third State, or to a group of States to which it belongs, or to all States, and the third State assents thereto. Its assent shall be presumed so long as the contrary is not indicated, unless the treaty otherwise provides.

2. A State exercising a right in accordance with paragraph 1 shall comply with the conditions for its exercise provided for in the treaty or established in conformity with the treaty.

Article 37. Revocation or modification of obligations or rights of third States. 1. When an obligation has arisen for a third State in conformity with article 35, the obligation may be revoked or modified only with the consent of the parties to the treaty and of the third State, unless it is established that they had otherwise agreed.

2. When a right has arisen for a third State in conformity with article 36, the right may not be revoked or modified by the parties if it is established that the right was intended not to be revocable or subject to modification without the consent of the third State.

Article 38. Rules in a treaty becoming binding on third States through international custom. Nothing in articles 34 to 37 precludes a rule set forth in a treaty from becoming binding upon a third State as a customary rule of international law, recognized as such.

Part IV · Amendment and modification of treaties

Article 39. General rule regarding the amendment of treaties. A treaty may be amended by agreement between the parties. The rules laid down in Part II apply to such an agreement except in so far as the treaty may otherwise provide.

Article 40. Amendment of multilateral treaties. 1. Unless the treaty otherwise provides, the amendment of multilateral treaties shall be governed by the following paragraphs.

2. Any proposal to amend a multilateral treaty as between all the parties must be notified to all the contracting States, each one of which shall have the right to take part in:

(a) the decision as to the action to be taken in regard to such proposal;

(b) the negotiation and conclusion of any agreement for the amendment of the treaty.

3. Every State entitled to become a party to the treaty shall also be entitled to become a party to the treaty as amended.

4. The amending agreement does not bind any State already a party to the treaty which does not become a party to the amending agreement; article 30, paragraph 4(b), applies in relation to such State.

5. Any State which becomes a party to the treaty after the entry into force of the amending agreement shall, failing an expression of a different intention by that State:

(a) be considered as a party to the treaty as amended; and

(b) be considered as a party to the unamended treaty in relation to any party to the treaty not bound by the amending agreement.

Article 41. Agreements to modify multilateral treaties between certain of the parties only. 1. Two or more of the parties to a multilateral treaty may conclude an agreement to modify the treaty as between themselves alone if:

(a) the possibility of such a modification is provided for by the treaty; or

(b) the modification in question is not prohibited by the treaty and:

(i) does not affect the enjoyment by the other parties of their rights under the treaty or the performance of their obligations;

(ii) does not relate to a provision, derogation from which is incompatible with the effective execution of the object and purpose of the treaty as a whole.

2. Unless in a case falling under paragraph 1(a) the treaty otherwise provides, the parties in question shall notify the other parties of their intention to conclude the agreement and of the modification to the treaty for which it provides.

Part V · Invalidity, termination and suspension of the operation of treaties

SECTION 1 · GENERAL PROVISIONS

Article 42. Validity and continuance in force of treaties. 1. The validity of a treaty or of the consent of a State to be bound by a treaty may be impeached only through the application of the present Convention.

2. The termination of a treaty, its denunciation or the withdrawal of a party, may take place only as a result of the application of the provisions of the treaty or of the present Convention. The same rule applies to suspension of the operation of a treaty.

Article 43. Obligations imposed by international law independently of a treaty. The invalidity, termination or denunciation of a treaty, the withdrawal of a party from it, or the suspension of its operation, as a result of the application of the present Convention or of the provisions of the treaty, shall not in any way impair the duty of any State to fulfil any obligation embodied in the treaty to which it would be subject under international law independently of the treaty.

Article 44. Separability of treaty provisions. 1. A right of a party, provided for in a treaty or arising under article 56, to denounce, withdraw from or suspend the operation of the treaty may be exercised only with respect to the whole treaty unless the treaty otherwise provides or the parties otherwise agree.

2. A ground for invalidating, terminating, withdrawing from or suspending the operation of a treaty recognized in the present Convention may be invoked only with respect to the whole treaty except as provided in the following paragraphs or in article 60.

3. If the ground relates solely to particular clauses, it may be invoked only with respect to those clauses where:

(a) the said clauses are separable from the remainder of the treaty with regard to their application;

(b) it appears from the treaty or is otherwise established that acceptance of those clauses was not an essential basis of the consent of the other party or parties to be bound by the treaty as a whole; and

(c) continued performance of the remainder of the treaty would not be unjust.

4. In cases falling under articles 49 and 50 the State entitled to invoke the fraud or corruption may do so with respect either to the whole treaty or, subject to paragraph 3, to the particular clauses alone.

5. In cases falling under articles 51, 52 and 53, no separation of the provisions of the treaty is permitted.

Article 45. Loss of a right to invoke a ground for invalidating, terminating, withdrawing from or suspending the operation of a treaty. A State may no longer invoke a ground for invalidating, terminating, withdrawing from or suspending the operation of a treaty under articles 46 to 50 or articles 60 and 62 if, after becoming aware of the facts:

(a) it shall have expressly agreed that the treaty is valid or remains in force or continues in operation, as the case may be; or

(b) it must by reason of its conduct be considered as having acquiesced in the validity of the treaty or in its maintenance in force or in operation, as the case may be.

Section 2 · Invalidity of treaties

Article 46. Provisions of internal law regarding competence to conclude treaties. 1. A State may not invoke the fact that its consent to be bound by a treaty has been expressed in violation of a provision of its internal law regarding competence to conclude treaties as invalidating its consent unless that violation was manifest and concerned a rule of its internal law of fundamental importance.

2. A violation is manifest if it would be objectively evident to any State conducting itself in the matter in accordance with normal practice and in good faith.

Article 47. Specific restrictions on authority to express the consent of a State. If the authority of a representative to express the consent of a State to be bound by a particular treaty has been made subject to a specific restriction, his omission to observe that restriction may not be invoked as invalidating the consent expressed by him unless the restriction was notified to the other negotiating States prior to his expressing such consent.

Article 48. Error. 1. A State may invoke an error in a treaty as invalidating its consent to be bound by the treaty if the error relates to a fact or situation which was assumed by that State to exist at the time when the treaty was concluded and formed an essential basis of its consent to be bound by the treaty.

2. Paragraph 1 shall not apply if the State in question contributed by its own conduct to the error or if the circumstances were such as to put that State on notice of a possible error.

3. An error relating only to the wording of the text of a treaty does not affect its validity; article 79 then applies.

Article 49. Fraud. If a State has been induced to conclude a treaty by the fraudulent conduct of another negotiating State, the State may invoke the fraud as invalidating its consent to be bound by the treaty.

Article 50. Corruption of a representative of a State. If the expression of a State's consent to be bound by a treaty has been procured through the corruption of its representative directly or indirectly by another negotiating State, the State may invoke such corruption as invalidating its consent to be bound by the treaty.

Article 51. Coercion of a representative of a State. The expression of a State's consent to be bound by a treaty which has been procured by the coercion of its representative through acts or threats directed against him shall be without any legal effect.

Article 52. Coercion of a State by the threat or use of force. A treaty is void if its conclusion has been procured by the threat or use of force in violation of the principles of international law embodied in the Charter of the United Nations.

Article 53. Treaties conflicting with a peremptory norm of general international law (jus cogens). A treaty is void if, at the time of its conclusion, it conflicts with a peremptory norm of general international law. For the purposes of the present Convention, a peremptory norm of general international law is a norm accepted and recognized by the international community of States as a whole as a norm from which no derogation is permitted and which can be modified only by a subsequent norm of general international law having the same character.

Section 3 · Termination and suspension of the operation of treaties

Article 54. Termination of or withdrawal from a treaty under its provisions or by consent of the parties. The termination of a treaty or the withdrawal of a party may take place:

(a) in conformity with the provisions of the treaty; or

(b) at any time by consent of all the parties after consultation with the other contracting States.

Article 55. Reduction of the parties to a multilateral treaty below the number necessary for its entry into force. Unless the treaty otherwise provides, a multilateral treaty does not terminate by reason only of the fact that the number of the parties falls below the number necessary for its entry into force.

Article 56. Denunciation of or withdrawal from a treaty containing no provision regarding termination, denunciation or withdrawal. 1. A treaty which contains no provision regarding its termination and which does not provide for denunciation or withdrawal is not subject to denunciation or withdrawal unless:

(a) it is established that the parties intended to admit the possibility of denunciation or withdrawal; or

(b) a right of denunciation or withdrawal may be implied by the nature of the treaty.

2. A party shall give not less than twelve months' notice of its intention to denounce or withdraw from a treaty under paragraph 1.

Article 57. Suspension of the operation of a treaty under its provisions or by consent of the parties. The operation of a treaty in regard to all the parties or to a particular party may be suspended:

(a) in conformity with the provisions of the treaty; or

(b) at any time by consent of all the parties after consultation with the other contracting States.

Article 58. Suspension of the operation of a multilateral treaty by agreement between certain of the parties only. 1. Two or more parties to a multilateral treaty may conclude an agreement to suspend the operation of provisions of the treaty, temporarily and as between themselves alone, if:

(a) the possibility of such a suspension is provided for by the treaty; or

(b) the suspension in question is not prohibited by the treaty and:

  (i) does not affect the enjoyment by the other parties of their rights under the treaty or the performance of their obligations;
  (ii) is not incompatible with the object and purpose of the treaty.

2. Unless in a case falling under paragraph 1(a) the treaty otherwise provides, the parties in question shall notify the other parties of their intention to conclude the agreement and of those provisions of the treaty the operation of which they intend to suspend.

Article 59. Termination or suspension of the operation of a treaty implied by conclusion of a later treaty. 1. A treaty shall be considered as terminated if all the parties to it conclude a later treaty relating to the same subject-matter and:

(a) it appears from the later treaty or is otherwise established that the parties intended that the matter should be governed by that treaty; or

(b) the provisions of the later treaty are so far incompatible with those of the earlier one that the two treaties are not capable of being applied at the same time.

2. The earlier treaty shall be considered as only suspended in operation if it appears from the later treaty or is otherwise established that such was the intention of the parties.

Article 60. Termination or suspension of the operation of a treaty as a consequence of its breach. 1. A material breach of a bilateral treaty by one of the parties entitles the other to invoke the breach as a ground for terminating the treaty or suspending its operation in whole or in part.

2. A material breach of a multilateral treaty by one of the parties entitles:

(a) the other parties by unanimous agreement to suspend the operation of the treaty in whole or in part or to terminate it either:

  (i) in the relations between themselves and the defaulting State; or
  (ii) as between all the parties;

(b) a party specially affected by the breach to invoke it as a ground for suspending the operation of the treaty in whole or in part in the relations between itself and the defaulting State;

(c) any party other than the defaulting State to invoke the breach as a ground for suspending the operation of the treaty in whole or in part with respect to itself if the treaty is of such a character that a material breach of its provisions by one party radically changes the position of every party with respect to the further performance of its obligations under the treaty.

3. A material breach of a treaty, for the purposes of this article, consists in:

(a) a repudiation of the treaty not sanctioned by the present Convention; or

(b) the violation of a provision essential to the accomplishment of the object or purpose of the treaty.

4. The foregoing paragraphs are without prejudice to any provision in the treaty applicable in the event of a breach.

5. Paragraphs 1 to 3 do not apply to provisions relating to the protection of the human person contained in treaties of a humanitarian character, in particular to provisions prohibiting any form of reprisals against persons protected by such treaties.

Article 61. Supervening impossibility of performance. 1. A party may invoke the impossibility of performing a treaty as a ground for terminating or withdrawing from it if the impossibility results from the permanent disappearance or destruction of an object indispensable for the execution of the treaty. If the impossibility is temporary, it may be invoked only as a ground for suspending the operation of the treaty.

2. Impossibility of performance may not be invoked by a party as a ground for terminating, withdrawing from or suspending the operation of a treaty if the impossibility is the result of a breach by that party either of an obligation under the treaty or of any other international obligation owed to any other party to the treaty.

Article 62. Fundamental change of circumstances. 1. A fundamental change of circumstances which has occurred with regard to those existing at the time of the conclusion of a treaty, and which was not foreseen by the parties, may not be invoked as a ground for terminating or withdrawing from the treaty unless:

(a) the existence of those circumstances constituted an essential basis of the consent of the parties to be bound by the treaty; and

(b) the effect of the change is radically to transform the extent of obligations still to be performed under the treaty.

2. A fundamental change of circumstances may not be invoked as a ground for terminating or withdrawing from a treaty:

(a) if the treaty establishes a boundary; or

(b) if the fundamental change is the result of a breach by the party invoking it either of an obligation under the treaty or of any other international obligation owed to any other party to the treaty.

3. If, under the foregoing paragraphs, a party may invoke a fundamental change of circumstances as a ground for terminating or withdrawing from a treaty it may also invoke the change as a ground for suspending the operation of the treaty.

Article 63. Severance of diplomatic or consular relations. The severance of diplomatic or consular relations between parties to a treaty does not affect the legal relations established between them by the treaty except in so far as the existence of diplomatic or consular relations is indispensable for the application of the treaty.

Article 64. Emergence of a new peremptory norm of general international law (jus cogens). If a new peremptory norm of general international law emerges, any existing treaty which is in conflict with that norm becomes void and terminates.

SECTION 4 · PROCEDURE

Article 65. Procedure to be followed with respect to invalidity, termination, withdrawal from or suspension of the operation of a treaty. 1. A party which, under the provisions of the present Convention, invokes either a defect in its consent to be bound by a treaty or a ground for impeaching the validity of a treaty, terminating it, withdrawing from it or suspending its operation, must notify the other parties of its claim. The notification shall indicate the measure proposed to be taken with respect to the treaty and the reasons therefor.

2. If, after the expiry of a period which, except in cases of special urgency, shall not be less than three months after the receipt of the notification, no party has raised any objection, the party making the notification may carry out in the manner provided in

article 67 the measure which it has proposed.

3. If, however, objection has been raised by any other party, the parties shall seek a solution through the means indicated in article 33 of the Charter of the United Nations.

4. Nothing in the foregoing paragraphs shall affect the rights or obligations of the parties under any provisions in force binding the parties with regard to the settlement of disputes.

5. Without prejudice to article 45, the fact that a State has not previously made the notification prescribed in paragraph 1 shall not prevent it from making such notification in answer to another party claiming performance of the treaty or alleging its violation.

Article 66. Procedures for judicial settlement, arbitration and conciliation. If, under paragraph 3 of article 65, no solution has been reached within a period of 12 months following the date on which the objection was raised, the following procedures shall be followed:

(a) any one of the parties to a dispute concerning the application or the interpretation of articles 53 or 64 may, by a written application, submit it to the International Court of Justice for a decision unless the parties by common consent agree to submit the dispute to arbitration;

(b) any one of the parties to a dispute concerning the application or the interpretation of any of the other articles in Part V of the present Convention may set in motion the procedure specified in the Annex to the Convention by submitting a request to that effect to the Secretary-General of the United Nations.

Article 67. Instruments for declaring invalid, terminating, withdrawing from or suspending the operation of a treaty. 1. The notification provided for under article 65 paragraph 1 must be made in writing.

2. Any act declaring invalid, terminating, withdrawing from or suspending the operation of a treaty pursuant to the provisions of the treaty or of paragraphs 2 or 3 of article 65 shall be carried out through an instrument communicated to the other parties. If the instrument is not signed by the Head of State, Head of Government or Minister for Foreign Affairs, the representative of the State communicating it may be called upon to produce full powers.

Article 68. Revocation of notifications and instruments provided for in articles 65 and 67. A notification or instrument provided for in articles 65 or 67 may be revoked at any time before it takes effect.

SECTION 5 · CONSEQUENCES OF THE INVALIDITY, TERMINATION OR SUSPENSION OF THE OPERATION OF A TREATY

Article 69. Consequences of the invalidity of a treaty. 1. A treaty the invalidity of which is established under the present Convention is void. The provisions of a void treaty have no legal force.

2. If acts have nevertheless been performed in reliance on such a treaty:

(a) each party may require any other party to establish as far as possible in their mutual relations the position that would have existed if the acts had not been performed;

(b) acts performed in good faith before the invalidity was invoked are not rendered unlawful by reason only of the invalidity of the treaty.

3. In cases falling under articles 49, 50, 51 or 52, paragraph 2 does not apply with respect to the party to which the fraud, the act of corruption or the coercion is imputable.

4. In the case of the invalidity of a particular State's consent to be bound by a multilateral treaty, the foregoing rules apply in the relations between that State and the parties to the treaty.

Article 70. Consequences of the termination of a treaty. 1. Unless the treaty otherwise provides or the parties otherwise agree, the termination of a treaty under its provisions or in accordance with the present Convention:

(a) releases the parties from any obligation further to perform the treaty;

(b) does not affect any right, obligation or legal situation of the parties created through the execution of the treaty prior to its termination.

2. If a State denounces or withdraws from a multilateral treaty, paragraph 1 applies in the relations between that State and each of the other parties to the treaty from the date when such denunciation or withdrawal takes effect.

Article 71. Consequences of the invalidity of a treaty which conflicts with a peremptory norm of general international law. 1. In the case of a treaty which is void under article 53 the parties shall:

(a) eliminate as far as possible the consequences of any act performed in reliance on any provision which conflicts with the peremptory norm of general international law; and

(b) bring their mutual relations into conformity with the peremptory norm of general international law.

2. In the case of a treaty which becomes void and terminates under article 64, the termination of the treaty:

(a) releases the parties from any obligation further to perform the treaty;

(b) does not affect any right, obligation or legal situation of the parties created through the execution of the treaty prior to its termination; provided that those rights, obligations or situations may thereafter be maintained only to the extent that their maintenance is not in itself in conflict with the new peremptory norm of general international law.

Article 72. Consequences of the suspension of the operation of a treaty. 1. Unless the treaty otherwise provides or the parties otherwise agree, the suspension of the operation of a treaty under its provisions or in accordance with the present Convention:

(a) releases the parties between which the operation of the treaty is suspended from the obligation to perform the treaty in their mutual relations during the period of the suspension;

(b) does not otherwise affect the legal relations between the parties established by the treaty.

2. During the period of the suspension the parties shall refrain from acts tending to obstruct the resumption of the operation of the treaty.

Part VI · Miscellaneous provisions

Article 73. Cases of State succession, State responsibility and outbreak of hostilities. The provisions of the present Convention shall not prejudge any question that may arise in regard to a treaty from a succession of States or from the international responsibility of a State or from the outbreak of hostilities between States.

Article 74. Diplomatic and consular relations and the conclusion of treaties. The severance or absence of diplomatic or consular relations between two or more States does not prevent the conclusion of treaties between those States. The conclusion of a treaty does not in itself affect the situation in regard to diplomatic or consular relations.

Article 75. Case of an aggressor State. The provisions of the present Convention are without prejudice to any obligation in relation to a treaty which may arise for an aggressor State in consequence of measures taken in conformity with the Charter of the United Nations with reference to that State's aggression.

Part VII · Depositaries, notifications, corrections and registration

Article 76. Depositaries of treaties. 1. The designation of the depositary of a treaty may be made by the negotiating States, either in the treaty itself or in some other manner. The depositary may be one or more States, an international organization or the chief administrative officer of the organization.

2. The functions of the depositary of a treaty are international in character and the depositary is under an obligation to act impartially in their performance. In particular, the fact that a treaty has not entered into force between certain of the parties or that a difference has appeared between a State and a depositary with regard to the performance of the latter's functions shall not affect that obligation.

Article 77. Functions of depositaries. 1. The functions of a depositary, unless otherwise provided in the treaty or agreed by the contracting States, comprise in particular:

(a) keeping custody of the original text of the treaty and of any full powers delivered to the depositary;

(b) preparing certified copies of the original text and preparing any further text of the treaty in such additional languages as may be required by the treaty and transmitting them to the parties and to the States entitled to become parties to the treaty;

(c) receiving any signatures to the treaty and receiving and keeping custody of any instruments, notifications and communications relating to it;

(d) examining whether the signature or any instrument, notification or communication relating to the treaty is in due and proper form and, if need be, bringing the matter to the attention of the State in question;

(e) informing the parties and the States entitled to become parties to the treaty of acts, notifications and communications relating to the treaty;

(f) informing the States entitled to become parties to the treaty when the number of signatures or of instruments of ratification, acceptance, approval or accession required for the entry into force of the treaty has been received or deposited;

(g) registering the treaty with the Secretariat of the United Nations;

(h) performing the functions specified in other provisions of the present Convention.

2. In the event of any difference appearing between a State and the depositary as to the performance of the latter's functions, the depositary shall bring the question to the attention of the signatory States and the contracting States or, where appropriate, of the competent organ of the international organization concerned.

Article 78. Notifications and communications. Except as the treaty or the present Convention otherwise provide, any notification or communication to be made by any State under the present Convention shall:

(a) if there is no depositary, be transmitted direct to the States for which it is intended, or if there is a depositary, to the latter;

(b) be considered as having been made by the State in question only upon its receipt

by the State to which it was transmitted or, as the case may be, upon its receipt by the depositary;

(c) if transmitted to a depositary, be considered as received by the State for which it was intended only when the latter State has been informed by the depositary in accordance with article 77, paragraph 1 (e).

Article 79. Correction of errors in texts or in certified copies of treaties. 1. Where, after the authentication of the text of a treaty, the signatory States and the contracting States are agreed that it contains an error, the error shall, unless they decide upon some other means of correction, be corrected:

(a) by having the appropriate correction made in the text and causing the correction to be initialled by duly authorized representatives;

(b) by executing or exchanging an instrument or instruments setting out the correction which it has been agreed to make; or

(c) by executing a corrected text of the whole treaty by the same procedure as in the case of the original text.

2. Where the treaty is one for which there is a depositary, the latter shall notify the signatory States and the contracting States of the error and of the proposal to correct it and shall specify an appropriate time-limit within which objection to the proposed correction may be raised. If, on the expiry of the time-limit:

(a) no objection has been raised, the depositary shall make and initial the correction in the text and shall execute a *procès-verbal* of the rectification of the text and communicate a copy of it to the parties and to the States entitled to become parties to the treaty;

(b) an objection has been raised, the depositary shall communicate the objection to the signatory States and to the contracting States.

3. The rules in paragraphs 1 and 2 apply also where the text has been authenticated in two or more languages and it appears that there is a lack of concordance which the signatory States and the contracting States agree should be corrected.

4. The corrected text replaces the

defective text *ab initio*, unless the signatory States and the contracting States otherwise decide.

5. The correction of the text of a treaty that has been registered shall be notified to the Secretariat of the United Nations.

6. Where an error is discovered in a certified copy of a treaty, the depositary shall execute a *procès-verbal* specifying the rectification and communicate a copy of it to the signatory States and to the contracting States.

Article 80. Registration and publication of treaties.
1. Treaties shall, after their entry into force, be transmitted to the Secretariat of the United Nations for registration or filing and recording, as the case may be, and for publication.

2. The designation of a depositary shall constitute authorization for it to perform the acts specified in the preceding paragraph.

Part VIII · Final provisions

Article 81. Signature. The present Convention shall be open for signature by all States Members of the United Nations or of any of the specialized agencies or of the International Atomic Energy Agency or parties to the Statute of the International Court of Justice, and by any other State invited by the General Assembly of the United Nations to become a party to the Convention, as follows: until 30 November 1969, at the Federal Ministry for Foreign Affairs of the Republic of Austria, and subsequently, until 30 April 1970, at United Nations Headquarters, New York.

Article 82. Ratification. The present Convention is subject to ratification. The instruments of ratification shall be deposited with the Secretary-General of the United Nations.

Article 83. Accession. The present Convention shall remain open for accession by any State belonging to any of the categories mentioned in article 81. The instruments of accession shall be deposited with the Secretary-General of the United Nations.

Article 84. Entry into force. 1. The present Convention shall enter into force on the thirtieth day following the date of deposit of the thirty-fifth instrument of ratification or accession.

2. For each State ratifying or acceding to the Convention after the deposit of the thirty-fifth instrument of ratification or accession, the Convention shall enter into force on the thirtieth day after deposit by such State of its instrument of ratification or accession.

Article 85. Authentic texts. The original of the present Convention, of which the Chinese, English, French, Russian and Spanish texts are equally authentic, shall be deposited with the Secretary-General of the United Nations.

IN WITNESS WHEREOF the undersigned Plenipotentiaries, being duly authorized thereto by their respective Governments, have signed the present Convention. DONE at Vienna, this twenty-third day of May, one thousand nine hundred and sixty-nine.

Annex

1. A list of conciliators consisting of qualified jurists shall be drawn up and maintained by the Secretary-General of the United Nations. To this end, every State which is a Member of the United Nations or a party to the present Convention shall be invited to nominate two conciliators, and the names of the persons so nominated shall constitute the list. The term of a conciliator, including that of any conciliator nominated to fill a casual vacancy, shall be five years and may be renewed. A conciliator whose term expires shall continue to fulfil any function for which he shall have been chosen under the following paragraph.

2. When a request has been made to the Secretary-General under article 66, the Secretary-General shall bring the dispute before a conciliation commission constituted as follows: The State or States constituting one of the parties to the dispute shall appoint:

(a) one conciliator of the nationality of that State or of one of those States, who may or may not be chosen from the list referred to in paragraph 1; and

(b) one conciliator not of the nationality of that State or of any of those States, who shall be chosen from the list.

The State or States constituting the other party to the dispute shall appoint two conciliators in the same way. The four conciliators chosen by the parties shall be appointed within sixty days following the date on which the Secretary-General receives the request. The four conciliators shall, within sixty days following the date of the last of their own appointments, appoint a fifth conciliator chosen from the list, who shall be chairman. If the appointment of the chairman or of any of the other conciliators has not been made within the period prescribed above for such appointment, it shall be made by the Secretary-General within sixty days following the expiry of that period. The appointment of the chairman may be made by the Secretary-General either from the list or from the membership of the International Law Commission. Any of the periods within which appointments must be made may be extended by agreement between the parties to the dispute. Any vacancy shall be filled in the manner prescribed for the initial appointment.

3. The Conciliation Commission shall decide its own procedure. The Commission, with the consent of the parties to the dispute, may invite any party to the treaty to submit to it its views orally or in writing. Decisions and recommendations of the Commission shall be made by a majority vote of the five members.

4. The Commission may draw the attention of the parties to the dispute to any measures which might facilitate an amicable settlement.

5. The Commission shall hear the parties, examine the claims and objections, and make proposals to the parties with a view to reaching an amicable settlement of the dispute.

6. The Commission shall report within twelve months of its constitution. Its report shall be deposited with the Secretary-General and transmitted to the parties to the dispute. The report of the Commission, including any conclusions stated therein regarding the facts or questions of law, shall not be binding upon the parties and it shall have no other character than that of recommendations submitted for the consideration of the parties in order to facilitate an amicable settlement of the dispute.

7. The Secretary-General shall provide the Commission with such assistance and facilities as it may require. The expenses of the Commission shall be borne by the United Nations.

I · The changing alliances and alignments before the First World War

The Bismarckian foundations: Germany's allies, 1879–1914

The core of the European alliance system that dominated the relations of the great powers before the First World War was created by Bismarck. Its bedrock was the *Dual Alliance with Austria-Hungary on 7 October 1879* (p. 36): article 1 promised that each power would aid the other with its whole strength if Russia attacked one of the two empires; article 2 provided that if another power attacked one of the allies the other would remain neutral unless the attacking country is joined by Russia. Bismarck's intention was to use this defensive alliance as a lever to bring Russia back into alliance with Germany and Austria-Hungary and so to dominate European diplomacy in the interests of peace between the great powers. The web of alliances with Berlin at its centre was intended to 'place a premium' on peace. Bismarck wished to prevent wars from breaking out over territorial and international disputes, particularly over the disposal of the Ottoman Emperor's European territories. No less serious concern later was the danger of war between the successor Balkan states on the one hand and Austria-Hungary and Russia, rivals for influence in the Balkans, on the other. Any such wars might spread and involve the German empire. In playing the role of 'honest broker' Bismarck was above all serving German national interests. He feared that the newly founded German empire, the most powerful state in the heart of Europe, would lead inevitably to a hostile counterbalance. His 'nightmare of coalitions' was that Germany's neighbours would ally with each other against Germany and encircle her. To prevent this from happening he allied Germany with Austria-Hungary, Italy and Russia, and isolated France which might otherwise be tempted to seek revenge for the defeat of 1871 and the loss of Alsace-Lorraine and act as the nucleus of an anti-German alliance group of nations.

During the 1890s the Bismarckian grand design progressively collapsed. Germany's allies had incompatible interests and national ambitions. Even before

Bismarck's fall in March 1890, the 'wire to St Petersburg' could scarcely be kept intact. Austria-Hungary, Russia and Germany could no longer be held together in the *Three Emperors' Alliance, originally concluded 18 June 1881, and renewed in 1884*. The separate *German-Russian* so-called *'Reinsurance Treaty', 18 June 1887*, was not renewed by Bismarck's successor in 1890. The link to St Petersburg was cut. The polarization of alliances and alignments began to take shape and gradually, though it is important to note not inevitably, hardened into the two alliance groupings that went to war in 1914.

The alliance treaties which survived Bismarck's fall were, first, the *Austro-German Alliance, renewed in 1883 and 1889 and on 1 June 1902* with the provision that it would be automatically renewed every three years thereafter unless one of the partners within one of the three-year periods entered into negotiations over the question whether the conditions the treaty was designed to meet still prevailed. The treaty remained in force in August 1914. It was a defensive alliance, the *casus foederis* only arose if Russia attacked Austria-Hungary. The *casus foederis* the treaty provided for did not actually arise in 1914 since it was Germany that declared war on Russia; Austria-Hungary remained at peace with Russia only for a short while longer as she was entitled to, but in reality had to join Germany in declaring war on Russia a few days later.

The second Bismarckian treaty to survive was the *Triple Alliance between Germany, Italy and Austria-Hungary, concluded on 20 May 1882* (p. 38). Italy wanted an ally in case she was attacked by France; for Austria-Hungary the value of an alliance with Italy was to ensure that Italy, with her own ambitions in the Balkans, would not stab Austria in the back in the event of conflict with Russia. Article 1 provided that the three parties to the treaty promised each other peace and friendship and undertook not to enter into an alliance or engagement directed at any one of their states. Article 2 promised Italy the help with all their forces of Germany and Austria-Hungary if attacked by France; Italy promised her aid if France attacked Germany. The absolute nature of these obligations was weakened by the phrase 'unprovoked aggression', that is, the *casus foederis* would only arise if the attack was 'unprovoked', which allowed the allies to make a judgement about the events that had led to the war. Article 3 provided that the *casus foederis* would arise if any one of the parties, without direct provocation on its part, was attacked by two or more great powers. Article 4 significantly did not contain the limitation of becoming operative only if the attack was unprovoked: it stated that, in the event of a war between one of the parties and one other (other than in the cases previously specified), the other parties had the option of remaining benevolently neutral or joining as allies in the war. This article therefore in practice should have covered Austria-Hungary if she found herself at war with Russia even if Austria had begun the war in defence of her security. The treaty was renewed on 20 February 1887, but Italy won additional support in North Africa and the Balkans from

Austria-Hungary and Germany in two separate additional treaties. With each renewal, the Italians sought a change of terms in their favour to back their colonial ambitions. The treaty was *renewed on 6 May 1891 and 28 June 1902*. By 1902, however, Italy was playing a double game, striking a bargain with France over North Africa, assuring France that Italy was not committed to go to war against France in any circumstances, whilst remaining committed to the Triple Alliance. Despite *subsequent renewals of the Triple Alliance in 1906 and finally on 5 December 1912* with the first five articles defining the *casus belli* unchanged, Italy's two allies Germany and Austria-Hungary knew that they could not rely on Italian loyalty. In August 1914 the Italians could claim article 3 did not apply since Germany had declared war on France and only article 4 applied requiring Italy to observe benevolent neutrality; on 4 May 1915 Italy repudiated the treaty and joined the Allied side.

By the outbreak of war in 1914, of the German alliances and agreements constructed by Bismarck, only the *Austro-German Alliance* survived. Worse still, a coalition of enemy great powers, Russia, Britain and France, had come into being.

Dual Alliance, Germany and Austria-Hungary, Vienna, 7 October 1879, ratified 21 October 1879

Inasmuch as their Majesties the Emperor of Austria, King of Hungary, and the German Emperor, King of Prussia, must consider it Their imperative duty as Monarchs to provide for the security of Their Empires and the peace of Their subjects, under all circumstances;

Inasmuch as the two Sovereigns, as was the case under the former existing relations of alliance, will be enabled by the close union of the two Empires to fulfil this duty more easily and more efficaciously;

Inasmuch as, finally, an intimate co-operation of Germany and Austria-Hungary can menace no one, but is rather calculated to consolidate the peace of Europe as established by the stipulations of Berlin;

Their Majesties the Emperor of Austria, King of Hungary, and the Emperor of Germany, while solemnly promising each other never to allow Their purely defensive Agreement to develop an aggressive tendency in any direction, have determined to conclude an Alliance of peace and mutual defence . . .

For this purpose Their Most Exalted Majesties have designated as Their Plenipotentiaries:

His Most Exalted Majesty the Emperor of Austria, King of Hungary, His Actual Privy Councillor, Minister of the Imperial Household and of Foreign Affairs, Lieutenant-Field-Marshal Count Julius Andrássy of Czik-Szent-Király and Kraszna-Horka, etc., etc.,

His most Exalted Majesty the German Emperor, His Ambassador Extraordinary and Plenipotentiary, Lieutenant-General Prince Henry VII of Reuss, etc., etc., who have met this day at Vienna, and, after the exchange of their full powers, found in good and due form, have agreed upon the following Articles:

Article I. Should, contrary to their hope, and against the loyal desire of the two High Contracting Parties, one of the two Empires be attacked by Russia, the High Contracting Parties are bound to come to the assistance one of the other with the whole war strength of their Empires, and accordingly only to conclude peace together and upon mutual agreement.

Article II. Should one of the High Contracting Parties be attacked by another Power, the other High Contracting Party binds itself hereby, not only not to support the aggressor against its high Ally, but to observe at least a benevolent neutral attitude towards its fellow Contracting Party.

Should, however, the attacking party in such a case be supported by Russia, either by an active co-operation or by military measures which constitute a menace to the Party attacked, then the obligation stipulated in Article I of this Treaty, for reciprocal assistance with the whole fighting force, becomes equally operative, and the conduct of the war by the two High Contracting Parties shall in this case also be in common until the conclusion of a common peace.

Article III. The duration of this Treaty shall be provisionally fixed at five years from the day of ratification. One year before the expiration of this period the two High Contracting Parties shall consult together concerning the question whether the conditions serving as the basis of the Treaty still prevail, and reach an agreement in regard to the further continuance or possible modification of certain details. If in the course of the first months of the last year of the Treaty no invitation has been received from either side to open these negotiations, the Treaty shall be considered as renewed for a further period of three years.

Article IV. This Treaty shall, in conformity with its peaceful character, and to avoid any misinterpretation, be kept secret by the two High Contracting Parties, and only communicated to a third Power upon a joint understanding between the two Parties, and according to the terms of a special Agreement.

The two High Contracting Parties venture to hope, after the sentiments expressed by the Emperor Alexander at the meeting at Alexandrovo, that the armaments of Russia will not in reality prove to be menacing to them, and have on that account no reason for making a communication at present; should, however, this hope, contrary to their expectations, prove to be erroneous, the two High Contracting Parties would consider it their loyal obligation to let the Emperor Alexander know, at least confidentially, that they must consider an attack on either of them as directed against both.

Article V. This Treaty shall derive its validity from the approbation of the two Exalted Sovereigns and shall be ratified within fourteen days after this approbation has been granted by Their Most Exalted Majesties . . .

In witness whereof the Plenipotentiaries have signed this Treaty with their own hands and affixed their arms. Done at Vienna, October 7, 1879.

Triple Alliance, Austria-Hungary, Germany, Italy, Vienna, 20 May 1882, ratified 30 May 1882

Their Majesties the Emperor of Austria, King of Bohemia, etc., and Apostolic King of Hungary, the Emperor of Germany, King of Prussia, and the King of Italy, animated by the desire to increase the guaranties of the general peace, to fortify the monarchical principle and thereby to assure the unimpaired maintenance of the social and political order in Their respective States, have agreed to conclude a Treaty which, by its essentially conservative and defensive nature, pursues only the aim of forestalling the dangers which might threaten the security of Their States and the peace of Europe.

To this end Their Majesties have appointed . . .

Article I. The High Contracting Parties mutually promise peace and friendship, and will enter into no alliance or engagement directed against any one of their States.

They engage to proceed to an exchange of ideas on political and economic questions of a general nature which may arise, and they further promise one another mutual support within the limits of their own interests.

Article II. In case Italy, without direct provocation on her part, should be attacked by France for any reason whatsoever, the two other Contracting Parties shall be bound to lend help and assistance with all their forces to the Party attacked.

This same obligation shall devolve upon Italy in case of any aggression without direct provocation by France against Germany.

Article III. If one, or two, of the High Contracting Parties, without direct provocation on their part, should chance to be attacked and to be engaged in a war with two or more Great Powers nonsignatory to the present Treaty, the *casus foederis* will arise simultaneously for all the High Contracting Parties.

Article IV. In case a Great Power nonsignatory to the present Treaty should threaten the security of the states of one of the High Contracting Parties, and the threatened Party should find itself forced on that account to make war against it, the two others bind themselves to observe towards their Ally a benevolent neutrality. Each of them reserves to itself, in this case, the right to take part in the war, if it should see fit, to make common cause with its Ally.

Article V. If the peace of any of the High Contracting Parties should chance to be threatened under the circumstances foreseen by the preceding Articles, the High Contracting Parties shall take counsel together in ample time as to the military measures to be taken with a view to eventual co-operation.

They engage henceforward, in all cases of common participation in a war, to conclude neither armistice, nor peace, nor treaty, except by common agreement among themselves.

Article VI. [Treaty to be kept secret]

Article VII. [Treaty to be in force for five years from date of ratification]

Article VIII. [Exchange of ratification]

The Imperial and Royal Government declares that the provisions of the secret treaty concluded May 20, 1882, between Austria-Hungary, Germany, and Italy, cannot, as had been previously agreed, in any case be regarded as directed against England.

The Dual Alliance: France and Russia

Rebuffed by Germany's refusal to renew the Reinsurance Treaty in 1890, Tsar Alexander III opted for alignment with republican France; neither France nor

Russia wished to be isolated confronting Germany, yet neither was keen to be dragged into a war over conflicts that concerned only the other. The first step was an *Exchange of Notes, 27 August 1891*, whereby the two countries would consult each other and reach an understanding on the measures to be adopted if peace were threatened. The relationship was strengthened by the conclusion of a draft *Military Convention drawn up by the Russian and French military staffs in August 1892*, it provided for specific numbers of troops to engage Germany so as to force Germany to fight on two fronts simultaneously. The *casus foederis* would arise if France were attacked by Germany or by Italy supported by Germany or if Germany attacked Russia or if Austria attacked Russia supported by Germany (article 1). This meant that France did not have to fight if Austria alone attacked Russia. But since mobilization would almost inevitably lead to war, this exemption might well not apply in practice since article 2 required Russia and France to mobilise if *any* of the Triple Alliance powers, that is Italy, or Austria or Germany mobilized. The delayed formal approval of the *Military Convention* by Tsar Alexander III was communicated in a *Note to the French on 27 December 1893* and the *French approval in response on 4 January 1894* (p. 40) marked the conclusion of a Franco–Russian alliance.

The wording of the alliance was modified on 9 August 1899: it was no longer to end with the ending of the Triple Alliance. Its purpose was to maintain the balance of power in Europe and peace; but the obligations of the Military Convention remained in force. After Britain had concluded an *Alliance with Japan on 30 January 1902* (p. 34), conflict threatened in China between Russia and Japan. *A Franco–Russian Declaration on 20 March 1902* extended the alliance to the Far East but only to the extent that if the aggressive actions of third powers or new troubles in China threatened French or Russian interests the two allies would consult how to react. A modification of significance to the Franco–Russian *Military Convention in April 1906* was that if Austria-Hungary or Italy mobilized alone, France and Russia need only consult on joint action rather than automatically mobilize. In September 1912 the French clarified their alliance commitment to the Russians in the event of conflict in the Balkans. France would not fight in a purely Balkan conflict but if there was a war between Russia and Austria-Hungary and Germany intervened the *casus foederis* would be established for France. This was a significant extension of the original terms of the Military Convention since it promised French military help to Russia against Austria-Hungary whichever power began such a war. With the German declaration of war on Russia on 1 August 1914, the *casus foederis* had arisen; the Germans anticipated a French declaration of war in compliance with the Franco–Russian alliance by declaring war on France on 3 August.

The Russian–French Alliance, 4 January 1894, based on the Draft Military Convention August 1892, approved by Russia and France, 27 December 1893 and 4 January 1894 respectively

France and Russia, being animated by an equal desire to preserve peace, and having no other object than to meet the necessities of a defensive war, provoked by an attack of the forces of the Triple Alliance against the one or the other of them, have agreed upon the following provisions:

1. If France is attacked by Germany, or by Italy supported by Germany, Russia shall employ all her available forces to attack Germany.

If Russia is attacked by Germany, or by Austria supported by Germany, France shall employ all her available forces to fight Germany.

2. In case the forces of the Triple Alliance, or of one of the Powers composing it, should mobilize, France and Russia, at the first news of the event and without the necessity of any previous concert, shall mobilize immediately and simultaneously the whole of their forces and shall move them as close as possible to their frontiers.

3. The available forces to be employed against Germany shall be, on the part of France, 1,300,000 men, on the part of Russia, 700,000 or 800,000 men.

These forces shall engage to the full, with all speed, in order that Germany may have to fight at the same time on the East and on the West.

4. The General Staffs of the Armies of the two countries shall co-operate with each other at all times in the preparation and facilitation of the execution of the measures above foreseen.

They shall communicate to each other, while there is still peace, all information relative to the armies of the Triple Alliance which is or shall be within their knowledge.

Ways and means of corresponding in times of war shall be studied and arranged in advance.

5. France and Russia shall not conclude peace separately.

6. The present Convention shall have the same duration as the Triple Alliance.

7. All the clauses above enumerated shall be kept rigorously secret.

Signed: OBRUCHEFF   BOISDEFFRE

Britain, France and Russia: the road to the Triple *Entente*, 1904–14

Nothing seemed less likely than an alliance or alignment among Britain, Russia and France in the 1890s. In west and north Africa, Britain and France were rivals for empire and at Fashoda in the Sudan in 1898 there was even a threat of war; Britain's imperial rivalry, the legendary 'Great Game', extended from Constantinople to Afghanistan and beyond to China. Britain had no territorial dispute of significance with any of the Triple Alliance powers and tended to look to Germany for support. Tentative moves for a closer alignment and co-operation with Germany 1898–1902, however, came to nothing. Britain's priority in 1901 was to protect her interests in China against Russia. But Germany was not willing to contemplate any alliance with provisions that would provide Britain with security of overstretched imperial interests. Britain next turned to Japan and concluded an *Alliance with Japan, 30 January 1902*. It obliged Britain to join Japan in a war with Russia only if a second power, i.e. France, also went to war with Japan. *On 12 August 1905, the Second Anglo–Japanese Alliance treaty* extended the agreement to India and the lands in proximity of India. Secondly, the alliance now became operative if any one power attacked unprovoked Japan or Britain. On 13 July 1911 the treaty was renewed for a further ten years.

Neither Britain nor France during the years 1902 to 1905 was willing to be drawn into Russia's and Japan's conflict in Manchuria and Korea. The seed was thereby sown that led to the agreement to settle Anglo–French imperial differences which became known as the *Anglo–French Entente, 8 April 1904* (p. 43). At the heart of that settlement was Britain's support for France's claim to predominance in Morocco and French support for Britain's similar claim in Egypt.

Almost a year later in March 1905 the Germans challenged the right of Britain and France to settle the Moroccan situation without them. They took advantage of Russia's temporary military eclipse after being defeated by the Japanese in the Russo–Japanese war.

The first Moroccan crisis was highlighted by Kaiser William II's dramatic landing at Tangier on 31 March 1905. The Germans demanded that the Moroccan question be submitted to an international conference which met at Algeçiras from 16 January to 31 March 1906. *The General Act of the Conference signed on 7 April 1906* gave France and Spain additional powers over the organization of the Moroccan police (chapter I) and placed restrictions on the importation of arms (chapter II), made provision for a state bank, the regulation of taxes and customs (III–IV) and other state services. Its true significance was temporarily to prevent France taking control of Morocco and to oblige France to take German views into account in any settlement. A settlement of the problem was postponed until the more serious second Moroccan crisis in 1911 when the Germans reinforced their demands for 'compensation' by sending the gunboat *Panther* to Agadir on 1 July 1911. It was settled by a *Franco–German Agreement on 4 November 1911*, Germany in practice agreeing to a French protectorate over Morocco provided equality of economic opportunities was preserved. In compensation the Germans received two strips of territory which were transferred to the German colony of Cameroon and gave them access to the Congo from the French colony of Congo. The French were now free to establish their Protectorate over Morocco forcing the Sultan to sign the *Treaty of Fez on 30 March 1912*.

The Franco–German conflicts over Morocco had wider international repercussions especially on the relations of Britain and France. While the Anglo–French *entente* never turned into an absolute commitment of an alliance with the undertaking of British military support in the event of a German attack on France, the threat of such an attack led to military conversations on co-operation between the French and British general staffs. They began in January 1906 in secrecy and were authorized by the British Foreign Secretary and Prime Minister without consulting the Cabinet. Anglo–French naval talks were additionally authorized by the Cabinet in July 1912. But despite repeated French pressure the *Entente* did not become an alliance before the outbreak of the 1914 war. An exchange of letters in November 1912 between the foreign secretary Sir Edward Grey and the French ambassador Paul Cambon merely promised consultation between the two governments if a third power launched an unprovoked attack or threatened the general peace.

From the outset, in 1903, Britain saw the benefit of an *entente* with France as easing the threat of France's ally Russia to Britain's imperial interests, especially the defence of India. France would use her influence in Russia so that the Franco–Russian alliance would not clash with the Anglo–French *Entente*. The extension of the Anglo–Japanese alliance in August 1905 did not provide adequate support for India's defence; the general settlement with Russia was not achieved until 1907, that is, after Russia's defeat by Japan. The essence of the *Anglo-Russian Convention, 31 August 1907* (p. 45) was that by agreeing to settlement of rivalries in Persia, Afghanistan and Tibet, the Russians undertook not to threaten India; it gave Britain a breathing space as long as she remained on good terms with Russia. For Russia the advantage lay in that she could pursue her European interests especially in the Balkans without fear of a threat from Britain in Asia. Persia was divided into spheres of interest, the northern to Russia, the centre including the Gulf was to be neutral, and the regions adjoining India, British. The Russians recognized that Afghanistan was outside their sphere of influence and that they would conduct relations with Afghanistan only through Britain; Chinese suzerainty over Tibet was recognized but it was accepted that Britain had a special interest in the maintenance of the status quo.

From 1909 onwards in Britain, the alignment with Russia and France was referred to as the *Triple Entente*. But the Russians were as unsuccessful as the French in turning it into an alliance with a commitment by Britain to go to war. To satisfy the Russians the British permitted Anglo-Russian naval talks in 1914 on the model of the French. Their significance was not strategic but psychological in that they increased German fears of 'encirclement'. Although the *Entente* with France did not commit Britain to enter the war as France's ally, a 'moral' commitment was felt by the foreign secretary Sir Edward Grey to exist because of agreed military and naval dispositions. The breach of Belgian neutrality by the Germans made the decision for war easier for the majority of the British Cabinet to accept. But even with a split in the Liberal Party, Asquith and Grey knew they could rely on the support of the Conservatives in opposition. The Liberal government survived resignations from the Cabinet and declared war on Germany on 4 August 1914.

Anglo–French Entente, 8 April 1904, Declaration between the United Kingdom and France respecting Egypt and Morocco

Article I. His Britannic Majesty's Government declare that they have no intention of altering the political status of Egypt.

The Government of the French Republic, for their part, declare that they will not obstruct the action of Great Britain in that country by asking that a limit of time be fixed for the British occupation or in any other manner, and that they give their assent to the draft Khedivial Decree annexed to the present. Arrangement, containing the guarantees considered necessary for the protection of the interests of the Egyptian bondholders, on the condition that, after its promulgation, it cannot be modified in any way without the consent of the Powers Signatory of the Convention of London of 1885.

It is agreed that the post of Director-General of Antiquities in Egypt shall continue, as in the past, to be entrusted to a French *savant*.

The French schools in Egypt shall continue to enjoy the same liberty as in the past.

Article II. The Government of the French Republic declare that they have no intention of altering the political status of Morocco.

His Britannic Majesty's Government, for their part, recognise that it appertains to France, more particularly as a Power whose dominions are conterminous for a great distance with those of Morocco, to preserve order in that country, and to provide assistance for the purpose of all administrative, economic, financial, and military reforms which it may require.

They declare that they will not obstruct the action taken by France for this purpose, provided that such action shall leave intact the rights which Great Britain, in virtue of Treaties, Conventions, and usage, enjoys in Morocco, including the right of coasting trade between the ports of Morocco, enjoyed by British vessels since 1901.

Article III. His Britannic Majesty's Government, for their part, will respect the rights which France, in virtue of Treaties, Conventions, and usage, enjoys in Egypt, including the right of coasting trade between Egyptian ports accorded to French vessels.

Article IV. The two Governments, being equally attached to the principle of commercial liberty both in Egypt and Morocco, declare that they will not, in those countries, countenance any inequality either in the imposition of customs duties or other taxes, or of railway transport charges.

The trade of both nations with Morocco and with Egypt shall enjoy the same treatment in transit through the French and British possessions in Africa. An Agreement between the two Governments shall settle the conditions of such transit and shall determine the points of entry.

This mutual engagement shall be binding for a period of thirty years. Unless this stipulation is expressly denounced at least one year in advance, the period shall be extended for five years at a time.

Nevertheless, the Government of the French Republic reserve to themselves in Morocco, and His Britannic Majesty's Government reserve to themselves in Egypt, the right to see that the concessions for roads, railways, ports, &c., are only granted on such conditions as will maintain intact the authority of the State over these great undertakings of public interest.

Article V. His Britannic Majesty's Government declare that they will use their influence in order that the French officials now in the Egyptian service may not be placed under conditions less advantageous than those applying to the British officials in the same service.

The Government of the French Republic, for their part, would make no objection to the application of analogous conditions to British officials now in the Moorish service.

Article VI. In order to insure the free passage of the Suez Canal, His Britannic Majesty's Government declare that they adhere to the stipulations of the Treaty of the 29th October, 1888, and that they agree to their being put in force. The free passage of the Canal being thus guaranteed, the execution of the last sentence of paragraph I as well as of paragraph 2 of Article VIII of that Treaty will remain in abeyance.

Article VII. In order to secure the free passage of the Straits of Gibraltar, the two Governments agree not to permit the erection of any fortifications or strategic works on that portion of the coast of Morocco comprised between, but not including, Melilla and the heights which command the right bank of the River Sebou.

This condition does not, however, apply to the places at present in the occupation of Spain on the Moorish coast of the Mediterranean.

Article VIII. The two Governments, inspired by their feeling of sincere friendship for Spain, take into special consideration the interests which that country derives from her geographical position and from her territorial possessions on the Moorish coast of the Mediterranean. In regard to these interests the French Government will come to an understanding with the Spanish Government.

The agreement which may be come to on the subject between France and Spain shall be communicated to His Britannic Majesty's Government.

Article IX. The two Governments agree to afford to one another their diplomatic support, in order to obtain the execution of the clauses of the present Declaration regarding Egypt and Morocco.

. . .

Secret Article I. In the event of either Government finding themselves constrained, by the force of circumstances, to modify their policy in respect to Egypt and Morocco, the engagements which they have undertaken towards each other by Articles IV, VI and VII of the Declaration of today's date would remain intact.

Secret Article II. His Britannic Majesty's Government have no present intention of proposing to the Powers any changes in the system of the Capitulations, or in the judicial organisation of Egypt.

In the event of their considering it desirable to introduce in Egypt reforms tending to assimilate the Egyptian legislative system to that in force in other civilised countries, the Government of the French Republic will not refuse to entertain any such proposals, on the understanding that His Britannic Majesty's Government will agree to entertain the suggestions that the Government of the French Republic may have to make to them with a view of introducing similar reforms in Morocco.

Secret Article III. The two Governments agree that a certain extent of Moorish territory adjacent to Melilla, Ceuta and other *Présides* should, whenever the Sultan ceases to exercise authority over it, come within the sphere of influence of Spain, and that the administration of the coast from Melilla as far as, but not including, the heights on the right bank of the Sebou shall be intrusted to Spain.

Nevertheless, Spain would previously have to give her formal assent to the provisions of Articles IV and VII of the Declaration of today's date, and undertake to carry them out.

She would also have to undertake not to alienate the whole or a part of the territories placed under her authority or in her sphere of influence.

Secret Article IV. If Spain, when invited to assent to the provisions of the preceding article, should think proper to decline, the Arrangement between France and Great Britain, as embodied in the Declaration of today's date, would be none the less applicable.

Secret Article V. Should the consent of the other Powers to the draft Decree mentioned in Article I of the Declaration of today's date not be obtained, the Government of the French Republic will not oppose the repayment at par of the Guaranteed, Privileged and Unified Debts after the 15th July, 1910.

Done at London, in duplicate, the 8th day of April, 1904 (L.S.) LANSDOWNE. (L.S.) PAUL CAMBON.

[Agreements were also concluded and signed on 8 April 1904 concerning delimita-tions of influence (1) a Declaration concerning Siam, Madagascar and the New Hebrides, (2) A Convertion concerning Newfoundland, and west and central Africa.]

Conventions between Russia and the United Kingdom relating to Persia, Afghanistan and Tibet, St Petersburg, 31 August 1907

The Governments of Great Britain and Russia having mutually engaged to respect the integrity and independence of Persia, and sincerely desiring the preservation of order throughout that country and its peaceful development, as well as the permanent establishment of equal advantages for the trade and industry of all other nations;

Considering that each of them has, for geographical and economic reasons, a special interest in the maintenance of peace and order in certain provinces of Persia adjoining, or in the neighbourhood of, the Russian frontier on the one hand, and the frontiers of Afghanistan and Baluchistan on the other; and being desirous of avoiding all cause of conflict between their respective interests in the above-mentioned provinces of Persia;

Have agreed on the following terms: –

I. Great Britain engages not to seek for herself, and not to support in favour of British subjects, or in favour of the subjects of third Powers, any Concessions of a political or commercial nature – such as Concessions for railways, banks, telegraphs, roads, transport, insurance, etc. – beyond a line starting from Kasri-Shirin, passing through Isfahan, Yezd, Kakhk, and ending at a point on the Persian frontier at the intersection of the Russian and Afghan frontiers, and not to oppose, directly or indirectly, demands for similar Concessions in this region which are supported by the Russian Government. It is understood that the above-mentioned places are included in the region in which Great Britain engages not to seek the Concessions referred to.

II. Russia, on her part, engages not to seek for herself and not to support, in favour of Russian subjects, or in favour of the subjects of third Powers, any Concessions of a political or commercial nature – such as Concessions for railways, banks, telegraphs, roads, transport, insurance, etc. – beyond a line going from the Afghan frontier by way of Gazik, Birjand, Kerman, and ending at Bender Abbas, and not to oppose, directly or indirectly, demands for similar Concessions in this region which are supported by the British Government. It is understood that the above-mentioned places are included in the region in which Russia engages not to seek the Concessions referred to.

III. Russia, on her part, engages not to oppose, without previous arrangement with Great Britain, the grant of any Concessions whatever to British subjects in the regions of Persia situated between the lines mentioned in Articles I and II. Great Britain undertakes a similar engagement as regards the grant of Concessions to Russian subjects in the same regions of Persia. All Concessions existing at present in the regions indicated in Articles I and II are maintained.

IV. [Regarding customs revenues, fisheries, posts and telegraph and loan service.]

V. [Agreement to be reached beforehand between Russia and Great Britain in the event of irregularities in the interest payments on loans.]

[Related documents were signed regarding Afghanistan and Tibet. The convention on Afghanistan stated that, to ensure secur-

ity on the frontiers in central Asia and lasting peace, Britain declared (Article 1) that it
had no intention of changing the political
status of Afghanistan and would exercise its
influence to prevent any threat to Russia
from the country. Russia recognized
Afghanistan as lying outside the Russian
sphere of influence and undertook that relations with Afghanistan would be conducted
through the intermediary of Britain. The
Russians also undertook to send no agents
to Afghanistan. Britain undertook (Article 2)
not to interfere in the internal government
of the country provided the Amir fulfilled
the engagements contracted towards Britain. Britain engaged not to annex or occupy
any part of the country. In the agreement
regarding Tibet, Britain and Russia recognized the suzerainty of China. Britain,
however, 'by reason of her geographical
position' was recognized by Russia as having a special interest in the maintenance of
the status quo in the country (preamble).
Britain and Russia undertook (Article 1) to
respect the territorial integrity of Tibet and
to refrain from interference in internal
affairs. British commercial agents, however,
were to be permitted direct relations with
the Tibetan authorities. It was agreed that
'the Buddhists, whether British or Russian
subjects, can enter into direct relations with
the Dalai Lama ... in Tibet on strictly
religious grounds' (Article 2). Britain and
Russia undertook not to secure any railway,
road, telegraph, or mining concessions in
Tibet (Article 4).]

The conflict in the Balkans 1895–1914

The Balkan conflict threatening to involve Russia, Austria-Hungary and Britain in war played a dominant role in European diplomacy for all but short periods of calm from 1878 to 1914. The Ottoman Empire was weakening in Europe; the emerging independent Balkan states contested the territories the Ottoman rulers were forced to give up; Russia and Austria-Hungary were rivals for influence and territory in the Balkans, and their ambitions also involved them in the struggles of the emerging Balkan nations; finally Britain, with its concern for the safety of the route to India, was determined, before 1914, to prevent Russia from controlling the Straits and dominating the seat of Ottoman rule, Constantinople. Italy and France were secondary players with ambitions and interests of their own in the closing years before the outbreak of war in 1914, Germany too broke with Bismarckian traditions and staked a claim in the future of the region.

Austria-Hungary and Russia

Austria-Hungary when opposing Russian ambition in the Balkans was dependent on the support of her allies. Their support was, however, conditional and uncertain. Her alliance with Germany was defensive, the alliance with Italy, a marriage of convenience. *The Alliances of Austria-Hungary with the Balkan states*, with *Serbia, 16 June 1881, renewed on 28 January 1889 and with Roumania, 30 October 1883, renewed on 13 July 1892, 30 September 1896, 4 April 1902 and 30 January 1913* were even less secure: The Roumanians were opposed to Hungarian rule over Transylvania with its large Roumanian ethnic population and Serbia was aggrieved over Austria-Hungary's occupation since 1878 of Bosnia-Herzegovina with its large

Slavic population. The *entente* with Britain, the *Mediterranean Agreements of 1887*, which also included Spain, ended in 1896 when the Austrians wanted to convert it into a military alliance in defence of Turkey; the British Prime Minister Lord Salisbury was averse to alliances and in any case at a time when the Turks were massacring Armenians (1895–96) felt British public opinion would not tolerate supporting Turkey in a war.

For the Russians, the Balkans and the future of the Ottoman Empire were as vital a question as for Austria-Hungary. The Ottoman Empire in the 1890s appeared on the verge of disintegration; the distribution of territorial spoils could not be left to chance or the possible chaos and conflict accompanying the final stages. Russia's principal concern was the future of the Straits. Simultaneously Russia was launching a forward policy in northern China. Amid such future uncertainties an understanding with Austria-Hungary was desirable. Austria-Hungary reciprocated, unsure of how much support she could expect from her allies. An *Exchange of Notes on 8 May 1897* was the basis of the *Austro-Hungarian and Russian Entente* concerning the Balkans. It left some areas of difference; there was no agreement about the Russian desire to change the rule of the Straits or the right of Austria-Hungary, awarded by the *Treaty of Berlin, 13 July 1878*, to change or militarize occupation of Bosnia-Herzegovina to annexation but there was agreement that both nations would try to maintain the status quo as long as possible and not interfere in the Balkan states; they also agreed that if the status quo proved impossible to maintain, they would seek no conquests for themselves but would agree on the future territorial frontiers of the Balkans and impose this on the other nations.

During the war between Greece and Turkey in 1897 Russia and Austria-Hungary co-operated to prevent its spread. The high point of the Austro–Russian *Entente* was reached during the years 1902–04. The Russians became embroiled in conflict and ultimately in war with Japan 1904–05 over the future of their po-sition in Manchuria and influence in Korea. Austria-Hungary faced difficulties at home, and her tenuous influence in Serbia weakened even more after the murder of Alexander I in June 1903 and the change of dynasties with the election of Peter Karadjordjević to the throne. A prime concern of Austria-Hungary was to prevent the enlargement of a hostile Serbia and Montenegro which threatened Austro-Hungary in Bosnia-Herzegovina. Austro–Russian relations also deteriorated from 1905 to 1908 in renewed Balkan rivalries.

Then in July 1908 there seemed to be a spectacular opportunity to improve relations. Foreign Minister Izvolsky proposed that the conservative 1897 agree-ment should be replaced by a deal between the two countries: Russia would adopt a benevolent attitude if Austria-Hungary chose to annex Bosnia-Herzegovina and the strategically important Ottoman Sanjak of Novibazar, and in return Austria-Hungary would benevolently support Russia in altering the rule of the Straits and

Bosphorus. The prevailing European settlement was that the passage of all foreign warships when Turkey was at peace was not permitted. It had been established by the *Straits Convention, 13 July 1841, concluded between Britain, Austria, France, Prussia, Russia and Turkey*. The Russians desired a revision to permit only Russian warships to pass through the Straits and Bosphorus in time of peace while continuing to prohibit the passage of all other warships.

No formal agreement or treaty was ever signed after *discussions between the Austrian Foreign Minister Aehrenthal and the Russian Izvolski* at the *Morovian Castle in Buchlau on 16 September 1908*. On 6 October 1908, Aehrenthal announced the Austrian annexation of Bosnia-Herzegovina unilaterally to a startled Europe. The Turks eventually agreed to accept the annexation on receiving compensation in a final settlement, the *Austro–Turkish Protocol of 26 February 1909*. Izvolski, unable to secure his side of the bargain in the rule of the Straits, was enraged; in the Balkans, Montenegro and Serbia were now set on a path of irreconcilable enmity with Austria-Hungary. The Austro–Russian *Entente* was replaced from 1908 to 1914 by open confrontation in the Balkans. In competing for influence Russia and Austria-Hungary were drawn into the maelstrom of the conflicts of Turkey and of the Balkan states for the legacy of what still remained of the Ottoman European and North African Empire.

The Italian–Turkish War, 1911–12

The first war for Ottoman territory did not have its origins in Turkey's Balkan territories but in Ottoman suzerainity over the North African territory of Libya. While France in 1911 was securing her dominance in Morocco, Italy too intended to claim her share of colonial rule in North Africa at Turkey's expense. The Turks were not simply going to accept further losses of their empire. The Young Turk revolution of 1908 placed a government in power in Constantinople that was determined to gain more control over their empire by centralizing power in Constantinople. *On 29 September 1911, Italy declared war on Turkey*. As Italian operations in Libya were going badly, the Italians bombarded the Straits and attacked the Dodecanese Islands in the Aegean, capturing Rhodes in May 1912. Faced with the growing threat of a combined attack by Bulgaria, Serbia and Greece, the Turks were anxious to negotiate peace with the Italians. *On 18 October 1912, the Treaty of Lausanne* was concluded between Italy and Turkey; under its terms Turkey ceded sovereignty over Tripolitania and Cyrenaica to Italy and undertook to withdraw its troops from Libya. As a guarantee for the completion of the Turkish evacuation the Italians were to hold the Dodecanese Islands and Rhodes; the Italians did not leave the islands after the Turkish evacuation and remained in possession of them until defeated in the Second World War. They were then, in 1946, united with Greece.

The First and Second Balkan Wars, 1912–14

The Young Turks' brutal efforts to suppress the insurrections of Catholic Albanians in 1910 and 1911 and attempts to centralize government in Constantinople raised the Balkan question once more. Bulgaria, Serbia and Greece were drawing together from 1911 to 1912 to take advantage of Turkey's difficulties at a time when she was at war with Italy. Greece wanted to expand to include the regions of Macedonia inhabited by ethnic Greeks and annex Crete. The Serbs were rivals for Macedonia but their main ambition for expansion was in the direction of Bosnia-Herzegovina, the Sanjak of Novibazar and Northern Albania. In Macedonia, Bulgaria and Serbia were rivals as well. A series of secret alliances were formed to divide up Ottoman lands in the Balkans. On *13 March 1912, Bulgaria,* which had proclaimed its full independence in 1908, *signed an Alliance* with Serbia, to attack Turkey and partition Macedonia. *The Greeks joined by signing an Alliance with Bulgaria, 29 May 1912,* undertaking to take the offensive in Macedonia and with the intention also of securing Crete; *on 6 October 1912 this was supplemented by a Montenegrin–Bulgarian alliance and on 24 October by a Montenegrin– Serbian alliance. The Balkan League* of states bound by series of these bilateral secret treaties agreed on attacking Turkey and presenting the great powers with a *fait accompli* but not on a final disposition of the spoils.

Montenegro on 8 October 1912 declared war on Turkey, followed on 18 October 1912 by Greece, Bulgaria and Serbia. On 28 November Albania declared its independence. The pretexts for the wars by the Balkan League were the Albanian insurrections, a Montenegrin frontier dispute with Turkey, and the demands for reforms in Macedonia where there were insurrectionary outbreaks against the Turks. But the Balkan League nations were determined to redraw the frontiers on ethnic lines favouring them and enlarging their territories while coming to the aid of their oppressed countrymen. Intense rivalry was sufficiently papered over to enable them jointly to fight Turkey.

The great powers, despite their own rivalries over the future of the Ottoman Empire, did not want to raise the question prematurely fearing the conflict that could result. In 1912–14 they were agreed on the lowest common denominator, the status quo. But they failed to control the Balkan nations. The intervention of Britain, France, Italy, Germany, Russia and Austria-Hungary to cool the crisis was ineffectual. Once the Balkan war began, the rival interests of Russia and Austria-Hungary continued to impede effective intervention and the preservation of the status quo in the Balkans. The defeat of Turkey led her to request the good offices of the powers. Meanwhile in November and December 1912 a serious crisis developed between Russia and Austria-Hungary when Russia backed Serb expansion into Albania as far as the Adriatic which was opposed by Austria-Hungary. Russia gave way. The great powers, *France, Britain, Russia, Germany, Austria-Hungary and Italy convened an Ambassadorial London Conference on 12 December 1912, after Bulgaria,*

Serbia and Montenegro (but not Greece) had signed an armistice with Turkey on 3 December 1912. The armistice was short-lived and *hostilities were resumed on 3 February 1913.* Despite attempts by the London Conference to gain control over events the powers could not jointly impose a territorial settlement on the warring Balkan states and Turkey after the *Balkan League and Turkey had agreed on preliminaries of peace on 30 May 1913. On 11 August 1913, the London Conference adjourned after recognizing Albanian independence.*

The Balkan crisis did not end, as the Balkan League allies predictably fell out over the division of the Ottoman territories given up by Turkey in the Treaty of London and as Turkey renewed fighting to recover lost territory. Roumania, which had not participated in the First Balkan War now wanted compensation in Silistria and an area of the Dobruja. The division between Serbia, Greece and Bulgaria of Macedonia was the most explosive issue. *Serbia and Bulgaria in their Alliance Treaty of 13 March 1912* had not definitively divided southern Macedonia. Now *Greece concluded an alliance with Serbia on 1 June 1913* for a different division, depriving Bulgaria of all but a small part of Macedonia. *The Second Balkan War* began when provoked by *Greece and Serbia, Bulgaria attacked the Serbs and Greeks in Macedonia during the night of 29/30 June 1913.* Then, because Roumanian claims in the Dobruja had not been met by Bulgaria, *Roumania attacked Bulgaria on 11 July 1913. A day later, on 12 July 1913, the Turks attacked Bulgaria,* advancing into Thrace and recapturing Adrianople. The Bulgarians, faced with all these enemies, were soon defeated.

There was an untidy end to the Balkan conflict. *On 30 July 1913, the Bulgarians secured an armistice with the Serbs, Greeks and Roumanians.* The Second Balkan War was ended by two treaties. *The Treaty of Bucharest, 10 August 1913, between Bulgaria, Serbia, Greece and Roumania and the Treaty of Constantinople between Bulgaria and Turkey of 29 September 1913.*

The outcome of the treaties was as follows: Bulgaria had to return Adrianople and a belt of territory on the right bank of the Maritsa River to Turkey; Bulgaria also retained only a small portion of Macedonia, having to give Salonica and Kavalla to Greece and Monastir and Ochrid to Serbia. The dream of a greater Bulgaria was shattered as she had gained neither Macedonia nor Thrace with the demise of the Ottoman Empire in Europe.

Greece extended her northern territory which now ran from Cape Stylos (in the Corfu Straits) to Lake Prespa and then to the lower Maritsa. Greece increased her territory by 68 per cent and her population from 2.7 million to 4.4 million. *Greece concluded peace with Turkey on 14 November 1913.*

Serbia extended her territory in Macedonia and partitioned with Montenegro the Sanjak of Novibazar, 7 November 1913. Serbia almost doubled her territory and increased her population from 2.9 to 4.5 million. *A peace was signed with Turkey on 14 March 1914.*

Turkey lost most of her Balkan territories but regained Adrianople and its surrounding land in the war with Bulgaria in 1913.

Roumania gained a small additional belt of territory in the northern Dobruja from Bulgaria.

The impact on the relations of Austria-Hungary and Russia of the two Balkan Wars was a major one and contributed to the outbreak of the First World War in 1914. The outcome of the two Balkan Wars realized Austria-Hungary's worst fears with the enlargement of Serbia. Austria-Hungary would tolerate no further increase of Serb power even as Serb clandestine organizations plotted the union of Bosnia-Herzegovina with Serbia. In October 1913 there was a renewed crisis over Serbia's claims to territory in northern Albania while Greece was claiming territories in southern Albania. This time Russia withdrew backing from Serbia and the crisis passed. Less than a year later, after the murder of Archduke Francis Ferdinand in Sarajevo neither Austria-Hungary nor Russia flinched when war once more threatened.

The Powers, China and the Pacific, 1898–1914

During the nineteenth century the powers competed for influence in China and forced on the Chinese 'unequal treaties' which would meet their demands to trade, to send in Christian missionaries and for bases and territory. After the First Opium War, the Sino–British treaty, *Treaty of Nanking, 29 August 1842*, became an example other nations followed. Among several provisions which diminished Chinese sovereignty was the cession in perpetuity of the island of Hong Kong to Britain. The Americans extracted trade privileges, the French and other western nations followed this lead. In December 1857 Britain and France went to war in China and new concessions were exacted. The Russians took advantage of China's defeat to seize all the Chinese territory north of the river Amur. Britain and France renewed the war in 1860, occupied Peking and burnt down the Summer Palace. The Chinese had to cede to Britain part of the Kowloon Peninsula opposite Hong Kong. The Russians also extended their territorial gains. The privileged legal status of foreigners in China established by these nineteenth-century treaties, extraterritoriality and most of the territorial seizures further augmented in 1898, remained legally in force until the Second World War (1939–45) and (in the case of Hong Kong) beyond.

Later nineteenth-century predators in China were the Germans and the Japanese. Japan went to war with China in 1894 over dominance of Korea. Japan's victory led her to impose crushing terms on China by the *Treaty of Shimoneseki on 17 April 1895*. Following western examples the Chinese had to recognize Korea's independence and cede Formosa (Taiwan), the Pescadores Islands and Liaotung Peninsula to Japan. But Japan was humiliated by the three-power intervention

(Russia, France and Germany) and had to return the Liaotung Peninsula to China. The west now increased pressure on China and extracted concessions. After November 1897 the imperialist pressure of the west and of Japan forced China to grant new concessions. The Germans seized Tsingtao and in March 1898 Kiaochow; the Russians, Port Arthur and Dairen and part of the Liaotung Peninsula; the British took Wei-hai-wei and they secured an extension of territory in Kowloon in 1899; the French secured Kwangchow Wan. After the defeat of the Boxer Uprising in 1900, a reaction to foreign imperialism, further humiliations were heaped on China by the *Final Protocol for the settlement of disturbances in China, 7 September 1901*, including article 6, a huge indemnity of 450 million Haikouan taels (1 tael = $0.79 or 3 shillings sterling) to be paid over thirty-nine years; to guarantee payment of this, the revenues of China's maritime customs, and other taxes were pledged; an edict was to be posted 'prohibiting forever, under pain of death, membership of any anti foreign society', the punishment of the perpetrators (article 2) and the erection of monuments to the murdered diplomats and expressions of regret (articles 1, 3 and 4); the occupation of strategic points by the allies between Peking and the sea (article 9) and the distruction of the Taku forts (article 8).

The continued Russian occupation of Manchuria after the relief of the foreign legations in Peking caused increasing Russo–Japanese tension; Japan and Russia were also locked in rivalry over the domination of Korea. The *Anglo–Japanese Alliance, 30 January 1902* (p. 54) assured Japan that if she fought Russia, she need not again fear facing a coalition of European powers alone; according to article 2, Britain and Japan would remain neutral if either power became involved 'in the defence of their respective interests; Japan's and Britain's special interests in China were designated in article 1 as were those of Japan' 'in a peculiar degree politically as well as commercially and industrially in Korea'. If another power or powers should join in hostilities against the ally, then Britain or Japan would assist militarily and make peace in common (article 3). *The Russo–Japanese War, 8 February 1904 to 5 September 1905*, profoundly altered the balance of power in the Pacific and China. President Theodore Roosevelt offered his mediation by the *Treaty of Portsmouth, New Hampshire, 5 September 1905* (p. 56). Russia and Japan agreed on peace terms; Russia recognized Japan's predominance in Korea; Russia's leasehold and all concessions in Liaotung were transferred to Japan and Russia agreed to withdraw from Manchuria. Russia also ceded to Japan the southern half of Sakhalin Island. Japan promised to observe the Open Door policy in China, a concession on which the United States insisted.

The Anglo–Japanese alliance was a major element in eastern Asia's international relations for twenty years. On *12 August 1905, the Anglo–Japanese Treaty of 1902 was 'replaced' by a new treaty*. This extended the aim to 'the consolidation and maintenance of the general peace in the regions of Eastern Asia and India'; the preservation of common interests of all powers in China 'by insuring the independence and integrity of the Chinese Empire' and equal commercial opportunities of all nations in China; 'the maintenance of the territorial rights of the High Contracting Parties in the regions of Eastern Asia and of India, and the defence of their special interests in the said regions'. The most significant change from the 1902 treaty was that if either Britain or Japan became involved in war with a *single* power in defence of the interests above 'by reason of unprovoked attack or aggressive action', the other would join the war unilaterally to assist their ally (article 2); Japan's paramountcy in Korea was recognized (article 3), and Britain's right on India's frontier 'to take such measures as she may find necessary for safeguarding her Indian possessions' (article 4); during a war between Japan and Russia, Britain would observe neutrality unless another power joined Russia against Japan (article 6); the treaty was to remain in force for ten years (article 8).

The alliance was renewed prematurely on 13 July 1911, for a further ten years. The original purpose of the alliance, protection from Russia of Britain's and Japan's interests in China and on the Indian frontier, was eroded during the decade after 1911 and replaced by Japan's ambitions in China which became a threat to British interests. But Britain's naval weakness in the Far East, the First World War and the force of historic ties, kept the alliance alive despite Japan's assertiveness in China. Increasing difficulty was caused by tension between the United States and Japan, over Japan's China policy, the potential of Japan's threat to the Philippines and America's racial exclusion policies. Britain made it clear that the provisions of the alliance to assist militarily did not apply in the event of a war between Japan and the United States. In the 1911 treaty this was provided for by the novel article 4, which excluded the obligation to go to war against a country with which 'either of the High Contracting Parties conclude a treaty of general arbitration'; although the United States was not specified, the article was intended to apply to the General Arbitration treaty being negotiated by Britain with the United States. *The Knox-Bryce Arbitration Treaty was concluded on 3 August 1911*. Requiring the ratification of the US Senate, it lapsed in March 1912 when the Senate's amendments proved unacceptable. Despite British efforts to renew the Anglo–Japanese alliance treaty in 1921, the opposition of the United States to it and Britain's desire to conclude a naval disarmament treaty which would include the United States and Japan, led to its demise and replacement by the *Four Power Treaty, 13 December 1921* (p. 136). It was agreed in the Four Power Treaty that the Anglo–Japanese alliance would end when ratifications were deposited in Washington. Although in practice defunct in December 1921, ratifications were exchanged only on 17 August 1923.

The United States had taken an interest in and conducted trade with China from the earliest days of the foundation of the republic. The American role as a significant colonial power in the Pacific, however, dated from the last years of the nineteenth century. Hawaii was annexed in August 1898, Guam and the

Philippines, when the *Treaty of Paris, which ended the Spanish-American-Cuban War of 1898, was ratified by the US Senate on 6 February 1899*. The danger of an imminent partition of China and American desire to preserve her trade led Secretary of State John Hay to send the *'Open Door Notes' to Britain, Russia, Germany, France and Japan, 6–17 November 1899*; these were followed by a *Circular on 3 July 1900* which was of great significance as it linked trade with American support for the integrity of China; it stated, 'The policy of the Government of the United States is to seek a solution which may bring about permanent safety and peace to China, preserve Chinese territorial and administrative entity, protect all rights guaranteed to friendly powers by treaty and international law, and safeguard for the world the principle of equal and impartial trade with all parts of the Chinese Empire.' Only Britain, France and Germany responded favourably.

America's weakness in the Pacific and the vulnerability of the Philippines induced the United States, despite underlying tensions and fears of war, to make expedient concessions to Japan in the *Taft-Katsura Memorandum, 29 July 1905* which conceded to Japan a free hand in Korea in return for a Japanese declaration that she had no aggressive designs on the Philippines. This was followed by an *Exchange of Notes on the Root-Takahira Agreement, 30 November 1908*, promising to maintain the 'existing status quo' in the region of the Pacific Ocean; to respect each other's territorial possessions; 'to preserve the common interests of all Powers in China, by supporting, by all pacific means at their disposal, the independence and integrity of China and the principle of equal opportunity for commerce and industry of all nations in that Empire'; if the status quo were threatened, the two governments would consult as to the useful measures to be taken. As only action by 'peaceful means' was referred to, the United States did not promise to defend China by military means; furthermore, Japan's territorial rights secured after the Russo–Japanese war were not challenged; the agreement did not refer to the 'territorial' integrity of China and the preservation of status quo was geographically linked to the 'region of the Pacific Ocean' and not the Chinese mainland. It represented a measure of American appeasement of Japanese ambitions in mainland Asia before the First World War.

Anglo–Japanese Alliance, 30 January 1902

The Governments of Great Britain and Japan, actuated solely by a desire to maintain the *status quo* and general peace in the extreme East, being, moreover, specially interested in maintaining the independence and territorial integrity of the Empire of China and the Empire of Corea, and in securing equal opportunities in those countries for the commerce and industry of all nations, hereby agree as follows: –

Article I. The High Contracting Parties having mutually recognized the independence of China and of Corea, declare themselves to be entirely uninfluenced by any aggressive tendencies in either country. Having in view, however, their special interests, of which those of Great Britain relate principally to China, while Japan, in addition to the interests which she possesses in China, is interested in a peculiar degree politically as well as commercially and industrially in Corea, the High Contracting Parties recognize that it will be admissible for either of them to take such measures as may be indispensable in order to safeguard those interests if threatened either by the aggressive action of any other Power, or by disturbances arising in China or Corea, and necessitating the intervention of either of the High Contracting Parties for the protection of the lives and property of its subjects.

Article II. If either Great Britain or Japan, in the defence of their respective interests as above described, should become involved in war with another Power, the other High Contracting Party will maintain a strict neutrality, and use its efforts to prevent other Powers from joining in hostilities against its ally.

Article III. If, in the above event, any other Power or Powers should join in hostilities against that ally, the other High Contracting Party will come to its assistance, and will conduct the war in common, and make peace in mutual agreement with it.

Article IV. The High Contracting Parties agree that neither of them will, without consulting the other, enter into separate arrangements with another Power to the prejudice of the interests above described.

Article V. Whenever, in the opinion of either Great Britain or Japan, the above-mentioned interests are in jeopardy, the two Governments will communicate with one another fully and frankly.

Article VI. The present Agreement shall come into effect immediately after the date of its signature, and remain in force for five years from that date.

In case neither of the High Contracting Parties should have notified twelve months before the expiration of the said five years the intention of terminating it, it shall remain binding until the expiration of one year from the day on which either of the High Contracting Parties shall have denounced it. But if, when the date fixed for its expiration arrives, either ally is actually engaged in war, the alliance shall, *ipso facto*, continue until peace is concluded.

Notes exchanged between the two Governments, January 30, 1902

Sir,

M. le Marquis,

IN reference to the Agreement concluded by us to-day on behalf of our respective Governments, I have the honour to inform you that the British/Japanese Government recognizes that the naval forces of Great Britain/Japan should, so far as possible, act in concert with those of Japan/Great Britain in time of peace, and agrees that mutual facilities shall be given for the docking and coaling of vessels of war of one country in the ports of the other, as well as other advantages conducing to the welfare and efficacy of the respective navies of the two Powers.

At the present moment Japan and Great Britain are each of them maintaining in the Extreme East a naval force superior in strength to that of any third Power. Great Britain/Japan has no intention of relaxing her efforts to maintain, so far as may be possible, available for concentration in the waters of the extreme East, a naval force superior to that of any third Power.

Treaty of Peace Between Japan and Russia, Portsmouth, New Hampshire, 5 September 1905

[translated from French version]

Article I. There shall henceforth be peace and amity between their Majesties the Emperor of Japan and the Emperor of all the Russias, and between their respective States and subjects.

Article II. The Imperial Russian Government, acknowledging that Japan possesses in Korea paramount political, military and economic interests, engages neither to obstruct nor to interfere with measures for guidance, protection and control which the Imperial Government of Japan may find necessary to take in Korea. It is understood that Russian subjects in Korea shall be treated in exactly the same manner as the subjects and citizens of other foreign Powers; that is to say, they shall be placed on the same footing as the subjects and citizens of the most favored nation. It is also agreed that, in order to avoid causes of misunderstanding, the two high contracting parties will abstain on the Russian-Korean frontier from taking any military measure which may menace the security of Russian or Korean territory.

Article III. Japan and Russia mutually engage: First. – To evacuate completely and simultaneously Manchuria, except the territory affected by the lease of the Liaotung Peninsula, in conformity with the provisions of the additional article I annexed to this treaty, and, Second.—To restore entirely and completely to the exclusive administration of China all portions of Manchuria now in occupation or under the control of the Japanese or Russian troops, with the exception of the territory above mentioned.

The Imperial Government of Russia declares that it has not in Manchuria any territorial advantages or preferential or exclusive concessions that impair the sovereignty of China or that are inconsistent with the principle of equal opportunity.

Article IV. Japan and Russia reciprocally engage not to obstruct any general measures common to all countries which China

may take for the development of the commerce or industry of Manchuria.

Article V. The Imperial Russian Government transfers and assigns to the Imperial Government of Japan, with the consent of the Government of China, the lease of Port Arthur, Talien [Dairen] and the adjacent territorial waters, and all rights, privileges and concessions connected with or forming part of such lease, and it also transfers and assigns to the Imperial Government of Japan all public works and properties in the territory affected by the above-mentioned lease.

The two contracting parties mutually engage to obtain the consent of the Chinese Government mentioned in the foregoing stipulation. The Imperial Government of Japan, on its part, undertakes that the property rights of Russian subjects in the territory above referred to shall be perfectly respected.

Article VI. The Imperial Russian Government engages to transfer and assign to the Imperial Government of Japan, without compensation and with the consent of the Chinese Government, the railway between Changchun and Port Arthur, and all the branches, together with all the rights, privileges and properties appertaining thereto in that region, as well as all the coal mines in said region belonging to or worked for the benefit of the railway. The two high contracting parties mutually engage to obtain the consent of the Government of China mentioned in the foregoing stipulation.

Article VII. Japan and Russia engage to exploit their respective railways in Manchuria exclusively for commercial and industrial purposes and not for strategic purposes. It is understood that this restrictiction does not apply to the railway in the territory affected by the lease of the Liaotung Peninsula.

Article VIII. The Imperial Governments of Japan and Russia with a view to promoting and facilitating intercourse and traffic will as soon as possible conclude a separate convention for the regulation of their connecting railway services in Manchuria.

Article IX. The Imperial Russian Government cedes to the Imperial Government of Japan in perpetuity and full sovereignty the southern portion of the Island of Sakhalin and all the islands adjacent thereto and the public works and properties thereon. The fiftieth degree of north latitude is adopted as the northern boundary of the ceded territory. The exact alignment of such territory shall be determined in accordance with the provisions of the additional article II annexed to this treaty.

Japan and Russia mutually agree not to construct in their respective possessions on the Island of Sakhalin or the adjacent islands any fortification or other similar military works. [. . .]

Article X. Russian subjects, inhabitants of the territory ceded to Japan, retain the right to sell their real property and return to their country, but if they prefer to remain in the ceded territory they will maintain protection of the full exercise of their industries and rights of property on condition of submitting to the Japanese laws and jurisdiction. Japan shall have full liberty to withdraw the right of residence in or to deport from such territory any inhabitants under political or administrative disability. She engages, however, that the property rights of such inhabitants shall be fully respected.

Article XI. [Fishing rights]

Article XII. [Commercial relations]

Article XIII. [Exchange of prisoners of war]

Article XIV. [Ratification]

Article XV. [Both English and French versions signed. French version to be authoritative in case of dispute.]

Sub-articles. In conformity with the provisions of articles 3 and 9 of the treaty of the peace between Japan and Russia of this date the undersigned plenipotentiaries have concluded the following additional articles:

Sub-article to Article III. The Imperial Governments of Japan and Russia mutually engage to commence the withdrawal of their military forces from the territory of Manchuria simultaneously and immediately after the treaty of peace comes into operation, and within a period of eighteen months after that date the armies of the two countries shall be completely withdrawn from Manchuria, except from the leased territory of the Liaotung Peninsula. The forces of the two countries occupying the front positions shall first be withdrawn.

The high contracting parties reserve to themselves the right to maintain guards to protect their respective railway lines in Manchuria. The number of such guards shall not exceed fifteen per kilometre and within that maximum number the commanders of the Japanese and Russian armies shall by common accord fix the number of such guards to be employed as small as possible while having in view the actual requirements.

The commanders of the Japanese and Russian forces in Manchuria shall agree upon the details of the evacuation in conformity with the above principles and shall take by common accord the measures necessary to carry out the evacuation as soon as possible, and in any case not later than the period of eighteen months.

Sub-article to Article IX. [Committee of delimitation for frontier on island of Sakhalin.]

The foregoing additional articles are to be considered ratified with the ratification of the treaty of peace to which they are annexed.

In witness whereof the respective plenipotentiaries have signed and affixed seals to the present treaty of peace.

Done at Portsmouth, New Hampshire, this fifth day of the ninth month of the thirty-eighth year of the Meijei, corresponding to the twenty-third day of August, one thousand nine hundred and five, (September 5, 1905.)

SERGEI WITTE
[Baron] ROSEN
JUTARO KOMURA
K. TAKAHIRA

The emergence of the United States as a world power

The Cuban-Spanish-American War of 1898 marked a significant stage in the emergence of the United States as a world power. US imperialism followed the classical path of expansion by strengthening her power in the Caribbean to keep out the imperialist European nations. *The Peace Treaty of Paris was ratified by the US Senate on 6 February 1899;* Cuba became a Protectorate of the United States and Puerto Rico passed into US possession. Outside the western hemisphere, Hawaii was annexed, and Guam and the Philippines passed into US possession. Possession of the Philippines far from strengthening US defence weakened the United States, unable to defend the Philippines if Japan chose to attack them.

In the Caribbean the United States after the war with Spain consolidated her position in Cuba by the *Platt Amendment, 2 March 1901* which provided for the intervention of the United States in Cuba for the preservation of Cuban independence, the maintenance of government adequate 'for the protection of life, property, and individual liberty'; the United States for its defence as well as that of Cuba established a naval base permanently at Guantánamo at the eastern tip of the island; Cuba was turned into a virtual US protectorate until Castro's overthrow of the pro-American dictator Batista in 1959. The United States was also determined to control the canal to be constructed across the central American Isthmus. The *Second Hay–Pauncefote Treaty with Britain was concluded on 18 November 1901 and an on 21 February 1902 the Senate ratified it* (p. 59). Britain gave up her rights under the Clayton–Bulwer Treaty of 1850, and agreed to the USA constructing and controlling the future isthmian canal under rules of neutrality on the model of the Suez Canal Convention of 1888. When Colombia failed to ratify a treaty granting the US full control over the strip of territory through which the canal was to pass *(Hay–Herrán Treaty, 22 January 1903)*, President Theodore Roosevelt intervened in Panama, recognized the revolutionary government on *18 November 1903, a new Canal Treaty*, the *Hay-Bunau-Varilla Treaty* granted to the United States in 'perpetuity' virtual sovereignty over the future canal zone for ten miles each side of the canal. The US Senate ratified the treaty on 23 February 1904.

United States claims to predominance in the Caribbean were asserted during the Venezuelan crisis in 1902, and US interventions occurred in the Dominican Republic, Haiti, Nicaragua and Mexico; the Danish West Indies (subsequently known as the US Virgin Islands) were purchased in 1917 for twenty-five million dollars.

In the Pacific, the United States sought to maintain both the Open Door to her trade in China and enunciated as its aim the territorial integrity of China; with Japan, the United States sought accommodation.

Towards the European powers, the United States before 1917 sought non-involvement in confrontations and war and maintained the principle of the freedom of the seas while building a large navy 'second to none'. Disputes with Britain and Canada were settled by arbitration treaties.

Treaty between Great Britain and the United States concerning the Trans-Isthmian Ship Canal between the Atlantic and Pacific Ocean 18 November 1901, ratified 21 February 1902 (Hay–Pauncefote Treaty)

Article I. The High Contracting Parties agree that the present Treaty shall supersede the afore-mentioned Convention of the 19th April, 1850. [Clayton–Bulwer]

II. It is agreed that the canal may be constructed under the auspices of the Government of the United States, either directly at its own cost, or by gift or loan of money to individuals or Corporations, or through subscription to or purchase of stock or shares, and that, subject to the provisions of the present Treaty, the said Government shall have and enjoy all the rights incident to such construction, as well as the exclusive right of providing for the regulation and management of the canal.

III. The United States adopts, as the basis of the neutralization of such ship-canal, the following Rules, substantially as embodied in the Convention of Constantinople, signed the 29th October, 1888, for the free navigation of the Suez Canal, that is to say:—

1. The canal shall be free and open to the vessels of commerce and of war of all nations observing these Rules, on terms of entire equality, so that there shall be no discrimination against any such nation, or its citizens or subjects, in respect of the conditions or charges of traffic or otherwise. Such conditions and charges of traffic shall be just and equitable.

2. The canal shall never be blockaded, nor shall any right of war be exercised nor any act of hostility be committed within it.

The United States, however, shall be at liberty to maintain such military police along the canal as may be necessary to protect it against lawlessness and disorder.

3. Vessels of war of a belligerent shall not revictual nor take any stores in the canal except so far as may be strictly necessary; and the transit of such vessels through the canal shall be effected with the least possible delay in accordance with the Regulations in force, and with only such intermission as may result from the necessities of the service.

Prizes shall be in all respects subject to the same Rules as vessels of war of the belligerents.

4. No belligerent shall embark or disembark troops, munitions of war, or warlike materials in the canal, except in case of accidental hindrance of the transit, and in such case the transit shall be resumed with all possible dispatch.

5. The provisions of this Article shall apply to waters adjacent to the canal, within three marine miles of either end. Vessels of war of a belligerent shall not remain in such waters longer than twenty-four hours at any one time except in case of distress, and in such case shall depart as soon as possible; but a vessel of war of one belligerent shall not depart within twenty-four hours from the departure of a vessel of war of the other belligerent.

6. The plant, establishments, buildings, and all work necessary to the construction,

maintenance, and operation of the canal shall be deemed to be part thereof, for the purposes of this Treaty, and in time of war, as in time of peace, shall enjoy complete immunity from attack or injury by belligerents, and from acts calculated to impair their usefulness as part of the canal.

IV. It is agreed that no change of territorial sovereignty or of the international relations of the country or countries traversed by the before-mentioned canal shall affect the general principle of neutralization or the obligation of the High Contracting Parties under the present Treaty.

[*V. Ratification*]

II · Secret agreements and treaties of the First World War

The outbreak of the First World War in August 1914 violated more than Belgian neutrality. The majority of the great territorial settlements of the nineteenth century, embodied in international treaties since 1815, were jeopardized. During the war international treaties ceased to be respected and the belligerents engaged in fierce bargaining to gain allies and to assure for themselves a favourable territorial settlement when the war was won. Each of the powers at war had vague and shifting 'war aims' often motivated by immediate military needs. Diplomacy in wartime was designed to support the military effort, to strengthen existing alliances and to make new allies. Secret agreements and undertakings between several allies or between one state and another were made throughout the war. They were sometimes inconsistent and could not all be reconciled with each other when the war ended, leaving a bitter legacy of dispute to the post-war world. Nor did any one state have full knowledge of the secret bargains that had been struck.

In the actual declaration of war, as distinct from mobilizations, the Central Powers took the initiative. Austria-Hungary declared war on Serbia on 28 July 1914. Germany declared war on Russia on 1 August, and on France on 3 August. The German invasion of Belgium on 4 August was followed by a British ultimatum and a British declaration of war on Germany on 4 August 1914.

Austria-Hungary remained at peace with Russia after Germany's declaration of war and was only prevailed upon to declare war on Russia on 6 August 1914. France and Britain declared war on Austria-Hungary on 12 August. Portugal declared its adherence to the British alliance in the autumn of 1914 and commenced military operations against Germany. Thus only in mid-August were the Central Powers – Austria-Hungary and Germany – at war with all the Allied *Entente* – France, Britain and Russia.

Japan did not join the grand alliance of Russia, Britain and France. It sent its own ultimatum to Germany on 15 August 1914 and declared war when it expired, basing its action on the Anglo–Japanese alliance. Japan did share one treaty in common with all the *Entente* Powers when on 19 October 1915 the Japanese government signed the *Declaration of London*, which had been concluded between Russia, France and Britain on 5 September 1914. This declaration stipulated that none of the signatories would conclude peace separately or demand conditions of peace without the previous agreement of the other signatories.

Italy, with Germany and Austria-Hungary, was a member of the Triple Alliance (last renewed in 1912) but declared its neutrality on 3 August 1914. Italy's obligations according to articles 2 and 3 of the Triple Alliance required Italy to fight in case of unprovoked aggression by France on Germany. This, the Italian government concluded, had not occurred since Germany had declared war on France. Moreover, in August 1914 the Italian government claimed that Austria-Hungary had not acted in accordance with article 7 of the Triple Alliance treaty when deciding to attack Serbia, for this article required previous consultation and agreement between Italy and Austria-Hungary based on reciprocal compensations.

The Central Powers, 1914–18

Germany secured a hasty secret alliance with *Turkey on 2 August 1914* (p. 63). It stipulated that the two powers would remain neutral in the conflict between Austria-Hungary and Serbia; but that if Russia intervened with active military measures Germany would intervene on the side of Austria-Hungary and the alliance with Turkey would become active. The German military mission was to exercise in the event of war an 'effective influence' over the Turkish army, and Germany undertook to defend Ottoman territory if it were threatened. Turkey did not enter the war straight away but took a number of steps against the *Entente* Powers: two German warships were sheltered and transferred to the Turkish navy in August, and on 26 September the Straits were closed, thus cutting the supply route to Russia. By the end of October 1914 Turkey actively entered the war on the side of Germany and Austria-Hungary and began operations against Russia. A new alliance was signed by Turkey and Germany in January 1915 and Austria-Hungary adhered to it in March 1915.

Bulgaria was induced in September 1915 to join the war on the side of Germany and Austria-Hungary by the promise of large territorial gains including Serbian Macedonia and a substantial grant of money. On *6 September 1915 Bulgaria signed a military agreement and an alliance treaty with Germany and Austria-Hungary* to join in a military offensive against Serbia, and in mid-October 1915 Bulgaria started fighting in accordance with this treaty.

Secret Treaty of Alliance between Germany and the Ottoman Empire, 2 August 1914

Article 1. The two Contracting Powers undertake to observe strict neutrality in the present conflict between Austria-Hungary and Serbia.

Article 2. In the event that Russia should intervene with active military measures and thus should create for Germany a *casus foederis* with respect to Austria-Hungary, this *casus foederis* would also come into force for Turkey.

Article 3. In the event of war, Germany will leave its Military Mission at the disposal of Turkey.
The latter, for its part, assures the said Military Mission effective influence over the general conduct of the army, in conformity with what has been agreed upon directly by His Excellency the Minister of War and His Excellency the Chief of the Military Mission.

Article 4. Germany obligates itself, by force of arms if need be, to defend Ottoman territory in case it should be threatened.

Article 5. This Agreement, which has been concluded with a view to protecting the two Empires from the international complications which may result from the present conflict, enters into force at the time of its signing by the above-mentioned plenipotentiaries and shall remain valid, with any analogous mutual agreements, until 31 December 1918.

[…]

[*Article 8.* The treaty to be secret unless signatories agree otherwise.]

The Allied and Associated Powers, 1914–18

Despite Italy's treaty engagement as a member of the Triple Alliance to remain benevolently neutral and not make alliances with the enemies of Germany and Austria-Hungary, Italy accepted the inducements of the Allies to join the war on their side. The promises of territorial expansion after the war held out to Italy were contained in the secret *Treaty of London, 26 April 1915* (p. 64). Italy was promised territory at the expense of the Austrian-Hungarian Empire, the Trentino, the South Tyrol, Istria and a third of Dalmatia, the sovereignty of the Dodecanese Islands which Italy already occupied, as well as a 'just share' of the Ottoman Empire in Asia in the event of its partial or total partition, taking into account Italy's special position in the province of Adalia. Italy was also promised compensation for British and French gains at the expense of Germany's colonies. On 23 May 1915 Italy declared war on Austria-Hungary.

Roumania, despite its treaty relations with Germany and Austria-Hungary before the war, also changed sides and abandoned neutrality in favour of joining the Allies. By *a secret treaty between Roumania, Britain, France, Italy and Russia signed on 17 August 1916* Roumania undertook to declare war and to attack Austria-Hungary and not to conclude a separate peace. Roumania was promised portions of Austria-Hungary, Transylvania, the Bukovina and Banat. But the value of these promises was made doubtful by a secret exchange of notes between Russia, Italy, France and Britain that Roumania's promised territorial gains would be granted only so far as the general situation at the end of the war allowed. In the event, the Allies were spared embarrassment, for by Roumania's separate peace signed at Bucharest on 7 May 1917 Roumania forfeited alliance claims.

The most important of the 'Associated Powers' entering the war during the first week of April 1917, side by side with the allied powers, was the United States. Germany had resumed unrestricted submarine warfare on 1 February 1917. President Wilson asked Congress on 2 April 1917 to recognize formally that a state of war existed between the United States and Germany. The House of Representatives passed a resolution for war and the Senate also on 6 April 1917. The United States declared war on Austria-Hungary several months later on 7 December 1917. In Europe, Greece was finally brought into the war by the Allies on their side on 2 July 1917 after they had blockaded the Greek coast and forced the abdication of King Constantine. China declared a state of war with Germany and Austria-Hungary in August 1917, thus complicating the intended settlement of Japanese claims at the expense of China.

Agreement between France, Russia, Britain and Italy (Treaty of London), 26 April 1915

Article I. A military convention shall be immediately concluded between the General Staffs of France, Great Britain, Italy and Russia. This convention shall settle the minimum number of military forces to be employed by Russia against Austria-Hungary in order to prevent that Power from concentrating all its strength against Italy, in the event of Russia deciding to direct her principal effort against Germany.

This military convention shall settle question of armistices, which necessarily comes within the scope of the Commanders-in-chief of the Armies.

Article 2. On her part, Italy undertakes to use her entire resources for the purpose of waging war jointly with France, Great Britain and Russia against all their enemies.

Article 3. The French and British fleets shall render active and permanent assistance to Italy until such time as the Austro-Hungarian fleet shall have been destroyed or until peace shall have been concluded.

A naval convention shall be immediately concluded to this effect between France, Great Britain and Italy.

Article 4. Under the Treaty of Peace, Italy shall obtain the Trentino, Cisalpine Tyrol with its geographical and natural frontier (the Brenner frontier), as well as Trieste, the counties of Gorizia and Gradisca, all Istria as far as the Quarnero and including Volosca and the Istrian islands of Cherso and Lussin, as well as the small islands of Plavnik, Unie, Canidole, Palazzuoli, San Pietro di Nembi, Asinello, Gruica, and the neighbouring islets . . . [frontier details]

Article 5. Italy shall also be given the province of Dalmatia within its present administrative boundaries, including to the north . . . [frontier details]

NOTE: The following Adriatic territory shall be assigned by the four Allied Powers to Croatia, Serbia and Montenegro:

In the Upper Adriatic, the whole coast from the bay of Volosca on the borders of

Istria as far as the northern frontier of Dalmatia, including the coast which is at present Hungarian and all the coast of Croatia, with the port of Fiume and the small ports of Novi and Carlopago, as well as the islands of Veglia, Pervichio, Gregorio, Goli and Arbe. And, in the Lower Adriatic (in the region interesting Serbia and Montenegro) the whole coast from Cape Planka as far as the River Drin, with the important harbours of Spalato, Ragusa, Cattaro, Antivari, Dulcigno and St Jean de Medua and the islands of Greater and Lesser Zirona, Bua, Solta, Brazza, Jaclian and Calamotta. The port of Durazzo to be assigned to the independent Moslem State of Albania.

Article 6. Italy shall receive full sovereignty over Valona, the islands of Saseno and surrounding territory of sufficient extent to assure defence of these points ... [frontier details]

Article 7. Should Italy obtain the Trentino and Istria in accordance with the provisions of Article 4, together with Dalmatia and the Adriatic islands within the limits specified in Article 5, and the Bay of Valona (Article 6), and if the central portion of Albania is reserved for the establishment of a small autonomous neutralized State, Italy shall not oppose the division of Northern and Southern Albania between Montenegro, Serbia and Greece, should France, Great Britain and Russia so desire. The coast from the southern boundary of the Italian territory of Valona (see Article 6) up to Cape Stylos shall be neutralized.

Italy shall be charged with the representation of the State of Albania in its relations with foreign Powers.

Italy agrees, moreover, to leave sufficient territory in any event to the east of Albania to ensure the existence of a frontier line between Greece and Serbia to the west of Lake Ochrida.

Article 8. Italy shall receive entire sovereignty over the Dodecanese Islands which she is at present occupying.

Article 9. Generally speaking, France, Great Britain and Russia recognize that Italy is interested in the maintenance of the balance of power in the Mediterranean and that, in the event of the total or partial partition of Turkey in Asia, she ought to obtain a just share of the Mediterranean region adjacent to the province of Adalia, where Italy has already acquired rights and interests which formed the subject of an Italo-British convention. The zone which shall eventually be allotted to Italy shall be delimited, at the proper time, due account being taken of the existing interests of France and Great Britain.

The interests of Italy shall also be taken into consideration in the event of the territorial integrity of the Turkish Empire being maintained and of alterations being made in the zones of interest of the Powers.

If France, Great Britain and Russia occupy any territories in Turkey in Asia during the course of the war, the Mediterranean region bordering on the Province of Adalia within the limits indicated above shall be reserved to Italy, who shall be entitled to occupy it.

Article 10. All rights and privileges in Libya at present belonging to the Sultan by virtue of the Treaty of Lausanne are transferred to Italy.

Article 11. Italy shall receive a share of any eventual war indemnity corresponding to her efforts and her sacrifices.

Article 12. Italy declares that she associates herself in the declaration made by France, Great Britain and Russia to the effect that Arabia and the Moslem Holy Places in Arabia shall be left under the authority of an independent Moslem Power.

Article 13. In the event of France and Great Britain increasing their colonial territories in Africa at the expense of Germany, those two Powers agree in principle that Italy may claim some equitable compensation, particularly as regards the settlement in her favour of the questions relative to the frontiers of the Italian colonies of Eritrea, Somaliland and Libya and the neighbouring colonies belonging to France and Great Britain.

Article 14. Great Britain undertakes to facilitate the immediate conclusion, under equitable conditions, of a loan of at least £50,000,000, to be issued on the London market.

Article 15. France, Great Britain and Russia shall support such opposition as Italy may make to any proposal in the direction of introducing a representative of the Holy See in any peace negotiations or negotiations for the settlement of questions raised by the present war.

Article 16. The present arrangement shall be held secret. The adherence of Italy to the Declaration of the 5th September 1914 shall alone be made public, immediately upon declaration of war by or against Italy.

After having taken act of the foregoing memorandum the representatives of France, Great Britain and Russia, duly authorized to that effect, have concluded the following agreement with the representative of Italy, also duly authorized by his Government:

France, Great Britain and Russia give their full assent to the memorandum presented by the Italian Government.

With reference to Articles 1, 2, and 3 of the memorandum which provide for military and naval cooperation between the four Powers, Italy declares that she will take the field at the earliest possible date and within a period not exceeding one month from the signature of these present . . .

[Signed] E. GREY, IMPERIALI, BENCKENDORFF, PAUL CAMBON.

Declaration by which France, Great Britain, Italy and Russia undertake not to conclude a separate peace during the course of the present European war

The Italian Government, having decided to participate in the present war with the French, British and Russian Governments, and to accede to the Declaration made at London, the 5th September 1914, by the three above-named Governments.

The undersigned, being duly authorized by their respective Governments, make the following declaration:

The French, British, Italian and Russian Governments mutually undertake not to conclude a separate peace during the course of the present war.

The four Governments agree that, whenever there may be occasion to discuss the terms of peace, none of the Allied Powers shall lay down any conditions of peace without previous agreement with each of the other Allies.

Declaration

The Declaration of the 26th April 1915, whereby France, Great Britain, Italy and Russia undertake not to conclude a separate peace during the present European war, shall remain secret.

After the declaration of war by or against Italy, the four Powers shall sign a new declaration in identical terms, which shall thereupon be made public.

The Ottoman Empire

The Allied Powers jointly and individually concluded a number of wartime treaties, agreements and understandings concerning the future of the Ottoman Empire. They proved impossible to reconcile when the war ended. Russia was promised Constantinople and the Straits at the time of the negotiations with Italy which had led to the *Treaty of London, 26 April 1915* (p. 64). An exchange of several diplomatic notes between Russia, Britain and France during March and April 1915 set out the attitude of the Allies: a *Russian Circular Telegram to France and Britain, 4 March 1915* (p. 68) contained extensive Russian demands for the annexation by Russia of Constantinople, the Straits, part of southern Thrace and part of the Adriatic shore. British replies in two *aides-mémoire*, both dated 12 March 1915, agreed in principle to the Russian acquisition of Constantinople and the Straits but made this dependent on a number of conditions, including some counter-concessions to Britain in the Ottoman Empire and Persia. The French reply in a note on 10 April 1915 agreed to the Russian proposal 'relating to Constantinople and the Straits', provided war was fought until victory and provided France and Britain realized their plans in the East and elsewhere. These conditional promises to Russia lapsed as Allied obligations when Russia concluded a separate armistice and peace with Germany in December 1917 and March 1918.

In the Ottoman Empire in Asia and the Middle East the Allies had made a number of promises to various factions, and came to agreements with each other which laid Britain and France open to charges of bad faith when engaged in peace-making from 1919 to 1923. Irreconcilable claims were embittered further when each party attempted to rely on wartime promises and undertakings. In April 1915 the secret *Treaty of London* between Italy, France, Russia and Britain (p. 68), as it applied to the Ottoman Empire, promised Italy the Dodecanese Islands and a share of the Mediterranean region of Anatolia adjacent to and including the province of Adalia. From *July 1915 to March 1916, Sir Henry McMahon, High Commissioner in Egypt, exchanged ten letters with the Sherif of Mecca* (p. 70) to encourage an Arab revolt against Ottoman rule; in return McMahon promised that the British would recognize and support the independence of the Arabs in regions demanded by the Sherif of Mecca, with some major reservations – the Mediterranean coastal strip west of Damascus, Hama, Homs and Aleppo (later Lebanon and the coastal region of French-mandated Syria) – and only in those areas where Britain was free to act without detriment to the interests of her ally, France. British interests required the Arabs to recognize Britain's special position in the provinces of Baghdad and Basra. The correspondence left the political area of Arab independence indefinite and ambiguous. Certain regions were excluded with some precision by their special mention, but Palestine was not specifically mentioned. In other regions the Arabs could assume support for independence, but the proviso that French interests would be taken into account by Britain left a very elastic loophole. The correspondence would lead the Arabs to suppose that Palestine would form part of the territory of Arab independence. But the promise to the Zionists contained in the *Balfour Declaration, 2 November 1917* (p. 75) of a 'national home for the Jewish people' could not easily be reconciled with Arab sovereignty in Palestine.

A tripartite agreement for the partition of the Ottoman Empire in Asia was worked out between France, Britain and Russia in exchanges of notes from April to October 1916, and is known as the *Sykes–Picot Agreement* (p. 71). The agreement created French and British spheres of interest; an 'independent' Arab state was foreseen as falling within French and British spheres of interest. In other specified regions more direct French and British administration was foreseen. Palestine became an international sphere of interest. The Russians sanctioned the Anglo-French partition, and in return France and Britain permitted Russian annexation in Turkish Armenia and Kurdistan. The secret Sykes–Picot Agreement was published by the Bolshevik government after the Russian revolution. The tripartite British, French, Italian *Agreement at St Jean de Maurienne, 19 April 1917* (p. 74) assigned to Italy a large region including Adalia and Smyrna for Italian administration, and a further zone of Italian influence to the north. This agreement, subject to Russia's consent, could only have been enforced on a completely prostrate Turkey and was incompatible with Greek and French ambitions in Asia Minor. In fact no effort was made to enforce it after 1919.

Secret Agreements between Russia, France and Britain concerning the Straits and Constantinople, 4 March–10 April 1915

Russian Memorandum to French and British Governments, 4 March 1915

The course of recent events leads His Majesty Emperor Nicholas to think that the question of Constantinople and of the Straits must be definitively solved, according to the time-honoured aspirations of Russia.

Every solution will be inadequate and precarious if the city of Constantinople, the western bank of the Bosphorus, of the Sea of Marmara and of the Dardanelles, as well as southern Thrace to the Enez-Midye line, should henceforth not be incorporated into the Russian Empire.

Similarly, and by strategic necessity, that part of the Asiatic shore that lies between the Bosphorus, the Sakarya River and a point to be determined on the Gulf of Izmit, and the islands of the Sea of Marmara, the Imbros Islands and the Tenedos Islands must be incorporated into the [Russian] Empire.

The special interests of France and of Great Britain in the above region will be scrupulously respected.

The Imperial Government entertains the hope that the above considerations will be sympathetically received by the two Allied Governments. The said Allied Governments are assured similar understanding on the part of the Imperial Government for the realization of plans which they may frame with reference to other regions of the Ottoman Empire or elsewhere.

British Memorandum to Russian Government, 12 March 1915

Subject to the war being carried on and brought to a successful conclusion, and to the desiderata of Great Britain and France in the Ottoman Empire and elsewhere being realized, as indicated in the Russian communication herein referred to, His Majesty's Government will agree to the Russian Government's *aide-mémoire* relative to Constantinople and the Straits, the text of which was communicated to His Britannic Majesty's Ambassador by his Excellency M. Sazonof on February 19th/March 4th instant.

British Memorandum (a comment on earlier memorandum) to Russian Government, 12 March 1915

His Majesty's Ambassador has been instructed to make the following observations with reference to the *aide-mémoire* which this Embassy had the honour of addressing to the Imperial Government on February 27/March 12, 1915.

The claim made by the Imperial Government in their *aide-mémoire* of February 19/March 4, 1915, considerably exceeds the desiderata which were foreshadowed by M. Sazonof as probable a few weeks ago. Before His Majesty's Government have had time to take into consideration what their own desiderata elsewhere would be in the final terms of peace, Russia is asking for a definite promise that her wishes shall be satisfied with regard to what is in fact the richest prize of the entire war. Sir Edward Grey accordingly hopes that M. Sazonof will realize that it is not in the power of His Majesty's Government to give a greater proof of friendship than that which is afforded by the terms of the above-mentioned *aide-mémoire*. That document involves a complete reversal of the traditional policy of His Majesty's Government, and is in direct opposition to the opinions and sentiments at one time universally held in England and which have still by no means died out. Sir Edward Grey therefore trusts that the Imperial Government will recognize that the recent general assurances given to M. Sazonof have been most loyally and amply fulfilled. In presenting the *aide-mémoire* now, His Majesty's Government believe and hope that a lasting friendship between Russia and Great Britain will be assured as soon as the proposed settlement is realized.

From the British *aide-mémoire* it follows that the desiderata of His Majesty's Government, however important they may be to British interests in other parts of the world, will contain no condition which could impair Russia's control over the territories described in the Russian *aide-mémoire* of February 19/March 4, 1915.

In view of the fact that Constantinople will always remain a trade *entrepôt* for South-Eastern Europe and Asia Minor, His Majesty's Government will ask that Russia shall, when she comes into possession of it, arrange for a free port for goods in transit to and from non-Russian territory. His Majesty's Government will also ask that there shall be commercial freedom for merchant ships passing through the Straits, as M. Sazonof has already promised.

Except in so far as the naval and military operations on which His Majesty's Government are now engaged in the Dardanelles may contribute to the common cause of the Allies, it is now clear that these operations, however successful, cannot be of any advantage to His Majesty's Government in the final terms of peace. Russia alone will, if the war is successful, gather the direct fruits of these operations. Russia should therefore, in the opinion of His Majesty's Government, not now put difficulties in the way of any Power which may, on reasonable terms, offer to cooperate with the Allies. The only Power likely to participate in the operations in the Straits is Greece. Admiral Carden has asked the Admiralty to send him more destroyers, but they have none to spare. The assistance of a Greek flotilla, if it could have been secured, would thus have been of inestimable value to His Majesty's Government.

To induce the neutral Balkan States to join the Allies was one of the main objects which His Majesty's Government had in view when they undertook the operations in the Dardanelles. His Majesty's Government hope that Russia will spare no pains to calm the apprehensions of Bulgaria and Roumania as to Russia's possession of the Straits and Constantinople being to their disadvantage. His Majesty's Government also hope that Russia will do everything in her power to render the cooperation of these two States an attractive prospect to them.

Sir E. Grey points out that it will

obviously be necessary to take into consideration the whole question of the future interests of France and Great Britain in what is now Asiatic Turkey; and, in formulating the desiderata of His Majesty's Government with regard to the Ottoman Empire, he must consult the French as well as the Russian Government. As soon, however, as it becomes known that Russia is to have Constantinople at the conclusion of the war, Sir E. Grey will wish to state that throughout the negotiations, His Majesty's Government have stipulated that the Mussulman Holy Places and Arabia shall under all circumstances remain under independent Mussulman dominion.

Sir E. Grey is as yet unable to make any definite proposal on any point of the British desiderata; but one of the points of the latter will be the revision of the Persian portion of the Anglo-Russian Agreement of 1907 so as to recognize the present neutral sphere as a British sphere.

Until the Allies are in a position to give to the Balkan States, and especially to Bulgaria and Roumania, some satisfactory assurance as to their prospects and general position with regard to the territories contiguous to their frontiers to the possession of which they are known to aspire; and until a more advanced stage of the agreement as to the French and British desiderata in the final peace terms is reached, Sir E. Grey points out that it is most desirable that the understanding now arrived at between the Russian, French, and British Governments should remain secret.

French *Note Verbal* to Russian Government, 10 April 1915

The Government of the [French] Republic will give its agreement to the Russian *aide-mémoire* addressed by M. Isvolsky to M. Delcassé on 6 March last, relating to Constantinople and the Straits, on condition that war shall be prosecuted until victory and that France and Great Britain realize their plans in the Orient as elsewhere, as it is stated in the Russian *aide-mémoire*.

Correspondence between Sir Henry McMahon and Sherif Hussayn: letter to Hussayn, 24 October 1915

... I regret that you should have received from my last letter the impression that I regarded the question of the limits and boundaries with coldness and hesitation; such was not the case ... I have realized, however, from your last letter that you regard this question as one of vital and urgent importance. I have, therefore, lost no time in informing the Government of Great Britain of the contents of your letter, and it is with great pleasure that I communicate to you on their behalf [i.e. that of the British Government] the following statement, which I am confident you will receive with satisfaction:

The two districts of Mersina and Alex-andretta and portions of Syria lying to the west of the districts of Damascus, Homs, Hama and Aleppo cannot be said to be purely Arab, and should be excluded from the limits demanded.

With the above modification, and without prejudice to our existing treaties with Arab chiefs, we accept those limits.

As for those regions lying within those frontiers wherein Great Britain is free to act without detriment to the interests of her ally, France, I am empowered in the name of the Government of Great Britain to give the following assurances and make the following reply to your letter:

1. Subject to the above modifications,

Great Britain is prepared to recognize and support the independence of the Arabs in all the regions within the limits demanded by the Sherif of Mecca.

2. Great Britain will guarantee the Holy Places against all external aggression and will recognize their inviolability.

3. When the situation admits, Great Britain will give to the Arabs her advice and will assist them to establish what may appear to be the most suitable forms of government in those various territories.

4. On the other hand, it is understood that the Arabs have decided to seek the advice and guidance of Great Britain only, and that such European advisers and officials as may be required for the formation of a sound form of administration will be British.

5. With regard to the *vilayets* of Baghdad and Basra, the Arabs will recognize that the established position and interests of Great Britain necessitate special administrative arrangements in order to secure these territories from foreign aggression, to promote the welfare of the local populations and to safeguard our mutual economic interests.

I am convinced that this declaration will assure you beyond all possible doubt of the sympathy of Great Britain towards the aspirations of her friends the Arabs and will result in a firm and lasting alliance, the immediate results of which will be the expulsion of the Turks from the Arab countries and the freeing of the Arab peoples from the Turkish yoke, which for so many years has pressed heavily upon them . . .

Tripartite (Sykes–Picot) Agreement for the partition of the Ottoman Empire by Britain, France and Russia, 26 April–23 October 1916

Grey to Cambon, French Ambassador in London, 16 May 1916

I have the honour to acknowledge the receipt of your Excellency's note of the 9th instant, stating that the French Government accept the limits of a future Arab State, or Confederation of States, and of those parts of Syria where French interests predominate, together with certain conditions attached thereto, such as they result from recent discussions in London and Petrograd on the subject.

I have the honour to inform your Excellency in reply that the acceptance of the whole project, as it now stands, will involve the abdication of considerable British interests, but, since His Majesty's Government recognize the advantage to the general cause of the Allies entailed in producing a more favourable internal political situation in Turkey, they are ready to accept the arrangement now arrived at, provided that the cooperation of the Arabs is secured, and that the Arabs fulfil the conditions and obtain the towns of Homs, Hama, Damascus, and Aleppo.

It is accordingly understood between the French and British Governments:

1. That France and Great Britain are prepared to recognize and protect ['protect' changed in August 1916 to 'uphold'] an independent Arab State or a Confederation of Arab States in the areas (A) and (B) marked on the annexed map, under the suzerainty of an Arab chief. That in area (A) France, and in area (B) Great Britain, shall have priority of right of enterprise and local loans. That in area (A) France, and in area (B) Great Britain, shall alone supply advisers or foreign functionaries at the request of the Arab State or Confederation of Arab States.

2. That in the blue area France, and in the red area Great Britain, shall be allowed

to establish such direct or indirect administration or control as they desire and as they may think fit to arrange with the Arab State or Confederation of Arab States.

3. That in the brown area there shall be established an international administration, the form of which is to be decided upon after consultation with Russia, and subsequently in consultation with the other Allies, and the representatives of the Shereef of Mecca.

4. That Great Britain be accorded (1) the ports of Haifa and Acre, (2) guarantee of a given supply of water from the Tigris and Euphrates in area (A) for area (B). His Majesty's Government, on their part, undertake that they will at no time enter into negotiations for the cession of Cyprus to any third Power without the previous consent of the French Government.

5. That Alexandretta shall be a free port as regards the trade of the British Empire, and that there shall be no discrimination in port charges or facilities as regards British shipping and British goods; that there shall be freedom of transit for British goods through Alexandretta and by railway through the blue area, whether those goods are intended for or originate in the red area, or (B) area, or area (A); and there shall be no discrimination, direct or indirect, against British goods on any railway or against British goods or ships at any port serving the areas mentioned.

That Haifa shall be a free port as regards the trade of France, her dominions and protectorates, and there shall be no discrimination in port charges or facilities as regards French shipping and French goods. There shall be freedom of transit for French goods through Haifa and by the British railway through the brown area, whether those goods are intended for or originate in the blue area, area (A), or area (B), and there shall be no discrimination, direct or indirect, against French goods on any railway, or against French goods or ships at any port serving the areas mentioned.

6. That in area (A) the Bagdad Railway shall not be extended southwards beyond Mosul, and in area (B) northwards beyond Samarra, until a railway connecting Bag-

dad with Aleppo via the Euphrates Valley has been completed, and then only with the concurrence of the two Governments.

7. That Great Britain has the right to build, administer, and be sole owner of a railway connecting Haifa with area (B), and shall have a perpetual right to transport troops along such a line at all times.

It is to be understood by both Governments that this railway is to facilitate the connection of Bagdad with Haifa by rail, and it is further understood that, if the engineering difficulties and expense entailed by keeping this connecting line in the brown area only make the project unfeasible, the French Government shall be prepared to consider that the line in question may also traverse the polygon Banias-Keis Marib-Salkhad Tell Otsda-Mesmie before reaching area (B).

8. For a period of twenty years the existing Turkish customs tariff shall remain in force throughout the whole of the blue and red areas, as well as in areas (A) and (B), and no increase in the rates of duty or conversion from *ad valorem* to specific rates shall be made except by agreement between the two powers.

There shall be no interior custom barriers between any of the above-mentioned areas. The customs duties leviable on goods destined for the interior shall be collected at the port of entry and handed over to the administration of the area of destination.

9. It shall be agreed that the French Government will at no time enter into any negotiations for the cession of their rights and will not cede such rights in the blue area to any third Power, except the Arab State or Confederation of Arab States, without the previous agreement of His Majesty's Government, who, on their part, will give a similar undertaking to the French Government regarding the red area.

10. The British and French Governments, as the protectors of the Arab State ['protectors of the Arab State' deleted August 1916], shall agree that they will not themselves acquire and will not consent to a third Power acquiring territorial possessions in the Arabian peninsula, or consent to a third Power installing a naval base either on the east coast, or on the islands, of the Red

Sea. This, however, shall not prevent such adjustment of the Aden frontier as may be necessary in consequence of recent Turkish aggression.

11. The negotiations with the Arabs as to the boundaries of the Arab State or Confederation of Arab States shall be continued through the same channel as heretofore on behalf of the two Powers.

12. It is agreed that measures to control the importation of arms into the Arab territories will be considered by the two Governments.

I have further the honour to state that, in order to make the agreement complete, His Majesty's Government are proposing to the Russian Government to exchange notes analogous to those exchanged by the latter and your Excellency's Government on the 26th April last. Copies of these notes will be communicated to your Excellency as soon as exchanged.

I would also venture to remind your Excellency that the conclusion of the present agreement raises, for practical consideration, the question of the claims of Italy to a share in any partition or rearrangement of Turkey in Asia, as formulated in Article 9 of the agreement of the 26th April, 1915, between Italy and the Allies.

His Majesty's Government further consider that the Japanese Government should be informed of the arrangements now concluded.

Grey to Benckendorff, Russian Ambassador in London, 23 May 1916

I have received from the French Ambassador in London copies of the notes exchanged between the Russian and French Governments on the 26th ultimo, by which your Excellency's Government recognize, subject to certain conditions, the arrangement made between Great Britain and France, relative to the constitution of an Arab State or a Confederation of Arab States, and to the partition of the territories of Syria, Cilicia, and Mesopotamia, provided that the cooperation of the Arabs is secured.

His Majesty's Government take note with satisfaction that your Excellency's Government concur in the limits set forth in that arrangement, and I have now the honour to inform your Excellency that His Majesty's Government, on their part, in order to make the arrangement complete, are also prepared to recognize the conditions formulated by the Russian Government and accepted by the French Government in the notes exchanged at Petrograd on the 26th ultimo.

In so far, then, as these arrangements directly affect the relations of Russia and Great Britain, I have the honour to invite the acquiescence of your Excellency's Government in an agreement on the following terms:

1. That Russia shall annex the regions of Erzeroum, Trebizond, Van, and Bitlis, up to a point subsequently to be determined on the littoral of the Black Sea to the west of Trebizond.

2. That the region of Kurdistan to the south of Van and of Bitlis between Mush, Sert, the course of the Tigris, Jezirehben-Omar, the crest-line of the mountains which dominate Amadia, and the region of Merga Var, shall be ceded to Russia; and that starting from the region of Merga Var, the frontier of the Arab State shall follow the crest-line of the mountains which at present divide the Ottoman and Persian Dominions. These boundaries are indicated in a general manner and are subject to modifications of detail to be proposed later by the Delimitation Commission which shall meet on the spot.

3. That the Russian Government undertake that, in all parts of the Ottoman territories thus ceded to Russia, any concessions accorded to British subjects by the Ottoman Government shall be maintained. If the Russian Government express the desire that such concessions should later be modified in order to bring them into harmony with the laws of the Russian Empire, this modification shall only take place in agreement with the British Government.

4. That in all parts of the Ottoman territories thus ceded to Russia, existing British rights of navigation and development, and

the rights and privileges of any British religious, scholastic, or medical institutions shall be maintained. His Majesty's Government, on their part, undertake that similar Russian rights and privileges shall be maintained in those regions which, under the conditions of this agreement, become entirely British, or in which British interests are recognized as predominant.

5. The two Governments admit in principle that every State which annexes any part of the Ottoman Empire is called upon to participate in the service of the Ottoman Debt.

Tripartite (St Jean de Maurienne) Agreement for the partition of the Ottoman Empire by Britain, France and Italy, 19 April–27 September 1917

The Agreement, London, 18 August 1917

Subject to Russia's assent.

1. The Italian Government adheres to the stipulations contained in Articles 1 and 2 of the Franco–British [Sykes–Picot] agreements of 9 and 16 May 1916. For their part, the Governments of France and of Great Britain cede to Italy, under the same conditions of administration and of interests, the green and 'C' zones as marked on the attached map . . .

2. Italy undertakes to make Smyrna a free port for the commerce of France, its colonies and its protectorates, and for the commerce of the British Empire and its dependencies. Italy shall enjoy the rights and privileges that France and Great Britain have reciprocally granted themselves in the ports of Alexandretta, of Haifa, and of St Jean d'Acre, in accordance with Article 5 of the said agreements. Mersina shall be a free port for the commerce of Italy, its colonies and its protectorates, and there shall be neither difference of treatment nor advantages in port rights which may be refused to the navy or the merchandise of Italy. There shall be free transit through Mersina, and by railroad across the *vilayet* of Adana, for Italian merchandise bound to and from the Italian zone. There shall be no difference of treatment, direct or indirect, at the expense of Italian merchandise or ships in any port along the coast of Cilicia serving the Italian zone.

3. The form of international administration in the yellow zone [same as Sykes–Picot brown zone] mentioned in Article 3 of the said agreements of 9 and 16 May shall be decided together with Italy.

4. Italy, in so far as she is concerned, approves the provisions on the ports of Haifa and of Acre contained in Article 4 of the same agreements.

5. Italy adheres, in that which relates to the green zone and zone 'C', to the two paragraphs of Article 8 of the Franco–British agreements concerning the customs régime that shall be maintained in the blue and red zones, and in zones 'A' and 'B'.

6. It is understood that the interests that each Power possesses in the zones controlled by the other Powers shall be scrupulously respected, but that the Powers concerned with these interests shall not use them as means for political action.

7. The provisions contained in Articles 10, 11 and 12 of the Franco–English agreements, concerning the Arabian Peninsula and the Red Sea, shall be considered as fully binding on Italy as if that Power were named in the articles with France and Great Britain as a Contracting Party.

8. It is understood that if, at the

conclusion of peace, the advantages embodied in the agreements contracted among the allied Powers regarding the allocation to each of a part of the Ottoman Empire cannot be entirely assured to one or more of the said Powers, then in whatever alteration or arrangement of provinces of the Ottoman Empire resulting from the war the maintenance of equilibrium in the Mediterranean shall be given equitable consideration, in conformity with Article 9 of the London agreement of 26 April 1915.

9. It has been agreed that the present memorandum shall be communicated to the Russian Government, in order to permit it to make its views known.

The Balfour Declaration (letter from Balfour to Lord Rothschild), 2 November 1917

I have much pleasure in conveying to you, on behalf of His Majesty's Government, the following declaration of sympathy with Jewish Zionist aspirations which has been submitted to, and approved by, the Cabinet:

His Majesty's Government view with favour the establishment in Palestine of a national home for the Jewish people, and will use their best endeavours to facilitate the achievement of this object, it being clearly understood that nothing shall be done which may prejudice the civil and religious rights of existing non-Jewish communities in Palestine, or the rights and political status enjoyed by Jews in any other country.

I should be grateful if you would bring this declaration to the knowledge of the Zionist Federation.

China, Japan and the Pacific

In August 1914 British policy vacillated on the desirability of invoking the Anglo–Japanese alliance and so ensuring Japan's entry into the war. Japan was expected to press its claims to take over the German lease of the port of Kiaochow and rights in the province of Shantung. Japan also sought possession of the German island colonies in the Pacific. Their future was of especial concern to two British Dominions, Australia and New Zealand, as well as to the United States. Japan decided the issue by declaring war on Germany after the expiration of its ultimatum of 15 August 1914. *Agreement between Japan and Britain was not finally reached until February 1917*, when Britain secretly agreed to support Japanese claims to those German islands which lay north of the Equator, the Marianas, Carolines and Marshalls, as well as to German concessions in Shantung; whilst Japan promised to support British claims south of the Equator, that is, for German Samoa, German New Guinea and Nauru. The French and Italian governments shortly after entered into similar agreements with Japan.

Japan was determined to strengthen and extend her interests and influence in China. Following the military occupation of Kiaochow Bay, on 18 January 1915

Japan presented to China *Twenty-One Demands*. They included the following: China was to give full assent to any agreement Japan might eventually make with Germany about the lease of Kiaochow and German rights in the province of Shantung; the Japanese were to be allowed to build an additional railway in the province and no land in it was to be alienated to any other country; an extension for a further ninety-nine years of the Japanese lease of Port Arthur and Dairen was to be granted; certain towns were to be opened to foreign trade; Japan demanded a recognition of her predominant position in southern Manchuria and eastern Inner Mongolia; China was not to cede or lease to any other Power any harbour, bay or island along the China coast; finally, 'seven wishes' comprised group V of the demands, including the proposal that the Chinese Government should employ Japanese political, military and financial advisers. After delivery of an ultimatum by Japan, *China and Japan signed two treaties and thirteen notes on 25 May 1915* based on the Twenty-One Demands, but the 'wishes' comprising group V were dropped. China had declared war on Germany in August 1917 and later at the peace conference refused to accept the validity of the agreements, declaring they had been signed under threat of coercion, and left without signing the Treaty of Versailles.

Japan's ally, Britain, and the neutral United States attempted to exercise a moderating influence on Japan in 1915. The United States was still committed to upholding the 'Open Door' and China's political and territorial integrity, but the US secretary of state, Bryan, in a note to the Japanese ambassador in Washington of 13 March 1915, had stated that the 'United States frankly recognizes that territorial contiguity creates special relations between Japan' with regard to Shantung, south Manchuria and east Mongolia. This attitude was confirmed by the *Lansing–Ishii Agreement, 2 November 1917* (p. 78). The United States tried to reconcile a recognition of Japan's special interests in China with China's territorial and political integrity.

In pursuing a forceful Chinese policy, Japan had acted in concert with Russia. Russia and Japan concluded four secret treaties and conventions between 1907 and 1916. The last of the treaties was the most extensive in scope, the *Russo–Japanese Treaty, 3 July 1916* (p. 77). Only two articles were made public and an additional secret convention stated that the two signatories had 'vital interests in China' and that they would cooperate to prevent China from falling under the political influence of any 'third power which entertains a hostile feeling against Japan and Russia'. The secret treaty was published and repudiated some eighteen months later by the Soviet Russian leaders after the revolution. The secret treaty is notable for extending the interest of Japan to the whole of China and for being presumably directed against the United States.

Secret Treaty of Alliance between Japan and Russia, Petrograd, 3 July 1916

The Russian Imperial Government and the Japanese Imperial Government, aiming to strengthen the firm friendship between them, established through the secret agreements of July 17/30, 1907, June 21/ July 4, 1910, and June 25/July 8, 1912, have agreed to supplement the aforesaid secret agreements with the following articles:

Article I. Both the high-contracting parties recognize that the vital interests of one and the other of them require the safeguarding of China from the political domination of any third Power whatsoever, having hostile designs against Russia or Japan: and therefore mutually obligate themselves, in the future at all times when circumstances demand, to enter into open-hearted dealings, based on complete trust, in order to take necessary measures with the object of preventing the possibility of occurrence of said state of affairs.

Article II. In the event, in consequence of measures taken by mutual consent of Russia and Japan, on the basis of the preceding article, a declaration of war is made by any third Power, contemplated by Article I of this agreement, against one of the contracting parties, the other party, at the first demand of its ally, must come to its aid. Each of the high-contracting parties herewith covenants, in the event such a condition arises, not to conclude peace with the common enemy, without preliminary consent therefor from its ally.

Article III. The conditions under which each of the high-contracting parties will lend armed assistance to the other side, by virtue of the preceding article, as well as the means by which such assistance shall be accomplished, must be determined in common by the corresponding authorities of one and the other contracting parties.

Article IV. It is requisite to have in view that neither one nor the other of the high-contracting parties must consider itself bound by Article II of this agreement to lend armed aid to its ally, unless it be given guarantees by its allies that the latter will give it assistance corresponding in character to the importance of the approaching conflict.

Article V. The present agreement shall have force from the time of its execution, and shall continue to be in force until July 1/14, of the year 1921.

In the event the other of the High-Contracting Parties does not deem it necessary twelve months prior to the end of said period, to declare its unwillingness to continue the present agreement in force, then the said agreement shall continue in force for a period of one year after the declaration of one of the Contracting. Parties disclaiming the said agreement.

Article VI. The present agreement must remain profoundly secret except to both of the High-Contracting Parties.

In witness whereof the persons invested with full power by both parties, have signed and affixed their seals to the present agreement at Petrograd on the 20th of June/July 3, of the year 1916, which corresponds in the Japanese calendar to the third day of the seventh month of the fifth year of the reign of Taisho.

(Signatures),   SAZONOFF.
MOTONO.

Exchange of Notes between Japan and the United States touching Questions of Mutual Interest relating to China, signed at Washington, 2 November 1917

[*The Secretary of State to the Ambassador Extraordinary and Plenipotentiary of Japan, on Special Mission.*]

DEPARTMENT OF STATE,
Washington, November 2, 1917.

Excellency:

I have the honor to communicate herein my understanding of the agreement reached by us in our recent conversations touching the questions of mutual interest to our Governments relating to the Republic of China.

In order to silence mischievous reports that have from time to time been circulated, it is believed by us that a public announcement once more of the desires and intentions shared by our two Governments with regard to China is advisable.

The Governments of the United States and Japan recognize that territorial propinquity creates special relations between countries, and, consequently, the Government of the United States recognizes that Japan has special interests in China, particularly in the part to which her possessions are contiguous.

The territorial sovereignty of China, nevertheless, remains unimpaired and the Government of the United States has every confidence in the repeated assurances of the Imperial Japanese Government that while geographical position gives Japan such special interests they have no desire to discriminate against the trade of other nations or to disregard the commercial rights heretofore granted by China in treaties with other powers.

The Governments of the United States and Japan deny that they have any purpose to infringe in any way the independence or territorial integrity of China and they declare, furthermore, that they always adhere to the principle of the so-called "Open Door" or equal opportunity for commerce and industry in China.

Moreover, they mutually declare that they are opposed to the acquisition by any Government of any special rights or privileges that would affect the independence or territorial integrity of China or that would deny to the subjects or citizens of any country the full enjoyment of equal opportunity in the commerce and industry of China.

I shall be glad to have Your Excellency confirm this understanding of the agreement reached by us.

Accept, Excellency, the renewed assurance of my highest consideration.

ROBERT LANSING

His Excellency
    Viscount KIKUJIRO ISHII,
        Ambassador Extraordinary and Plenipotentiary of Japan, on Special Mission.

[*The Ambassador Extraordinary and Plenipotentiary of Japan, on Special Mission, to the Secretary of State.*]

THE SPECIAL MISSION OF JAPAN,
Washington, November 2, 1917.

SIR: I have the honor to acknowledge the receipt of your note of to-day, communicating to me your understanding of the agreement reached by us in our recent conversations touching the questions of mutual interest to our Governments relating to the Republic of China.

I am happy to be able to confirm to you, under authorization of my Government, the understanding in question set forth in the following terms:

In order to silence mischievous reports that have from time to time been circulated, it is believed by us that a public announcement once more of the desires and intentions shared by our two Governments with regard to China is advisable.

The Governments of Japan and the United States recognize that territorial propinquity creates special relations between countries, and, consequently, the Government of the United States recognizes that

Japan has special interests in China, particularly in the part to which her possessions are contiguous.

The territorial sovereignty of China, nevertheless, remains unimpaired and the Government of the United States has every confidence in the repeated assurances of the Imperial Japanese Government that while geographical position gives Japan such special interests they have no desire to discriminate against the trade of other nations or to disregard the commercial rights heretofore granted by China in treaties with other Powers.

The Governments of Japan and the United States deny that they have any purpose to infringe in any way the independence or territorial integrity of China and they declare, furthermore, that they always adhere to the principle of the so-called "Open Door" or equal opportunity for commerce and industry in China.

Moreover, they mutually declare that they are opposed to the acquisition by any government of any special rights or privileges that would affect the independence or territorial integrity of China or that would deny to the subjects or citizens of any country the full enjoyment of equal opportunity in the commerce and industry of China.

I take this opportunity to convey to you, Sir, the assurances of my highest consideration.

K. Ishii
Ambassador Extraordinary and Plenipotentiary of Japan on Special Mission.

Honorable Robert Lansing,
Secretary of State.

The Treaty of Brest-Litovsk: Eastern and Central Europe, 1917–18

The Europe of the inter-war years began to take shape in the autumn of 1917 and the spring of 1918 with the victory of the Central Powers over Russia and Roumania. The signature on *3 March 1918 of the Treaty of Brest-Litovsk* (p. 83) was of lasting importance, even though the treaty itself was formally abrogated after the defeat of the Central Powers (the abandonment of Brest-Litovsk had been one of the conditions of the Allied armistice on 11 November 1918).

The peace of Brest-Litovsk marked the break-up of the Russian Empire, the first of the three pre-war multinational empires to collapse (the Hapsburg Monarchy and the Ottoman Empire were the others). During the war the Germans had encouraged nationalism as a weapon against the Tsarist Russian Empire and had supported non-Russian ethnic groups as a means of limiting Soviet Russian power. The Ukraine had already been recognized as an independent state by the Central Powers in February 1918, but German and Austro-Hungarian armies under the Supreme Command remained in occupation of the 'border' territories from the Baltic to the Caucasus, and occupied the Ukraine defeating the advancing Bolshevik forces. At the request of the Finnish government, German armed forces in April and May 1918 helped the White Finns achieve victory over the Bolsheviks in the Finnish civil war. Towards the independence of the Baltic States and Poland, Germany maintained a reserved and equivocal attitude. The defeat of Tsarist Russia had been the first condition of the independence of the Russian borderlands; the subsequent defeat of Germany was the second condition; and before some of these states attained independence during the inter-war years, the defeat of Soviet Russia in 1919 and 1920 had become just as necessary (see pp. 87–8).

Roumania also accepted defeat and concluded the *Peace of Bucharest on 7 May 1918* with the Central Powers. The treaty deprived Roumania of the southern part of the Dobruja which was incorporated in Bulgaria; Roumania also lost territory to Hungary but retained Bessarabia. Bessarabia had only been incorporated in Rumania in April 1918, a month before the Peace of Bucharest. Bessarabia was beyond the control of the Bolsheviks in 1917 and 1918; it had been proclaimed independent by its leaders and voted for incorporation with Roumania on 8 April 1918. This was recognized by the Central Powers but not by Soviet Russia. With the Allied victory, Roumania regained the southern Dobruja and much more than the territory lost to Hungary; Roumania also kept Bessarabia.

For Lenin and the Bolshevik leaders, Brest-Litovsk was a bitter peace. Russia was deprived of one-third of her population and her westward expansion during the previous three centuries was lost. But what was far more important, as Lenin understood, was that Bolshevik power had survived and was consolidated in the heart of Russia. The Bolsheviks survived by only a narrow margin and could not have withstood Germany's determination to destroy them. But the Germans, desiring peace with some established government and fearing that the opponents of the Bolsheviks might fight on, had been keen to preserve Bolshevik control in Petrograd. Lenin had bought time. Russia's losses he regarded as temporary. They would last until the war among the imperialist powers had been turned into an international class war with the spread of revolution outward from Russia.

The armistice and peace negotiations between Russia and Germany were bizarre. On 8 November 1917 the 'Workers' and 'Peasants' government proposed to all warring peoples and their governments to begin at once negotiations leading, 'to a just and democratic peace . . . an immediate peace without annexations . . . and without indemnities . . . ' ; any nation within the boundaries of a certain state, 'by free voting and completely free from the presence of the troops of the annexing stronger State and without the least pressure' should have the right to determine its own future. On 26 November Trotsky formally applied to the German High Command for an immediate armistice leading to a democratic peace without annexations or indemnities. Britain, France and the United States tried without success to prevent the new Russia from leaving the war. But Russia's enemies, Bulgaria, Turkey, Austria-Hungary, thoroughly exhausted by the war, welcomed the opportunity to end it in the east. The German High Command too, though victorious, wanted to bring the war in Russia to a rapid end so as to gain advantage of the raw materials and grain from the vast regions they occupied and to transfer troops to the west for the decisive battles ahead. The armistice negotiations opened in Brest-Litovsk on 3 December 1917. The Russians now made demands which included the proposition that no German troops should be withdrawn to other fronts; as orders for this had already been issued, the Germans appeared to agree but added the proviso, except for the orders already issued. The Russians attempted to spin out the negotiations as time, they believed, was on their side; propaganda and war weariness, they hoped, would set all peoples and soldiers against their own imperialist governments responsible for the war. *On 15 December 1917 an armistice was concluded.*

The Bolsheviks now stepped up their propaganda as the Germans had carelessly permitted 'exchanges of views'. Formal peace negotiations between Russia and the Central Powers opened on 20 December 1917. The Russian delegation did not behave like a defeated power and used time day after day to make new demands and to distribute propaganda. *On 9 February 1918 the Germans and their allies Turkey, Bulgaria and Austria-Hungary signed a separate peace treaty with Ukraine at Brest-Litovsk.* Most importantly, in the preamble the Central Powers recognized Ukrainian independence and article 2 defined the frontiers of Ukraine leaving detailed delimitation to a mixed commission 'after taking the wishes of the inhabitants into consideration'. The contracting parties mutually renounced repayment of their war costs (article 5). The expected gain for the Central Powers was the opening of Ukraine's grain harvest to Austria-Hungary and Germany as both countries were suffering from severe food shortages; economic relations were set out in article 7. This peace treaty was a severe blow to the Russian delegation. On 10 February 1918, without a treaty agreed, Trotsky, who now led the Russian delegation, broke off further discussion declaring, 'we are going out of the war' and that the Russian armies would simply be demobilized and would stop fighting. Trotsky miscalculated that the German people would not permit the generals to start the war again. Lenin however doubted Trotsky's optimism. On 18 February 1918 the Germans renewed their offensive declaring the armistice at an end. The Russians were powerless to resist.

On 24 February the Bolsheviks now had to accept much harsher terms of a dictated peace. On 28 February the Russian delegation reached Brest-Litovsk. The Germans insisted on continuing their advance until a peace treaty was actually concluded; only three days, from 1 to 3 March 1918, were allowed for the Russians to accept or reject the terms of the Central Powers. Under protest of duress, declaring that self-determination of the Russian border states was a pretence and a cloak for German control, the Russians signed the *Peace of Brest-Litovsk on 3 March 1918.* Article 2 prohibited further propaganda. Territorially Germany continued her occupation of vast regions of the Russian Empire, the line ran from Narva through Mohilev to Rostov. Article 3 simply stated that the occupied lands 'will no longer be subject to Russian sovereignty'; Germany and Austria-Hungary would decide their future 'in agreement with their populations', a formula that was vague enough to permit many interpretations; article 6 obliged Russia to recognize the Treaty concluded between the Central Powers and Ukraine, thus compelling Russia to accept the loss of the Ukraine; Estonia and Livonia (Latvia) not yet occupied by the Germans was included in the territories which would 'no longer be subject to Russian sovereignty'; Germany and Austria-Hungary would 'determine the future status of these territories in agreement with their populations' (article 3); eastern Anatolia would be returned to Turkey; the districts of Ardahan, Kars and Batum were also lost. It was a draconian peace.

The Treaty of Brest-Litovsk was ratified on 29 March 1918. By the summer of 1918 Germany in the west was hard pressed and, although the Bolsheviks were themselves confronting civil war and the dissolution of the territory they controlled, they attempted to exploit Germany's weakness in negotiations for *Treaties supplementing the Peace of Brest-Litovsk. These were signed in Berlin on 27 August 1918.* The pretence of no indemnities was abandoned and Russia agreed on reparations of 6 billion marks (a 120 million gold rouble instalment was paid); Russia had to renounce sovereignty over Livonia and Estonia (the Baltic States, Estonia, Latvia, and Lithuania, declared their independence 1917–18), and Russia had to accept the independence of Georgia; but Germany made large concessions too, handing back Baku, agreeing to evacuate White Russia, the Black Sea territory, Rostov and the Don Basin region and promising not to encourage separatist movements in Russia. German territorial moderation was influenced by the wish to secure imports from Russia and revive trade (article 8). A secret Exchange of Notes accompanied the agreements: the most important points were that Germany undertook to prevent Ukraine from supporting separatist movements in Russia and to expel allied troops from northern Russia with the help of the Finns if the Russians could not do so, with a promise to evacuate this territory after peace was concluded and to help Russia defeat General Alexeiev's volunteer army and the Czech legion.

The Russians had broken their undertaking to their Allies not to conclude a separate peace. From this undertaking they had not been released. Yet their sacrifices for the Allied cause had exceeded that of any other single nation. During the armistice negotiations a vain attempt had also been made by the Russians to stipulate that no German troops should be transferred to the western front; but the Russians were powerless to prevent such transfers. Even so, a large German army remained in the east until November 1918, regarded by the German High Command as too unreliable or ill-equipped for use on the western front.

On 11 November 1918 the Allied Armistice conditions required all German troops to withdraw within the frontiers of Germany as of 1 August 1914 with one notable exception. The Bolshevik threat added a proviso: German troops in territories which had formed a part of Russia in 1914 were to withdraw only 'as soon as the Allies shall consider this desirable having regard to the interior conditions of those territories', which required them to stay. *On 13 November 1918 the Soviets repudiated the Treaty of Brest-Litovsk, and in the west it was annulled by article 116 of the Treaty of Versailles* The final disposition of the Russian Empire's western territories was decided by war and negotiation (see Chapter VI).

Peace Treaty between Russia and Germany, Austria-Hungary, Bulgaria and Turkey (Treaty of Brest-Litovsk), 3 March 1918

Article I. Germany, Austria-Hungary, Bulgaria, and Turkey, for the one part, and Russia for the other part, declare that the state of war between them has ceased. They are resolved to live henceforth in peace and amity with one another.

Article II. The Contracting Parties will refrain from any agitation or propaganda against the Government or the public and military institutions of the other party. In so far as this obligation devolves upon Russia, it holds good also for the territories occupied by the Powers of the Quadruple Alliance.

Article III. The territories lying to the west of the line agreed upon by the Contracting Parties which formerly belonged to Russia, will no longer be subject to Russian sovereignty; the line agreed upon is traced on the map submitted as an essential part of this Treaty of Peace (Annex I). The exact fixation of the line will be established by a Russo-German Commission.

No obligations whatever toward Russia shall devolve upon the territories referred to, arising from the fact that they formerly belonged to Russia.

Russia refrains from all interference in the internal relations of these territories. Germany and Austria-Hungary propose to determine the future status of these territories in agreement with their population.

Article IV. As soon as a general peace is concluded and Russian demobilization is carried out completely, Germany will evacuate the territory lying to the east of the line designated in paragraph I of Article III in so far as Article VI does not determine otherwise.

Russia will do all within her power to ensure the immediate evacuation of the provinces of Eastern Anatolia and their lawful return to Turkey.

The districts of Ardahan, Kars, and Batum will likewise and without delay be cleared of Russian troops. Russia will not interfere in the reorganization of the national and international relations of these districts, but leave it to the population of these districts to carry out this reorganization in agreement with the neighbouring States, especially with Turkey.

Article V. Russia will, without delay, carry out the full demobilization of her army inclusive of those units recently organized by the present Government.

Furthermore, Russia will either bring her warships into Russian ports and there detain them until the day of the conclusion of a general peace, or disarm them forthwith. Warships of the States which continue in a state of war with the Powers of the Quadruple Alliance, in so far as they are within Russian sovereignty, will be treated as Russian warships . . .

Article VI. Russia obligates herself to conclude peace at once with the Ukrainian People's Republic and to recognize the treaty of peace between that State and the Powers of the Quadruple Alliance. The Ukrainian territory will, without delay, be cleared of Russian troops and the Russian Red Guard. Russia is to put an end to all agitation or propaganda against the Government or the public institutions of the Ukrainian People's Republic.

Estonia and Livonia will likewise, without delay, be cleared of Russian troops and the Russian Red Guard. The eastern boundary of Estonia runs, in general, along the river Narva. The eastern boundary of Livonia crosses, in general, lakes Peipus and Pskov, to the south-western corner of the latter, then across Lake Luban in the direction of Livenhof on the Dvina. Estonia and Livonia will be occupied by a German police force until security is ensured by proper national institutions and until public order has been established. Russia will liberate at once all arrested or deported inhabitants of Estonia and Livonia, and ensures the safe return of all deported Estonians and Livonians.

Finland and the Aaland Islands will

immediately be cleared of Russian troops and the Russian Red Guard, and the Finnish ports of the Russian fleet and of the Russian naval forces. So long as the ice prevents the transfer of warships into Russian ports, only limited forces will remain on board the warships. Russia is to put an end to all agitation or propaganda against the Government or the public institutions of Finland.

The fortresses built on the Aaland Islands are to be removed as soon as possible. As regards the permanent non-fortification of these islands as well as their further treatment in respect to military and technical navigation matters, a special agreement is to be concluded between Germany, Finland, Russia, and Sweden; there exists an understanding to the effect that, upon Germany's desire, still other countries bordering upon the Baltic Sea would be consulted in this matter.

Article VII. In view of the fact that Persia and Afghanistan are free and independent States, the Contracting Parties obligate themselves to respect the political and economic independence and the territorial integrity of these States.

Article VIII. The prisoners of war of both parties will be released to return to their homeland. The settlement of the questions connected therewith will be effected through the special treaties provided for in Article XII.

Article IX. The Contracting Parties mutually renounce compensation for their war expenses, i.e. of the public expenditures for the conduct of the war, as well as compensation for war losses, i.e. such losses as were caused them and their nationals within the war zones by military measures, inclusive of all requisitions effected in enemy country.

Article X. Diplomatic and consular relations between the Contracting Parties will be resumed immediately upon the ratification of the Treaty of Peace. As regards the reciprocal admission of consuls, separate agreements are reserved.

Article XI. As regards the economic relations between the Powers of the Quadruple Alliance and Russia the regulations contained in Appendices II–V are determinative, namely Appendix II for the Russo-German, Appendix III for the Russo-Austro-Hungarian, Appendix IV for the Russo-Bulgarian, and Appendix V for the Russo-Turkish relations.

Supplementary Treaty of Peace between Russia and the Central Powers, Berlin, 27 August 1918

Guided by the wish to solve certain political questions which have arisen in connection with the Peace Treaty of March 3–7, 1918, between Germany, Austria-Hungary, Bulgaria, and Turkey, for the one part, and Russia, for the other part, in the spirit of friendly understanding and mutual conciliation, and, in so doing, to promote the restoration of good and confidential relations between the two Empires, for which a way was paved by the conclusion of peace, the German Imperial Government and the Government of the Russian Socialist Federal Soviet Republic have agreed to conclude a supplementary treaty to the Peace Treaty with this object, and have . . . agreed to the following provisions:

[*Article 1.* Demarcation of frontiers.]

[*Article 2.* Frontier commission.]

Article 3. Germany will evacuate the territory occupied by her east of Beresina, even before the conclusion of general peace, in proportion as Russia makes the cash payments stipulated in Article 2 of the Russo-German Financial Agreement of this date; further provisions as to this, particularly the fixing of the individual sectors to be evacuated, are left to the Commission referred to in Article 2, paragraph 1, of this Supplementary Treaty.

The Contracting Parties reserve the right to make further agreements with regard to the effecting of the evacuation of the occupied territory west of the Beresina before the conclusion of general peace, in accordance with the fulfilment by Russia of the remaining financial obligations undertaken by her.

Part II · Separatist movements in the Russian Empire

Article 4. In so far as is not otherwise prescribed in the Peace Treaty or in this Supplementary Treaty, Germany will in no wise interfere in the relations between the Russian Empire and parts of its territory, and will thus in particular neither cause nor support the formation of independent States in those territories.

Part III · North Russian territory

Article 5. Russia will at once employ all the means at her disposal to expel the Entente forces from North Russian territory in observance of her neutrality.

Germany guarantees that during these operations there shall be no Finnish attack of any kind on Russian territory, particularly on St Petersburg.

Article 6. When the Entente forces shall have evacuated North Russian territory, the local Russian coast shipping within the three-mile limit from the north coast, and the fishing boats within a stretch of thirty miles along this coast shall be relieved of the barred zone menace. The German naval command shall have an opportunity, in a way to be further agreed upon, of convincing itself that this concession shall not be taken advantage of to forward contraband goods.

Part IV · Estonia, Livonia, Courland, and Lithuania

Article 7. Russia, taking account of the condition at present existing in Estonia and Livonia, renounces sovereignty over these regions, as well as all interference in their internal affairs. Their future fate shall be decided in agreement with their inhabitants . . .

[*Article 13.* Recognition of Georgia's independence.]
[In a Financial Agreement concluded at the same time, Russia agreed to pay Germany 6,000 million marks as compensation for losses to Germany caused by Russian measures.]

Decree of the All-Russian Central Executive Committee of the Soviets on the cancellation of the Brest-Litovsk Treaty, 13 November 1918

To all peoples of Russia, to the population of all occupied regions and territories:

The All-Russian Central Executive Committee of the Soviets hereby declares solemnly that the conditions of peace with Germany signed at Brest on March 3, 1918, are null and void. The Brest-Litovsk treaty (and equally the annexed agreement signed at Berlin on August 27, and ratified by the

All-Russian Central Executive Committee on September 6, 1918), in their entirety and in all their articles, are herewith declared as annulled. All obligations assumed under the Brest-Litovsk treaty and dealing with the payment of contributions or the cession of territory or regions, are declared void . . .

III · The peace settlements, 1919–23

The armed conflict of the First World War came to an end with the separate signatures of armistices between the belligerents. Turkey signed an armistice at Mudros on 30 October 1918, Austria-Hungary on 3 November 1918 and Germany on 11 November 1918.

In the west the armistice conditions of 11 November 1918 between the Allies and Germany provided for an orderly withdrawal of the German army from occupied territories and also from the right and left banks of the Rhine. But the conditions of the German armistice did not provide for the German evacuation of all occupied Tsarist territory. Territories in Central and Eastern Europe that had once formed part of the Tsarist Russian Empire of 1914 were not to be evacuated by German troops, according to article 12 of the armistice, until 'the Allies think the moment suitable, having regard to the internal situation of these territories'. Thus the Allies enlisted German help to prevent the spread of Bolshevism until they were ready to intervene; article 16 reserved to the Allies 'free access to the territories evacuated by the Germans on their eastern frontier, either through Danzig or by the Vistula, in order to convey supplies to the population of these territories or for the purpose of maintaining order'. Similarly anti-Bolshevik terms had been included in the Austro-Hungarian armistice of 3 November 1918. In the Turkish armistice the Allies assured themselves of strategic access to the Black Sea; they asserted their right to occupy the forts of the Dardanelles and Bosphorus and provided for an Allied occupation of Batum and Baku; they also claimed the general right to occupy any strategic point 'in the event of a situation arising which threatens the security of the Allies'. In December 1918 and January 1919 the Allies, referring to article 12 of the German armistice, strenuously objected to German withdrawals in southern Russia, the Ukraine and from Estonia, 'Livonia and Courland' (Latvia, Lithuania). The Allies feared that they would not be able to reinforce German and anti-Bolshevik forces fast enough to maintain their *cordon sanitaire*. During the course of 1918 the provisional independent governments of Estonia and Latvia were reorganized by the Allies though under foreign occupation. The Allies attempted to stop the Bolshevik advance in the Baltic and in Central Europe, and as the peace conference opened in January 1919 the Germans assisted by dispatching the *Free Corps* troops to the Baltic.

During the *Paris Peace Conference* four of the five great powers, Britain, France, Italy and the United States (but not Japan) in their negotiations and discussions ranged over the international problems of the whole world, but did not settle all the world's problems; only the Covenant of the League of Nations was intended to be of universal application. The frontiers and peace treaties settled by the peace conference were those that concerned the Allied and Associated Powers on the one hand and the defeated enemy states, Germany, Austria, Hungary, Bulgaria and Turkey, on the other. Excluded from the territorial peace settlements were Russia and the frontiers of Russia and its neighbours. The failure of Allied intervention and the outcome of the Civil War determined the fate of Russia. Russia's frontiers were dealt with separately in negotiations and treaties between Russia on the one hand, and Finland, Estonia, Latvia, Lithuania, Poland and Turkey on the other, after continued fighting in eastern and central Europe during 1919 and 1920. Thus the territorial peace settlements of the Allied and Associated Powers did not cover the whole of Europe.

THE ORGANIZATION OF THE PARIS PEACE CONFERENCE

The Peace Conference of Paris opened on 18 January 1919 and officially ended on 21 January 1920. Thirty-two nations, enemies of Germany or one of its allies, sent plenipotentiaries; included were five Latin American States which had severed diplomatic relations with Germany. The following states were represented: United States; Britain; Canada; Australia; South Africa; New Zealand; India; France; Italy; Japan; Belgium; Bolivia; Brazil; China; Cuba; Czechoslovakia; Ecuador; Greece; Guatemala; Haiti; the Hejaz; Honduras; Liberia; Nicaragua; Panama; Peru; Portugal; Poland; Rumania; Kingdom of the Serbs, Croats and Slovenes (Yugoslavia); Siam; Uruguay. The Council of Ten (see below) accepted separate representation for the Dominions, Canada, South Africa, Australia, New Zealand and India. Much expert research had been undertaken on the subjects with which the peace conference would have to deal, but little thought had been given to the actual organization and procedure of the conference itself. The order in which issues were to be raised and resolved was never settled, or rather the approach adopted was pragmatic; issues were decided as and when they should prove ready for discussion. Consequently the major political settlements were reached in detail by a piecemeal process and not according to an overall design and plan. The second Plenary Session of the conference established the main special commissions to examine specific issues. The crucial bargaining, however, was not conducted by all the participating nations, but only by the 'Big Five', Britain, France, Italy, Japan and the United States, which with two plenipotentiaries each formed the Council of Ten. This great power directorate promised to consult the smaller states when their interests were affected and established a large number of expert territorial commissions to deal with frontier questions.

After 24 March 1919 the Council of Ten gave way to a smaller, more informal, Council of Four of Wilson, Lloyd George, Clemenceau and Orlando. In the fourth week of April when Fiume was not awarded to Italy, Orlando left the Council of Four in protest, so the decisions were then left to the remaining three. The Treaty of Versailles, 28 June 1919, formally concluded the League of Nations and the German aspects of the peace settlements, and Wilson returned to the United States. Negotiations continued on the other peace treaties, with the United States playing a decreasing role after the rejection of them by the Senate on 19 November 1919 and 19 March 1920. The United States concluded separate peace treaties with Germany, Austria and Hungary in August 1921.

The Treaty of Versailles: the peace settlement with Germany

THE ARMISTICE

Germany did not 'surrender unconditionally' in November 1918. On 4 October 1918 Prime Minister Max von Baden, the German Chancellor, sought an armistice on the basis of the Fourteen Points in an appeal to President Wilson. Only after exchanging three notes with the German government did Wilson, on 23 October, formally consult the Allies, who meantime were alarmed at the prospect of bilateral US–German negotiations for peace. The biggest obstacle did not prove to be the Fourteen Points as far as they applied to Germany, but American insistence of 'absolute freedom of navigation upon the seas, outside territorial waters' in time of peace and war. Britain strenuously resisted and maintained her national right to blockade and interruption in 1918 as she had done in 1812. Agreement was finally reached between the United States and the Allies on 4 November which accepted peace on the Fourteen Points, together with Wilson's subsequent addresses and pronouncements of principles and two further provisos, one concerning reparations, the other leaving open the question of the freedom of the seas for the peace conference. This marked the first official acceptance of Wilson's unilateral proclamation of war aims in *the Fourteen Points, 8 January 1918* (p. 98) which he had delivered in his address to a joint session of Congress. Independently, in a speech three days earlier on 5 January 1918, Lloyd George had defined British war aims, which closely resembled all but one of Wilson's Fourteen Points, namely the second point on the freedom of the seas. Germany accepted the terms agreed by the Allies and the United States together with the military terms decided upon by the commander in the field; the armistice was signed on 11 November 1918.

THE TERRITORIAL TERMS

In the west, Alsace-Lorraine was returned to France and Germany's request for a plebiscite was rejected; the Saar was placed under an International Commission of the League and it was agreed that a plebiscite would be held at the end of fifteen years (in 1935 the Saar opted for Germany with Germany then able to repurchase mines); the mines of the Saar passed into French ownership as part of the reparations for damage to French mines; three small territories became Belgian – Moresent, Eupen and Malmédy.

French demands for the strategic frontier of the Rhine caused a crisis among the Big Four in March and April 1919. France only acquiesced to German sovereignty continuing over the territories of both banks of the Rhine on two conditions agreed to by the Allies and the United States. First, Allied troops were to occupy German territory west of the Rhine and some bridgeheads across the Rhine in three zones, to be evacuated at five-year intervals provided Germany fulfilled the treaty conditions of Versailles. In June 1919, a concession was made to Germany that if it gave proof of goodwill and satisfactory guarantees of fulfilling its obligations, the projected fifteen-year occupation might be shortened; the German territory west of the Rhine, moreover, was demilitarized (no troops or fortifications permitted in the demilitarized zone) as well as a strip of territory running 50 kilometres east of the Rhine. Second, France received a *Treaty of Guarantee* from the United States and Britain of military support if Germany attacked France. The *Treaties of Guarantee were signed on 28 June 1919* (p. 112), at the same time as the Treaty of Versailles, but the coming into force of the British treaty depended on the prior ratification by the Senate of the United States. Thus when Senate rejected the Versailles Treaty, the US Treaty of Guarantee with France and the British Treaty of Guarantee with France lapsed also.

In the north, on the Danish–German frontier, it was agreed that a new frontier would be fixed according to a plebiscite of the population of Schleswig; the predominantly Danish-speaking northern part of Schleswig chose to join Denmark in 1920, and southern Schleswig stayed in Germany.

In the east, Germany lost large territories to the new Polish state. To allow Poland an outlet to the sea the Polish 'corridor' was created which separated Germany from the east Prussian territories. The province of Posen (Poznan) was also placed under Polish sovereignty together with Upper Silesia; the German-speaking town of Danzig was made a Free City under the supervision of the League, but with Poland enjoying special rights, a customs union and control of foreign affairs. German protests in June 1919 modified the final terms of the German eastern frontier significantly in that the final disposition of Upper Silesia was to be dependent on plebiscites held in that region. In July 1920 the territory of East Prussia was considerably enlarged southwards as a result of plebiscites in the Allenstein and Marienwerder zones; in March 1921 about two-thirds of the area of Upper Silesia voted for Germany, and only about one-third became Polish, though it contained the greater mineral wealth. The settlement of the Polish–German frontier in 1920 and 1921 left a German minority of more than one million in Poland and a Polish minority in excess of half a million in Germany. Germany lost Memel and its district with its half-German-speaking and half-Lithuanian population, which Lithuania seized in 1923. Germany also lost a small piece of Silesian territory to Czechoslovakia.

Germany was obliged to give up all her colonies. The African colonies were divided in the form of different classes of mandates under the League of Nations between Britain, South Africa, France and Belgium (except for some small areas annexed by France and Portugal); Australia, New Zealand, Britain and Japan took over the Pacific territories. Japanese insistence on acquiring Germany's special privileges in the Chinese province of Shantung caused great difficulty at the peace conference as China was an ally that had declared war on Germany; but secret British, French and Italian wartime promises secured Japan the necessary support at the peace conference. China thereupon refused to sign the Treaty of Versailles.

REPARATIONS

The question of reparations proved among the most contentious issues of the peace conference. Too large a sum might lead the Germans to refuse to sign the treaty, and a sum likely to prove within Germany's reasonable capacity to pay would not satisfy public opinion in France and Britain, on which the British and French prime ministers negotiating in Paris were dependent. No total sum was stated in the treaty nor any limit to the years of payment; instead a Reparations Commission was set up to determine by 1 May 1921 the total of Germany's obligations. The inability to fix a relatively moderate sum made the earlier hard-won agreement secured by Wilson that Germany should only pay for civilian damage, not the whole of the war costs, of little practical importance. The famous War Guilt clause (article 231) came to symbolize the injustices of the Treaty of Versailles. The wording was ill-considered and in subsequent years helped to undermine credibility in the treaty. It was not intended to be considered by itself, but was the first article in the reparations section; in article 232 German liability was limited, and 'complete reparation for all such loss and damage', that is the whole of the war costs, would not be demanded. To make the concession of requiring reparations only for civilian damage (and pensions) more palatable, it was agreed that the Allies should assert, and Germany should be obliged to accept, German responsibility with its allies for 'all the loss and damage . . . as a consequence of the war imposed upon them by the aggression of Germany and her allies'.

FOOD SUPPLIES AND THE BLOCKADE

A loosely coordinated Allied relief effort under Herbert Hoover as Director-General began to function early in 1919, and brought food and relief to the peoples of eastern Europe facing starvation. The bulk of food supplies and services came from the United States, and Britain also made a major contribution, but Germany was excluded from the relief grants. The blockade was maintained against Germany, a later potent propaganda plank used by the Nazis to discredit all the proceedings of Versailles. The French demanded immediate reparations payments and the handing over of the German merchant fleet. This was made an additional condition of renewing the armistice on 16 January 1919. At first Germany refused, but Allied agreement was eventually reached, in Brussels on 14 March 1919, on German payments in foreign securities for food and the surrender of the German merchant fleet; before the end of the month food supplies began to reach the Germans. The blockade was relaxed but not finally raised until 12 July 1919, after the German ratification of the peace treaty.

MILITARY LIMITATIONS

The provisions of the treaty made Germany virtually defenceless; her armed forces were sufficient only for the internal preservation of law and order. The German army was limited to 100,000 men, and to prevent the training of more men, the period of service was set for twelve years for all but officers, who would have to serve twenty-five years. The German navy was limited and permitted no submarines; Germany was permitted no air force, and the armaments industry was placed under the severest restraint and Allied control and inspection. The demilitarization and occupation of the Rhineland completed Germany's military impotence in facing French military strength. To make these clauses more palatable to Germany, the intention of general disarmament among all the powers was expressed in the treaty.

OTHER PROVISIONS

Among the many other provisions of the treaty the more important were those concerning Russia, Germany had to renounce the Treaty of Brest-Litovsk and the Treaty of Bucharest, and acknowledge the right to independence of all the territories of the Russian Empire as it existed on 1 August 1914; Russia retained rights to reparations from Germany. Germany also had to recognize the frontiers and accept all treaties the Allies might conclude with present and future states, existing or coming into existence, whose territories had once formed part of the Russian Empire of 1914 (articles 116 and 117). But the provisions for the trial of 'war criminals', including the Kaiser, proved largely inoperative. The rights of the German minority in Poland were safeguarded not in the Treaty of Versailles itself but in a treaty signed the same day, *the Minorities Treaty between the Allied and Associated Powers and Poland, 28 June 1919* (p. 113). It served as the model for treaties dealing with German and other minorities in Czechoslovakia, Yugoslavia, Roumania and Greece.

The draft peace treaty was presented to the German representatives, who were summoned for this purpose to the Trianon Palace, on 7 May 1919. After German written protests had been considered, and a few amendments made, the most significant being the plebiscite in Upper Silesia, *the Treaty of Peace was signed at Versailles on 28 June 1919* (p. 100).

Peace treaties with Austria, Bulgaria and Hungary, 1919–20

The crucial decisions affecting the territorial distributions of central and eastern Europe had been taken before the signature of the Versailles Treaty, indeed in many cases before the peace conference opened in Paris. Thus the Allies and the United States were committed to confirming the new multinational succession states of the Austro-Hungarian Empire, which had broken up in the aftermath of defeat: these were Czechoslovakia and Yugoslavia. Military action too, either against the defeated forces of Austria and Hungary or to fill the vacuum left by their departure, created a number of situations by force which later proved completely or partially irrevocable and were recognized by the Allies. The Hungarian *Banat* was occupied after the armistice with Hungary by Serbian troops in November 1918, and Roumania claimed the whole region at the peace conference in vain. The Roumanians in turn occupied the whole of Transylvania and even Budapest during the spring and summer of 1919. The Italians seized disputed Fiume in September 1919, and the Czechoslovaks in the previous autumn occupied the whole of historic Bohemia and Moravia, including large German-speaking minorities. The Poles and Czechs clashed in the district of Teschen and the Poles occupied the mainly Ukrainian-Ruthenian ethnic region of eastern Galicia, which had formed part of Austria. The actual boundaries contained in the peace treaties with Austria, Hungary and Bulgaria were thus drawn largely as a result of territorial awards eventually made to the neighbouring states, of territory for the most part already occupied by them, after investigation by the Territorial Claims Commissions set up by the Council of Ten.

The Treaty of St Germain with Austria, 10 September 1919, was modelled on the Treaty of Versailles, as were the other peace treaties. The Covenant of the League of Nations was integrally included in the peace treaties, and the war responsibility and reparations clauses were similar in form to the German treaty. Austria was limited militarily and permitted an army of no more than 30,000 officers and men. Austria was expressly forbidden union with Germany. The South Tyrol, with a German-speaking population of some 240,000, was handed over to Italy, giving Italy the Brenner pass frontier promised in the Allied *Treaty of London, April 1915* (p. 64); Bohemia and Moravia merged into Czechoslovakia; Bukovina was acquired by Roumania. Owing to disputes among the Allies, other areas were ceded by Austria to the Allies for disposition by them; these regions included the northern Adriatic and Galicia. In the Klagenfurth district of Carinthia a plebiscite in October 1920 decided for Austria against Yugoslavia. Austria received a small area from Hungary, and most of the 'Burgenland', but in a smaller part of 'Burgenland' a plebiscite favoured Hungary. Apart from these small areas, populations were transferred and frontiers redrawn without benefit of plebiscites. These cessions of territory left independent Austria with little more than a quarter of the territory that had formed the Austrian half of the pre-war Dual Monarchy.

The Treaty of Trianon with Hungary, 4 June 1920, was only signed several months after the formal end of the Paris Peace Conference. Peacemaking was in part delayed by the revolution and setting up of the Bolshevik government of Béla Kun from March 1919 to August 1919. The Kun régime collapsed after attacking and being defeated by the Roumanians who were occupying western Hungary (Transylvania) and now advanced to occupy Budapest; the Roumanians could not be induced to withdraw from some of the territory until the autumn of 1919. Historic Hungary had in practice been dismembered before the presentation of the peace treaty to the Hungarian delegates. Almost one-third of the Hungary of 1918, Transylvania and two-thirds of Banat, was ceded to Roumania, and this demarcation left about two million Magyars, mainly in south-east Transylvania, as a minority in post-war Rumania; Croatia-Slovakia and one-third of the Banat were ceded to Yugoslavia; Slovakia, Ruthenia and the region of Pressburg (Bratislava) with some 700,000 Magyars to Czechoslovakia; Fiume eventually to Italy; the greater part of the Burgenland to Austria; and finally to Poland and Czechoslovakia the small areas of Ostrava and Spis in northern Slovakia. Altogether Hungary lost rather more than two-thirds of its territory. Apart from the plebiscites permitted in two small regions, the transfer of population in Hungary was also decided upon without plebiscites. Hungary was limited to a professional army of 35,000 officers and men, and in common with the other peace treaties, the League Covenant and other clauses such as war responsibility and reparations were included. An unusual feature of the treaty was an accompanying letter from the French Prime Minister, Millerand, promising that if the treaty contained any injustice which it would be in the general interest to remove, the Frontier Delimitation Commission might suggest revisions to the League of Nations. This as it turned out raised Hungarian hopes in vain.

The Treaty of Neuilly with Bulgaria, 27 November 1919. By the armistice terms Bulgaria had to withdraw its troops to the pre-war frontier. The territorial terms required Bulgaria to return the southern Dobruja to Roumania regardless of ethnic considerations; and to cede to Yugoslavia most of the four small regions occupied by Serbia in 1918. To the Allies, Bulgaria had to cede nearly the whole of western Thrace thus losing Bulgaria's Aegean littoral; the Allies transferred this territory to Greece by treaty on 10 August 1920, and at the same time a treaty was signed with Turkey. Reparations were required and the Bulgarian army was limited to 33,000 professionals.

Allied disputes and settlements

The peace treaties of St Germain, Neuilly and Trianon, whilst they settled the reduced frontiers of Austria, Bulgaria and Hungary, did not determine the final division of all the ceded territories among the various Allies. The principal disputes occurred over:

1. FIUME

Italy was scarcely reconciled to a compact Yugoslav state along the Adriatic which would prove an obstacle to Italian Balkan ambitions. In addition to the Italian-speaking Trieste region, a part of Austrian domains of the Dual Monarchy, Italy also claimed Fiume, once part of Hungary, which the Yugoslavs desired as their major seaport. Italy had been excluded from Fiume in the Treaty of London, and Orlando's claim was resisted by the others in the Council of Four, causing an Allies crisis in April 1919 and the departure for a time of the Italians from the Peace Conference of Paris. In September 1919 d'Annunzio with Italian 'volunteers' seized the city and drove out the inter-Allied force of occupation. Allied efforts secured no agreement. Eventually by the *Yugoslav–Italian Treaty of Rapallo, 12 November 1920*, the Italian–Yugoslav frontier dispute was settled and Fiume made a Free City; Italy finally acquired Fiume together with a small strip of territory so that Fiume and the rest of Italy were contiguous.

2. THE BANAT

This territory ceded by Hungary had been promised by the Allies in a secret treaty to Roumania in 1916, but Roumania's separate peace treaty with the Central Powers at Bucharest in 1918 had voided the Allied promise. In November 1918 the

Serbians occupied the Banat. The Allied decision in June 1919 to partition the Banat between Yugoslavia and Roumania was rejected by Roumania until Allied pressure forced Roumania to give way in December 1919.

3. ALBANIA

Italy and Greece desired Albanian territory and planned its partition in 1919 and 1920. Yugoslavia too made territorial claims. Long drawn-out negotiations ended in the recognition of Albanian independence, though Albania's frontiers were not finally agreed until 1926.

4. TESCHEN

The *Teschen* dispute was resolved largely in Czechoslovakia's favour, the incorporation of Galicia in Poland was finally acknowledged and the still uncertain frontier between Austria and Hungary settled by plebiscites.

The League of Nations

The devastation of two great European wars encouraged the victors on both occasions to try to find a better way of conducting diplomacy. After the Napoleonic Wars, the Vienna settlement of 1815 was accompanied by the cooperation of the great powers known as the 'Concert of Europe', and the First World War led in 1920 to the *League of Nations* (p. 100) whose aim it was to allow states great and small to find security with justice. Within ten years of the foundation of the League it could be seen that these high hopes were unlikely to be fulfilled. Britain, France and the United States were not willing to check aggression by risking war in the 1930s; no one else could. The League had been weakened at the outset by the Senate's rejection of the peace treaties which meant that the United States could not become a member. But this was not the cause of its failure since the US was frequently ready to cooperate.

The League provided both the rules of conduct between nations and new diplomatic machinery intended to ensure that these rules would be observed. The strength of the League ultimately depended on its members and not on the procedures written into the Covenant. But the will to uphold and strengthen the purposes of the League was lacking when the state to be disciplined was a great power. The sacrifices required of the other great powers in such a situation were not made. Support for the principles and rules of the League came second when weighed against individual national interests.

The immediate origins of the League are to be found in the advocacy of British and American statesmen, notably the former President Taft, President Wilson,

Lord Robert Cecil and Sir Edward Grey. Organized groups of private citizens advocating a new international order after the war were influential in persuading the British and American leaders at Paris that the creation of an international organization was likely to win strong political support in their own countries.

Various drafts reflecting the French, American and British points of view on how to best 'organize' peace were considered at Paris in January and February 1919 by the League Commission, and the text of a completed draft of the Covenant was submitted to the Plenary Session of the peace conference on 14 February 1919. President Wilson then explained to the members of that session that *the Covenant* was based on two principles: (1) that 'no nation shall go to war with any other nation until every other possible means of settling the dispute shall have been full and fairly tried'; and (2) that 'under no circumstances shall any nation seek forcibly to disturb the territorial settlement to be arrived at as the consequence of this peace or to interfere with the political independence of any of the States of the world'.

The League came into existence when the Treaty of Versailles entered into force on 10 January 1920, and was an association of states each retaining its sovereignty. The institutions of the League provided the machinery for working out agreed policies. Its two major purposes were the achievement of international security through collective action, and international cooperation for social and economic welfare. The following articles of the Covenant should be especially noted. In article 10 members subscribed to a mutual guarantee of the political independence and territorial integrity of all member states. This was really no more than a declaration of intent, a moral commitment; military support for a victim of aggression was not automatic. The drafting of article 10 was ambiguous. Any military obligations which might have arisen were in any case made optional when in 1923 an interpretive resolution of article 10 was adopted by the League which left it to each state to decide how far it was bound to contribute military force to fulfil its obligations.

Articles 12 to 17 provided the League with fact-finding and some arbitral functions. Here too are to be found the sanctions which could be adopted against the aggressor. These sanctions emphasized economic pressure which it was believed would be effective and left the ultimate military obligations of member states obscure.

The Geneva Protocol of 1924 attempted to strengthen the League by filling in the 'gaps' of the existing Covenant. The Covenant as it stood did not cover all possible situations of aggression and victimization. If the Council of the League, for instance, should fail to reach unanimous agreement on its report on a dispute, or if for any reason that seemed sufficient to it the Council did not report on a dispute, then League sanctions could not be invoked and one state could make war on another with impunity. In any case an individual state desiring to go to war was obliged only to observe a three-month cooling-off period; thereafter the Council was not bound to impose sanctions if the two states involved in a conflict refused to accept the report of the Council, or the decision of the Court of Arbitrators. The Geneva Protocol sought to ensure that all disputes would be settled by some means other than war. Sanctions would, according to the Geneva Protocol, be imposed on any state resorting to war. Without the adoption of the Protocol, sanctions could only be imposed when a state was found to be at war in breach of the Covenant. Although the Geneva Protocol was agreed to and recommended to members by the League, the British Conservative government in 1925 rejected it as it was unwilling to accept a widening of obligations.

The League was ineffective during the decade of aggression 1931–41, but its record of promoting international and social collaboration through such bodies as the Health Organization, World Economic Conferences and the International Labour Organization was notable. Through the League was devised the mandate system for providing a period of European 'tutelage' over emerging non-European nations or former colonies. The League also sought to ensure the rights of minorities and to carry out humanitarian work for refugees.

By November 1920 there were forty-two members of the League, ten more than the Allied states original signatories of the treaties of peace. But the United States never became a member. Germany was admitted in 1926 and the USSR in 1934. Those great powers who planned or carried out aggression left the League one by one in the 1930s: Nazi Germany in 1933, Japan in the same year, Italy in 1937 and the USSR was expelled in December 1939 after its attack on Finland. In April 1946, after the establishment of the United Nations, the League was dissolved by resolution of the UN Assembly which, however, provided for the continuation of some of its functions.

President Wilson's Fourteen Points, 8 January 1918

We entered this war because violations of right had occurred which touched us to the quick and made the life of our own people impossible unless they were corrected and the world secure once for all against their recurrence. What we demand in this war, therefore, is nothing peculiar to ourselves. It is that the world be made fit and safe to live in; and particularly that it be made safe for every peace-loving nation which, like our own, wishes to live its own life, determine its own institutions, be assured of justice and fair dealing by the other peoples of the world as against force and selfish aggression. All the peoples of the world are in effect partners in this interest, and for our own part we see very clearly that unless justice be done to others it will not be done to us. The programme of the world's peace, therefore, is our programme; and that programme, the only possible programme, as we see it, is this:

I. Open covenants of peace, openly arrived at, after which there shall be no private international understandings of any kind but diplomacy shall proceed always frankly and in the public view.

II. Absolute freedom of navigation upon the seas, outside territorial waters, alike in peace and in war, except as the seas may be closed in whole or in part by international action for the enforcement of international covenants.

III. The removal, so far as possible, of all economic barriers, and the establishment of an equality of trade conditions among all the nations consenting to the peace and associating themselves for its maintenance.

IV. Adequate guarantees given and taken that national armaments will be reduced to the lowest point consistent with domestic safety.

V. A free, open-minded, and absolutely impartial adjustment of all colonial claims, based upon a strict observance of the principle that in determining all such questions of sovereignty the interests of the populations concerned must have equal weight with the equitable claims of the Government whose title is to be determined.

VI. The evacuation of all Russian territory and such a settlement of all questions affecting Russia as will secure the best and freest cooperation of the other nations of the world in obtaining for her an unhampered and unembarrassed opportunity for the independent determination of her own political development and national policy and assure her of a sincere welcome into the society of free nations under institutions of her own choosing; and, more than a welcome, assistance also of every kind that she may need and may herself desire. The treatment accorded Russia by her sister nations in the months to come will be the acid test of their good will, of their comprehension of her needs as distinguished from their own interests, and of their intelligent and unselfish sympathy.

VII. Belgium, the whole world will agree, must be evacuated and restored, without any attempt to limit the sovereignty which she enjoys in common with all other free nations. No other single act will serve as this will serve to restore confidence among the nations in the laws which they have themselves set and determined for the government of their relations with one another. Without this healing act the whole structure and validity of international law is forever impaired.

VIII. All French territory should be freed and the invaded portions restored, and the wrong done to France by Prussia in 1871 in the matter of Alsace-Lorraine, which has unsettled the peace of the world for nearly fifty years, should be righted, in order that peace may once more be made secure in the interest of all.

IX. A readjustment of the frontiers of Italy should be effected along clearly recognizable lines of nationality.

X. The peoples of Austria-Hungary, whose place among the nations we wish to see safeguarded and assured, should be accorded the freest opportunity of autonomous development.

XI. Rumania, Serbia, and Montenegro should be evacuated; occupied territories restored; Serbia accorded free and secure access to the sea; and the relations of the several Balkan States to one another determined by friendly counsel along historically established lines of allegiance and nationality; and international guarantees of the political and economic independence and territorial integrity of the several Balkan States should be entered into.

XII. The Turkish portions of the present Ottoman Empire should be assured a secure sovereignty, but the other nationalities which are now under Turkish rule should be assured an undoubted security of life and an absolutely unmolested opportunity of autonomous development, and the Dardanelles should be permanently opened as a free passage to the ships and commerce of all nations under international guarantees.

XIII. An independent Polish State should be erected which should include the territories inhabited by indisputably Polish populations, which should be assured a free and secure access to the sea, and whose political and economic independence and territorial integrity should be guaranteed by international covenant.

XIV. A general association of nations

must be formed under specific covenants for the purpose of affording mutual guarantees of political independence and territorial integrity to great and small States alike.

In regard to these essential rectifications of wrong and assertions of right we feel ourselves to be intimate partners of all the Governments and peoples associated together against the Imperialists. We cannot be separated in interest or divided in purpose. We stand together until the end . . . .

Treaty of Peace between the Allied and Associated Powers and Germany (Treaty of Versailles), 28 June 1919

Part I · The Covenant of the League of Nations

THE HIGH CONTRACTING PARTIES,

In order to promote international cooperation and to achieve international peace and security

by the acceptance of obligations not to resort to war,

by the prescription of open, just and honourable relations between nations,

by the firm establishment of the understandings of international law as the actual rule of conduct among Governments, and

by the maintenance of justice and a scrupulous respect for all treaty obligations in the dealings of organized peoples with one another,

Agree to this Covenant of the League of Nations.

Article 1. The original Members of the League of Nations shall be those of the Signatories which are named in the Annex to this Covenant and also such of those other States named in the Annex as shall accede without reservation to this Covenant. Such accession shall be effected by a declaration deposited with the Secretariat within two months of the coming into force of the Covenant. Notice thereof shall be sent to all other Members of the League.

Any fully self-governing State, Dominion or Colony not named in the Annex may become a Member of the League if its admission is agreed to by two-thirds of the Assembly, provided that it shall give effective guarantees of its sincere intention to observe its international obligations, and shall accept such regulations as may be prescribed by the League in regard to its military, naval and air forces and armaments.

Any Member of the League may, after two years' notice of its intention so to do, withdraw from the League, provided that all its international obligations and all its obligations under this Covenant shall have been fulfilled at the time of its withdrawal.

Article 2. The action of the League under this Covenant shall be effected through the instrumentality of an Assembly and of a Council, with a permanent Secretariat.

Article 3. The Assembly shall consist of Representatives of the Members of the League.

The Assembly shall meet at stated intervals and from time to time as occasion may require at the Seat of the League or at such other place as may be decided upon.

The Assembly may deal at its meetings with any matter within the sphere of action of the League or affecting the peace of the world.

At meetings of the Assembly each Member of the League shall have one vote, and may have not more than three Representatives.

Article 4. The Council shall consist of Representatives of the Principal Allied and Associated Powers, together with Representatives of four other Members of the League. These four Members of the League shall be selected by the Assembly from time to time in its discretion. Until the appointment of the Representatives of the four Members of the League first selected by the Assembly, Representatives of Belgium, Brazil, Spain and Greece shall be members of the Council.

With the approval of the majority of the Assembly, the Council may name additional Members of the League whose Representatives shall always be members of the Council; the Council with like approval may increase the number of Members of the League to be selected by the Assembly for representation on the Council.

The Council shall meet from time to time as occasion may require, and at least once a year, at the Seat of the League, or at such other place as may be decided upon.

The Council may deal at its meetings with any matter within the sphere of action of the League or affecting the peace of the world.

Any Member of the League not represented on the Council shall be invited to send a Representative to sit as a member at any meeting of the Council during the consideration of matters specially affecting the interests of that Member of the League.

At meetings of the Council, each Member of the League represented on the Council shall have one vote, and may have not more than one Representative.

Article 5. Except where otherwise expressly provided in this Covenant or by the terms of the present Treaty, decisions at any meeting of the Assembly or of the Council shall require the agreement of all the Members of the League represented at the meeting.

All matters of procedure at meetings of the Assembly or of the council, including the appointment of Committees to investigate particular matters, shall be regulated by the Assembly or by the Council and may be decided by a majority of the Members of the League represented at the meeting.

The first meeting of the Assembly and the first meeting of the Council shall be summoned by the President of the United States of America.

*Article 6.*The permanent Secretariat shall be established at the Seat of the League. The Secretariat shall comprise a Secretary-General and such secretaries and staff as may be required.

The first Secretary-General shall be the person named in the Annex; thereafter the Secretary-General shall be appointed by the Council with the approval of the majority of the Assembly.

The secretaries and staff of the Secretariat shall be appointed by the Secretary-General with the approval of the Council.

The Secretary-General shall act in that capacity at all meetings of the Assembly and of the Council.

The expenses of the Secretariat shall be borne by the Members of the League in accordance with the apportionment of the expenses of the International Bureau of the Universal Postal Union.

Article 7. The Seat of the League is established at Geneva.

The Council may at any time decide that the Seat of the League shall be established elsewhere.

Article 8. The Members of the League recognize that the maintenance of peace requires the reduction of national armaments to the lowest point consistent with national safety and the enforcement by common action of international obligations.

The Council, taking account of the geographical situation and circumstances of each State, shall formulate plans for such reduction for the consideration and action of the several Governments . . .

[*Article 9*. Permanent Commission to be set up to advise Council on the execution of Articles 1-8.]

Article 10. The Members of the League undertake to respect and preserve as against external aggression the territorial integrity and existing political independence of all Members of the League. In case of any such aggression or in case of any threat or danger of such aggression the

Council shall advise upon the means by which this obligation shall be fulfilled.

Article 11. Any war or threat of war, whether immediately affecting any of the Members of the League or not, is hereby declared a matter of concern to the whole League, and the League shall take any action that may be deemed wise and effectual to safeguard the peace of nations. In case any such emergency should arise the Secretary-General shall on the request of any Member of the League forthwith summon a meeting of the Council.

It is also declared to be the friendly right of each Member of the League to bring to the attention of the Assembly or of the Council any circumstance whatever affecting international relations which threatens to disturb international peace or the good understanding between nations upon which peace depends.

Article 12. The Members of the League agree that if there should arise between them any dispute likely to lead to a rupture, they will submit the matter either to arbitration or to inquiry by the Council, and they agree in no case to resort to war until three months after the award by the arbitrators or the report by the Council.

In any case under this Article the award of the arbitrators shall be made within a reasonable time, and the report of the Council shall be made within six months after the submission of the dispute.

Article 13. The Members of the League agree that whenever any dispute shall arise between them which they recognize to be suitable for submission to arbitration and which cannot be satisfactorily settled by diplomacy, they will submit the whole subject-matter to arbitration.

Disputes as to the interpretation of a treaty, as to any question of international law, as to the existence of any fact which if established would constitute a breach of any international obligation, or as to the extent and nature of the reparation to be made for any such breach, are declared to be among those which are generally suitable for submission to arbitration.

For the consideration of any such dispute the court of arbitration to which the case is referred shall be the court agreed on by the parties to the dispute or stipulated in any convention existing between them.

The Members of the League agree that they will carry out in full good faith any award that may be rendered, and that they will not resort to war against a Member of the League which complies therewith. In the event of any failure to carry out such an award, the Council shall propose what steps should be taken to give effect thereto.

Article 14. The Council shall formulate and submit to the Members of the League for adoption plans for the establishment of a Permanent Court of International Justice. The Court shall be competent to hear and determine any dispute of an international character which the parties thereto submit to it. The Court may also give an advisory opinion upon any dispute or question referred to it by the Council or by the Assembly.

Article 15. If there should arise between Members of the League any dispute likely to lead to a rupture, which is not submitted to arbitration in accordance with Article 13, the Members of the League agree that they will submit the matter to the Council. Any party to the dispute may effect such submission by giving notice of the existence of the dispute to the Secretary-General, who will make all necessary arrangements for a full investigation and consideration thereof.

For this purpose the parties to the dispute will communicate to the Secretary-General as promptly as possible, statements of their case, with all the relevant facts and papers, and the Council may forthwith direct the publication thereof.

The Council shall endeavour to effect a settlement of the dispute, and if such efforts are successful, a statement shall be made public giving such facts and explanations regarding the dispute and the terms of settlement thereof as the Council may deem appropriate.

If the dispute is not thus settled, the Council either unanimously or by a majority vote shall make and publish a report containing a statement of the facts of the dispute and the recommendations which are deemed just and proper in regard thereto.

Any Member of the League represented on the Council may make public a statement of the facts of the dispute and of its conclusions regarding the same.

If a report by the Council is unanimously agreed to by the members thereof other than the Representatives of one or more of the parties to the dispute, the Members of the League agree that they will not go to war with any party to the dispute which complies with the recommendations of the report.

If the Council fails to reach a report which is unanimously agreed to by the members thereof, other than the Representatives of one or more of the parties to the dispute, the Members of the League reserve to themselves the right to take such action as they shall consider necessary for the maintenance of right and justice.

If the dispute between the parties is claimed by one of them, and is found by the Council, to arise out of a matter which by international law is solely within the domestic jurisdiction of that party, the Council shall so report, and shall make no recommendation as to its settlement.

The Council may in any case under this Article refer the dispute to the Assembly. The dispute shall be so referred at the request of either party to the dispute, provided that such request be made within fourteen days after the submission of the dispute to the Council.

In any case referred to the Assembly, all the provisions of this Article and of Article 12 relating to the action and powers of the Council shall apply to the action and powers of the Assembly, provided that a report made by the Assembly, if concurred in by the Representatives of those Members of the League represented on the Council and of a majority of the other Members of the League, exclusive in each case of the Representatives of the parties to the dispute, shall have the same force as a report by the Council concurred in by all the members thereof other than the Representatives of one or more of the parties to the dispute.

Article 16. Should any Member of the League resort to war in disregard of its covenants under Articles 12, 13 or 15, it shall *ipso facto* be deemed to have committed an act of war against all other Members of the League, which hereby undertake immediately to subject it to the severance of all trade or financial relations, the prohibition of all intercourse between their nationals and the nationals of the covenant-breaking State, and the prevention of all financial, commercial or personal intercourse between the nationals of the covenant-breaking State and the nationals of any other State, whether a Member of the League or not.

It shall be the duty of the Council in such case to recommend to the several Governments concerned what effective military, naval or air force the Members of the League shall severally contribute to the armed forces to be used to protect the covenants of the League.

The Members of the League agree, further, that they will mutually support one another in the financial and economic measures which are taken under this Article, in order to minimize the loss and inconvenience resulting from the above measures, and that they will mutually support one another in resisting any special measures aimed at one of their number by the covenant-breaking State, and that they will take the necessary steps to afford passage through their territory to the forces of any of the Members of the League which are cooperating to protect the covenants of the League.

Any Member of the League which has violated any covenant of the League may be declared to be no longer a Member of the League by a vote of the Council concurred in by the Representatives of all the other Members of the League represented thereon.

Article 17. In the event of a dispute between a Member of the League and a State which is not a Member of the League, or between States not Members of the League, the State or States not Members of the League shall be invited to accept the obligations of Membership in the League for the purposes of such dispute, upon such conditions as the Council may deem just. If such invitation is accepted, the provisions of Articles 12 to 16 inclusive shall be applied . . .

Article 18. Every treaty or international engagement entered into hereafter by any Member of the League shall be forthwith registered with the Secretariat and shall as soon as possible be published by it. No such treaty or international engagement shall be binding until so registered.

Article 19. The Assembly may from time to time advise the reconsideration by Members of the League of treaties which have become inapplicable and the consideration of international conditions whose continuance might endanger the peace of the world.

Article 20. The Members of the League severally agree that this Covenant is accepted as abrogating all obligations or understanding *inter se* which are inconsistent with the terms thereof, and solemnly undertake that they will not hereafter enter into any engagements inconsistent with the terms thereof.

In case any Member of the League shall, before becoming a Member of the League, have undertaken any obligations inconsistent with the terms of this Covenant, it shall be the duty of such Member to take immediate steps to procure its release from such obligations.

Article 21. Nothing in this Covenant shall be deemed to affect the validity of international engagements, such as treaties of arbitration or regional understandings like the Monroe Doctrine, for securing the maintenance of peace.

Article 22. To those colonies and territories which as a consequence of the late war have ceased to be under the sovereignty of the States which formerly governed them and which are inhabited by peoples not yet able to stand by themselves under the strenuous conditions of the modern world, there should be applied the principle that the well-being and development of such peoples form a sacred trust of civilization and that securities for the performance of

this trust should be embodied in this Covenant.

The best method of giving practical effect to this principle is that the tutelage of such peoples should be entrusted to advanced nations who by reason of their resources, their experience or their geographical position can best undertake this responsibility, and who are willing to accept it, and that this tutelage should be exercised by them as Mandatories on behalf of the League.

The character of the mandate must differ according to the stage of the development of the people, the geographical situation of the territory, its economic conditions and other similar circumstances.

Certain communities formerly belonging to the Turkish Empire have reached a stage of development where their existence as independent nations can be provisionally recognized subject to the rendering of administrative advice and assistance by a Mandatory until such time as they are able to stand alone. The wishes of these communities must be a principal consideration in the selection of the Mandatory.

Other peoples, especially those of Central Africa, are at such a stage that the Mandatory must be responsible for the administration of the territory under conditions which will guarantee freedom of conscience and religion, subject only to the maintenance of public order and morals, the prohibition of abuses such as the slave trade, the arms traffic and the liquor traffic, and the prevention of the establishment of fortifications or military and naval bases and of military training of the natives for other than police purposes and the defence of territory, and will also secure equal opportunities for the trade and commerce of other Members of the League.

There are territories, such as South-west Africa and certain of the South Pacific Islands, which, owing to the sparseness of their population, or their small size, or their remoteness from the centres of civilization, or their geographical contiguity to the territory of the Mandatory, and other circumstances, can be best administered under the laws of the Mandatory as integral portions of its territory, subject to the safeguards above mentioned in the interests of the indigenous population.

In every case of mandate, the Mandatory shall render to the Council an annual report in reference to the territory committed to its charge.

The degree of authority, control, or administration to be exercised by the Mandatory shall, if not previously agreed upon by the Members of the League, be explicitly defined in each case by the Council.

A permanent Commission shall be constituted to receive and examine the annual reports of the Mandatories and to advise the Council on all matters relating to the observance of the mandates.

Article 23. Subject to and in accordance with the provisions of international conventions existing or hereafter to be agreed upon, the Members of the League:

(*a*) will endeavour to secure and maintain fair and humane conditions of labour for men, women, and children, both in their own countries and in all countries to which their commercial and industrial relations extend, and for that purpose will establish and maintain the necessary international organizations;

(*b*) undertake to secure just treatment of the native inhabitants of territories under their control;

(*c*) will entrust the League with the general supervision over the execution of agreements with regard to the traffic in women and children, and the traffic in opium and other dangerous drugs;

(*d*) will entrust the League with the general supervision of the trade in arms and ammunition with the countries in which the control of this traffic is necessary in the common interest;

(*e*) will make provision to secure and maintain freedom of communications and of transit and equitable treatment for the commerce of all Members of the League. In this connection, the special necessities of the regions devastated during the war of 1914-1918 shall be borne in mind;

(*f*) will endeavour to take steps in matters of international concern for the prevention and control of disease.

[*Article 24.* International bureaux to be placed under League if parties consent.]

[*Article 25.* Encouragement of Red Cross.]

Article 26. Amendments to this Covenant will take effect when ratified by the Members of the League whose Representatives compose the Council and by a majority of the Members of the League whose Representatives compose the Assembly.

No such amendment shall bind any Members of the League which signifies its dissent therefrom, but in that case it shall cease to be a Member of the League.

Part II · Boundaries of Germany

Article 27. The boundaries of Germany will be determined as follows ... [see pp. 90-91].

Part III · Political clauses for Europe

SECTION I · BELGIUM

Article 31. Germany, recognizing that the Treaties of April 19, 1839, which established the status of Belgium before the war, no longer conform to the requirements of the situation, consents to the abrogation of the said treaties and undertakes immediately to recognize and to observe whatever conventions may be entered into by the Principal Allied and Associated Powers, or by any of them, in concert with the Governments of Belgium and of the Netherlands, to replace the said Treaties of 1839. If her formal adhesion should be required to such conventions or to any of their stipulations, Germany undertakes immediately to give it.

Article 32. Germany recognizes the full sovereignty of Belgium over the whole of the contested territory of Moresnet (called *Moresnet neutre*).

. . .

[*Article 40.* Germany renounces all rights in Luxembourg.]

Section III · Left bank of the Rhine

Article 42. Germany is forbidden to maintain or construct any fortifications either on the left bank of the Rhine or on the right bank to the west of a line drawn 50 kilometres to the east of the Rhine.

Article 43. In the area defined above the maintenance and the assembly of armed forces, either permanently or temporarily, and military manœuvres of any kind, as well as the upkeep of all permanent works for mobilization, are in the same way forbidden.

Article 44. In case Germany violates in any manner whatever the provisions of Articles 42 and 43, she shall be regarded as committing a hostile act against the Powers signatory of the present Treaty and as calculated to disturb the peace of the world.

Section IV · Saar Basin

Article 45. As compensation for the destruction of the coal mines in the north of France and as part payment towards the total reparation due from Germany for the damage resulting from the war, Germany cedes to France in full and absolute possession, with exclusive rights of exploitation, unencumbered and free from all debts and charges of any kind, the coal mines situated in the Saar Basin as defined in Article 48.

. . .

Article 49. Germany renounces in favour of the League of Nations, in the capacity of trustee, the government of the territory defined above.

At the end of fifteen years from the coming into force of the present Treaty the inhabitants of the said territory shall be called upon to indicate the sovereignty under which they desire to be placed.

Section V · Alsace-Lorraine

The High Contracting Parties, recognizing the moral obligation to redress the wrong done by Germany in 1871 both to the rights of France and to the wishes of the population of Alsace and Lorraine, which were separated from their country in spite of the solemn protest of their representatives at the Assembly of Bordeaux,

Agree upon the following Articles:

Article 51. The territories which were ceded to Germany in accordance with the Preliminaries of Peace signed at Versailles on February 26, 1871, and the Treaty of Frankfurt of May 10, 1871, are restored to French sovereignty as from the date of the Armistice of November 11, 1918.

The provisions of the Treaties establishing the delimitation of the frontiers before 1871 shall be restored.

. . .

Section VI · Austria

Article 80. Germany acknowledges and will respect strictly the independence of Austria, within the frontiers which may be fixed in a Treaty between that State and the Principal Allied and Associated Powers; she agrees that this independence shall be inalienable, except with the consent of the Council of the League of Nations.

Section VII · Czecho-Slovak State

Article 81. Germany, in conformity with the action already taken by the Allied and Associated Powers, recognizes the complete independence of the Czecho-Slovak State which will include the autonomous territory of the Ruthenians to the south of the Carpathians. Germany hereby recognizes the frontiers of this State as determined by the Principal Allied and Associated Powers and the other interested States.

. . .

Section VIII · Poland

Article 87. Germany, in conformity with the action already taken by the Allied and Associated Powers, recognizes the complete independence of Poland, and renounces in her favour all rights and title over the territory bounded by the Baltic Sea, the eastern frontier of Germany as laid down in Article 27 of Part II (Boundaries of Germany) of the present Treaty up to a point situated about 2 kilometres to the east of Lorzendorf, then a line to the acute angle which the northern boundary of Upper Silesia makes about 3 kilometres north-west of Simmenau, then the boundary of Upper Silesia to its meeting point with the old frontier between Germany and Russia, then this frontier to the point where it crosses the course of the Niemen, and then the northern frontier of East Prussia as laid down in Article 28 of Part II aforesaid.

The provisions of this Article do not, however, apply to the territories of East Prussia and the Free City of Danzig, as defined in Article 28 of Part II (Boundaries of Germany) and in Article 100 of Section XI (Danzig) of this Part.

The boundaries of Poland not laid down in the present Treaty will be subsequently determined by the Principal Allied and Associated Powers . . . .

Article 89. Poland undertakes to accord freedom of transit to persons, goods, vessels, carriages, wagons and mails in transit between East Prussia and the rest of Germany over Polish territory, including territorial waters, and to treat them at least as favourably as the persons, goods, vessels, carriages, wagons and mails respectively of Polish or of any other more favoured nationality, origin, importation, starting point, or ownership as regards facilities, restrictions and all other matters.

Goods in transit shall be exempt from all customs or other similar duties.

Freedom of transit will extend to telegraphic and telephonic services under the conditions laid down by the conventions referred to in Article 98.

. . .

Article 93. Poland accepts and agrees to embody in a Treaty with the Principal Allied and Associated Powers such provisions as may be deemed necessary by the said Powers to protect the interests of inhabitants of Poland who differ from the majority of the population in race, language or religion.

Poland further accepts and agrees to embody in a Treaty with the said Powers such provisions as they may deem necessary to protect freedom of transit and equitable treatment of the commerce of other nations.

Section IX · East Prussia

Article 94. In the area between the southern frontier of East Prussia, as described in Article 28 of Part II (Boundaries of Germany) of the present Treaty, and the line described below, the inhabitants will be called upon to indicate by a vote the State to which they wish to belong . . . .

Section X · Memel

Article 99. Germany renounces in favour of the Principal Allied and Associated Powers all rights and title over the territories included between the Baltic, the north-eastern frontier of East Prussia as defined in Article 28 of Part II (Boundaries of Germany) of the present Treaty and the former frontier between Germany and Russia.

Germany undertakes to accept the settlement made by the Principal Allied and Associated Powers in regard to these territories, particularly in so far as concerns the nationality of the inhabitants.

Section XI · Free City of Danzig

Article 100. Germany renounces in favour of the Principal Allied and Associated Powers all rights and title over the territory comprised within the following limits . . . .

Article 102. The Principal Allied and Associated Powers undertake to establish the town of Danzig, together with the rest of the territory described in Article 100, as a Free City. It will be placed under the protection of the League of Nations.

Article 103. A constitution for the Free City of Danzig shall be drawn up by the duly appointed representatives of the Free City in agreement with a High Commissioner to be appointed by the League of Nations. This constitution shall be placed under the guarantee of the League of Nations.

The High Commissioner will also be entrusted with the duty of dealing in the first instance with all differences arising between Poland and the Free City of Danzig in regard to this Treaty or any arrangements or agreements made thereunder.

The High Commissioner shall reside at Danzig.

Article 104. The Principal Allied and Associated Powers undertake to negotiate a Treaty between the Polish Government and the Free City of Danzig, which shall come into force at the same time as the establishment of the said Free City, with the following objects:

(1) To effect the inclusion of the Free City of Danzig within the Polish customs frontiers, and to establish a free area in the port;

(2) To ensure to Poland without any restriction the free use and service of all waterways, docks, basins, wharves and other works within the territory of the Free City necessary for Polish imports and exports;

(3) To ensure to Poland the control and administration of the Vistula and of the whole railway system within the Free City, except such street and other railways as serve primarily the needs of the Free City, and of postal, telegraphic and telephonic communication between Poland and the port of Danzig;

(4) To ensure to Poland the right to develop and improve the waterways, docks, basins, wharves, railways and other works and means of communication mentioned in this Article, as well as to lease or purchase through appropriate processes such land and other property as may be necessary for these purposes;

(5) To provide against any discrimination within the Free City of Danzig to the detriment of citizens of Poland and other persons of Polish origin or speech;

(6) To provide that the Polish Government shall undertake the conduct of the foreign relations of the Free City of Danzig as well as the diplomatic protection of citizens of that city when abroad.

SECTION XIV · RUSSIA AND RUSSIAN STATES

Article 116. Germany acknowledges and agrees to respect as permanent and inalienable the independence of all the territories which were part of the former Russian Empire on August 1, 1914.

In accordance with the provisions of Article 259 of Part IX (Financial Clauses) and Article 292 of Part X (Economic Clauses) Germany accepts definitely the abrogation of the Brest-Litovsk Treaties and of all other treaties, conventions and agreements entered into by her with the Maximalist Government in Russia.

The Allied and Associated Powers formally reserve the rights of Russia to obtain from Germany restitution and reparation based on the principles of the present Treaty.

Article 117. Germany undertakes to recognize the full force of all treaties or agreements which may be entered into by the Allied and Associated Powers with States now existing or coming into existence in future in the whole or part of the former Empire of Russia as it existed on August 1, 1914, and to recognize the frontiers of any such States as determined therein.

Part IV · German rights and interests outside Germany

Article 118. In territory outside her European frontiers as fixed by the present Treaty, Germany renounces all rights, titles and privileges whatever in or over territory which belonged to her or to her allies, and all rights, titles and privileges whatever their origin which she held as against the Allied and Associated Powers.

Germany hereby undertakes to recognize and to conform to the measures which may be taken now or in the future by the Principal Allied and Associated Powers, in agreement where necessary with third Powers, in order to carry the above stipulation into effect.

In particular Germany declares her acceptance of the following Articles relating to certain special subjects.

SECTION I · GERMAN COLONIES

Article 119. Germany renounces in favour of the Principal Allied and Associated Powers all her rights and titles over her oversea possessions . . . .

[*Article 128.* Germany renounces all rights acquired in 1901 in China.]

[*Article 138*. Germany renounces all rights in Liberia.]

[*Article 141*. Germany renounces all rights in Morocco.]

[*Article 147*. Germany renounces all rights in Egypt.]

SECTION VIII · SHANTUNG

Article 156. Germany renounces, in favour of Japan, all her rights, title and privileges – particularly those concerning the territory of Kiaochow, railways, mines and submarine cables – which she acquired in virtue of the Treaty concluded by her with China on March 6, 1898, and of all other arrangements relative to the Province of Shantung . . . .

Part V · Military, naval and air clauses

In order to render possible the initiation of a general limitation of the armaments of all nations, Germany undertakes strictly to observe the military, naval and air clauses which follow.

SECTION I · MILITARY CLAUSES

Chapter I: Effectives and cadres of the German army

Article 159. The German military forces shall be demobilized and reduced as prescribed hereinafter.

Article 160. 1. By a date which must not be later than March 31, 1920, the German army must not comprise more than seven divisions of infantry and three divisions of cavalry.

After that date the total number of effectives in the army of the States constituting Germany must not exceed one hundred thousand men, including officers and establishments of depots. The army shall be devoted exclusively to the maintenance of order within the territory and to the control of the frontiers.

. . .

Chapter II: Armament, munitions and material

Article 164. Up till the time at which Germany is admitted as a member of the League of Nations the German army must not possess an armament greater than the amounts fixed in Table No. II annexed to this Section . . . .

Article 173. Universal compulsory military service shall be abolished in Germany.

The German army may only be constituted and recruited by means of voluntary enlistment.

Article 174. The period of enlistment for non-commissioned officers and privates must be twelve consecutive years . . . .

Article 175. The officers who are retained in the army must undertake the obligation to serve in it up to the age of forty-five years at least . . . .

Chapter IV: Fortifications

Article 180. All fortified works, fortresses and field works situated in German territory to the west of a line drawn 50 kilometres to the east of the Rhine shall be disarmed and dismantled . . . .

[*Article 181*. Naval limitation to six battleships and thirty smaller warships; no submarines.]

[*Article 198*. No military or naval air force.]

SECTION IV · INTER-ALLIED COMMISSIONS OF CONTROL

Article 203. All the military, naval and air clauses contained in the present Treaty, for the execution of which a time limit is prescribed, shall be executed by Germany under the control of Inter-Allied Commissions specially appointed for this purpose by the Principal Allied and Associated Powers . . . .

Part VIII · Reparation

SECTION I · GENERAL PROVISIONS

Article 231. The Allied and Associated Governments affirm and Germany accepts the responsibility of Germany and her allies for causing all the loss and damage to which the Allied and Associated Governments and their nationals have been subjected as a consequence of the war imposed upon them by the aggression of Germany and her allies.

Article 232. The Allied and Associated Governments recognize that the resources of Germany are not adequate, after taking into account permanent diminutions of such resources which will result from other provisions of the present Treaty, to make complete reparation for all such loss and damage.

The Allied and Associated Governments, however, require, and Germany undertakes, that she will make compensation for all damage done to the civilian population of the Allied and Associated Powers and to their property during the period of the belligerency of each as an Allied or Associated Power against Germany by such aggression by land, by sea and from the air, and in general all damage as defined in Annex I hereto.

In accordance with Germany's pledges, already given, as to complete restoration for Belgium, Germany undertakes, in addition to the compensation for damage elsewhere in this Part provided for, as a consequence of the violation of the Treaty of 1839, to make reimbursement of all sums which Belgium has borrowed from the Allied and Associated Governments up to November 11, 1918, together with interest at the rate of five per cent (5%) per annum on such sums. This amount shall be determined by the Reparation Commission . . . .

Article 233. The amount of the above damage for which compensation is to be made by Germany shall be determined by an Inter-Allied Commission, to be called the *Reparation Commission* and constituted in the form and with the powers set forth hereunder and in Annexes II to VII inclusive hereto.

This Commission shall consider the claims and give to the German Government a just opportunity to be heard.

The findings of the Commission as to the amount of damage defined as above shall be concluded and notified to the German Government on or before May 1, 1921, as representing the extent of that Government's obligations.

The Commission shall concurrently draw up a schedule of payments prescribing the time and manner for securing and discharging the entire obligation within a period of thirty years from May 1, 1921. If, however, within the period mentioned, Germany fails to discharge her obligations, any balance remaining unpaid may, within the discretion of the Commission, be postponed for settlement in subsequent years, or may be handled otherwise in such manner as the Allied and Associated Governments, acting in accordance with the procedure laid down in this Part of the present Treaty, shall determine.

. . .

Part IX · Financial clauses

Article 248. Subject to such exceptions as the Reparation Commission may approve, a first charge upon all the assets and revenues of the German Empire and its constituent States shall be the cost of reparation and all other costs arising under the present Treaty or any treaties or agreements supplementary thereto or under arrangements concluded between Germany and the Allied and Associated Powers during the Armistice or its extensions . . . .

Article 249. There shall be paid by the German Government the total cost of all armies of the Allied and Associated Governments in occupied German territory from the date of the signature of the Armistice of November 11, 1918, including the keep of men and beasts, lodging and billeting, pay and allowances, salaries and wages, bedding, heating, lighting, clothing, equipment, harness and saddlery, armament and rolling stock, air services, treatment of sick and wounded, veterinary and remount services, transport service of all sorts (such as by rail, sea or river, motor lorries), communications and correspondence, and in general the cost of all administrative or technical services the working of which is necessary for the training of troops and for keeping their numbers up to strength and preserving their military efficiency.

The cost of such liabilities under the above heads so far as they relate to purchases or requisitions by the Allied and Associated Governments in the occupied territories shall be paid by the German Government to the Allied and Associated Governments in marks at the current or agreed rate of exchange. All other of the above cost shall be paid in gold marks.

· · ·

Part XIV · Guarantees

SECTION I · WESTERN EUROPE

Article 428. As a guarantee for the execution of the present Treaty by Germany, the German territory situated to the west of the Rhine, together with the bridgeheads, will be occupied by Allied and Associated troops for a period of fifteen years from the coming into force of the present Treaty.

Article 429. If the conditions of the present Treaty are faithfully carried out by Germany, the occupation referred to in Article 428 will be successively restricted as follows:

(i) At the expiration of five years there will be evacuated: the bridgehead of Cologne and the territories north of a line running along the Ruhr, then along the railway Jülich, Düren, Euskirchen, Rheinbach, thence along the road Rheinbach to Sinzig, and reaching the Rhine at the confluence with the Ahr; the roads, railways and places mentioned above being excluded from the area evacuated.

(ii) At the expiration of ten years there will be evacuated: the bridgehead of Coblenz and the territories north of a line to be drawn from the intersection between the frontiers of Belgium, Germany and Holland, running about 4 kilometers south of Aix-la-Chapelle, then to and following the crest of Forst Gemünd, then east of the railway of the Urft Valley, then along Blankenheim, Valdorf, Dreis, Ulmen to and following the Moselle from Bremm to Nehren, then passing by Kappel and Simmern, then following the ridge of the heights between Simmern and the Rhine and reaching this river at Bacharach; all the places, valleys, roads and railways mentioned above being excluded from the area evacuated.

(iii) At the expiration of fifteen years there will be evacuated: the bridgehead of Mainz, the bridgehead of Kehl and the remainder of the German territory under occupation.

If at that date the guarantees against unprovoked aggression by Germany are not considered sufficient by the Allied and Associated Governments, the evacuation of the occupying troops may be delayed to the extent regarded as necessary for the purpose of obtaining the required guarantees.

Article 430. In case either during the occupation or after the expiration of the fifteen years referred to above the Reparation Commission finds that Germany refuses to observe the whole or part of her obligations under the present Treaty with regard to reparation, the whole or part of the areas specified in Article 429 will be reoccupied immediately by the Allied and Associated forces.

Article 431. If before the expiration of the period of fifteen years Germany complies with all the undertakings resulting from the present Treaty, the occupying forces will be withdrawn immediately.

Article 432. All matters relating to the occupation and not provided for by the present Treaty shall be regulated by subsequent agreements, which Germany hereby undertakes to observe.

SECTION II · EASTERN EUROPE

Article 433. As a guarantee for the execution of the provisions of the present Treaty, by which Germany accepts definitely the abrogation of the Brest-Litovsk Treaty, and of all treaties, conventions and agreements entered into by her with the Maximalist Government in Russia, and in order to ensure the restoration of peace and good government in the Baltic Provinces and Lithuania, all German troops at present in the said territories shall return to within the frontiers of Germany as soon as the Governments of the Principal Allied and

Associated Powers shall think the moment suitable, having regard to the internal situation of these territories. These troops shall abstain from all requisitions and seizures and from any other coercive measures, with a view to obtaining supplies intended for Germany, and shall in no way interfere with such measures for national defence as may be adopted by the Provisional Governments of Estonia, Latvia and Lithuania.

No other German troops shall, pending the evacuation or after the evacuation is complete, be admitted to the said territories.

Part XV · Miscellaneous provisions

Article 434. Germany undertakes to recognize the full force of the Treaties of Peace and Additional Conventions which may be concluded by the Allied and Associated Powers with the Powers who fought on the side of Germany and to recognize whatever dispositions may be made concerning the territories of the former Austro-Hungarian Monarchy, of the Kingdom of Bulgaria and of the Ottoman Empire, and to recognize the new States within their frontiers as there laid down.

Treaty between France and Great Britain (Treaty of Guarantee), 28 June 1919

Assistance to France in the event of unprovoked aggression by Germany

Article I. In case the following stipulations relating to the Left Bank of the Rhine contained in the Treaty of Peace with Germany signed at Versailles the 28th day of June, 1919, by the British Empire, the French Republic, and the United States of America among other Powers:

> ARTICLE 42. Germany is forbidden to maintain or construct any fortifications either on the left bank of the Rhine or on the right bank to the west of a line drawn 50 kilometers to the east of the Rhine.
> ARTICLE 43. In the area defined above the maintenance and assembly of armed forces, either permanently, or temporarily, and military manœuvres of any kind, as well as the upkeep of all permanent works for mobilization, are in the same way forbidden.
> ARTICLE 44. In case Germany violates in any manner whatsoever the provisions of Articles 42 and 43, she shall be regarded as committing a hostile act against the Powers signatory of the present Treaty and as calculated to disturb the peace of the world.

may not at first provide adequate security and protection to France, Great Britain agrees to come immediately to her assistance in the event of any unprovoked movement of aggression against her being made by Germany.

Article 2. The present Treaty, in similar terms with the Treaty of even date for the same purpose concluded between the French Republic and the United States of America, a copy of which Treaty is annexed hereto, will only come into force when the latter is ratified.

Article 3. The present Treaty must be submitted to the Council of the League of Nations and must be recognized by the Council, acting if need be by a majority, as an engagement which is consistent with the Covenant of the League; it will continue in force until on the application of one of the Parties to it the Council, acting if need be by a majority, agree that the League itself affords sufficient protection.

Article 4. The present Treaty shall before ratification by His Majesty be submitted to Parliament for approval.

It shall before ratification by the

President of the French Republic be submitted to the French Chambers for approval.

Article 5. The present Treaty shall impose no obligation upon any of the Dominions of the British Empire unless and until it is approved by the Parliament of the Dominion concerned.

The present Treaty shall be ratified, and shall, subject to Articles 2 and 4, come into force at the same time as the Treaty of Peace with Germany of even date comes into force for the British Empire and the French Republic.

In Faith Whereof the above-named plenipotentiaries have signed the present Treaty, drawn up in the English and French languages.

Done in duplicate at Versailles, on the twenty-eighth day of June, 1919.

(Seal) D. LLOYD GEORGE
(Seal) ARTHUR JAMES BALFOUR
(Seal) G. CLEMENCEAU
(Seal) S. PICHON

Treaty between the Allied and Associated Powers and Poland on the protection of minorities, 28 June 1919

Article 2. Poland undertakes to assure full and complete protection of life and liberty to all inhabitants of Poland without distinction of birth, nationality, language, race or religion.

All inhabitants of Poland shall be entitled to the free exercise, whether public or private, of any creed, religion or belief, whose practices are not inconsistent with public order or public morals.

Article 3. Poland admits and declares to be Polish nationals *ipso facto* and without the requirement of any formality German, Austrian, Hungarian or Russian nationals habitually resident at the date of the coming into force of the present Treaty in territory which is or may be recognized as forming part of Poland, but subject to any provisions in the Treaties of Peace with Germany or Austria respectively relating to persons who became resident in such territory after a specified date.

Nevertheless, the persons referred to above, who are over eighteen years of age will be entitled under the conditions contained in the said Treaties to opt for any other nationality which may be open to them. Option by a husband will cover his wife and option by parents will cover their children under eighteen years of age . . . .

Article 7. All Polish nationals shall be equal before the law and shall enjoy the same civil and political rights without distinction as to race, language or religion.

Differences of religion, creed or confession shall not prejudice any Polish national in matters relating to the enjoyment of civil or political rights, as for instance admission to public employments, functions and honours, or exercise of professions and industries.

No restriction shall be imposed on the free use by any Polish national of any language in private intercourse, in commerce, in religion, in the press or in publications of any kind, or at public meetings . . . .

Article 8. Polish nationals who belong to racial, religious or linguistic minorities shall enjoy the same treatment and security in law and in fact as the other Polish nationals. In particular they shall have an equal right to establish, manage and control at their own expense charitable, religious and social institutions, schools and other educational establishments, with the right to use their own language and to exercise their religion freely therein.

Article 9. Poland will provide in the public educational system in towns and districts in which a considerable proportion of Polish nationals of other than Polish speech are residents adequate facilities for ensuring that in the primary schools the instruction shall be given to the children of such Polish nationals through the medium of their own language. This provision shall not prevent the Polish Government from making the teaching of the Polish language obligatory in the said schools.

. . .

Article 11. Jews shall not be compelled to perform any act which constitutes a violation of their Sabbath, not shall they be placed under any disability by reason of their refusal to attend courts of law or to perform any legal business on their Sabbath. This provision however shall not exempt Jews from such obligations as shall be imposed upon all other Polish citizens for the necessary purposes of military service, national defence or the preservation of public order . . . .

The Allies, Turkey and Greece, 1920–23

The Allies planned the partition of Turkey at the peace conference. Not only were the subject national groups to be taken from the Ottoman Empire, but Turkey proper was to be placed under the tutelage of the western powers. In the Middle East, the wartime inter-Allied agreements and promises to the Arabs and Zionists made the disposition of this part of the Ottoman Empire the subject of protracted negotiations. The problems of Asia Minor were only considered intermittently at Paris during the spring of 1919. It was decided at Paris to internationalize the Straits and to assist and encourage autonomous governments among the liberated subject peoples. The mandate system was devised to reconcile autonomous national development and great power influence and supervision both in the Middle East and in respect to the German colonies. France claimed the mandate for the whole of Syria. Lloyd George wished to restrict the French mandate to the coastal region as determined in the *Sykes–Picot Agreement* of 1916 (p. 71). A mandate for Armenia and the Straits was offered at Paris to the United States, but Wilson could give no decision before his return to Washington in June 1919, and Congress did not formally refuse the mandate until a year later. The peace settlement was further delayed by the claims of Italy and Greece. In April 1919, the Italians had landed troops in Antalya (Adalia) in Asia Minor, and in May 1919, the Greeks landed troops in Izmir (Smyrna). An Allied force had been in occupation of the Straits in accordance with the terms of the Armistice of Mudros, 30 October 1918, and in March 1920 occupied Constantinople. The peace terms were presented to the practically captive Sultan's government in May 1920 and the Sultan's government concluded the *Treaty of Sèvres with the Allies on 10 August 1920* (p. 118). In European Turkey, eastern Thrace was ceded to Greece and most of the Aegean islands; the Straits were left under nominal Turkish sovereignty, but the waterway was internationalized, demilitarized and was to be open to all merchant ships and warships in peace and in war (a reversal of the régime established by the Straits Convention of 1841); it was to be run by a Commission of ten powers under the League of Nations framework. Smyrna and district in western Anatolia was to be administered by Greece for five years, followed by a plebiscite. In eastern Anatolia, Armenia was granted independence and its frontiers were to be decided later; Kurdistan was permitted autonomy; Turkey lost Syria which became a French mandate, Palestine and Mesopotamia which became British mandates, and the Arabian peninsula which was granted independence as the Kingdom of Hejaz. Turkish finances were placed under British, French and Italian supervision.

These onerous terms were signed by the Sultan's government which was increasingly losing control of the country to the Turkish Nationalists led by Mustafa Kemal. Kemal and the Nationalist Assembly in Ankara rejected the terms. Kemal and the reorganized Turkish army concluded *a treaty with Bolshevik Russia on 16 March 1921* (p. 121), and crushed Armenia. The Moscow treaty with Soviet Russia settled Turkey's eastern frontier without reference to the Allies and rejected the validity of any treaty imposed on Turkey.

Kemal's growing strength decided the Allies against attempting to enforce the Treaty of Sèvres by force. The United States had withdrawn its support altogether. In June 1921 Italy began to evacuate Asia Minor. France and Turkey concluded the *Treaty of Ankara, 20 October 1921*. Hostilities between France and Kemal's troops ceased; a new frontier was drawn between Syria and Turkey more favourable to Turkey than that of Sèvres. France recognized Kemal's government of the Grand National Assembly. By the treaty Allied unity and the Treaty of Sèvres was shattered as France concluded a separate peace.

The Greek army in Asia Minor was decisively defeated in August 1922 and Kemal's troops entered Izmir on 9 September. In the Straits Allied unity had crumbled when French and Italian garrisons were withdrawn in September 1922. The British remained alone, guarding the Straits at Chanak with the Turks in October 1922 determined to regain control. The consequent Chanak crisis was resolved by negotiation and the *Armistice of Mudanya* between Turkey, Italy, France and Britain on *11 October 1922* (on 14 October the Greeks acceded to it): by the terms of the armistice eastern Thrace as far as the Maritsa river and Adrianople was handed by the Greeks to the Nationalist Turks, and Turkish sovereignty over Istanbul (Constantinople) and the Straits was recognized.

The final settlement was worked out at the *Conference of Lausanne, 21 November 1922–24 February 1923 and 23 April–24 July 1923*. The ambiguous position of the Turkish Nationalists and the Sultan was resolved by the abolition of the Sultanate on 1 November 1922. During the course of the conference, agreement was reached in January 1923 on a compulsory exchange of Greek and Turkish minorities and a convention signed to this effect by *Greece and Turkey, 30 January 1923*. After protracted negotiations the conference ended with the signature by Turkey of the *Treaty of Lausanne, 24 July 1923* (p. 123). Many of the onerous terms of the Treaty of Sèvres were abandoned. Turkey alone among ex-enemy states was not required to pay reparations. The special legal privileges which the 'civilized' western nations had enjoyed in their dealings with the Ottoman Empire, known as the capitulations, were abolished. Few restrictions on national Turkish sovereignty remained. The treaty settled the boundaries of Turkey, and, with the restoration of eastern Thrace, Turkey's frontier in Europe was restored to what it had been in 1914 (with the exception of a small piece of territory ceded to Bulgaria). Greece retained all but two of the former Turkish Aegean islands, which were near the mouth of the Dardanelles and which were returned to Turkey. (The Dodecanese Islands were retained by Italy.) British sovereignty over Cyprus was confirmed. The frontier between British-mandated Iraq and Turkey was not finally settled; the key region of Mosul had been left for later settlement, eventually reached in 1926 when Mosul was given to Iraq.

The question of the Straits was settled by the *Straits Convention* (p. 125) which formed an annex to the treaty. A demilitarized zone was established on both the Asian and European shores, but the Turks were permitted to garrison Istanbul; the security of the Straits and the demilitarized zones and free navigation was guaranteed by the signatories of the convention and more especially by France, Britain, Italy and Japan; the Soviet Union signed but did not ratify the convention. The passage of merchant vessels was guaranteed through the Straits in time of peace or war, and if Turkey itself was at war; the passage of warships in time of peace was limited by tonnage and number, and to a maximum force for each country not exceeding 'the most powerful fleet of the littoral Powers of the Black Sea', at such a time. In time of war, Turkey being neutral, warships of belligerents could pass through the Straits without practical limitations (this marked the great change of rule from that established by the Straits Convention of 1841). In time of war, *Turkey being a belligerent*, the passage of neutral warships was permitted, limited by the same provision as for warships in time of peace.

The rule of the Straits established by the Treaty of Lausanne lasted until 1936 when it was replaced by the *Montreux Convention, 20 July 1936* (p. 128). This treaty restored Turkish sovereignty over the Straits, subject to certain conditions. It permitted the Black Sea powers *in time of peace* to send warships through the Straits subject to certain restrictions (articles 11–14); other naval powers could pay courtesy visits to Turkish ports in the Straits (article 17). The total tonnage any Black Sea power could have in the Black Sea was limited by article 18, but the limitations were only relative and flexible. Thus the Black Sea states, including the Soviet Union, enjoyed considerable advantages of egress denied to the other powers desiring to enter the Black Sea. In time of war, Turkey being neutral, warships of belligerents were *not* permitted to pass through the Straits unless assisting the victim of aggression within the framework of the League of Nations (article 19). If Turkey itself were at war, or threatened with war, the passage of warships was left to its discretion (articles 20 and 21). Turkish control of the Straits was restored; the International Straits Commission's work was handed over to the Turkish government (article 24) and the demilitarized zones abolished, allowing Turkey to guard the Straits (this was done by omitting the relevant articles of the Treaty of Lausanne).

The settlement in the Middle East

The settlement of the territories of the former Ottoman Empire outside the Asian frontiers of Turkey was modified by the *Treaty of Lausanne in 1923* (p. 123) which made the full application of the secret inter-Allied wartime agreements of Italian, French and British spheres of influence in Anatolia and Asia Minor impossible to fulfil. At the *Conference of San Remo, April 1920*, the former Ottoman province of Syria was divided between French and British mandates and the Arabian peninsula proper permitted independent Arab government. The outcome of the various Allied decisions and actions for the Middle East was as follows.

1. *Under British influence and/or jurisdiction.* Palestine, where Britain was given full control by the mandate; Transjordan granted its own government by a treaty with Britain in 1928, with British influence over finance, foreign policy and defence. Britain received the mandate for Mesopotamia, renamed Iraq; Iraq became a kingdom in 1921, and gained independence by the *Anglo–Iraq Alliance Treaty, 30 June 1930*, which terminated the British mandate; but Britain retained special rights for the defence of Iraq as well as air bases. Iraq was admitted to the League of Nations in October 1932. Egypt was pronounced independent by Britain on 1 March 1922, but here too Britain retained special rights including the presence of British troops to defend Egypt and the Suez Canal; Britain also reserved to itself the continuing control of the Sudan. A new *Anglo–Egyptian Alliance Treaty, 26 August 1936*, brought the British military occupation of Egypt to an end, but Britain was permitted to continue stationing forces in 'Egyptian territory in the vicinity of the Canal' to defend the Canal. Iran (Persia) was an independent state, but British influence was exerted through controlling interests in the oil industry. Britain had special treaty arrangements with Sheiks in the Persian Gulf. Britain also concluded the *Jedda Treaty, 20 May 1927*, with the independent kingdom of Hejaz and Nejd (renamed Saudi Arabia after 1932). Aden was a Crown colony and British influence predominated over the Aden Protectorate.

2. *Under French influence.* The history of these territories before 1939 is in this sense simpler in that the French mandate was maintained. France had received the mandate of Syria, which the French did not confine to the coastal regions but extended to the interior by military action in July 1920. The French divided their mandate into the State of Syria (1924) and the Lebanon (1920). Draft alliance

treaties between France and Syria, 9 September 1936, making provisions for the ending of the mandates but preserving special French rights were not signed owing to the fall of the French government that had negotiated the treaty. The independent states of Syria and Lebanon were proclaimed by the 'Free French' in 1941 after replacing the Vichy authorities during the Second World War. The admission of Syria and Lebanon to the UN, at the foundation of the organization, internationally confirmed the end of the French mandates, and French troops withdrew in 1946.

Treaty of Peace between the Allied and Associated Powers and Turkey (Treaty of Sèvres), 10 August 1920

[Part I · Covenant of the League of Nations]

Part II · Frontiers of Turkey

Article 27. I. In Europe, the frontiers of Turkey will be laid down as follows:

1. *The Black Sea*: From the entrance of the Bosphorus to the point described below.
2. *With Greece*: From a point to be chosen on the Black Sea near the mouth of the Biyuk Dere, situated about 7 kilometres north-west of Podima, south-westwards to the most north-westerly point of the limit of the basin of the Istranja Dere (about 8 kilometres north-west of Istranja),

a line to be fixed on the ground passing through Kapilja Dagh and Uchbunar Tepe;

thence south-south-eastwards to a point to be chosen on the railway from Chorlu to Chatalja about 1 kilometre west of the railway station of Sinekli,

a line following as far as possible the western limit of the basin of the Istranja Dere;

thence south-eastwards to a point to be chosen between Fener and Kurfali on the watershed between the basins of those rivers which flow into Biyuk Chekmeje Geul, on the north-east, and the basin of those rivers which flow direct into the Sea of Marmora on the south-west,

a line to be fixed on the ground passing south of Sinekli;

thence south-eastwards to a point to be chosen on the Sea of Marmora about 1 kilometre south-west of Kalikratia,

a line following as far as possible this watershed.

3. *The Sea of Marmora:* From the point defined above to the entrance of the Bosphorus.

II. In Asia, the frontier of Turkey will be laid down as follows:

1. *On the West and South:* From the entrance of the Bosphorus into the Sea of Marmora to a point described below, situated in the eastern Mediterranean Sea in the neighbourhood of the Gulf of Alexandretta near Karatash Burun,

the Sea of Marmora, the Dardanelles, and the Eastern Mediterranean Sea; the islands of the Sea of Marmora, and those which are situated within a distance of 3 miles from the coast, remaining Turkish, subject to the provisions of Section IV and Articles 84 and 122, Part III (Political Clauses).

2. *With Syria:* From a point to be chosen on the eastern bank of the outlet of the Hassan Dede, about 3 kilometres north west of Karatash Burun, north-eastwards

to a point to be chosen on the Djaihun Irmak about 1 kilometre north of Babeli,

a line to be fixed on the ground passing north of Karatash;

thence to Kesik Kale,

the course of the Djaihun Irmak upstream;

thence north-eastwards to a point to be chosen on the Djaihun Irmak about 15 kilometres east-southeast of Karsbazar,

a line to be fixed on the ground passing north of Kara Tepe;

thence to the bend in the Djaihun Irmak situated west of Duldul Dagh,

the course of the Djaihun Irmak upstream;

thence in a general south-easterly direction to a point to be chosen on Emir Musi Dagh about 15 kilometres south-south-west of Giaour Geul,

a line to be fixed on the ground at a distance of about 18 kilometres from the railway, and leaving Duldul Dagh to Syria;

thence eastwards to a point to be chosen about 5 kilometres north of Urfa,

a generally straight line from west to east to be fixed on the ground passing north of the roads connecting the towns of Baghche, Aintab, Biridjik, and Urfa and leaving the last three named towns to Syria;

thence eastwards to the south-western extremity of the bend in the Tigris about 6 kilometres north of Azekh (27 kilometres west to Djezire-ibn-Omar),

a generally straight line from west to east to be fixed on the ground leaving the town of Mardin to Syria;

thence to a point to be chosen on the Tigris between the point of confluence of the Khabur Su with the Tigris and the bend in the Tigris situated about 10 kilometres north of this point,

the course of the Tigris downstream, leaving the island on which is situated the town of Djezire-ibn-Omar to Syria.

3. *With Mesopotamia:* Thence in a general easterly direction to a point to be chosen on the northern boundary of the *vilayet* of Mosul,

a line to be fixed on the ground;

thence eastwards to the point where it meets the frontier between Turkey and Persia,

the northern boundary of the *vilayet* of Mosul, modified, however, so as to pass south of Amadia.

4. *On the East and the North-east:* From the point above defined to the Black Sea, the existing frontier between Turkey and Persia, then the former frontier between Turkey and Russia, subject to the provisions of Article 89.

5. *The Black Sea.*

Part III · Political clauses

SECTION I · CONSTANTINOPLE

Article 36. Subject to the provisions of the present Treaty, the High Contracting Parties agree that the rights and title of the Turkish Government over Constantinople shall not be affected, and that the said Government and His Majesty the Sultan shall be entitled to reside there and to maintain there the capital of the Turkish State.

Nevertheless, in the event of Turkey failing to observe faithfully the provisions of the present Treaty, or of any treaties or conventions supplementary thereto, particularly as regards the protection of the rights of racial, religious or linguistic minorities, the Allied Powers expressly reserve the right to modify the above provisions, and Turkey hereby agrees to accept any dispositions which may be taken in this connection.

SECTION II · STRAITS

Article 37. The navigation of the Straits, including the Dardanelles, the Sea of Marmora and the Bosphorus, shall in future be open, both in peace and war, to every vessel of commerce or of war and to military and commercial aircraft, without distinction of flag.

These waters shall not be subject to blockade, nor shall any belligerent right be exercised nor any act of hostility be committed within them, unless in pursuance of a decision of the Council of the League of Nations.

Article 38. The Turkish Government recognizes that it is necessary to take further measures to ensure the freedom of navigation provided for in Article 37, and accordingly delegates, so far as it is concerned, to a Commission to be called the 'Commission of the Straits', and hereinafter referred to as 'the Commission', the control of the waters specified in Article 39.

The Greek Government, so far as it is concerned, delegates to the Commission the same powers and undertakes to give it in all respects the same facilities.

Such control shall be exercised in the name of the Turkish and Greek Governments respectively, and in the manner provided in this Section.

Article 39. The authority of the Commission will extend to all the waters between the Mediterranean mouth of the Dardanelles and the Black Sea mouth of the Bosphorus, and to the waters within three miles of each of these mouths.

This authority may be exercised on shore to such extent as may be necessary for the execution of the provisions of this Section.

Article 40. The Commission shall be composed of representatives appointed respectively by the United States of America (if and when that Government is willing to participate), the British Empire, France, Italy, Japan, Russia (if and when Russia becomes a member of the League of Nations), Greece, Roumania, and Bulgaria and Turkey (if and when the two latter States become members of the League of Nations). Each Power shall appoint one representative. The representatives of the United States of America, the British Empire, France, Italy, Japan and Russia shall each have two votes. The representatives of Greece, Roumania, and Bulgaria and Turkey shall each have one vote. Each Commissioner shall be removable only by the Government which appointed him.

Article 42. The Commission will exercise the powers conferred on it by the present Treaty in complete independence of the local authority. It will have its own flag, its own budget and its separate organization.

Article 43. Within the limits of its jurisdiction as laid down in Article 39 the Commission will be charged with the following duties:

(*a*) the execution of any works considered necessary for the improvement of the channels or the approaches to harbours;

(*b*) the lighting and buoying of the channels;

(*c*) the control of pilotage and towage;

(*d*) the control of anchorages;

(*e*) the control necessary to assure the application in the ports of Constantinople and Haidar Pasha of the régime prescribed in Articles 335 to 344, Part XI (Ports, Waterways and Railways) of the present Treaty;

(*f*) the control of all matters relating to wrecks and salvage;

(*g*) the control of lighterage.

Article 44. In the event of the Commission finding that the liberty of passage is being interfered with, it will inform the representatives at Constantinople of the Allied Powers providing the occupying forces provided for in Article 178. These representatives will thereupon concert with the naval and military commanders of the said forces such measures as may be deemed necessary to preserve the freedom of the Straits. Similar action shall be taken by the said representatives in the event of any external action threatening the liberty of passage of the Straits.

. . .

Article 48. In order to facilitate the execution of the duties with which it is entrusted by this Section, the Commission shall have power to organize such a force of special police as may be necessary. This force shall be drawn so far as possible from the native population of the zone of the Straits and islands referred to in Article 178, Part V (Military, Naval and Air Clauses), excluding the islands of Lemnos, Imbros, Samothrace, Tenedos and Mitylene. The said force shall be commanded by foreign police officers appointed by the Commission.

[Provision for autonomy, and later on, if people were considered ready, independence.]

SECTION IV · SMYRNA

Article 65. The provisions of this Section will apply to the city of Smyrna and the adjacent territory defined in Article 66, until the determination of their final status in accordance with Article 83.

Article 66. The geographical limits of the territory adjacent to the city of Smyrna will be laid down as follows . . . .

[*Articles 69–71.* The city of Smyrna and territory defined in Article 66 to remain under Turkish sovereignty. Turkey however transfers to the Greek Government the exercise of her rights over these territories. Greek Government will be responsible for administration and will maintain such military forces necessary for order and public security.]

[*Article 72.* A local parliament to be set up; electoral system to ensure proportional representation of all sections of the population including linguistic, racial and religious minorities.]

. . .

Article 83. When a period of five years shall have elapsed after the coming into force of the present Treaty the local parliament referred to in Article 72 may, by a majority of votes, ask the Council of the League of Nations for the definitive incorporation in the Kingdom of Greece of the city of Smyrna and the territory defined in Article 66. The Council may require, as a preliminary, a plebiscite under conditions which it will lay down.

In the event of such incorporation as a result of the application of the foregoing paragraph, the Turkish sovereignty referred to in Article 69 shall cease. Turkey hereby renounces in that event in favour of Greece all rights and title over the city of Smyrna and the territory defined in Article 66.

Section V · Greece

Article 84. Without prejudice to the frontiers of Bulgaria laid down by the Treaty of Peace signed at Neuilly-sur-Seine on November 27, 1919, Turkey renounces in favour of Greece all rights and title over the territories of the former Turkish Empire in Europe situated outside the frontiers of Turkey as laid down by the present Treaty.

The islands of the Sea of Marmora are not included in the transfer of sovereignty effected by the above paragraph.

Turkey further renounces in favour of Greece all her rights and title over the islands of Imbros and Tenedos . . . .

Treaty of Friendship between Russia and Turkey, 16 March 1921

The Government of the Russian Socialist Federal Soviet Republic and the Government of the Grand National Assembly of Turkey, sharing as they do the principles of the liberty of nations, and the right of each nation to determine its own fate, and taking into consideration, moreover, the common struggle undertaken against imperialism, foreseeing that the difficulties arising for the one would render worse the position of the other, and inspired by the desire to bring about lasting good relations and uninterrupted sincere friendship between themselves, based on mutual interests, have decided to sign an agreement to assure amicable and fraternal relations between the two countries . . . .

Article I. Each of the Contracting Parties agrees not to recognize any peace treaty or other international agreement imposed upon the other against its will. The Government of the R.S.F.S.R. agrees not to recognize any international agreement relating to Turkey which is not recognized by the National Government of Turkey, at present represented by the Grand National Assembly.

The expression 'Turkey' in the present Treaty is understood to mean the territories included in the Turkish National Pact on the 28th January 1920, elaborated and proclaimed by the Ottoman Chamber of Deputies in Constantinople, and communicated to the press and to all foreign Governments.

The north-east frontier of Turkey is fixed as follows: [frontier definition]

Article II. Turkey agrees to cede to Georgia the right of suzerainty over the town and the port of Batum, and the territory situated to the north of the frontier mentioned in Article I, which formed a part of the district of Batum, on the following conditions:

(a) The population of the localities specified in the present Article shall enjoy a generous measure of autonomy, assuring to each community its cultural and religious rights, and allowing them to enact agrarian laws in accordance with the wishes of the population of the said districts.

(b) Turkey will be granted free transit for all Turkish imports and exports through the port of Batum, without payment of taxes and customs duties and without delays. The right of making use of the port of Batum without special expenses is assured to Turkey.

Article III. Both Contracting Parties agree that the Nakhichevan district, with the boundaries shown in Annex I (C) to the present Treaty, shall form an autonomous territory under the protection of Azerbaijan, on condition that the latter cannot transfer this protectorate to any third State . . . .

Article IV. The Contracting Parties, establishing contact between the national movement for the liberation of the Eastern peoples and the struggle of the workers of Russia for a new social order, solemnly recognize the right of these nations to freedom and independence, also their right to choose a form of government according to their own wishes.

Article V. In order to assure the opening of the Straits to the commerce of all nations, the Contracting Parties agree to entrust the final elaboration of an international agreement concerning the Black Sea to a conference composed of delegates of the littoral States, on condition that the decisions of the above-mentioned conference shall not be of such a nature as to diminish the full sovereignty of Turkey or the security of Constantinople, her capital.

Article VI. The Contracting Parties agree that the treaties concluded heretofore between the two countries do not correspond with their mutual interests, and therefore agree that the said treaties shall be considered as annulled and abrogated.

The Government of the R.S.F.S.R. declares that it considers Turkey to be liberated from all financial and other liabilities based on agreements concluded between Turkey and the Tsarist Government.

Article VII. The Government of the R.S.F.S.R., holding that the Capitulations régime is incompatible with the full exercise of sovereign rights and the national development of any country, declares this régime and any rights connected therewith to be null and void.

Article VIII. The Contracting Parties undertake not to tolerate in their respective territories the formation and stay of organizations or associations claiming to be the Government of the other country or of a part of its territory and organizations whose aim is to wage warfare against the other State.

Russia and Turkey mutually accept the same obligation with regard to the Soviet Republic of the Caucasus.

'Turkish territory', within the meaning of this Article, is understood to be territory under the direct civil and military administration of the Government of the Grand National Assembly of Turkey.

Article IX. To secure uninterrupted communication between the two countries, both Contracting Parties undertake to carry out urgently, and in agreement one with the other, all necessary measures for the security and development of the railway lines, telegraph and other means of communication, and to assure free movement of persons and goods between the two countries. It is agreed that the regulations in force in each country shall be applied as regards the movement, entry and exit of travellers and goods.

Article X. The nationals of the Contracting Parties residing on the territory of the other shall be treated in accordance with the laws in force in the country of their residence, with the exception of those connected with national defence, from which they are exempt . . . .

Article XI. The Contracting Parties agree to treat the nationals of one of the parties residing in the territory of the other in accordance with the most-favoured-nation principles.

This Article will not be applied to citizens of the Soviet Republics allied with Russia, nor to nationals of Mussulman States allied with Turkey.

Article XII. Any inhabitant of the territories forming part of Russia prior to 1918, and over which Turkish sovereignty has been acknowledged by the Government of the R.S.F.S.R., in the present Treaty, shall be free to leave Turkey and to take with him all his goods and possessions or the proceeds of their sale. The population of the territory of Batum, sovereignty over which has been granted to Georgia by Turkey, shall enjoy the same right.

Article XIII. Russia undertakes to return, at her own expense within three months, to the north-east frontier of Turkey all Turkish prisoners of war and interned civilians in the Caucasus and in European Russia, and those in Asiatic Russia within six months, dating from the signature of the present Treaty . . . .

Article XIV. The Contracting Parties agree to conclude in as short a time as possible a consular agreement and other arrangements regulating all economic, financial and other questions which are necessary for the establishment of friendly relations between the two countries, as set forth in the preamble to the present Treaty.

Article XV. Russia undertakes to take the necessary steps with the Transcaucasian Republics with a view to securing the recognition by the latter, in their agreement with Turkey, of the provisions of the present Treaty which directly concern them.

[*Article XVI.* Ratification.]

Treaty of Peace with Turkey (Treaty of Lausanne), 24 July 1923

The British Empire, France, Italy, Japan, Greece, Roumania and the Serb-Croat-Slovene State,

of the one part,

and Turkey,

of the other part;

Being united in the desire to bring to a final close the state of war which has existed in the East since 1914 . . . have agreed as follows:

Part I · Political clauses

Article I. From the coming into force of the present Treaty, the state of peace will be definitely re-established between the British Empire, France, Italy, Japan, Greece, Roumania and the Serb-Croat-Slovene State of the one part, and Turkey of the other part, as well as between their respective nationals . . . .

SECTION I · TERRITORIAL CLAUSES

Article 2. From the Black Sea to the Ægean the frontier of Turkey is laid down as follows . . . .

[*Article 3.* The frontier from the Mediterranean to the frontier of Persia.]

[*Articles 4–11*. Frontier delimitation, work of the Boundary Commission.]

[*Article 12*. Greek sovereignty over islands in Eastern Mediterranean confirmed. Unless provision to contrary, Turkey to retain sovereignty over islands less than 3 miles from Asiatic coast.]

[*Article 13*. Greece undertakes not to fortify Mytilene, Chios, Samos and Nikaria.]

. . .

Article 15. Turkey renounces in favour of Italy all rights and title over the following islands: Stampalia (Astrapalia), Rhodes (Rhodos), Calki (Kharki), Scarpanto, Casos (Casso), Piscopis (Tilos), Misiros (Nisyros), Calimnos (Kalymnos), Leros, Patmos, Lipsos (Lipso), Simi (Symi), and Cos (Kos), which are now occupied by Italy, and the islets dependent thereon, and also over the island of Castellorizzo . . . .

Article 16. Turkey hereby renounces all rights and title whatsoever over or respecting the territories situated outside the frontiers laid down in the present Treaty and the islands other than those over which her sovereignty is recognized by the said Treaty, the future of these territories and islands being settled or to be settled by the parties concerned.

The provisions of the present Article do not prejudice any special arrangements arising from neighbourly relations which have been or may be concluded between Turkey and any limitrophe countries.

Article 17. The renunciation by Turkey of all rights and titles over Egypt and over the Soudan will take effect as from the 5th November 1914.

. . .

Article 20. Turkey hereby recognizes the annexation of Cyprus proclaimed by the British Government on the 5th November 1914.

. . .

[*Article 22*. Turkey renounces rights in Libya.]

. . .

[*Article 28*. Abolition of Capitulations is accepted.]

SECTION III · PROTECTION OF MINORITIES

Article 37. Turkey undertakes that the stipulations contained in Articles 38 to 44 shall be recognized as fundamental laws, and that no law, no regulation, nor official action shall conflict or interfere with these stipulations, nor shall any law, regulation, nor official action prevail over them.

Article 38. The Turkish Government undertakes to assure full and complete protection of life and liberty to all inhabitants of Turkey without distinction of birth, nationality, language, race or religion.

[*Article 39–44*. Non-Moslem Turkish citizens to enjoy equal political and civil rights as Moslem Turkish citizens.]

[*Article 45*. The same rights as in Articles 39 to 44 to be enjoyed by Moslem majority in Greece.]

Part II · Financial clauses

[*Article 46–58*. These deal with the Ottoman Public Debt. Article 58 states that Turkey and the Allied Powers, except Greece, renounce all financial claims arising from war and conflict since 1 August 1914.]

Convention regarding the régime of the Straits (Lausanne Convention), 24 July 1923

Article 1. The High Contracting Parties agree to recognize and declare the principle of freedom of transit and of navigation by sea and by air in the Strait of the Dardanelles, the Sea of Marmora and the Bosphorus, hereinafter comprised under the general term of the 'Straits'.

Article 2. The transit and navigation of commercial vessels and aircraft, and of war vessels and aircraft in the Straits in time of peace and in time of war shall henceforth be regulated by the provisions of the attached Annex.

Annex · *Rules for the Passage of Commercial Vessels and Aircraft, and of War Vessels and Aircraft through the Straits . . .*

I. MERCHANT VESSELS, INCLUDING HOSPITAL SHIPS, YACHTS AND FISHING VESSELS AND NON-MILITARY AIRCRAFT

[In time of peace: freedom of passage. In time of war, Turkey being neutral: freedom of passage. In time of war, Turkey being belligerent: freedom of passage for neutrals, Turkey being permitted the right of search of contraband. Turkey may take whatever measures regarded as necessary to prevent use of Straits by enemy ships.]

2. WARSHIPS, INCLUDING FLEET AUXILIARIES, TROOPSHIPS, AIRCRAFT CARRIERS AND MILITARY AIRCRAFT

(a) *In time of peace.* Complete freedom of passage by day and by night under any flag, without any formalities, or tax, or charge whatever, but subject to the following restrictions as to the total force:

The maximum force which any one Power may send through the Straits into the Black Sea is not to be greater than that of the most powerful fleet of the littoral Powers of the Black Sea existing in that sea at the time of passage; but with the proviso that the Powers reserve to themselves the right to send into the Black Sea, at all times and under all circumstances, a force of not more than three ships, of which no individual ship shall exceed 10,000 tons.

Turkey has no responsibility in regard to the number of war vessels which pass through the Straits.

In order to enable the above rule to be observed, the Straits Commission provided for in Article 10 will, on the 1st January and 1st July of each year, enquire of each Black Sea littoral Power the number of each of the following classes of vessel which such Power possesses in the Black Sea: battleships, battlecruisers, aircraft carriers, cruisers, destroyers, submarines, or other types of vessels as well as naval aircraft; distinguishing between the ships which are in active commission and the ships with reduced complements, the ships in reserve and the ships undergoing repairs or alterations.

The Straits Commission will then inform the Powers concerned that the strongest naval force in the Black Sea comprise: battleships, battle-cruisers, aircraft carriers, cruisers, destroyers, submarines, aircraft and units of other types which may exist. The Straits Commission will also immediately inform the Powers concerned when, owing to the passage into or out of the Black Sea of any ship of the strongest Black Sea force, any alteration in that force has taken place.

The naval force that may be sent through the Straits into the Black Sea will be calculated on the number and type of the ships of war in active commission only.

(b) *In time of war, Turkey being neutral.* Complete freedom of passage by day and by night under any flag, without any formalities, or tax, or charge whatever, under the same limitations as in paragraph 2 (a).

However, these limitations will not be applicable to any belligerent Power to the prejudice of its belligerent rights in the Black Sea.

The rights and duties of Turkey as a neutral Power cannot authorize her to take any measures liable to interfere with navigation through the Straits, the waters of which, and the air above which, must remain entirely free in time of war, Turkey being neutral, just as in time of peace.

Warships and military aircraft of belligerents will be forbidden to make any capture, to exercise the right of visit and search, or to carry out any other hostile act in the Straits.

As regards revictualling and carrying out repairs, war vessels will be subject to the terms of the Thirteenth Hague Convention of 1907, dealing with maritime neutrality.

Military aircraft will receive in the Straits similar treatment to that accorded under the Thirteenth Hague Convention of 1907 to warships, pending the conclusion of an international convention establishing the rules of neutrality for aircraft.

(c) *In time of war, Turkey being belligerent.* Complete freedom of passage for neutral warships, without any formalities, or tax, or charge whatever, but under the same limitations as in paragraph 2 (a).

The measures taken by Turkey to prevent enemy ships and aircraft from using the Straits are not to be of such a nature as to prevent the free passage of neutral ships and aircraft, and Turkey agrees to provide the said ships and aircraft with either the necessary instructions or pilots for the above purpose.

Neutral military aircraft will make the passage of the Straits at their own risk and peril, and will submit to investigation as to their character. For this purpose aircraft are to alight on the ground or on the sea in such areas as are specified and prepared for this purpose by Turkey.

3. (a) The passage of the Straits by submarines of the Powers at peace with Turkey must be made on the surface . . . .

(c) The right of military and non-military aircraft to fly over the Straits, under the conditions laid down in the present rules, necessitates for aircraft:

(i) Freedom to fly over a strip of territory of 5 kilometres wide on each side of the narrow parts of the Straits;

(ii) Liberty, in the event of a forced landing, to alight on the coast or on the sea in the territorial waters of Turkey.

. . .

Article 3. With a view to maintaining the Straits free from any obstacle to free passage and navigation, the provisions contained in Articles 4 to 9 will be applied to the waters and shores thereof as well as to the islands situated therein, or in the vicinity.

Article 4. The zones and islands indicated below shall be demilitarized:

1. Both shores of the Straits of the Dardanelles and the Bosphorus over the extent of the zones delimited below [*Dardanelles; Bosphorus*].

2. All the islands in the Sea of Marmora, with the exception of the island of Emir Ali Adasi.

3. In the Ægean Sea, the islands of Samothrace, Lemnos, Imbros, Tenedos and Rabbit Islands.

Article 5. A Commission composed of four representatives appointed respectively by the Governments of France, Great Britain, Italy and Turkey shall meet within 15 days of the coming into force of the present Convention to determine on the spot the boundaries of the zone laid down in Article 4 (1) . . . .

Article 6. Subject to the provisions of Article 8 concerning Constantinople, there shall exist, in the demilitarized zones and islands, no fortifications, no permanent artillery organization, no submarine engines of war other than submarine vessels, no military aerial organization, and no naval base.

No armed forces shall be stationed in the demilitarized zones and islands except the police and *gendarmerie* forces necessary for the maintenance of order . . . .

Article 7. No submarine engines of war other than submarine vessels shall be installed in the waters of the Sea of Marmora.

The Turkish Government shall not install any permanent battery or torpedo tubes, capable of interfering with the passage of the Straits, in the coastal zone of the European shore of the Sea of Marmora or in the coastal zone on the Anatolian shore situated to the east of the demilitarized zone of the Bosphorus as far as Darije.

Article 8. At Constantinople, . . . there may be maintained for the requirements of the capital, a garrison with maximum strength of 12,000 men . . . .

Article 9. If, in case of war, Turkey, or Greece, in pursuance of their belligerent rights, should modify in any way the provisions of demilitarization prescribed above, they will be bound to re-establish as soon as peace is concluded the régime laid down in the present Convention.

Article 10. There shall be constituted at Constantinople an International Commission composed in accordance with Article 12 and called the 'Straits Commission'.

Article 11. The Commission will exercise its functions over the waters of the Straits.

Article 12. The Commission shall be composed of a representative of Turkey, who shall be President, and representatives of France, Great Britain, Italy, Japan, Bulgaria, Greece, Roumania, Russia, and the Serb-Croat-Slovene State, in so far as these Powers are signatories of the present Convention, each of these Powers being entitled to representation as from its ratification of the said Convention.

The United States of America, in the event of their acceding to the present Convention, will also be entitled to have one representative on the Commission.

Under the same conditions any independent littoral States of the Black Sea which are not mentioned in the first paragraph of the present Article will possess the same right.

[*Article 14–16.* Duties of Commission to see provisions of treaties are observed.]

Article 17. The terms of the present Convention will not infringe the right of Turkey to move her fleet freely in Turkish waters.

Article 18. The High Contracting Parties, desiring to secure that the demilitarization of the Straits and of the contiguous zones shall not constitute an unjustifiable danger to the military security of Turkey, and that no act of war should imperil the freedom of the Straits or the safety of the demilitarized zones, agree as follows:

Should the freedom of navigation of the Straits of the security of the demilitarized zones be imperilled by a violation of the provisions relating to freedom of passage, or by a surprise attack or some act of war or threat of war, the High Contracting Parties, and in any case France, Great Britain, Italy and Japan, acting in conjunction, will meet such violation, attack, or other act of war or threat of war, by all the means that the Council of the League of Nations may decide for this purpose.

So soon as the circumstance which may have necessitated the action provided for in the preceding paragraph shall have ended, the régime of the Straits as laid down by the terms of the present Convention shall again be strictly applied.

The present provision, which forms an integral part of those relating to the demilitarization and to the freedom of the Straits, does not prejudice the rights and obligations of the High Contracting Parties under the Covenant of the League of Nations.

Convention regarding the régime of the Straits (Montreux Convention), 20 July 1936

Article 1. The High Contracting Parties recognize and affirm the principle of freedom of transit and navigation by sea in the Straits.

The exercise of this freedom shall henceforth be regulated by the provisions of the present Convention.

SECTION I · MERCHANT VESSELS

Article 2. In time of peace, merchant vessels shall enjoy complete freedom of transit and navigation in the Straits, by day and by night, under any flag and with any kind of cargo, without any formalities, except as provided in Article 3 below. No taxes or charges other than those authorized by Annex I to the present Convention shall be levied by the Turkish authorities on these vessels when passing in transit without calling at a port in the Straits . . . .

[*Article 3.* Sanitary regulations.]

Article 4. In time of war, Turkey not being belligerent, merchant vessels, under any flag or with any kind of cargo, shall enjoy freedom of transit and navigation in the Straits subject to the provisions of Articles 2 and 3.

Pilotage and towage remain optional.

Article 5. In time of war, Turkey being belligerent, merchant vessels not belonging to a country at war with Turkey shall enjoy freedom of transit and navigation in the Straits on condition that they do not in any way assist the enemy.

Such vessels shall enter the Straits by day and their transit shall be effected by the route which shall in each case be indicated by the Turkish authorities.

Article 6. Should Turkey consider herself to be threatened with imminent danger of war, the provisions of Article 2 shall nevertheless continue to be applied except that vessels must enter the Straits by day and that their transit must be effected by the route which shall, in each case, be indicated by the Turkish authorities . . . .

SECTION II · VESSELS OF WAR

Article 11. Black Sea Powers may send through the Straits capital ships of a tonnage greater than that laid down in the first paragraph of Article 14, on condition that these vessels pass through the Straits singly, escorted by not more than two destroyers.

Article 12. Black Sea Powers shall have the right to send through the Straits, for the purpose of rejoining their base, submarines constructed or purchased outside the Black Sea, provided that adequate notice of the laying down or purchase of such submarines shall have been given to Turkey.

Submarines belonging to the said Powers shall also be entitled to pass through the Straits to be repaired in dockyards outside the Black Sea on condition that detailed information on the matter is given to Turkey.

In either case, the said submarines must travel by day and on the surface, and must pass through the Straits singly.

[*Article 13.* Details of notification to Turkish authorities of transit of warships.]

Article 14. The maximum aggregate tonnage of all foreign naval forces which may be in course of transit through the Straits shall not exceed 15,000 tons, except in the cases provided for in Article 11 . . . .

The forces specified in the preceding paragraph shall not, however, comprise more than nine vessels.

Vessels, whether belonging to Black Sea or non-Black Sea Powers, paying visits to a port in the Straits, in accordance with the provisions of Article 17, shall not be included in this tonnage.

Neither shall vessels of war which have suffered damage during their passage through the Straits be included in this tonnage; such vessels, while undergoing repair, shall be subject to any special provisions relating to security laid down by Turkey.

[*Article 15.* Prohibition against use of aircraft by warships in transit.]

[*Article 16*. Except in case of damage, transit to be accomplished without delay.]

Article 17. Nothing in the provisions of the preceding Articles shall prevent a naval force of any tonnage or composition from paying a courtesy visit of limited duration to a port in the Straits, at the invitation of the Turkish Government. Any such force must leave the Straits by the same route as that by which it entered, unless it fulfils the conditions required for passage in transit through the Straits as laid down by Articles 10, 14 and 18.

Article 18. 1. The aggregate tonnage which non-Black Sea Powers may have in that sea in time of peace shall be limited as follows:

(a) Except as provided in paragraph (b) below, the aggregate tonnage of the said Powers shall not exceed 30,000 tons;

(b) If at any time the tonnage of the strongest fleet in the Black Sea shall exceed by at least 10,000 tons the tonnage of the strongest fleet in that sea at the date of the signature of the present Convention, the aggregate tonnage of 30,000 tons mentioned in paragraph (a) shall be increased by the same amount, up to a maximum of 45,000 tons. For this purpose, each Black Sea Power shall, in conformity with Annex IV to the present Convention, inform the Turkish Government, on the 1st January and the 1st July of each year, of the total tonnage of its fleet in the Black Sea; and the Turkish Government shall transmit this information to the other High Contracting Parties and to the Secretary General of the League of Nations;

(c) The tonnage which any one non-Black Sea Power may have in the Black Sea shall be limited to two-thirds of the aggregate tonnage provided for in paragraphs (a) and (b) above;

(d) In the event, however, of one or more non-Black Sea Powers desiring to send naval forces into the Black Sea, for a humanitarian purpose, the said forces, which shall in no case exceed 8,000 tons altogether, shall be allowed to enter the Black Sea without having to give the notification provided for in Article 13 of the present Convention, provided an authorization is obtained from the Turkish Government . . . .

2. Vessels of war belonging to non-Black Sea Powers shall not remain in the Black Sea more than twenty-one days, whatever be the object of their presence there.

Article 19. In time of war, Turkey not being belligerent, warships shall enjoy complete freedom of transit and navigation through the Straits under the same conditions as those laid down in Articles 10 to 18.

Vessels of war belonging to belligerent Powers shall not, however, pass through the Straits except in cases arising out of the application of Article 25 of the present Convention, and in cases of assistance rendered to a State victim of aggression in virtue of a treaty of mutual assistance binding Turkey, concluded within the framework of the Covenant of the League of Nations, and registered and published in accordance with the provisions of Article 18 of the Covenant.

In the exceptional cases provided for in the preceding paragraph, the limitations laid down in Articles 10 to 18 of the present Convention shall not be applicable.

Notwithstanding the prohibition of passage laid down in paragraph 2 above, vessels of war belonging to belligerent Powers, whether they are Black Sea Powers or not, which have become separated from their bases, may return thereto.

Vessels of war belonging to belligerent Powers shall not make any capture, exercise the right of visit and search, or carry out any hostile act in the Straits.

Article 20. In time of war, Turkey being belligerent, the provisions of Articles 10 to 18 shall not be applicable; the passage of warships shall be left entirely to the discretion of the Turkish Government.

Article 21. Should Turkey consider herself to be threatened with imminent danger of war she shall have the right to apply the provisions of Article 20 of the present Convention.

Vessels which have passed through the Straits before Turkey has made use of the powers conferred upon her by the preceding paragraph, and which thus find themselves separated from their bases, may return thereto. It is, however, understood that Turkey may deny this right to vessels of war belonging to the State whose attitude has given rise to the application of the present Article.

Should the Turkish Government make use of the powers conferred by the first paragraph of the present Article, a notification to that effect shall be addressed to the High Contracting Parties and to the Secretary-General of the League of Nations.

If the Council of the League of Nations decide by a majority of two-thirds that the measures thus taken by Turkey are not justified, and if such should also be the opinion of the majority of the High Contracting Parties signatories to the present Convention, the Turkish Government undertakes to discontinue the measures in question as also any measures which may have been taken under Article 6 of the present Convention.

Protocol

At the moment of signing the Convention bearing this day's date, the undersigned plenipotentiaries declare for their respective Governments that they accept the following provisions:

1. Turkey may immediately remilitarize the zone of the Straits as defined in the Preamble to the said Convention.

2. As from the 15th August, 1936, the Turkish Government shall provisionally apply the régime specified in the said Convention.

3. The present Protocol shall enter into force as from this day's date.

SECTION III · AIRCRAFT

[*Article 23*. Turkish Government to indicate routes for civil aircraft between Mediterranean and Black Sea.]

Article 24. The functions of the International Commission set up under the Convention relating to the régime of the

Straits of the 24th July 1923, are hereby transferred to the Turkish Government.

The Turkish Government undertake to collect statistics and furnish information concerning the application of Articles 11, 12, 14 and 18 of the present Convention.

They will supervise the execution of all the provisions of the present Convention relating to the passage of vessels of war through the Straits.

As soon as they have been notified of the intended passage through the Straits of a foreign naval force the Turkish Government shall inform the representatives at Angora of the High Contracting Parties of the composition of that force, its tonnage, the date fixed for its entry into the Straits, and, if necessary, the probable date of its return.

The Turkish Government shall address to the Secretary-General of the League of Nations and to the High Contracting Parties an annual report giving details regarding the movements of foreign vessels of war through the Straits and furnishing all information which may be of service to commerce and navigation, both by sea and by air, for which provision is made in the present Convention.

Article 25. Nothing in the present Convention shall prejudice the rights and obligations of Turkey, or of any of the other High Contracting Parties members of the League of Nations, arising out of the Covenant of the League of Nations.

SECTION V · FINAL PROVISIONS

Article 26. The present Convention shall be ratified as soon as possible . . . .

[*Article 27*. After entry into force, Convention open to accession by any signatory of Treaty of Lausanne, 1923.]

Article 28. The present Convention shall remain in force for twenty years from the date of its entry into force.

The principle of freedom of transit and navigation affirmed in Article 1 of the present Convention shall however continue without limit of time.

If, two years prior to the expiry of the

said period of twenty years, no High Contracting Party shall have given notice of denunciation to the French Government the present Convention shall continue in force until two years after such notice shall have been given. Any such notice shall be communicated by the French Government to the High Contracting Parties.

In the event of the present Convention being denounced in accordance with the provisions of the present Article, the High Contracting Parties agree to be represented at a conference for the purpose of concluding a new Convention.

Article 29. At the expiry of each period of five years from the date of the entry into force of the present Convention each of the High Contracting Parties shall be entitled to initiate a proposal for amending one or more of the provisions of the present Convention . . . .

Should it be found impossible to reach an agreement on these proposals through the diplomatic channel, the High Contracting Parties agree to be represented at a conference to be summoned for this purpose.

Such a conference may only take decisions by a unanimous vote, except as regards cases of revision involving Articles 14 and 18, for which a majority of three-quarters of the High Contracting Parties shall be sufficient.

The said majority shall include three-quarters of the High Contracting Parties which are Black Sea Powers, including Turkey . . . .

China, Japan and the Pacific: the Washington Conference, 1921–22

The Paris Peace Conference had assigned to Japan mandates of Germany's Pacific island colonies north of the Equator; Japan had also secured German rights in Shantung. Apart from thus disposing of German assets, no general settlement between the powers concerning their future relationships in China and the Pacific was reached in Paris. These problems were the subject of the negotiations at the *Washington Conference, November 1921–February 1922.* Of the powers with interests in the Pacific only Soviet Russia was not invited. Three major treaties were concluded. A treaty on the *limitation of naval armaments, 6 February 1922, between the British Empire, France, Italy, Japan and the United States* (p. 132) limited and set proportions between the signatories of warships of the largest tonnage, mainly battleships, as follows: Britain – 5, United States – 5, Japan – 3, France – 1·7, and Italy – 1·7. A ten-year 'naval holiday' on the construction of capital ships apart from specific exceptions was to be followed by only limited construction until 1936. The disadvantage of the proportions to Japan was counterbalanced by an agreement in the treaty limiting the construction of new naval bases or the expansion of existing bases in the Pacific, but excluding Hawaii. A *Nine Power Treaty concerning China was signed on 6 February 1922 by the British Empire, France, Italy, Japan, the United States, China, Netherlands, Belgium and Portugal* (p. 135). Its purpose was to bolster up the integrity and independence of China, particularly threatened by the special rights demanded by Japan during the First World War. Japan made some concessions in Shantung, and the signatories promised to respect the sovereignty and integrity of China and the 'Open Door', but China did not secure the withdrawal of Japanese troops from Manchuria or the recognition of Chinese sovereignty over Manchuria. Nor was China's unequal status abolished. The foreign powers maintained special rights; by a separate treaty the Chinese were permitted to raise their customs tariff over whose rates the foreign powers retained control. The powers were unwilling to give up their existing rights, and only promised not to extend them. The third treaty to be signed was the *Four Power Treaty relating to insular possessions and insular dominions in the Pacific Ocean between the British Empire, France, the United States and Japan, 13 December 1921* (p. 136). This Four Power Treaty replaced the alliance relationship between Britain and Japan (last renewed in 1911). The four powers undertook to respect the rights of each other in their 'insular possessions and insular dominions in the region of the Pacific Ocean', whereby any American recognition of Japan's position in China and Siberia was avoided. The treaty also contained provision for conferences between the signatories to resolve disputes and frank exchanges if the rights of the signatories were threatened by other powers.

Treaty between the United States, the British Empire, France, Italy and Japan limiting naval armament, 6 February 1922

The United States of America, the British Empire, France, Italy and Japan;

Desiring to contribute to the maintenance of the general peace, and to reduce the burdens of competition in armament . . .

Have agreed as follows:

Chapter I: General provisions relating to the limitation of naval armament

Article I. The Contracting Powers agree to limit their respective naval armament as provided in the present Treaty.

Article II. The Contracting Powers may retain respectively the capital ships which are specified in Chapter II, Part 1. On the coming into force of the present Treaty, but subject to the following provisions of this Article, all other capital ships, built or building, of the United States, the British Empire and Japan shall be disposed of as prescribed in Chapter II, Part 2.

In addition to the capital ships specified in Chapter II, Part 1, the United States may

complete and retain two ships of the *West Virginia* class now under construction. On the completion of these two ships the *North Dakota* and *Delaware* shall be disposed of as prescribed in Chapter II, Part 2.

The British Empire may, in accordance with the replacement table in Chapter II, Part 3, construct two new capital ships not exceeding 35,000 tons (35,560 metric tons) standard displacement each. On the completion of the said two ships the *Thunderer, King George V, Ajax* and *Centurion* shall be disposed of as prescribed in Chapter II, Part 2.

Article III. Subject to the provisions of Article II, the Contracting Powers shall abandon their respective capital ship building programmes, and no new capital ships shall be constructed or acquired by any of the Contracting Powers except replacement tonnage which may be constructed or acquired as specified in Chapter II, Part 3.

Ships which are replaced in accordance

with Chapter II, Part 3, shall be disposed of as described in Part 2 of that Chapter.

Article IV. The total capital ship replacement tonnage of each of the Contracting Powers shall not exceed in standard displacement, for the United States 525,000 tons (533,400 metric tons); for the British Empire 525,000 tons (533,400 metric tons); for France 175,000 tons (177,800 metric tons); for Italy 175,000 tons (177,800 metric tons); for Japan 315,000 tons (320,040 metric tons).

Article V. No capital ship exceeding 35,000 tons (35,560 metric tons) standard displacement shall be acquired by, or constructed by, for, or within the jurisdiction of, any of the Contracting Powers.

Article VI. No capital ship of any of the Contracting Powers shall carry a gun with a caliber in excess of 16 inches (406 millimetres).

Article VII. The total tonnage for aircraft carriers of each of the Contracting Powers shall not exceed in standard displacement, for the United States 135,000 tons (137,160 metric tons); for the British Empire 135,000 tons (137,160 metric tons); for France 60,000 tons (60,960 metric tons); for Italy 60,000 tons (60,960 metric tons); for Japan 81,000 tons (82,296 metric tons).

Article VIII. The replacement of aircraft carriers shall be effected only as prescribed in Chapter II, Part 3, provided, however, that all aircraft carrier tonnage in existence or building on November 12, 1921, shall be considered experimental, and may be replaced, within the total tonnage limit prescribed in Article VII, without regard to its age.

Article IX. No aircraft carrier exceeding 27,000 tons (27,432 metric tons) standard displacement shall be acquired by, or constructed by, for or within the jurisdiction of, any of the Contracting Powers.

However, any of the Contracting Powers may, provided that its total tonnage allowance of aircraft carriers is not thereby exceeded, build not more than two aircraft carriers, each of a tonnage of not more than 33,000 tons (33,528 metric tons) standard displacement, and in order to effect economy any of the Contracting Powers

may use for this purpose any two of their ships, whether constructed or in course of construction, which would otherwise be scrapped under the provisions of Article II . . . [limitation on armament].

[*Article X.* Armament limitation: calibre of guns.]

Article XI. No vessel of war exceeding 10,000 tons (10,160 metric tons) standard displacement, other than a capital ship or aircraft carrier shall be acquired by, or constructed by, for, or within the jurisdiction of, any of the Contracting Powers. Vessels not specifically built as fighting ships nor taken in time of peace under government control . . . shall not be within the limitations of this Article.

. . .

Article XV. No vessel of war constructed within the jurisdiction of any of the Contracting Powers for a non-Contracting Power shall exceed the limitations as to displacement and armament prescribed by the present Treaty for vessels of a similar type which may be constructed by or for any of the Contracting Powers; provided, however, that the displacement for aircraft carriers constructed for a non-Contracting Power shall in no case exceed 27,000 tons (27,432 metric tons) standard displacement.

Article XIX. The United States, the British Empire and Japan agree that the *status quo* at the time of the signing of the present Treaty, with regard to fortifications and naval bases, shall be maintained in their respective territories and possessions specified hereunder:

(1) The insular possessions which the United States now holds or may hereafter acquire in the Pacific Ocean, except (a) those adjacent to the coast of the United States, Alaska and the Panama Canal Zone, not including the Aleutian Islands, and (b) the Hawaiian Islands;

(2) Hongkong and the insular possessions which the British Empire now holds or may hereafter acquire in the Pacific Ocean, east of the meridian 110° east longitude, except (a) those adjacent to the coast of Canada, (b) the Commonwealth of Australia and its Territories, and (c) New Zealand;

(3) The following insular territories and possessions of Japan in the Pacific Ocean, to wit: the Kurile Islands, the Bonin Islands, Amami-Oshima, the Loo-choo Islands, Formosa and the Pescadores, and any insular territories or possessions in the Pacific Ocean which Japan may hereafter acquire.

The maintenance of the *status quo* under the foregoing provisions implies that no new fortifications or naval bases shall be established in the territories and possessions specified, that no measures shall be taken to increase the existing naval facilities for the repair and maintenance of naval forces, and that no increase shall be made in the coast defences of the territories and possessions above specified. This restriction, however, does not preclude such repair and replacement of worn-out weapons and equipment as is customary in naval and military establishments in time of peace.

Article XX. The rules for determining tonnage displacement prescribed in Chapter II, Part 4, shall apply to the ships of each of the Contracting Powers.

Chapter III: Miscellaneous provisions

Article XXI. If during the term of the present Treaty the requirements of the national security of any Contracting Power in respect of naval defence are, in the opinion of that Power, materially affected by any change of circumstances, the Contracting Powers will, at the request of such Power, meet in conference with a view to the reconsideration of the provisions of the Treaty and its amendment by mutual agreement.

In view of possible technical and scientific developments, the United States, after consultation with the other Contracting Powers, shall arrange for a conference of all the Contracting Powers which shall convene as soon as possible after the expiration of eight years from the coming into force of the present Treaty to consider what changes, if any, in the Treaty may be necessary to meet such developments.

Article XXII. Whenever any Contracting Power shall become engaged in a war which in its opinion affects the naval defence of its national security, such Power may after notice to the other Contracting Powers suspend for the period of hostilities its obligations under the present Treaty other than those under Articles XIII and XVII, provided that such Power shall notify the other Contracting Powers that the emergency is of such a character as to require such suspension.

The remaining Contracting Powers shall in such case consult together with a view to agreement as to what temporary modifications if any should be made in the Treaty as between themselves. Should such consultation not produce agreement, duly made in accordance with the constitutional methods of the respective Powers, any one of said Contracting Powers may, by giving notice to the other Contracting Powers, suspend for the period of hostilities its obligations under the present Treaty, other than those under Articles XIII and XVII.

On the cessation of hostilities the Contracting Powers will meet in conference to consider what modifications, if any, should be made in the provisions of the present Treaty.

Article XXIII. The present Treaty shall remain in force until December 31, 1936, and in case none of the Contracting Powers shall have given notice two years before that date of its intention to terminate the Treaty, it shall continue in force until the expiration of two years from the date on which notice of termination shall be given by one of the Contracting Powers, whereupon the Treaty shall terminate as regards all the Contracting Powers . . . .

[*Article XXIV.* Ratification.]

Treaty between the United States, Belgium, the British Empire, China, France, Italy, Japan, the Netherlands and Portugal (Nine Power Treaty) concerning China, 6 February 1922

The United States of America, Belgium, the British Empire, China, France, Italy, Japan, the Netherlands and Portugal:

Desiring to adopt a policy designed to stabilize conditions in the Far East, to safeguard the rights and interests of China, and to promote intercourse between China and the other Powers upon the basis of equality of opportunity . . .

Have agreed as follows:

Article I. The Contracting Powers, other than China, agree:

1. To respect the sovereignty, the independence, and the territorial and administrative integrity of China;

2. To provide the fullest and most unembarrassed opportunity to China to develop and maintain for herself an effective and stable government;

3. To use their influence for the purpose of effectually establishing and maintaining the principle of equal opportunity for the commerce and industry of all nations throughout the territory of China;

4. To refrain from taking advantage of conditions in China in order to seek special rights or privileges which would abridge the rights of subjects or citizens of friendly States, and from countenancing action inimical to the security of such States.

Article II. The Contracting Powers agree not to enter into any treaty, agreement, arrangement, or understanding, either with one another, or individually or collectively, with any Power or Powers, which would infringe or impair the principles stated in Article I.

Article III. With a view to applying more effectually the principles of the Open Door or equality of opportunity in China for the trade and industry of all nations, the Contracting Powers, other than China, agree that they will not seek, nor support their respective nationals in seeking:

(a) Any arrangement which might purport to establish in favour of their interests any general superiority of rights with respect to commercial or economic development in any designated region of China;

(b) Any such monopoly or preference as would deprive the nationals of any other Power of the right of undertaking any legitimate trade or industry in China, or of participating with the Chinese Government, or with any local authority, in any category of public enterprise, or which by reason of its scope, duration or geographical extent is calculated to frustrate the practical application of the principle of equal opportunity.

It is understood that the foregoing stipulations of this Article are not to be so construed as to prohibit the acquisition of such properties or rights as may be necessary to the conduct of a particular commercial, industrial, or financial undertaking or to the encouragement of invention and research.

China undertakes to be guided by the principles stated in the foregoing stipulations of this Article in dealing with applications for economic rights and privileges from Governments and nationals of all foreign countries, whether parties to the present Treaty or not.

Article IV. The Contracting Powers agree not to support any agreements by their respective nationals with each other designed to create Spheres of Influence or to provide for the enjoyment of mutually exclusive opportunities in designated parts of Chinese territory.

Article V. China agrees that, throughout the whole of the railways in China, she will not exercise or permit unfair discrimination of any kind . . . .

Article VI. The Contracting Powers, other than China, agree fully to respect China's rights as a neutral in time of war to which

China is not a party; and China declares that when she is a neutral she will observe the obligations of neutrality.

Article VII. The Contracting Powers agree that, whenever a situation arises which in the opinion of any one of them involves the application of the stipulations of the present Treaty, and renders desirable discussion of such application, there shall be full and frank communication between the Contracting Powers concerned.

Article VIII. Powers not signatory to the present Treaty, which have Governments recognized by the signatory Powers and which have treaty relations with China, shall be invited to adhere to the present Treaty. To this end the Government of the United States will make the necessary communications to non-signatory Powers and will inform the Contracting Powers of the replies received. Adherence by any Power shall become effective on receipt of notice thereof by the Government of the United States.

[*Article IX.* Ratification.]

Declaration by China

China, upon her part, is prepared to give an undertaking not to alienate or lease any portion of her territory or littoral to any Power.

Treaty between the United States, the British Empire, France and Japan (Four Power Treaty) relating to their insular possessions and insular dominions in the Pacific Ocean, 13 December 1921

The United States of America, the British Empire, France and Japan,

With a view to the preservation of the general peace and the maintenance of their rights in relation to their insular possessions and insular dominions in the region of the Pacific Ocean, have determined to conclude a Treaty to this effect and have agreed as follows:

Article I. The High Contracting Parties agree as between themselves to respect their rights in relation to their insular possessions and insular dominions in the region of the Pacific Ocean.

If there should develop between any of the High Contracting Parties a controversy arising out of any Pacific question and involving their said rights which is not satisfactorily settled by diplomacy and is likely to affect the harmonious accord now happily subsisting between them, they shall invite the other High Contracting Parties to a joint conference to which the whole subject will be referred for consideration and adjustment.

Article II. If the said rights are threatened by the aggressive action of any other Power, the High Contracting Parties shall communicate with one another fully and frankly in order to arrive at an understanding as to the most efficient measures to be taken, jointly or separately, to meet the exigencies of the particular situation.

Article III. This Treaty shall remain in force for ten years from the time it shall take effect, and after the expiration of said period it shall continue to be in force subject to the right of any of the High Contracting Parties to terminate it upon twelve months' notice.

Article IV. This Treaty shall be ratified as soon as possible in accordance with the constitutional methods of the High Contracting Parties . . .

[In ratifying this Treaty the United States resolved ... 'The United States understands that under the statement in the preamble or under the terms of this Treaty there is no commitment to armed force, no alliance, no obligation to join in any defense.']

Declaration accompanying the Treaty

In signing the Treaty this day between the United States of America, the British Empire, France and Japan, it is declared to be the understanding and intent of the signatory Powers:

1. That the Treaty shall apply to the mandated islands in the Pacific Ocean; provided, however, that the making of the Treaty shall not be deemed to be an assent on the part of the United States of America to the mandates and shall not preclude agreements between the United States of America and the Mandatory Powers respectively in relation to the mandated islands.

2. That the controversies to which the second paragraph of Article I refers shall not be taken to embrace questions which according to principles of international law lie exclusively within the domestic jurisdiction of the respective Powers.

Supplementary Agreement

... The term 'insular possessions and insular dominions' used in the aforesaid Treaty shall, in its application to Japan, include only Karafuto (or the southern portion of the island of Sakhalin), Formosa and the Pescadores, and the islands under the mandate of Japan . . . .

IV · France, Britain, Italy and Germany, 1921–33

Within six years of the signature of the Treaty of Versailles, the relationship between Germany and the victorious western powers who had dictated the peace terms to Germany had profoundly changed. The terms imposed on Germany were being significantly changed and softened. The question of reparations bedevilled Germany's relations with the west. The huge total sum demanded in 1921 was progressively abandoned during the decade of the 1920s. The treaties of Locarno of 1925 established a new relationship and signified the practical abandonment of the policy of imposing the terms of Versailles by military sanction. The Rhineland was evacuated completely five years ahead of time in June 1930 and effective means of supervising German armaments by Allied control were abandoned in 1927. The Pact of Paris in 1928 symbolized the idealistic and optimistic side of great power diplomacy in this era, but the reservations added to it indicate an underlying sense of realism. By the end of the decade and the beginning of the 1930s disarmament had become largely a question of which powers were to disarm and which to *rearm*. The 1930s became increasingly dominated by Hitler, but the abandonment of parts of the Versailles settlement had already occurred before he came to power.

The reparations question

German 'reparations' in theory were intended to make good the civilian damage caused by Germany in France, Belgium, Britain and elsewhere and were expected to burden the German people for more than half a century. In the event the burden lasted only a decade and brought no benefit to those who received these sums. No sensible settlement of post-war finance was politically possible in the early 1920s. The debt the Allies owed each other was huge, as was the debt of some 11 billion dollars the Allied nations owed the United States. To be in a position to pay their debts the Allies created 'credits' by imposing reparations plans on the defeated Germans; France and Britain had to collect reparations if the debts to the United States were to be paid. But the Allied nations were not allowing Germany such conditions of international trade as would have permitted the Germans to make sustained large payments from surpluses earned by exports. Largely private loans to German industry and the German government totalling more than 5 billion dollars provided a means to pay the reparations of almost 4.7 billion dollars, and these payments enabled the Allies to service the debts to the United States. (Note: to convert the dollar amount to pounds sterling divide by five.) The Allies' other 'creditor' was Soviet Russia whose leaders were pressed at the Genoa Conference and elsewhere to honour the debts of the Tsarist Empire. In turn the Soviet leaders were promised, as part of a deal, a share in German reparations according to Article 116 of the Treaty of Versailles. In the event the threats and counterthreats to collect debts and enforce reparations payments brought the German and Russians together, and they concluded the *Treaty of Rapallo* (p. 181).

'The Treaty of Versailles had empowered the Reparations Commission to collect 5,000 million dollars before 1 May 1921 and then to announce the total amount Germany would have to meet. Disputes on this liability led to an Allied ultimatum in March 1921 and an extension of Allied occupation to Düsseldorf and two other German towns, and subsequently the declaration that Germany was in default. The Reparations Commission finally worked out the German bill at about 33,000 million dollars, a huge and unrealistic sum. More important were the details of the annual payment plan worked out at the *Second London Conference, 30 April–5 May 1921*, involving reparations at an annual rate of about 500 million dollars, and in addition an amount equivalent to 26 per cent of German exports. A little over a year later, on 31 August 1922, Germany's inability to pay was recognized by the Allies. The policy of meeting Allied claims, the declared intention of the German Foreign Minister, Walter Rathenau, proved impossible to realize as far as reparations were concerned.

Under the London payment plan of 1921 Germany had paid a total of about 3 billion gold marks in gold and goods (the Germans claimed that they had paid all that was due) and then made no further payment. The response of France and Belgium was to occupy the Ruhr, the centre of German industry, in January 1923. Some financial order was restored in 1924 by the *Dawes Plan* (p. 140) which began with a loan and called for payments rising annually to 2.5 billion Reichsmarks. In May and June 1930, just after the *Young Plan* (p. 141) came into force, the occupation of the last zone of the Rhineland was ended prematurely. The Young Plan scaled down Germany's repayments to 1,900 million Reichsmarks. Under the Young Plan the ultimate total payment would have worked out to about a third of the original total fixed in 1921. In 1931, a year of deepening economic depression,

President Hoover proposed and gained acceptance of a one-year moratorium of all inter-government debts including Germany's reparation payments. Finally at the *Lausanne Conference, June–July 1932*, German reparations were reduced to a sum more important psychologically than financially.

Of the total reparations fixed by the Reparations Commission in 1921 as 132,000 million gold marks (33 billion dollars) the Germans had 'paid' a little more than one-tenth (the precise figures remain in dispute), and during the same period had obtained foreign loans attracted by a high interest rate well in excess of the payments made in reparation; the loans had been subscribed by American and Allied investors; in 1934 Hitler repudiated them. The huge total sum arrived at in 1921 was intended more as a political gesture to appease public opinion than as the kind of reparations the experts had the slightest expectations of ever collecting. Reality brought the reparations chapter to a virtual close in 1932–33 amid worldwide depression. Hitler's version of the history of reparations served Nazi propaganda in the years that followed.

Agreement between the Reparations Commission and the German Government (Dawes Plan), 9 August 1924

The Contracting Parties

Being desirous of carrying into effect the plan for the discharge of reparation obligations and other pecuniary liabilities of Germany under the Treaty of Versailles proposed to the Reparation Commission on April 9, 1924, by the First Committee of Experts appointed by the Commission (which plan is referred to in this agreement as the Experts' [Dawes] Plan) and of facilitating the working of the Experts' Plan by putting into operation such additional arrangements as may hereafter be made between the German Government and the Allied Governments at the Conference now being held in London, in so far as the same

may lie within the respective spheres of action of the Reparation Commission and the German Government;

And the Reparation Commission acting in virtue not only of the powers conferred upon it by the said treaty but also of the authority given to it by the Allied Governments represented at the said Conference in respect of all payments by Germany dealt with in the Experts' Plan but not comprised in Part VIII of the said treaty;

Hereby agree as follows:

1. The German Government undertakes to take all appropriate measures for carrying into effect the Experts' Plan and for ensuring its permanent operation . . . .

Protocol concerning approval in principle of Report of Experts on Reparations (Young Plan), 31 August 1929

The representatives of Germany, Belgium, France, Great Britain, Italy and Japan, meeting at Geneva on the 16 September 1928, expressed their determination to make a complete and final settlement of the question of reparations and, with a view to attaining this object, provided for the constitution of a Committee of Financial Experts.

With this object the Experts met at Paris and their report was made on the 7 June 1929. Approval in principle was given to this report by The Hague Protocol of the 31 August 1929 . . . .

Article I. The Experts' Plan of the 7 June 1929, together with this present Agreement and the Protocol of the 31 August 1929 (all of which are hereinafter described as the New Plan) is definitely accepted as a complete and final settlement, so far as Germany is concerned, of the financial questions resulting from the war. By their acceptance the signatory Powers undertake the obligations and acquire the rights resulting for them respectively from the New Plan.

The German Government gives the creditor Powers the solemn undertaking to pay the annuities for which the New Plan provides in accordance with the stipulations contained therein.

. . .

Article 8. With a view to facilitating the successful working of the New Plan the German Government declares spontaneously that it is firmly determined to make every possible effort to avoid a declaration of postponement and not to have recourse thereto until it has come to the conclusion in good faith that Germany's exchange and economic life may be seriously endangered by the transfer in part or in full of the postponable portion of the annuities. It remains understood that Germany alone has authority to decide whether occasion has arisen for declaring a postponement as provided by the New Plan.

[In Annex III, Germany undertook to make annual payments beginning in 1929 and ending in 1988; these varied each year but averaged about 1,700 million Reichsmarks.]

The treaties of Locarno, 16 October 1925

France had emerged a victorious ally in 1918, but physically Germany remained potentially the preponderant power in Europe. At the peace conference the French had only been prevailed upon to abandon plans of detaching large parts of Germany by the promise of a guarantee of security and the alliance offered to France by the United States and Britain. This treaty never came into force, for the Senate repudiated Wilson's policy of global involvement (p. 90). Then the League of Nations' security procedures were hedged by so many qualifications that the French never placed undue faith in them. When the clarification and stiffening of measures against aggression embodied in the *Geneva Protocol of 1924* (p. 97) was abandoned in 1925, the writing was on the wall. In a great power conflict the League was unlikely to prove effective. What France desired above all was a British alliance, but British support could only be secured conditionally. This the French had to accept as better than nothing. The attraction to France of a

German proposal for a security pact to cover the Rhine area was that Britain promised to support such a settlement. On French insistence the scope of the treaties was enlarged to include some arrangements for eastern Europe. The British government favoured the treaties signed at Locarno as they appeared to solve a number of problems simultaneously: France would be promised support only conditionally on following a defensive policy in Europe; the reduction of Franco–German tension would contribute to general pacification, yet British commitments would remain strictly limited whilst allowing her the diplomatic initiative. But the Dominions were not bound and the British government signed on behalf of the United Kingdom alone, not for the British Empire. In Anglo–French relations the Locarno relationship remained important until the eve of the Second World War. The architects of the Locarno complex of treaties were Aristide Briand, Austen Chamberlain and Gustav Stresemann.

For the German governments of the Weimar Republic, Locarno represented the exchange of a German undertaking to accept the Versailles territorial settlement in the west for the concrete advantages that a growing sense of French security would lead to the recovery of German sovereignty, to the relaxation of Allied control over German armaments, and above all, to the early evacuation of all the parts of the Rhineland occupied by the Allies. But Germany was not reconciled to the 1922 frontier with Poland. An alignment with Soviet Russia had been established at *Rapallo, 16 April 1922* (p. 181) and was maintained after the signature of the Locarno treaties, with the *Treaty of Berlin, 24 April 1926* (p. 182). Germany made it clear that when it entered the League of Nations and took its permanent seat on the Council as promised at Locarno, and achieved in the autumn of 1926, Article 16 would not bind Germany to fight Soviet Russia or oblige the German government to permit armed forces passing across German territory to aid the victim of aggression. Germany had no intention of protecting 'Versailles' Poland. Nor would Germany guarantee its own eastern frontiers with Poland and Czechoslovakia as being permanent; only an arbitration agreement between these states and Germany in case of dispute was concluded. Its enforcement was not guaranteed by Britain and Italy; there was no reference in their preamble to the Treaty of Mutual Guarantee.

There were altogether five *Locarno treaties concluded on 16 October 1925* (p. 144): the Treaty of Mutual Guarantee and four arbitration treaties between Germany, Poland, Czechoslovakia, Belgium and France. The *Treaty of Mutual Guarantee* (p. 145) was signed by Britain, France, Germany, Belgium and Italy. These powers guaranteed the territorial status quo resulting from the frontiers between France and Germany and Germany and Belgium. They also guaranteed the demilitarization of the Rhine as provided in articles 42 and 43 of the Treaty of Versailles. Germany, France and Belgium mutually undertook not to invade each other or to resort to force (article 2). But this stipulation did not apply 'to a flagrant breach of

Articles 42 or 43 of the said Treaty of Versailles, if such breach constitutes an unprovoked act of aggression and by reason of the assembly of armed forces in the demilitarized zone immediate action is necessary': in such a case France could resort to force. If France, Belgium or Germany claimed a violation of the treaty had been committed, or a breach of articles 42 or 43 of the Treaty of Versailles had been or was being committed, the question was to be brought to the League of Nations; and if the League found a violation to have been committed, the guaranteeing powers (Britain and Italy) would each come to the assistance of the victim. But the guaranteeing powers would anticipate the League decision and come to the immediate assistance of the victim in a case of 'flagrant violation' of article 2, or if Germany 'flagrantly' violated articles 42 and 43 concerning the demilitarized Rhineland, and the guaranteeing powers (Britain and Italy) were satisfied 'that this violation constitutes an unprovoked act of aggression and that by reason either of the crossing of the frontier or of the outbreak of hostilities or of the assembly of the armed forces in the demilitarized zone immediate action is necessary' (article 4). Articles 2 and 4 had been very carefully worded and were the subject of lengthy negotiation. The actual commitment of Britain and Italy remained imprecise and would depend on their own decision whether the treaty had merely been violated or 'flagrantly' violated. There was thus no automatic commitment to go to war. There was no doubt Britain would do so if Germany actually invaded or attacked France. For French security the demilitarized Rhineland was of capital importance. The Versailles treaty regarded *any* violation as a 'hostile act'. The new treaty only promised the help of Britain and Italy if their view of the violation was flagrant. The diplomatic discussions preceding the Locarno treaty indicated that Britain would not regard Germany taking some military defensive measures as a 'flagrant violation' though they clearly were a violation of Versailles. Britain's view appears to have been that only if a German military build-up in the Rhineland was clearly an offensive step leading to the invasion of France or Belgium would the case of 'flagrant violation' be made out. The result for France was therefore a weakening of the terms imposed on Germany at Versailles, but also a strengthening of security in that military help was promised by Britain in certain circumstances without having to await the doubtful processes of the League of Nations. This undertaking was the substitute for the failed *Treaty of Guarantee of 28 June 1919* (p. 112). The French still retained another guarantee – the Allies remained in occupation of the three Rhineland zones, and would evacuate only one zone, the Cologne zone, towards the end of 1926.

Besides the Treaty of Mutual Guarantee, Germany signed *Arbitration Treaties with France and Belgium* (p. 147). These in turn were guaranteed by the Treaty of Mutual Guarantee. Germany also signed an *Arbitration Treaty with Poland and with Czechoslovakia* (p. 150) virtually identical in wording to the German–French and

German–Belgian arbitration treaties, but vitally different in that these two treaties were not related to or covered by the Treaty of Mutual Guarantee. This meant not only that Britain and Italy would not guarantee to come to the aid of the victim by reason of a violation of the arbitration clauses, but it also meant that there was no undertaking by Germany to accept the frontiers as settled in 1922, so that any violation of that frontier would not automatically place Germany in the wrong. Further, although Germany undertook not to resort to force from the start but to accept arbitration, the Germans made it clear at the time that this did not mean that under certain conditions force would not be employed eventually. France had been unable to secure an extension of a guarantee of the status quo in the east. France signed new alliance treaties with Czechoslovakia and Poland on the same day as the Locarno treaties, but it was clear that these alliances did not fall within the multinational framework of the latter. The French ability to fulfil its commitments to Poland and Czechoslovakia had in fact been weakened.

Pact of Locarno, 16 October 1925

Final Protocol of the Locarno Conference, 1925

The representatives of the German, Belgian, British, French, Italian, Polish, and Czechoslovak Governments, who have met at Locarno from the 5th to 16th October 1925, in order to seek by common agreement means for preserving their respective nations from the scourge of war and for providing for the peaceful settlement of disputes of every nature which might eventually arise between them,

Have given their approval to the draft treaties and conventions which respectively affect them and which, framed in the course of the present conference, are mutually interdependent:

Treaty between Germany, Belgium, France, Great Britain, and Italy (Annex A).
Arbitration Convention between Germany and Belgium (Annex B).

Arbitration Convention between Germany and France (Annex C).
Arbitration Treaty between Germany and Poland (Annex D).
Arbitration Treaty between Germany and Czechoslovakia (Annex E).

These instruments, hereby initialed *ne varietur*, will bear today's date, the representatives of the interested parties agreeing to meet in London on the 1st December next, to proceed during the course of a single meeting to the formality of the signature of the instruments which affect them.

The Minister for Foreign Affairs of France states that as a result of the draft arbitration treaties mentioned above, France, Poland, and Czechoslovakia have also concluded at Locarno draft agreements in order reciprocally to assure to themselves the benefit of the said treaties. These agreements will be duly deposited at the League of Nations, but M. Briand holds copies forthwith at the disposal of the Powers represented here.

The Secretary of State for Foreign Affairs of Great Britain proposes that, in reply to certain requests for explanations concerning Article 16 of the Covenant of the League of Nations presented by the Chancellor and the Minister for Foreign Affairs of Germany, a letter, of which the draft is similarly attached (Annex F) should be addressed to them at the same time as the formality of signature of the above-mentioned instruments takes place. This proposal is agreed to.

The representatives of the Governments represented here declare their firm conviction that the entry into force of these treaties and conventions will contribute greatly to bring about a moral relaxation of the tension between nations, that it will help powerfully towards the solution of many political or economic problems in accordance with the interests and sentiments of peoples, and that, in strengthening peace and security in Europe, it will hasten on effectively the disarmament provided for in Article 8 of the Covenant of the League of Nations.

They undertake to give their sincere cooperation to the work relating to disarmament already undertaken by the League of Nations and to seek the realization thereof in a general agreement.

[Signed] Luther, Stresemann, Vandervelde, Briand, Chamberlain, Mussolini, Skrzynski, Benes.

Treaty of Mutual Guarantee between the United Kingdom, Belgium, France, Germany and Italy, Locarno, 16 October 1925

The Heads of State of Germany, Belgium, France, Britain, and Italy . . .

Anxious to satisfy the desire for security and protection which animates the peoples upon whom fell the scourge of the war of 1914–18;

Taking note of the abrogation of the treaties for the neutralization of Belgium, and conscious of the necessity of ensuring peace in the area which has so frequently been the scene of European conflicts;

Animated also with the sincere desire of giving to all the signatory Powers concerned supplementary guarantees within the framework of the Covenant of the League of Nations and the treaties in force between them;

Have determined to conclude a Treaty with these objects, and have . . . agreed as follows:

Article 1. The High Contracting Parties collectively and severally guarantee, in the manner provided in the following Articles, the maintenance of the territorial *status quo* resulting from the frontiers between Germany and Belgium and between Germany and France and the inviolability of the said frontiers as fixed by or in pursuance of the Treaty of Peace signed at Versailles on the 28th June 1919, and also the observance of the stipulations of Articles 42 and 43 of the said treaty concerning the demilitarized zone.

Article 2. Germany and Belgium, and also Germany and France, mutually undertake that they will in no case attack or invade each other or resort to war against each other.

This stipulation shall not, however, apply in the case of:

1. The exercise of the right of legitimate defence, that is to say, resistance to a violation of the undertaking contained in the previous paragraph or to a flagrant breach of Articles 42 or 43 of the said Treaty of Versailles, if such breach constitutes an unprovoked act of aggression and by reason of the assembly of armed

forces in the demilitarized zone immediate action is necessary.

2. Action in pursuance of Article 16 of the Covenant of the League of Nations.

3. Action as the result of a decision taken by the Assembly or by the Council of the League of Nations or in pursuance of Article 15, paragraph 7, of the Covenant of the League of Nations, provided that in this last event the action is directed against a State which was the first to attack.

Article 3. In view of the undertakings entered into in Article 2 of the present Treaty, Germany and Belgium and Germany and France undertake to settle by peaceful means and in the manner laid down herein all questions of every kind which may arise between them and which it may not be possible to settle by the normal methods of diplomacy:

Any question with regard to which the parties are in conflict as to their respective rights shall be submitted to judicial decision, and the parties undertake to comply with such decision.

All other questions shall be submitted to a Conciliation Commission. If the proposals of this commission are not accepted by the two parties, the question shall be brought before the Council of the League of Nations, which will deal with it in accordance with Article 15 of the Covenant of the League.

The detailed arrangements for effecting such peaceful settlement are the subject of special agreements signed this day.

Article 4. 1. If one of the High Contracting Parties alleges that a violation of Article 2 of the present Treaty or a breach of Articles 42 or 43 of the Treaty of Versailles has been or is being committed, it shall bring the question at once before the Council of the League of Nations.

2. As soon as the Council of the League of Nations is satisfied that such violation or breach has been committed, it will notify its findings without delay to the Powers signatory of the present Treaty, who severally agree that in such case they will each of them come immediately to the assistance of the Power against whom the act complained of is directed.

3. In case of a flagrant violation of Article 2 of the present Treaty or of a flagrant breach of Articles 42 or 43 of the Treaty of Versailles by one of the High Contracting Parties, each of the other Contracting Parties hereby undertakes immediately to come to the help of the party against whom such a violation or breach has been directed as soon as the said Power has been able to satisfy itself that this violation constitutes an unprovoked act of aggression and that by reason either of the crossing of the frontier or of the outbreak of hostilities or of the assembly of armed forces in the demilitarized zone immediate action is necessary. Nevertheless, the Council of the League of Nations, which will be seized of the question in accordance with the first paragraph of this Article, will issue its findings, and the High Contracting Parties undertake to act in accordance with the recommendations of the Council provided that they are concurred in by all the members other than the representatives of the parties which have engaged in hostilities.

Article 5. The provisions of Article 3 of the present Treaty are placed under the guarantee of the High Contracting Parties as provided by the following stipulations:

If one of the Powers referred to in Article 3 refuses to submit a dispute to peaceful settlement or to comply with an arbitral or judicial decision and commits a violation of Article 2 of the present Treaty or a breach of Articles 42 or 43 of the Treaty of Versailles, the provisions of Article 4 shall apply.

Where one of the Powers referred to in Article 3 without committing a violation of Article 2 of the present Treaty or a breach of Articles 42 or 43 of the Treaty of Versailles, refuses to submit a dispute to peaceful settlement or to comply with an arbitral or judicial decision, the other party shall bring the matter before the Council of the League of Nations, and the Council shall propose what steps shall be taken; the High Contracting Parties shall comply with these proposals.

Article 6. The provisions of the present Treaty do not affect the rights and obligations of the High Contracting Parties under the Treaty of Versailles or under arrangements supplementary thereto, including the agreements signed in London on the 30th August 1924.

Article 7. The present Treaty, which is designed to ensure the maintenance of peace, and is in conformity with the Covenant of the League of Nations, shall not be interpreted as restricting the duty of the League to take whatever action may be deemed wise and effectual to safeguard the peace of the world.

Article 8. The present Treaty shall be registered at the League of Nations in accordance with the Covenant of the League. It shall remain in force until the Council, acting on a request of one or other of the High Contracting Parties notified to the other signatory Powers three months in advance, and voting at least by a two-thirds majority, decides that the League of Nations ensures sufficient protection to the High Contracting Parties; the Treaty shall cease to have effect on the expiration of a period of one year from such decision.

Article 9. The present Treaty shall impose no obligation upon any of the British Dominions, or upon India, unless the Government of such Dominion, or of India, signifies its acceptance thereof.

Article 10. The present Treaty shall be ratified as soon as possible.

It shall enter into force as soon as all the ratifications have been deposited and Germany has become a member of the League of Nations . . . .

Arbitration Convention between Germany and France, 16 October 1925

[An identical Arbitration Convention was concluded between Germany and Belgium.]

The undersigned duly authorized,

Charged by their respective Governments to determine the methods by which, as provided in Article 3 of the Treaty concluded this day between Germany, Belgium, France, Great Britain, and Italy, a peaceful solution shall be attained of all questions which cannot be settled amicably between Germany and Belgium,

Have agreed as follows:

Part I

Article 1. All disputes of every kind between Germany and France with regard to which the parties are in conflict as to their respective rights, and which it may not be possible to settle amicably by the normal methods of diplomacy, shall be submitted for decision either to an arbitral tribunal or to the Permanent Court of International Justice, as laid down hereafter. It is agreed that the disputes referred to above include in particular those mentioned in Article 13 of the Covenant of the League of Nations.

This provision does not apply to disputes arising out of events prior to the present Convention and belonging to the past.

Disputes for the settlement of which a special procedure is laid down in other conventions in force between Germany and France shall be settled in conformity with the provisions of those conventions.

Article 2. Before any resort is made to arbitral procedure or to procedure before the Permanent Court of International Justice, the dispute may, by agreement between the parties, be submitted, with a view to amicable settlement, to a permanent international commission styled the Permanent Conciliation Commission, constituted in accordance with the present Convention.

Article 3. In the case of a dispute the occasion of which, according to the municipal law of one of the parties, falls within the competence of the national courts of such party, the matter in dispute shall not be submitted to the procedure laid down in the present Convention until a judgement with final effect has been pronounced, within a reasonable time, by the competent national judicial authority.

Article 4. The Permanent Conciliation Commission mentioned in Article 2 shall be composed of five members, who shall be appointed as follows, that is to say: the German Government and the French Government shall each nominate a commissioner chosen from among their respective nationals, and shall appoint, by common agreement, the three other commissioners from among the nationals of third Powers; these three commissioners must be of different nationalities, and the German and French Governments shall appoint the president of the Commission from among them.

The commissioners are appointed for three years, and their mandate is renewable. Their appointment shall continue until their replacement and, in any case, until the termination of the work in hand at the moment of the expiry of their mandate . . . .

Article 5. The Permanent Conciliation Commission shall be constituted within three months from the entry into force of the present Convention . . . .

Article 6. The Permanent Conciliation Commission shall be informed by means of a request addressed to the president by the two parties acting in agreement or, in the absence of such agreement, by one or other of the parties.

The request, after having given a summary account of the subject of the dispute, shall contain the invitation to the Commission to take all necessary measures with a view to arrive at an amicable settlement.

If the request emanates from only one of the parties, notification thereof shall be made without delay to the other party.

Article 7. Within fifteen days from the date when the German Government or the French Government shall have brought a dispute before the Permanent Conciliation Commission either party may, for the examination of the particular dispute, replace its commissioner by a person possessing special competence in the matter . . . .

Article 8. The task of the Permanent Conciliation Commission shall be to elucidate questions in dispute, to collect with that object all necessary information by means of inquiry or otherwise, and to endeavour to bring the parties to an agreement. It may, after the case has been examined, inform the parties of the terms of settlement which seem suitable to it, and lay down a period within which they are to make their decision.

At the close of its labours the Commission shall draw up a report stating, as the case may be, either that the parties have come to an agreement and, if need arises, the terms of the agreement, or that it has been impossible to effect a settlement.

The labours of the Commission must, unless the parties otherwise agree, be terminated within six months from the day on which the Commission shall have been notified of the dispute.

[*Article 9.* Commission shall lay down its own procedure failing any provision to the contrary.]

[*Article 10.* President chooses meeting place in absence of agreement by parties to the contrary.]

[*Article 11.* Work of Permanent Conciliation Commission not public unless agreement by parties to the contrary.]

[*Article 12.* The parties shall be represented by agents before the Commission; agents may be assisted by experts; Commission may obtain oral evidence from agents, experts and with the consent of their Government from any person they regard as useful.]

Article 13. Unless otherwise provided in the present Convention, the decisions of the Permanent Conciliation Commission shall be taken by a majority.

Article 14. The German and French Governments undertake to facilitate the labours of the Permanent Conciliation Commission . . . to allow it to proceed in their territory and in accordance with their law to the summoning and hearing of witnesses or experts, and to visit the localities in question.

[*Article 15.* Salary of Commissioners.]

Article 16. In the event of no amicable agreement being reached before the Permanent Conciliation Commission the dispute shall be submitted by means of a special agreement either to the Permanent Court of International Justice under the conditions and according to the procedure laid down by its statute or to an arbitral tribunal under the conditions and according to the procedure laid down by the Hague Convention of the 18th October 1907, for the Pacific Settlement of International Disputes.

If the parties cannot agree on the terms of the special arrangement after a month's notice one or other of them may bring the dispute before the Permanent Court of International Justice by means of an application.

Part II

Article 17. All questions on which the German and French Governments shall differ without being able to reach an amicable solution by means of the normal methods of diplomacy the settlement of which cannot be attained by means of a judicial decision as provided in Article 1 of the present Convention, and for the settlement of which no procedure has been laid down by other conventions in force between the parties, shall be submitted to the Permanent Conciliation Commission, whose duty it shall be to propose to the parties an acceptable solution and in any case to present a report.

The procedure laid down in Articles 6–15

of the present Convention shall be applicable.

Article 18. If the two parties have not reached an agreement within a month from the termination of the labours of the Permanent Conciliation Commission the question shall, at the request of either party, be brought before the Council of the League of Nations, which shall deal with it in accordance with Article 15 of the Covenant of the League.

GENERAL PROVISION

Article 19. In any case, and particularly if the question on which the parties differ arises out of acts already committed or on the point of commission, the Conciliation Commission or, if the latter has not been notified thereof, the arbitral tribunal or the Permanent Court of International Justice, acting in accordance with Article 41 of its statute, shall lay down within the shortest possible time the provisional measures to be adopted. It shall similarly be the duty of the Council of the League of Nations, if the question is brought before it, to ensure that suitable provisional measures are taken. The German and French Governments undertake respectively to accept such measures, to abstain from all measures likely to have a repercussion prejudicial to the execution of the decision or to the arrangements proposed by the Conciliation Commission or by the Council of the League of Nations, and in general to abstain from any sort of action whatsoever which may aggravate or extend the dispute.

Article 20. The present Convention continues applicable as between Germany and France even when other Powers are also interested in the dispute.

Article 21. The present Convention shall be ratified. Ratifications shall be deposited at Geneva with the League of Nations at the same time as the ratifications of the treaty concluded this day between Germany, Belgium, France, Great Britain, and Italy.

It shall enter into and remain in force under the same conditions as the said treaty . . . .

Arbitration Treaty between Germany and Poland, 16 October 1925

[An identical treaty was concluded between Germany and Czechoslovakia.

The terms of this treaty are the same as the Arbitration Convention with two exceptions. Article 22 states that the treaty is in conformity with the Covenant and does not affect the rights of members of the League. But the crucial difference lies in the preamble which does not refer to the Treaty of Mutual Guarantee. This link with the four Guaranteeing Powers is absent; compare with the preamble of the German–French Arbitration Convention.]

Preamble

The President of the German Empire and the President of the Polish Republic;

Equally resolved to maintain peace between Germany and Poland by assuring the peaceful settlement of differences which might arise between the two countries;

Declaring that respect for the rights established by treaty or resulting from the law of nations is obligatory for international tribunals;

Agreeing to recognize that the rights of a State cannot be modified save with its consent;

And considering that sincere observance of the methods of peaceful settlement of international disputes permits of resolving, without recourse to force, questions which may become the cause of division between States;

Have decided to embody in a treaty their common intentions in this respect, and have named as their plenipotentiaries the following . . .

Who, having exchanged their full powers, found in due and good form, are agreed upon the following Articles . . .

Collective Note to Germany regarding Article 16 of the Covenant of the League of Nations

The German delegation has requested certain explanations in regard to Article 16 of the Covenant of the League of Nations.

We are not in a position to speak in the name of the League, but in view of the discussions which have already taken place in the Assembly and in the commissions of the League of Nations, and after the explanations which have been exchanged between ourselves, we do not hesitate to inform you of the interpretation which, in so far as we are concerned, we place upon Article 16.

In accordance with that interpretation the obligations resulting from the said Article on the Members of the League must be understood to mean that each State Member of the League is bound to cooperate loyally and effectively in support of the Covenant and in resistance to any act of aggression to an extent which is compatible with its military situation and takes its geographical position into account.

The Pact of Paris, 27 August 1928

A treaty attempting to 'outlaw' war was first drafted by France and the United States on the initiative of Briand. This draft, the *Briand–Kellogg Pact*, fifteen nations were invited to sign on *27 August 1928* under its official title of the *Pact of Paris* (p. 151). Other nations quickly adhered and by 1933 sixty-five governments had pledged themselves to observe its provisions.

During the course of negotiations the French government, generally followed by other states, made four reservations: (1) the treaty was not to be effective unless it secured universal adherence or until some special further agreement had been reached; (2) each country retained the right of legitimate defence; (3) if one country violated its pledge then the others would be automatically released from theirs; (4) the treaty was not to interfere with French treaty obligations under the League, Locarno or her neutrality treaties. Specifically, in respect to Article 1 Britain reserved her right to act in the Empire and would not allow interference in these regions of the world. The US Senate Foreign Relations Committee understood that by the treaty the right of self-defence was not curtailed nor the right to maintain the Monroe Doctrine. The Soviet Union sent a long protest at its exclusion from the discussions, but together with the Baltic states signed a declaration adhering to the treaty. The reservations undermined the credibility of the Pact of Paris.

The treaty was a self-denying undertaking containing no sanctions against countries in breach of it. The aggressors of the 1930s, Japan, Italy, Germany and the Soviet Union, were not restrained by it though they were all signatories. The treaty was based on the hope that the forces of moral diplomacy and the weight of world public opinion were powerful influences restraining the use of force. The events of the next two decades falsified that hope.

Pact of Paris (Briand–Kellogg Pact), 27 August 1928

[The Heads of State of the United States, Belgium, Czechoslovakia, Britain, Germany, Italy, Japan and Poland. . . .]

Deeply sensible of their solemn duty to promote the welfare of mankind; persuaded that the time has come when a frank renunciation of war as an instrument of national policy should be made, to the end that the peaceful and friendly relations now existing between their peoples may be perpetuated;

Convinced that all changes in their relations with one another should be sought only by pacific means and be the result of a peaceful and orderly process, and that any signatory Power which shall hereafter seek to promote its national interests by resort to war should be denied the benefits furnished by this Treaty;

Hopeful that, encouraged by their example, all the other nations of the world will join in this humane endeavour and, by adhering to the present Treaty as soon as it comes into force, bring their peoples within the scope of its beneficent provisions, thus uniting the civilized nations of the world in a common renunciation of war as an instrument of their national policy;

Have decided to conclude a treaty, . . . and . . . have agreed upon the following Articles:

Article I. The High Contracting Parties solemnly declare, in the names of their respective peoples, that they condemn recourse to war for the solution of international controversies and renounce it as an instrument of national policy in their relations with one another.

Article II. The High Contracting Parties agree that the settlement or solution of all disputes or conflicts, of whatever nature or of whatever origin they may be, which may arise among them, shall never be sought except by pacific means.

[*Article III*. Ratification] . . .
This Treaty shall, when it has come into effect as prescribed in the preceding paragraph, remain open as long as may be necessary for adherence by all the other Powers of the world . . . .

Protocol concluded between the Soviet Union, Estonia, Latvia, Poland and Rumania on 9 February 1929, giving effect to the treaty renouncing war

The Government of the Estonian Republic, the President of the Latvian Republic, the President of the Polish Republic, His Majesty the King of Rumania and the Central Executive Committee of U.S.S.R.; animated by the desire to contribute to the maintenance of the existing peace between their countries and for the purpose of putting into force without delay, between the peoples of those countries, the Treaty for the Renunciation of War as an Instrument of National Policy, signed at Paris on August 27, 1928; have decided to achieve this purpose by means of the present Protocol and have . . . agreed as follows:

Article I. The Treaty for the Renunciation of War as an Instrument of National Policy, signed at Paris on August 27, 1928, a copy of which is attached to the present Protocol as an integral part of this instrument, shall come into force between the Contracting Parties after the ratification of the said Treaty of Paris of 1928 by the competent legislative bodies of the respective Contracting Parties.

Article II. The entry into force, in virtue of the present Protocol of the Treaty of Paris of 1928 in the reciprocal relations between the parties to the present Protocol shall be valid independently of the entry into force of the Treaty of Paris of 1928 as provided in Article III of the last-named Treaty.

Article III. The present Protocol shall be ratified by the competent legislative bodies of the Contracting Parties, in conformity with the requirements of their respective constitutions . . . .

Disarmament

As an essential part of the general post-war settlement the Allies and Associated Powers worked for a reduction of armaments and the diminution of armament rivalries on land and on the sea. In accordance with articles 8 and 9 of the Covenant a Permanent Advisory Commission of the League was set up in May 1920. In the following year the *Naval Limitation Treaty* was negotiated at the *Washington Conference, 1921–22* (p. 132). Little other progress was made, but with the signature of the Locarno treaties the Council of the League took a fresh initiative in setting up a Preparatory Commission in December 1925, which it was intended should be followed by a Disarmament Conference. Progress was frustrated by national assessments of security needs. Eventually in *1930 the London Naval Conference led to a Naval Treaty, 22 April 1930*, which extended to other than capital ships the provisions of the naval limitations of the Washington Treaty of 1922. But only three groups of powers ratified the treaty: Britain and the Dominions, Japan, and the United States. Italian claims for parity with France frustrated the intention of including these two European states. The general Disarmament Conference sponsored by the Council of the League did not meet until February 1932. The various phases of the conference revealed the growing international conflicts and produced only one tangible result, the banning of chemical and bacteriological warfare. In October 1933 Nazi Germany withdrew from the conference; thereafter it dragged on for a few months longer to its inevitable practical failure and adjournment in May 1934.

Japan gave notice of termination of the Washington Treaty of 6 February 1922, and this treaty as well as provisions in the Naval Treaty of 22 April 1930 concerning naval limitation expired on 31 December 1936. A Naval Conference as provided by the treaty of 1930 met in London in December 1935, but Japan withdrew. *A Naval Treaty was signed between the United States, France, Great Britain and the Dominions on 25 March 1936* which provided for little more than consultation. In December 1938, subject to certain provisions, Italy acceded, but with the outbreak of war in September 1939 the treaty was suspended. In practice the naval conference of 1936 marked the end of the search for disarmament which had been pursued during the inter-war years.

Treaty between Britain and Dominions, France, Italy, Japan and the United States for the limitation and reduction of naval armament, London, 22 April 1930

. . .

Part I

Desiring to prevent the dangers and reduce the burdens inherent in competitive armaments, and

Desiring to carry forward the work begun by the Washington Naval Conference and to facilitate the progressive realization of general limitation and reduction of armaments,

Have resolved to conclude a Treaty for the limitation and reduction of naval armament, and have accordingly appointed as their plenipotentiaries . . .

Article 1. The High Contracting Parties agree not to exercise their rights to lay down the keels of capital ship replacement tonnage during the years 1931–1936 inclusive as provided in Chapter II, Part 3, of the Treaty for the Limitation of Naval Armament signed between them at Washington on the 6th February 1922, and referred to in the present Treaty as the Washington Treaty.

This provision is without prejudice to the disposition relating to the replacement of ships accidentally lost or destroyed contained in Chapter II, Part 3, Section I, paragraph (c) of the said Treaty.

France and Italy may, however, build the replacement tonnage which they were entitled to lay down in 1927 and 1929 in accordance with the provisions of the said Treaty.

Article 2. 1. The United States, the United Kingdom of Great Britain and Northern Ireland and Japan shall dispose of the following capital ships as provided in this Article . . . .

[U.S. – 3, U.K. – 5, and Japan – 1 named ship.]

2. Subject to any disposal of capital ships which might be necessitated, in accordance with the Washington Treaty, by the building by France or Italy of the replacement tonnage referred to in Article 1 of the present Treaty, all existing capital ships mentioned in Chapter II, Part 3, Section II of the Washington Treaty and not designated above to be disposed of may be retained during the term of the present Treaty.

[*Articles 3 and 4.* Definition of aircraft carrier; no aircraft carrier to be constructed of less than 10,000 tons.]

[*Article 5.* Restriction on armament of aircraft carriers.]

[*Article 7.* Limitation on submarine construction.]

. . .

Part III

The President of the United States of America, His Majesty the King of Great Britain, Ireland and the British Dominions beyond the Seas, Emperor of India, and His Majesty the Emperor of Japan, have agreed as between themselves to the provisions of this Part III:

Article 14. The naval combatant vessels of the United States, the British Commonwealth of Nations and Japan, other than capital ships, aircraft carriers and all vessels exempt from limitation under Article 8, shall be limited during the term of the present Treaty as provided in this Part III, and, in the case of special vessels, as provided in Article 12.

Article 15. For the purpose of this Part III the definition of the cruiser and destroyer categories shall be as follows . . . .

Article 16. 1. The completed tonnage in the cruiser, destroyer and submarine categories which is not to be exceeded on the 31st December 1936, is given in the following table . . . .

2. Vessels which cause the total tonnage in any category to exceed the figures given . . . [*Cruisers:* U.S. tonnage, 323,500 tons; British Commonwealth, 339,000 tons; Japan, 208,850 tons. *Destroyers:* U.S. tonnage, 150,000 tons; British Commonwealth, 150,000 tons; Japan, 105,500 tons. *Submarines:* U.S. tonnage, 52,700 tons; British Commonwealth, 52,700 tons; Japan, 52,700 tons] shall be disposed of gradually during the period ending on the 31st December 1936.

3. The maximum number of cruisers of sub-category (a) shall be as follows: for the United States, 18; for the British Commonwealth of Nations, 15; for Japan, 12 . . . .

Article 21. If, during the term of the present Treaty, the requirements of the national security of any High Contracting Party in respect of vessels of war limited by Part III of the present Treaty are in the opinion of that Party materially affected by new construction of any Power other than those who have joined in Part III of this Treaty, that High Contracting Party will notify the other Parties to Part III as to the increase required to be made in its tonnages within one or more of the categories of such vessels of war, . . . and shall be entitled to make such increase. Thereupon the other Parties to Part III of this Treaty shall be entitled to make a proportionate increase in the category or categories specified . . .

Part IV

[Accepted rules of international law.]

[*Article 23.* Treaty shall remain in force until 31 December 1936. New Conference to meet in 1935.]

The Four Power Pact, 7 June 1933

In a speech at Turin in October 1932, Mussolini proposed a Four Power Pact between the four great European powers, Italy, France, Germany and Britain. Its main purpose was to be the consideration of the revision of the peace treaties in a way agreed to by the four powers, who would then 'induce' other countries to 'adopt the same policy of peace'. Germany would have been the principal beneficiary. It was intended that the revision of the treaties, such as gradual rearmament, would be brought about through agreement and not unilaterally by Hitler's Germany. The Little *Entente* powers had most to lose from any revision of the peace treaties and they objected violently. The Four Power Pact was only signed on 7 June 1933 after France had secured substantial amendment to the original draft. The pact was never ratified and in its emasculated form proved of little influence even in the immediate months after its signature.

Four Power Pact between Italy, Britain, France and Germany, Rome, 7 June 1933

[This was not ratified and did not enter into force.]

. . .

Article 1. The High Contracting Parties will consult together as regards all questions which appertain to them. They undertake to make every effort to pursue, within the framework of the League of Nations, a policy of effective cooperation between all Powers with a view to the maintenance of peace.

Article 2. In respect of the Covenant of the League of Nations, and particularly Articles 10, 16 and 19, the High Contracting Parties decide to examine between themselves and without prejudice to decisions which can only be taken by the regular organs of the League of Nations, all proposals relating to methods and procedure calculated to give due effect to these Articles.

Article 3. The High Contracting Parties undertake to make every effort to ensure the success of the Disarmament Conference and, should questions which particularly concern them remain in suspense on the conclusion of that Conference, they reserve the right to re-examine these questions between themselves in pursuance of the present Agreement with a view to ensuring their solution through the appropriate channels.

Article 4. The High Contracting Parties affirm their desire to consult together as regards all economic questions which have a common interest for Europe and particularly for its economic restoration, with a view to seeking a settlement within the framework of the League of Nations . . . .

[*Article 5.* Agreement concluded for ten years.]

[*Article 6.* Ratification.]

V · France and her eastern allies, 1921–39

Even at the time of victory in January 1919, when the French Premier Georges Clemenceau became host to the peace conference and Paris was the centre of world diplomacy, the French never lost sight of the fact that France was in a position of fundamental weakness in post-war Europe. With more than 4 million dead and maimed and a huge debt of 34 billion gold francs, as well as the physical destruction of much of northern France, French statesmen did not face the future with much confidence. The recovery of a Germany that contained 20 million more Germans than Frenchmen as well as the capacity of the industrial Ruhr basin could once more place France internationally on the defensive, contemplating the possibility of a third German invasion. French foreign policy was thus designed to fulfil two complementary objectives: to find a way of permanently reducing Germany's future power and to retain and gain new allies to ensure a preponderance of strength over a revived Germany. The League of Nations was the third prop, but successive French governments were loath to place much reliance on it.

The search for firm alliances in the west, that is with Britain and the United States, proved elusive during the years 1919–24; only in the Locarno peace framework could France in 1925 secure British promises of help (p. 144). In the east the position had totally changed with Imperial Russia's defeat and the Bolshevik revolution. At the end of the war the Czechs were in a good position to occupy and claim all the lands which were to become the Republic of Czechoslovakia.

French alliances with Czechoslovakia and Poland, 1921–25

The Czechs looked to the French as their allies. The position of the Polish frontiers, on the other hand, remained unsettled in the east and the west; what is more, the Poles were in bitter dispute over the Teschen territory with the Czechs. For the French there appeared to be the alternative policy of making a revived Russia France's major ally. As long as the civil war continued in Russia and the overthrow of the Bolshevik Russian forces remained a possibility, France would not back Poland's policy of annexing more Russian territory as this would have earned France the enmity of the White Russians. And so Poland owed its national survival in the war with Bolshevik Russia (1920–21) to its own strength rather than to French help.

With the *Treaty of Riga, 18 March 1921* (p. 176) which settled the Russian–Polish frontier, and with the consolidation of Soviet power, the French reviewed their eastern policy during the winter of 1920–21. The French government now in 1921 concluded that a strong Poland linked in military alliance with France would prove a barrier to Bolshevik Russia and the best check on Germany. The alternative of attempting to gain the alliance of Soviet Russia was not adopted in the 1920s. Franco–Polish cooperation was seen by France as making an essential contribution to post-war European stability. *On 19 February 1921 Poland and France signed an Alliance Treaty, and on 21 February a secret Military Convention* (p. 158). These two agreements were coupled with a secret Polish–French economic agreement, not finally concluded until 6 February 1922, which provided that in return for a French loan of 400 million francs Poland would purchase all its war materials in France. The commercial agreements also gave France preferential treatment in bilateral trade, especially in the Polish oil industry.

At the time of concluding the alliance there remained widespread French misgivings on the extensive commitments assumed. By limiting the *casus foederis* to unprovoked aggression the French hoped to guard against an 'adventurous' Polish policy at the expense of Russia. The military commitment was nevertheless far-reaching.

The Czechs felt themselves more secure than the Poles. When the *Franco–Czechoslovak Alliance was signed on 25 January 1924* (p. 159) it was the Czechs not the French who refused an additional secret military convention. The Czech government wished to retain freedom of action and to follow an independent foreign policy in the Danubian regions. The Franco–Czech alliance was thus much more imprecise and flexible than the Franco–Polish treaties, and Franco–Czech military consultation and cooperation was provided for only by a secret exchange of letters and not by treaty.

Revised alliance treaties with Poland and Czechoslovakia were signed by France on 16 October 1925, at the time of the conclusion of the *Locarno Treaties* (p. 144). To reconcile French obligations under the Locarno Treaties with commitments to Poland and Czechoslovakia, France's eastern allies, was difficult even though the new alliance treaties did not supersede the old. France could no longer act in defence of Poland by invading Germany from the west. Poland and Czechoslovakia would first have to turn to the League of Nations. In practice France was tying its hands to the views taken by Britain and Italy, the Locarno guarantors of the Franco–German frontier. In practice too, Poland and Czechoslovakia followed, perhaps realistically, independent foreign policies and did not rely for sole support on the French alliance. In 1925, with the signature of the Locarno Treaties, the French alliances and the Balkan alignments the European diplomatic pattern of the inter-war years was emerging from the uncertainties of the years immediately following Germany's collapse in 1918.

Political Agreement between France and Poland, 19 February 1921

The Polish Government and the French Government, both desirous of safeguarding, by the maintenance of the Treaties which both have signed or which may in future be recognized by both Parties, the peace of Europe, the security of their territories and their common political and economic interests, have agreed as follows:

1. In order to coordinate their endeavours towards peace, the two Governments undertake to consult each other on all questions of foreign policy which concern both States, so far as those questions affect the settlement of international relations in the spirit of the Treaties and in accordance with the Covenant of the League of Nations.

2. In view of the fact that economic restoration is the essential preliminary condition of the re-establishment of international order and peace in Europe, the two Governments shall come to an understanding in this regard, with a view to concerted action and mutual support.

They will endeavour to develop their economic relations, and for this purpose will conclude special agreements and a Commercial Treaty.

3. If, notwithstanding the sincerely peaceful views and intentions of the two Contracting States, either or both of them should be attacked without giving provocation, the two Governments shall take concerted measures for the defence of their territory and the protection of their legitimate interests, within the limits specified in the preamble.

4. The two Governments undertake to consult each other before concluding new agreements which will affect their policy in Central and Eastern Europe.

5. The present Agreement shall not come into force until the commercial agreements now in course of negotiation have been signed.

Secret Military Convention between France and Poland, 21 February 1921

[This summary is based on the reconstruction of this military treaty from manuscript sources by Piotr S. Wandycz, *France and her Eastern Allies 1919–1925*, Minneapolis, University of Minnesota Press, 1962, pp. 394–5.]

[*Article 1.* If the situation of Germany should become menacing to the extent that there is a threat of war against one of the two signatories, and especially if Germany mobilizes or if the maintenance of the Treaty of Versailles necessitates joint action by the signatories, then the two signatories undertake to strengthen their military preparations in such a way as to be in a position to provide effective and speedy assistance to each other and to act in common. If Germany attacks one of the two countries they are bound to afford assistance to each other following an agreement between them.

Article 2. If Poland is threatened or attacked by Soviet Russia, France undertakes to hold Germany in check by action as necessary on land and sea and to aid Poland in defence against the Soviet army as detailed below.

Article 3. If the eventualities foreseen in Articles 1 and 2 arise, direct French help to Poland will consist of sending to Poland war equipment and a technical mission, but not French troops, and securing the lines of sea communication between France and Poland.

. . .

Article 5. Poland undertakes with French help to develop its war indemnity according to a particular plan so as to be able to equip the Polish army as necessary.

Article 6. Provision for continuous consultations between the general staffs of the two countries to fulfil the provisions of this treaty.

Article 7. Measures to be taken to ensure the effectiveness of the French military mission in Poland.

Article 8. This Agreement will only come into force when the commercial agreement is concluded.]

Treaty of Alliance between France and Czechoslovakia, 25 January 1924

The President of the French Republic and the President of Czechoslovak Republic,

Being earnestly desirous of upholding the principle of international agreements which was solemnly confirmed by the Covenant of the League of Nations,

Being further desirous of guarding against any infraction of the peace, the maintenance of which is necessary for the political stability and economic restoration of Europe,

Being resolved for this purpose to ensure respect for the international juridical and political situation created by the Treaties of which they were both signatories,

And having regard to the fact that, in order to attain this object, certain mutual guarantees are indispensable for security against possible aggression and for the protection of their common interests,

Have appointed as their plenipotentiaries:

For the President of the French Republic:
M. Raymond Poincaré, *President of the Council, Minister for Foreign Affairs*;

For the President of the Czechoslovak Republic:
M. Eduard Beneš, *Minister for Foreign Affairs*,

Who, after examining their full powers, which were found in good and due form, have agreed to the following provisions:

Article 1. The Governments of the French Republic and of the Czechoslovak Republic undertake to concert their action in all matters of foreign policy which may threaten their security or which may tend to subvert the situation created by the Treaties of Peace of which both parties are signatories.

Article 2. The High Contracting Parties shall agree together as to the measures to be adopted to safeguard their common interests in case the latter are threatened.

Article 3. The High Contracting Parties, being fully in agreement as to the importance, for the maintenance of the world's peace, of the political principles laid down in Article 88 of the Treaty of Peace of St Germain-en-Laye of September 10, 1919, and in the Protocols of Geneva dated October 4, 1922, of which instruments they both are signatories, undertake to consult each other as to the measures to be taken in case there should be any danger of an infraction of these principles.

Article 4. The High Contracting Parties, having special regard to the declarations made by the Conference of Ambassadors on February 3, 1920, and April 1, 1921, on which their policy will continue to be based, and to the declaration made on November 10, 1921, by the Hungarian Government to the Allied diplomatic representatives, undertake to consult each other in case their interests are threatened by a failure to observe the principles laid down in the aforesaid declarations.

Article 5. The High Contracting Parties solemnly declare that they are in complete agreement as to the necessity, for the maintenance of peace, of taking common action in the event of any attempt to restore the Hohenzollern dynasty in Germany, and they undertake to consult each other in such a contingency.

Article 6. In conformity with the principles laid down in the Covenant of the League of Nations, the High Contracting Parties agree that if in future any dispute should arise between them which cannot be settled by friendly agreement and through diplomatic channels, they will submit such dispute either to the Permanent Court of International Justice or to such other arbitrator or arbitrators as they may select.

Article 7. The High Contracting Parties undertake to communicate to each other all agreements affecting their policy in Central Europe which they may have previously concluded, and to consult one another before concluding any further agreements. They declare that, in this matter, nothing in the present Treaty is contrary to the above agreements, and in particular to the Treaty of Alliance between France and Poland, or to the Conventions and Agreements concluded by Czechoslovakia with the Federal Republic of Austria, Roumania, the Kingdom of the Serbs, Croats and Slovenes, or to the Agreement effected by an exchange of notes on February 8, 1921, between the Italian Government and the Czechoslovak Government.

Article 8. The present Treaty shall be communicated to the League of Nations in conformity with Article 18 of the Covenant.

The present Treaty shall be ratified and the instruments of ratification shall be exchanged at Paris as soon as possible.

In faith whereof the respective plenipotentiaries, being duly empowered for this purpose, have signed the present Treaty and have thereto affixed their seals.

Done at Paris, in duplicate, on January 25, 1924.

[Signed] R. POINCARÉ, DR EDUARD BENEŠ

Treaty of Understanding between France and Yugoslavia, 11 November 1927

[This treaty is similar in text to the Treaty of Friendship between France and Rumania, 10 June 1926. Rumania also signed a Treaty of Friendship with Italy, 16 September 1926.]

. . .

Article 1. France and the Kingdom of the Serbs, Croats and Slovenes reciprocally undertake to refrain from all attacks or invasions directed against one another and in no circumstances to resort to war against one another . . . [unless in virtue of League obligations]

[*Article 2.* Pacific settlement of disputes.]

. . .

Article 5. The High Contracting Parties agree to take counsel together in the event of any modification, or attempted modification, of the political status of European countries and, subject to any resolutions which may be adopted in such case by the Council or Assembly of the League of Nations, to come to an understanding as to the attitude which they should respectively observe in such an eventuality.

Article 6. The High Contracting Parties declare that nothing in this Treaty is to be interpreted as contradicting the stipulations of the treaties at present in force which have been signed by France or the Kingdom of the Serbs, Croats and Slovenes, and which concern their policy in Europe. They undertake to exchange views on questions affecting European policy in order to coordinate their efforts in the cause of peace, and for this purpose to communicate to each other henceforward any treaties or agreements which they may conclude with third Powers on the same subject. Such treaties or agreements shall invariably be directed to aims which are compatible with the maintenance of peace.

Treaty of Mutual Guarantee between France and Poland, Locarno, 16 October 1925

[This treaty is identical in text to the Treaty of Mutual Guarantee between France and Czechoslovakia, 16 October 1925.]

The President of the French Republic and the President of the Polish Republic;

Equally desirous to see Europe spared from war by a sincere observance of the undertakings arrived at this day with a view to the maintenance of general peace,

Have resolved to guarantee their benefits to each other reciprocally by a treaty concluded within the framework of the Covenant of the League of Nations and of the treaties existing between them . . . and . . . have agreed on the following provisions:

Article 1. In the event of Poland or France being injured by a failure to observe the undertakings arrived at this day between them and Germany with a view to the maintenance of general peace, France, and reciprocally Poland, acting in application of Article 16 of the Covenant of the League of Nations, undertake to lend each other immediately aid and assistance, if such a failure is accompanied by an unprovoked resort to arms.

In the event of the Council of the League of Nations, when dealing with a question brought before it in accordance with the said undertakings, being unable to succeed in making its report accepted by all its members other than the representatives of the parties to the dispute, and in the event of Poland or France being attacked without provocation, France, or reciprocally Poland, acting in application of Article 15, paragraph 7, of the Covenant of the League of Nations, will immediately lend aid and assistance.

Article 2. Nothing in the present Treaty shall affect the rights and obligations of the High Contracting Parties as members of the League of Nations, or shall be interpreted as restricting the duty of the League to take whatever action may be deemed wise and effectual to safeguard the peace of the world.

Article 3. The present Treaty shall be registered with the League of Nations, in accordance with the Covenant.

Article 4. The present Treaty shall be ratified. The ratifications will be deposited at Geneva with the League of Nations at the same time as the ratification of the Treaty concluded this day between Germany, Belgium, France, Great Britain, and Italy, and the ratification of the Treaty concluded at the same time between Germany and Poland.

It will enter into force and remain in force under the same conditions as the said Treaties.

The Little *Entente* states and the Polish-Roumanian Alliance, 1920–39

The peace settlements did not mark an end to the frontier problems of the states of the Danube region. The diplomatic relations of the nations were largely influenced by three sometimes contradictory considerations.

1. The 'successor states' carved out of the Austro-Hungarian Monarchy, namely Czechoslovakia and Yugoslavia together with Roumania, which had acquired much former Hungarian territory as well as Bulgarian territory, stood for the maintenance of the peace treaties, and tended to combine against Germany, Hungary, Austria and Bulgaria, countries that might desire to 'revise' these settlements. 2. Soviet Russia was not only feared by Roumania, which had received formerly Russian Bessarabia; for ideological reasons the spread of revolution was feared by all the states on its borders, and they tended to combine against the Bolsheviks. The Czechs were the most friendly to Soviet Russia. 3. Finally, just as before 1914 the smaller states of the Balkans were bound to react to the ambitions of those great powers who pursued an active Balkan policy during the inter-war period, especially France, Italy, and in the 1930s, Germany.

It was the uncertainty of French policy in the Balkans and French advances to Hungary in 1920 which first led some of the Balkan states to band together in a joint defence of their interests. In the summer of 1920 Yugoslavia, Czechoslovakia and Roumania began to negotiate the series of treaties which formed the *Little Entente: a defensive alliance between Czechoslovakia and Yugoslavia, 14 August 1920*, directed against Hungarian revisionist plans; a *treaty between Czechoslovakia and Roumania, 5 June 1921*, aimed at preventing Hungarian and Bulgarian revisionism, based on a *convention* directed only against Hungary of *23 April 1921*; finally a *treaty between Yugoslavia and Roumania, 7 June 1921*, directed against both Bulgaria and Hungary (pp. 164–65). Thus the basis of the Little *Entente* was the determination to maintain the Treaty of Neuilly (p. 95) and the Treaty of Trianon (p. 94).

The Polish government was not well disposed to the Little *Entente*, which tended to give diplomatic leadership to the Czechs. No lasting friendship and cooperation could be established between the Czechs and Poles during the inter-war years. The Roumanians, however, were not only afraid of Hungarian and Bulgarian irredentism (hence their partnership in the *Little* Entente) but also of Russian hostility over the loss of Bessarabia. As the Little *Entente* was not directed against Russia, *the Poles and Roumanians signed a separate Alliance Treaty, 3 March 1921* (p. 165), providing for help if either state was attacked by Russia. This treaty was renewed and extended by the *Treaty of Guarantee, 26 March 1926*, which stipulated immediate help to the ally in the event of unprovoked attack contrary to articles 12, 13 and 15 of the Covenant of the League of Nations (p. 166).

The Little *Entente* states and Roumania and Poland wished by their align-ments to create a stable and strong central and Danubian Europe. They were prepared to make agreements with great power neighbours France, Italy, Ger-many and even the Soviet Union, in order to strengthen their security and independence. Thus the inter-war period saw the conclusion not only of treaties with France but also between *Italy and Yugoslavia* (January 1924), *Czechoslovakia and Italy* (July 1924), *France and Roumania* (January 1926), *Italy and Roumania* (September 1926) and *France and Yugoslavia* (November 1927).

These agreements had their effects on the relations of the Danubian states and Poland in the inter-war period, but from the moment of crisis in the autumn of 1938 onwards they counted for very little. Czechoslovakia was not preserved by the Little *Entente* in 1938–39, nor did Poland receive aid from Roumania in Sep-tember 1939 when invaded by Germany and Russia. Yugoslavia was invaded by Germany in April 1941 and was left to fend for itself; Roumania, with Greece the recipient of a unilateral *Anglo–French Guarantee of March 1939* (p. 223), joined the Germans in their war against the Soviet Union in 1941. Though France had been the principal great power seeking allies in eastern and central Europe in the 1920s, the majority of French leaders came to look upon the eastern connections in the 1930s as more of a liability and obstacle to effective 'appeasement' than a source of strength.

Alliance between Yugoslavia and Czechoslovakia, 14 August 1920

Firmly resolved to maintain the peace obtained by so many sacrifices, and provided for by the Covenant of the League of Nations, as well as the situation created by the Treaty concluded at Trianon on June 4, 1920, between the Allied and Associated Powers on the one hand, and Hungary on the other, the President of the Czechoslovak Republic and His Majesty the King of the Serbs, Croats, and Slovenes have agreed to conclude a defensive Convention . . . and have agreed as follows:

Article 1. In case of an unprovoked attack on the part of Hungary against one of the High Contracting Parties, the other party agrees to assist in the defence of the party attacked, in the manner laid down by the arrangement provided for in Article 2 of the present Convention.

Article 2. The competent Technical Authorities of the Czechoslovak Republic and the Kingdom of the Serbs, Croats, and Slovenes shall decide, by mutual agreement, upon the provisions necessary for the execution of the present Convention.

Article 3. Neither of the High Contracting Parties shall conclude an alliance with a third Power without preliminary notice to the other.

Article 4. The present Convention shall be valid for two years from the date of the exchange of ratifications. On the expiration of this period, each of the Contracting Parties shall have the option of denouncing the present Convention. It shall, however, remain in force for six months after the date of denunciation.

Alliance between Rumania and Czechoslovakia, 23 April 1921

Firmly resolved to maintain the peace obtained by so many sacrifices, and provided for by the Covenant of the League of Nations, as well as the situation created by the Treaty concluded at Trianon on June 4, 1920, between the Allied and Associated Powers on the one hand, and Hungary on the other, the President of the Czechoslovak Republic and His Majesty the King of Rumania, have agreed to conclude a defensive Convention . . . and have agreed as follows:

Article 1. In case of an unprovoked attack on the part of Hungary against one of the High Contracting Parties, the other party agrees to assist in the defence of the party attacked, in the manner laid down by the arrangement provided for in Article 2 of the present Convention.

Article 2. The competent Technical Authorities of the Czechoslovak Republic and Rumania shall decide by mutual agreement and in a Military Convention to be concluded, upon the provisions necessary for the execution of the present Convention.

Article 3. Neither of the High Contracting Parties shall conclude an alliance with a third Power without preliminary notice to the other.

Article 4. For the purpose of coordinating their efforts to maintain peace, the two Governments undertake to consult together on questions of foreign policy concerning their relations with Hungary.

Article 5. The present Convention shall be valid for two years from the date of the exchange of ratifications. On the expiration of this period, each of the Contracting Parties shall have the option of denouncing the present Convention. It shall, however, remain in force for six months after the date of denunciation.

Alliance between Yugoslavia and Rumania, 7 June 1921

Firmly resolved to maintain the peace obtained by so many sacrifices, and the situation created by the Treaty concluded at Trianon on June 4, 1920, between the Allied and Associated Powers on the one hand, and Hungary on the other, as well as the Treaty concluded at Neuilly on November 27, 1919, between the same Powers and Bulgaria, His Majesty the King of the Serbs, Croats, and Slovenes and His Majesty the King of Rumania have agreed to conclude a defensive Convention . . . and have concluded the following Articles:

Article 1. In case of an unprovoked attack on the part of Hungary or of Bulgaria, or of these two Powers, against one of the two High Contracting Parties, with the object of destroying the situation created by the Treaty of Trianon or the Treaty of Neuilly, the other Party agrees to assist in the defence of the Party attacked, in the man-

ner laid down by Article 2 of this Convention.

Article 2. The Technical Authorities of the Kingdom of the Serbs, Croats, and Slovenes and of the Kingdom of Rumania shall decide by mutual agreement, in a Military Convention to be concluded as soon as possible, upon the provisions necessary for the execution of the present Convention.

Article 3. Neither of the High Contracting Parties shall conclude an alliance with a third Power without preliminary notice to the other.

Article 4. With the object of associating their efforts to maintain peace, the two Governments bind themselves to consult together on questions of foreign policy concerning their relations with Hungary and Bulgaria.

Alliance between Poland and Rumania, 3 March 1921

Being firmly resolved to safeguard a peace which was gained at the price of so many sacrifices, the Chief of the State of the Polish Republic and His Majesty the King of Rumania have agreed to conclude a Convention for a defensive alliance . . . .

Article 1. Poland and Rumania undertake to assist each other in the event of their being the object of an unprovoked attack on their present eastern frontiers.

Accordingly, if either State is the object of an unprovoked attack, the other shall consider itself in a state of war and shall render armed assistance.

Article 2. In order to coordinate their efforts to maintain peace, both Governments undertake to consult together on such questions of foreign policy as concern their relations with their eastern neighbours.

Article 3. A military Convention shall determine the manner in which either country shall render assistance to the other should the occasion arise.

This Convention shall be subject to the same conditions as the present Convention as regards duration and denunciation.

Article 4. If, in spite of their efforts to maintain peace, the two States are compelled to enter on a defensive war under the terms of Article I, each undertakes not to negotiate nor to conclude an armistice or a peace without the participation of the other State.

Article 5. The duration of the present Convention shall be five years from the date of its signature, but either Government shall be at liberty to denounce it after two years, on giving the other State six months' notice.

Article 6. Neither of the High Contracting Parties shall be at liberty to conclude an alliance with a third Power without having previously obtained the assent of the other party.

Alliances with a view to the maintenance of treaties already signed jointly by both Poland and Rumania are excepted from this provision.

Such alliances must, however, be notified.

The Polish Government hereby declares that it is acquainted with the agreements entered into by Rumania with other States with a view to upholding the Treaties of Trianon and Neuilly, which agreements may be transformed into treaties of alliance.

The Rumanian Government hereby declares that it is acquainted with the agreements entered into by Poland with the French Republic.

Treaty of Guarantee between Poland and Rumania, 26 March 1926

The President of the Polish Republic and His Majesty the King of Rumania, noting with satisfaction the consolidation of the guarantees for the general peace of Europe, and anxious to satisfy the desire for peace by which the peoples are animated, desirous of seeing their country spared from war, and animated also with the sincere desire of giving to their peoples supplementary guarantees within the framework of the Covenant of the League of Nations and of the treaties of which they are signatories, have determined to conclude a Treaty with this object . . . .

Article 1. Poland and Rumania undertake each to respect and preserve against external aggression the territorial integrity and existing political independence of the other.

Article 2. In the event of Poland or Rumania, contrary to the undertakings imposed by Articles 12, 13, and 15 of the Covenant of the League of Nations, being attacked without provocation, Poland and reciprocally Rumania, acting in application of Article 16 of the Covenant of the League of Nations, undertake to lend each other immediately aid and assistance.

In the event of the Council of the League of Nations, when dealing with a question brought before it in accordance with the provisions of the Covenant of the League of Nations, being unable to secure the acceptance of its report by all its Members other than the representatives of the parties to the dispute, and in the event of Poland or Rumania being attacked without provocation, Poland or reciprocally Rumania, acting in application of Article 15, paragraph 7, of the Covenant of the League of Nations, will immediately lend aid and assistance to the other country.

Should a dispute of the kind provided for in Article 17 of the Covenant of the League of Nations arise, and Poland or Rumania be attacked without provocation, Poland and reciprocally Rumania undertake to lend each other immediately aid and assistance.

The details of application of the above provisions shall be settled by technical agreements.

Article 3. If, in spite of their efforts to maintain peace, the two States are compelled to enter on a defensive war under the terms of Articles 1 and 2, each undertakes not to negotiate or conclude an armistice or a peace without the participation of the other State.

Article 4. In order to coordinate their efforts to maintain peace, both Governments undertake to consult together on such questions of foreign policy as concern both Contracting Parties.

Article 5. Neither of the High Contracting Parties shall be at liberty to conclude an alliance with a third Power without having previously consulted the other party.

Alliances with a view to the maintenance of treaties already signed jointly by both Poland and Rumania are excepted from this provision.

Such alliances must, however, be notified.

Article 6. The High Contracting Parties undertake to submit all disputes which may arise between them or which it may not have been possible to settle by the ordinary methods of diplomacy, to conciliation or arbitration. The details of this procedure of pacific settlement shall be laid down in a special convention to be concluded as soon as possible.

Article 7. The present Treaty shall remain in force for five years from the date of its signature, but either of the two Governments shall be entitled to denounce it after two years, upon giving six months' notice.

[*Article 8.* Ratification.]

Protocol

The Convention of Defensive Alliance which expires on April 3, 1926, being recognized to have had results beneficial to the cause of peace, the undersigned plenipotentiaries, holding full powers, found in good and due form, from the President of the Polish Republic and from His Majesty the King of Rumania, respectively, have agreed to conclude a Treaty of Guarantee for a further period of five years . . . .

[The Treaty of Guarantee was concluded again on 15 January 1931.]

Supplementary Agreement to the Treaties of Friendship and Alliance between the States of the Little Entente, 27 June 1930

[Czechoslovakia, Rumania and Yugoslavia . . .] Being desirous of strengthening still further the ties of friendship and alliance which exist between the States of the Little Entente,

Wishing to supplement the organization of the political cooperation and of the defence of the common interests of their three States by means of a fixed procedure,

Have resolved to confirm the present practice and the present procedure of close cooperation between their States by defining them with greater precision . . . .

Article 1. The Ministers for Foreign Affairs of the Little Entente shall meet whenever circumstances make it necessary. They shall in any case meet at least once a year. Compulsory ordinary meetings shall be held, in turn, in each of the three States at a place selected beforehand. There shall also be an optional ordinary meeting at Geneva during the Assemblies of the League of Nations.

Article II. The compulsory meeting shall be presided over by the Minister for Foreign Affairs of the State in which it is held. That Minister is responsible for fixing the date and selecting the place of the meeting. He draws up its agenda and is responsible for the preparatory work connected with the decisions to be taken. Until the regular meeting of the following year he is considered as President for the time being.

Article III. In all the questions which are discussed and in all the measures which are taken in regard to the relations of the States of the Little Entente between themselves, the principle of the absolute equality of the three States shall be rigorously respected. That principle shall also be respected more particularly in the relations of these States with other States or with a group of States, or with the League of Nations.

Article IV. According to the necessities of the situation, the three Ministers for Foreign Affairs may decide, by common agreement, that in regard to any particular question the representation or the defence of the point of view of the States of the Little Entente shall be entrusted to a single delegate or to the delegation of a single State.

Article V. An extraordinary meeting may be convened by the President for the time being when the international situation or an international event requires it.

Article VI. The present Agreement shall enter into force immediately. It shall be ratified and the exchange of ratifications shall take place at Prague as soon as possible . . . .

Pact of Organization of the Little Entente, 16 February 1933

. . . Desirous of maintaining and organizing peace;

Firmly determined to strengthen economic relations with all States without distinction and with the Central European States in particular,

Anxious that peace shall be safeguarded in all circumstances, that progress in the direction of the real stabilization of conditions in Central Europe shall be assured and that the common interests of their three countries shall be respected,

Determined, with this object, to give an organic and stable basis to the relations of friendship and alliance existing between the three States of the Little Entente, and,

Convinced of the necessity of bringing about such stability on the one hand by the complete unification of their general policy and on the other by the creation of a directing organ of this common policy, namely, the group of the three States of the Little Entente, thus forming a higher international unit, open to other States under conditions to be agreed upon in each particular case . . .

Article 1. A Permanent Council of the States of the Little Entente, composed of the Ministers for Foreign Affairs of the three respective countries or of the special delegates appointed for the purpose, shall be constituted as the directing organ of the common policy of the group of the three States. Decisions of the Permanent Council shall be unanimous.

Article 2. The Permanent Council, apart from its normal intercourse through the diplomatic channel, shall be required to meet at least three times a year. One obligatory annual meeting shall be held in the three States in turn, and another shall be held at Geneva during the Assembly of the League of Nations.

Article 3. The President of the Permanent Council shall be the Minister for Foreign Affairs of the State in which the obligatory annual meeting is held. He shall take the initiative in fixing the date and the place of meeting, shall arrange its agenda and shall draw up the questions to be decided. He shall continue to be President of the Permanent Council until the first obligatory meeting of the following year.

Article 4. In all questions that may be discussed, as in all decisions that may be reached, whether in regard to the relations of the States of the Little Entente among themselves or in regard to their relations with other States, the principle of the absolute equality of the three States of the Little Entente shall be rigorously respected.

Article 5. According to the exigencies of the situation, the Permanent Council may decide that in any given question the representation or the defence of the point of view of the States of the Little Entente shall be entrusted to a single delegate or to the delegation of a single State.

Article 6. Every political treaty of any one State of the Little Entente, every unilateral act changing the existing political situation of one of the States of the Little Entente in relation to an outside State, and every economic agreement involving important political consequences shall henceforth require the unanimous consent of the Council of the Little Entente.

The existing political treaties of each State of the Little Entente with outside States shall be progressively unified as far as possible.

Article 7. An Economic Council of the States of the Little Entente shall be constituted for the progressive coordination of the economic interests of the three States, whether among themselves or in their relations with other States. It shall be composed of specialists and experts in economic, commercial and financial matters and shall act as an auxiliary advisory organ of the Permanent Council in regard to its general policy.

Article 8. The Permanent Council shall be empowered to establish other stable or temporary organs, commissions or committees for the purpose of studying and preparing the solution of special questions or groups of questions for the Permanent Council.

Article 9. A Secretariat of the Permanent Council shall be created. Its headquarters shall be established in each case for one year in the capital of the President in office of the Permanent Council. A section of the Secretariat shall function permanently at the seat of the League of Nations at Geneva.

Article 10. The common policy of the Permanent Council shall be inspired by the general principles embodied in all the great international instruments relating to post-war policy, such as the Covenant of the League of Nations, the Pact of Paris, the General Act of Arbitration, any Conventions concluded in regard to disarmament, and the Locarno Pacts. Furthermore, nothing in the present Pact shall be construed as contrary to the principles or provisions of the Covenant of the League of Nations.

Article 11. The Conventions of Alliance between Roumania and Czechoslovakia of April 23, 1921, between Roumania and Yugoslavia of June 7, 1921, and between Czechoslovakia and Yugoslavia of August 31, 1922, which were extended on May 21, 1929, and are supplemented by the provisions of the present Pact, as well as the Act of Conciliation, Arbitration and Judicial Settlement signed by the three States of the Little Entente at Belgrade on May 21, 1929, are hereby renewed for an indefinite period.

Article 12. The present Pact shall be ratified and the exchange of ratifications shall take place at Prague not later than the next obligatory meeting . . . .

Pact of Balkan Entente between Turkey, Greece, Roumania and Yugoslavia, 9 February 1934

Article 1. Greece, Roumania, Turkey and Yugoslavia mutually guarantee the security of each and all of their Balkan frontiers.

Article 2. The High Contracting Parties

undertake to concert together in regard to the measures to be taken in contingencies liable to affect their interests as defined by the present Agreement. They undertake not to embark upon any political action in relation to any other Balkan country not a signatory of the present Agreement without previous mutual consultation, nor to incur any political obligation to any other Balkan country without the consent of the other Contracting Parties.

Article 3. The present Agreement shall come into force on the date of its signature by the Contracting Parties . . .

Protocol: Annex of the Pact, 9 February 1934

In proceeding to sign the Pact of Balkan Entente, the four Ministers for Foreign Affairs of Greece, Roumania, Yugoslavia, and Turkey have seen fit to define as follows the nature of the undertakings assumed by their respective countries, and to stipulate explicitly that the said definitions form an integral part of the Pact.

1. Any country committing one of the acts of aggression to which Article 2 of the London Conventions of July 3rd and 4th, 1933, relates shall be treated as an aggressor.

2. The Pact of Balkan Entente is not directed against any Power. Its object is to guarantee the security of the several Balkan frontiers against any aggression on the part of any Balkan State.

3. Nevertheless, if one of the High Contracting Parties is the victim of aggression on the part of any other non-Balkan Power, and a Balkan State associates itself with such aggression, whether at the time or subsequently, the Pact of Balkan Entente shall be applicable in its entirety in relation to such Balkan State.

4. The High Contracting Parties undertake to conclude appropriate Conventions for the furtherance of the objects pursued by the Pact of Balkan Entente. The negotiation of such Conventions shall begin within six months.

5. As the Pact of Balkan Entente does not conflict with previous undertakings, all previous undertakings and all Conventions based on previous treaties shall be applicable in their entirety, the said undertakings and the said treaties having all been published.

6. The words 'Firmly resolved to ensure the observance of the contractual obligations already in existence', in the Preamble to the Pact, shall cover the observance by the High Contracting Parties of existing treaties between Balkan States, to which one or more of the High Contracting Parties is a signatory party.

7. The Pact of Balkan Entente is a defensive instrument; accordingly, the obligations on the High Contracting Parties which arise out of the said Pact shall cease to exist in relation to a High Contracting Party becoming an aggressor against any other country within the meaning of Article 2 of the London Conventions.

8. The maintenance of the territorial situation in the Balkans as at present established is binding definitively on the High Contracting Parties. The duration of the obligations under the Pact shall be fixed by the High Contracting Parties in the course of the two years following the signature of the Pact, or afterwards. During the two years in question the Pact cannot be denounced. The duration of the Pact shall be fixed at not less than five years, and may be longer. If, two years after the signature of the same, no duration has been fixed, the Pact of Balkan Entente shall *ipso facto* remain in force for five years from the expiry of the two years after the signature thereof. On the expiry of the said five years, or of the period on which the High Contracting Parties have agreed for its duration, the Pact of Balkan Entente shall be renewed automatically by tacit agreement for the period for which it was previously in force, failing denunciation by any one of the High Contracting Parties one year before the date of its expiry; provided always that no denunciation or notice of denunciation shall be admissible, whether in the first period of the Pact's validity (namely, seven or more than seven years) or in any subsequent period fixed automatically by tacit agreement, before the year preceding the date on which the Pact expires.

9. The High Contracting Parties shall inform each other as soon as the Pact of Balkan Entente is ratified in accordance with their respective laws.

Balkan Entente between Turkey, Greece, Rumania and Yugoslavia, 9 February 1934, and Bulgaria, 31 July 1938

Whereas Bulgaria is an adherent of the policy of consolidation of peace in the Balkans, and is desirous of maintaining relations of good neighbourhood and full and frank collaboration with the Balkan States, and

Whereas the States of the Balkan Entente are animated by the same pacific spirit in relation to Bulgaria and the same desire of cooperation,

Now therefore the undersigned:

His Excellency Monsieur Georges KIOS-SÉIVANOV, President of the Council of Ministers, Bulgarian Minister for Foreign Affairs and Public Worship, of the one part, and

His Excellency Monsieur Jean METAXAS, President of the Council of Ministers, Greek Minister for Foreign Affairs, acting in his capacity as President in Office of the Permanent Council of the Balkan Entente, in the name of all the Members of the Balkan Entente, of the other part,

Hereby declare, on behalf of the States which they represent, that the said States undertake to abstain in their relations with one another from any resort to force, in accordance with the agreements to which they have severally subscribed in respect of non-aggression, and are agreed to waive the application in so far as they are concerned of the provisions contained in Part IV (Military, Naval and Air clauses) of the Treaty of Neuilly, as also of the provisions contained in the Convention respecting the Thracian Frontier, signed at Lausanne, July 24th, 1923.

VI · The Soviet Union and her neighbours, 1919–37

The years from 1918 to 1921 saw an astonishing transformation of Bolshevik Russia's fortunes. In the spring of 1918 the control of the Bolsheviks over Russia's territory had shrunk to only a shadow of the former empire. Russia was occupied on the one hand by the Germans who could still advance at will, and also by Allied 'intervention'. But even after Germany's collapse in November 1918, Soviet Russia's troubles were far from over. Allied 'intervention' continued; Soviet Russia simultaneously fought and survived both the civil war and the Polish War.

The first task facing the Soviet leaders was to achieve settled frontiers and to secure Soviet power within them. Taking advantage of Russia's weakness, the Poles early in 1919 had occupied as much territory eastwards as they could, whilst from Siberia, Admiral Kolchak's anti-Bolshevik forces were pushing into European Russia. Kolchak was defeated but the Poles could not be simultaneously resisted. That autumn of 1919 Yudenich advanced from his Baltic base and threatened Moscow. But early in 1920 the Red Army defeated the White Russian forces and Wrangel's last stand in the Crimea during 1920–21 proved but an epilogue to the civil war. Allied intervention, never effective, ceased for all practical purposes. During the spring of 1920 the Poles, led by Marshal Joseph Pilsudski, posed the greatest threat to Russia. In April 1920 Pilsudski negotiated an agreement with the hard pressed anti-Bolshevik régime of what remained of the independent State of the Ukraine. The Poles advanced and reached Kiev in May 1920. The Russian counter-attack came within reach of Warsaw in August, but Pilsudski was able to counter-attack in turn and to force the Red Army to withdraw. In October 1920 an armistice brought the war to an end, and the *Treaty of Riga, 18 March 1921* (p. 176), settled the frontiers of the two states until 1939. That same year, 1920, Soviet Russia recognized the independence of the three Baltic Republics, Estonia, Latvia and Lithuania, and also of Finland. Russia concluded with Finland the *Treaty of Dorpat, 14 October 1920* (p. 174). Not until the spring of 1921 did Soviet Russia win a measure of international recognition with the signature of the *Anglo–Soviet Trade Agreement, 16 March 1921* (p. 178). Soviet foreign policy was designed to achieve two complementary objectives: to strengthen and broaden the Soviet base and to weaken the 'capitalist' opposition.

Treaty of Peace between Latvia and Soviet Russia, 11 August 1920

[Similar treaties were concluded with the other Baltic States.]

Russia on the one hand, and Latvia on the other, being strongly desirous of bringing to an end the present state of war between them, and of bringing about a final settlement of all the questions arising from the former subjection of Latvia to Russia, have decided to commence negotiations for peace and to conclude as soon as possible a lasting, honourable and just peace . . . and have agreed on the following terms:

Article I. The state of war between the Contracting Parties shall cease from the date of the coming into force of the present Treaty.

Article II. By virtue of the principle proclaimed by the Federal Socialist Republic of the Russian Soviets, which establishes the right of self-determination for all nations, even to the point of total separation from the States with which they have been incorporated, and in view of the desire expressed by the Latvian people to possess an independent national existence, Russia unreservedly recognizes the independence and sovereignty of the Latvian State and voluntarily and irrevocably renounces all sovereign rights over the Latvian people and territory which formerly belonged to Russia under the then existing constitutional law as well as under international treaties, which, in the sense here indicated, shall in future cease to be valid. The previous status of subjection of Latvia to Russia shall not entail any obligation towards Russia on the part of the Latvian people or territory.

Article III. The State frontier between Russia and Latvia shall be fixed as follows: . . .

Article IV. The two Contracting Parties undertake:

1. To forbid any army to remain on either territory except their own army or that of friendly States with which one of the Contracting Parties has concluded a military convention, but which are not in a *de facto* state of war with either Contracting Party; and also to forbid, within the limits of their respective territory, the mobilization and recruiting of any personnel intended for the armies of States, organizations or groups, for purposes of armed conflict against the other Contracting Party . . . .

2. Not to permit the formation or residence in their territory of organizations or groups of any kind claiming to represent the Government of all or part of the territory of the other Contracting Party; or of representatives or officials of organizations or groups having as their object the overthrow of the Government of the other Contracting Party.

3. To forbid Governments in a *de facto* state of war with the other party, and organizations and groups having as their object military action against the other Contracting Party, to transport through

their ports or their territory anything which might be used for military purposes against the other Contracting Party, in particular, military forces belonging to these States, organizations or groups; material of war; technical military stores belonging to artillery, supply services, engineers or air services.

4. To forbid, except in cases provided for by international law, passage through or navigation in their territorial waters of all warships, gunboats, torpedo boats, etc., belonging either to organizations and groups whose object is military action against the other Contracting Party, or to Governments which are in state of war with the other Contracting Party and which aim at military action against the other Contracting Party. This provision shall come into force as soon as such intentions are known to the Contracting Party to whom the said territorial waters and ports belong.

Article V. The two parties mutually undertake not to claim the expenses of the war from each other. By this is understood the expenses incurred by the State for the conduct of the war, and likewise any compensations for losses occasioned by the war, that is, losses occasioned to themselves or to their subjects by military operations, including all kinds of requisitions made by one of the Contracting Parties in the territory of the other.

Article VI. In view of the fact that it is necessary to apportion in an equitable manner among the States of the world the obligation to make good the damages caused by the World War of 1914–17 to States that

have been ruined, or to portions of States on whose territory military operations have taken place, the two Contracting Parties undertake to do all in their power to secure an agreement among all States in order to establish an international fund, which would be used to cover the sums intended for the reparation of damages due to the war.

Independently of the creation of this international fund, the Contracting Parties consider it necessary that Russia and all new States constituting independent Republics in what was formerly Russian territory should render each other, as far as possible, mutual support to make good from their own resources the damage caused by the World War, and undertake to do all in their power to secure this agreement between the above-mentioned Republics.

Article VII. Prisoners of war of both parties shall be repatriated as soon as possible. The method of exchange of prisoners is laid down in the Annex to this present Article. NOTE: All captives who are not serving voluntarily in the army of the Government which has made them prisoners shall be considered as prisoners of war.

ANNEX TO ARTICLE VII

I. Prisoners of the two Contracting Parties shall be repatriated unless, with the consent of the Government on whose territory they are, they express the desire to remain in the country in which they are or to proceed to any other country . . . .

Treaty of Peace between Finland and Soviet Russia (Treaty of Dorpat), 14 October 1920

Whereas Finland declared its independence in 1917, and Russia has recognized the independence and the sovereignty of

Finland within the frontiers of the Grand Duchy of Finland,

The Government of the Republic of Finland, and the Government of the Federal Socialist Republic of Soviet Russia,

Actuated by a desire to put an end to the war which has arisen between their States, to establish mutual and lasting peace relations and to confirm the situation which springs from the ancient political union of Finland and Russia,

Have resolved to conclude a Treaty with this object in view, and have agreed on the following provisions:

Article I. From the date upon which this Treaty shall come into force, a state of war shall cease to exist between the Contracting Powers, and the two Powers shall mutually undertake to maintain, for the future, an attitude of peace and goodwill towards one another.

Article II. The frontier between the States of Russia and of Finland shall be as follows . . .

. . .

Article VI. 1. Finland guarantees that she will not maintain, in the waters contiguous to her seaboard in the Arctic Ocean, warships or other armed vessels, other than armed vessels of less than 100 tons displacement, which Finland may keep in these waters in any number, and of a maximum number of fifteen warships and other armed vessels, each with a maximum displacement of 400 tons.

Finland also guarantees that she will not maintain, in the above-mentioned waters, submarines or armed airplanes.

2. Finland also guarantees that she will not establish on the coast in question naval ports, bases or repairing stations of greater size than are necessary for the vessels mentioned in the preceding paragraph and for their armament.

. . .

Article VIII. 1. The right of free transit to and from Norway through the territory of Pechenga shall be guaranteed to the State of Russia and to its nationals . . . .

. . .

Article XII. The two Contracting Powers shall on principle support the neutralization of the Gulf of Finland and of the whole Baltic Sea, and shall undertake to cooperate in the realization of this object.

Article XIII. Finland shall militarily neutralize the following of her islands in the Gulf of Finland: Sommaro (Someri), Nervo (Narvi), Seitskar (Seiskari), Peninsaari, Lavansaari, Stora Tyterskar (Suuri Tytarsaari), Lilla Tyterskar (pieni Tytarsaari) and Rodskar . . . .

Article XIV. As soon as this Treaty comes into force, Finland shall take measures for the military neutralization of Hogland under an international guarantee . . . .

. . .

Article XVI. . . . Russia shall, however, have the right to send Russian war vessels into the navigable waterways of the interior by the canals along the southern bank of Ladoga and even, should the navigation of these canals be impeded, by the southern part of Ladoga.

2. Should the Gulf of Finland and the Baltic Sea be neutralized, the Contracting Powers mutually undertake to neutralize Ladoga also.

. . .

Article XXIV. The Contracting Powers will exact no indemnity whatsoever from one another for war expenses.

Finland will take no share in the expenses incurred by Russia in the World War of 1914–1918.

Article XXV. Neither of the Contracting Powers is responsible for the public debts and other obligations of the other Power.

Article XXVI. The debts and other obligations of the Russian State and of Russian governmental institutions towards the State of Finland and the Bank of Finland, and, similarly, the debts and obligations of the State of Finland and Finnish governmental institutions towards the Russian State and its governmental institutions, shall be regarded as mutually liquidated . . . .

Treaty of Peace between Poland and Soviet Russia (Treaty of Riga), 18 March 1921

Poland of the one hand and Russia and the Ukraine of the other, being desirous of putting an end to the war and of concluding a final, lasting and honourable peace based on a mutual understanding and in accordance with the peace preliminaries signed at Riga on October 12, 1920, have decided to enter into negotiations and have appointed for this purpose as plenipotentiaries . . . and have agreed to the following provisions:

Article I. The two Contracting Parties declare that a state of war has ceased to exist between them.

Article II. The two Contracting Parties, in accordance with the principle of national self-determination, recognize the independence of the Ukraine and of White Ruthenia and agree and decide that the eastern frontier of Poland, that is to say, the frontier between Poland on the one hand, and Russia, White Ruthenia and the Ukraine on the other, shall be as follows . . . [details].

Article III. Russia and the Ukraine abandon all rights and claims to the territories situated to the west of the frontier laid down by Article II of the present Treaty. Poland, on the other hand, abandons in favour of the Ukraine and of White Ruthenia all rights and claims to the territory situated to the east of this frontier. The two Contracting Parties agree that, in so far as the territory situated to the west of the frontier fixed in Article II of the present Treaty includes districts which form the subject of a dispute between Poland and Lithuania, the question of the attribution of these districts to one of those two States is a matter which exclusively concerns Poland and Lithuania.

Article IV. Poland shall not, in view of the fact that a part of the territories of the Polish Republic formerly belonged to the Russian Empire, be held to have incurred any debt or obligation towards Russia, except as provided in the present Treaty.

Similarly, no debt or obligation shall be regarded as incurred by Poland towards White Ruthenia or the Ukraine and vice versa except as provided in the present Treaty, owing to the fact that these countries formerly belonged to the Russian Empire.

Article V. Each of the Contracting Parties mutually undertakes to respect in every way the political sovereignty of the other party, to abstain from interference in its internal affairs, and particularly to refrain from all agitation, propaganda or interference of any kind, and not to encourage any such movement.

Each of the Contracting Parties undertakes not to create or protect organizations which are formed with the object of encouraging armed conflict against the other Contracting Party or of undermining its territorial integrity, or of subverting by force its political or social institutions, nor yet such organizations as claim to be the Government of the other party or of a part of the territories of the other party. The Contracting Parties therefore, undertake to prevent such organizations, their official representatives and other persons connected therewith, from establishing themselves on their territory, and to prohibit military recruiting and the entry into their territory and transport across it of armed forces, arms, munitions and war material of any kind destined for such organizations.

Article VI. 1. All persons above the age of 18 who, at the date of the ratification of the present Treaty are within the territory of Poland and on August 1 1914 were nationals of the Russian Empire and are, or have the right to be, included in the registers of the permanent population of the former Kingdom of Poland, or have been included in the registers of an urban or rural commune, or of one of the class organizations in the territories of the former Russian Empire which formed part of Poland, shall have the right of opting for Russian or Ukrainian nationality. A similar declaration by nationals of the former Russian Empire of all other categories who are within Polish territory at the date of the ratification of the present Treaty shall not be necessary.

2. Nationals of the former Russian Empire above the age of 18 who at the date of the ratification of the present Treaty are within the territory of Russia and of the Ukraine and are, or have the right to be, included in the register of the permanent population of the former Kingdom of Poland, or have been included in the registers of an urban or rural commune, or of one of the class organizations in the territories of the former Russian Empire which formed part of Poland, shall be considered as Polish citizens if they express such a desire in accordance with the system of opting laid down in this Article. Persons above the age of 18 who are within the territory of Russia and of the Ukraine shall also be considered as Polish citizens if they express such a desire, in accordance with the system of opting laid down in this Article, and if they provide proofs that they are descendants of those who took part in the Polish struggle for independence between 1830 and 1865, or that they are descendants of persons who have for at least three generations been continuously established in the territory of the former Polish Republic, or if they show that they have by their actions, by the habitual use of the Polish language and by their method of educating their children, given effective proof of their attachment to Polish nationality . . . .

Article VII. I. Russia and the Ukraine undertake that persons of Polish nationality in Russia, the Ukraine and White Ruthenia shall, in conformity with the principles of the equality of peoples, enjoy full guarantees of free intellectual development, the use of their national language and the exercise of their religion. Poland undertakes to recognize the same rights in the case of persons of Russian, Ukrainian and White Ruthenian nationality in Poland . . . .

. . .

3. The churches and religious associations in Russia, the Ukraine and White Ruthenia, of which Polish nationals are members, shall, so far as is in conformity with the domestic legislation of these countries, have the right of independent self-administration in domestic matters . . . .

Article VIII. The two Contracting Parties mutually abandon all claims to the repayment of war expenses, that is to say all the expenses incurred by the State during the war, and of the indemnities for damages caused by the war, that is to say, for damages caused to them or to their nationals in the theatre of war as a result of the war or of military measures taken during the Polish-Russian-Ukrainian War.

Soviet treaties, 1921–27

Soviet treaties fall into distinctive groups: treaties of peace with Russia's neighbours, Poland, the Baltic Republics and Finland, all formerly part of the Russian Empire and now recognized as independent states with mutually agreed and delimited frontiers.

The need for recognition and trade led Soviet Russia to make a number of treaties and agreements with the west. The first breakthrough came with the signature of the *Anglo–Soviet Trade Agreement, 16 March 1921* (p. 178), whereby Soviet Russia secured *de facto* recognition from the world's most important 'capitalist state'. Soviet Russia gradually gained international recognition throughout the world including the United States (1933). While the Russian Soviet government on the one hand signed treaties in which conditions were to be created for normalizing relations between the Soviet Union and its neighbours, the Russian

Communist Party on the other sought to organize world revolution with the help of the Comintern.

The first congress of the Third International held in Moscow in March 1919 served Lenin's purpose in that it created an organization around which could be grouped a worldwide international socialist movement under the control of the Russian Communist Party. Its aim was to promote revolution abroad. The second congress met in July 1920, and during its course Lenin laid down the conditions which had to be met before a communist group could be admitted to the Third International. By the time of the meeting of the third congress (June–July 1921) it had become evident that world revolution was no longer imminent, but the efforts to promote it were not abandoned: revolution was merely delayed.

Alliances and treaties with anti-colonial and nationalist movements were concluded by *Soviet Russia and Iran on 26 February 1921* which, as one Soviet historian recently wrote, 'struck a powerful blow at imperialism and its colonial system'. Two days later came the signature of a *Soviet Treaty with Afghanistan, 28 February 1921*, whereby the Soviets intended to weaken the British position in India; and a month later the remarkable Soviet *coup* was completed with the signature of the *Soviet–Turkish Treaty of Friendship, 16 March 1921* (p. 115). These treaties were confirmed by the signatures of the *Soviet–Turkish Treaty of Non-Aggression and Neutrality, 17 December 1925*, and similar treaties with *Afghanistan, 31 August 1926*, and *Iran, 1 October 1927*.

Trade Agreement between Britain and the Soviet Union, London, 16 March 1921

Whereas it is desirable in the interests both of Russia and of the United Kingdom that peaceful trade and commerce should be resumed forthwith between these countries, and whereas for this purpose it is necessary pending the conclusion of a formal general Peace Treaty between the Governments of these countries by which their economic and political relations shall be regulated in the future that a preliminary Agreement should be arrived at between the Government of the United Kingdom and the Government of the Russian Socialist Federal Soviet Republic, hereinafter referred to as the Russian Soviet Government.

The aforesaid parties have accordingly entered into the present Agreement for the resumption of trade and commerce between the countries.

The present Agreement is subject to the fulfilment of the following conditions, namely:

(a) That each party refrains from hostile action or undertakings against the other and from conducting outside of its own borders any official propaganda direct or indirect against the institutions of the British Empire or the Russian Soviet Republic respectively, and more particularly that the Russian Soviet Government refrains from any attempt by military or diplomatic or any other form of action or propaganda to encourage any of the peoples of Asia in any form of hostile action against British interests or the British Empire, especially in India and in the Independent State of Afghanistan. The British Government gives a similar particular undertaking to the Russian Soviet Government in respect of the countries which formed part of the former Russian Empire and which have now become independent.

(b) That all British subjects in Russia are immediately permitted to return home, and that all Russian citizens in Great Britain or other parts of the British Empire who desire to return to Russia are similarly released.

It is understood that the term 'conducting any official propaganda' includes the giving by either party of assistance or encouragement to any propaganda conducted outside its own borders.

The parties undertake to give forthwith all necessary instructions to their agents and to all persons under their authority to conform to the stipulations undertaken above.

Article I. Both parties agree not to impose or maintain any form of blockade against each other and to remove forthwith all obstacles hitherto placed in the way of the resumption of trade between the United Kingdom and Russia in any commodities which may be legally exported from or imported into their respective territories to or from any other foreign country, and do not exercise any discrimination against such trade, as compared with that carried on with any other foreign country or to place any impediments in the way of banking, credit and financial operations for the purpose of such trade, but subject always to legislation generally applicable in the respective countries. It is understood that nothing in this Article shall prevent either party from regulating the trade in arms and ammunition under general provisions of law which are applicable to the import of arms and ammunition from, or their export to foreign countries . . . .

. . .

Article IV. Each party may nominate such number of its nationals as may be agreed from time to time as being reasonably necessary to enable proper effect to be given to this Agreement, having regard to the conditions under which trade is carried on in its territories, and the other party shall permit such persons to enter its territories, and to sojourn and carry on trade there, provided that either party may restrict the admittance of any such persons into any specified areas, and may refuse admittance to or sojourn in its territories to any individual who is *persona non grata* to itself, or who does not comply with this Agreement or with the conditions precedent thereto . . . .

. . .

Article XIII. The present Agreement shall come into force immediately and both parties shall at once take all necessary measures to give effect to it. It shall continue in force unless and until replaced by the Treaty contemplated in the preamble so long as the conditions laid down both in the Articles of the Agreement and in the preamble are observed by both sides. Provided that at any time after the expiration of twelve months from the date on which the Agreement comes into force either party may give notice to terminate the provisions of the preceding Articles, and on the expiration of six months from the date of such notice those Articles shall terminate accordingly . . . .

Provided also that in the event of the infringement by either party at any time of any of the provisions of this Agreement or of the conditions referred to in the preamble, the other party shall immediately be free from the obligations of the Agreement. Nevertheless it is agreed that before taking any action inconsistent with the Agreement the aggrieved party shall give the other party a reasonable opportunity of furnishing an explanation or remedying the default . . . .

Declaration of Recognition of Claims

At the moment of signature of the preceding Trade Agreement both parties declare that all claims of either party or of its nationals against the other party in respect of property or rights or in respect of obligations incurred by the existing or former Governments of either country shall be equitably dealt with in the formal general Peace Treaty referred to in the preamble.

In the meantime and without prejudice to the generality of the above stipulation the Russian Soviet Government declares that it recognizes in principle that it is liable to pay compensation to private persons who have supplied goods or services to Russia for which they have not been paid. The detailed mode of discharging this liability shall be regulated by the Treaty referred to in the preamble.

The British Government hereby makes a corresponding declaration.

It is clearly understood that the above declarations in no way imply that the claims referred to therein will have preferential treatment in the aforesaid Treaty as compared with any other classes of claims which are to be dealt with in that Treaty.

Relations between the Soviet Union and Germany

Germany and Russia, once in the relationship of victor and vanquished when Brest-Litovsk was signed, had both become defeated powers after November 1918. The war had gravely weakened the two countries. Nevertheless Russia and Germany remained potentially great powers. Thus despite their entirely different political complexions there was a community of interest which brought Russia and Germany together in the 1920s. Their collaboration involved some limited secret military cooperation and limited economic assistance for Russia; joint enmity towards Poland within its post-war frontiers was the basis. In 1922 the *Genoa Conference* of major European powers met to reconstruct the economy of Europe and to revive world trade. It proved abortive. The most important result was that two of the participants, Soviet Russia and Germany, unable to persuade the western powers to make sufficient concessions, signed a treaty with each other at the neighbouring resort of Rapallo. The significance of the *Treaty of Rapallo, 16 April 1922* (p. 181) lay in the fact that both Soviet Russia and Germany broke out of diplomatic isolation. Their cooperation was based not on an identity of views or genuine friendship but on self-interest. The Locarno reconciliation with the west and Germany's entry into the League of Nations in 1926 was carefully dovetailed by Stresemann to harmonize with Germany's undertakings to Soviet Russia. Thus Germany would not be automatically obliged to join in any action against Russia under Article 16, because it need only do so to an extent that was compatible with its military situation and geographical location, a phrase that left Germany the decision. Weimar Germany reaffirmed its relationship with Soviet Russia by the *Treaty of Berlin, 24 April 1926* (p. 182); but the relative position of the two countries had changed. Locarno meant that Germany was no longer exclusively reliant on the Soviet Union for support (p. 141). The Soviet Union attempted to extend the principle of neutrality and non-aggression treaties to the Baltic States. All these efforts failed except for a *treaty with Lithuania, 28 September*

1926. On *25 January 1929, Germany and the Soviet Union concluded a Conciliation Convention* (pp. 185–86).

The consequences of the world depression of 1929 ended the collaboration between the Weimar Republic and Soviet Russia. From 1930 to 1933 the German communists combined with the nazis to undermine the Weimar Republic. In this they succeeded.

A NOTE ON SECRET GERMAN SOVIET–MILITARY COOPERATION

Several secret military agreements were concluded between German industrialists, the German army (with the knowledge of some ministers of the Weimar Government) and the Soviet Union. The first of these was a provisional agreement, 15 March 1922, which provided the finance for Junkers to build an aeroplane factory in the Soviet Union. German troops were sent for training to the Soviet Union in 1922; munitions and poison gas were manufactured in Russia. The agreements were not formal treaties, but nevertheless were concrete arrangements to further what were then regarded by the German military as the mutual and parallel interests of Germany and the Soviet Union; they both looked on post-Versailles Poland as the enemy. By 1926 relatively little was actually achieved in providing Germany with armaments. The most important advantage for Germany was the provision of training facilities for German pilots. After 1929 a tank school trained some German troops in the Soviet Union; there were some joint German–Soviet poison gas experiments, and a number of German officers participated in Soviet manœuvres. These agreements broke the military terms of the Versailles treaty. They were, however, much more limited than the rumoured 'secret treaties' of extensive military cooperation, which did not exist.

Treaty between Germany and Soviet Russia (Treaty of Rapallo)
regarding the solution of general problems, 16 April 1922

The German Government, represented by Reichsminister Dr Walther Rathenau, and the Government of R.S.F.S.R., represented by People's Commissar Chicherin, have agreed upon the following provisions:

Article I. The two Governments agree that all questions resulting from the state of war between Germany and Russia shall be settled in the following manner:

(a) Both Governments mutually renounce repayment for their war expenses and for damages arising out of the war, that is to say, damages caused to them and their nationals in the zone of the war operations by military measures, including all requisitions effected in a hostile country. They renounce in the same way repayment for civil damages inflicted on civilians, that is to say, damages caused to the nationals of the two countries by exceptional war legislation or by violent measures taken by any authority of the State of either side.

(b) All legal relations concerning questions of public or private law resulting from the state of war, including the question of the treatment of merchant ships which fell into the hands of the one side or the other during the war, shall be settled on the basis of reciprocity.

(c) Germany and Russia mutually renounce repayment of expenses incurred for prisoners of war. The German Government also renounces repayment of expenses for soldiers of the Red Army interned in Germany. The Russian Government, for its part, renounces repayment of the sums Germany has derived from the sale of Russian army material brought into Germany by these interned troops.

Article II. Germany renounces all claims resulting from the enforcement of the laws and measures of the Soviet Republic as it has affected German nationals or their private rights or the rights of the German State itself, as well as claims resulting from measures taken by the Soviet Republic or its authorities in any other way against subjects of the German State or their private rights, provided that the Soviet Republic shall not satisfy similar claims by any third State.

Article III. Consular and diplomatic relations between Germany and the Federal Soviet Republic shall be resumed immediately. The admission of consuls to both countries shall be arranged by special agreement.

Article IV. Both Governments agree, further, that the rights of the nationals of either of the two parties on the other's territory as well as the regulation of commercial relations shall be based on the most-favoured-nation principle. This principle does not include rights and facilities granted by the Soviet Government to another Soviet State or to any State that formerly formed part of the Russian Empire.

Article V. The two Governments undertake to give each other mutual assistance for the alleviation of their economic difficulties in the most benevolent spirit. In the event of a general settlement of this question on an international basis, they undertake to have a preliminary exchange of views. The German Government declares itself ready to facilitate, as far as possible, the conclusion and the execution of economic contracts between private enterprises in the two countries.

Article VI. Article I, paragraph (b), and Article IV of this agreement will come into force after the ratification of this document. The other Articles will come into force immediately.

Treaty of Berlin between the Soviet Union and Germany, Berlin, 24 April 1926

The German Government and the Government of the Union of Socialist Soviet Republics, being desirous of doing all in their power to promote the maintenance of general peace,

And being convinced that the interests of the German people and of the peoples of the Union of Socialist Soviet Republics demand constant and trustful cooperation,

Having agreed to strengthen the friendly relations existing between them by means

THE SOVIET UNION AND HER NEIGHBOURS, 1919-37

of a special Treaty ... have agreed upon the following provisions:

Article 1. The relations between Germany and the Union of Socialist Soviet Republics shall continue to be based on the Treaty of Rapallo.

The German Government and the Government of the Union of Socialist Soviet Republics will maintain friendly contact in order to promote an understanding with regard to all political and economic questions jointly affecting their two countries.

Article 2. Should one of the Contracting Parties, despite its peaceful attitude, be attacked by one or more third Powers, the other Contracting Party shall observe neutrality for the whole duration of the conflict.

Article 3. If on the occasion of a conflict of the nature mentioned in Article 2, or at a time when neither of the Contracting Parties is engaged in warlike operations, a coalition is formed between third Powers with a view to the economic or financial boycott of either of the Contracting Parties, the other Contracting Party undertakes not to adhere to such coalition.

Article 4. The present Treaty shall be ratified and the instruments of ratification shall be exchanged at Berlin.

It shall enter into force on the date of the exchange of the instruments of ratification and shall remain in force for five years. The two Contracting Parties shall confer in good time before the expiration of this period with regard to the future development of their political relations.

In faith whereof the plenipotentiaries have signed the present Treaty.

Exchange of Notes, 24 April 1926

(a) HERR STRESEMANN TO M. KRESTINSKI

With reference to the negotiations upon the Treaty signed this day between the German Government and the Government of the Union of Socialist Soviet Republics, I have the honour, on behalf of the German Government, to make the following observations:

(1) In the negotiation and signature of the Treaty, both Governments have taken the view that the principle laid down by them in Article 1, paragraph 2, of the Treaty, of reaching an understanding on all political and economic questions affecting the two countries, will contribute considerably to the maintenance of peace. In any case the two Governments will in their deliberations be guided by the need for the maintenance of the general peace.

(2) In this spirit also the two Governments have approached the fundamental questions which are bound up with the entry of Germany into the League of Nations. The German Government is convinced that Germany's membership of the League cannot constitute an obstacle to the friendly development of the relations between Germany and the Union of Socialist Soviet Republics. According to its basic idea, the League of Nations is designed for the peaceful and equitable settlement of international disputes. The German Government is determined to cooperate to the best of its ability in the realization of this idea. If, however, though the German Government does not anticipate this, there should at any time take shape within the League, contrary to that fundamental idea of peace, any efforts directed exclusively against the Union of Socialist Soviet Republics, Germany would most energetically oppose such efforts.

(3) The German Government also proceeds upon the assumption that this fundamental attitude of German policy towards the Union of Socialist Soviet Republics cannot be adversely influenced by the loyal observance of the obligations, arising out of Articles 16 and 17 of the Covenant of the League and relating to the application of sanctions, which would devolve upon Germany as a consequence of her entry into the League of Nations. By the terms of these Articles, the application of sanctions against the Union of Socialist Soviet Republics would come into consideration, in the absence of other causes, only if the Union of Socialist Soviet Republics entered upon a war of aggression against a third State. It is to be borne in mind that the question whether the Union

of Socialist Soviet Republics is the aggressor in the event of a conflict with a third State could only be determined with binding force for Germany with her own consent; and that, therefore, an accusation to this effect levelled by other Powers against the Union of Socialist Soviet Republics and regarded by Germany as unjustified, would not oblige Germany to take part in measures of any kind instituted on the authority of Article 16. With regard to the question whether, in a concrete case, Germany would be in a position to take part in the application of sanctions at all, and to what extent, the German Government refers to the Note of December 1, 1925, on the interpretation of Article 16 addressed to the German Delegation on the occasion of the signing of the Treaties of Locarno.

(4) In order to create a secure basis for disposing without friction of all questions arising between them, the two Governments regard it as desirable that they should immediately embark upon negotiations for the conclusion of a general treaty for the peaceful solution of any conflicts that may arise between them, when special attention shall be given to the possibilities of the procedure of arbitration and conciliation.

I avail myself of this opportunity to renew to Your Excellency the assurance of my highest consideration.

(b) M. KRESTINSKI TO HERR STRESEMANN

. . . I have the honour, on behalf of the Union of Socialist Soviet Republics, to make the following reply:

(1) In the negotiation and signature of the Treaty, both Governments have taken the view that the principle laid down by them in Article 1, paragraph 2, of the Treaty, of reaching an understanding on all political and economic questions jointly affecting the two countries, will contribute considerably to the maintenance of peace. In any case the two Governments will in their deliberations be guided by the need for the maintenance of the general peace.

(2) The Government of the Union of Socialist Soviet Republics takes note of the explanation contained in Sections 2 and 3 of your Note concerning the fundamental questions connected with Germany's entry into the League of Nations.

(3) In order to create a secure basis for disposing without friction of all questions arising between them, the two Governments regard it as desirable that they should immediately embark upon negotiations for the conclusion of a general treaty for the peaceful solution of any conflicts that may arise between them, when special attention shall be given to the possibilities of the procedure of arbitration and conciliation . . . .

Treaties of non-aggression and mutual assistance in Europe, 1926–36

The years after 1926 marked a new stage in Soviet policy. Within the Soviet Union, Stalin emerged as sole dictator and the organs of the state were transformed to a fully totalitarian system. Stalin embarked on a policy of industrialization, on collectivization of agriculture regardless of human life, and on a policy of terror against all probable and improbable opponents. Internationally the Soviet Union, despite its recognition and entry into the League of Nations in 1934, felt itself increasingly isolated and in danger. All was now subordinated to the security of the state. The virulent hatred of the Nazis for the Bolsheviks cut the links between the Soviet Union and Germany. These had been weakening since Locarno.

The Soviet Union engaged in vigorous diplomatic activity to assure its safety from attack and to prevent a hostile coalition of powers coming into being. From 1926 to 1937 the Soviet Union concluded a large number of non-aggression treaties. Stalin acquiesced for the time being in the existence of the 'Buffer States', Poland, the Baltic states and Finland. The most important *non-aggression treaty was that concluded with Poland, 25 July 1932* (p. 187); similar treaties were concluded with *France, 29 November 1932* (p. 190), and *Finland, 21 January 1932* (p. 191), *Latvia, 5 February 1932, Estonia, 4 May 1932, and Lithuania in 1926* (p. 185).

The failure to obtain an eastern Locarno, whereby France and Russia would have guaranteed the independence of the buffer states, led the Russians to sign with France a *Treaty of Mutual Assistance, 2 May 1935* (p. 194). Although the clauses of the treaty suggest a complete and effective alliance, appearances are misleading. The obligation to go to war was not automatic; the League of Nations had first to recognize the fact of aggression under Article 16 of the Covenant. There were no detailed military provisions; geography ensured that since Russia and Germany lacked a common frontier, Russia could not help France as long as Germany and Russia respected Polish and Baltic neutrality; similarly France could not 'attack' Germany without a breach of Locarno. The treaty was not ratified for almost a year and entered into force on 27 March 1936. The *Soviet Union also signed a Mutual Assistance Treaty with Czechoslovakia, 16 May 1935* (p. 196), but it contained the provision that it would only become operative if France first came to the help of the Czechs. Once more geography denied Soviet Russia the possibility of giving direct military help without passing through hostile Poland or Roumania. Despite these agreements Czechoslovakia was sacrificed to Hitler at Munich in September 1938 (without Soviet participation at the conference but also without any real chance of Soviet help for Czechoslovakia during the crisis).

Treaty of Non-Aggression concluded between the Soviet Union and Lithuania, 28 September 1926

Article 1. The relations between the Union of Socialist Soviet Republics and the Lithuanian Republic shall continue to be based on the Treaty of Peace between Lithuania and Russia, concluded at Moscow on July 12, 1920, all provisions of which shall retain their force and inviolability.

Article 2. The Lithuanian Republic and the Union of Socialist Soviet Republics undertake to respect in all circumstances each other's sovereignty and territorial integrity and inviolability.

Article 3. Each of the two Contracting Parties undertakes to refrain from any act of aggression whatsoever against the other party.

Should one of the Contracting Parties, despite its peaceful attitude, be attacked by one or several third Powers, the other Contracting Party undertakes not to support the said third Power or Powers against the Contracting Party attacked.

Article 4. If, on the occasion of a conflict of the type mentioned in Article 3, second paragraph, or at a time when neither of the Contracting Parties is engaged in warlike operations, a political agreement directed against one of the Contracting Parties is concluded between third Powers, or a coalition is formed between third Powers with a view to the economic or financial boycott of either of the Contracting Parties, the other Contracting Party undertakes not to adhere to such agreement or coalition.

Article 5. Should a dispute arise between them, the Contracting Parties undertake to appoint conciliation commissions if it should not prove possible to settle the dispute by diplomatic means.

The composition of the said commissions, their rights and the procedure they shall observe shall be settled in virtue of a separate agreement to be concluded between the two parties.

. . .

Conciliation Convention between Germany and the Soviet Union, 25 January 1929

The Central Executive Committee of U.S.S.R. and the President of the German Reich, animated by a desire further to strengthen the friendly relations which exist between the two countries, have decided, in execution of the Agreement reached in the Exchange of Notes of April 24, 1926, to conclude an Agreement for a procedure of conciliation, and . . . have agreed upon the following terms:

Article I. Disputes of all kinds, particularly differences of opinion which arise regarding the interpretation of the bilateral treaties which exist between the two Contracting Parties or regarding past or future agreements concerning their elucidation or execution, shall, in the event of difficulties arising over their solution through diplomatic channels, be submitted to a procedure of conciliation in accordance with the following provisions.

Article II. The procedure of conciliation shall be before a Conciliation Commission.

The Conciliation Commission shall not be permanent, but shall be formed expressly for each meeting. It shall meet once a year in the middle of the year, in ordinary session, the exact date of which shall be arranged each year by agreement between the two Governments.

There shall be extraordinary sessions whenever in the opinion of the two Governments special need arises.

The meetings of the Conciliation Commission shall be held alternately in Moscow and Berlin. The place of the first meeting shall be decided by lot.

A session shall ordinarily last not longer than fourteen days.

. . .

Article V. The task of the Conciliation Commission shall be to submit to the two Governments a solution of the questions laid before it which shall be fair and acceptable to both parties, with special regard to the avoidance of possible future differences of opinion between the two parties on the same question.

Should the Conciliation Commission in the course of a session fail to agree upon a recommendation regarding any question on the agenda, the question shall be laid before an extraordinary session of the Conciliation Commission, which must, however, meet not later than four months after the first meeting. Otherwise the matter shall be dealt with through diplomatic channels.

The results of each session of the Conciliation Commission shall be submitted to the two Governments for approval in the form of a report.

The report, or parts of it, shall be published only by agreement between the two Governments.

. . .

[In an additional Protocol, it was stated that the Soviet Union could not accept any provision for the appointment of a Chairman;

the possibility was not excluded in special cases.]

[NOTE: This Convention and the Agreement of Neutrality and Non-Aggression of 24 April 1926 were prolonged by a Protocol concluded 24 June 1931.]

Pact of Non-Aggression between the Soviet Union and Poland, 25 July 1932

The President of the Polish Republic of the one part, and the Central Executive Committee of U.S.S.R. of the other part; desirous of maintaining the present state of peace between their countries and convinced that the maintenance of peace between them constitutes an important factor in the work of preserving universal peace; considering that the Treaty of Peace of March 18, 1921 constitutes, now as in the past, the basis of their reciprocal relations and undertakings; convinced that the peaceful settlement of international disputes and the exclusion of all that might be contrary to the normal condition of relations between States are the surest means of arriving at the goal desired; declaring that none of the obligations hitherto assumed by either of the parties stands in the way of peaceful development of their mutual relations or is incompatible with the present Pact; have decided to conclude the present Pact with the object of amplifying and completing the Pact for the Renunciation of War signed at Paris on August 27, 1928, and put into force by the Protocol signed at Moscow on February 9, 1929; . . . and have agreed on the following provisions:

Article I. The two Contracting Parties, recording the fact that they have renounced war as an instrument of national policy in their mutual relations, reciprocally undertake to refrain from taking any aggressive action against or invading the territory of

the other party, either alone or in conjunction with other Powers.

Any act of violence attacking the integrity and inviolability of the territory or the political independence of the other Contracting Party shall be regarded as contrary to the undertakings contained in the present Article, even if such acts are committed without declaration of war and avoid all warlike manifestations as far as possible.

Article II. Should one of the Contracting Parties be attacked by a third State or by a group of other States, the other Contracting Party undertakes not to give aid or assistance, either directly or indirectly, to the aggressor State during the whole period of the conflict.

Should one of the Contracting Parties commit an act of aggression against a third State, the other Contracting Party shall have the right to denounce the present Pact without notice.

Article III. Each of the Contracting Parties undertakes not to be a party to any agreement openly hostile to the other party from the point of view of aggression.

Article IV. The undertakings provided for in Articles I and II of the present Pact shall in no case limit or modify the international rights and obligations of each Contracting Party under agreements concluded by it before the coming into force of the present Pact, so far as the said agreements contain no aggressive elements.

Article V. The two Contracting Parties, desirous of settling and solving, exclusively by peaceful means, any disputes and differences, of whatever nature or origin, which may arise between them, undertake to submit questions at issue, which it has not been possible to settle within a reasonable period by diplomacy, to a procedure of conciliation, in accordance with the provisions of the Convention for the application of the procedure of conciliation which constitutes an integral part of the present Pact and shall be signed separately and ratified as soon as possible simultaneously with the Pact of Non-Aggression.

Article VI. The present Pact shall be ratified as soon as possible, and the instruments of ratification shall be exchanged at Warsaw within thirty days following the ratification by Poland and U.S.S.R., after which the Pact shall come into force immediately.

Article VII. The Pact is concluded for three years. If it is not denounced by one of the Contracting Parties, after previous notice of not less than six months before the expiry of that period, it shall be automatic-ally renewed for a further period of two years.

Article VIII. The present Pact is drawn up in Polish and Russian, both texts being authentic.

Protocol of Signature (I)

The Contracting Parties declare that Article VII of the Pact of July 25, 1932 may not be interpreted as meaning that the expiry of the time limit of denunciation before the expiry of the time period under Article VII could have as a result the limitation or cancellation of the obligations arising out of the Pact of Paris of 1928.

Protocol of Signature (II)

On signing the Pact of Non-Aggression this day, the two parties, having exchanged their views on the draft Conciliation Convention submitted by the Soviet Party, declare that they are convinced that there is no essential difference of opinion between them.

Protocol prolonging the Pact of Non-Aggression, 25 July 1932, with Final Protocol, 5 May 1934

The Central Executive Committee of U.S.S.R. and the President of the Republic of Poland; being desirous of providing as firm a basis as possible for the development of the relations between their countries; being desirous of giving each other fresh proof of the unchangeable character and solidity of the pacific and friendly relations happily established between them; moved by the desire to contribute to the consolidation of world peace and to the stability and peaceful development of international relations in Eastern Europe; noting that the conclusion on July 25, 1932 at Moscow of the Treaty between U.S.S.R. and the Republic of Poland has had a beneficial influence on the development of their relations and on the solution of the above-mentioned problems; have decided to sign the present Protocol and have . . . agreed on the following provisions:

Article I. In modification of the provisions of Article VII of the Treaty of Non-Aggression concluded at Moscow on July 25, 1932 between U.S.S.R. and the Republic of Poland concerning the date and manner in which that Treaty shall cease to have effect, the two Contracting Parties decide that it shall remain in force until December 31, 1945.

Each of the High Contracting Parties

shall be entitled to denounce the Treaty by giving notice to that effect six months before the expiry of the above-mentioned period. If the Treaty is not denounced by either of the Contracting Parties, its period of validity shall be automatically prolonged for two years; similarly, the Treaty shall be regarded as prolonged on each occasion for a further period of two years, if it is not denounced by either of the Contracting Parties in the manner provided for in the present Article.

Article II. The present Protocol is drawn up in duplicate, each copy being in the Russian and Polish languages and both texts being equally authentic.

The present Protocol shall be ratified as soon as possible, and the instruments of ratification shall be exchanged between the Contracting Parties at Warsaw.

The present Protocol shall come into force on the date of the exchange of the instruments of ratification.

Final Protocol

In connection with the signature on this date of the Protocol prolonging the Treaty of Non-Aggression between the U.S.S.R. and the Republic of Poland of July 25, 1932, each of the High Contracting Parties, having again examined all the provisions of the Peace Treaty concluded at Riga on March 18, 1921, which constitutes the basis of their mutual relations, declares that it has no obligations and is not bound by any declarations inconsistent with the provisions of the said Peace Treaty in particular of Article III thereof.

Consequently, the Government of U.S.S.R. confirms that the Note from the People's Commissar, G. V. Chicherin, of September 28, 1926, to the Lithuanian Government cannot be interpreted to mean that that Note implied any intention on the part of the Soviet Socialist Government to interfere in the settlement of the territorial questions mentioned therein.

Joint Soviet–Polish Statement, 26 November 1938

A series of conversations recently held between the U.S.S.R. People's Commissar for Foreign Affairs, M. Litvinov, and the Polish Ambassador in Moscow, M. Grzybowski, has led to the following statement:

1. Relations between the Polish Republic and U.S.S.R. are and will continue to be based to the fullest extent on all the existing Agreements, including the Polish–Soviet Pact of Non-Aggression dated July 25, 1932. This Pact, concluded for five years and extended on May 5, 1934 for a further period ending December 31, 1945, has a basis wide enough to guarantee the inviolability of peaceful relations between the two States.

2. Both Governments are favourable to the extension of their commercial relations.

3. Both Governments agree that it is necessary to settle a number of current and longstanding matters that have arisen in connection with the various Agreements in force and, in particular, to dispose of the various frontier incidents that have recently been occurring.

Protocol of Signature

. . .

2. The High Contracting Parties declare that subsequent denunciation of the present Treaty before its termination or annulment shall neither cancel nor restrict the undertakings arising from the Pact for the Renunciation of War signed at Paris on August 27, 1928.

Pact of Non-Aggression between the Soviet Union and France, 29 November 1932

[A Conciliation Convention was signed at the same time.]

The President of the French Republic and the Central Executive Committee of U.S.S.R.; animated by the desire to consolidate peace; convinced that it is in the interests of both High Contracting Parties to improve and develop relations between the two countries; mindful of the international undertakings which they have previously assumed and none of which, they declare, constitutes an obstacle to the pacific development of their mutual relations or is inconsistent with the present Treaty; desirous of confirming and defining, so far as concerns their respective relations, the General Pact of August 27, 1928 for the renunciation of war; . . . have agreed on the following provisions:

Article I. Each of the High Contracting Parties undertakes with regard to the other not to resort in any case, whether alone or jointly with one or more third Powers, either to war or to any aggression by land, sea or air against that other party, and to respect the inviolability of the territories which are placed under the party's sovereignty or which it represents in external relations or for whose administration it is responsible.

Article II. Should either High Contracting Party be the object of aggression by one or more third Powers, the other High Contracting Party undertakes not to give aid or assistance, either directly or indirectly, to the aggressor or aggressors during the period of the conflict.

Should either High Contracting Party resort to aggression against a third Power, the other High Contracting Party may denounce the present Treaty without notice.

Article III. The undertakings set forth in Articles I and II above shall in no way limit or modify the rights or obligations of each Contracting Party under agreements concluded by it before the coming into force of the present Treaty, each Party hereby declaring further that it is not bound by any agreement involving an obligation for it to participate in aggression by a third State.

Article IV. Each of the High Contracting Parties undertakes, for the duration of the present Treaty, not to become a party to any international agreement of which the effect in practice would be to prevent the purchase of goods from or the sale of goods or the granting of credits to the other party, and not to take any measure which would result in the exclusion of the other party from any participation in its foreign trade.

Article V. Each of the High Contracting Parties undertakes to respect in every connection the sovereignty or authority of the other party over the whole of that party's territories as defined in Article I of the present Treaty, not to interfere in any way in its internal affairs, and to abstain more particularly from action of any kind calculated to promote or encourage agitation, propaganda or attempted intervention designed to prejudice its territorial integrity or to transform by force the political or social régime of all or part of its territories.

Each of the High Contracting Parties undertakes in particular not to create, protect, equip, subsidize or admit in its territory either military organizations for the purpose of armed combat with the other party or organizations assuming the role of government or representing all or part of its territories.

Article VI. The High Contracting Parties having already recognized, in the General Pact of August 27, 1928 for the renunciation of war, that the settlement or solution of all disputes or conflicts, of whatever nature or of whatever origin they may be, which may arise among them, shall never be sought except by pacific means, confirm that provision, and, in order to give effect to it, annex to the present Treaty a Convention relating to conciliation procedure.

Article VII. The present Treaty, of which the French and Russian texts shall both be authentic, shall be ratified, and the ratifications thereof shall be exchanged at Moscow. It shall enter into effect on the date of the said exchange and shall remain in force for the period of one year as from the date on which either High Contracting Party shall have notified the other of its intention to denounce it. Such notification may not, however, be given before the expiry of a period of two years from the date of the entry into force of the present Treaty.

Treaty of Non-Aggression between the Soviet Union and Finland, 21 January 1932

The Central Executive Committee of U.S.S.R. on the one part, and the President of the Republic of Finland on the other part, actuated by the desire to contribute to the maintenance of general peace; being convinced that the conclusion of the undertakings mentioned below and the pacific settlement of any dispute whatsoever between U.S.S.R. and the Republic of Finland is in the interests of both High Contracting Parties and will contribute towards the development of friendly and neighbourly relations between the two countries; declaring that none of the international obligations which they have hitherto assumed debars the pacific development of their mutual relations or is incompatible with the present Treaty; being desirous of confirming and completing the General Pact of August 27, 1928 for the renunciation of war; have resolved to conclude the present Treaty . . . and have agreed upon the following provisions:

Article I. 1. The High Contracting Parties mutually guarantee the inviolability of the frontiers existing between U.S.S.R. and the Republic of Finland, as fixed by the Treaty of Peace concluded at Dorpat on October 14, 1920, which shall remain the firm foundation of their relations, and reciprocally undertake to refrain from any act of aggression directed against each other.

2. Any act of violence attacking the integrity and inviolability of the territory or the political independence of the other High Contracting Party shall be regarded as an act of aggression, even if it is committed without declaration of war and avoids warlike manifestations.

PROTOCOL TO ARTICLE 1. In conformity with the provisions of Article IV of the present Treaty, the Agreement of June 1, 1922 regarding measures ensuring the inviolability of the frontiers shall not be affected by the provisions of the present Treaty and shall continue to remain fully in force.

Article II. 1. Should either High Contracting Party be the object of aggression on the part of one or more third Powers, the other High Contracting Party undertakes to maintain neutrality throughout the duration of the conflict.

2. Should either High Contracting Party resort to aggression against a third Power, the other High Contracting Party may denounce the present Treaty without notice.

Article III. Each of the High Contracting Parties undertakes not to become a party to any treaty, agreement or convention which is openly hostile to the other party or contrary, whether formally or in substance, to the present Treaty.

Article IV. The obligations mentioned in the preceding Articles of the present Treaty may in no case affect or modify the international rights or obligations of the High Contracting Parties under agreements concluded or undertakings assumed before the coming into force of the present Treaty, in so far as such agreements contain no elements of aggression within the meaning of the present Treaty.

Article V. The High Contracting Parties declare that they will always endeavour to settle in a spirit of justice any disputes of whatever nature or origin which may arise between them, and will resort exclusively to pacific means of settling such disputes. For this purpose, the High Contracting Parties undertake to submit any disputes which may arise between them after the signature of the present Treaty, and which it may not have been possible to settle through diplomatic proceedings within a reasonable time, to a procedure of conciliation before a joint conciliation commission whose powers, composition and working shall be fixed by a special supplementary Convention, which shall form an integral part of the present Treaty and which the High Contracting Parties undertake to conclude as soon as possible and in any event before the present Treaty is ratified. Conciliation procedure shall also be applied in the event of any dispute as to the application or interpretation of a Convention concluded between the High Contracting Parties, and particularly the question whether the mutual undertaking as to non-aggression has or has not been violated.

[*Articles VI and VII.* Ratification.]

[*Article VIII.* Treaty concluded for three years, automatically renewed for a further two years unless six months' notice of termination is given.]

Convention concluded between the Soviet Union, Afghanistan, Estonia, Latvia, Persia, Poland and Rumania regarding the definition of aggression, 3 July 1933

[A similar Convention was concluded by the Soviet Union, Rumania, Turkey and Yugoslavia on 4 July 1933.]

. . .

Article II. Accordingly, the aggressor in an international conflict shall, subject to the agreement in force between the parties to the dispute, be considered to be that State which is the first to commit any of the following actions:

1. Declaration of war upon another State;

2. Invasion by its armed forces, with or without a declaration of war, of the territory of another State;

3. Attack by its land, naval or air forces, with or without a declaration of war, on the territory, vessels or aircraft of another State;

4. Naval blockade of the coasts or ports of another State;

5. Provision of support to armed bands formed in its territory which have invaded the territory of another State, or refusal, notwithstanding the request of the invaded State, to take in its own territory all the measures in its power to deprive those bands of all assistance or protection.

No political, military, economic or other considerations may serve as an excuse or justification for the aggression referred to in Article II. (For examples, see Annex.)

Annex

The High Contracting Parties signatories of the Convention relating to the definition of aggression; desiring, subject to the express reservation that the absolute validity of the rule laid down in Article III of that Convention shall be in no way restricted, to furnish certain indications for determining the aggressor; declare that no act of aggression within the meaning of Article II of that Convention can be justified on either of the following grounds, among others:

A. The internal condition of a State: e.g. its political, economic or social structure; alleged defects in its administration; disturbances due to strikes, revolutions, counter-revolutions or civil war.

B. The international conduct of a State:

e.g. the violation or threatened violation of the material or moral rights or interests of a foreign State or its nationals; the rupture of diplomatic or economic relations; economic or financial boycotts; disputes relating to economic, financial or other obligations towards foreign States; frontier incidents not forming any of the cases of aggression specified in Article II.

The High Contracting Parties further agree to recognize that the present Convention can never make legitimate any violations of international law that may be implied in the circumstances comprised in the above list.

Baltic Entente between Lithuania, Estonia and Latvia, 3 November 1934

Article 1. In order to coordinate their efforts in the cause of peace, the three Governments undertake to confer together on questions of foreign policy which are of common concern and to afford one another mutual political and diplomatic assistance in their international relations.

Article 2. For the purpose set forth in Article 1, the High Contracting Parties hereby decide to institute periodical conferences of the Ministers for Foreign Affairs of the three countries, to take place at regular intervals, at least twice a year, in the territories of each of the three States in turn. At the request of one of the High Contracting Parties and by joint agreement, extraordin-

ary conferences may be held in the territory of one of the three States or elsewhere . . .

Article 3. The High Contracting Parties recognize the existence of the specific problems which might make a concerted attitude with regard to them difficult. They agree that such problems constitute an exception to the undertakings laid down in Article 1 of the present Treaty.

Article 4. The High Contracting Parties shall endeavour to settle amicably and in a spirit of justice and equity any questions in respect of which their interests may clash and also to do so in the shortest possible time . . . .

Treaty of Mutual Assistance between the Soviet Union and France, 2 May 1935

The Central Executive Committee of U.S.S.R. and the President of the French Republic, being desirous of strengthening peace in Europe and of guaranteeing its benefits to their respective countries by securing a fuller and stricter application of those provisions of the Covenant of the League of Nations which are designed to maintain the national security, territorial integrity and political independence of States; determined to devote their efforts to the preparation and conclusion of a European agreement for that purpose and in the meantime to promote, as far as lies in their power, the effective application of the provisions of the Covenant of the League of Nations; have resolved to conclude a Treaty to this end and have appointed as their plenipotentiaries . . . and have agreed upon the following provisions:

Article I. In the event of France or U.S.S.R. being threatened with or in danger of aggression on the part of any European State, U.S.S.R. and reciprocally France undertake mutually to proceed to an immediate consultation as regards the measures to be taken for the observance of the provisions of Article X of the Covenant of the League of Nations.

Article II. Should, in the circumstances specified in Article XV, paragraph 7, of the Covenant of the League of Nations, France or U.S.S.R. be the object, notwithstanding the sincerely peaceful intentions of both countries, of an unprovoked aggression on the part of a European State, U.S.S.R. and reciprocally France shall immediately come to each other's aid and assistance.

Article III. In consideration of the fact that under Article XVI of the Covenant of the League of Nations any member of the League which resorts to war in disregard of its covenants under Articles XII, XIII or XV of the Covenant is *ipso facto* deemed to have committed an act of war against all other members of the League, France and reciprocally U.S.S.R. undertake, in the

event of one of them being the object, in these conditions and notwithstanding the sincerely peaceful intentions of both countries, of an unprovoked aggression on the part of a European State, immediately to come to each other's aid and assistance in application of Article XVI of the Covenant.

The same obligation is assumed in the event of France or U.S.S.R. being the object of an aggression on the part of a European State in the circumstances specified in Article XVII, paragraphs 1 and 3, of the Covenant of the League of Nations.

Article IV. The undertakings stipulated above being consonant with the obligations of the High Contracting Parties as members of the League of Nations, nothing in the present Treaty shall be interpreted as restricting the duty of the latter to take any action that may be deemed wise and effectual to safeguard the peace of the world, or as restricting the obligations resulting for the High Contracting Parties from the Covenant of the League of Nations.

[*Article V.* Ratification to be exchanged as soon as possible. Treaty to remain in force for five years unless denounced by either party giving at least one year's notice; at end of five years the Treaty to continue indefinitely, each party being at liberty to terminate it with one year's notice.]

Protocol of Signature

Upon proceeding to the signature of the Franco-Soviet Treaty of Mutual Assistance of today's date the plenipotentiaries have signed the following Protocol, which shall be included in the exchange of ratifications of the Treaty.

1. It is agreed that the effect of Article III is to oblige each Contracting Party immediately to come to the assistance of the other by immediately complying with the recommendations of the Council of the League of Nations as soon as they have

been issued in virtue of Article XVI of the Covenant. It is further agreed that the two Contracting Parties will act in concert to insure that the Council shall issue the said recommendations with all the speed required by the circumstances, and that should the Council nevertheless, for whatever reason, issue no recommendation or fail to reach a unanimous decision, effect shall none the less be given to the obligation to render assistance. It is also agreed that the undertakings to render assistance mentioned in the present Treaty refer only to the case of an aggression committed against either Contracting Party's own territory.

2. It being the common intention of the two Governments in no way to contradict, by the present Treaty, undertakings previously assumed toward third States by France and by U.S.S.R. in virtue of published treaties, it is agreed that effect shall not be given to the provisions of the said Treaty in a manner which, being incompatible with treaty obligations assumed by one of the Contracting Parties, would expose that party to sanctions of an international character.

3. The two Governments, deeming it desirable that a regional agreement should be concluded aiming at organizing security between Contracting States, and which might moreover embody or be accompanied by pledges of mutual assistance, recognize their right to become parties by mutual consent, should occasion arise, to similar agreements in any form, direct or indirect, that may seem appropriate, the obligations under these various agreements to take the place of those assumed under the present Treaty.

4. The two Governments place on record the fact that the negotiations which have resulted in the signature of the present Treaty were originally undertaken with a view to supplementing a security agreement embracing the countries of north-eastern Europe, namely, U.S.S.R., Germany, Czechoslovakia, Poland and the Baltic States which are neighbours of U.S.S.R.; in addition to that agreement, there was to have been concluded a treaty of assistance between U.S.S.R. and France and Germany, by which each of those three States was to have undertaken to come to the assistance of any one of them which might be the object of aggression on the part of any other of those three States. Although circumstances have not hitherto permitted the conclusion of those agreements, which both parties continue to regard as desirable, it is nonetheless the case that the undertakings stipulated in the Franco–Soviet Treaty of Assistance are to be understood as intended to apply only within the limits contemplated in the three-party agreement previously planned. Independently of the obligations assumed under the present Treaty, it is further recalled that, in accordance with the Franco–Soviet Pact of Non-Aggression signed on November 29, 1932, and moreover, without affecting the universal character of the undertakings assumed in the Pact, in the event of either party becoming the object of aggression by one or more third European Powers not referred to in the above-mentioned three-party agreement, the other Contracting Party is bound to abstain, during the period of the conflict, from giving any aid or assistance, either direct or indirect, to the aggressor or aggressors, each party declaring further that it is not bound by any assistance agreement which would be contrary to this undertaking.

Treaty of Mutual Assistance between the Soviet Union and Czechoslovakia, 16 May 1935

The President of the Czechoslovak Republic and the Central Executive Committee of the U.S.S.R.; being desirous of strengthening peace in Europe and of guaranteeing its benefits to their respective countries by securing a fuller and stricter application of those provisions of the Covenant of the League of Nations which are designed to maintain the national security, territorial integrity and political independence of States; determined to devote their efforts to the preparation and conclusion of a European agreement for that purpose, and in the meantime to promote, as far as lies in their power, the effective application of the provisions of the Covenant of the League of Nations; have resolved to conclude a Treaty to this end and have appointed as their plenipotentiaries:

The President of the Czechoslovak Republic: Eduard Beneš, Minister for Foreign Affairs;

The Central Executive Committee of U.S.S.R.: Sergei Alexandrovsky, Envoy Extraordinary and Minister Plenipotentiary of the U.S.S.R.;

. . . and have agreed upon the following provisions:

Article I. In the event of the Czechoslovak Republic or U.S.S.R. being threatened with, or in danger of, aggression on the part of any European State, U.S.S.R. and reciprocally the Czechoslovak Republic undertake mutually to proceed to an immediate consultation as regards the measures to be taken for the observance of the provisions of Article X of the Covenant of the League of Nations.

Article II. Should, in the circumstances specified in Article XV, paragraph 7, of the Covenant of the League of Nations, the Czechoslovak Republic or U.S.S.R. be the object, notwithstanding the sincerely peaceful intentions of both countries, of an unprovoked aggression on the part of a European State, U.S.S.R. and reciprocally the Czechoslovak Republic shall immediately come to each other's aid and assistance.

Article III. In consideration of the fact that under Article XVI of the Covenant of the League of Nations any member of the League which resorts to war in disregard of its covenants under Articles XII, XIII or XV of the Covenant is *ipso facto* deemed to have committed an act of war against all other members of the League, the Czechoslovak Republic and reciprocally U.S.S.R. undertake, in the event of one of them being the object, in these conditions and notwithstanding the sincerely peaceful intentions of both countries, of an unprovoked aggression on the part of a European State, immediately to come to each other's aid and assistance in application of Article XVI of the Covenant.

The same obligation is assumed in the event of the Czechoslovak Republic or U.S.S.R. being the object of an aggression on the part of a European State in the circumstances specified in Article XVII, paragraphs 1 and 3, of the Covenant of the League of Nations.

Article IV. Without prejudice to the preceeding provisions of the present Treaty, it is stipulated that should either of the High Contracting Parties become the object of an aggression on the part of one or more third Powers in conditions not giving ground for aid or assistance within the meaning of the present Treaty, the other High Contracting Party undertakes not to lend, for the duration of the conflict, aid or assistance, either directly or indirectly, to the aggressor or aggressors. Each High Contracting Party further declares that it is not bound by any other agreement for assistance which is incompatible with the present undertaking.

Article V. The undertaking stipulated above being consonant with the obligations of the High Contracting Parties as members of the League of Nations, nothing in the present Treaty shall be interpreted as restricting the duty of the latter to take any action that may be deemed wise and effectual to safeguard the peace of the world or as restricting the obligations resulting for the High Contracting Parties from the Covenant of the League of Nations.

Article VI. The present Treaty, both the Czechoslovak and the Russian texts whereof shall be equally authentic, shall be ratified and the instruments of ratification shall be exchanged at Moscow as soon as possible. It shall be registered with the Secretariat of the League of Nations.

It shall take effect as soon as the ratifications have been exchanged and shall remain in force for five years. If it is not denounced by either of the High Contracting Parties giving notice thereof at least one year before the expiry of that period, it shall remain in force indefinitely, each of the High Contracting Parties being at liberty to terminate it at a year's notice by a declaration to that effect.

Protocol of Signature

Upon proceeding to the signature of the Treaty of Mutual Assistance between the Czechoslovak Republic and U.S.S.R. of today's date, the plenipotentiaries have signed the following Protocol, which shall be included in the exchange of ratifications of the Treaty.

I. It is agreed that the effect of Article III is to oblige each Contracting Party immediately to come to the assistance of the other by immediately complying with the recommendations of the Council of the League of Nations as soon as they have been issued in virtue of Article XVI of the Covenant. It is further agreed that the two Contracting Parties will act in concert to ensure that the Council shall issue the said recommendations with all the speed required by the circumstances and that, should the Council nevertheless, for whatever reason, issue no recommendation or fail to reach a unanimous decision, effect shall none the less be given to the obligation to render assistance. It is also agreed that the undertakings to render assistance mentioned in the present Treaty refer only to the case of an aggression committed against either Contracting Party's own territory.

II. The two Governments declare that the undertakings laid down in Articles I, II and III of the present Treaty, concluded with a view of promoting the establishment in Eastern Europe of a regional system of security, inaugurated by the Franco–Soviet Treaty of May 2, 1935, will be restricted within the same limits as were laid down in paragraph 4 of the Protocol of signature of the said Treaty. At the same time, the two Governments recognize that the undertaking to render mutual assistance will operate between them only in so far as the conditions laid down in the present Treaty may be fulfilled and in so far as assistance may be rendered by France to the party victim of the aggression.

III. The two Governments, deeming it desirable that a regional agreement should be concluded aiming at organizing security between Contracting States, and which might moreover embody or be accompanied by pledges of mutual assistance, recognize their right to become parties by mutual consent, should occasion arise, to similar agreements in any form, direct or indirect, that may seem appropriate; the obligations under these various agreements to take the place of those resulting from the present Treaty.

Soviet treaties in eastern Asia

In 1919 in Eastern Asia, Soviet Russia felt itself threatened by allied and Japanese intervention, by occupation and by support given to anti–Bolshevik forces. Attempts to win over China by denouncing Tsarist imperialism were not very successful. The Chinese, taking advantage of Russian impotence, had regained control of the Chinese Eastern Railway and over autonomous Outer Mongolia. By April 1920 the Soviet position improved. Only the Japanese remained a strong foreign force on Russian soil. A Soviet-supported revolution brought Outer Mongolia back under Soviet protection. Russo–Chinese relations in the 1920s varied from normalization, advanced by the *Agreement of 31 May 1924 concerning the Chinese Eastern Railway*, to the all but declared war in 1929 as a result of Soviet attempts to establish Soviet influence in China. In the 1920s good relations were established between Russia and Japan, marked especially by the *Convention between Japan and the Soviet Union concerning their general relationship, 20 January 1925* (see below).

But the 1930s saw a reversal of Russia's Far Eastern policies. With Japanese aggression in China and Japan's growing expansionism, the Soviet Union gave support to China. The change in this relationship with China is marked by the signature of a *Treaty of Non-Aggression between the U.S.S.R. and the Republic of China, 21 August 1937* (p. 202). Despite the agreement reached between the Soviet Union with Japan's puppet state of Manchukuo for the sale of the *Chinese Eastern Railway, 23 March 1935* (p. 200), Soviet–Japanese relations remained very strained. With the *Mongolian People's Republic the Soviet Union concluded a Mutual Assistance Treaty, 12 March 1936* (p. 201).

Convention between Japan and the Soviet Union, Peking, 20 January 1925

Japan and U.S.S.R., desiring to promote relations of good neighbourhood and economic cooperation between them, have resolved to conclude a Convention embodying basic rules in regulation of such relations and, to that end, have agreed as follows:

Article I. The High Contracting Parties agree that with the coming into force of the present Convention, diplomatic and consular relations shall be established between them.

Article II. U.S.S.R. agrees that the Treaty of Portsmouth of September 5, 1905, shall remain in force.

It is agreed that the treaties, conventions and agreements other than the said Treaty of Portsmouth, which were concluded between Japan and Russia prior to November 7, 1917, shall be re-examined at a conference to be subsequently held between the Governments of the High Contracting Parties and are liable to revision or annulment as altered circumstances may require.

Article III. The Governments of the High Contracting Parties agree that upon the coming into force of the present Convention, they shall proceed to the revision of the Fishery Convention of 1907, taking into consideration such changes as may have taken place in the general conditions since the conclusion of the said Fishery Convention.

Pending the conclusion of a convention so revised, the Government of U.S.S.R. shall maintain the practice established in 1924 relating to the lease of fishery lots to Japanese subjects.

Article IV. The Governments of the High Contracting Parties agree that upon the coming into force of the present Convention, they shall proceed to the conclusion of a treaty of commerce and navigation in conformity with the principles hereunder mentioned, and that, pending the conclusion of such a treaty, the general intercourse between the two countries shall be regulated by those principles . . . .

Article V. The High Contracting Parties solemnly affirm their desire and intention to live in peace and amity with each other, scrupulously to respect the undoubted right of a State to order its own life within its own jurisdiction in its own way, to refrain and to restrain all persons in any governmental service for them, and all organizations in receipt of any financial assistance from them, from any act overt or covert liable in any way whatsoever to endanger the order and security in any part of the territories of Japan or U.S.S.R.

It is further agreed that neither Contracting Party shall permit the presence in the territories under its jurisdiction: (a) of organizations or groups pretending to be the Government for any part of the territories of the other party, or (b) of alien subjects or citizens who may be found to be actually carrying on political activities for such organizations or groups.

Article VI. In the interest of promoting economic relations between the two countries, and taking into consideration the needs of Japan with regard to natural resources, the Government of U.S.S.R. is willing to grant to Japanese subjects, companies and associations, concessions for the exploitation of minerals, forests and other natural resources in all the territories of U.S.S.R.

[*Article VII.* Ratification.]

Protocol A

Japan and U.S.S.R., in proceeding this day to the signature of the Convention embodying basic rules of the relations between them, have deemed it advisable to regulate certain questions in relation to the said Convention, and have, through their respective plenipotentiaries, agreed upon the following stipulations:

Article I. Each of the High Contracting Parties undertakes to place in the possession of the other party the movable and immovable property belonging to the embassy under consulates of such other party and actually existing within its own territories. . . .

Article II. It is agreed that all questions of the debts due to the Government of subjects of Japan on account of public loans and treasury bills issued by the former Russian Governments, to wit, by the Imperial Government of Russia and the Provisional Government which succeeded it, are reserved for adjustment at subsequent negotiations between the Government of Japan and the Government of U.S.S.R.: provided that in the adjustment of such question, the Government or subjects of Japan shall not, all other conditions being equal, be placed in any position less favourable than that which the Government of U.S.S.R. may accord to the Government or nationals of any other country on similar questions.

It is also agreed that all questions relating to claims of the Government of either party to the Government of the other, or of the nationals of either party to the Government of the other, are reserved for adjustment at subsequent negotiations between the Government of Japan and the Government of U.S.S.R.

Article III. In view of climatic conditions in Northern Sakhalin preventing the immediate homeward transportation of Japanese troops now stationed there, these troops shall be completely withdrawn from the said region by May 15, 1925.

Such withdrawal shall be commenced as soon as climatic conditions will permit, and any and all districts in Northern Sakhalin so evacuated by Japanese troops shall immediately thereupon be restored in full sovereignty to the proper authorities of U.S.S.R . . . .

Article IV. The High Contracting Parties mutually declare that there actually exists no treaty or agreement of military alliance nor any other secret agreement which either of them has entered into with any third party and which constitutes an infringement upon, or a menace to, the sovereignty, territorial rights or national safety of the other Contracting Party.

Article V. The present Protocol is to be considered as ratified with the ratification of the Convention embodying basic rules of the relations between Japan and U.S.S.R., signed under the same date.

Protocol B

The High Contracting Parties have agreed upon the following as the basis for the concession contracts to be concluded within five months from the date of the complete evacuation of Northern Sakhalin by Japanese troops, as provided for in Article III of Protocol A signed this day between the plenipotentiaries of Japan and of U.S.S.R.

Article 1. The Government of U.S.S.R. agrees to grant to Japanese concerns recommended by the Government of Japan the concession for the exploitation of 50 per cent, in area, of the oil fields in Northern Sakhalin which are mentioned in the Memorandum submitted to the representative of the Union by the Japanese representative on August 29, 1924 . . . .

Article 2. The Government of U.S.S.R. also agrees to authorize Japanese concerns recommended by the Government of Japan to prospect oil fields, for a period of from five to ten years, on the eastern coast of Northern Sakhalin over an area of one thousand square versts to be selected within one year after the conclusion of the concession contracts, and in case oil fields shall have been established in consequence of such prospecting by the Japanese, the concession for the exploitation of 50 per cent, in area, of the oil fields so established shall be granted to the Japanese.

Article 3. The Government of U.S.S.R. agrees to grant to Japanese concerns recommended by the Government of Japan the concession for the exploitation of coal fields on the western coast of Northern Sakhalin over a specific area which shall be determined in the concession contracts.

The Government of U.S.S.R. further agrees to grant to such Japanese concerns the concession regarding coal fields in the Doue district over a specific area to be determined in the concession contracts.

With regard to the coal fields outside the specific areas mentioned in the preceding two paragraphs, it is also agreed that should the Government of U.S.S.R. decide to offer them for foreign concession, Japanese concerns shall be afforded equal opportunity in the matter of such concession.

Article 4. The period of the concession for the exploitation of oil and coal fields stipulated in the preceding paragraphs shall be from forty to fifty years.

Article 5. As royalty for the said concessions, the Japanese concessionaires shall make over annually to the Government of U.S.S.R., in case of coal fields, from 5 to 8 per cent of their gross output and, in case of oil fields, from 5 to 15 per cent of their gross output . . . .

Declaration

In proceeding this day to the signature of the Convention embodying basic rules of the relations between U.S.S.R. and Japan, the undersigned plenipotentiary of U.S.S.R. has the honour to declare that the recognition by the Government of U.S.S.R. of the validity of the Treaty of Portsmouth of September 5, 1905 does not in any way signify that the Government of the Union shares with the former Tsarist Government the political responsibility for the conclusion of the said Treaty.

. . .

Agreement on the sale of Chinese Eastern Railway to Manchukuo, Tokyo, 23 March 1935

Manchukuo and U.S.S.R., being desirous of settling the question of the North Manchuria Railway (Chinese Eastern Railway) and thus to contribute to the safeguarding of peace in the Far East, have resolved to conclude an Agreement for the cession to Manchukuo of the rights of U.S.S.R. concerning the North Manchuria Railway (Chinese Eastern Railway), and have . . . agreed upon the following Articles:

Article I. The Government of U.S.S.R. will cede to the Government of Manchukuo all the rights it possesses over the North Manchuria Railway (Chinese Eastern Railway), in consideration of which the Government of Manchukuo will pay to the Government of U.S.S.R. the sum of one hundred and forty million (140,000,000) yen in Japanese currency.

Article II. All the rights of the Government of U.S.S.R. concerning the North Manchuria Railway (Chinese Eastern Railway) will pass to the Government of Manchukuo

upon the coming into force of the present Agreement, and at the same time the North Manchuria Railway (Chinese Eastern Railway) will be placed under the complete occupation and the sole management of the Government of Manchukuo.

Article III. I. Upon the coming into force of the present Agreement, the senior members of the administration of the North Manchuria Railway (Chinese Eastern Railway) who are citizens of U.S.S.R. will be released from their duties. The said senior members of the administration of the railway will hand over all the archives, records, papers and documents of whatever description in their charge to their respective successors in the new administration of the railway . . . [administrative and financial details].

Protocol of Mutual Assistance between the Mongolian People's Republic and the Soviet Union, Ulan Bator, 12 March 1936

The Governments of U.S.S.R. and the Mongolian People's Republic, taking into consideration the unalterable friendship that has existed between their countries since the liberation of the territory of the Mongolian People's Republic in 1921, with the support of the Red Army, from the White Guard detachments and the military forces with which the latter were connected and which invaded Soviet Territory, and desirous of supporting the cause of peace in the Far East and further strengthening the friendly relations between their countries, have decided to set forth in the form of the present Protocol the gentlemen's agreement existing between them since November 27, 1934, providing for mutual assistance in every possible manner in the matter of averting and preventing the danger of military attack and for support in the event of an attack by any third party on U.S.S.R. or the Mongolian People's Repub-

lic, and for these purposes have signed the present Protocol.

Article I. In the event of the threat of an attack on the territory of the Mongolian or Soviet Socialist Republics by a third country, the Governments of U.S.S.R. and the Mongolian People's Republic undertake to confer immediately regarding the situation and to adopt all measures that may be necessary for the protection and safety of their territories.

Article II. The Governments of U.S.S.R. and the Mongolian People's Republic undertake, in the event of a military attack on one of the Contracting Parties, to render each other every assistance, including military assistance.

Article III. The Governments of U.S.S.R. and the Mongolian People's Republic are in full understanding that the troops of either country will be sent into the territory of the other in accordance with a mutual agreement and in accordance with Articles I and II of this Protocol, and will immediately be withdrawn from that territory as soon as the period of necessity is over, as took place in 1925 when Soviet troops retired from the territory of the Mongolian People's Republic.

. . .

Treaty of Non-Aggression between China and the Soviet Union, Moscow, 21 August 1937

The National Government of the Republic of China and the Government of U.S.S.R., animated by the desire to contribute to the maintenance of general peace, to consolidate the amicable relations now existing between them on a firm and lasting basis, and to confirm in a more precise manner the obligations mutually undertaken under the Treaty for the Renunciation of War, signed in Paris on August 27, 1928, have resolved to conclude the present Treaty and have . . . agreed on the following Articles:

Article I. The two High Contracting Parties solemnly reaffirm that they condemn recourse to war for the solution of international controversies, and that they renounce it as an instrument of national policy in their relations with each other, and, in pursuance of this pledge, they undertake to refrain from any aggression against each other either individually or jointly with one or more other Powers.

Article II. In the event that either of the High Contracting Parties should be subjected to aggression on the part of one or more third Powers, the other High Contracting Party obligates itself not to render assistance of any kind, either directly or indirectly to such third Power or Powers at any time during the entire conflict, and also to refrain from taking any action or entering into any agreement which may be used by the aggressor or aggressors to the disadvantage of the parties subjected to aggression.

Article III. The provisions of the present Treaty shall not be so interpreted as to affect or modify the rights and obligations arising, in respect of the High Contracting Parties, out of bilateral or multilateral treaties or agreements to which the High Contracting Parties are signatories and which were concluded prior to the entering into force of the present Treaty,

Article IV. The present Treaty is drawn up in duplicate in English. It comes into force on the day of signature by the above-mentioned plenipotentiaries and shall remain in force for a period of five years. Either of the High Contracting Parties may inform the other six months before the expiration of the period of its desire to terminate the Treaty. In case both parties fail to do so in time, the Treaty shall be considered as being automatically extended for a period of two years after the expiration of the first period. Should neither of the High Contracting Parties inform the other six months before the expiration of the two-year period of its desire to terminate the Treaty, it shall continue in force for another period of two years, and so on successively.

VII · The collapse of the territorial settlements of Versailles, 1931–37

The security of post-Versailles Europe rested on certain assumptions: a military balance that favoured France and Britain, and the maintenance of the provisions of the Versailles Treaty. The Germany of the Weimar Republic had already succeeded in weakening the control and constraints imposed by the Versailles Treaty. By 1930, the Allies had evacuated the Rhineland ahead of time, German armaments were no longer closely controlled and Germany was no longer diplomatically isolated. But all this had been achieved by governments which were determined to avoid another collision with France and Britain and which did not openly flout the provisions of the Versailles Treaty. With the coming to power of Hitler, German policy was set on a revolutionary Nazi course. Hitler rejected pre-1914 concepts of the successful national state expanding through piecemeal territorial conquests. To re-establish Germany as an equal great power, to 'rectify' the eastern frontier – these were not just ends he had in view; for Hitler they were stepping stones to creating a new European order, and beyond that a new world order based on race.

From 1933 to 1938 Hitler laid the foundation for his wars of conquest: he openly defied the disarmament restrictions of Versailles, he remilitarized the Rhineland in 1936, and prepared the way for undermining the independence of Austria and Czechoslovakia through support of local Nazi movements. The ambitions of Japan in Asia and Italy in Africa, and the international division caused by the Spanish Civil War, Italy's conquest of Abyssinia, western suspicion of Soviet ideological policies, and the effect of economic depression, all provided Hitler with opportunities for ruthless exploitation. The credibility of the League of Nations was shattered in the 1930s: it could not check aggression by the adoption of 'procedures' when the European powers and the United States lacked either the will or the means to do so. Such was the case when Japan decided to dominate Manchuria by force.

War in Manchuria, 1931–33: the League, China and Japan

Manchuria played an important role in the great power rivalries of eastern Asia during the first half of the twentieth century. No Chinese central government was able to gain complete control over this great region before the 1950s. From 1900 to 1904 Russia exerted predominant control; after the Russo–Japanese war, Japan secured what were formerly Russian privileges in the south, whilst Russian influence remained in the north. Even when in 1925, after the death of Sun Yat-sen, Chiang Kai-shek successfully asserted control over the greater part of China, the warlord Chang Hsueh-liang was able to maintain his power and local auton-omy in Manchuria. The warlord also tried to lessen Soviet and Japanese influence by regaining control over the railway lines (the Soviet, Chinese Eastern Railway and the Japanese South Manchurian railway) running through the province. The Japanese reacted forcefully. Japanese troops in Manchuria took matters into their own hands. During the night of *18–19 September 1931 the Mukden incident* marked the beginning of the Japanese military occupation of southern Manchuria and fight-ing spread to the north. In September 1932 Japan signed a treaty giving *de jure* recognition to a puppet state, Manchukuo, which had been set up the previous February.

On 21 September 1931 the Chinese appealed to the League under Article II. But at the League Palace of Nations in Geneva, effective action, it was believed, would depend on securing the practical cooperation of the United States against Japan. This the United States would not contemplate. Secretary of State Stimson, in a Note of 7 January 1932, would go no further than enunciating an American doctrine of non-recognition of situations created in defiance of specific treaty engagements.

The conflict in China spread to Shanghai in January 1932. The Chinese now also invoked articles 10 and 15 of the League Covenant, which in the event of a breach being found would bring the sanction article (19) into force (p. 96).

The League was unable to bring about a Japanese withdrawal in compliance with a League resolution and so break the deadlock, and on 21 November 1931 it accepted a Japanese proposal to send to Manchuria a Commission of Enquiry. Lord Lytton headed the commission, which left in February 1932. On 11 March 1932 the League issued a declaration similar to the non-recognition doctrine first formulated by Stimson. But the League did not proceed to sanc-tions. Instead of sanctions, it postponed concrete action by deciding to wait for the report of the Lytton Commission. The Lytton Report, when finally laid before the League on 1 October 1932, found that Japan had no valid reason for invading Manchuria and envisaged as a solution some form of Manchurian autonomy under Chinese sovereignty. To achieve a solution Lytton recommended a League effort at conciliation. While the League attempted to find a way out along these lines, in January the Japanese 1933 extended their aggression against China. In February 1933 at Geneva, meantime, the principles of the Lytton Report were accepted. The only action the League took against Japanese aggression was juridical in that it refused to recognize the State of Manchukuo. In protest, on 27 March 1933 the Japanese announced their intention of leaving the League. Soon after, China, abandoning all hope of practical help, acknowledged defeat. *On 31 May 1933 the Chinese and Japanese concluded the Tangku Truce* which provided for Chinese withdrawal from a demilitarized zone of 5,000 square miles on the Chinese side of the Great Wall. The League had thus failed to preserve one of its members from aggression by another member, which was a great power. Collective security in the face of aggression had proved ineffective.

In the 1930s Japan moved away from her traditional alignment with Britain and began to turn to Nazi Germany. As a further step to gain ascendancy over China, and also in order to warn off the Soviet Union, Japan signed the German-inspired *Anti-Comintern Pact, 25 November 1936* (see below).

Agreement (Anti-Comintern) between Japan and Germany, Berlin, 25 November 1936

The Imperial Government of Japan and the Government of Germany,

In cognizance of the fact that the object of the Communistic International (the so-called Komintern) is the disintegration of, and the commission of violence against, existing States by the exercise of all means at its command;

Believing that the toleration of interference by the Communistic International in the internal affairs of nations not only endangers their internal peace and social welfare, but threatens the general peace of the world;

Desiring to cooperate for defence against communistic disintegration, have agreed as follows:

Article I. The High Contracting States agree that they will mutually keep each other informed concerning the activities of the Communistic International, will confer upon the necessary measures of defence, and will carry out such measures in close cooperation.

Article II. The High Contracting States will jointly invite third States whose internal peace is menaced by the disintegrating work of the Communistic International, to adopt defensive measures in the spirit of the present Agreement or to participate in the present Agreement.

Article III. The Japanese and German texts are each valid as the original text of this

Agreement. The Agreement shall come into force on the day of its signature and shall remain in force for the term of five years. The High Contracting States will, in a reasonable time before the expiration of the said term, come to an understanding upon the further manner of their cooperation . . . .

Supplementary Protocol to the Agreement guarding against the Communistic International

On the occasion of the signature this day of the Agreement guarding against the Communistic International the undersigned plenipotentiaries have agreed as follows:

(a) The competent authorities of both High Contracting States will closely cooperate in the exchange of reports on the activities of the Communistic International and on measures of information and defence against the Communistic International.

(b) The competent authorities of both High Contracting States will, within the framework of the existing law, take stringent measures against those who at home or abroad work on direct or indirect duty of the Communistic International or assist its disintegrating activities.

(c) To facilitate the cooperation of the competent authorities of the two High Contracting States as set out in (a) above, a standing committee shall be established. By this committee the further measures to be adopted in order to counter the disintegrating activities of the Communistic International shall be considered and conferred upon . . . .

Germany's military revival, 1933–36

The coming to power of Hitler as Chancellor on 30 January 1933 marked the beginning of a German policy that destroyed the European territorial settlements of Versailles in the west, the east and central Europe within the space of eight years, and substituted for these settlements the continental hegemony of Germany. The years from 1933 to the spring of 1939 are therefore more notable for the breach of treaties than for the conclusion of new ones. Hitler utilized the Disarmament Conference to further his plan to rearm while others disarmed and, unable to gain the approval of Britain and France, withdrew from the conference and the *League of Nations on 14 October 1933*. He followed this by proclaiming his peaceful intention towards Poland and towards any frontier revisions in the east, and a *German–Polish Treaty was concluded on 26 January 1934* (p. 207) renouncing the use of force for ten years. An Austrian Nazi *coup*, involving the assassination of the Austrian Chancellor Dollfuss on 25 July 1934, failed. Mussolini was still acting as the protector of Austrian independence.

In *January 1935 a plebiscite was held in the Saar which voted to return to Germany*; this was Germany's first, albeit legal, increase of territory since the peace settlements. In the spring of 1935 Hitler risked the open repudiation of the military clauses of the Versailles Treaty, announcing on 9 March 1935 that a German air force was in existence, and a week later on 16 March he declared that Germany would resume complete freedom in establishing offensive forces and announced the introduction of conscription. At the *Stresa Conference, 11–14 April 1935*, Britain, France and Italy condemned Germany's unilateral repudiation of her Versailles obligations, and their resolution to this effect was carried unanimously by the League Council. But three months later Britain agreed to German naval rearmament, though the British government hoped it would be limited by the terms of the *Anglo–German Naval Agreement, 18 June 1935* (p. 208). Meantime *France and the Soviet Union had signed the Pact of Mutual Assistance, 2 May 1935* (p. 194). The Franco–Soviet treaty was ratified by the French Chamber of Deputies almost a year later on 27 February 1936; this gave Hitler the pretext to make a crucial breach in the Versailles military limitations on Germany, and on 7 March 1936 he remilitarized the Rhineland. He justified his action by a *Note on 7 March 1936* denouncing the Locarno pact as incompatible with the Franco–Soviet pact; that denunciation was coupled with proposals for various new peace pacts.

Declaration of Non-Aggression between Germany and Poland, 26 January 1934

The Governments of Germany and Poland consider that the time has arrived to introduce a new phase in the political relations between Germany and Poland by a direct understanding between State and State. They have therefore decided to lay the foundation for the future development of these relations in the present Declaration.

Both Governments base their action on the fact that the maintenance and guarantee of a permanent peace between their countries is an essential condition for the general peace of Europe. They are therefore determined to base their mutual relations on the principles contained in the Pact of Paris of the 27th August 1928, and desire to define more precisely the application of these principles in so far as the relations between Germany and Poland are concerned.

In so doing each of the two Governments declares that the international obligations hitherto undertaken by it towards a third party do not hinder the peaceful development of their mutual relations, do not conflict with the present Declaration

and are not affected by this Declaration. In addition both Governments state that the present Declaration does not extend to questions which, in accordance with international law, are to be regarded exclusively as internal concerns of either of the two States.

Both Governments announce their intention to reach direct understanding on questions of any nature whatsoever concerning their mutual relations. Should any disputes arise between them and agreement thereon not be reached by direct negotiations, they will in each particular case, on the basis of mutual agreement, seek a solution by other peaceful means, without prejudice to the possibility of applying, if necessary, such modes of procedure as are provided for such cases by other agreements in force between them. In no circumstances, however, will they proceed to use force in order to settle such disputes.

The guarantee of peace created by these principles will facilitate for both Governments the great task of finding for political, economic and cultural problems solutions based upon just and equitable adjustment of the interests of both parties.

Both Governments are convinced that the relations between their countries will in this manner fruitfully develop and will lead to the establishment of good neighbourly relations, contributing to the well-being not only of their two countries but also of the other nations of Europe.

The present Declaration shall be ratified and the instruments of ratification shall be exchanged at Warsaw as soon as possible. The Declaration is valid for a period of ten years, reckoned from the date of the exchange of the instruments of ratification.

If it is not denounced by either of the two Governments six months before the expiration of this period, it will continue in force, but can then be denounced by either Government at any time on giving six months' notice.

Done in duplicate in the German and Polish languages.

Berlin, January 26, 1934

For the German Government:
C. Freiherr von Neurath

For the Polish Government:
Józef Lipski

Anglo–German Naval Agreement, 18 June 1935 (Exchange of Notes)

Your Excellency,

1. During the last few days the representatives of the German Government and His Majesty's Government in the United Kingdom have been engaged in conversations, the primary purpose of which has been to prepare the way for the holding of a general conference on the subject of the limitation of naval armaments. I have now much pleasure in notifying your Excellency of the formal acceptance by His Majesty's Government in the United Kingdom of the proposal of the German Government discussed at those conversations that the future strength of the German navy in relation to the aggregate naval strength of the Members of the British Commonwealth of Nations should be in the proportion of 35:100. His Majesty's Government in the United Kingdom regard this proposal as a contribution of the greatest importance to the cause of future naval limitation. They further believe that the agreement which they have now reached with the German Government, and which they regard as a permanent and definite agreement as from today between the two Governments will facilitate the conclusion of a general agreement on the subject of naval limita-

tion between all the naval Powers of the world.

2. His Majesty's Government in the United Kingdom also agreed with the explanations which were furnished by the German representatives in the course of the recent discussions in London as to the method of application of this principle. These explanations may be summarized as follows:

(a) The ratio of 35:100 is to be a permanent relationship, i.e. the total tonnage of the German fleet shall never exceed a percentage of 35 of the aggregate tonnage of the naval forces, as defined by treaty, of the Members of the British Commonwealth of Nations, or, if there should in future be no treaty limitations of this tonnage, a percentage of 35 of the aggregate of the actual tonnages of the Members of the British Commonwealth of Nations.

(b) If any future general treaty of naval limitation should not adopt the method of limitation by agreed ratios between the fleets of different Powers, the German Government will not insist on the incorporation of the ratio mentioned in the preceding sub-paragraph in such future general treaty, provided that the method therein adopted for the future limitation of naval armaments is such as to give Germany full guarantees that this ratio can be maintained.

(c) Germany will adhere to the ratio 35:100 in all circumstances, e.g. the ratio will not be affected by the construction of other Powers. If the general equilibrium of naval armaments, as normally maintained in the past, should be violently upset by any abnormal and exceptional construction by other Powers, the German Government reserve the right to invite His Majesty's Government in the United Kingdom to examine the new situation thus created.

(d) The German Government favour, in the matter of limitation of naval armaments, that system which divides naval vessels into categories, fixing the maximum tonnage and/or armament for vessels in each category, and allocates the tonnage to be allowed to each Power by categories of vessels. Consequently, in principle, and subject to (f) below, the German Government are prepared to apply the 35 per cent ratio to the tonnage of each category of vessel to be maintained, and to make any variation of this ratio in a particular category or categories dependent on the arrangements to this end that may be arrived at in a future general treaty on naval limitation, such arrangements being based on the principle that any increase in one category would be compensated for by a corresponding reduction in others. If no general treaty on naval limitation should be concluded, or if the future general treaty should not contain provision creating limitation by categories, the manner and degree in which the German Government will have the right to vary the 35 per cent ratio in one or more categories will be a matter for settlement by agreement between the German Government and His Majesty's Government in the United Kingdom, in the light of the naval situation then existing.

(e) If, and for so long as, other important naval Powers retain a single category for cruisers and destroyers, Germany shall enjoy the right to have a single category for these two classes of vessel, although she would prefer to see these classes in two categories.

(f) In the matter of submarines, however, Germany, while not exceeding the ratio of 35:100 in respect of total tonnage, shall have the right to possess a submarine tonnage equal to the total submarine tonnage possessed by the Members of the British Commonwealth of Nations. The German Government, however, undertake that, except in the circumstances indicated in the immediately following sentence, Germany's submarine tonnage shall not exceed 45 per cent of the total of that possessed by the Members of the British Commonwealth of Nations. The German Government reserve the right, in the event of a situation arising which in their opinion makes it necessary for Germany to avail herself of her right to a percentage of submarine tonnage exceeding the 45 per cent above mentioned, to give notice to this effect to His Majesty's Government in the United Kingdom, and agree that the matter shall be the subject of friendly discussion before the German Government exercise that right.

(g) Since it is highly improbable that the calculation of the 35 per cent ratio should give for each category of vessels tonnage figures exactly divisible by the maximum individual tonnage permitted for ships in that category, it may be necessary that adjustments should be made in order that Germany shall not be debarred from utilizing her tonnage to the full. It has consequently been agreed that the German Government and His Majesty's Government in the United Kingdom will settle by common accord what adjustments are necessary for this purpose, and it is understood that this procedure shall not result in any substantial or permanent departure from the ratio 35:100 in respect of total strengths.

3. With reference to sub-paragraph (c) of the explanations set out above, I have the honour to inform you that His Majesty's Government in the United Kingdom have taken note of the reservation and recognize the right therein set out, on the understanding that the 35:100 ratio will be maintained in default of agreement to the contrary between the two Governments.

4. I have the honour to request your Excellency to inform me that the German

Government agree that the proposal of the German Government has been correctly set out in the preceding paragraphs of this note.

[On 10 December 1938 Germany for-

mally exercised its option to build submarines up to the strength of the British and Commonwealth number, having in fact already laid down submarines in breach of the 1935 treaty. On 27 April 1939 Hitler denounced the treaty.]

The formation of the Rome–Berlin Axis: Abyssinia, Spain and Austria, 1935–38

Mussolini planned to dominate Abyssinia as a first step on the road to making Italy a world power. The Duce prepared the way by seeking agreement with France. On *7 January 1935* Laval, the French Foreign Minister, and Mussolini signed a *secret agreement in Rome* intended to settle Italian–French colonial disputes and designed to facilitate the united front against Germany. The Stresa Conference in April 1935 was the public affirmation of this unity of purpose. It was shortlived. The Anglo–German Naval Agreement of 18 June 1935 (p. 208) shattered Anglo–French solidarity. The French paid a price: the Franco–Italian understanding of 7 January 1935 was interpreted by Mussolini as giving him practically a free hand in his dealings with Abyssinia as far as France was concerned. After months of tension, *Italy invaded Abyssinia on 3 October 1935*. The League Council on 7 October 1935 in its report condemned Italy for aggression. Member states were now obliged to apply the sanctions of Article 16. But the League followed a 'double policy': economic sanctions were gradually applied, but France and Britain were encouraged to seek a settlement of the Abyssinian–Italian conflict, it being understood that this would involve the loss of some Abyssinian territory. In December 1935 the British Foreign Secretary, Sir Samuel Hoare, and Pierre Laval agreed on a plan to end the conflict, to be put to the belligerents. The Hoare–Laval plan envisaged widespread concessions to Italy at Abyssinia's expense, but it was received with such disapproval by public opinion in Britain that Prime Minister Baldwin had to disavow it. Conciliation efforts were dead. Mussolini proceeded with the conquest of Abyssinia. On 5 May 1936 Addis Ababa fell and Italy proclaimed the annexation of Abyssinia. Meantime sanctions were not effectively applied by the League. A decision on oil sanctions was constantly postponed – the one sanction that might have hurt Italy's military effort – and the Suez Canal was not closed to Italy. Collective security through the adoption of sanctions in the face of aggression had completely failed.

The *de jure* recognition of Italy's conquest of Abyssinia by the most important of the western democracies, Britain, followed some two years later when on 16 November 1938 the British Government brought into force an *Anglo–Italian Agreement, concluded on 16 April 1938* and concerned with Italian intervention in Spain where another war – the civil war – was being fought. In accordance with the agreement, Italy promised to withdraw her troops from Spain, but only when the war was over; then the agreement would come into force.

The civil war had begun in mid-July 1936 with a military revolt led by General Franco against the Spanish government. The Italians provided substantial help for General Franco through 'volunteer' troops, planes and armaments, with the Germans supplying armaments and the fighters and bombers that formed the 'Condor Legion', which fought under German command. Russia sent arms and planes to Republican Spain. An International Bridge of some 18,000, including large volunteer contingents from France, Italy, Germany, Austria and Britain, fought for the Republic. Officially, Britain, France, as well as Italy, Germany and Russia accepted a policy of neutrality and non-intervention in the Spanish civil war by the end of August 1936. During the months when it functioned, the ban was openly flouted by Italy, Germany and the Soviet Union. But two Anglo–Italian agreements were concluded: on 2 January 1937, in the so-called 'Gentleman's Agreement', Italy and Britain disclaimed any desire to see modified the status quo as regards national sovereignty of territories in the Mediterranean region; and an agreement in March 1937 provided for the withdrawal of volunteers and the setting-up of an international blockade to report on breaches of the agreements reached on non-intervention. The policy of non-intervention was a failure. But when 'pirate' submarines, actually Italian submarines aiding Franco, attacked neutral ships including British ones, a conference of Mediterranean and Black Sea Powers met at Nyon, and *on 14 September 1937 signed the Agreement of Nyon* (p. 214) to defend neutral ships by sinking at sight suspicious submarines. The governments effectively defended their own ships and interests. The Italians were Franco's main ally and helped him to win the civil war by the spring of 1939.

March 1938 marked the demise of Austria, a member of the League of Nations, as a result of a German military invasion and a German proclamation of Anschluss or union with Germany. The way to Nazi dominance had been prepared by the *Austro–German Agreement, 11 July 1936* (p. 212). It committed Germany to a promise of respecting Austrian independence, but the Austrian government was gravely weakened by having to admit Nazi sympathizers into the government itself, by opening Austria to Nazi propaganda, and by conceding that Austrian foreign policy would be based on the principle that Austria was a 'German state'.

Austrian independence had rested partly on Italian support. The growing intimacy of Germany and Italy, partly the consequence of Italy's Abyssinian and Spanish policies, undermined Austria's independence. Italian–German cooperation was first set out in the *October Protocol, 1936*, on a number of issues. On 1 November 1936 in a speech at Milan, Mussolini referred to the existence of a Rome–Berlin axis. The treaty ties between Italy and Germany were drawn closer when Italy *on 6 November 1937 joined the Anti-Comintern Pact signed a year earlier by Germany and Japan* (p. 216) and they culminated in an *Italian–German alliance, The*

Pact of Steel, 22 May 1939 (p. 226). Between the signatures by Italy of the Anti-Comintern Pact and the Pact of Steel occurred the loss of Austrian independence, and this time without Italian protest.

Rome Protocol between Italy, Austria and Hungary, 17 March 1934

The Head of the Government of His Majesty the King of Italy,

The Federal Chancellor of the Republic of Austria,

The President of the Royal Council of Ministers of Hungary,

Being anxious to contribute to the maintenance of peace and to the economic reconstruction of Europe on the basis of respect for the independence and rights of every State;

Being convinced that cooperation in this direction between the three Governments is likely to create a genuine basis for wider cooperation with other States;

Undertake, with a view to achieving the above-mentioned purposes:

To confer together on all problems which particularly concern them, and on problems of a general character, with a view to pursuing, in the spirit of the existing treaties of friendship between Italy and Austria, Italy and Hungary and Austria and Hungary, which are based on a recognition of the existence of numerous common interests, a concordant policy directed towards the promotion of effective cooperation between the States of Europe and particularly between Italy, Austria and Hungary.

To this end, the three Governments shall proceed to hold joint consultations whenever at least one of them deems it desirable.

[A further Protocol for the Development of Economic Relations was also concluded on 17 March 1934.]

Additional Protocol, 23 March 1936

[Reaffirmed Protocol of 17 March 1934 and specifically to consult with each other before undertaking any important negotiation on Danubian questions with any other State. A permanent organ composed of foreign ministers of three states was to be established for consultation.]

'Gentlemen's' Agreement between Austria and Germany, 11 July 1936

CONFIDENTIAL!

Convinced that the mutually expressed desire for the re-establishment of normal and friendly relations between the German Reich and the Federal State of Austria requires a series of preliminary stipulations on the part of the two Governments, both Governments approve the following confidential Gentlemen's Agreement:

I. Regulation of the treatment of Reich-Germans in Austria and of Austrian nationals in the Reich

Associations of their nationals in either country shall not be hindered in their activities so long as they comply with the policies established in their bylaws in conformity with the laws in force and do not interfere in the internal political affairs of the other country, nor, in particular, endeavour to influence citizens of the other State by means of propaganda.

II. Mutual cultural relations

All factors decisive for the formation of public opinion of both countries shall serve the purpose of re-establishing normal and friendly relations. With the thought that both countries belong within the German cultural orbit, both parties pledge themselves immediately to renounce any aggressive utilization of radio, motion picture, newspaper, and theatrical facilities against the other party . . . .

III. The Press

Both parties shall influence their respective Press to the end that it refrain from exerting any political influence on conditions in the other country and limit its objective criticism of conditions in the other country to an extent not offensive to public opinion in the other country. This obligation also applies to the *émigré* Press in both countries.

The gradual elimination of prohibitions on the importation of newspapers and printed matter of the other party is envisaged by both parties, in relation to the gradual *détente* in mutual relations aimed at in this Agreement. Newspapers admitted shall, in any criticism of the internal political situation in the other country, adhere particularly strictly to the principle enunciated in paragraph I . . . .

IV. Emigré problems

Both parties agree in their desire to contribute by reciprocal concessions to the speediest possible satisfactory solution of the problem of the Austrian National Socialist exiles in the Reich.

The Austrian Government will proceed to the examination of this problem as soon as possible and will announce the result to a joint commission to be composed of representatives of the competent Ministries so that an agreement may be put into effect.

V. National insignia and national anthems

Each of the two Governments declares that within the scope of existing laws, it will place the nationals of the other party on an equal footing with nationals of third States in regard to the display of the national insignia of their country.

The singing of national anthems shall – in addition to official occasions – be permitted to nationals of the other party at closed meetings attended by these nationals exclusively.

VI. Economic relations

The Government of the German Reich, putting aside considerations of Party policy, is prepared to open the way for normal economic relations between the German Reich and Austria, and this readiness extends to the re-establishment of routine border crossing [*der Kleine Grenzverkehr*]. Discrimination against persons and areas, if not based upon purely economic considerations will not be undertaken.

VII. Tourist traffic

The restrictions on tourist traffic imposed by both sides because of the tension which had arisen between the two States shall be lifted. This understanding shall not affect restrictions based on the legislation of both countries for the protection of foreign exchange . . . .

VIII. Foreign policy

The Austrian Government declares that it is prepared to conduct its foreign policy in the light of the peaceful endeavours of the

German Government's foreign policy. It is agreed that the two Governments will from time to time enter into an exchange of views on the problems of foreign policy affecting both of them. The Rome Protocols of 1934 and the Supplementary Protocols of 1936, as well as the position of Austria with regard to Italy and Hungary as parties to these Protocols, are not affected thereby.

enjoy the personal confidence of the Federal Chancellor and whose selection he reserves to himself. It is agreed, in this connection, that persons trusted by the Federal Chancellor shall be charged with the task of arranging, in accordance with a plan worked out with the Federal Chancellor, for the internal pacification of the National Opposition and for its participation in the shaping of the political will in Austria.

IX. AUSTRIAN DECLARATION ON DOMESTIC POLICY IN RELATION TO THIS *MODUS VIVENDI*

The Federal Chancellor declares that he is prepared:

(a) To grant a far-reaching political amnesty, from which persons who have committed serious public crimes shall be excluded.

Also covered by this amnesty shall be persons who have not yet been sentenced by judicial decree or penalized by administrative process.

These provisions shall also be duly applied to *émigrés*.

(b) For the purpose of promoting a real pacification, to appoint at the appropriate moment, contemplated for the near future, representatives of the so-called 'National Opposition in Austria' to participate in political responsibility; they shall be men who

X. PROCEDURE FOR OBJECTIONS AND COMPLAINTS

For the handling of objections and complaints which may arise in connection with the above Gentlemen's Agreement, as well as in order to guarantee a progressive *détente* within the framework of the preceding agreements, there shall be established a joint commission composed of three representatives of the Foreign Ministry of each country. Its task shall be to discuss at regular meetings the operation of the Agreement as well as any supplements thereto which may be required.

SCHUSCHNIGG
Federal Chancellor

VIENNA, 11 July 1936

Nyon Agreement between Britain, Bulgaria, Egypt, France, Greece, Rumania, Turkey, U.S.S.R. and Yugoslavia, Nyon, 14 September 1937

Whereas arising out of the Spanish conflict attacks have been repeatedly committed in the Mediterranean by submarines against merchant ships not belonging to either of the conflicting Spanish parties; and

Whereas these attacks are violations of the rules of international law referred to in Part IV of the Treaty of London of April

22, 1930 with regard to the sinking of merchant ships and constitute acts contrary to the most elementary dictates of humanity, which should be justly treated as acts of piracy; and

Whereas without in any way admitting the right of either party to the conflict in Spain to exercise belligerent rights or to interfere with merchant ships on the high seas even if the laws of warfare at sea are observed and without prejudice to the right of any participating Power to take such action as may be proper to protect its merchant shipping from any kind of interference on the high seas or to the possibility of further collective measures being agreed upon subsequently, it is necessary in the first place to agree upon certain special collective measures against piratical acts by submarines:

In view thereof the undersigned, being authorized to this effect by their respective Governments, have met in conference at Nyon between the 9th and the 14th September 1937, and have agreed upon the following provisions which shall enter immediately into force:

I. The participating Powers will instruct their naval forces to take the action indicated in paragraphs II and III below with a view to the protection of all merchant ships not belonging to either of the conflicting Spanish parties.

II. Any submarine which attacks such a ship in a manner contrary to the rules of international law referred to in the International Treaty for the Limitation and Reduction of Naval Armaments signed in London on April 22, 1930, and confirmed in the Protocol signed in London on November 6, 1936, shall be counterattacked and, if possible, destroyed.

III. The instruction mentioned in the preceding paragraph shall extend to any submarine encountered in the vicinity of a position where a ship not belonging to either of the conflicting Spanish parties has recently been attacked in violation of the rules referred to in the preceding paragraph in circumstances which give valid grounds for the belief that the submarine was guilty of the attack.

IV. In order to facilitate the putting into force of the above arrangements in a practical manner, the participating Powers have agreed upon the following arrangements:

1. In the western Mediterranean and in the Malta Channel, with the exception of the Tyrrhenean Sea, which may form the subject of special arrangements, the British and French fleets will operate both on the high seas and in the territorial waters of the participating Powers, in accordance with the division of the area agreed upon between the two Governments.

2. In the eastern Mediterranean:

(a) Each of the participating Powers will operate in its own territorial waters;

(b) On the high seas with the exception of the Adriatic Sea, the British and French fleets will operate up to the entrance to the Dardanelles, in those areas where there is reason to apprehend danger to shipping in accordance with the division of the area agreed upon between the two Governments. The other participating Governments possessing a sea border on the Mediterranean, undertake, within the limit of their resources, to furnish these fleets any assistance that may be asked for; in particular, they will permit them to take action in their territorial waters and to use such of their ports as they shall indicate.

3. It is further understood that the limits of the zones referred to in sub-paragraphs 1 and 2 above, and their allocation shall be subject at any time to revision by the participating Powers in order to take account of any change in the situation.

V. The participating Powers agree that, in order to simplify the operation of the above-mentioned measures, they will for their part restrict the use of their submarines in the Mediterranean in the following manner:

(a) Except as stated in (b) and (c) below, no submarine will be sent to sea within the Mediterranean.

(b) Submarines may proceed on passage after notification to the other participating Powers, provided that they proceed on the surface and are accompanied by a surface ship.

(c) Each participating Power reserves for purposes of exercises certain areas defined in Annex I hereto in which its submarines are exempt from the restrictions mentioned in (a) or (b).

The participating Powers further undertake not to allow the presence in their respective territorial waters of any foreign submarines except in case of urgent distress, or where the conditions prescribed in sub-paragraph (b) above are fulfilled.

VI. The participating Powers also agree that, in order to simplify the problem involved in carrying out the measures above described, they may severally advise their merchant shipping to follow certain main routes in the Mediterranean agreed upon between them and defined in Annex II hereto.

VII. Nothing in the present Agreement restricts the right of any participating Power to send its surface vessels to any part of the Mediterranean . . . .

Protocol concluded by Italy, Germany and Japan (Anti-Comintern Pact), Rome, 6 November 1937

The Italian Government, the Government of the German Reich, and the Imperial Government of Japan,

Considering that the Communist International continues constantly to imperil the civilized world in the Occident and Orient, disturbing and destroying peace and order,

Considering that only close collaboration looking to the maintenance of peace and order can limit and remove that peril,

Considering that Italy – who with the advent of the Fascist régime has with inflexible determination combated that peril and rid her territory of the Communist International – has decided to align herself against the common enemy along with Germany and Japan, who for their part are animated by like determination to defend themselves against the Communist International,

Have, in conformity with Article II of the Agreement against the Communist International concluded at Berlin on November 25, 1936, by Germany and Japan, agreed upon the following:

Article 1. Italy becomes a party to the Agreement against the Communist International and to the Supplementary Protocol concluded on November 25, 1936, between Germany and Japan, the text of which is included in the Annex to the present Protocol.

Article 2. The three Powers signatory to the present Protocol agree that Italy will be considered as an original signatory to the Agreement and Supplementary Protocol mentioned in the preceding Article, the signing of the present Protocol being equivalent to the signature of the original text of the aforesaid Agreement and Supplementary Protocol.

Article 3. The present Protocol shall constitute an integral part of the above-mentioned Agreement and Supplementary Protocol.

Article 4. The present Protocol is drawn up in Italian, Japanese, and German, each text being considered authentic. It shall enter into effect on the date of signature.

In testimony whereof, etc. . . . .

[signed]   CIANO,   VON   RIBBENTROP, HOTTA.

VIII · From peace to world war in Europe and Asia, 1937–41

During the short space of eighteen months, from March 1938 to September 1939, Hitler plunged Europe from one crisis to another, each time 'breaking his word' that he had made his last territorial demand. When each crisis is examined in isolation there seems some merit in Germany's arguments: why should the Austrians of the Sudeten German-speaking population of Czechoslovakia be denied the right of self-determination; the 'rectification' of Germany's eastern frontier was an objective followed by the 'European' Stresemann in the 1920s before Hitler made his demands concerning the Polish corridor and Danzig; was it not time to remove the last vestiges of discrimination against Germany imposed by the Versailles *Diktat*? Reasonable western statesmen would surely prefer diplomatic adjustments, even some sacrifice on the part of the 'artificially' created post-Versailles states, to world war.

To begin with, Neville Chamberlain, leading the French Daladier government, was prepared to follow the path of apparent reason in preference to the human and material destruction that another world war would entail. But the cumulative impact of Hitler's aggressions of 1938–39 and the realization that he was launched on a policy of aggression without foreseeable 'diplomatic' limits led to a fundamental change of British policy in 1939 which carried France with it. The door to diplomatic agreements for a settlement of all European questions would not be closed; Hitler should be offered all possible enticements to choose diplomacy rather than force; he would hopefully also be deterred by an alliance against Germany; but if neither inducements nor deterrents could influence him then Britain was prepared for war rather than allow Hitler the hegemony of continental Europe. But where would the Soviet Union fit into this new pattern of diplomacy? No one in Britain or Germany knew for certain until Stalin made his choice in August 1939.

In Asia, Japan had resumed fighting in China in July 1937 and an 'undeclared war' began. The sympathy of the western democracies was with China, but the more immediate threat of Germany in Europe decided France and Britain to preserve a policy of limiting help to China to an extent that would allow peaceful relations to be preserved with Japan. The outbreak of war in Europe only strengthened this resolve. After the fall of France in June 1940, Britain agreed to the closure of the Burma supply route to China, but reopened it in October 1940. From then on, British policy followed in the wake of American policy in the Pacific. United States resistance to Japanese expansion in South-east Asia finally led to the Japanese decision to start war advantageously with the surprise attack on Pearl Harbor, 7 December 1941. For the USSR, fighting a war for survival since June 1941, the absolute need to avoid having to face a second front in Asia as well overrode all other considerations; and so it remained loyal to the Neutrality Pact it had concluded with Japan in April 1941.

Europe, 1938–39

GERMAN EXPANSION

The German proclamation of the *Austrian Anschluss on 13 March 1938* for the first time during the Nazi era extended German sovereignty by the threat and use of force. When the opportunity was offered, Hitler assumed control over the whole of Austria. With similar opportunism Hitler broke up Czechoslovakia in October 1938 by annexing the so-called mainly German-speaking Sudeten areas. In the following March he partitioned what was left of the country and created an 'independent' puppet state of Slovakia.

The first transfer of Czech territory in October 1938 was given a semblance of international sanction at the *Four Power Conference at Munich, 29–30 September 1938*. Germany, Italy, France and Britain participated in this 'settlement'. The Czechoslovak government was not represented and only acquiesced in the decisions of Munich in the face of the German threat of force, and since without the help of her western ally, France, military resistance would have been hopeless. The extent of Soviet help too would have been uncertain and in any case probably ineffective. (See p. 159 for the terms of the Franco–Czech alliance and p. 196 for the Franco–Soviet and Czech-Soviet treaties of 1935.) A number of documents were signed at Munich: *the Munich Four Power Agreement, 29–30 September 1938* (p. 220), which provided for the occupation of the Sudetenland in stages from 1–10 October 1938; a *conditional guarantee* for the remainder of Czechoslovakia after Polish and Hungarian claims had been settled; and an *Anglo-German Declaration* (p. 221) of pacific intent. Not to be outdone the Daladier government concluded a *Franco-German Agreement on 6 December 1938*. It recognized mutual frontiers and thus the Germans appeared to abandon claims to Alsace-Lorraine; it promised consultations between France and Germany on questions of mutual interest, while their 'relations' with other states were not affected. The use of the word 'relations' in place of existing 'alliances' seemed to point to a French desire to play down the alliances without abandoning them.

The validity of the Four Power Agreement was challenged by the Czechoslovak government, in exile during the Second World War, on the grounds that Czech assent to the occupation had been obtained under duress. Of the original signatories which later declared the treaty to be invalid, the French National Committee did so in 1942 and the French Provisional Government reaffirmed this in 1944, and post-fascist Italy declared the treaty invalid from the beginning in 1944. The wartime British government would not repudiate the legality of the original Munich Agreements but only bound itself in 1942 to regard the treaty as no longer in force due to the Germans having broken it. The German government in 1997 laid the ghost of Munich finally to rest (p. 447). The Soviet Union, not a signatory of Munich, was the first great power to declare to the Czechoslovak government that it had not recognized the Munich settlement at the time or since.

The guarantee given at Munich never became operative as the British and French governments decided that they would only honour it in the event of Hitler's aggression if Italy also did so. Despite a visit by Chamberlain to Mussolini in January 1939 there was not the slightest chance that Italy would side against her Axis partner. When a political crisis in autonomous Slovakia gave Hitler his next opportunity, he ordered German troops on 15 March 1939 to occupy the remnants of the Czech state, and set up the Protectorate of Bohemia and Moravia on 16 March 1939. *On 23 March 1939 a German–Slovak treaty* was signed which described Slovakia as an independent state but under the protection of Germany, with closely subservient Slovak policies in matters of the army, foreign policy and economic and financial affairs; Germany was given the right to station troops in Slovakia and undertook to protect the independence of its satellite.

Poland and Hungary also benefited from the breakup of Czechoslovakia (October 1938–March 1939). Poland secured the territory of Teschen, 1–2 October 1938, after the Czechoslovak government accepted a peremptory demand for its cession. Hungary, by the *First Vienna Award, 2 November 1938*, an arbitral judgement given by Germany and Italy, re-acquired the ethnic strip of Magyar territory along the Hungarian borders with Slovakia and Ruthenia, which left the rest of Slovakia and Ruthenia autonomous. *Hungary* formally joined the Axis powers when adhering *on 26 February 1939 to the Anti-Comintern Pact*, and two weeks later on 14–15 March 1939, with German encouragement, the Hungarians annexed Ruthenia (also known as 'Carpatho-Ukraine') at the same time as the Wehrmacht marched into Czechoslovakia.

Hitler made his first aggressive move in the Baltic the day after entering

Czechoslovakia, by sending an ultimatum to Lithuania on 16 March 1939 demanding the cession of the Memelland. Lithuania accepted on 19 March 1939. Hitler entered Memel from the sea on 23 March 1939 when the treaty of cession was formally signed. His next objective was the Free City of Danzig together with an extra-territorial corridor linking East Prussia to the rest of Germany. Mussolini now sprang his surprise by *annexing Albania to Italy on 7 April 1939*.

The Munich Agreement between Germany, Britain, Italy and France, Munich, 29 September 1938

Germany, the United Kingdom, France and Italy, taking into consideration the agreement which has been already reached in principle for the cession to Germany of the Sudeten German territory, have agreed on the following terms and conditions governing the said cession and the measures consequent thereon, and by this Agreement they each hold themselves responsible for the steps necessary to secure its fulfilment:

1. The evacuation will begin on 1st October.

2. The United Kingdom, France and Italy agree that the evacuation of the territory shall be completed by 10th October without any existing installations having been destroyed, and that the Czechoslovak Government will be held responsible for carrying out the evacuation without damage to the said installations.

3. The conditions governing the evacuation will be laid down in detail by an international commission composed of representatives of Germany, the United Kingdom, France, Italy and Czechoslovakia.

4. The occupation by stages of the predominantly German territory by German troops will begin on 1st October. The four territories marked on the attached map will be occupied by German troops in the following order: the territory marked No. I on the 1st and 2nd October; the territory marked No. II on the 2nd and 3rd October; the territory marked No. III on the 3rd, 4th and 5th October; the territory marked No. IV on the 6th and 7th October. The remaining territory of preponderatingly German character will be ascertained by the aforesaid international commission forthwith and be occupied by German troops by the 10th October.

5. The international commission referred to in paragraph 3 will determine the territories in which a plebiscite is to be held. These territories will be occupied by international bodies until the plebiscite has been completed. The same commission will fix the conditions in which the plebiscite is to be held, taking as a basis the conditions of the Saar plebiscite. The commission will also fix a date, not later than the end of November, on which the plebiscite will be held.

6. The final determination of the frontier will be carried out by the international commission. This commission will also be entitled to recommend to the four Powers – Germany, the United Kingdom, France and Italy – in certain exceptional cases minor modifications in the strictly ethnographical determination of the zones which are to be transferred without plebiscite.

7. There will be a right of option into and out of the transferred territories, the option to be exercised within six months from the date of this Agreement. A German–Czechoslovak commission shall determine the details of the option, consider

ways of facilitating the transfer of population and settle questions of principle arising out of the said transfer.

8. The Czech Government will, within a period of four weeks from the date of this Agreement, release from their military and police forces any Sudeten Germans who may wish to be released, and the Czech Government will, within the same period, release Sudeten German prisoners who are serving terms of imprisonment for political offences.

Munich, September 29, 1938

Annex

His Majesty's Government in the United Kingdom and the French Government have entered into the above agreement on the basis that they stand by the offer, contained in paragraph 6 of the Anglo-French proposals of 19th September, relating to an international guarantee of the new boundaries of the Czech State against unprovoked aggression.

When the question of the Polish and Hungarian minorities in Czechoslovakia has been settled, Germany and Italy, for their part, will give a guarantee to Czechoslovakia.

Munich, September 29, 1938

Declaration

The heads of the Governments of the four Powers declare that the problems of the Polish and Hungarian minorities in Czechoslovakia, if not settled within three months by agreement between the respective Governments, shall form the subject of another meeting of the heads of the Governments of the four Powers here present.

Munich, September 29, 1938

Supplementary Declaration

All questions which may arise out of the transfer of the territory shall be considered as coming within the terms of reference of the international commission.

Munich, September 29, 1938

The four heads of Governments here present agree that the international commission provided for in the Agreement signed by them today shall consist of the Secretary of State in the German Foreign Office, the British, French and Italian Ambassadors accredited in Berlin, and a representative to be nominated by the Government of Czechoslovakia.

Munich, September 29, 1938

Anglo-German Declaration, Munich, 30 September 1938

We, the German Führer and Chancellor and the British Prime Minister, have had a further meeting today and are agreed in recognizing that the question of Anglo-German relations is of the first importance for the two countries and for Europe.

We regard the agreement signed last night and the Anglo-German Naval Agreement as symbolic of the desire of our two peoples never to go to war with one another again.

We are resolved that the method of consultation shall be the method adopted to deal with any other questions that may concern our two countries, and we are determined to continue our efforts to remove possible sources of difference and thus to contribute to assure the peace of Europe.

(Signed) A. HITLER
(Signed) NEVILLE CHAMBERLAIN

THE ANGLO-FRENCH RESPONSE

These sudden violent changes created great uncertainty throughout Europe. Roumania was already more in the German than western orbit, having signed a number of economic agreements with Germany in December 1938 and on 23 March 1939; but Roumania also felt her territorial integrity threatened by Hungary, Bulgaria and Germany during the crisis of mid-March 1939. Poland was threatened by a Slovakia under German control and by Hitler's ambitions in the Baltic. Against the background of general diplomatic confusion, and fearing a complete collapse of central and eastern Europe to Nazi aggression, there began the British attempt, in association with France, to call a halt to further German territorial expansion by force. On *31 March 1939 Chamberlain announced a provisional Anglo-French guarantee of Poland* (p. 223). After Italy seized Albania on 7 April 1939, this guarantee was extended to the Balkans when on *13 April 1939 an Anglo-French guarantee of Greece and Rumania was announced*. Turkey was brought into the Anglo-French alignment when on 12 May 1939 the British and Turkish governments issued a declaration that they would cooperate in the event of aggression leading to war in the Mediterranean; the two governments also said that they would conclude a long-term treaty (for the Anglo-French-Turkish Treaty, 19 October 1939, see p. 232). The long drawn-out diplomatic exchanges and negotiations between France, Britain and the Soviet Union from March 1939 to August 1939 led to no result.

The refusal of the Polish government to give in to the substance of German demands and Britain's determination to stand by Poland led to a more definitive alliance, the *Anglo-Polish Agreement of Mutual Assistance, 25 August 1939* (p. 223).

THE AXIS

Germany bound Italy more closely to its side when Hitler finally persuaded Mussolini to conclude a military alliance, the *Pact of Steel, 22 May 1939* (p. 226), but in a secret memorandum to Hitler a week later Mussolini stated that Italy would not be ready for war until after the end of 1942. On the eve of Germany's attack on Poland, on 25 August 1939, Mussolini replied to Hitler that he could not take military action before the end of 1942 unless sufficient arms and raw materials were provided for Italy. Hitler preferred to do without immediate Italian military help when he attacked Poland on 1 September 1939, having already purchased Soviet acquiescence. Secretly the Soviet Union negotiated with Germany in Berlin whilst simultaneously negotiating with France and Britain in Moscow. The *German–Soviet Non-Aggression Pact was signed on 23 August 1939* (p. 229), and a secret protocol was signed the same day which outlined the German and Soviet spheres of interests and paved the way for Soviet annexations of territory in the Baltic and central Europe. The German invasion of Poland on 1 September 1939 was followed on 3 September 1939 by British and French ultimatums and declarations of war.

Statement by Chamberlain in the House of Commons concerning the guarantee to Poland, 31 March 1939

The Prime Minister [Mr Chamberlain]: The Right Hon. Gentleman the Leader of the Opposition asked me this morning whether I could make a statement as to the European situation. As I said this morning, His Majesty's Government have no official confirmation of the rumours of any projected attack on Poland and they must not, therefore, be taken as accepting them as true.

I am glad to take this opportunity of stating again the general policy of His Majesty's Government. They have constantly advocated the adjustment, by way of free negotiation between the parties concerned, of any differences that may arise between them. They consider that this is the natural and proper course where differences exist. In their opinion there should be no question incapable of solution by peaceful means, and they would see no justification for the substitution of force or threats of force for the method of negotiation.

As the House is aware, certain consultations are now proceeding with other Governments. In order to make perfectly clear the position of His Majesty's Government in the meantime before those consultations are concluded, I now have to inform the House that during that period, in the event of any action which clearly threatened Polish independence, and which the Polish Government accordingly considered it vital to resist with their national forces, His Majesty's Government would feel themselves bound at once to lend the Polish Government all support in their power. They have given the Polish Government an assurance to this effect.

I may add that the French Government have authorized me to make it plain that they stand in the same position in this matter as do His Majesty's Government.

Agreement of Mutual Assistance between Britain and Poland, London, 25 August 1939

The Government of the United Kingdom of Great Britain and Northern Ireland and the Polish Government:

Desiring to place on a permanent basis the collaboration between their respective countries resulting from the assurances of mutual assistance of a defensive character which they have already exchanged;

Have resolved to conclude an Agreement for that purpose and have . . . agreed on the following provisions:

Article 1. Should one of the Contracting Parties become engaged in hostilities with a European Power in consequence of aggression by the latter against that Contracting Party, the other Contracting Party will at once give the Contracting Party engaged in hostilities all the support and assistance in its power.

Article 2. 1. The provisions of Article I will also apply in the event of any action by a European Power which clearly threatened, directly or indirectly, the independence of one of the Contracting Parties, and was of such a nature that the party in question considered it vital to resist it with its armed forces.

2. Should one of the Contracting Parties become engaged in hostilities with a European Power in consequence of action by that Power which threatened the independence or neutrality of another European State in such a way as to constitute a clear menace to the security of that Contracting

Party, the provisions of Article 1 will apply, without prejudice, however, to the rights of the other European State concerned.

Article 3. Should a European Power attempt to undermine the independence of one of the Contracting Parties by processes of economic penetration or in any other way, the Contracting Parties will support each other in resistance to such attempts. Should the European Power concerned thereupon embark on hostilities against one of the Contracting Parties, the provisions of Article 1 will apply.

Article 4. The methods of applying the undertakings of mutual assistance provided for by the present Agreement are established between the competent naval, military and air authorities of the Contracting Parties.

Article 5. Without prejudice to the foregoing undertakings of the Contracting Parties to give each other mutual support and assistance immediately on the outbreak of hostilities, they will exchange complete and speedy information concerning any development which might threaten their independence and, in particular, concerning any development which threatened to call the said undertakings into operation.

Article 6. 1. The Contracting Parties will communicate to each other the terms of any undertakings of assistance against aggression which they have already given or may in future give to other States.

2. Should either of the Contracting Parties intend to give such an undertaking after the coming into force of the present Agreement, the other Contracting Party shall, in order to ensure the proper functioning of the Agreement, be informed thereof.

3. Any new undertaking which the Contracting Parties may enter into in future shall neither limit their obligations under the present Agreement nor indirectly create new obligations between the Contracting Party not participating in these undertakings and the third State concerned.

Article 7. Should the Contracting Parties be engaged in hostilities in consequence of the application of the present Agreement, they will not conclude an armistice or treaty of peace except by mutual agreement.

Article 8.1. The present Agreement shall remain in force for a period of five years.

2. Unless denounced six months before the expiry of this period it shall continue in force, each Contracting Party having thereafter the right to denounce it at any time by giving six months' notice to that effect.

3. The present Agreement shall come into force on signature.

In faith whereof the above-named plenipotentiaries have signed the present Agreement and have affixed thereto their seals.

Done in English in duplicate at London, the 25th August 1939. A Polish text shall subsequently be agreed upon between the Contracting Parties and both texts will then be authentic.

(L.S.)   HALIFAX
(L.S.)   EDWARD RACZYŃSKI

Secret Protocol

The Polish Government and the Government of the United Kingdom of Great Britain and Northern Ireland are agreed upon the following interpretation of the Agreement of Mutual Assistance signed this day as alone authentic and binding:

1. (a) By the expression 'a European Power' employed in the Agreement is to be understood Germany.

(b) In the event of action within the meaning of Articles 1 or 2 of the Agreement by a European Power other than Germany, the Contracting Parties will consult together on the measures to be taken in common.

2. (a) The two Governments will from time to time determine by mutual agreement the hypothetical cases of action by Germany coming within the ambit of Article 2 of the Agreement.

(b) Until such time as the two Governments have agreed to modify the following provisions of this paragraph, they will consider: that the case contemplated by paragraph 1 of Article 2 of the Agreement is that of the Free City of Danzig; and that the cases contemplated by paragraph 2 of Article 2 are Belgium, Holland, Lithuania.

(c) Latvia and Estonia shall be regarded by the two Governments as included in the list of countries contemplated by paragraph 2 of Article 2 from the moment that an undertaking of mutual assistance between the United Kingdom and a third State covering those two countries enters into force.

(d) As regards Roumania, the Government of the United Kingdom refers to the guarantee which it has given to that country; and the Polish Government refers to the reciprocal undertakings of the Roumano–Polish alliance which Poland has never regarded as incompatible with her traditional friendship for Hungary.

3. The undertaking mentioned in Article 6 of the Agreement, should they be entered into by one of the Contracting Parties with a third State, would of necessity be so framed that their execution should at no time prejudice either the sovereignty or territorial inviolability of the other Contracting Party.

4. The present Protocol constitutes an integral part of the Agreement signed this day, the scope of which it does not exceed.

In faith whereof the undersigned, being duly authorized, have signed the present Protocol.

Done in English in duplicate, at London, the 25th August 1939. A Polish text will subsequently be agreed upon between the Contracting Parties and both texts will then be authentic.

(Signed)   HALIFAX
(Signed)   EDWARD RACZYŃSKI

Protocol of Mutual Assistance between Poland and France, 4 September 1939

Article 1. The Polish Government and the French Government, desiring to assure the full efficacy of the Polish–French Alliance, and having especially in view the present situation of the League of Nations, agree to confirm that their mutual obligations of assistance in the event of aggression by a third Power continue to be founded on the Agreements of Alliance in force.

At the same time they declare that henceforth they interpret the said Agreements as embodying the following obligations: The undertaking of the two Contracting Parties mutually to render all aid and assistance in their power at once and from the outbreak of hostilities between one of the Contracting Parties and a European Power in consequence of that Power's aggression against the said Contracting Party, equally applies to the case of any action by a European Power which manifestly directly or indirectly threatens the independence of one of the Contracting Parties, and is of such a nature that the Party in question considers it vital to resist that aggression with its armed forces.

Should one of the Contracting Parties become engaged in hostilities with a European Power in consequence of action by that Power which threatened the independence or neutrality of another European State in such a way as to constitute a clear menace to the security of that Contracting Party, the provisions of Article 1 will apply, without prejudice, however, to the rights of the other European State concerned.

Article 2. The methods of applying the undertakings of mutual assistance provided for by the present Agreement are established between the competent military, naval, and air authorities of the Contracting Parties.

Article 3. 1. The Contracting Parties will

communicate to each other the terms of any undertakings of assistance against aggression which they have already given or may in the future give to other States.

2. Should either of the Contracting Parties intend to give such an undertaking after the coming into force of the present Agreement, the other Contracting Party shall, in order to ensure proper functioning of the Agreement, be informed thereof.

3. Any new undertaking which the Contracting Parties may enter into in the future shall neither limit their obligations under the present Agreement nor indirectly create new obligations between the Contracting Party not participating in those undertakings and the third State concerned.

Article 4. Should the Contracting Parties be engaged in hostilities in consequence of the application of the present Agreement, they will not conclude an armistice or treaty of peace except by mutual agreement.

The present Protocol, constituting an integral part of the Polish-French Agreements of 1921 and 1925, shall remain in force as long as the said Agreements.

Alliance between Germany and Italy (Pact of Steel), 22 May 1939

The German Chancellor and His Majesty the King of Italy and Albania, Emperor of Ethiopia, deem that the time has come to strengthen the close relationship of friendship and homogeneity, existing between National Socialist Germany and Fascist Italy, by a solemn pact.

Now that a safe bridge for mutual aid and assistance has been established by the common frontier between Germany and Italy fixed for all time, both Governments reaffirm the policy, the principles and objectives of which have already been agreed upon by them, and which has proved successful, both for promoting the interests of the two countries and also for safeguarding peace in Europe.

Firmly united by the inner affinity between their ideologies and the comprehensive solidarity of their interests, the German and Italian nations are resolved in future also to act side by side and with united forces to secure their living space and to maintain peace.

Following this path, marked out for them by history, Germany and Italy intend, in the midst of a world of unrest and disintegration, to serve the task of safeguarding the foundations of European civilization.

In order to lay down these principles in a pact there have been appointed plenipotentiaries ... and they have agreed on the following terms.

Article 1. The High Contracting Parties will remain in continuous contact with each other in order to reach an understanding on all questions affecting their common interests or the general European situation.

Article II. Should the common interests of the High Contracting Parties be endangered by international events of any kind whatsoever, they will immediately enter into consultations on the measures to be taken for the protection of these interests.

Should the security or other vital interests of one of the High Contracting Parties be threatened from without, the other High Contracting Party will afford the threatened party full political and diplomatic support in order to remove this threat.

Article III. If, contrary to the wishes and hopes of the High Contracting Parties, it should happen that one of them became involved in warlike complications with another Power or Powers, the other High Contracting Party would immediately come to its assistance as an ally and support it with all its military forces on land, at sea and in the air.

Article IV. In order to ensure in specific cases the speedy execution of the obligations of alliance undertaken under Article III, the Governments of the two High Contracting Parties will further intensify their collaboration in the military field, and in the field of war economy.

In the same way the two Governments will remain in continuous consultation also on other measures necessary for the practical execution of the provisions of this Pact.

For the purposes indicated in paragraphs 1 and 2 above, the two Governments will set up commissions which will be under the direction of the two Foreign Ministers.

Article V. The High Contracting Parties undertake even now that, in the event of war waged jointly, they will conclude an armistice and peace only in full agreement with each other.

Article VI. The two High Contracting Parties are aware of the significance that attaches to their common relations with Powers friendly to them. They are resolved to maintain these relations in the future also and together to shape them in accordance with the common interests which form the bonds between them and these Powers.

Article VII. This Pact shall enter into force immediately upon signature. The two High Contracting Parties are agreed in laying down that its first term of validity shall be for ten years. In good time before the expiry of this period, they will reach agreement on the extension of the validity of the Pact.

In witness whereof the plenipotentiaries have signed this Pact and affixed thereto their seals.

Done in duplicate in the German and the Italian languages, both texts being equally authoritative.

Berlin, May 22, 1939, in the XVIIth year of the Fascist Era.

JOACHIM V. RIBBENTROP
GALEAZZO CIANO

Trade Agreement between the Soviet Union and Germany, 19 August 1939

[The contents of this agreement can be derived from the German Foreign Ministry Memorandum of 29 August 1939 below.]

Memorandum

The German–Soviet Trade Agreement concluded on August 19 covers the following:

1. Germany grants the Soviet Union a merchandise credit of 200 million Reichsmarks. The financing will be done by the German Golddiskontbank . . . [at an actual rate of interest of 4½ per cent].

2. The credit will be used to finance Soviet orders in Germany. The Soviet Union will make use of it to order the industrial products listed in schedule A of the Agreement. They consist of machinery and industrial installations. Machine tools up to the very largest dimensions form a considerable part of the deliveries. And armaments in the broader sense (such as optical supplies, armour plate and the like) will, subject to examination of every single item, be supplied in smaller proportion.

3. The credit will be liquidated by Soviet raw materials, which will be selected by agreement between the two Governments. The annual interest will likewise be paid from the proceeds of Soviet merchandise, that is, from the special accounts kept in Berlin.

4. In order that we might secure an immediate benefit from the Credit Agreement, it was made a condition from the beginning that the Soviet Union bind itself to the delivery, starting immediately, of certain raw materials as current business. It was possible so to arrange these raw-material commitments of the Russians that our wishes were largely met. The Russian commitments of raw materials are contained in schedule C. They amount to 180 million Reichsmarks: half to be delivered in each of the first and second years following the conclusion of the Agreement. It is a question, in particular, of lumber, cotton, feed grain, oil cake, phosphate, platinum, raw furs, petroleum, and other goods which for us have a more or less gold value.

5. Since these Soviet deliveries made as current business are to be compensated by German counterdeliveries, certain German promises of delivery had to be made to the Russians. The German industrial products to be supplied in current business as counterdeliveries for Russian raw materials are listed in schedule B. This schedule totals 120 million Reichsmarks and comprises substantially the same categories of merchandise as schedule A.

6. From the welter of difficult questions of detail which arose during the negotiations, the following might also be mentioned: guaranteeing of the rate of exchange of the Reichsmark. The complicated arrangement arrived at appears in the Confidential Protocol signed on August 26 of this year. In order not to jeopardize the conclusion of the Agreement on August 19 of this year, the question was laid aside and settled afterwards. The questions of the liquidation of the old credits, the shipping clause, an emergency clause for the event of inability to deliver of either party, the arbitration procedure, the price clause, etc., were settled satisfactorily despite the pressure of time.

7. The Agreement, which has come into being after extraordinary difficulties, will undoubtedly give a decided impetus to German–Russian trade. We must try to build anew on this foundation and, above all, try to settle a number of questions which could not heretofore be settled, because of the low ebb which had been reached in our trade relations. The framework now set up represents a minimum. Since the political climate is favourable, it may well be expected that it will be exceeded considerably in both directions, both in imports and exports.

8. Under the Agreement, the following movement of goods can be expected for the next few years:

Exports to the U.S.S.R.

200 million Reichsmarks credit deliveries, schedule 'A'.
120 mill. RM. deliveries as current business, schedule 'B'.
X mill. RM. unspecified deliveries on current business.

Imports from the U.S.S.R.

180 mill. RM. raw material deliveries, schedule 'C'.
200 mill. RM. repayment of 1935 credit.
approx. 100 mill. RM. capitalized interest from present and last credit.
X mill. RM. unspecified deliveries of Soviet goods under German–Soviet Trade Agreement of Dec. 19, 1938.

The movement of goods envisaged by the Agreement might therefore reach a total of more than 1 billion Reichsmarks for the next few years, not including liquidation of the present 200 million credit by deliveries of Russian raw materials beginning in 1946.

9. Apart from the economic imports of the Treaty, its significance lies in the fact that the negotiations also served to renew political contacts with Russia and that the Credit Agreement was considered by both sides as the first decisive step in the reshaping of political relations.

Treaty of Non-Aggression between Germany and the Soviet Union, Moscow, 23 August 1939

The Government of the German Reich and

The Government of the Union of Soviet Socialist Republics

Desirous of strengthening the cause of peace between Germany and the U.S.S.R., and proceeding from the fundamental provisions of the Neutrality Agreement concluded in April 1926 between Germany and the U.S.S.R., have reached the following Agreement:

Article 1. Both High Contracting Parties obligate themselves to desist from any act of violence, any aggressive action, and any attack on each other, either individually or jointly with other Powers.

Article II. Should one of the High Contracting Parties become the object of belligerent action by a third Power, the other High Contracting Party shall in no manner lend its support to this third Power.

Article III. The Governments of the two High Contracting Parties shall in the future maintain continual contact with one another for the purpose of consultation in order to exchange information on problems affecting their common interests.

Article IV. Neither of the two High Contracting Parties shall participate in any grouping of Powers whatsoever that is directly or indirectly aimed at the other party.

Article V. Should disputes or conflicts arise between the High Contracting Parties over problems of one kind or another, both parties shall settle these disputes or conflicts exclusively through friendly exchange of opinion or, if necessary, through the establishment of arbitration commissions.

Article VI. The present Treaty is concluded for a period of ten years, with the proviso that, in so far as one of the High Contracting Parties does not denounce it one year prior to the expiration of this period, the validity of this Treaty shall automatically be extended for another five years.

Article VII. The present Treaty shall be ratified within the shortest possible time. The ratifications shall be exchanged in Berlin. The Agreement shall enter into force as soon as it is signed.

Secret Additional Protocol

On the occasion of the signature of the Non-Aggression Pact between the German Reich and the Union of Socialist Soviet Republics the undersigned plenipotentiaries of each of the two parties discussed in strictly confidential conversations the question of the boundary of their respective spheres of influence in Eastern Europe. These conversations led to the following conclusions:

Article 1. In the event of a territorial and political rearrangement in the areas belonging to the Baltic States (Finland, Estonia, Latvia, Lithuania), the northern boundary of Lithuania shall represent the boundary of the spheres of influence of Germany and the U.S.S.R. In this connection the interest of Lithuania in the Vilna area is recognized by each party.

Article 2. In the event of a territorial and political rearrangement of the areas belonging to the Polish State the spheres of influence of Germany and the U.S.S.R. shall be bounded approximately by the line of the rivers Narew, Vistula, and San.

The question of whether the interests of both parties make desirable the maintenance of an independent Polish State and how such a State should be bounded can only be definitely determined in the course of further political developments.

In any event both Governments will resolve this question by means of a friendly agreement.

Article 3. With regard to south-eastern Europe attention is called by the Soviet side to its interest in Bessarabia. The German side declares its complete political disinterestedness in these areas.

Article 4. This Protocol shall be treated by both parties as strictly secret.

  Moscow, August 23, 1939

For the Government
of the German Reich:
  v. RIBBENTROP

Plenipotentiary of the
Government of the U.S.S.R.
  V. MOLOTOV

Allied diplomacy, 1939–41

In September 1939 war did not immediately engulf all of Europe. The countries which declared war on Germany were Britain and the Dominions (with the exception of Eire) and France; Poland had no choice as she was attacked by Germany without a declaration of war. But Germany's ally Italy, with Hitler's consent, remained neutral. Portugal, Britain's ally, with British consent declared its neutrality on the outbreak of war. On the Allied side the earliest effort at diplomacy in wartime was to win the support of Turkey.

TURKEY

On 19 October 1939 Britain, France and Turkey concluded a Tripartite Treaty (p. 232). Five months earlier (12 May 1939) an Anglo-Turkish declaration had foreshadowed a long-term treaty to meet aggression in the Mediterranean region. The treaty now concluded on 19 October 1939 provided for a promise of British and French help if Turkey was attacked by a European power; the three powers, France and Britain on the one hand and Turkey on the other, promised mutual assistance if a European power committed an act of aggression leading to a war which involved the signatories; Turkey promised aid if Britain and France were at war in consequence of their guarantees to Greece and Roumania, but could remain benevolently neutral if a war involving Britain and France was the result of events outside the Mediterranean region, as was the case over Poland. Thus in practice the application of the alliance was limited to aggression by Germany or Italy in the Balkans; an important additional clause provided that the obligations Turkey undertook were not to have the effect of compelling her to go to war with the USSR. When Italy entered the war on 10 June 1940 during the final phase of the French collapse, Turkey disavowed the Tripartite Treaty, claiming that France could no longer fulfil it, and declared its intention to remain non-belligerent. The Italian and German attacks on Greece in 1941 did not alter Turkey's stand. After Germany's threat had lessened through military failure, Turkey broke off diplomatic relations on 2 August 1944 but did not declare war until 23 February 1945.

THE UNITED STATES AND THE EUROPEAN WAR

On 11 December 1941, four days after the Japanese attack on Pearl Harbor (7 December 1941), Germany and Italy declared war on the United States. By a number of agreements made during the period of American neutrality (September 1939 to December 1941) the United States had provided crucial help for the Allied cause even before becoming an ally. On 4 November 1939 Roosevelt approved the revised *Neutrality Act* which repealed the embargo on the export of munitions to belligerents, though American supplies to the Allies before the fall of France were not large. The German conquests of Denmark, Norway, the Netherlands, Belgium and France in the spring and summer of 1940 led to increasing American help and to a tremendous expansion of the American armaments industry. *The Anglo-American Destroyer–Naval Base Agreement, 2 September 1940*, gave Britain fifty American First World War destroyers in exchange for leasing to the United States naval bases in the British islands of the western Atlantic, in the Caribbean and in British Guiana. *The Lend–Lease Act, 11 March 1941*, passed Congress with the stated purpose of promoting the defence of the United States by providing all-out material aid to any country whose defence the President regarded as vital to the defence of the United States, on whatever terms the President regarded as proper. In August 1941 Churchill and Roosevelt met and set out their principles of present and future policy in the *Atlantic Charter, published on 14 August 1941* (p. 234). On 17 November 1941 Congress further revised the Neutrality Acts. American merchant ships could now carry arms to belligerent ports (British ports) and so be armed.

The German victories in Europe also raised the possibility that German aggression might expand to the western hemisphere. Pan-American solidarity in the event of the war reaching the American Republics was strengthened at the *Panama Conference, 23 September–3 October 1939* (p. 331). This created a neutral belt of several hundred miles from the coastline of the American Republics, foreshadowed the United States revision of the neutrality legislation and affirmed the no-transfer principle. The Declaration of Panama said: 'In case any geographic region of America subject to the jurisdiction of a non-American state should be obliged to change its sovereignty and there should result therefrom a danger to the security of the American continent, a consultative meeting such as the one now being held will be convoked with the urgency that the case may require.' With the German occupation of France, Belgium, the Netherlands, Norway and Denmark, the danger envisaged had come near and on 18 June 1940 the United States Congress affirmed that it would not acquiesce in any transfer of sovereignty from one non-American state to another of territory in the American hemisphere. The Pan-American Conference met again in Havana on 21 July 1940. The no-transfer principle was reaffirmed by resolution and the *Act of Havana, which came into force on*

8 January 1942 (p. 341). It provided in case of necessity that the republics in collective trusteeship would administer any such territory that was threatened. The Havana Conference also passed a resolution that an act of aggression against one republic would be treated as an act of aggression against all, which would lead to consultation on measures of common defence.

New allies and the collapse of France

In 1940 Britain lost the war on the continent of Europe and gained new allies, not by their choice but because they became victims of German aggression. Germany extended the war in the west by attacking Denmark and Norway on 9 April 1940. Denmark was occupied virtually without resistance and Norway, despite Allied attempts to create a front in the central and northern regions of the country, fell a few weeks later.

Germany opened her military offensive against France a month later on 10 May 1940 by crossing three neutral frontiers, the Netherlands, Belgium and Luxembourg. All three governments after the complete military collapse refused to sign an armistice with Germany, and transferred themselves to London to join there the Polish and Norwegian governments in exile. After the defeat of the British and French armies Marshal Pétain formed a new government which sought an armistice from the Germans. The *Franco-German armistice was signed on 22 June 1940* and became effective three days later. It divided France into an occupied zone of northern France and the Atlantic coastline and an unoccupied zone. The 'Free French' under de Gaulle continued to fight on the Allied side but were not recognized as a fully-fledged government in exile. Meantime Italy had declared war on France and Britain on 10 June 1940 during the closing stages of the German campaign in France. Italy's contribution to the growing number of Allied powers was to follow up her short campaign in France by attacking *Greece on 28 October 1940*. Greece now joined the war against Italy. Italian military ineptitude brought about German intervention when *Germany attacked Greece on 6 April 1941*.

Treaty of Mutual Assistance between Britain, France and Turkey, 19 October 1939

Article 1. In the event of Turkey being involved in hostilities with a European

Power in consequence of aggression by that Power against Turkey, France and the

United Kingdom will cooperate effectively with Turkey and will lend her all aid and assistance in their power.

Article 2.1. In the event of an act of aggression by a European Power leading to war in the Mediterranean area in which France and the United Kingdom are involved, Turkey will collaborate effectively with France and the United Kingdom and will lend them all aid and assistance in her power.

2. In the event of an act of aggression by a European Power leading to war in the Mediterranean area in which Turkey is involved, France and the United Kingdom will collaborate effectively with Turkey and will lend her all aid and assistance in their power.

Article 3. So long as the guarantees given by France and the United Kingdom to Greece and Roumania by their respective Declarations of the 13th April 1939 remain in force, Turkey will cooperate effectively with France and the United Kingdom and will lend them all aid and assistance in her power, in the event of France and the United Kingdom being engaged in hostilities in virtue of either of the said guarantees.

Article 4. In the event of France and the United Kingdom being involved in hostilities with a European Power in consequence of aggression committed by that Power against either of those States without the provisions of Articles 2 or 3 being applicable, the High Contracting Parties will immediately consult together.

It is nevertheless agreed that in such an eventuality Turkey will observe at least a benevolent neutrality towards France and the United Kingdom.

Article 5. Without prejudice to the provisions of Article 3 above, in the event of either:

1. Aggression by a European Power against another European State which the Government of one of the High Contracting Parties had, with the approval of that State, undertaken to assist in maintaining its independence or neutrality against such aggression, or

2. Aggression by a European Power which while directed against another European State, constituted, in the opinion of the Government of one of the High Contracting Parties, a menace to its own security, the High Contracting Parties will immediately consult together with a view to such common action as might be considered effective.

Article 6. The present Treaty is not directed against any country, but is designed to assure France, the United Kingdom and Turkey of mutual aid and assistance in resistance to aggression should the necessity arise.

Article 7. The provisions of the present Treaty are equally binding as bilateral obligations between Turkey and each of the two other High Contracting Parties.

Article 8. If the High Contracting Parties are engaged in hostilities in consequence of the operation of the present Treaty, they will not conclude an armistice or peace except by common agreement.

Article 9. The present Treaty shall be ratified and the instruments of ratification shall be deposited simultaneously at Angora as soon as possible. It shall enter into force on the date of this deposit.

The present Treaty is concluded for a period of fifteen years. If none of the High Contracting Parties has notified the two others of its intention to terminate it six months before the expiration of the said period, the Treaty will be renewed by tacit consent for a further period of five years, and so on.

Protocol No. 1

The undersigned plenipotentiaries state that their respective Governments agree that the Treaty of today's date shall be put into force from the moment of its signature.

The present Protocol shall be considered as an integral part of the Treaty concluded today between France, the United Kingdom and Turkey.

Protocol No. 2

At the moment of signature of the Treaty between France, the United Kingdom and Turkey, the undersigned plenipotentiaries, duly authorized to this effect, have agreed as follows:

The obligations undertaken by Turkey in virtue of the above-mentioned Treaty cannot compel that country to take action having as its effect, or involving as its consequence, entry into armed conflict with the Soviet Union.

Declaration of Principles known as the Atlantic Charter, made public on 14 August 1941

Joint Declaration of the President of the United States of America and the Prime Minister, Mr Churchill, representing His Majesty's Government in the United Kingdom, being met together, deem it right to make known certain common principles in the national policies of their respective countries on which they base their hopes for a better future for the world.

First, their countries seek no aggrandizement, territorial or other;

Second, they desire to see no territorial changes that do not accord with the freely expressed wishes of the peoples concerned;

Third, they respect the right of all peoples to choose the form of government under which they will live; and they wish to see sovereign rights and self-government restored to those who have been forcibly deprived of them;

Fourth, they will endeavour, with due respect for their existing obligations, to further the enjoyment by all States, great or small, victor or vanquished, of access, on equal terms, to the trade and to the raw materials of the world which are needed for their economic prosperity;

Fifth, they desire to bring about the fullest collaboration between all nations in the economic field with the object of securing, for all, improved labour standards, economic advancement and social security;

Sixth, after the final destruction of the Nazi tyranny, they hope to see established a peace which will afford to all nations the means of dwelling in safety within their own boundaries, and which will afford assurance that all the men in all the lands may live out their lives in freedom from fear and want;

Seventh, such a peace should enable all men to traverse the high seas and oceans without hindrance;

Eighth, they believe that all of the nations of the world, for realistic as well as spiritual reasons must come to the abandonment of the use of force. Since no future peace can be maintained if land, sea or air armaments continue to be employed by nations which threaten, or may threaten, aggression outside of their frontiers, they believe, pending the establishment of a wider and permanent system of general security, that the disarmament of such nations is essential. They will likewise aid and encourage all other practicable measures which will lighten for peace-loving peoples the crushing burden of armaments.

The Axis powers and the Soviet Union, 1939–41: the Winter War

For Germany and Poland the Second World War began on 1 September 1939 when the Wehrmacht and the Luftwaffe crossed the Polish frontier. Just a week earlier the Soviet Union and Germany announced a *Treaty of Non-Aggression, 23 August 1939* (p. 229). After Hitler's virulent anti-Bolshevik tirades, such a treaty marked a reversal of what the public could have anticipated. Equally, communists throughout Europe were thrown into confusion. An additional *secret protocol* marked out German and Soviet 'spheres of influence' and envisaged the partition of Poland and other territories within each sphere according to the convenience of each signatory. On 17 September 1939, seventeen days after Germany's attack on Poland, with the Polish armies routed but still fighting the Germans, Soviet troops crossed Poland's eastern frontier. The detailed division of Poland was laid down in the *German–Soviet Boundary and Friendship Treaty, 28 September 1939* (p. 237), to which were added one confidential and two secret protocols. These political treaties were accompanied by German–Soviet economic agreements. The first economic agreement, the *German–Soviet Trade Agreement, was concluded on 19 August 1939* (p. 227). Six months later a comprehensive and extensive *German–Soviet Commercial Agreement was signed on 11 February 1940* (p. 239).

Having concluded these political and economic agreements which apparently ensured that Germany and the Soviet Union could count on the neutrality of one state towards the other, Germany and the Soviet Union pursued their separate expansionist policies. Germany attacked Denmark and Norway on 9 April 1940 and the Netherlands, Belgium and Luxembourg on 10 May 1940.

The Soviet Union, in accordance with the German–Soviet Boundary and Friendship Treaty on 28 September 1939, had secured German agreement that Lithuania fell within her sphere of interest. Stalin was now determined to assure Soviet predominance in the Baltic states of Lithuania, Estonia and Latvia as well as Finland. Under threat of force a *Soviet–Estonian Mutual Assistance Pact was concluded on 28 September 1939*, which, whilst formally preserving Estonian sovereignty, made military bases available to the Soviet Union in Estonia and permitted the Soviet Union to station troops in these bases. *Latvia signed a similar pact with the Soviet Union on 5 October 1939* (p. 240). *Lithuania* was also forced to sign a pact with the Soviet Union permitting the stationing of the Red Army in Lithuania, but on *10 October 1939* received a 'consolation prize': Vilna and its region was transferred from occupied Poland to Lithuania. The Soviet Union wished to control the foreign and military affairs of the Baltic to strengthen Soviet security. Independent governments continued to function in the Baltic states until mid-June 1940. Then, after unremitting pressure and when already under Soviet control, the Baltic states 'requested' incorporation in the Soviet Union. Lithuania was accordingly 'admitted' to the Soviet Union on 1 August 1940, Latvia on 5 August 1940, Estonia on 8 August 1940, and these states became Republics of the Soviet Union. This marked the extinction of the three Baltic states as sovereign nations until 1991.

In October 1939 Finland refused Soviet demands which involved frontier changes and the abandonment of the Mannerheim line of fortifications across the Karelian isthmus. After fruitless negotiations the Soviet Union began the invasion of Finland on 30 November 1939. The Winter War lasted unexpectedly long with strong Finnish resistance, but after three months of fighting Finland was forced to sue for peace. *On 12 March 1940 a Finnish–Soviet Peace Treaty was signed* which accepted Soviet demands for frontier changes and bases.

The Soviet Union next moved to increase the security of her southern frontier by demanding from Roumania on 26 June 1940 Bessarabia and northern Bukovina. The Roumanians accepted, on German advice, and by 1 July 1940 this region had been completely occupied by Soviet troops. The Hungarians now also wished to recover territory lost after the First World War (p. 94) and threatened to use force if Roumania did not hand back Transylvania; the Bulgarians demanded from Roumania frontier concessions in the Dobruja. Hitler imposed a settlement by the *Second Vienna Award, 30 August 1940*, partitioning Transylvania, which left Roumania about three-fifths and gave Hungary the remainder. *Roumania ceded the southern Dobruja to Bulgaria on 7 September 1940*. In its new frontiers Hitler now gave a *German guarantee to Roumania* at the request of the Roumanians, who on 1 July 1940 had formally denounced the *Anglo-French guarantee of April 1939* (see p. 222). In September 1940 German troops began to occupy Roumania at 'Roumania's request', as Hitler assured the Russians. Russo–German relations deteriorated. In November 1940 Hitler secretly prepared for war in the Balkans and an attack on Russia, Bulgaria and Greece. Meantime, not to be outdone by Germany in the Balkans Mussolini attacked Greece on 28 October 1940.

Faced with the hostile great powers, Italy, Germany and Russia, the still independent Balkan states attempted to strengthen their security by diplomacy and by appeasing Hitler. In November 1940 the Bulgarians promised to cooperate with the three Axis powers, Germany, Italy and Japan who had concluded the *Tripartite Pact of 27 September 1940* (p. 241). Hungary signed a *Protocol of Adherence to the Tripartite Pact, 20 November 1940*, but according to its terms the Hungarians were left some freedom in choosing what action to take to help the Axis partners. *Roumania adhered to the Tripartite Pact on 23 November 1940 and Slovakia on 24 November 1940*. On 12 December 1940 the *Hungarian–Yugoslav Pact* apparently reconciled these two states. On the following day, 13 December 1940, Hitler issued military directives for a German attack on Greece and on 18 December 1940 for an attack on the Soviet Union. Germany strengthened her position by securing Bulgarian acquiescence to a virtual German military occupation during February 1941. *Bulgaria* next concluded a *Non-Aggression Pact with Turkey on 17 February 1942*.

The aggressive policies of Germany and Italy had thrown the Balkan states (all of which, apart from Greece, had remained at peace) into such a state of great alarm that they vied for German friendship. On *1 March 1941 Bulgaria openly adhered to the Tripartite Pact*. Finally, *on 25 March 1941 Yugoslavia adhered to the Tripartite Pact,* receiving assurances from Germany that her sovereignty and territorial integrity would be respected. This pro-Axis policy resulted in a popular uprising in Yugoslavia: the military leaders took charge, the Prince Regent was deposed, and a new government was formed. To gain time the new Yugoslav government forwarded to Berlin protestations of friendship for Italy and Germany. Hitler responded to the Yugoslav *coup* by ordering a German surprise attack on Yugoslavia and on Greece, which commenced on 6 April 1941. Three days later the Hungarians also crossed the Yugoslav frontier. On 17 April 1941 the Yugoslav army surrendered. The government under King Peter left the country, while in Yugoslavia the struggle was continued in the mountains. By the end of May 1941 the Germans had conquered Greece and Crete.

Hitler could now dispose of the spoils of victory. Yugoslavia was partitioned between Germany, Italy, Hungary and Bulgaria; an 'independent kingdom' of Croatia was allowed to exist under Italian control; what was left of Serbia became another 'independent state' under German occupation. Greece was deprived of western Thrace and eastern Macedonia, which was handed to Bulgaria; Italy took the Ionian Islands and enlarged Albania at the Greeks' expense. The remainder of Greece was placed under mainly Italian occupation after a formal Greek military surrender to the Germans had been signed on 23 April 1941.

Having gained complete dominance in the Balkans, Hitler was now ready to take his most momentous step in expanding the war in Europe by next launching an attack on the Soviet Union. But Yugoslavia's resistance had postponed the original time set for the attack: instead of in May, it could only begin on 22 June 1941. Hitler was joined by allies. Italy and Roumania declared war on Russia on 22 June 1941, Slovakia on 23 June 1941, Finland on 25 June 1941 and Hungary on 27 June 1941. Only Bulgaria (practically under German control) remained neutral, together with Turkey. With the onset of winter, the Soviet Union avoided the defeat predicted both by the Allies and the Axis in 1941.

Boundary and Friendship Treaty between the Soviet Union and Germany, Moscow, 28 September 1939

The Government of the German Reich and the Government of the U.S.S.R. consider it as exclusively their task, after the collapse of the former Polish State, to re-establish peace and order in these territories and to assure to the peoples living there a peaceful life in keeping with their national character. To this end, they have agreed upon the following:

Article I. The Government of the German Reich and the Government of the U.S.S.R.

determine as the boundary of their respective national interests in the territory of the former Polish State the line marked on the attached map, which shall be described in more detail in a Supplementary Protocol.

Article II. Both parties recognize the boundary of the respective national interests established in Article I as definitive and shall reject any interference of third Powers in this settlement.

Article III. The necessary reorganization of public administration will be effected in the areas west of the line specified in Article I by the Government of the German Reich, in the areas east of this line by the Government of the U.S.S.R.

Article IV. The Government of the German Reich and the Government of the U.S.S.R. regard this settlement as a firm foundation for a progressive development of the friendly relations between their peoples.

Article V. This Treaty shall be ratified and the ratifications shall be exchanged in Berlin as soon as possible. The Treaty becomes effective upon signature.

Confidential Protocol

[Provided that Germans and people of German descent may leave territories under Soviet jurisdiction for Germany, and Ukrainians and White Russians may leave German territories for Soviet Union.]

Secret Supplementary Protocol

The undersigned plenipotentiaries declare the agreement of the Government of the German Reich and the Government of U.S.S.R. on the following:

The Secret Supplementary Protocol signed on August 23, 1939 shall be amended in Item 1 to the effect that the territory of the Lithuanian State falls in the sphere of influence of U.S.S.R., while, on the other hand, the province of Lublin and parts of the province of Warsaw fall in the sphere of influence of Germany (cf. the map attached to the Frontier and Friendship Treaty

signed today). As soon as the Government of U.S.S.R. takes special measures on Lithuanian territory to protect its interests, the present German–Lithuanian frontier, for the purpose of a natural and simple frontier delineation, will be rectified in such a way that the Lithuanian territory situated to the south-west of the line marked on the attached map will fall to Germany.

Further it is declared that the Economic Agreements now in force between Germany and Lithuania will not be affected by the measures of the Soviet Union referred to above.

Secret Supplementary Protocol

The undersigned plenipotentiaries, on concluding the German–Russian Frontier and Friendship Treaty, have declared their agreement on the following:

Neither party will tolerate in its territories Polish agitation that affects the territories of the other party. Both parties will suppress in their territories all beginnings of such agitation and will inform each other concerning suitable measures for this purpose.

Declaration

After the Government of the German Reich and the Government of U.S.S.R. have, by means of the Treaty signed today, definitively settled the problems arising from the collapse of the Polish State and have thereby created a sure foundation for a lasting peace in Eastern Europe, they mutually express their conviction that it would serve the true interests of all peoples to put an end to the state of war existing at present between Germany on the one side, and England and France on the other. Both Governments will therefore direct their common efforts, jointly with other friendly Powers if occasion arises, towards attaining this goal as soon as possible.

Should, however, the efforts of the two Governments remain fruitless, this would demonstrate the fact that England and France are responsible for the continuation of the war, whereupon, in case of the continuation of the war, the Governments of Germany and of U.S.S.R. will engage in mutual consultations with regard to necessary measures.

Commercial Agreement between the Soviet Union and Germany, 11 February 1940

[Information based on German Foreign Ministry Memorandum below.]

Memorandum

The Agreement is based on the correspondence – mentioned in the Preamble – between the Reich Minister for Foreign Affairs and the Chairman of the Council of People's Commissars, Molotov, dated September 28, 1939. The Agreement represents the first great step towards the economic programme envisaged by both sides and is to be followed by others.

1. The Agreement covers a period of twenty-seven months, i.e. the Soviet deliveries, which are to be made within eighteen months, will be compensated by German deliveries in turn within twenty-seven months. The most difficult point of the correspondence of September 28, 1939, namely, that the Soviet raw material deliveries are to be compensated by German industrial deliveries over a *longer period*, is thereby settled in accordance with our wishes . . . .

2. The Soviet deliveries. According to the Agreement, the Soviet Union shall within the first twelve months deliver raw materials in the amount of approximately 500 million Reichsmarks.

In addition, the Soviets will deliver raw materials contemplated in the Credit Agreement of August 19, 1939, for the same period, in the amount of approximately 100 million Reichsmarks.

The most important raw materials are the following:

1,000,000 tons of grain for cattle, and of legumes, in the amount of 120 million Reichsmarks

900,000 tons of mineral oil in the amount of approximately 115 million Reichsmarks

100,000 tons of cotton in the amount of approximately 90 million Reichsmarks

500,000 tons of phosphates

100,000 tons of chrome ores

500,000 tons of iron ore

300,000 tons of scrap iron and pig iron

2,400 kg of platinum

Manganese ore metals, lumber, and numerous other raw materials.

. . . [Stalin also promised to purchase raw materials in third countries for Germany.]

Pact of Mutual Assistance between the Soviet Union and Latvia, Moscow, 5 October 1939

[Pacts of Mutual Assistance were also concluded with Estonia, 28 September 1939, and Lithuania, 10 October 1939.] The Presidium of the Supreme Soviet of U.S.S.R. on the one hand, and the President of the Latvian Republic on the other, for the purpose of developing the friendly relations created by the Peace Treaty of August 11, 1920, which were based on the recognition of the independent statehood and noninterference in the internal affairs of the other party; recognizing that the Peace Treaty of August 11, 1920 and the Agreement of February 5, 1932 concerning nonaggression and the amicable settlement of conflicts, continue to be the firm basis of their mutual relations and obligations; convinced that a definition of the precise conditions ensuring mutual safety is in accordance with the interests of both Contracting Parties; have considered it necessary to conclude between them the following Mutual Assistance Pact . . .

Article I. Both Contracting Parties undertake to render each other every assistance, including military, in the event of a direct attack, or threat of attack, on the part of any European Great Power, with respect to the sea borders of the Contracting Parties on the Baltic Sea, or their land borders through the territory of the Estonian or Latvian Republics, or also the bases referred to in Article III.

Article II. The Soviet Union undertakes to render assistance on preferential conditions to the Latvian army in the form of armaments and other war materials.

Article III. In order to ensure the safety of U.S.S.R. and to consolidate her own independence, the Latvian Republic grants to the Union the right to maintain in the cities of Liapaja (Libava) and Ventspils (Vindava) naval bases and several airfields

for aviation purposes on leasehold at a reasonable rental. The locations of the bases and airfields shall be exactly specified and their boundaries determined by mutual agreement.

For the purpose of protecting the Straits of Irbe, the Soviet Union is given the right to establish on the same conditions a coast artillery base between Ventspils and Pitrags.

For the purpose of protecting the naval bases, the airfields and the coast artillery base, the Soviet Union has the right to maintain at its own expense on the areas set aside for bases and airfields a strictly limited number of Soviet land and air forces, the maximum number of which is to be fixed by special agreement.

Article IV. Both Contracting Parties undertake not to enter into any alliances or to participate in any coalitions directed against one of the Contracting Parties.

Article V. The entry into force of the present Pact must in no way affect the sovereign rights of the Contracting Parties, in particular their political structure, their economic and social system, and their military measures.

The areas set aside for the bases and airfields (Article III) remain in the territory of the Latvian Republic.

Article VI. The present Pact goes into force with the exchange of documents of ratification. The exchange of documents will take place in the City of Riga within six days after the signing of the present Pact.

The present Pact shall remain in force for a period of ten years, and in the event that one of the Contracting Parties does not consider it necessary to denounce it prior to the expiration of such period, it will automatically remain in force for the following ten years.

Treaty of Non-Aggression between Germany and Turkey, 18 June 1941

Article 1. The Turkish Republic and the German Reich undertake to respect mutually the inviolability and integrity of their territories, and to abstain from all action aimed directly or indirectly against one another.

Article 2. The Turkish Republic and the German Reich undertake to enter into friendly contact in the future in regard to all matters involving their mutual interests with a view to reaching an agreement for their solution.

Article 3. The present Treaty which shall enter into force on the date of its signature shall be valid for a period of ten years. The High Contracting Parties shall in due time reach an agreement on the matter of its prolongation.

The present Treaty shall be ratified and the ratifications shall be exchanged in Berlin as soon as possible . . . .

Three Powers Pact between Germany, Italy and Japan, Berlin, 27 September 1940

The Governments of Germany, Italy and Japan, considering it as the condition precedent of any lasting peace that all nations of the world be given each its own proper place, have decided to stand by and cooperate with one another in regard to their efforts in Greater East Asia and the regions of Europe respectively wherein it is their prime purpose to establish and maintain a new order of things calculated to promote mutual prosperity and welfare of the peoples concerned.

Furthermore it is the desire of the three Governments to extend cooperation to such nations in other spheres of the world as may be inclined to put forth endeavours along lines similar to their own, in order that their ultimate aspirations for world peace may thus be realized. Accordingly the Governments of Germany, Italy and Japan have agreed as follows:

Article 1. Japan recognizes and respects the leadership of Germany and Italy in the establishment of a new order in Europe.

Article 2. Germany and Italy recognize and respect the leadership of Japan in the establishment of a new order in Greater East Asia.

Article 3. Germany, Italy and Japan agree to cooperate in their efforts on the aforesaid lines. They further undertake to assist one another with all political, economic and military means when one of the three Contracting Parties is attacked by a Power at present not involved in the European War or in the Sino-Japanese Conflict.

Article 4. With a view to implementing the present Pact, joint technical commissions the members of which are to be appointed by the respective Governments of Germany, Italy and Japan will meet without delay.

Article 5. Germany, Italy and Japan affirm that the aforesaid terms do not in any way affect the political status which exists at present as between each of the three Contracting Parties and Soviet Russia.

Article 6. The present Pact shall come into effect immediately upon signature and shall remain in force for ten years from the date of its coming into force.

At proper time before the expiration of the said term the High Contracting Parties shall, at the request of any one of them, enter into negotiations for its renewal . . . .

Agreement between Germany, Italy and Japan on the joint prosecution of the war, Berlin, 11 December 1941

In their unshakeable determination not to lay down arms until the common war against the United States of America and Britain has been brought to a successful conclusion, the German Government, the Italian Government, and the Japanese Government have agreed upon the following provisions:

Article 1. Germany, Italy and Japan jointly and with every means at their disposal will pursue the war forced upon them by the United States of America and Britain to a victorious conclusion.

Article 2. Germany, Italy, and Japan undertake not to conclude an armistice or peace with the United States of America or Britain except in complete mutual agreement.

Article 3. After victory has been achieved Germany, Italy, and Japan will continue in closest cooperation with a view to establishing a new and just order along the lines of the Tripartite Agreement concluded by them on September 27, 1940.

Article 4. The present Agreement will come into force with its signature, and will remain valid as long as the Tripartite Pact of September 27, 1940.

The High Contracting Parties will in good time before the expiry of this term of validity enter into consultation with each other as to the future development of their cooperation, as provided under Article 3 of the present Agreement.

Asia: Japan, Russia and China, 1937–41

In July 1937 Japan resumed an 'undeclared war' against China. During the two years from the renewed invasion of China by Japan in the summer of 1937 until the outbreak of war in Europe in September 1939, fighting not only spread through China but the tension between Russia and Japan increased to the point of open fighting on the borders of Manchuria.

On 21 August 1937 the Soviet Union and China signed a Non-Aggression Pact (p. 202). But Japan's diplomatic position was strengthened when in November 1937 Italy joined the *German–Japanese Anti–Comintern Pact* (p. 216). China's appeal to the League resulted in no effective support. In 1938 the Soviet Union began to provide credit and send war supplies to free China. By the summer of 1938 fierce fighting broke out between Japanese and Soviet troops over the border, near the junction of Manchuria, Korea and the Soviet Union. Although a truce was concluded the tension continued. From May to September 1939 serious clashes occurred between Japanese and Soviet troops on the Mongolian–Manchurian border. The Soviet Union appeared encircled and threatened by two Axis Powers – Germany and Japan. The alignment of the Axis against the Soviet Union was suddenly broken by the signature of the *German–Soviet Non-Aggression Pact* in August 1939 (p. 229). The Soviet Union, while continuing in 1939 and 1940 to aid China with supplies, also sought some accommodation with Japan. Japan meanwhile strengthened her ties with Italy and Germany after Germany's military successes in France, and concluded the *Tripartite Pact on 27 September 1940* (p. 241). For Japan, Indo-China and the Dutch East Indies were assuming new importance in the autumn of 1940. This Japanese drive southwards, partly to ensure for herself the raw materials essential for war, brought her into conflict with the United States. For Japan a settlement with the Soviet Union thus became more desirable. It was achieved when *Japan and the Soviet Union concluded a Neutrality Pact on 13 April 1941.*

Asia: the United States, Britain and Japan, 1940–41

Japan extended her influence in Asia and the Pacific as Germany, the Axis partner, spread over the continent of Europe. After unrelenting Japanese military pressure the Japanese and Vichy government reached a *Franco–Japanese Agreement on Indo-China by an exchange of notes, 30 August 1940*. France recognized Japan's predominance in eastern Asia, special economic privileges in Indo-China and, most important, special military facilities to enable Japan to bring the war with China to an end; Japan recognized French sovereignty over Indo-China and Indo-China's territorial integrity. After further tension leading to the brink of conflict, a *Franco–Japanese Military Agreement concerning Indo-China was signed on 22 September 1940* which permitted the Japanese the use of three airfields in Tonkin and the right to station 6,000 troops on them, as well as the right to send up to 25,000 men through Tonkin to attack China.

   Japan also supported Thailand (Siam). Thailand began to acquire Cambodian territory in Indo-China. This local conflict was brought to a halt by Japan on terms favourable to Japanese interests. The *Thailand–Franco–Japanese treaties of 9 May 1941* gave to Thailand about one-third of Cambodia and part of Laos on the west bank of the Mekong; Japan guaranteed the French–Thailand settlement, and Thailand and the Vichy French government in Indo-China undertook to conclude no agreements which could involve them in political, economic or military collaboration with another country against Japan. *On 29 July 1941 the Japanese extended their occupation over southern Indo-China*, having extracted an agreement from Vichy France under threat of using force. Japan had further strengthened her position for moving southwards by signing the *Tripartite Pact of 27 September 1940 with Italy and Germany* (p. 241) and the *Japanese–Soviet Pact of Neutrality of 13 April*

1941. But Japanese efforts to bring the Dutch East Indies into her Greater East Asia sphere from February 1940 to December 1941 met with Dutch resistance. The Dutch authorities would not consent to allowing Japan a privileged economic position which she wanted so as to be able to assure her vital oil supplies and other minerals. Japan was also faced with strong American diplomatic and economic opposition. The extension of the Japanese occupation of southern Indo-China in July 1941 provided bases against Britain in Malaya and the Dutch East Indies. But the alarm felt at Japanese expansion by the United States led to a number of American measures intended to hinder further Japanese expansion; the United States adopted financial and oil restrictions and also increased military aid to China.

Though there were American–Japanese negotiations for a general settlement, these were broken off by the Japanese attack at dawn on the American fleet at *Pearl Harbor on 7 December 1941*. About an hour and a half earlier, under cover of darkness, Japanese troops began landing on the British Malay coast. At 6 a.m. Japan declared war on Britain and the United States, but owing to the international dateline the day of Pearl Harbor was 8 December 1941 in Tokyo and Malaya. Japan's surprise attack was followed by *German and Italian declarations of war on the United States on 11 December 1941*. The United States had now become a full ally of Britain and the Allied nations both in Asia and Europe.

IX · The Grand Alliance, 1941–45

Britain, the United States and the Soviet Union, June 1941–June 1942

In a broadcast on the evening of 22 June 1941, Winston Churchill promised help to Russians fighting for their homeland in the cause of 'free men and free people' everywhere. Military supplies from Britain and America began to reach the Soviet Union in appreciable quantities in the autumn of 1941. The Anglo–Soviet alliance against Germany was first placed on a formal basis by the brief *Anglo–Soviet Agreement of 12 July 1941*, in which the two powers undertook to render each other assistance and support in the war against 'Hitlerite Germany', and not to negotiate an armistice or peace treaty except by mutual agreement. From the first, relations between the Soviet Union and Britain, and later the United States, were made difficult by Stalin's insistent demand that Russia's allies should engage the Germans on the continent of Europe. His call for a second front was not fully satisfied until the Allied landings in France in June 1944. As a result of Russian pressure, however, *Britain declared war on Finland, Hungary and Rumania on 6 December 1941*. Bulgaria had not joined in the German war against the Soviet Union, but to show a theoretical loyalty to the Axis declared war on Britain and the United States on 13 December 1941.

An *Anglo–Soviet–Iranian Treaty was concluded on 29 January 1942* (p. 247) which promised Britain and Russia all facilities to defend Iran from aggression, and Britain and Russia promised to respect Persian independence and integrity and to withdraw not later than six months after the war. Negotiations for a full Anglo–Soviet alliance were long drawn-out. Stalin's suspicions of Britain's resolution to relieve German military pressure in Russia, and Russian territorial demands in the post-war European settlement, were the major obstacles. Russia wished recognition of her right to the Baltic states and to Poland up to the Curzon line, with possible minor frontier readjustments. But Britain, and later the United States, had agreed to postpone all questions of the new frontiers until after the war. Finally the Russian denial of, and Poland's insistence on, her claim to the right of restoration within her pre-1939 frontiers could not be reconciled; Britain gave support to Poland in 1941, declaring in a *Note to the Polish Government, 30 July 1941* (p. 248), that it recognized none of the changes of territory brought about in Poland by the Soviet Union or Germany since August 1939. The fundamental differences between the Allies are reflected in the difficulties the negotiators faced in attempting to reach agreement and to conclude treaties.

With Japan's attack on Pearl Harbor on 7 December 1941, and Germany's and Italy's declaration of war on the United States on 11 December 1941, Britain, the United States and Russia became allies in the war against Germany and Italy, but only Britain and the United States were allies in the war against Japan. In the drafting of a comprehensive alliance between the powers at war this was a further cause of difficulty. Such a comprehensive alliance was first set out in negotiations in Washington and took the form of the *United Nations Declaration of 1 January 1942* (p. 248). The 'United Nations' declaration, a phrase originating with Roosevelt, was intended to circumvent the right of the United States Senate to pass by a two-thirds majority treaties of alliance negotiated with foreign powers. The Free French did not sign despite the loophole which would have allowed 'appropriate authorities which are not Governments' to adhere. The Joint Declaration listed the Allied nations in alphabetical order, but placed at the head were the United States, Britain, the USSR and China. In this way these four nations were treated differently from the rest thus setting out their status as 'Great Powers'.

In the spring of 1942, Britain and the Soviet Union concluded the negotiation of an alliance treaty begun the previous autumn. The Soviet Union agreed to the omission of a clause defining specific frontiers, such as her rights to all territory included in Soviet Russia on 22 June 1941. The Russians at the time were anxious to hasten the opening of a 'second front' against Germany in France.

The *Anglo–Soviet Alliance of 26 May 1942* (p. 249) appeared momentous at the time because it provided a bond between the Soviet Union and Britain, a great 'capitalistic' imperial power. The treaty was intended to outlast the German war for it was given a duration of twenty years. It repeated the undertakings of the agreement of 12 July 1941 (mutual assistance, no separate peace), but went further in a second part which set out some of the principles of post-war cooperation. The signatories envisaged an organization of states for the preservation of peace; Britain and the Soviet Union also declared that they would 'take into account' the interests of the United Nations and not seek 'territorial aggrandizement for themselves'. Stalin, of course, did not regard the incorporation in the Soviet Union of eastern Poland in 1939 and the Baltic states in 1940 as 'aggrandizement', since he claimed the populations concerned had opted for the Soviet Union. Churchill had been ready in March 1942 to go further and to breach the principle of no frontier discussions by accepting Russia's claim to her 1940 frontiers (including the Baltic states, Bessarabia, Bukovina and Finnish conquests), except for territories which had been Polish in 1939. In the event the Soviet Union accepted the treaty without territorial clauses.

Alliance Treaty between Britain, the Soviet Union and Iran, 29 January 1942

Article 1. His Majesty The King of Great Britain, Ireland and the British Dominions beyond the Seas, Emperor of India, and the Union of Soviet Socialist Republics (hereinafter referred to as the Allied Powers) jointly and severally undertake to respect the territorial integrity, sovereignty and political independence of Iran.

Article 2. An alliance is established between the Allied Powers on the one hand and His Imperial Majesty The Shahinshah of Iran on the other.

Article 3. (i) The Allied Powers jointly and severally undertake to defend Iran by all means at their command from all aggression on the part of Germany or any other Power.

(ii) His Imperial Majesty The Shahinshah undertakes:

(a) To cooperate with the Allied Powers with all the means at his command and in every way possible, in order that they may be able to fulfil the above undertaking. The assistance of the Iranian forces shall, however, be limited to the maintenance of internal security on Iranian territory;

(b) To secure to the Allied Powers, for the passage of troops or supplies from one Allied Power to the other or for other similar purposes, the unrestricted right to use, maintain, guard and, in case of military necessity, control in any way that they may require, all means of communication throughout Iran, including railways, roads, rivers, aerodromes, ports, pipelines and telephone, telegraph and wireless installations . . . .

Article 4. (i) The Allied Powers may maintain in Iranian territory land, sea and air forces in such number as they consider necessary. The location of such forces shall be decided in agreement with the Iranian Government so long as the strategic situation allows . . . .

Article 5. The forces of the Allied Powers shall be withdrawn from Iranian territory not later than six months after all hostilities between the Allied Powers and Germany and her associates have been suspended by the conclusion of an armistice or armistices, or on the conclusion of peace between them, whichever date is the earlier. The expression 'associates' of Germany means all other Powers which have engaged or may in the future engage in hostilities against either of the Allied Powers.

Article 6. (i) The Allied Powers undertake in their relations with foreign countries not to adopt an attitude which is prejudicial to the territorial integrity, sovereignty or political independence of Iran, nor to conclude treaties inconsistent with the provisions of the present Treaty. They undertake to consult the Government of His Imperial Majesty the Shahinshah in all matters affecting the direct interests of Iran.

(ii) His Imperial Majesty the Shahinshah undertakes not to adopt in his relations with foreign countries an attitude which is inconsistent with the alliance . . . .

Note issued by the Foreign Office in London on non-recognition of any territorial changes in Poland since August 1939

London, 30 July 1941

1. An agreement between the Republic of Poland and the Soviet Union was signed in the Secretary of State's room at the Foreign Office on July 30. General Sikorski, Polish Prime Minister, signed for Poland; M. Maisky, Soviet Ambassador, signed for the Soviet Union. Mr Churchill and Mr Eden were present.

2. The agreement is being published.

3. After the signature of the agreement, Mr Eden handed to General Sikorski an official Note in the following terms:

> On the occasion of the signature of the Polish–Soviet Agreement of today, I desire to take this opportunity of informing you that in conformity with the provision of the Agreement of Mutual Assistance between the United Kingdom and Poland of the 25th August 1939, His Majesty's Government in the United Kingdom have entered into no undertakings towards the Union of Socialist Soviet Republics which affect the relations between that country and Poland. I also desire to assure you that His Majesty's Government do not recognize any territorial changes which have been effected in Poland since August 1939.

General Sikorski handed to Mr Eden the following reply:

> The Polish Government take note of your letter dated July 30 and desire to express sincere satisfaction at the statement that His Majesty's Government in the United Kingdom do not recognize any territorial changes which have been effected in Poland since August 1939. This corresponds with the view of the Polish Government which, as they have previously informed His Majesty's Government, have never recognized any territorial changes effected in Poland since the outbreak of the war.

Declaration by the United Nations, 1 January 1942

The Governments signatory hereto,

Having subscribed to a common programme of purposes and principals embodied in the Joint Declaration of the President of the United States of America and the Prime Minister of the United Kingdom of Great Britain and Northern Ireland dated August 14, 1941, known as the Atlantic Charter,

Being convinced that complete victory over their enemies is essential to defend life, liberty, independence and religious freedom, and to preserve human rights and justice in their own lands as well as in other lands, and that they are now engaged in a common struggle against savage and brutal forces seeking to subjugate the world,

Declare:

(i) Each Government pledges itself to employ its full resources, military or economic, against those members of the Tripartite Pact and its adherents with which such Government is at war.

(ii) Each Government pledges itself to cooperate with the Governments signatory hereto and not to make a separate armistice or peace with the enemies.

The foregoing Declaration may be adhered to by other nations which are, or may be, rendering material assistance and contributions in the struggle for victory over Hitlerism.

Alliance between Britain and the Soviet Union, London, 26 May 1942

His Majesty The King of Great Britain, Ireland, and the British Dominions beyond the Seas, Emperor of India, and the Presidium of the Supreme Council of the Union of Soviet Socialist Republics;

Desiring to confirm the stipulations of the Agreement between His Majesty's Government in the United Kingdom and the Government of the Union of Soviet Socialist Republics for joint action in the war against Germany, signed at Moscow on the 12th July 1941, and to replace them by a formal treaty;

Desiring to contribute after the war to the maintenance of peace and to the prevention of further aggression by Germany or the States associated with her in acts of aggression in Europe;

Desiring, moreover, to give expression to their intention to collaborate closely with one another as well as with the other United Nations at the peace settlement and during the ensuing period of reconstruction on the basis of the principles enunciated in the declaration made on the 14th August 1941 by the President of the United States of America and the Prime Minister of Great Britain to which the Government of the Union of Soviet Socialist Republics has adhered;

Desiring, finally, to provide for mutual assistance in the event of an attack upon either High Contracting Party by Germany or any of the States associated with her in acts of aggression in Europe . . . .

Have decided to conclude a Treaty for that purpose and have appointed as their plenipotentiaries:

His Majesty The King of Great Britain, Ireland, and the British Dominions beyond the Seas, Emperor of India,

For the United Kingdom of Great Britain and Northern Ireland:

The Right Honourable Anthony Eden, M.P., His Majesty's Principal Secretary of State for Foreign Affairs,

The Presidium of the Supreme Council of the Union of Soviet Socialist Republics:

M. Vyacheslav Mikhailovich Molotov, People's Commissar for Foreign Affairs,

Who, having communicated their full powers, found in good and due form, have agreed as follows:

Part I

Article I. In virtue of the alliance established between the United Kingdom and the Union of Soviet Socialist Republics the High Contracting Parties mutually undertake to afford one another military and other assistance and support of all kinds in the war against Germany and all those States which are associated with her in acts of aggression in Europe.

Article II. The High Contracting Parties undertake not to enter into any negotiations with the Hitlerite Government or any other Government in Germany that does not clearly renounce all aggressive intentions, and not to negotiate or conclude except by mutual consent any armistice or peace treaty with Germany or any other State associated with her in acts of aggression in Europe.

Part II

Article III. (1) The High Contracting Parties declare their desire to unite with other likeminded States in adopting proposals for common action to preserve peace and resist aggression in the post-war period.

(2) Pending the adoption of such proposals, they will after the termination of hostilities take all the measures in their power to render impossible a repetition of aggression and violation of the peace by Germany or any of the States associated with her in acts of aggression in Europe.

Article IV. Should one of the High Contracting Parties during the post-war period become involved in hostilities with Germany or any of the States mentioned in Article III (2) in consequence of an attack by that State against that party, the other High Contracting Party will at once give to the Contracting Party so involved in hostilities all the military and other support and assistance in his power.

This Article shall remain in force until the High Contracting Parties, by mutual agreement, shall recognize that it is superseded by the adoption of the proposals contemplated in Article III (I). In default of the adoption of such proposals, it shall remain in force for a period of twenty years, and thereafter until terminated by either High Contracting Party, as provided in Article VIII.

Article V. The High Contracting Parties, having regard to the interests of the security of each of them, agree to work together in close and friendly collaboration after the re-establishment of peace for the organization of security and economic prosperity in Europe. They will take into account the interests of the United Nations in these objects, and they will act in accordance with the two principles of not seeking territorial aggrandizement for themselves and of non-interference in the internal affairs of other States.

Article VI. The High Contracting Parties agree to render one another all possible economic assistance after the war.

Article VII. Each High Contracting Party undertakes not to conclude any alliance and not to take part in any coalition directed against the other High Contracting party.

Article VIII. The present Treaty is subject to ratification in the shortest possible time and the instruments of ratification shall be exchanged in Moscow as soon as possible.

It comes into force immediately on the exchange of the instruments of ratification and shall thereupon replace the Agreement between the Government of the Union of Soviet Socialist Republics and His Majesty's Government in the United Kingdom, signed at Moscow on the 12th July 1941.

Part I of the present Treaty shall remain in force until the re-establishment of peace between the High Contracting Parties and Germany and the Powers associated with her in acts of aggression in Europe.

Part II of the present Treaty shall remain in force for a period of twenty years. Thereafter, unless twelve months' notice has been given by either party to terminate the Treaty at the end of the said period of twenty years, it shall continue in force until twelve months after either High Contracting Party shall have given notice to the other in writing of his intention to terminate it.

In witness whereof the above-named plenipotentiaries have signed the present Treaty and have affixed thereto their seals.

Done in duplicate in London on the 26th day of May, 1942, in the English and Russian languages, both texts being equally authentic.

(L.S.) ANTHONY EDEN
(L.S.) V. MOLOTOV

Poland, Czechoslovakia and the Soviet Union, 1941–44

The Polish government in exile in London, headed by General Władysław Sikorski, fought uncompromisingly for Poland's pre-war frontiers. With the entry of the USSR into the war the Polish government with equal urgency wished to secure the release of Polish prisoners placed into camps by the Russians. Polish–Soviet diplomatic relations were resumed with the signature of the *Polish–Soviet Treaty of 30 July 1941*. Though the Soviet Union in this treaty declared that the German–Soviet treaties of 1939 relating to Polish territory had 'lost their validity' Stalin did not abandon his claim to the Polish territory then seized.

The *Anglo–Soviet Agreement of 12 July 1941* had been accompanied by a *British Note to the Polish Government of 30 July 1941* (p. 248) in which the British government declared that, in conformity with the Anglo–Polish alliance of 1939, it had entered into no undertaking towards the USSR affecting Polish–Soviet relations, and that His Majesty's Government did not recognize any territorial changes which had been effected in Poland since August 1939.

On 14 August 1941 a Polish–Soviet Military Agreement was concluded providing for the organization of a Polish army in the USSR Poles kept in camps in Russia were to be released. The USSR was to assist in the arming of Polish units who would fight in the Soviet Union under Polish command, but this would be sub-ordinated operationally under the High Command of the USSR In December 1941 General Sikorski visited Moscow, and a *Polish–Soviet Declaration of Friendship and Mutual Assistance was signed on 4 December 1941*. But from 1941 to 1943 Polish Soviet relations were embittered by Russia's claim to have irrevocably annexed the region of pre-war Poland occupied in 1939, and by Russian insistence that according to Soviet law the permanent inhabitants of those lands were Soviet citizens. The Poles were also dissatisfied with the treatment of Poles released from Russian camps, and individual cases of maltreatment. Polish officers and men continued to be missing. Soviet–Polish relations were close to breaking point when the Germans broadcast on 13 April 1943 that they had discovered a mass grave of some 10,000 Polish officers in Katyn, near Smolensk, and accused the Russians of their murder. The Polish government requested the International Red Cross to investigate, and on 25 April 1943 the Russians severed relations with the Polish government, declaring that the Germans had massacred the missing Polish officers and that in accusing the Russians the Polish government in London was acting in collusion with Hitler. The problem of Poland continued to present a major difficulty in the way of Allied cooperation to the end of the war.

The Czechoslovak government in exile chose a different course from the Polish government in dealing with the Soviet Union. Soviet–Czech military cooperation against Germany was provided for in the *Czechoslovak–Soviet Agreement of 18 July 1941*. Beneš had been disillusioned by the Munich settlement in 1938 and would no longer rely solely on the friendship of the western powers. He was determined to win Russia's friendship and to secure from all the Allies a declaration that since the Munich settlement had been imposed by threat of force on Czechoslovakia it was invalid. The British government would only agree to declare that since the Germans had subsequently broken it, the Munich treaty was no longer binding. The Soviet government, on the other hand, recognized the Czechoslovak government in exile and Czechoslovakia in its 1937 frontiers, and also declared the Munich settlement as illegal and void. A *Soviet–Czechoslovak Treaty of Friendship and Alliance was signed on 12 December 1943* (p. 253). Beneš, in Moscow for the signature of the treaty, was also confronted with Russian demands for aligning the post-war Czech economy with the Soviet economy, which he consented to in an additional agreement. *On 8 May 1944 a further Soviet–Czechoslovak Agreement regarding the administration of liberated Czechoslovak territories* was concluded. The Soviet advance into Czechoslovakia began in the autumn of 1944, but too late to prevent the Germans crushing a national uprising in Slovakia. Czech administrators were only permitted to function with Soviet consent and the Czechoslovak government had to accept the 'wish' of the Ruthenians to accede to the Soviet Union. With the acquisition of this strategically vital territory together with the eastern Polish territories, the Soviet Union gained a common frontier with Hungary and Czechoslovakia.

Agreement between Poland and the Soviet Union, 30 July 1941

The Government of the Republic of Poland and the Government of the Union of Soviet Socialist Republics have concluded the present Agreement and decided as follows:

1. The Government of the Union of Soviet Socialist Republics recognizes that the Soviet–German treaties of 1939 relative to territorial changes in Poland have lost their validity. The Government of the Republic of Poland declares that Poland is not bound by any Agreement with any third State directed against the U.S.S.R.

2. Diplomatic relations will be restored between the two Governments upon the signature of this Agreement and an exchange of Ambassadors will follow immediately.

3. The two Governments mutually undertake to render one another aid and support of all kinds in the present war against Hitlerite Germany.

4. The Government of the Union of Soviet Socialist Republics expresses its consent to the formation on the territory of the Union of Soviet Socialist Republics of a Polish army under a commander appointed by the Government of the Republic of Poland, in agreement with the Government of the Union of Soviet Socialist Republics. The Polish army on the territory of the

Union of Soviet Socialist Republics will be subordinated in operational matters to the Supreme Command of the U.S.S.R. on which there will be a representative of the Polish army. All details as to command, organization and employment of this force will be settled in a subsequent agreement.

5. This Agreement will come into force immediately upon its signature and without ratification. The present Agreement is drawn up in two copies, each of them in the Russian and Polish languages. Both texts have equal force.

Secret Protocol

1. Various claims both of public and private nature will be dealt with in the course of further negotiations between the two Governments.

2. This Protocol enters into force simultaneously with the Agreement of the 30th of July, 1941.

Protocol

1. As soon as diplomatic relations are re-established the Government of the Union of Soviet Socialist Republics will grant

amnesty to all Polish citizens who are at present deprived of their freedom on the territory of the U.S.S.R. either as prisoners of war or on other adequate grounds.

2. The present Protocol comes into force simultaneously with the Agreement of July 30, 1941.

Treaty of Friendship and Mutual Assistance and Post-War Cooperation between the Soviet Union and Czechoslovakia, Moscow, 12 December 1943

The Presidium of the Supreme Soviet of the Union of Soviet Socialist Republics and the President of the Czechoslovakian Republic, desiring to modify and supplement the Treaty of Mutual Assistance existing between the Union of Soviet Socialist Republics and the Czechoslovakian Republic and signed in Prague on May 16, 1935, and to confirm the terms of the Agreement between the Government of the Union of Soviet Socialist Republics and the Government of the Czechoslovakian Republic concerning joint action in the war against Germany, signed July 18, 1941, in London; desiring to cooperate after the war to maintain peace and to prevent further aggression on the part of Germany and to assure permanent friendship and peaceful post-war cooperation between them, have resolved to conclude for this purpose a Treaty and ... have agreed to the following:

Article 1. The High Contracting Parties, having agreed mutually to join in a policy of permanent friendship and friendly post-war cooperation, as well as of mutual assistance, engage to extend to each other military and other assistance and support of all kinds in the present war against Germany and against all those States which are associated with it in acts of aggression in Europe.

Article 2. The High Contracting Parties engage not to enter during the period of the present war into any negotiations with the Hitler Government or with any other

Government in Germany which does not clearly renounce all aggressive intentions, and not to carry on negotiations and not to conclude without mutual agreement any armistice or other treaty of peace with Germany or with any other State associated with it in acts of aggression in Europe.

Article 3. Affirming their pre-war policy of peace and mutual assistance, expressed in the treaty signed at Prague on May 16, 1935, the High Contracting Parties, in case one of them in the period after the war should become involved in military action with Germany, which might resume its policy of 'Drang nach Osten', or with any other State which might join with Germany directly or in any other form in such a war, engage to extend immediately to the other Contracting Party thus involved in military action all manner of military and other support and assistance at its disposal.

Article 4. The High Contracting Parties, having regard to the security interests of each of them, agree to close and friendly cooperation in the period after the restoration of peace and agree to act in accordance with the principles of mutual respect for their independence and sovereignty, as well as of non-interference in the internal affairs of the other State. They agree to develop their economic relations to the fullest possible extent and to extend to each other all possible economic assistance after the war.

Article 5. Each of the High Contracting Parties engages not to conclude any alliance and not to take part in any coalition directed against the other High Contracting Party.

Article 6. The present Treaty shall come into force immediately after signature and shall be ratified within the shortest possible time; the exchange of ratifications will take place in Moscow as soon as possible.

The present Treaty shall remain in force for a period of twenty years from the date of signature, and if one of the High Contracting Parties at the end of this period of twenty years does not give notice of its desire to terminate the Treaty twelve months before its expiration, it will continue to remain in force for the following five years and for each ensuing five-year period unless one of the High Contracting Parties gives notice in writing twelve months before the expiration of the current five-year period of its intention to terminate it.

Protocol

On the conclusion of the Treaty of Friendship, Mutual Assistance and Post-War Cooperation between the Union of Soviet Socialist Republics and the Czechoslovakian Republic the High Contracting Parties undertake that, in the event that any third country bordering on the U.S.S.R. or the Czechoslovakian Republic and constituting in this war an object of German aggression desires to subscribe to this Treaty, it will be given the opportunity, upon the joint agreement of the Governments of the U.S.S.R. and the Czechoslovakian Republic, to adhere to this Treaty, which will thus acquire the character of a tripartite agreement.

By Authority of the Presidium of the Supreme Council of the U.S.S.R.
V. MOLOTOV

By Authority of the President of the Czechoslovakian Republic
Z. FIERLINGER

The Allies and France, 1941–45

France and Germany signed an *armistice on 22 June 1940.* On 28 June 1940 the British government recognized General de Gaulle as the 'Leader of all Free Frenchmen, wherever they may be, who rally to him in support of the Allied cause'. The future of the French fleet, still in the control of the new French government of Marshal Pétain, and of the French colonial empire remained in doubt, though Britain received French assurances that the fleet would not be allowed to fall into the hands of the Germans. But the British government was not prepared to trust these assurances and there resulted the British bombardment on French warships at Mers-el-Kebir on 3 July 1940. Britain and Vichy France broke direct diplomatic links, but avoided a complete breach. The United States and Vichy France remained in normal diplomatic relations after the armistice which precluded the recognition of de Gaulle's movement as the government of France in exile. By the end of August 1940 the French African colonial territories of Chad and the Cameroons rallied to de Gaulle and became the nucleus of 'Free France'. The French empire in North Africa and Indo-China remained loyal to Vichy France. On 8 June 1941 an Anglo-French force was sent to the French mandated territory of Syria, which remained loyal to Vichy. The Free French issued a proclamation declaring Syria and the Lebanon 'sovereign and independent peoples'. After heavy fighting *Syria* passed into Anglo-Free French wartime control with the *armistice of 14 July 1941*. In the autumn of 1941, the Free French movement was strengthened by the creation and British recognition of a Free French National Committee. But the United States continued to remain in full diplomatic relations with Vichy France after entering the war in December 1941. In July 1942 it recognized the French National Committee without breaking with Vichy, and by Allied agreement the Free French movement called itself the 'Fighting French', implying leadership of all Frenchmen fighting the Germans whether in 'Free' French territories or in metropolitan Vichy France.

Throughout 1942 the United States and Britain continued, for what appeared to be compelling military reasons, to treat Vichy France as a legitimate government to ensure that the French fleet should remain in French hands and to avoid driving the Vichy North African territory into open opposition. In May 1942 British troops began the occupation of Vichy France Madagascar, without prior reference to General de Gaulle for fear of driving the Vichy colonial authorities into active opposition. Madagascar was a curtain raiser for North Africa where the Anglo-American allies were prepared to negotiate with the Vichy French authorities, ignoring the claims of the Free French National Committee to represent all French interests. Operation Torch was the name given to the Anglo-American invasion of French North Africa which had remained loyal to Vichy. General de Gaulle and the Free French did not participate in the landings, and the operation was kept secret from them. The Allies pinned their hopes on General Giraud, who had escaped from a German prisoner-of-war camp in April 1942, to rally French North Africa to the Allied cause. The Allied landings began on 8 November 1942 near Algiers, Oran and Casablanca. Three days later, on 11 November, the Germans militarily occupied 'Unoccupied France', but the Vichy French commanders succeeded in scuttling the French fleet at Toulon. Contrary to expectations General Giraud had little influence. Admiral Darlan, who was visiting Algiers, as the highest ranking representative of Vichy commanded the French forces. *It was with the Vichy French administration under Darlan that the Allies reached agreement on 17 November 1942*, accepting Darlan's authority and securing the ending of French military resistance to the Allied operations. With the assassination of Darlan on 23 December 1942, Giraud assumed political leadership. Although General de Gaulle met General Giraud at the Casablanca conference in January 1943, Giraud maintained Vichy legality; *not until 3 June 1943 was an agreement signed fixing Giraud's and de Gaulle's authorities in a new French Committee of National Liberation* under their joint presidency. With the exception of the Soviet government, Britain and the United States refused to recognize the National Committee as legitimately representing the interests of all France. The French Committee of National Liberation began to change its composition in November 1943, admitting French political parties and representatives of the resistance and dropping Giraud step by step. On 15 May 1944 the French Committee of National Liberation changed its name to Provisional Government of the Republic of France under de Gaulle's leadership, General Giraud having resigned on 14 April 1944. But General Eisenhower, the Supreme Allied Commander, refused to recognize de Gaulle's authority before D-Day, 6 June 1944, when the Allies began their assault on German-occupied France. Only on 11 July 1944 were the Americans prepared to recognize de Gaulle and his committee as the *de facto* representatives of the French people. Full recognition was awarded by Great Britain, the United States and the Soviet Union to General de Gaulle as the head of the Provisional Government of France on 23 October 1944. *An Alliance Treaty between the Soviet Union and France was concluded on 10 December 1944* (see below). The treaty was to last twenty years and, unless ended with notice of one year, 'indefinitely'. It was directed exclusively against the resurgence of German aggression and both countries undertook to obstruct any measures that would make reviewed aggression possible. The onset of the cold war and the Franco–German *rapprochement* made this treaty unreal within ten years. France was invited to become a member of the European Advisory Commission and the fifth permanent member of the proposed Security Council of the United Nations organization (p. 301).

Treaty of Alliance and Mutual Assistance between the Soviet Union and the French Republic, Moscow, 10 December 1944

The Presidium of the Supreme Soviet of the Union of Soviet Socialist Republics and the Provisional Government of the French Republic, determined to prosecute jointly and to the end the war against Germany, convinced that once victory is achieved, the re-establishment of peace on a stable basis and its prolonged maintenance in the future will be conditioned upon the existence of close collaboration between them and with all the United Nations; having resolved to collaborate in the cause of the creation of an international system of security for the effective maintenance of general peace and for ensuring the harmonious development of relations between nations; desirous of confirming the mutual obligations resulting from the exchange of letters of September 20, 1941, concerning joint actions in the war against Germany; convinced that the conclusion of an alliance between the U.S.S.R. and France corresponds to the sentiments and interests of both peoples, the demands of war, and the requirements of peace and economic reconstruction in full conformity with the aims which the United Nations have set themselves, have decided to conclude a Treaty to this effect and appointed as their plenipotentiaries . . .

Article I. Each of the High Contracting Parties shall continue the struggle on the side of the other party and on the side of the United Nations until final victory over Germany. Each of the High Contracting Parties undertakes to render the other party aid and assistance in this struggle with all the means at its disposal.

Article II. The High Contracting Parties shall not agree to enter into separate negotiations with Germany or to conclude without mutual consent any armistice or peace treaty either with the Hitler Government or with any other Government or authority set up in Germany for the purpose of the continuation or support of the policy of German aggression.

Article III. The High Contracting Parties undertake also, after the termination of the present war with Germany, to take jointly all necessary measures for the elimination of any new threat coming from Germany, and to obstruct such actions as would make possible any new attempt at aggression on her part.

Article IV. In the event either of the High Contracting Parties finds itself involved in military operations against Germany, whether as a result of aggression committed by the latter or as a result of the operation of the above Article III, the other party shall at once render it every aid and assistance within its power.

Article V. The High Contracting Parties undertake not to conclude any alliance and not to take part in any coalition directed against either of the High Contracting Parties.

Article VI. The High Contracting Parties agree to render each other every possible economic assistance after the war, with a view to facilitating and accelerating reconstruction of both countries, and in order to contribute to the cause of world prosperity.

Article VII. The present Treaty does not in any way affect obligations undertaken previously by the High Contracting Parties in regard to third States in virtue of published treaties.

Article VIII. The present Treaty, whose Russian and French texts are equally valid, shall be ratified and ratification instruments shall be exchanged in Paris as early as possible. It comes into force from the moment of the exchange of ratification instruments and shall be valid for twenty years. If the Treaty is not denounced by either of the High Contracting Parties at least one year before the expiration of this term, it shall remain valid for an unlimited time; each of the Contracting Parties will be able to terminate its operation by giving notice to that effect one year in advance . . . .

On the authorization of the Presidium of the Supreme Soviet of the U.S.S.R.

MOLOTOV

On the authorization of the Provisional Government of the French Republic

BIDAULT

The Allies and Italy, 1943–45

The Allies landed in Sicily on 10 July 1943; on 25 July 1943 Mussolini fell from power and was replaced by Marshal Pietro Badoglio, who secretly negotiated a military armistice accepting the Allied terms of surrender on 3 September 1943. The *Italian armistice* required Italy to withdraw her armed forces from the war, established an Allied Military Government under the Allied Commander-in-Chief over all parts of Italy, and bound the Italian government at a later time to accept the political and economic conditions demanded by the Allies. The armistice was publicly announced on *8 September 1943* to coincide with the Allied seaborne invasion of Italy at Salerno. More detailed armistice conditions were signed on *29 September 1943*. On 13 October 1943 the King of Italy declared war on Germany, and Italy was granted the status of co-belligerency. Italy became a battleground of the Allied forces and the Germans, who militarily occupied central and northern Italy over which Mussolini's Republic of Salò claimed legal control. The Italian Peace Treaty was eventually signed in February 1947, nearly two years after the German surrender in May 1945.

X · The wartime conferences and the surrender of Japan, 1943-45

The conferences

The Allied conferences from 1943 to 1945 attempted to reconcile the wartime military policies of the Allies with an agreed programme of post-war settlements in Europe and Asia. For the sake of the maximum possible degree of military cooperation which was necessary to defeat the powerful and fanatically tenacious German war effort, fundamental Allied differences were not allowed to develop into major rifts. At the Yalta Conference the great power interests of Britain, the United States and the Soviet Union largely determined the post-war settlements not only of defeated enemies but also of the smaller Allies. At Yalta, the Big Three displayed at least an outward show of unanimity of purpose and wartime comradeship. By the time of the Potsdam Conference a few months later the Allied differences which developed into the 'cold war' were already strongly in evidence.

The thirteen major Allied conferences of this period fall into two divisions: (1) predominantly Anglo-American, and (2) three power conferences between the Soviet Union, Britain and the United States, sometimes with other countries present. The table on pages 262–3 summarizes their sequence.

The first two important conferences of 1943 endeavoured to coordinate British and United States diplomacy and did not involve the Russians. From a political point of view the *Conference of Casablanca* (Churchill, Roosevelt, Combined Chiefs of Staff) *14–25 January 1943* was notable for the attempt made to bring together Generals Giraud and de Gaulle; also for the 'unconditional surrender' call as the only terms the Allies would offer their enemies. The phrase 'unconditional surrender' had been under discussion, but was omitted from the final communiqué, though publicly announced in a press conference given by President Roosevelt.

Research which was to lead to the making of the atomic bomb was the subject

259

of a secret Anglo-American agreement at the *Quebec Conference of August 1943*, not disclosed until 1954. The exclusive possession of the bomb with its secrets, and the unknown possible application of atomic energy after the war, made the know-ledge of the secrets one of the most prized assets of power in the war and in the post-war world. These secrets were not shared with the Soviet Union. *The Agreement on Anglo-American–Canadian collaboration and development of atomic research was signed on 19 August 1943* by Churchill and Roosevelt. It set out the policy of pooling in the United States the scientists and resources to speed the project. The two countries undertook not to use the atomic bomb against each other; they also agreed not to use it against another country without each others' consent; they agreed not to communicate any information to another country without their mutual consent. Britain disclaimed any 'post-war advantages of an industrial or commercial character' beyond what the president of the United States considered fair and just and for the welfare of the world. Allocation of materials, all policy, and interchange of information was to be the function of a Combined Policy Committee of the three American, two British and one Canadian officials. Infor-mation about large-scale plants was to become the subject of later agreements. The first atomic bomb was dropped on Hiroshima on 6 August 1945 and the second on Nagasaki on 9 August 1945. The post-war operation of this secret executive agreement caused Anglo-American differences of opinion in 1945 and 1946 after Roosevelt's death; its existence was unknown to Congress. The Ameri-can desire to preserve secrecy and military nuclear monopoly led to the passing of the McMahon Act in 1946 which made the wartime agreement in practice inoperative.

At the *Conference of Foreign Ministers at Moscow* (Molotov, Eden, Hull, Deane) *18–30 October 1943*, agreement was reached on a *Four Power Declaration of General Security* whereby the United States, Great Britain, the Soviet Union and China agreed to help establish a general international organization for the maintenance of peace and security, and to continue their collaboration in peace as in war. The confer-ence also agreed to set up a *European Advisory Commission* with headquarters in London to consider all specific questions concerning the surrender terms and their execution; the commission was empowered to make recommendations but could exercise no mandatory authority. An *Advisory Council for Italy* was also estab-lished but exercised little influence. The Foreign Ministers agreed that Austria should be re-established as an independent state after the war. A decision on cooperating in the punishment of individuals responsible for atrocities was also reached. At the end of the conference an official communiqué was issued together with four *Declarations on General Security, Italy, Austria, and German Atrocities, 30 October 1943.*

The Cairo Conference took place on 22–26 November 1943 (Roosevelt, Churchill, Chi-ang Kai-shek). The Russians would not attend since they were not at war with

Japan. Besides military strategy in the Far East, the post-war settlement there was discussed. The final communiqué outlined the territorial peace terms the three Allies would impose on Japan, and promised Korea independence in due course.

Roosevelt and Churchill next flew to Persia to participate with the Russians in the *Teheran Conference* (Churchill, Roosevelt, Stalin, Eden, Hopkins, Combined Chiefs of Staff) *28 November–1 December 1943*. The military situation in Europe and the Far East was discussed. Stalin declared the Soviet Union would join in the war against Japan after victory over Germany. There were exploratory discussions concerning the future of France, Germany and Poland. Roosevelt initiated a discussion on the establishment of a post-war international organization to preserve peace and security. It was agreed that 'Overlord', the Anglo-American invasion of northern France, would take place on 1 May 1944. Turkey and Italy were discussed. No formal written agreement was reached on the Soviet Union's and Poland's western frontiers, though Churchill agreed to the Curzon line as a basis and to the acquisition by Poland of German territory east of the Oder river. A declaration promised to Iran independence and territorial integrity. A communiqué on the results of the conference was published on 6 December 1943.

More than a year elapsed after the conclusion of the Teheran Conference until Churchill, Roosevelt and Stalin met again at Yalta in February 1945. Meantime Roosevelt and Churchill and the Combined Chiefs of Staff had met at *Quebec, 11– 19 September 1944* to discuss future policy towards Germany; Churchill flew to Moscow to discuss post-war spheres of influence, the Balkans and Poland, with Stalin; Harriman attended as an observer from 9–20 October 1944. Shortly before Yalta, the Combined Chiefs of Staff, Churchill, Eden and Stettinius met at *Malta, 30 January–3 February 1945*, to examine military strategy and the Anglo-American zones of occupation, and briefly discuss Italy and China.

The 'Big Three' meeting at *Yalta* (Churchill, Roosevelt, Stalin, Chiefs of Staff, Molotov, Stettinius, Eden, Hopkins) *4–11 February 1945* (p. 267) was the most crucial of the war in moulding the reconstruction of the post-war world. Roosevelt was anxious to secure a firm Russian undertaking to join in the war against Japan. He acceded to Stalin's condition that the Soviet Union should resume her old rights in China lost as a result of the Russo-Japanese war of 1904–5. Despite the difficulties of China's rights, *a secret tripartite agreement was signed on 11 February 1945* concerning Russia's participation in the war against Japan (p. 270); this agreement was only published a year after its signature on 11 February 1946. Allied policy towards Germany led to discussions and agreements at Yalta. The European Advisory Commission had reached agreed recommendations which formed the basis of the awards at Yalta on the zones of occupation, on Berlin and on the form of Allied control. At Yalta agreement was also reached to allow the French a zone of occupation and to admit France as an equal member of the Allied Control Commission for Germany. A decision on reparations was referred to a

The major wartime conferences

Date	Place	Participants	Subjects discussed
14–25 January 1943	Casablanca	Britain, US	Reconciling rival French leaders on the allied side; 'unconditional surrender' call; Far Eastern and European strategy.
19–24 August 1943	Quebec	Britain, US, Canada	Atomic research and use of atomic bomb; 'second front' in Europe; Far Eastern strategy; Italian surrender.
18–30 October 1943	Moscow	Britain, US, USSR (Foreign Ministers)	United Nations; Austria; surrender terms; war criminals.
22–6 November 1943	Cairo	Britain, US, China	Japanese surrender terms; Far Eastern settlement; Far Eastern military strategy.
28 November–1 December 1943	Teheran	Britain, US, USSR	European and Far Eastern strategy; Russia and Japan; United Nations; Turkey; Italy; Russia's frontiers; Poland; Germany's eastern frontier.
1–22 July 1944	Bretton Woods	44 countries	International finance and trade.
21 August–7 October 1944	Dumbarton Oaks	Britain, US, USSR, China (China participated 29 September–7 October)	United Nations

Date	Location	Participants	Topics
11–19 September 1944	Quebec	Britain, US, Canada	Germany; military strategy in Europe and in war against Japan.
9–20 October 1944	Moscow	Britain, USSR (with US observer)	Balkan 'spheres of influence'; Poland; Soviet entry into war against Japan.
30 January–3 February 1945	Malta	Britain, US	Military strategy; occupation zones in Germany; Italy; China.
4–11 February 1945	Yalta	Britain, US, USSR	Post-war policies: Germany, United Nations, Poland, liberated Europe, Russia, Japan and China.
25 April–26 June 1945	San Francisco	50 countries	United Nations
17 July–2 August 1945	Potsdam	Britain, US, USSR	Draft peace treaties; Germany; Poland; Japan.

Reparations Commission to be set up in Moscow. The decisions concerning Allied treatment of Germany reached at Yalta lacked precision and were vague, since practical details were not worked out. They were summarized in Protocols III, IV, V and VI of the Proceedings of the Conference. Protocol I set out the agreement reached on the setting up of a world organization of the United Nations, and more especially on the voting formula for the Security Council; it was agreed to call a United Nations Conference at San Francisco on 25 April 1945 (p. 268).

The future of Poland was a most contentious and difficult issue at Yalta, and no precise conclusions were reached on post-war Polish boundaries (though the Curzon line with some small digressions in Poland's favour was referred to as Poland's eastern frontier). Nor was there agreement over the 'reconstruction' of the Polish government. The ambiguous Declaration on Poland was embodied in Protocol VII. A number of other important post-war problems were set out in Protocols IX to XIV. Finally, the Declaration on Liberated Europe, Protocol II, is noteworthy as an attempt, on American initiative, to commit the Soviet Union to the restoration of democratic national self-government to the states occupied by the Russian armies at the close of the war.

By the time of the next Big Three meeting at Potsdam in July 1945 the war in Europe was over. Admiral Dönitz, who had succeeded Hitler, authorized the acceptance of Germany's unconditional surrender, and the instrument of surrender was signed at Eisenhower's headquarters in Rheims on 7 May 1945; Stalin insisted on a second capitulation in Berlin on 9 May 1945 a day after the fighting had ended. Before the Potsdam meeting the agreements reached at Yalta were being differently interpreted by the Allies. Russian pressure for the establishment of a communist government on 6 March 1945 was regarded by the western Allies as in breach of the Declaration of Liberated Europe. On 10 March 1945, Stalin assigned to Roumania the part of Transylvania which Hitler had awarded to Hungary. Allied disputes over the future Polish government continued. On 12 April 1945 Roosevelt died and Truman was sworn in as President. Serious Allied differences over the control of Austria, deep suspicion of Russian intentions in Poland, problems in occupied Germany, hard-won agreement over the establishment of an international organization and the reparations question were all part of the diplomatic confrontation during the immediate aftermath of the end of the war in Europe. Some differences were patched up. The Charter of the United Nations was signed on 26 June 1945 (p. 309). The British government and the United States recognized a reorganized Soviet-sponsored Polish Provisional government of National Unity on 5 July 1945. The machinery of Allied control over Germany was established, and the zones of occupation brought under the respective military control of the USSR, France, Britain and the United States. The Polish western frontier had not been finally settled at Yalta; the Russians handed over German territory as far as the rivers Oder and the western Neisse to Polish administration. The Potsdam Conference was to settle future Allied policies, to lay the foundation for definitive peace settlements and to reach agreed policies on the treatment of Germany.

The Potsdam Conference, 17 July–2 August 1945 (p. 271) – *Attlee, Churchill* (prime minister until 26 July when the general election brought Attlee and the Labour Party to power), *Stalin, Truman, Bevin, Byrnes, Eden, Molotov* – appeared to get off to a good start with an agreement on an American proposal that a Council of Foreign Ministers should be set up to prepare drafts of peace treaties with the ex-enemy states in Europe and Asia (this body replaced the European Advisory Commission); London was chosen as the permanent seat of the council. The French had not been invited to Potsdam but were to be represented on the Council of Foreign Ministers. Germany's frontiers were not established with finality, though it was agreed that the frontiers of 1937 should be taken as the basis for discussion, which excluded Austria, the territory taken from Czechoslovakia at Munich, as well as German-occupied Poland. The Polish question led to acrimonious debate, particularly the extent of Polish expansion eastward at Germany's expense, the Russians and Britain and the United States differing later as to what had been settled. The agreement left under the Polish administration the territory assigned to them by the Russians, adding that it was not 'considered as part of the Soviet zone of occupation of Germany'; while the final delimitation of Poland's western frontier was reserved until the conclusion of a German peace treaty. Soviet claims to about half of East Prussia including Königsberg were accepted, by Britain and the United States who undertook to support the Soviet Union when a peace conference assembled. Agreement was reached on the treatment of Austria. But Soviet insistence that immediate recognition be granted to the Soviet-sponsored Armistice governments of Hungary, Bulgaria and Roumania proved unacceptable to the three western powers, as did western insistence on supervised genuinely free elections. In practice these three countries were left in Soviet control. The western interpretation of the Yalta Declaration on Liberated Europe could not be realized. Many questions remained unsettled, such as the Turkish Straits and the Italian colonies. On the central problem of the treatment of Germany, agreements were reached which reflected paper compromises. The idea of partitioning Germany into a number of states was dropped. Supreme authority in Germany was to be exercised by the Commanders-in-Chief of the British, French, American and Russian armed forces each in their own zones, whilst for Germany as a whole they were to act jointly as members of the Control Council. Principles governing the treatment of the whole of Germany leading to disarmament, de-nazification and demilitarization were agreed. But policies in practice differed widely between the Russian and western zones of occupation. Similarly, it was agreed that Germany was to be treated as a single economic unit with a living standard for the German people *not exceeding* the average of other Europeans, but again control of German industry was exercised differently in each zone, as was the collection of reparations despite agreement on general principles. The differing views of the Russians and western powers on reparations and the German frontiers proved amongst the most intractable problems of the conference. The decisions concerning Germany in practice undermined the general principle of treating occupied Germany as a whole, and confirmed the divisions of Germany especially as between the Russian and western zones. A major problem was the settlement of German refugees, several million of whom were either fleeing or were being expelled from Polish-occupied Germany, from the Sudetenland, East Prussia and Hungary. Their expulsion was accepted at Potsdam as necessary but it was supposed to be carried out in an 'orderly and humane manner'.

The surrender of Japan, 14 August 1945

The British and American delegations at Potsdam agreed, on behalf of the nations at war with Japan, on a declaration calling upon Japan to submit to surrender 'unconditionally', and published the *Potsdam Declaration on 26 July 1945*. In practice this declaration outlined surrender conditions. On 6 and 9 August 1945 atomic bombs were dropped on Hiroshima and Nagasaki. On 8 August 1945 the Soviet Union declared war on Japan, to take effect the following day when the Russian armies began occupying Manchuria. On 10 August the Japanese acceptance of the conditions of the Potsdam Declaration was received by the Americans, but Japan's acceptance was conditional on the Allies agreeing that the prerogatives of the emperor as a sovereign ruler were not prejudiced. The Americans replied on 11 August 1945 that the emperor would be subject to the Supreme Commander and that the 'ultimate form of government of Japan shall, in accordance with the Potsdam Declaration, be established by the freely expressed will of the Japanese people'. On these conditions the Japanese surrendered on 14 August 1945. The formal instrument of surrender was signed on 2 September 1945 in Tokyo Bay. Japanese armies throughout Asia surrendered to the military Commander-in-Chief in each region. The Japanese armies in Manchuria, Korea north of the 38th parallel, the Kuriles and Sakhalin surrendered to the Russians. The Soviet Union regularized the hasty Russian invasion of Manchuria by concluding the *Sino–Soviet Treaty of Friendship on 14 August 1945* (p. 277).

Report of the Crimea Conference (Yalta Conference), 11 February 1945

For the past eight days Winston S. Church-ill, Prime Minister of Great Britain, Frank-lin D. Roosevelt, President of the United States of America, and Marshal J. V. Stalin, Chairman of the Council of People's Commissars of the Union of Soviet Social-ist Republics, have met with the Foreign Secretaries, Chiefs of Staff and other advisers in the Crimea.

In addition to the three Heads of Gov-ernment, the following took part in the Conference . . .

The following statement is made by the Prime Minister of Great Britain, the Presi-dent of the United States of America, and the Chairman of the Council of People's Commissars of the Union of Soviet Social-ist Republics, on the results of the Crimea Conference.

I. THE DEFEAT OF GERMANY

We have considered and determined the military plans of the three Allied Powers for the final defeat of the common enemy. The military staffs of the three Allied nations have met in daily meetings throughout the Conference. These meetings have been most satisfactory from every point of view and have resulted in closer coordination of the military effort of the three Allies than ever before. The fullest information has been interchanged. The timing, scope and coordination of new and even more power-ful blows to be launched by our armies and air forces into the heart of Germany from the East, West, North and South have been fully agreed and planned in detail.

Our combined military plans will be made known only as we execute them, but we believe that the very close working part-nership among the three staffs attained at this Conference will result in shortening the war. Meetings of the three staffs will be con-tinued in the future whenever the need arises.

Nazi Germany is doomed. The German people will only make the cost of their defeat heavier to themselves by attempting to continue a hopeless resistance.

II. THE OCCUPATION AND CONTROL OF GERMANY

We have agreed on common policies and plans for enforcing the unconditional sur-render terms which we shall impose together on Nazi Germany after German armed resistance has been finally crushed. These terms will not be made known until the final defeat of Germany has been accomplished. Under the agreed plan, the forces of the Three Powers will each occupy a separate zone of Germany. Coordinated administration and control has been pro-vided for under the plan through a central Control Commission consisting of the Supreme Commanders of the Three Powers with headquarters in Berlin. It has been agreed that France should be invited by the Three Powers, if she should so desire, to take over a zone of occupation, and to participate as a fourth member of the Control Commission. The limits of the French zone will be agreed by the four Governments concerned through their rep-resentatives on the European Advisory Commission.

It is our inflexible purpose to destroy German militarism and Nazism and to ensure that Germany will never again be able to disturb the peace of the world. We are determined to disarm and disband all German armed forces; break up for all time the German General Staff that has repeat-edly contrived the resurgence of German militarism; remove or destroy all German military equipment; eliminate or control all German industry that could be used for military production; bring all war criminals to just and swift punishment and exact rep-aration in kind for the destruction wrought by the Germans; wipe out the Nazi party, Nazi laws, organizations and institutions, remove all Nazi and militarist influences from public office and from the cultural and economic life of the German people; and take in harmony such other measures in Germany as may be necessary to the future peace and safety of the world. It is not our purpose to destroy the people of Germany, but only when Nazism and militarism have been extirpated, will there be hope for a decent life for Germans, and a place for them in the comity of nations.

III. REPARATION BY GERMANY

We have considered the question of the damage caused by Germany to the Allied nations in this war and recognized it as just that Germany be obliged to make compensation for this damage in kind to the greatest extent possible. A Commission for the Compensation of Damage will be established. The Commission will be instructed to consider the question of the extent and methods for compensating damage caused by Germany to the Allied countries. The Commission will work in Moscow.

IV. UNITED NATIONS CONFERENCE

We are resolved upon the earliest possible establishment with our Allies of a general international organization to maintain peace and security. We believe that this is essential, both to prevent aggression and to remove the political, economic and social causes of war through the close and continuing collaboration of all peace-loving peoples.

The foundations were laid at Dumbarton Oaks. On the important question of voting procedure, however, agreement was not there reached. The present Conference has been able to resolve this difficulty.

We have agreed that a Conference of United Nations should be called to meet at San Francisco in the United States on the 25th April 1945, to prepare the charter of such an organization, along the lines proposed in the informal conversations at Dumbarton Oaks.

The Government of China and the Provisional Government of France will be immediately consulted and invited to sponsor invitations to the Conference jointly with the Governments of the United States,

Great Britain and the Union of Soviet Socialist Republics. As soon as the consultation with China and France has been completed, the text of the proposals on voting procedure will be made public.

V. DECLARATION ON LIBERATED EUROPE

We have drawn up and subscribed to a Declaration on Liberated Europe. This Declaration provides for concerting the policies of the Three Powers and for joint action by them in meeting the political and economic problems of liberated Europe in accordance with democratic principles. The text of the Declaration is as follows:

The Premier of the Union of Soviet Socialist Republics, the Prime Minister of the United Kingdom, and the President of the United States of America have consulted with each other in the common interests of the peoples of their countries and those of liberated Europe. They jointly declare their mutual agreement to concert during the temporary period of instability in liberated Europe the policies of their three Governments in assisting the peoples liberated from the domination of Nazi Germany and the peoples of the former Axis satellite States of Europe to solve by democratic means their pressing political and economic problems.

The establishment of order in Europe and the rebuilding of national economic life must be achieved by processes which will enable the liberated peoples to destroy the last vestiges of Nazism and Fascism and to create democratic institutions of their own choice. This is a principle of the Atlantic Charter – the right of all peoples to choose the form of government under which they will live – the restoration of sovereign rights and self-government to those peoples who have been forcibly deprived of them by the aggressor nations.

To foster the conditions in which the liberated peoples may exercise those rights, the three Governments will jointly assist the people in any European liberated State or former Axis satellite State in Europe where in their judgement conditions require: (a) to establish conditions of internal peace; (b) to carry out emergency measures for the relief of distressed peoples; (c) to form interim governmental authorities broadly representative of all democratic elements in the population and pledged to the earliest possible establishment through free elections of Governments responsive to the will of the people; and (d) to facilitate where necessary the holding of such elections.

The three Governments will consult the other United Nations and provisional authorities or other Governments in Europe when matters of direct interest to them are under consideration.

When, in the opinion of the three Governments, conditions in any European liberated State or any former Axis satellite State in Europe make such action necessary, they will immediately consult together on the measures necessary to discharge the joint responsibilities set forth in this Declaration.

By this Declaration we reaffirm our faith in the principles of the Atlantic Charter, our pledge in the Declaration by the United Nations, and our determination to build in cooperation with other peace-loving nations a world order under law, dedicated to peace, security, freedom and the general well-being of all mankind.

In issuing this Declaration, the Three Powers express the hope that the Provisional Government of the French Republic may be associated with them in the procedure suggested.

VI. POLAND

We came to the Crimea Conference resolved to settle our differences about Poland. We discussed fully all aspects of the question. We reaffirm our common desire to see established a strong, free independent and democratic Poland. As a result of our discussions we have agreed on the conditions in which a new Polish Provisional Government of National Unity may be formed in such a manner as to command recognition by the three major Powers.

The agreement reached is as follows:

A new situation has been created in Poland as a result of her complete liberation by the Red Army. This calls for the establishment of a Polish Provisional Government which can be more broadly based than was possible before the recent liberation of western Poland. The Provisional Government which is now functioning in Poland should therefore be reorganized on a broader democratic basis with the inclusion of democratic leaders from Poland itself and from Poles abroad. This new Government should then be called the Polish Provisional Government of National Unity.

M. Molotov, Mr Harriman and Sir A. Clark Kerr are authorized as a Commission to consult in the first instance in Moscow with members of the present Provisional Government and with other Polish democratic leaders from within Poland and from abroad, with a view to the reorganization of the present Government along the above lines. This Polish Provisional Government of National Unity shall be pledged to the holding of free and unfettered elections as soon as possible on the basis of universal suffrage and secret ballot. In these elections all democratic and anti-Nazi parties shall have the right to take part and to put forward candidates.

When a Polish Provisional Government of National Unity has been properly formed in conformity with the above, the Government of the Union of Soviet Socialist Republics, which now maintains diplomatic relations with the present Provisional Government of Poland, and the Government of the United Kingdom and the Government of the United States will establish diplomatic relations with the new Polish Government of National Unity, and will exchange Ambassadors by whose reports the respective Governments will be kept informed about the situation in Poland.

The three Heads of Government consider that the eastern frontier of Poland should follow the Curzon line with digressions from it in some regions of 5 to 8 kilometres in favour of Poland. They recognize that Poland must receive substantial accessions of territory in the north and west. They feel that the opinion of the new Polish Provisional Government of National Unity should be sought in due course on the extent of these accessions and that the final delimitation of the western frontier of

Poland should thereafter await the Peace Conference.

VII. *Yugoslavia*

We have agreed to recommend to Marshal Tito and Dr Subasić that the Agreement between them should be put into effect immediately, and that a new Government should be formed on the basis of that Agreement.

We also recommend that as soon as the new Government has been formed it should declare that:

(i) The Anti-Fascist Assembly of National Liberation (Avnoj) should be extended to include members of the last Yugoslav Parliament (Skupshtina) who have not compromised themselves by collaboration with the enemy, thus forming a body to be known as a temporary Parliament; and

(ii) Legislative acts passed by the Assembly of National Liberation will be subject to subsequent ratification by a Constituent Assembly.

There was also a general review of other Balkan questions.

VIII. MEETINGS OF FOREIGN SECRETARIES

Throughout the Conference, besides the daily meetings of the Heads of Governments, and the Foreign Secretaries, separate meetings of the three Foreign Secretaries, and their advisers, have also been held daily.

These meetings have proved of the utmost value and the Conference agreed that permanent machinery should be set up for regular consultation between the three Foreign Secretaries. They will, therefore, meet as often as may be necessary, probably about every three or four months. These meetings will be held in rotation in the three capitals, the first meeting being held in London, after the United Nations Conference on World Organization.

IX. UNITY FOR PEACE AS FOR WAR

Our meeting here in the Crimea has reaffirmed our common determination to maintain and strengthen in the peace to come that unity of purpose and of action which has made victory possible and certain for the United Nations in this war. We believe that this is a sacred obligation which our Governments owe to our peoples and to all the peoples of the world.

Only with continuing and growing cooperation and understanding among our three countries, and among all the peace-loving nations, can the highest aspiration of humanity be realized – a secure and lasting peace which will, in the words of the Atlantic Charter 'Afford assurance that all the men in all the lands may live out their lives in freedom from fear and want'.

Victory in this war and establishment of the proposed international organization will provide the greatest opportunity in all history to create in the years to come the essential conditions of such a peace.
(Signed)
WINSTON S. CHURCHILL
FRANKLIN D. ROOSEVELT
J. V. STALIN
11th February 1945

Yalta Agreement on the Kuriles and entry of the Soviet Union in the war against Japan, 11 February 1945 (released 11 February 1946)

The leaders of the three Great Powers – the Soviet Union, the United States of America and Great Britain – have agreed that in two or three months after Germany has surrendered and the war in Europe has terminated the Soviet Union shall enter into the war against Japan on the side of the Allies on condition that:

1. The *status quo* in Outer Mongolia (The Mongolian People's Republic) shall be preserved;

2. The former rights of Russia violated by the treacherous attack of Japan in 1904 shall be restored, viz:

(a) the southern part of Sakhalin as well as all the islands adjacent to it shall be returned to the Soviet Union,

(b) the commercial port of Dairen shall be internationalized, the pre-eminent interests of the Soviet Union in this port being safeguarded and the lease of Port Arthur as a naval base of the U.S.S.R. restored,

(c) the Chinese-Eastern Railroad and the South-Manchurian Railroad which provides an outlet to Dairen shall be jointly operated by the establishment of a joint Soviet-Chinese Company, it being understood that the pre-eminent interests of the Soviet Union shall be safeguarded and that China shall retain full sovereignty in Manchuria;

3. The Kuril islands shall be handed over to the Soviet Union.

It is understood that the agreement concerning Outer Mongolia and the ports and railroads referred to above will require concurrence of Generalissimo Chiang Kai-shek. The President will take measures in order to obtain this concurrence on advice from Marshal Stalin.

The Heads of the three Great Powers have agreed that these claims of the Soviet Union shall be unquestionably fulfilled after Japan has been defeated.

For its part the Soviet Union expresses its readiness to conclude with the National Government of China a pact of friendship and alliance between the U.S.S.R. and China in order to render assistance to China with its armed forces for the purpose of liberating China from the Japanese yoke.

February 11, 1945

J. STALIN
FRANKLIN D. ROOSEVELT
WINSTON S. CHURCHILL

Potsdam Conference Protocol, 2 August 1945

The Berlin Conference of the three Heads of Government of the U.S.S.R., U.S.A., and U.K., which took place from July 17 to August 2, 1945, came to the following conclusions:

I · Establishment of a Council of Foreign Ministers

A. The Conference reached the following agreement for the establishment of a Council of Foreign Ministers to do the necessary preparatory work for the peace settlements:

1. There shall be established a Council composed of the Foreign Ministers of the United Kingdom, the Union of Soviet Socialist Republics, China, France, and the United States.

2. (i) The Council shall normally meet in London which shall be the permanent seat of the joint Secretariat which the Council will form . . . .

3. (i) As its immediate important task, the Council shall be authorized to draw up, with a view to their submission to the United Nations, treaties of peace with Italy, Rumania, Bulgaria, Hungary and Finland, and to propose settlements of territorial questions outstanding on the termination of the war in Europe. The Council shall be utilized for the preparation of a peace settlement for Germany to be accepted by the Government of Germany when a Government adequate for the purpose is established.

(ii) For the discharge of each of these tasks the Council will be composed of the Members representing those States which were signatory to the terms of surrender imposed upon the enemy State concerned. For the purposes of the peace settlement for Italy, France shall be regarded as a signatory to the terms of surrender for Italy. Other Members will be invited to participate when matters directly concerning them are under discussion.

(iii) Other matters may from time to time be referred to the Council by agreement between the Member Governments.

4. (i) Whenever the Council is considering a question of direct interest to a State not represented thereon, such State should be invited to send representatives to participate in the discussion and study of that question.

(ii) The Council may adapt its procedure to the particular problems under consideration. In some cases it may hold its own preliminary discussions prior to the participation of other interested States. In other cases, the Council may convoke a formal conference of the States chiefly interested in seeking a solution of the particular problem.

B. It was agreed that the three Governments should each address an identical invitation to the Governments of China and France to adopt this text and to join in establishing the Council . . . .

[It was agreed to recommend that the European Advisory Commission be dissolved.]

II · The principles to govern the treatment of Germany in the initial control period

A · POLITICAL PRINCIPLES

1. In accordance with the Agreement on Control Machinery in Germany, supreme authority in Germany is exercised, on instructions from their respective Governments, by the Commanders-in-Chief of the armed forces of the United States of America, the United Kingdom, the Union of Soviet Socialist Republics, and the French Republic, each in his own zone of occupation, and also jointly, in matters affecting Germany as a whole, in their capacity as members of the Control Council.

2. So far as is practicable, there shall be uniformity of treatment of the German population throughout Germany.

3. The purposes of the occupation of Germany by which the Control Council shall be guided are:

(i) The complete disarmament and demilitarization of Germany and the elimination or control of all German industry that could be used for military production . . . .

(ii) To convince the German people that they have suffered a total military defeat and that they cannot escape responsibility for what they have brought upon themselves, since their own ruthless warfare and the fanatical Nazi resistance have destroyed German economy and made chaos and suffering inevitable.

(iii) To destroy the National Socialist Party and its affiliated and supervised organizations, to dissolve all Nazi institutions, to ensure that they are not revived in any form, and to prevent all Nazi and militarist activity or propaganda.

(iv) To prepare for the eventual reconstruction of German political life on a democratic basis and for eventual peaceful cooperation in international life by Germany.

4. All Nazi laws which provided the basis of the Hitler régime or established discriminations on grounds of race, creed, or political opinion shall be abolished. No such discriminations, whether legal, administrative or otherwise, shall be tolerated.

5. War criminals and those who have participated in planning or carrying out Nazi enterprises involving or resulting in atrocities or war crimes shall be arrested and brought to judgement. Nazi leaders, influential Nazi supporters and high officials of Nazi organizations and institutions and any other persons dangerous to the occupation or its objectives shall be arrested and interned.

6. All members of the Nazi Party who have been more than nominal participants in its activities and all other persons hostile to Allied purposes shall be removed from public and semi-public office, and from positions of responsibility in important

private undertakings. Such persons shall be replaced by persons who, by their political and moral qualities, are deemed capable of assisting in developing genuine democratic institutions in Germany.

7. German education shall be so controlled as completely to eliminate Nazi and militarist doctrines and to make possible the successful development of democratic ideas.

8. The judicial system will be reorganized in accordance with the principles of democracy, of justice under law, and of equal rights for all citizens without distinction of race, nationality or religion.

9. The administration in Germany should be directed towards the decentralization of the political structure and the development of local responsibility. To this end:

(i) local self-government shall be restored throughout Germany on democratic principles and in particular through elective councils as rapidly as is consistent with military security and the purposes of military occupation;

(ii) all democratic political parties with rights of assembly and of public discussion shall be allowed and encouraged throughout Germany;

(iii) representative and elective principles shall be introduced into regional, provincial and State (*Land*) administration as rapidly as may be justified by the successful application of these principles in local self-government;

(iv) for the time being, no central German Government shall be established. Notwithstanding this, however, certain essential central German administrative departments, headed by State Secretaries, shall be established, particularly in the fields of finance, transport, communications, foreign trade and industry. Such departments will act under the direction of the Control Council.

10. Subject to the necessity for maintaining military security, freedom of speech, press and religion shall be permitted, and religious institutions shall be respected. Subject likewise to the maintenance of military security, the formation of free trade unions shall be permitted.

B. ECONOMIC PRINCIPLES

11. In order to eliminate Germany's war potential, the production of arms, ammunition and implements of war as well as all types of aircraft and sea-going ships shall be prohibited and prevented. Production of metals, chemicals, machinery and other items that are directly necessary to a war economy shall be rigidly controlled and restricted to Germany's approved post-war peacetime needs to meet the objectives stated in paragraph 15. Productive capacity not needed for permitted production shall be removed in accordance with the reparations plan recommended by the Allied Commission on Reparations and approved by the Governments concerned or if not removed shall be destroyed.

12. At the earliest practicable date, the German economy shall be decentralized for the purpose of eliminating the present excessive concentration of economic power as exemplified in particular by cartels, syndicates, trusts and other monopolistic arrangements.

13. In organizing the German economy, primary emphasis shall be given to the development of agriculture and peaceful domestic industries.

14. During the period of occupation Germany shall be treated as a single economic unit. To this end common policies shall be established in regard to:

(a) mining and industrial production and its allocation;

(b) agriculture, forestry and fishing;

(c) wages, prices and rationing;

(d) import and export programmes for Germany as a whole;

(e) currency and banking, central taxation and customs;

(f) reparation and removal of industrial war potential;

(g) transportation and communications.

In applying these policies account shall be taken, where appropriate, of varying local conditions.

15. Allied controls shall be imposed upon the German economy but only to the extent necessary . . . .

16. In the imposition and maintenance of economic controls established by the

Control Council, German administrative machinery shall be created and the German authorities shall be required to the fullest extent practicable to proclaim and assume administration of such controls . . . .

17. Measures shall be promptly taken:

(a) to effect essential repair of transport;

(b) to enlarge coal production;

(c) to maximize agricultural output; and

(d) to effect emergency repair of housing and essential utilities.

18. Appropriate steps shall be taken by the Control Council to exercise control and the power of disposition over German-owned external assets not already under the control of United Nations which have taken part in the war against Germany.

19. Payment of reparations should leave enough resources to enable the German people to subsist without external assistance. In working out the economic balance of Germany the necessary means must be provided to pay for imports approved by the Control Council in Germany. The proceeds of exports from current production and stocks shall be available in the first place for payment for such imports . . . .

III · Reparations from Germany

1. Reparation claims of the U.S.S.R. shall be met by removals from the zone of Germany occupied by the U.S.S.R., and from appropriate German external assets.

2. The U.S.S.R. undertakes to settle the reparation claims of Poland from its own share of reparations.

3. The reparation claims of the United States, the United Kingdom and other countries entitled to reparations shall be met from the Western zones and from appropriate German external assets.

4. In addition to the reparations to be taken by the U.S.S.R. from its own zone of occupation, the U.S.S.R. shall receive additionally from the Western zones:

(a) Fifteen per cent of such usable and complete industrial capital equipment, in the first place from the metallurgical, chemical and machine manufacturing industries as is unnecessary for the German peace economy and should be removed from the Western zones of Germany, in exchange for an equivalent value of food, coal, potash, zinc, timber, clay products, petroleum products, and such other commodities as may be agreed upon.

(b) Ten per cent of such industrial capital equipment as is unnecessary for the German peace economy and should be removed from the Western zones, to be transferred to the Soviet Government on reparations account without payment or exchange of any kind in return.

Removals of equipment as provided in (a) and (b) above shall be made simultaneously . . . .

8. The Soviet Government renounces all claims in respect of reparations to shares of German enterprises which are located in the Western zones of Germany as well as to German foreign assets in all countries except those specified in paragraph 9 below.

9. The Governments of the U.K. and U.S.A. renounce all claims in respect of reparations to shares of German enterprises which are located in the Eastern zone of occupation in Germany, as well as to German foreign assets in Bulgaria, Finland, Hungary, Rumania and Eastern Austria . . . .

IV · Disposal of the German Navy and Merchant Marine

A. The following principles for the distribution of the German Navy were agreed:

1. The total strength of the German Surface Navy, excluding ships sunk and those taken over from Allied Nations, but including ships under construction or repair, shall be divided equally among the U.S.S.R., U.K., and U.S.A. . . .

The German Merchant Marine, surrendered to the Three Powers and wherever located, shall be divided equally among the U.S.S.R., the U.K., and the U.S.A.

V · City of Koenigsberg and the adjacent area

The Conference examined a proposal by the Soviet Government to the effect that pending the final determination of territorial questions at the peace settlement, the section of the western frontier of the Union of Soviet Socialist Republics which is adjacent to the Baltic Sea should pass from a point on the eastern shore of the Bay of Danzig to the east, north of Braunsberg-Goldap, to the meeting point of the frontiers of Lithuania, the Polish Republic and East Prussia.

The Conference has agreed in principle to the proposal of the Soviet Government concerning the ultimate transfer to the Soviet Union of the City of Koenigsberg and the area adjacent to it as described above subject to expert examination of the actual frontier.

The President of the United States and the British Prime Minister have declared that they will support the proposal of the Conference at the forthcoming peace settlement.

VI · War criminals

[Trials to begin at earliest possible date.]

VII · Austria

The Conference examined a proposal by the Soviet Government on the extension of the authority of the Austrian Provisional Government to all of Austria.

The three Governments agreed that they were prepared to examine this question after the entry of the British and American forces into the city of Vienna.

It was agreed that reparations should not be exacted from Austria.

VIII · Poland

A · DECLARATION

We have taken note with pleasure of the agreement reached among representative Poles from Poland and abroad which has made possible the formation, in accordance with the decisions reached at the Crimea Conference, of a Polish Provisional Government of National Unity recognized by the Three Powers. The establishment by the British and United States Governments of diplomatic relations with the Polish Provisional Government of National Unity has resulted in the withdrawal of their recognition from the former Polish Government in London, which no longer exists.

The British and United States Governments have taken measures to protect the interest of the Polish Provisional Government of National Unity as the recognized Government of the Polish State in the property belonging to the Polish State located in their territories and under their control, whatever the form of this property may be. They have further taken measures to prevent alienation to third parties of such property. All proper facilities will be given to the Polish Provisional Government of National Unity for the exercise of the ordinary legal remedies for the recovery of any property belonging to the Polish State which may have been wrongfully alienated.

The Three Powers are anxious to assist the Polish Provisional Government of National Unity in facilitating the return to Poland as soon as practicable of all Poles abroad who wish to go, including members of the Polish armed forces and the Merchant Marine. They expect that those Poles who return home shall be accorded personal and property rights on the same basis as all Polish citizens.

The Three Powers note that the Polish Provisional Government of National Unity, in accordance with the decisions of the Crimea Conference, has agreed to the holding of free and unfettered elections as soon as possible on the basis of universal suffrage and secret ballot in which all democratic and anti-Nazi parties shall have the right to take part and to put forward candidates, and that representatives of the Allied press shall enjoy full freedom to report to the world upon developments in Poland before and during the elections.

B · WESTERN FRONTIER OF POLAND

In conformity with the agreement on Poland reached at the Crimea Conference the three Heads of Government have sought the opinion of the Polish Provisional

Government of National Unity in regard to the accession of territory in the north and west which Poland should receive. The President of the National Council of Poland and members of the Polish Provisional Government of National Unity have been received at the Conference and have fully presented their views. The three Heads of Government reaffirm their opinion that the final delimitation of the western frontier of Poland should await the peace settlement.

The three Heads of Government agree that, pending the final determination of Poland's western frontier, the former German territories east of a line running from the Baltic Sea immediately west of Swinamunde, and thence along the Oder river to the confluence of the western Neisse river and along the western Neisse to the Czechoslovak frontier, including that portion of East Prussia not placed under the administration of the Union of Soviet Socialist Republics in accordance with the understanding reached at this Conference and including the area of the former Free City of Danzig, shall be under the administration of the Polish State and for such purposes should not be considered as part of the Soviet zone of occupation in Germany.

IX · Conclusion of peace treaties and admission to the United Nations Organization

The three Governments consider it desirable that the present anomalous position of Italy, Bulgaria, Finland, Hungary and Rumania should be terminated by the conclusion of peace treaties. They trust that the other interested Allied Governments will share these views . . . .

As regards the admission of other States into the United Nations Organization, Article 4 of the Charter of the United Nations declares that:

1. Membership in the United Nations is open to all other peace-loving States who accept the obligations contained in the present Charter and, in the judgement of the Organization, are able and willing to carry out these obligations.

2. The admission of any such State to membership in the United Nations will be effected by a decision of the General Assembly upon the recommendation of the Security Council.

The three Governments, so far as they are concerned, will support applications for membership from those States which have remained neutral during the war and which fulfil the qualifications set out above.

The three Governments feel bound however to make it clear that they for their part would not favour any application for membership put forward by the present Spanish Government, which having been founded with the support of the Axis Powers, does not, in view of its origins, its nature, its record and its close association with the aggressor States, possess the qualifications necessary to justify such membership.

X · Territorial trusteeship

The Conference examined a proposal by the Soviet Government on the question of trusteeship territories as defined in the decision of the Crimea Conference and in the Charter of the United Nations Organization.

After an exchange of views on this question it was decided that the disposition of any former Italian colonial territories was one to be decided in connection with the preparation of a peace treaty for Italy and that the question of Italian colonial territory would be considered by the September Council of Ministers of Foreign Affairs.

XI · Revised allied control commission procedure in Rumania, Bulgaria and Hungary

[Revision of procedures will be undertaken.]

XII · Orderly transfer of German populations

The three Governments, having considered the question in all its aspects, recognize that the transfer to Germany of German populations, or elements thereof, remaining in Poland, Czechoslovakia and Hungary, will have to be undertaken. They agree that any transfers that take place should be effected in an orderly and humane manner . . . .

XIII · Oil equipment in Rumania

[Commission of experts to investigate.]

XIV · Iran

It was agreed that Allied troops should be withdrawn immediately from Teheran, and that further stages of the withdrawal of troops from Iran should be considered at the meeting of the Council of Foreign

Ministers to be held in London in September 1945.

XV · International zone of Tangier

[Agreement to be reached.]

XVI · The Black Sea Straits

The three Governments recognized that the convention concluded at Montreux should be revised as failing to meet present-day conditions.

It was agreed that as the next step the matter should be the subject of direct conversations between each of the three Governments and the Turkish Government.

. . .

[Signed] Stalin, Truman, Attlee.

Treaty of Friendship and Alliance between China and the Soviet Union, Moscow, 14 August 1945

I · Treaty of Friendship and Alliance

The President of the National Government of the Republic of China and the Praesidium of the Supreme Soviet of the Union of Soviet Socialist Republics,

Being desirous of strengthening the friendly relations which have always prevailed between the Republic of China and the Soviet Union, by means of an alliance and by good neighbourly post-war collaboration;

Determined to assist each other in the struggle against aggression on the part of the enemies of the United Nations in this World War and to collaborate in the common war against Japan until that country's unconditional surrender;

Expressing their unswerving resolve to collaborate in maintaining peace and security for the benefit of the peoples of both

countries and of all peace-loving nations . . . have agreed as follows:

Article 1. The High Contracting Parties undertake jointly with the other United Nations to prosecute the war against Japan until final victory is achieved. The High Contracting Parties mutually undertake to afford one another all necessary military and other assistance and support in this war.

Article 2. The High Contracting Parties undertake not to enter into separate negotiations with Japan or conclude, except by mutual consent, any armistice or peace treaty either with the present Japanese Government or any other Government or authority set up in Japan that does not clearly renounce all aggressive intentions.

Article 3. On the conclusion of the war

against Japan, the High Contracting Parties undertake to carry out jointly all the measures in their power to render impossible a repetition of aggression and violation of the peace by Japan.

Should either of the High Contracting Parties become involved in hostilities with Japan in consequence of an attack by the latter against that party, the other High Contracting Party will at once render to the High Contracting Party so involved in hostility all the military and other support and assistance in its power.

This Article shall remain in force until such time as, at the request of both High Contracting Parties, responsibility for the prevention of further aggression by Japan is placed upon the 'United Nations' Organization.

Article 4. Each High Contracting Party undertakes not to conclude any alliance and not to take part in any coalition directed against the other Contracting Party.

Article 5. The High Contracting Parties, having regard to the interests of the security and economic development of each of them, agree to work together in close and friendly collaboration after the re-establishment of peace and to act in accordance with the principles of mutual respect for each other's sovereignty and territorial integrity and non-intervention in each other's internal affairs.

Article 6. The High Contracting Parties agree to afford one another all possible economic assistance in the post-war period in order to facilitate and expedite the rehabilitation of both countries and to make their contribution to the prosperity of the world.

Article 7. Nothing in this Treaty should be interpreted in such a way as to prejudice the rights and duties of the High Contracting Parties as Members of the Organization of the 'United Nations'.

Article 8. The present Treaty is subject to ratification in the shortest possible time. The instruments of ratification shall be exchanged in Chungking as soon as possible.

The Treaty comes into force immediately upon ratification, and shall remain in force for thirty years. Should neither of the High Contracting Parties make, one year before the date of the Treaty's expiry, a statement of its desire to denounce it, the Treaty will remain in force for an unlimited period, provided that each High Contracting Party may invalidate it by announcing its intention to do so to the other Contracting Party one year in advance.

. . .

Exchange of Notes

No. 1

In connection with the signing on this date of the Treaty of Friendship and Alliance between China and the Union of Soviet Socialist Republics, I have the honour to place on record that the following provisions are understood by both Contracting Parties as follows:

1. In accordance with the spirit of the above-mentioned Treaty and to implement its general idea and its purposes, the Soviet Government agrees to render China moral support and assist her with military supplies and other material resources, it being understood that this support and assistance will go exclusively to the National Government as the Central Government of China.

2. During the negotiations on the ports of Dairen and Port Arthur and on the joint operation of the Chinese Changchun Railway, the Soviet Government regarded the Three Eastern Provinces as part of China and again affirmed its respect for the complete sovereignty of China over the Three Eastern Provinces and recognition of their territorial and administrative integrity.

3. With regard to recent events in Sinkiang, the Soviet Government confirms that, as stated in Article 5 of the Treaty of Friendship and Alliance, it has no intention of interfering in the internal affairs of China.

. . .

No. 3
In view of the frequently manifested desire for independence of the people of Outer Mongolia, the Chinese Government states that, after the defeat of Japan, if this desire is confirmed by a plebiscite of the people of Outer Mongolia, the Chinese Government will recognize the independence of Outer Mongolia within her existing frontiers . . . .

II · Agreement between the Chinese Republic and the Union of Soviet Socialist Republics on the Chinese Changchun Railway, signed at Moscow on 14 August 1945

The President of the National Government of the Republic of China and the Praesidium of the Supreme Soviet of the U.S.S.R. being desirous of strengthening, on the basis of complete regard for the rights and interests of each of the two parties, friendly relations and economic ties between the two countries, have agreed as follows:

Article 1. After the expulsion of the Japanese armed forces from the Three Eastern Provinces of China, the main trunk lines of the Chinese Eastern Railway and the South Manchurian Railway leading from the station of Manchouli to the station of Pogranichnaya and from Harbin to Dairen and Port Arthur, shall be combined to form a single railway system to be known as 'Chinese Changchun Railway', and shall become the joint property of the U.S.S.R. and the Chinese Republic and be jointly exploited by them. Only such lands and branch lines shall become joint property and be jointly exploited as were constructed by the Chinese Eastern Railway while it was under Russian and joint Soviet-Chinese management, and by the South Manchurian Railway while under Russian management, and which are intended to serve the direct needs of those railways. Ancillary undertakings directly serving the needs of those railways and constructed during the above-mentioned periods shall also be included. All other railway branch lines, ancillary undertakings and lands will be the exclusive property of the Chinese

Government. The joint exploitation of the above-mentioned railways shall be effected by a single administration under Chinese sovereignty as a purely commercial transport undertaking.

[*Articles 2–18*. Details of administration.]

III · Agreement on the Port of Dairen, signed at Moscow on 14 August 1945

Whereas a Treaty of Friendship and Alliance has been concluded between the Chinese Republic and the Union of Soviet Socialist Republics, and whereas the U.S.S.R. has guaranteed to respect the sovereignty of China over the Three Eastern Provinces as an inalienable part of China, the Chinese Republic, in order to protect the interests of the Union of Soviet Socialist Republics in Dairen as a port for the import and export of goods, hereby agrees:
1. To proclaim Dairen a free port, open to the trade and shipping of all countries.
2. The Chinese Government agrees to allocate docks and warehouse accommodation in the said free port to be leased to the U.S.S.R. under a separate agreement.

Protocol

1. The Government of China when requested to do so by the Soviet Union shall grant the Soviet Union, freely and without consideration, a thirty years' lease of one-half of all harbour installations and equipment, the other half of the harbour installations and equipment remaining the property of China.

. . .

IV · Agreement on Port Arthur, signed at Moscow on 14 August 1945

In accordance with the Sino-Soviet Treaty of Friendship and Alliance and as an addition thereto, both Contracting Parties have agreed on the following:
1. In order to strengthen the security of China and the U.S.S.R. and prevent a

repetition of aggression on the part of Japan, the Government of the Chinese Republic agrees to the joint use by both Contracting Parties of Port Arthur as a naval base . . . .

V · Agreement on relations between the Soviet Commander-in-Chief and the Chinese administration following the entry of Soviet forces into the territory of the three Eastern Provinces of China in connection with the present joint war against Japan, signed at Moscow on 14 August 1945

The President of the National Government of the Chinese Republic and the Praesidium of the Supreme Soviet of the Union of Soviet Socialist Republics, being desirous that after the entry of Soviet forces into the territory of the Three Eastern Provinces of China in connection with the present joint war of China and the U.S.S.R. against Japan, relations between the Soviet Commander-in-Chief and the Chinese administration conform with the spirit of friendship and alliance existing between both countries, have agreed on the following:

1. After the entry, as a result of military operations, of Soviet troops into the territory of the Three Eastern Provinces of China, the supreme authority and responsibility in the zone of military activity in all matters relating to the conduct of the war shall, during the period necessary for conducting such operations, be vested in the Commander-in-Chief of the Soviet Armed Forces.

2. A representative of the National Government of the Chinese Republic and a staff shall be appointed in any recaptured territory, who shall:

(a) Organize and control, in accordance with the laws of China, the administration on the territory freed from the enemy;

(b) Assist in establishing cooperation in restored territories between the Chinese armed forces, whether regular or irregular, and the Soviet armed forces;

(c) Ensure the active collaboration of the Chinese administration with the Soviet Commander-in-Chief and, in particular, issue corresponding instructions to the local authorities, being guided by the requirements and desires of the Soviet Commander-in-Chief.

3. A Chinese Military Mission shall be appointed to the Headquarters of the Soviet Commander-in-Chief for the purpose of maintaining contact between the Soviet Commander-in-Chief and the representative of the National Government of the Chinese Republic.

4. In zones that are under the supreme authority of the Soviet Commander-in-Chief, the administration of the National Government of the Chinese Republic for restored territories shall maintain contact with the Soviet Commander-in-Chief through a representative of the National Government of the Chinese Republic.

5. As soon as part of a recaptured territory ceases to be a zone of direct military operations, the National Government of the Chinese Republic shall assume complete power in respect of civil affairs and shall render the Soviet Commander-in-Chief all assistance and support through its civil and military organs.

6. All members of the Soviet armed forces on Chinese territory shall be under the jurisdiction of the Soviet Commander-in-Chief. All Chinese citizens whether civil or military, shall be under Chinese jurisdiction . . .

Minutes

At the fifth meeting between Generalissimo Stalin and Mr T. V. Soong, President of the Executive Yuan, which took place on 11 July 1945, the question of the evacuation of Soviet forces from Chinese territory after participation of the U.S.S.R. in the war against Japan was discussed. Generalissimo Stalin declined to include in the Agreement on the Entry of Soviet Forces into the Territory of the Three Eastern Provinces any provision for the evacuation of Soviet troops within three months following the defeat of Japan. Generalissimo Stalin stated, however, that the Soviet forces would begin to be withdrawn within three weeks after the capitulation of Japan.

Mr T. V. Soong asked how much time would be required to complete the evacuation. Generalissimo Stalin stated that in his opinion the evacuation of troops could be completed within a period of not exceeding two months. Mr T. V. Soong again asked whether the evacuation would really be completed within three months. Generalissimo Stalin stated that three months would be a maximum period sufficient for the completion of the withdrawal of troops.

XI · The peace treaties, 1945–51

Peacemaking in Europe

Peace treaties among some of the belligerents of the Second World War were signed, after much wrangling, within a few years after the end of the war, but the attempt to arrive at a final peace treaty and comprehensive settlement with Germany was, after much argument, tacitly abandoned (see Chapter XV).

The Potsdam Conference laid down the procedures to be followed to arrive at peace settlements and charged the Council of Foreign Ministers to draft peace treaties immediately with Italy, Rumania, Bulgaria, Hungary and Finland. A peace settlement for Germany was expected to take longer to conclude since in 1945 the time seemed distant and uncertain when a German government could be re-established that could accept and sign a peace treaty with the Allies. Not all members of the Council of Foreign Ministers were to participate in the drafting of peace terms but only those representing states signatory to the terms of surrender of the enemy state concerned. China thus had a voice only in the far eastern settlements. France was entitled to participate in the Italian treaty and, it was understood, would participate in any eventual treaty with Germany. The United States would play no part in the treaty with Finland. The great powers would draft the treaties and then submit them to the other allies for approval. The special position of the great powers in their peacemaking role was thus emphasized as it had been at the earlier peace conferences at Vienna in 1814–15 and at Paris in 1919.

During the eighteen months after the end of the war there were six major rounds of Allied negotiations: the Council of Foreign Ministers in London (September–October 1945), the Foreign Ministers Meeting of the USSR, USA and Great Britain in Moscow (December 1945), the Council of Foreign Ministers Meetings in Paris (April–May 1946 and June–July 1946), followed by the Paris Peace Conference of twenty-one nations (29 July–15 October 1946) and a final Council of Foreign Ministers Meeting in New York (4 November–12 December 1946). From these negotiations there emerged the drafts of peace treaties with Italy, Rumania, Bulgaria, Hungary and Finland. Peace treaties with these States were formally concluded in February 1947.

THE ITALIAN PEACE TREATY, 10 FEBRUARY 1947 (p. 285)

Eleven headings and seventeen annexes made up the treaty between Italy on the one hand and the Allied and Associated Powers on the other. The preamble acknowledged that the Fascist régime was overthrown not only in consequence of Allied victory but also 'with the assistance of the democratic elements of the Italian people'. Territorially Italy was re-established in its frontiers of 1 January 1938 with a number of important exceptions. The Fascist conquests of Albania and Ethiopia were annulled, the Dodecanese were ceded to Greece, and some Italian islands in the Adriatic were transferred to Greece and to Yugoslavia. There were also territorial adjustments involving Italian cessions along the boundary between Italy and France.

It was the eastern frontier of Italy that caused the greatest diplomatic difficulties. The larger part of the Venezia Giulia peninsula including Fiume was ceded to Yugoslavia by the peace treaty. Trieste with a small hinterland, formerly Italian, was set up as the Free Territory of Trieste under the guarantee of the Security Council of the UN. The Free Territory was divided into Zone A, comprising mainly the city of Trieste, to be administered by Britain and the United States, and Zone B under Yugoslav administration. Britain and the United States after 1948 gradually handed their Trieste zone over to the Italians. By October 1954 a settlement was reached between the Four Powers (USSR, US, Great Britain and France), Yugoslavia and Italy whereby nearly all of Zone A reverted to Italy while Zone B, with a small addition, was ceded to Yugoslavia; Trieste retained its status as a free port and the rights of ethnic minorities were safeguarded.

The Italians retained the south Tyrolean region of Bolzano which led to disturbances among some of its German-speaking population and to differences with Austria. A comprehensive Italian–Austrian settlement of these differences in principle was reached on 30 November 1969 after long negotiations.

The future of the Italian African colonies of Libya, Eritrea and Somaliland was not settled by the peace treaty. The treaty provided that if the four powers failed to reach agreement within one year of the coming into force of the peace treaty, then the matter was to be referred to the General Assembly of the United Nations. Under the auspices of the UN, Libya became independent in December 1951, an autonomous Eritrea was federated to Ethiopia in 1952, and in 1950 Somaliland became a UN trust territory under Italian administration, leading to the independence of Somalia in 1960 formed by unifying previously British and Italian administered Somalilands.

The Italian navy, army and air force were limited until modified 'by agreement between the Allied and Associated Powers and Italy or, after Italy becomes a member of the United Nations, by agreement between the Security Council and Italy'.

The political clauses of the Italian peace treaty included provisions for human rights and fundamental freedoms, and specifically an obligation that fascist and other anti-democratic organizations would not be permitted to revive. The treaty also provided for the trial of war criminals. Military clauses limited Italian armaments so that Italy would not again be able to wage aggressive war, but it was foreseen that the military clauses might later be relaxed 'in whole or in part by agreement between the Allied and Associated Powers and Italy' (Article 46), or secondly if an agreement were reached between Italy and the Security Council once Italy had been admitted to membership of the UN. Allied troops were to be withdrawn from Italy by December 1947. Reparations were exacted: the Soviet Union was to receive some 100 million dollars over a period of seven years; other reparation payments were to be paid to Yugoslavia (125 million dollars), Greece (105 million dollars), Ethiopia (25 million dollars) and Albania (5 million dollars). France, Britain and the US agreed to forgo their reparations claims.

The Peace Treaties with Romania, Hungary, Bulgaria and Finland, 10 February 1947

These were all concluded at the same time as the Italian treaty, on 10 February 1947, and followed it in their form and structure. The political clauses of these treaties guaranteed human rights and the elimination of fascist organizations. In 1949 Great Britain and the United States complained that the peoples of Romania, Hungary and Bulgaria were not enjoying the fundamental freedoms so guaranteed. The military clauses placed limitations on the armed forces of the defeated states. Reparations were paid as follows: Romania and Finland to pay 300 million dollars each to the Soviet Union; Hungary to pay 200 million dollars to the Soviet Union, and 100 million dollars each to Czechoslovakia and Yugoslavia; Bulgaria to pay 45 million dollars to Greece and 25 million dollars to Yugoslavia. The re-establishment of international control over, and freedom of navigation along the Danube was not finally settled in the peace treaties but became a matter of serious dispute between the Soviet Union and the western powers. On 18 August 1948 the Soviet Union took the lead in establishing a *Danube Commission* comprising Bulgaria, Czechoslovakia, Hungary, Romania, the Ukraine, the USSR and Yugoslavia, but excluding Austria and the western powers. The United States, Great Britain and France refused to recognize this commission for it deprived Greece, Britain, France, Italy and Belgium of their rights under earlier treaties. Austria joined the Commission in 1959 and West Germany followed in 1963.

The peace treaties brought about a number of territorial changes. *Bulgaria* was recognized within its frontiers of 1 January 1941; by this settlement Bulgaria retained the southern Dobruja acquired by an earlier Axis treaty from Romania in September 1940. But Bulgaria returned Serbian territory to Yugoslavia and western Thrace to Greece.

Hungary was required to return northern Transylvania, acquired in August 1940, to Romania. Hungary had to return to Czechoslovakia southern Slovakia, which had been secured after the Munich Conference in 1938, and also to cede additional Hungarian territory across the Danube opposite Bratislava to Czechoslovakia.

Romania: the cession of Bessarabia and northern Bukovina to the USSR, first occupied by Russia in June 1940, was confirmed in 1947. The Soviet Union retained a special right in 1947 to maintain enough troops in Romania and Hungary to safeguard its communications with the Red Army in the Soviet zone of Austria until the conclusion of a treaty with Austria.

Finland confirmed the cession of three territories originally ceded to the Soviet Union in 1940: the province of Petsamo, an area along the central portion of the Soviet–Finnish frontier, and the province of the Karelian isthmus in south-eastern Finland. The Soviet Union renounced its right to the lease of the Hango Peninsula, but secured instead a fifty-year lease of the Porkkala–Udd area as a naval base to protect the entrance to the Gulf of Finland; this lease was terminated by Russia in 1955.

By 1947 the first phase of peacemaking in Europe was complete. The next such treaty, the Austrian State Treaty, was not signed until 1955.

Peace Treaty between the Allies and Italy, 10 February 1947

Part I · Territorial clauses

SECTION I · FRONTIERS

Article 1. The frontiers of Italy shall, subject to the modifications set out in Articles 2, 3, 4, 11 and 22, be those which existed on January 1, 1938. These frontiers are traced on the maps attached to the present Treaty (Annex I). In case of a discrepancy between the textual description of the frontiers and the maps, the text shall be deemed to be authentic.

Article 2. The frontier between Italy and France, as it existed on January 1, 1938, shall be modified as follows:

1. *Little St Bernard Pass . . .*
2. *Mont Cenis Plateau . . .*

3. *Mont Thabor-Chaberton . . .*

4. *Upper Valleys of the Tinée, Vesubie and Roya . . .*

Article 3. The frontier between Italy and Yugoslavia shall be fixed as follows . . .

SECTION V · GREECE (special clause)

Article 14. 1. Italy hereby cedes to Greece in full sovereignty the Dodecanese Islands indicated hereafter, namely Stampalia (Astropalia), Rhodes (Rhodos), Calki (Kharki), Scarpanto, Casos (Casso), Piscopis (Tilos), Misiros (Nisyros), Calimnos (Kalymnos), Leros, Patmos, Lipsos (Lipso), Simi (Symi), Cos (Kos) and Castellorizo, as well as the adjacent islets.

2. These islands shall be and shall remain demilitarized . . . .

Part II · Political clauses

SECTION I · GENERAL CLAUSES

Article 15. Italy shall take all measures necessary to secure to all persons under Italian jurisdiction, without distinction as to race, sex, language or religion, the enjoyment of human rights and of the fundamental freedoms, including freedom of expression, of press and publication, of religious worship, of political opinion and of public meeting.

Article 16. Italy shall not prosecute or molest Italian nationals, including members of the armed forces, solely on the ground that during the period from June 10, 1940, to the coming into force of the present Treaty, they expressed sympathy with or took action in support of the cause of the Allied and Associated Powers.

Article 17. Italy, which, in accordance with Article 30 of the Armistice Agreement, has taken measures to dissolve the Fascist organizations in Italy, shall not permit the resurgence on Italian territory of such organizations, whether political, military or semi-military, whose purpose it is to deprive the people of their democratic rights.

Article 18. Italy undertakes to recognize the full force of the Treaties of Peace with Romania, Bulgaria, Hungary and Finland

and other agreements or arrangements which have been or will be reached by the Allied and Associated Powers in respect of Austria, Germany and Japan for the restoration of peace.

. . .

SECTION III · FREE TERRITORY OF TRIESTE

Article 21. 1. There is hereby constituted the Free Territory of Trieste, consisting of the area lying between the Adriatic Sea and the boundaries defined in Articles 4 and 22 of the present Treaty. The Free Territory of Trieste is recognized by the Allied and Associated Powers and by Italy, which agree that its integrity and independence shall be assured by the Security Council of the United Nations.

2. Italian sovereignty over the area constituting the Free Territory of Trieste, as above defined, shall be terminated upon the coming into force of the present Treaty.

3. On the termination of Italian sovereignty, the Free Territory of Trieste shall be governed in accordance with an instrument for a provisional régime drafted by the Council of Foreign Ministers and approved by the Security Council. This Instrument shall remain in force until such date as the Security Council shall fix for the coming into force of the Permanent Statute which shall have been approved by it. The Free Territory shall thenceforth be governed by the provisions of such Permanent Statute. The texts of the Permanent Statute and of the Instrument for the Provisional Régime are contained in Annexes VI and VII.

4. The Free Territory of Trieste shall not be considered as ceded territory within the meaning of Article 19 and Annex XIV of the present Treaty.

5. Italy and Yugoslavia undertake to give to the Free Territory of Trieste the guarantees set out in Annex IX.

Article 22. The frontier between Yugoslavia and the Free Territory of Trieste shall be fixed as follows . . .

SECTION IV · ITALIAN COLONIES

Article 23. 1. Italy renounces all right and title to the Italian territorial possessions in

Africa, i.e. Libya, Eritrea and Italian Somaliland.

2. Pending their final disposal, the said possessions shall continue under their present administration.

3. The final disposal of these possessions shall be determined jointly by the Governments of the Soviet Union, of the United Kingdom, of the United States of America, and of France within one year from the coming into force of the present Treaty, in the manner laid down in the joint declaration of February 10, 1947, issued by the said Governments, which is reproduced in Annex XI.

SECTION V · SPECIAL INTERESTS OF CHINA

Article 24. Italy renounces in favour of China all benefits and privileges resulting from the provisions of the final Protocol signed at Pekin on September 7, 1901, and all annexes, notes and documents supplementary thereto . . .

SECTION VI · ALBANIA

Article 27. Italy recognizes and undertakes to respect the sovereignty and independence of the State of Albania.

Article 28. Italy recognizes that the Island of Saseno is part of the territory of Albania and renounces all claims thereto.

SECTION VII · ETHIOPIA

Article 33. Italy recognizes and undertakes to respect the sovereignty and independence of the State of Ethiopia.

Article 34. Italy formally renounces in favour of Ethiopia all property (apart from normal diplomatic or consular premises), rights, interests and advantages of all kinds acquired at any time in Ethiopia by the Italian State, as well as all para-statal property as defined in paragraph 1 of Annex XIV of the present Treaty.

Italy also renounces all claims to special interests or influence in Ethiopia.

Article 35. Italy recognizes the legality of all measures which the Government of Ethio-

pia has taken or may hereafter take in order to annul Italian measures respecting Ethiopia taken after October 3, 1935, and the effects of such measures.

Article 36. Italian nationals in Ethiopia will enjoy the same juridical status as other foreign nationals, but Italy recognizes the legality of all measures of the Ethiopian Government annulling or modifying concessions or special rights granted to Italian nationals, provided such measures are taken within a year from the coming into force of the present Treaty.

Article 37. Within eighteen months from the coming into force of the present Treaty, Italy shall restore all works of art, religious objects, archives and objects of historical value belonging to Ethiopia or its nationals and removed from Ethiopia to Italy since October 3, 1935.

Article 38. The date from which the provisions of the present Treaty shall become applicable as regards all measures and acts of any kind whatsoever entailing the responsibility of Italy or of Italian nationals towards Ethiopia, shall be held to be October 3, 1935.

SECTION VIII · INTERNATIONAL AGREEMENTS

Article 39. Italy undertakes to accept any arrangements which have been or may be agreed for the liquidation of the League of Nations, the Permanent Court of International Justice and also the International Financial Commission in Greece.

Article 40. Italy hereby renounces all rights, titles and claims deriving from the mandate system or from any undertakings given in connection therewith, and all special rights of the Italian State in respect of any mandated territory.

Article 41. Italy recognizes the provisions of the Final Act of August 31, 1945, and of the Franco-British Agreement of the same date on the Statute of Tangier, as well as all provisions which may be adopted by the Signatory Powers for carrying out these instruments.

Article 42. Italy shall accept and recognize

any arrangements which may by made by the Allied and Associated Powers concerned for the modification of the Congo Basin Treaties with a view to bringing them into accord with the Charter of the United Nations.

Article 43. Italy hereby renounces any rights and interests she may possess by virtue of Article 16 of the Treaty of Lausanne signed on July 24, 1923.

Section IX · BILATERAL TREATIES

Article 44. 1. Each Allied or Associated Power will notify Italy, within a period of six months from the coming into force of the present Treaty, which of its pre-war bilateral treaties with Italy it desires to keep in force or revive. Any provisions not in conformity with the present Treaty shall, however, be deleted from the above-mentioned treaties.

2. All such treaties so notified shall be registered with the Secretariat of the United Nations in accordance with Article 102 of the Charter of the United Nations.

3. All such treaties not so notified shall be regarded as abrogated.

Part III · War criminals

Article 45. 1. Italy shall take all necessary steps to ensure the apprehension and surrender for trial of:

(a) Persons accused of having committed, ordered or abetted war crimes and crimes against peace or humanity;

(b) Nationals of any Allied or Associated Power accused of having violated their national law by treason or collaboration with the enemy during the war.

2. At the request of the United Nations Government concerned, Italy shall likewise make available as witnesses persons within its jurisdiction, whose evidence is required for the trial of the persons referred to in paragraph 1 of this Article.

3. Any disagreement concerning the application of the provisions of paragraphs 1 and 2 of this Article shall be referred by any of the Governments concerned to the Ambassadors in Rome of the Soviet Union, of the United Kingdom, of the United States of America, and of France, who will reach agreement with regard to the difficulty.

Part IV · Naval, military and air clauses

SECTION I · DURATION OF APPLICATION

Article 46. Each of the military, naval and air clauses of the present Treaty shall remain in force until modified in whole or in part by agreement between the Allied and Associated Powers and Italy or, after Italy becomes a member of the United Nations, by agreement between the Security Council and Italy.

SECTION II · GENERAL LIMITATIONS

Article 47. 1. (a) The system of permanent Italian fortifications and military installations along the Franco-Italian frontier, and their armaments, shall be destroyed or removed . . .

Article 48. 1. (a) Any permanent Italian fortifications and military installations along the Italo-Yugoslav frontier, and their armaments, shall be destroyed or removed . . .

SECTION III · LIMITATION OF THE ITALIAN NAVY

Article 59. 3. The total standard displacement of the war vessels, other than battleships, of the Italian Navy, including vessels under construction after the date of launching, shall not exceed 67,500 tons.

4. Any replacement of war vessels by Italy shall be effected within the limit of tonnage given in paragraph 3. There shall be no restriction on the replacement of auxiliary vessels.

5. Italy undertakes not to acquire or lay down any war vessels before January 1, 1950, except as necessary to replace any vessel, other than a battleship, accidentally lost, in which case the displacement of the new vessel is not to exceed by more than 10 per cent the displacement of the vessel lost.

6. The terms used in this Article are, for

the purposes of the present Treaty, defined in Annex XIII A.

Article 60. 1. The total personnel of the Italian Navy, excluding any naval air personnel, shall not exceed 25,000 officers and men . . . .

Section IV · LIMITATION OF THE ITALIAN ARMY

Article 61. The Italian Army, including the Frontier Guards, shall be limited to a force of 185,000 combat, service and overhead personnel and 65,000 . . .

SECTION V · LIMITATION OF THE ITALIAN AIR FORCE

Article 64. 1. The Italian Air Force, including any naval air arm, shall be limited to a force of 200 fighter and reconnaissance aircraft and 150 transport, air-sea rescue, training (school type) and liaison aircraft. These totals include reserve aircraft. All aircraft except for fighter and reconnaissance aircraft shall be unarmed. The organization and armament of the Italian Air Force as well as their deployment throughout Italy shall be designed to meet only tasks of an internal character, local defence of Italian frontiers and defence against air attack.

2. Italy shall not possess or acquire any aircraft designed primarily as bombers with internal bomb-carrying facilities.

Article 65. 1. The personnel of the Italian Air Force, including any naval air personnel, shall be limited to a total of 25,000 effectives, which shall include combat, service and overhead personnel.

· · ·

SECTION VII · PREVENTION OF GERMAN AND JAPANESE REARMAMENT

Article 68. Italy undertakes to cooperate fully with the Allied and Associated Powers with a view to ensuring that Germany and Japan are unable to take steps outside German and Japanese territories towards rearmament.

· · ·

Part V · Withdrawal of Allied forces

Article 73. 1. All armed forces of the Allied and Associated Powers shall be withdrawn from Italy as soon as possible and in any case not later than ninety days from the coming into force of the present Treaty.

2. All Italian goods for which compensation has not been made and which are in possession of the armed forces of the Allied and Associated Powers in Italy at the coming into force of the present Treaty shall be returned to the Italian Government within the same period of ninety days or due compensation shall be made.

3. All bank and cash balances in the hands of the forces of the Allied and Associated Powers at the coming into force of the present Treaty which have been supplied free of cost by the Italian Government shall similarly be returned or a corresponding credit given to the Italian Government.

Part VI · Claims arising out of the war

SECTION 1 · REPARATION

Article 74. A. *Reparation for the Union of Soviet Socialist Republics* 1. Italy shall pay the Soviet Union reparation in the amount of $100,000,000 during a period of seven years from the coming into force of the present Treaty. Deliveries from current industrial production shall not be made during the first two years.

2. Reparation shall be made from the following sources:

(a) A share of the Italian factory and tool equipment designed for the manufacture of war material, which is not required by the permitted military establishments, which is not readily susceptible of conversion to civilian purposes and which will be removed from Italy pursuant to Article 67 of the present Treaty;

(b) Italian assets in Roumania, Bulgaria and Hungary, subject to the exceptions specified in paragraph 6 of Article 79;

(c) Italian current industrial production, including production by extractive industries.

3. The quantities and types of goods to be delivered shall be the subject of agree-

ments between the Governments of the Soviet Union and of Italy, and shall be selected and deliveries shall be scheduled in such a way as to avoid interference with the economic reconstruction of Italy and the imposition of additional liabilities on other Allied or Associated Powers. Agreements concluded under this paragraph shall be communicated to the Ambassadors in Rome of the Soviet Union, of the United Kingdom, of the United States of America, and of France.

4. The Soviet Union shall furnish to Italy on commercial terms the materials which are normally imported into Italy and which are needed for the production of these goods. Payments for these materials shall be made by deducting the value of the materials furnished from the value of the goods delivered to the Soviet Union.

5. The four Ambassadors shall determine the value of the Italian assets to be transferred to the Soviet Union.

6. The basis of calculation for the settlement provided in this Article will be the United States dollar at its gold parity on July 1, 1946, i.e. $35 for one ounce of gold.

B. *Reparation for Albania, Ethiopia, Greece and Yugoslavia.* 1. Italy shall pay reparation to the following States:

Albania in the amount of	$5,000,000
Ethiopia in the amount of	$25,000,000
Greece in the amount of	$105,000,000
Yugoslavia in the amount of	$125,000,000

These payments shall be made during a period of seven years from the coming into force of the present Treaty. Deliveries from current industrial production shall not be made during the first two years.

2. Reparation shall be made from the following sources:

(a) A share of the Italian factory and tool equipment designed for the manufacture of war material, which is not required by the permitted military establishments, which is not readily susceptible of conversion to civilian purposes and which will be removed from Italy pursuant to Article 67 of the present Treaty;

(b) Italian current industrial production, including production by extractive industries;

(c) All other categories of capital goods or services, excluding Italian assets which, under Article 79 of the present Treaty, are subject to the jurisdiction of the States mentioned in paragraph 1 above. Deliveries under this paragraph shall include either or both of the passenger vessels *Saturnia* and *Vulcania*, if, after their value has been determined by the four Ambassadors, they are claimed within ninety days by one of the States mentioned in paragraph 1 above. Such deliveries may also include seeds.

3. The quantities and types of goods and services to be delivered shall be the subject of agreements between the Governments entitled to receive reparation and the Italian Government, and shall be selected and deliveries shall be scheduled in such a way as to avoid interference with the economic reconstruction of Italy and the imposition of additional liabilities on other Allied or Associated Powers.

4. The States entitled to receive reparation from current industrial production shall furnish to Italy on commercial terms the materials which are normally imported into Italy and which are needed for the production of these goods. Payment for these materials shall be made by deducting the value of the materials furnished from the value of the goods delivered.

5. The basis of calculation for the settlement provided in this Article will be the United States dollar at its gold parity on July 1, 1946, i.e. $35 for one ounce of gold.

6. Claims of the States mentioned in paragraph 1 of part B of this Article, in excess of the amounts of reparation specified in that paragraph, shall be satisfied out of the Italian assets subject to their respective jurisdictions under Article 79 of the present Treaty.

. . .

D. *Reparation for other States.* 1. Claims of the other Allied and Associated Powers shall be satisfied out of the Italian assets subject to their respective jurisdictions under Article 79 of the present Treaty.

2. The claims of any State which is receiving territories under the present Treaty and which is not mentioned in part

B of this Article shall also be satisfied by the transfer to the said State, without payment, of the industrial installations and equipment situated in the ceded territories and employed in the distribution of water, and the production and distribution of gas and electricity, owned by any Italian company whose *siège social* is in Italy or is transferred to Italy, as well as by the transfer of all other assets of such companies in ceded territories.

3. Responsibility for the financial obligations secured by mortgages, *liens* and other charges on such property shall be assumed by the Italian Government.

E. *Compensation for property taken for reparation purposes.* The Italian Government undertakes to compensate all natural or juridical persons whose property is taken for reparation purposes under this Article.

SECTION II · RESTITUTION BY ITALY

Article 75. 1. Italy accepts the principles of the United Nations Declaration of January 5, 1943, and shall return, in the shortest possible time, property removed from the territory of any of the United Nations.

2. The obligation to make restitution applies to all identifiable property at present in Italy which was removed by force or duress by any of the Axis Powers from the territory of any of the United Nations, irrespective of any subsequent transactions by which the present holder of any such property has secured possession.

3. The Italian Government shall return the property referred to in this Article in good order and, in this connection, shall bear all costs in Italy relating to labour, materials and transport.

Peacemaking in eastern Asia

The British and American delegations at Potsdam agreed, on behalf of the nations at war with Japan, on a declaration calling upon Japan to surrender 'unconditionally', and published the *Potsdam Declaration on 26 July 1945*. In effect this declaration outlined surrender conditions. On 6 and 9 August 1945 atomic bombs were dropped on Hiroshima and Nagasaki. On 8 August 1945 the Soviet Union declared war on Japan, to take effect the following day when the Russian armies began occupying Manchuria. On 10 August the Japanese acceptance of the conditions of the Potsdam Declaration was received by the Americans, but Japan's acceptance was conditional on the Allies agreeing that the prerogatives of the Emperor as a sovereign ruler were not prejudiced. The Americans replied on 11 August 1945 that the Emperor would be subject to the Supreme Commander and that the 'ultimate form of government of Japan shall, in accordance with the Potsdam Declaration, be established by the freely expressed will of the Japanese people'. On these conditions the Japanese surrendered on 14 August 1945. The formal instrument of surrender was signed on 2 September 1945 in Tokyo Bay. Japanese armies throughout Asia surrendered to the military Commander-in-Chief in each region. The Japanese armies in Manchuria, Korea north of the 38th parallel, the Kuriles and Sakhalin surrendered to the Russians. The Soviet Union regularized the hasty Russian invasion of Manchuria by concluding the *Sino-Soviet Treaty of Friendship on 14 August 1945*.

After Japan's surrender to the Allies, General Douglas MacArthur as Supreme Allied Commander headed the predominantly American occupation forces of

Japan. The Emperor, a Japanese Government and Diet, under the overall authority and supervision of the Supreme Commander, governed the country. The
seven Allied Powers which had been at war with Japan were represented on the
Far Eastern Commission in Washington, which came into being in the spring of 1946
together with an Allied Council in Tokyo. In practice the United States, represented by General MacArthur, maintained its predominant influence in carrying
through the occupation policies of the Allies with the broad objectives of dem-
ocratizing and demilitarizing Japan. In 1946 a new constitution was promulgated
for Japan. Its preamble pledged the people to maintain the high ideals of the
democratic constitution, dedicated to peaceful cooperation among nations and
the blessings of liberty. The Emperor's powers were limited to those of a constitutional monarch; henceforth he became only symbolic head of state and his
position derived 'from the will of the people with whom resides sovereign power'.
In Article 9 of the constitution war was renounced and no armed forces were to
be maintained. 'Aspiring sincerely to an international peace based on justice and
order, the Japanese people forever renounce war as a sovereign right of the nation
and the threat or use of force as means of settling territorial disputes. In order to
accomplish the aim of the preceding paragraph, land, sea, and air forces, as well
as other war potential, will never be maintained. The right of belligerency of the
State will not be recognized.'

The surrender limited Japanese sovereignty from north to south, to the island
of Honshu, Hokkaido, Kyushu and Shikoku, together with some minor islands.
The Kurile islands and southern Sakhalin were administered by the Soviet Union.
In Korea, Japanese forces north of latitude 38° surrendered to the Russians and
south of the line to the Americans, thus creating two military zones. Soviet forces
withdrew from North Korea in October 1948 after the establishment of a communist North Korean Government; the United States withdrew from South
Korea in June 1949 where a Government was also established under UN auspices. Formosa and the Pescadores were handed over to China; the Ryukyu
Islands including Okinawa were placed under US administration, and the Japanese trusteeship of Germany's former Pacific islands became a United Nations
trust territory under American administration.

In preparing a peace treaty for Japan, the Soviet Union and the western
powers were soon in dispute. A breach occurred over the rejection in January 1950
of the Soviet demand that the nationalist Chinese representative on the Far Eastern Commission be replaced by the representative of the People's Republic of
China, and the consequent Soviet withdrawal from the Far Eastern Commission.
The years 1949 and 1950 brought about far-reaching changes in eastern Asia and
fundamental reappraisals of great power diplomacy. In 1949 the communist
Chinese defeated the nationalist Chinese, who withdrew to Taiwan (Formosa). On
25 June 1950 the Korean War began, involving the North Koreans and eventually

Chinese 'volunteers' on the one side, and the South Koreans and the United States and UN allies, who came to the defence of South Korea, on the other. For the United States these events led to basic policy decisions to maintain a line of defence including Taiwan, Japan and South Korea. In the midst of the Korean War, the United States resolved to conclude a peace treaty with Japan even if Soviet approval could not be won, and to convert a defeated enemy into a willing ally. President Harry Truman sent Ambassador John Foster Dulles to America's principal allies to work out an agreed draft peace treaty. Then, on the basis of an Anglo-American draft, the United States and Britain invited fifty allied nations which had declared war on Japan to a Peace Conference at San Francisco to meet in September 1951. The Soviet Union was included in the invitation, but neither nationalist nor communist China (the three associated States of Indo-China on the other hand received an invitation). India, Burma and Yugoslavia declined the invitation. The Soviet Union attended, but refused to sign the treaty.

The Japanese Peace Treaty of 8 September 1951 (p. 294), negotiated substantially in advance before the San Francisco conference opened, was thus signed by the majority of nations at war with Japan but not by the USSR nor either of the Chinas. The territorial terms corresponded to the dispositions at the end of the war, and Japan renounced its rights to all territories surrendered by the armistice of 2 September 1945, and all special privileges in China. The peace treaty established that in principle Japan should pay reparations, but left amounts to later bilateral negotiations. Japan agreed to follow the principles of the UN Charter as well as internationally accepted fair practices in trade and commerce. Sovereignty and independence were restored to Japan, and the occupation régime was to end ninety days after the treaty became effective; but the treaty did not prevent the stationing of foreign troops in consequence of a treaty made by Japan with one or more Allied Powers. Comparing the Japanese peace treaty with the European peace treaties already negotiated, there is one marked feature of difference in the absence from the Japanese treaty of military clauses restricting the military forces of Japan. As was noted earlier, the Japanese constitution of 1946 forbade the maintenance of any Japanese armed forces. Article 5 of the peace treaty promised Japanese assistance in action taken in accordance with the UN Charter (the Korean War), and the Allied Powers who were signatories confirmed Japan's 'inherent right of individual or collective self-defence' referred to in Article 51 of the Charter of the United Nations, which permitted Japan to enter voluntarily into collective security arrangements.

The result of these arrangements was the transformation of Japan from an occupied vassal of the United States into a valued American ally in the western powers' confrontation with the Soviet Union and communist China. On the same day as the Japanese Peace Treaty was signed, *the United States signed a Security Treaty with Japan* (see p. 369). The constitutional bar on the maintenance of armed forces was circumvented after 1950 by the formation of a 'Self-Defence Force'.

The *Nationalist Chinese (Taiwan) signed a Peace Treaty with Japan on 28 April 1952*, but (in large measure as a consequence) no agreement between Japan and communist China was reached until the 1970s. Although the Soviet Union resumed diplomatic relations with Japan in 1956, no peace treaty between the two powers was ever signed. Soviet retention after 1945 of the formerly Japanese-governed Kurile islands as well as the southern half of Sakhalin island (gained by Japan from Russia in 1905) developed in the 1970s into a minor but persistent irritant in Soviet–Japanese relations.

Treaty of Peace with Japan, San Francisco, 8 September 1951

Whereas the Allied Powers and Japan are resolved that henceforth their relations shall be those of nations which, as sovereign equals, cooperate in friendly association to promote their common welfare and to maintain international peace and security, and are therefore desirous of concluding a Treaty of Peace which will settle questions still outstanding as a result of the existence of a state of war between them;

Whereas Japan for its part declares its intention to apply for membership in the United Nations and in all circumstances to conform to the principles of the Charter of the United Nations; to strive to realize the objectives of the Universal Declaration of Human Rights; to seek to create within Japan conditions of stability and well-being as defined in Articles 55 and 56 of the Charter of the United Nations and already initiated by post-surrender Japanese legislation; and in public and private trade and commerce to conform to internationally accepted fair practices;

Whereas the Allied Powers welcome the intentions of Japan set out in the foregoing paragraph;

The Allied Powers and Japan have therefore determined to conclude the present Treaty of Peace, and have accordingly appointed the undersigned plenipotentiar-

ies, who, after presentation of their full powers, found in good and due form, have agreed on the following provisions:

Chapter I: Peace

Article 1. (a) The state of war between Japan and each of the Allied Powers is terminated as from the date on which the present Treaty comes into force between Japan and the Allied Power concerned as provided for in Article 23.

(b) The Allied Powers recognize the full sovereignty of the Japanese people over Japan and its territorial waters.

Chapter II: Territory

Article 2. (a) Japan, recognizing the independence of Korea, renounces all right, title and claim to Korea, including the islands of Quelpart, Port Hamilton and Dagelet.

(b) Japan renounces all right, title and claim to Formosa and the Pescadores.

(c) Japan renounces all rights, title and claim to the Kurile islands, and to that portion of Sakhalin and the islands adjacent to it over which Japan acquired sovereignty as a consequence of the Treaty of Portsmouth of September 5, 1905.

(d) Japan renounces all right, title and

claim in connection with the League of Nations Mandate System, and accepts the action of the United Nations Security Council of April 2, 1947, extending the trusteeship system to the Pacific islands formerly under mandate to Japan.

(e) Japan renounces all claim to any right or title to or interest in connection with any part of the Antarctic area, whether deriving from the activities of Japanese nationals or otherwise.

(f) Japan renounces all right, title and claim to the Spratly islands and to the Paracel islands.

. . .

Chapter III: Security

Article 5. (a) Japan accepts the obligations set forth in Article 2 of the Charter of the United Nations, and in particular the obligations.

(i) to settle its international disputes by peaceful means in such a manner that international peace and security, and justice, are not endangered;

(ii) to refrain in its international relations from the threat or use of force against the territorial integrity or political independence of any State or in any other manner inconsistent with the Purposes of the United Nations;

(iii) to give the United Nations every assistance in any action it takes in accordance with the Charter and to refrain from giving assistance to any State against which the United Nations may take preventive or enforcement action.

(b) The Allied Powers confirm that they will be guided by the principles of Article 2 of the Charter of the United Nations in their relations with Japan.

(c) The Allied Powers for their part recognize that Japan as a sovereign nation possesses the inherent right of individual or collective self-defense referred to in Article 51 of the Charter of the United Nations and that Japan may voluntarily enter into collective security arrangements.

Article 6. (a) All occupation forces of the Allied Powers shall be withdrawn from Japan as soon as possible after the coming into force of the present Treaty, and in any case not later than ninety days thereafter.

Nothing in this provision shall, however, prevent the stationing or retention of foreign armed forces in Japanese territory under or in consequence of any bilateral or multilateral agreements which have been or may be made between one or more of the Allied Powers, on the one hand, and Japan on the other.

(b) The provisions of Article 9 of the Potsdam Proclamation of July 26, 1945, dealing with the return of Japanese military forces to their homes, to the extent not already completed, will be carried out.

. . .

Chapter IV: Political and economic clauses

. . .

Article 10. Japan renounces all special rights and interests in China, including all benefits and privileges resulting from the provisions of the final Protocol signed at Peking on September 7, 1901, and all annexes, notes and documents supplementary thereto, and agrees to the abrogation in respect to Japan of the said Protocol, annexes, notes and documents.

Article 11. Japan accepts the judgements of the International Military Tribunal for the Far East and of other Allied War Crimes Courts both within and outside Japan, and will carry out the sentences imposed thereby upon Japanese nationals imprisoned in Japan. The power to grant clemency, to reduce sentences and to parole with respect to such prisoners may not be exercised except on the decision of the Government or Governments which imposed the sentence in each instance, and on the recommendation of Japan. In the case of persons sentenced by the International Military Tribunal for the Far East, such power may not be exercised except on the decision of a majority of the Governments represented on the Tribunal, and on the recommendation of Japan.

Article 12. [Trade arrangements] . . . (c) In respect to any matter, however, Japan shall be obliged to accord to an Allied Power national treatment, or most-favored-nation treatment, only to the extent that the Allied Power concerned accords Japan national treatment or most-favored-nation treatment, as the case may be, in respect of the same matter.

. . .

Chapter V: Claims and property

Article 14. (a) It is recognized that Japan should pay reparations to the Allied Powers for the damage and suffering caused by it during the war. Nevertheless it is also recognized that the resources of Japan are not presently sufficient, if it is to maintain a viable economy, to make complete reparation for all such damage and suffering and at the same time meet its other obligations.
   Therefore,
   (i) Japan will promptly enter into negotiations with Allied Powers so desiring, whose present territories were occupied by Japanese forces and damaged by Japan, with a view to assisting to compensate those countries for the cost of repairing the damage done, by making available the services of the Japanese people in production, salvaging and other work for the Allied Powers in question. Such arrangements shall avoid the imposition of additional liabilities on other Allied Powers, and, where the manufacturing of raw materials is called for, they shall be supplied by the Allied Powers in question, so as not to throw any foreign exchange burden upon Japan . . . .
   (b) Except as otherwise provided in the present Treaty, the Allied Powers waive all reparations claims of the Allied Powers, other claims of the Allied Powers and their nationals arising out of any actions taken by Japan and its nationals in the course of the prosecution of the war, and claims of the Allied Powers for direct military costs of occupation.

. . .

Article 16. As an expression of its desire to indemnify those members of the armed forces of the Allied Powers who suffered undue hardships while prisoners of war of Japan, Japan will transfer its assets and those of its nationals in countries which were neutral during the war, or which were at war with any of the Allied Powers, or, at its option, the equivalent of such assets, to the International Committee of the Red Cross which shall liquidate such assets and distribute the resultant fund to appropriate national agencies, for the benefit of former prisoners of war and their families on such basis as it may determine to be equitable . . . .

Chapter VII: Final clauses

Article 23. (a) The present Treaty shall be ratified by the States which sign it, including Japan, and will come into force for all the States which have then ratified it, when instruments of ratification have been deposited by Japan and by a majority, including the United States of America as the principal occupying Power . . . .

Article 26. Japan will be prepared to conclude with any State which signed or adhered to the United Nations Declaration of January 1, 1942, and which is at war with Japan, or with any State which previously formed a part of the territory of a State named in Article 23, which is not a signatory of the present Treaty, a bilateral treaty of peace on the same or substantially the same terms as are provided for in the present Treaty, but this obligation on the part of Japan will expire three years after the first coming into force of the present Treaty. Should Japan make a peace settlement or war claims settlement with any State granting that State greater advantages than those provided by the present Treaty, those same advantages shall be extended to the parties to the present Treaty.

XII · The United Nations

The United Nation and its specialized agencies

As early as 1941, with the Axis powers seemingly at the height of their power, discussions began on the formation of a new world organization to replace the defunct League of Nations. Winston Churchill was keen to associate the United States with an international organization as successor to the League to provide more effective 'collective security'. When Roosevelt and Churchill met to draw up the *Atlantic Charter, 14 August 1941* (p. 234), Roosevelt would not accept such a far-reaching objective and insisted on a vaguer reference merely calling for the abandonment of the use of force and for disarmament, 'pending the establishment of a wider and permanent system of general security' (point 8); there was, however, more specific emphasis on the 'fullest collaboration between all nations in the economic field' (point 5). The priorities of the United States at this early stage became clear when in 1942 the USA proposed the establishment of an international fund to stabilize currencies and of a bank to assist post-war reconstruction. These aims were realized internationally at the *Bretton Woods Conference* in July 1944 (see p. 324).

Following Anglo-American talks in Washington, and after consultation with the USSR, the three major allies (together with twenty-three minor allies who were invited to sign 'on a take-it-or-leave-it basis') issued the *United Nations Declaration 1 January 1942*. This pledged the signatories to continue to fight together until the final defeat of the Axis powers; although the declaration made no mention of an international organization, the use of the term 'United Nations' marked the first embryonic stage of development of the wartime alliance into a universal body. The name appears to have been devised by President Roosevelt.

At the Allied meetings in Moscow and Teheran in the autumn of 1943 support was declared for the establishment of an international organization for the maintenance of peace and international security. Britain, the United States, Russia and

China agreed to work out the functions and powers of an international world organization at a meeting in Washington held in two parts, with the Soviet Union, not then at war with Japan, leaving the conference to make way for a second stage with China's participation. Accordingly the *Dumbarton Oaks Conference took place in two phases from 21 August to 28 September 1944 and from 29 September to 7 October 1944.* The communiqué after the conference on 9 October 1944 published 'Proposals for the Establishment of a General International Organization', which outlined the main structure of the United Nations; but on a crucial question of whether one of the great powers holding a permanent seat on the Security Council could exercise a veto on a dispute involving itself, no final agreement was reached. It was, however, agreed that a permanent member of the Security Council could exercise a veto on issues in which his country was not directly involved. The proposals left open to later agreement three contentious issues: the voting procedures of Security Council, the membership of the organization and the question of trusteeship and colonial territories. At the Yalta Conference in February 1945 the Big Three reached agreement on an American proposal for the voting procedure on the Security Council whereby the veto would not apply to every issue before it; procedural questions or the peaceful adjustments of disputes would not be subject to the veto; but the unanimity of all the permanent members would be required in all decisions involving enforcement measures. Nevertheless the wording of this agreement proved too imprecise to prevent later dispute. On the question of UN membership it was agreed that three Soviet representatives would be admitted, one for the USSR and one each for Ukraine and Byelorussia. All the states that had declared war on the Axis by 1 March 1945 were also to be founder members. It was further agreed that a Drafting Conference should convene at San Francisco on 25 April 1945 and that China and France should be invited together with the Big Three.

The San Francisco Conference of 25 April–26 June 1945 was attended by foreign ministers of the great powers and their delegations, as well as by delegations of countries at war with Germany. But Poland was not represented, as the Russian-sponsored Polish government was not recognized by the western powers. The Soviet Union, for its part, objected unsuccessfully to the participation of Argentina.

The most bitter dispute of the conference, which even threatened the founding of the international organization, concerned the voting procedure of the proposed Security Council. This procedure was complicated by the distinction drawn between the different types of decisions the Security Council would be asked to reach.

1. It was accepted by the delegates at San Francisco that each of the permanent members, that is, the 'Five', Britain, France, China, Russia and the United States, whether a party to a dispute or not, would have to concur if any sanctions including military action were decided on to meet aggression.

Each of the 'Big Five' thus held a veto against action involving enforcement. The Charter of the United Nations (p. 309), in article 51, however, safeguarded the rights of nations to defend themselves or to defend a member of the United Nations in regional alliances 'until' the Security Council took appropriate action. This safeguarded nations in the event that the Security Council through disagreement was unable to act. Individual or collective self-defence was acknowledged as an 'inherent right', but 'enforcement action' (Chapter VII) under any other circumstances required 'the authorization of the Security Council' (article 53).

2. Questions of *procedure* in the event of a dispute being brought before the Security Council were to be decided by a majority of seven members out of eleven (after 1965, nine out of the fifteen).

3. The third category would arise when the Security Council discussed a dispute, and reached and recorded conclusions about it intended to facilitate a peaceful settlement but not involving enforcement action. Such decisions or resolutions were called '*substantive*', and in article 27.3 it was agreed that they would require the affirmative vote of nine members including the unanimity of the permanent members of the Security Council, but that in decisions under Chapter VI, the Pacific Settlement of disputes, articles 33 to 38, and 52.3, any permanent members themselves involved in the dispute could not vote. In other words, a permanent member in these circumstances could exercise a veto only if his country was not involved in the dispute.

The trouble was, and remains, one of defining 'procedural' or 'substantive', and what precisely constitutes 'enforcement action'. The widest interpretation of the veto held by the Soviet Union in 1945 was not in the end accepted by the conference, but the freedom of the Security Council to work for the *peaceful resolution* of disputes was also curtailed.

The standing military force to be placed at the disposal of the Security Council, as envisaged in article 43 of the Charter, does not exist, for this article has never been implemented. Consequently the Security Council cannot itself enforce military sanctions as was apparently intended, but can only *recommend* that member states furnish troops to an *ad hoc* force, to preserve peace or to resist aggression. Economic sanctions can be invoked by the Security Council and were for the first time in December 1966 against the régime of Southern Rhodesia.

The Charter was unanimously adopted on 26 June 1945. By 24 October 1945, the 'Big Five' (Britain, China, France, the Soviet Union and the United States) and a majority of other signatory states ratified it and it was brought into force. It established the United Nations Organization whose members are sovereign states. In 1965 Indonesia withdrew and sought to organize a rival body; this failed and Indonesia soon returned. By 1986 membership had grown from the original 51 member states to a total of 159, primarily as a result of the adhesion of former colonial states. The two German states became members in 1973 reducing from two seats to one upon German reunification in 1990. In 1971 the People's Republic of China finally took over the Chinese seat from the nationalist Republic of China (Taiwan), the latter subsequently finding itself excluded from the organization. Membership of the United Nations by sovereign states became nearly universal by the 1980s. Among important states only the two Koreas and Switzerland remained non-members though all three had observer status. The former headquarters of the League of Nations, the Palais des Nations in Geneva, became, with the consent of the Swiss Federal Government, the European offices of the UN (whose main headquarters are located in New York). South Korea and North Korea were admitted in 1991. By 1999 the organization had 185 members. The success of the UN in achieving virtual universality of membership contrasted strikingly with the limited membership of the League of Nations between the wars. Even such disparate entities as the Holy See (the Vatican) and the Palestine Liberation Organization were granted observer status. With the exception of Taiwan no state has been excluded from membership of the organization, although South Africa, one of the original members, was effectively prevented from participating in the General Assembly from 1973 to 1993.

STRUCTURE OF THE UNITED NATIONS

The United Nations is not a centralized organization with clearly linked parts. It is a highly complex web of bodies where each one may act quite independently of the other, each with its own bureaucracy, rules and governors. This has led to duplication and interagency competition for resources. Attempts at reforms have so far failed to tackle all the problems as UN activities have expanded.

The United Nations can be divided into five parts: the *General Assembly*, the *Security Council*, and the *Trusteeship Council*, the *International Court of Justice* and the *Secretary General together with the Secretariat*. They act autonomously.

The *Trusteeship Council* was established under Chapter XIII of the Charter to supervise the eleven territories under trusteeship. By 1994 with Palau choosing free association with the United States, there were no colonial territories left which had not opted for independence or association with another country. The Trusteeship Council has therefore ceased to be of significance.

The *Security Council* is for all practical purposes independent (officially autonomous) and the most important organ of the UN. It is not controlled by the General Assembly.

The *General Assembly* is charged with all UN activities that are not assigned to the Security Council or to the Trusteeship Council and specifically with human rights. Every member state is a member of the General Assembly which debates and passes resolutions, initiates studies, and considers reports from the Security Council and other UN organs. Among its effective powers are consideration of the UN budget and apportionment of members' contributions, though in practice it cannot compel them to pay; both the United States and the Soviet Union were among states that withheld part of their contributions.

The *International Court of Justice* is a body of fifteen independent judges regardless of nationality who are elected for nine-year terms by the General Assembly and Security Council acting independently. Its competence is defined as dealing with cases only between states which refer disputes to the Court, interpretation of a treaty, and any question of international law. It played only a minor role as the Soviet Union would not accept its jurisdiction until 1980 and many states made reservations. In 1993 more attention came to be focused on the role of the UN in international law with the establishment of a separate *War Crimes Tribunal* at the Hague motivated by the atrocities committed in the Yugoslav conflicts (p. 897).

Finally, the *Secretary-General and the Secretariat*: The Secretary-General represents the UN, acts as mediator and diplomat in international disputes, consults with world leaders and may launch wide-ranging initiatives for the world community. He may be entrusted with missions by policy-making bodies or he may decide to act independently. Under article 99 he can bring to the attention of the Security Council any matter which he regards as threatening peace and security. The Secretary-General is appointed by the General Assembly on the recommendation of the Security Council (article 97), where any one of the five permanent members can veto a proposed candidate. He can initiate agendas and is supported by a secretariat of more than 14,000 international civil servants.

The *Security Council* is built around the nucleus of five permanent members and ten countries (originally six) elected by the General Assembly for a two-year term, and since 1965 on an agreed geographical basis. The complex voting procedure of the Security Council has been discussed. Under the Charter, the Security Council has primary responsibility in all questions of peace and security (article 24.1). The Security Council can make recommendations to settle disputes (article 36). Under Chapter VI, 'Pacific Settlements of Disputes', the Security Council may investigate whether a dispute, if continued, is likely to endanger international peace and security (article 34) and 'recommend appropriate procedures or methods of adjustment' (article 36). The Security Council can try to impose settlements under Chapter VII, 'Action with Respect to Threats to Peace, Breaches of the Peace, and Acts of Aggression'. Crucially, however, the Security Council has to determine first 'the existence of any threat to the peace, breach of the peace, or act of aggression' *before* it can act. If it fails to do so, as, for example, when Iraq attacked Iran in 1980, the start of eight years of bloody war, it cannot act. Under articles 41 and 42 escalating sanctions from economic, to demonstrations, blockade or armed force can be resorted to and under article 43, 'All members of the United Nations . . . undertake to make available to the Security Council, on its call . . . armed forces, assistance and facilities'. Article 48 requires that the action necessary to carry out the decisions of the Security Council 'shall be taken by all members of the United Nations or by some of them, as the Security Council may determine'.

After Korea, the first major operation undertaken by the UN was in the Congo in 1960. The Congo operation proved costly and was objected to by France and the United States; it put a damper on ambitions for further UN military intervention. The cold war made it difficult to reach the necessary accord in the Security Council between the five permanent members. In following their national interests, member nations have frequently been reluctant to appeal to the UN and preferred to act by 'old-fashioned' inter-state diplomacy. Finally it was in practice impossible to act if one of the five permanent members was the aggressor, or one of the five permanent members was closely allied to or supported the aggressor.

Many bloody conflicts occurred not between but within existing states, in Algeria, in Tibet, the massacres in Burundi and Rwanda in 1993 and 1994 to cite a few. Such conflicts could be considered to fall under article 2.7 as being of domestic concern and so not subject to UN action. But article 2.7 also adds, 'This principle shall not prejudice the application of enforcement measures under Chapter VII'. Under Chapter VI, article 34, moreover, concerned with the 'Pacific Settlement of Disputes', the Security Council also has a clear right to 'investigate' in order to determine whether the maintenance of peace and security is endangered. If the Security Council wishes to intervene therefore, as it did against South Africa whose *apartheid* policies were condemned, it can do so by determining that international peace and security are threatened, but it has more usually failed to act.

A change appeared to be heralded when the Security Council acted promptly after Iraq's invasion of Kuwait on 2 August 1990 and invoked Chapter VII. But by the time military action began in January 1991, it was not under the command of the UN but in accord with article 51 which permitted collective self-defence 'until the Security Council has taken measures necessary to maintain international peace and security' (p. 316); consequently the war was fought by a US-led regional alliance. The Gulf War opened the way to claiming the right that overriding humanitarian concerns justify intervention in the domestic affairs of a state despite the first part of article 2.7. In April 1991 the Security Council created safe havens under allied military protection within Iraq's borders to protect the Kurds. After Iraq's defeat she accepted the conditions of a UN cease-fire which included supervision of its terms. The destruction of Iraq's weapons of mass destruction was required to be verified by a UN mission of inspectors; meanwhile sanctions were to be continued. When, after years of difficulty the UN inspectors were ordered out of Iraq in the winter of 1998, the divisions among the permanent members of the Security Council on how to react left the UN in 1999 without an agreed way to proceed.

UN peace-keeping activities after 1992 during the breakup of Yugoslavia also revealed limits. The UN Protection Force (UNPROFOR) in Croatia and Bosnia, despatched after long delay in 1992, provided essential food supplies and saved many lives, but the UN reluctance to use force in any situation but the self-defence of UN troops permitted widespread atrocities to occur under the eyes of the UN. In July 1995 Srebrenica which had been declared by the UN a 'safe area' was overrun by Serb forces and its civilian male population was massacred. The fighting in Bosnia was eventually halted only in the autumn of 1995 by NATO intervention and the military and diplomatic lead of the United States (see p. 900). The ineffectualness of the Security Council to prevent the escalation of 'ethnic cleansing' in ex-Yugoslavia had been exposed and was later repeated in Kosovo in 1999 where UN sanctions short of force proved insufficient to halt the expulsion of ethnic Albanians from the province.

Peace-keeping forces have been sent to maintain armistices and cease-fire lines; they do not stop ongoing fighting but generally come in after agreement to end it has been reached; this usually requires the consent of contending parties and of any country on whose territory they are to be stationed. When President Nasser in 1967 withdrew permission for the peace-keeping force in the Sinai Desert, it had to withdraw and the fuse was lit for the 'Six Day War'. Peace-keeping forces therefore assist in 'freezing' conflicts and prevent renewed fighting only for as long as the parties in dispute are so disposed.

Peace-keeping forces responsible to the Security Council were set up in the Middle East (the United Nations Truce Supervision Organization, UNTSO) to maintain the 1949 armistice between Israel and her Arab neighbours. In the conflict between India and Pakistan over Kashmir, a united Nations Military Observer Group for India and Pakistan (UNMOGIP) was set up in 1949. In Korea, the United Nations Military Command was set up in July 1950, and it has supervised the armistice line between South and North Korea since July 1953. United Nations forces were sent to Egypt during the Suez crisis of 1956. A United Nations Peace-keeping Force in Cyprus (UNFICYP) was set up in March 1964 to help prevent communal strife between the Greeks and the Turks on the island. By 1999, the UN had deployed peace-keepers or observers in fifty separate operations around the world. Some of these, such as those in Kashmir and Cyprus have lasted for several decades and their missions show no sign yet of ending. Others were short-lived – for example, the peace-keeping operation in the Aouzou Strip between Libya and Chad in 1994 which lasted for little over a month. These 'peace-keepers' have fulfilled a valuable function even though the title 'peace-keepers' does not always mean that they can fulfil this function. They have sought to stabilize civil conflicts by supervising elections in Mozambique 1993–94 and in Angola 1992–93 and 1995 without ending the conflict; nor could the UN bring peace to Somalia. From 1992 to 1993 the UN mounted a large and costly effort to end through elections decades of war in Cambodia. In East Timor an unarmed UN mission supervised an independent referendum in September 1999, but was powerless to stop the killing that followed until belatedly Indonesia agreed to accept UN Peace-keepers.

The Security Council has not played the role of a world government able to enforce peace and security. Nations have more often negotiated with each other outside the formal procedures of the Security Council but then resorted frequently to the Security Council to legitimize the outcome. Thus the UN has provided a useful and in some respects indispensable additional channel in relations between nations. Had the Security Council attempted much more, the UN probably would not have survived.

THE SPECIALIZED AGENCIES OF THE UN

The following are some of the most significant bodies under the UN umbrella. Their functions frequently overlap in the areas of development of the Third World, the enhancement of living conditions of the poorest, social protection, human rights, and other issues of global concern. In this listing they range from the humanitarian to the regulation of global technical services:

The *United Nations Relief and Rehabilitation Administration (UNRRA)* was established in November 1943 and ceased operations in March 1949. Its main purpose was to provide relief, especially food, to regions devastated by war and to stave off famine and social collapse. Financed mainly by the US during the early years, UNRRA personnel and aid were dispatched to Italy, Greece, Poland and Yugoslavia as well as China. Foreign aid was granted to parts of eastern Europe including the Soviet republics of Ukraine and Byelorussia. UNRRA had provided help for several million refugees before ceasing its operations which were taken over for a time by the International Refugee Organization and then by the UN High Commissioner for Refugees.

The *United Nations Relief and Works Agency for Palestine Refugees in the Near East*, established in 1949, assumed responsibility for housing, education, feeding and medical care of Palestinian refugees who fled what became Israel in 1948.

The position of *UN High Commissioner for Human Rights* was established by the General Assembly in 1993. The Commissioner's mission is 'to ensure the universal enjoyment of all human rights by giving practical effect to the will and resolve of the world community'. Since some members of the General Assembly and the Security Council are themselves human rights abusers, the Commissioner often faces insuperable problems.

The *Department of Humanitarian Affairs (DHA) and the Office of the UN Disaster Relief Coordinator (UNDRO)*, intended as a focal point for relief efforts by different agencies, has also had difficulty fulfilling its brief. The UN has not generally been the principal provider of disaster emergency relief. International responses have more usually been made by voluntary organizations or by governments. The establishment of the DHA in 1992 marked a fresh effort by the UN to coordinate relief effectively. The Emergency Relief Coordinator chairs an inter-agency Standing Committee in the field of humanitarian relief consisting of the United Nations Development Programme, UNICEF, World Food Programme, FAO, WHO, UN High Commissioner for Refugees and major humanitarian organizations, each with their own budget. There is much overlap. It is a daunting task with inadequate resources.

The *Office of the United Nations High Commissioner for Refugees* (UNHCR) was established in 1951. At first intended to provide short-term assistance for refugees especially in Europe after the Second World War, it has had to deal with long-term refugee problems since the 1960s. The protection of the rights of refugees, including the right to residence or to return home, has been impossible to implement where governments refuse to do so. It is one of the organizations which is a provider of emergency relief, food and shelter as well as longer term care. The early distinction between providing relief only once a refugee has crossed the borders and not within their own state borders, has become blurred as humanitarian relief came to be provided to internally displaced refugees in Bosnia and Herzegovina, Somalia, Sri Lanka and Azerbaijan to mention only some, and most recently to Kosovo refugees who had left the province. The scale of refugees and displaced persons is so large that in 1995 there were more than 27 million refugees. UNHCR cannot be expected to cope with and implement its stated aims adequately on the resources made available to the UN and in the face of policies pursued by governments creating the problem.

The *World Health Organization* (WHO) is a specialized agency to combat disease on a global scale. Efforts to develop international law by treaty in this sphere stretched back at least to the mid-nineteenth century. In 1851 the first International Sanitary Conference met in Paris and tried, but failed to produce an international sanitary convention. The first *International Sanitary Convention*, limited to cholera, was not agreed until 1892. It was followed by other international health agreements. In 1902 the International Sanitary Bureau was established in Washington. It was followed in 1907 by *l'Office International d'Hygiène Publique* in Paris. The League of Nations set up its own Health Organization side by side with the Paris body in 1919. The World Health Organization was established following a conference in New York in 1946. It set four main goals:

- to give worldwide guidance in the field of health
- to set global standards for health
- to cooperate with governments in strengthening national health programmes
- to develop and transfer appropriate health technology, information and standards.

The WHO has done particularly valuable work in 'primary health care and disease prevention'. The WHO adopted a number of new international medical agreements – now known as International Health Regulations. One major achievement was the worldwide eradication of smallpox by 1977. Other major scourges such as polio, guinea-worm disease and leprosy also approached extinction, but tuberculosis and malaria remain great killers and AIDS is the most recent of the pandemics which the WHO has not the resources to combat. The expense of drugs to prolong life is so costly as to make them practically unavailable to patients in Africa and the poorest countries.

The *International Labour Organization* (ILO) was established in 1919 by the Treaty of Versailles as an associated organization of the League of Nations. In 1946 it became a specialized agency of the United Nations, keeping its headquarters in Geneva. It was concerned internationally with establishing agreed conditions of labour and also with social security, economic planning and full employment.

The *United Nations Children's Fund* (UNICEF) was founded in 1946 to aid mothers and children in need as a result of war or from other causes, especially in developing countries. It is financed by voluntary contributions.

The *United Nations Educational, Scientific and Cultural Organization* (UNESCO) was founded in 1946. It promoted many international educational and cultural projects, including a campaign against illiteracy and the saving of the Abu Simbel temple sculptures on the upper Nile. Nearly all states joined UNESCO. South Africa, however, withdrew in 1956. In 1984 the USA, the organization's largest financial contributor, withdrew, complaining of politicization of the organization's activities. Britain and Singapore withdrew in 1985 and other countries followed suit. In 1988, however, a reform process began and most of the countries that had withdrawn subsequently returned. By 1995 UNESCO had 184 members.

The undeveloped poor countries of Africa, Latin America and Asia at the *United Nations Conference on Trade and Development* (UNCTAD) in 1964 saw themselves at a disadvantage in relations with the western industrialized world and criticized the western dominated World Bank and the International Monetary Fund (see below) for not addressing the problems of the poor nations sufficiently from the perspective of their needs in their relations with the industrial nations. They combined in an informal 'Group of 77' to press their case and coordinate action in UN bodies where their votes carried equal weight. They sought trade concessions from the developed countries and a change in liberal trade relations placing them into a position of dependency. They demanded a 'New International Economic Order' (1973). Its aims were to secure more favourable terms of trade, a link between the price of commodities exported and goods imported, control over trans-national corporations, technology transfer to accelerate industrialization, aid and debt reduction. UNCTAD established a secretariat in Geneva. Over time some progress was achieved on commodity support, aid and debt rescheduling.

But its more radical agenda to change the world economic order met with no success. The *World Bank* and the *IMF*, dominated by the industrialized west, carried far more weight in the development of the economies of Africa, Asia and Latin American countries than any other UN organization.

The *United Nations Development Programme* (UNDP) created in 1965 was the UN's largest multilateral provider of grants. The UNDP receives its funds from contributors of member states and other sources and its executive board approves major programmes and makes policy decisions. It then allocates funds to the special agencies in whose sector, technical, agricultural, educational and so on a particular project falls. The operational activities in developing countries are handled by the specialized agencies. In one year, for example, in 1985, more than 5,000 projects were undertaken, some of great value, others less so. During 1999, the UNDP sponsored projects in 174 countries. The top-down structure carries heavy administrative costs. The projects – even where vital and essential – do not form a coherent overall approach to development. Coordination of operational units also remains a problem, though repeated attempts have been made to strengthen it.

The *United Nations Industrial Development Organization* was established by the UN General Assembly in 1966. Its mandate was to help developing countries (later also 'transitional economies', i.e. those moving from communist to free-market systems) to 'pursue sustainable industrial development', and to coordinate UN activities.

The *Food and Agricultural Organization* (FAO) established in 1945 set as its aim the raising of living standards by improving production and distribution of agricultural produce. The FAO also established a warning system after the famine in Africa in 1973 and 1974. But the continued decline of food production actually led to devastating famines in the mid-1980s. By 1999 the FAO claimed to be the largest autonomous agency within the UN, with 175 member states and a biennial budget for 1998–99 of $650 million which is not nearly adequate to meet global needs.

The UN Charter made disarmament and the regulation of armaments one of the principal concerns of the organization. The UN set up a series of commissions and committees on the subject from 1946 onwards. But during most of the cold war period disarmament negotiations conducted under UN auspices yielded few tangible results. More substantial advances were negotiated by the major powers at conferences set up especially for the purpose (see Chapter XXIII), but the UN plays a significant role in monitoring nuclear proliferation.

The *International Atomic Energy Agency* (IAEA) was set up, with headquarters in Vienna, in 1957, on the initiative of US President Eisenhower in his 'Atoms for Peace' speech to the UN General Assembly. The *IAEA Statute was approved on 23 October 1956* by the Conference on the Statute of the International Atomic Energy Agency, which was held at the headquarters of the United Nations. It came into force on 29 July 1957. The IAEA's mandate was to promote the use of atomic energy for peace, health and prosperity, and to ensure that help under the programme is not misused for military purposes. Nuclear safety became a more active concern of the IAEA after the Chernobyl disaster in 1986 and its inspections and other actions to prevent nuclear arms proliferation more rigorous in the 1990s. By 1999 the IAEA had 137 member states, a staff of 2,221, and formal agreements with forty partner organizations. It was responsible for enforcing 221 safeguards agreements in the member states (plus Taiwan). The IAEA was responsible for a number of major international agreements.

The *International Civil Aviation Organization* was founded in 1947, following the coming into force of the *Convention on International Civil Aviation, 7 December 1944*, agreed at a conference of fifty-two states in Chicago. The Convention set international standards for air navigation and practice. The Agency was particularly concerned with efforts towards air safety. By 1997 185 'Contracting States' participated in the ICAO.

The *International Maritime Organization* was established by means of a *Convention adopted under the auspices of the United Nations in Geneva on 17 March 1948* although it did not begin to function until 1959. Its headquarters were established in London. It was responsible for 'measures to improve the safety of international shipping and to prevent marine pollution from ships' and it was also involved in 'legal matters, including liability and compensation issues and the facilitation of international maritime traffic'. According to its official description, its chief concern in its early years was to develop international treaties and other legislation concerning safety and marine pollution prevention. By the late 1970s, however, this work had been largely completed. After that IMO concentrated on keeping legislation up to date and ensuring that it is ratified by as many countries as possible. This has been so successful that many Conventions now apply to more than 98 per cent of world merchant shipping tonnage. Among the treaties agreed under the auspices of the IMO were the *International Convention for the Safety of Life at Sea (SOLAS), 1960 and 1974, International Regulations for Preventing Collisions at Sea (COLREG), 1972*, the *Convention on the International Maritime Satellite Organization (INMARSAT), 1976*, the *Torremolinos International Convention for the Safety of Fishing Vessels (SVF), 1977*, and the *International Convention on Maritime Search and Rescue (SAR)*, 1979. The IMO also took the lead in developing international law for the prevention of marine pollution, leading to a number of treaties (see p. 879). By 1999 the IMO had 157 member states.

The *International Telecommunication Union* (ITU) had its origins in the *International Telegraph Union*, founded as a result of the first *International Telegraph Convention, 17 May 1865*, agreed by twenty countries. The ITU assumed responsibility for drawing up international legislation on telegraphy and, from 1885, also for telephony. Following the *International Radiotelegraph Conference held in 1906*, the first *International*

Radiotelegraph Convention was signed. With the start of sound broadcasting in the 1920s, the ITU became responsible for allocating waveband frequencies. In 1934 the organization's title was changed to reflect the broadening of its scope of activity. In 1947 its headquarters moved from Berne to Geneva. From 1963 it became responsible for allocating frequencies. In 1999 the ITU had 188 members.

The *Universal Postal Union* (UPU) was the idea of a German postal official, Heinrich von Stephan. In 1874, the Swiss government convened a conference of twenty-two countries at Berne. This led to the *Treaty of Berne, 9 October 1874*, which established the General Postal Union (the name changed in 1878). The UPU set agreed rates and rules for international postage and sought to eliminate barriers to the free flow of mail. The UPU became a specialized agency of the UN in 1948.

The *World Intellectual Property Organization* (WIPO) was set up under the *Convention Establishing the World Intellectual Property Organization* signed at *Stockholm on 14 July 1967 (amended 28 September 1979)*. It became responsible for industrial property (trade marks, industrial design and appellations of origin) and copyright law. It was responsible for administering a number of international agreements in the field, including the *Paris Convention for the Protection of Industrial Property of 20 March 1983*, the *International Convention for the Protection of Performers, Producers of Phonograms and Broadcasting Organizations, Rome 26 October 1961*, the *Treaty on Intellectual Property in Respect of Integrated Circuits, Washington, 26 May 1989*, and the *Trademark Law Treaty, Geneva, 27 October 1994*. By 1999 the WIPO had 171 members.

The World Meteorological Organization (WMO), with 185 members by 1999, was established under the terms of the *World Meteorological Convention*, adopted at a conference in *Washington in 1947*. The WMO began operations in 1951 and was based in Geneva.

The *International Law Commission* was established to prepare 'drafts on topics of international law which can then be incorporated into conventions and opened for ratification by States'.

Charter of the United Nations, 26 June 1945

[The text reproduced here includes subsequent amendments to Articles 23, 27, 61 and 109.]

WE THE PEOPLES OF THE UNITED NATIONS

DETERMINED

to save succeeding generations from the scourge of war, which twice in our lifetime has brought untold sorrow to mankind, and to reaffirm faith in fundamental human rights, in the dignity and worth of the human person, in the equal rights of men and women and of nations large and small, and to establish conditions under which justice and respect for the obligations arising from treaties and other sources of international law can be maintained, and to promote social progress and better standards of life in larger freedom,

AND FOR THESE ENDS

to practice tolerance and live together in peace with one another as good neighbours, and to unite our strength to maintain international peace and security, and to ensure, by the acceptance of principles and the institution of methods, that armed force shall not be used, save in the common interest, and to employ international machinery for the promotion of the economic and social advancement of all peoples,

HAVE RESOLVED TO COMBINE OUR EFFORTS TO ACCOMPLISH THESE AIMS.

Accordingly, our respective Governments, through representatives assembled in the city of San Francisco, who have exhibited their full powers found to be in good and due form, have agreed to the present Charter of the United Nations and do hereby establish an international organization to be known as the United Nations.

Chapter I

PURPOSES AND PRINCIPLES

Article 1. The Purposes of the United Nations are:

1. To maintain international peace and security, and to that end: to take effective collective measures for the prevention and removal of threats to the peace, and for the suppression of acts of aggression or other breaches of the peace, and to bring about by peaceful means, and in conformity with the principles of justice and international law, adjustment or settlement of international disputes or situations which might lead to a breach of the peace;

2. To develop friendly relations among nations based on respect for the principle of equal rights and self-determination of peoples, and to take other appropriate measures to strengthen universal peace;

3. To achieve international co-operation in solving international problems of an economic, social, cultural, or humanitarian character, and in promoting and encouraging respect for human rights and for fundamental freedoms for all without distinction as to race, sex, language, or religion; and

4. To be a centre for harmonizing the actions of nations in the attainment of these common ends.

Article 2. The Organization and its Members, in pursuit of the Purposes stated in Article 1, shall act in accordance with the following Principles.

1. The Organization is based on the principle of the sovereign equality of all its Members.

2. All Members, in order to ensure to all of them the rights and benefits resulting from membership, shall fulfil in good faith the obligations assumed by them in accordance with the present Charter.

3. All Members shall settle their international disputes by peaceful means in such a manner that international peace and security, and justice, are not endangered.

4. All Members shall refrain in their international relations from the threat or use of force against the territorial integrity or political independence of any state, or in any other manner inconsistent with the Purposes of the United Nations.

5. All Members shall give the United Nations every assistance in any action it takes in accordance with the present Charter, and shall refrain from giving assistance to any state against which the United Nations is taking preventive or enforcement action.

6. The Organization shall ensure that states which are not Members of the United Nations act in accordance with these Principles so far as may be necessary for the maintenance of international peace and security.

7. Nothing contained in the present Charter shall authorize the United Nations to intervene in matters which are essentially within the domestic jurisdiction of any state or shall require the Members to submit such matters to settlement under the present Charter; but this principle shall not prejudice the application of enforcement measures under Chapter VII.

Chapter II

MEMBERSHIP

Article 3. The original Members of the United Nations shall be the states which, having participated in the United Nations Conference on International Organization at San Francisco, or having previously signed the Declaration by United Nations of 1 January 1942, sign the present Charter and ratify it in accordance with Article 110.

Article 4. 1. Membership in the United Nations is open to other peace-loving states which accept the obligations contained in the present Charter and, in the judgment of the Organization, are able and willing to carry out these obligations.

2. The admission of any such state to membership in the United Nations will be effected by a decision of the General Assembly upon the recommendation of the Security Council.

Article 5. A Member of the United Nations against which preventive or enforcement action has been taken by the Security Council may be suspended from the exercise of the rights and privileges of membership by the General Assembly upon the recommendation of the Security Council. The exercise of these rights and privileges may be restored by the Security Council.

Article 6. A Member of the United Nations which has persistently violated the Principles contained in the present Charter may be expelled from the Organization by the General Assembly upon the recommendation of the Security Council.

Chapter III

ORGANS

Article 7. 1. There are established as the principal organs of the United Nations: a General Assembly, a Security Council, an Economic and Social Council, a Trusteeship Council, an International Court of Justice, and a Secretariat.

2. Such subsidiary organs as may be found necessary may be established in accordance with the present Charter.

Article 8. The United Nations shall place no restrictions on the eligibility of men and women to participate in any capacity and under conditions of equality in its principal and subsidiary organs.

Chapter IV

THE GENERAL ASSEMBLY

Composition

Article 9. 1. The General Assembly shall consist of all the Members of the United Nations.

2. Each Member shall have not more than five representatives in the General Assembly.

Functions and powers

Article 10. The General Assembly may discuss any questions or any matters within the scope of the present Charter or relating to the powers and functions of any organs provided for in the present Charter, and, except as provided in Article 12, may make recommendations to the Members of the United Nations or to the Security Council or to both on any such questions or matters.

Article 11. 1. The General Assembly may consider the general principles of co-operation in the maintenance of international peace and security, including the principles governing disarmament and the regulation of armaments, and may make recommendations with regard to such principles to the Members or to the Security Council or to both.

2. The General Assembly may discuss any questions relating to the maintenance of international peace and security brought before it by any Member of the United Nations, or by the Security Council, or by a state which is not a Member of the United Nations in accordance with Article 35, paragraph 2, and, except as provided in Article 12, may make recommendations with regard to any such questions to the state or states concerned or to the Security Council or to both. Any such question on which action is necessary shall be referred to the Security Council by the General Assembly either before or after discussion.

3. The General Assembly may call the attention of the Security Council to situations which are likely to endanger international peace and security.

4. The powers of the General Assembly set forth in this Article shall not limit the general scope of Article 10.

Article 12. 1. While the Security Council is exercising in respect of any dispute or situation the functions assigned to it in the present Charter, the General Assembly shall not make any recommendation with regard to that dispute or situation unless the Security Council so requests.

2. The Secretary-General, with the consent of the Security Council, shall notify the General Assembly at each session of any matters relative to the maintenance of international peace and security which are being dealt with by the Security Council and similarly notify the General Assembly, or the Members of the United Nations if the General Assembly is not in session, immediately the Security Council ceases to deal with such matters.

Article 13. 1. The General Assembly shall initiate studies and make recommendations for the purpose of:

a. promoting international co-operation in the political field and encouraging the progressive development of international law and its codification;

b. promoting international co-operation in the economic, social, cultural, educational, and health fields, and assisting in the realization of human rights and fundamental freedoms for all without distinction as to race, sex, language, or religion.

2. The further responsibilities, functions and powers of the General Assembly with respect to matters mentioned in paragraph 1(b) above are set forth in Chapters IX and X.

Article 14. Subject to the provisions of Article 12, the General Assembly may recommend measures for the peaceful adjustment of any situation, regardless of origin, which it deems likely to impair the general welfare or friendly relations among nations, including situations resulting from a violation of the provisions of the present Charter setting forth the Purposes and Principles of the United Nations.

Article 15. 1. The General Assembly shall receive and consider annual and special reports from the Security Council; these reports shall include an account of the measures that the Security Council has decided upon or taken to maintain international peace and security.

2. The General Assembly shall receive and consider reports from the other organs of the United Nations.

Article 16. The General Assembly shall perform such functions with respect to the international trusteeship system as are assigned to it under Chapters XII and XIII, including the approval of the trusteeship agreements for areas not designated as strategic.

Article 17. 1. The General Assembly shall consider and approve the budget of the Organization.

2. The expenses of the Organization shall be borne by the Members as apportioned by the General Assembly.

3. The Assembly shall consider and approve any financial and budgetary arrangements with specialized agencies referred to in Article 57 and shall examine the administrative budgets of such specialized agencies with a view to making recommendations to the agencies concerned.

Voting

Article 18. 1. Each member of the General Assembly shall have one vote.

2. Decisions of the General Assembly on important questions shall be made by a two-thirds majority of the members present and voting. These questions shall include: recommendations with respect to the maintenance of international peace and security, the election of the non-permanent members of the Security Council, the election of the members of the Economic and Social Council, the election of members of the Trusteeship Council in accordance with paragraph 1(c) of Article 86, the admission of new Members to the United Nations, the suspension of the rights and privileges of

membership, the expulsion of Members, questions relating to the operation of the trusteeship system, and budgetary questions.

3. Decisions on other questions, including the determination of additional categories of question to be decided by a two-thirds majority, shall be made by a majority of the members present and voting.

Article 19. A Member of the United Nations which is in arrears in the payment of its financial contributions to the Organization shall have no vote in the General Assembly if the amount of its arrears equals or exceeds the amount of the contributions due from it for the preceding two full years. The General Assembly may, nevertheless, permit such a Member to vote if it is satisfied that the failure to pay is due to conditions beyond the control of the Member.

Procedure

Article 20. The General Assembly shall meet in regular annual sessions and in such special sessions as occasion may require. Special sessions shall be convoked by the Secretary-General at the request of the Security Council or of a majority of the Members of the United Nations.

Article 21. The General Assembly shall adopt its own rules of procedure. It shall elect its President for each session.

Article 22. The General Assembly may establish such subsidiary organs as it deems necessary for the performance of its functions.

Chapter V

THE SECURITY COUNCIL

Composition

Article 23. 1. The Security Council shall consist of fifteen Members of the United Nations. The Republic of China, France, the Union of Soviet Socialist Republics, the United Kingdom of Great Britain and Northern Ireland, and the United States of America shall be permanent members of the Security Council. The General

Assembly shall elect ten other Members of the United Nations to be non-permanent members of the Security Council, due regard being specially paid, in the first instance to the contribution of Members of the United Nations to the maintenance of international peace and security and to the other purposes of the Organization, and also to equitable geographical distribution.

2. The non-permanent members of the Security Council shall be elected for a term of two years. In the first election of the non-permanent members after the increase of the membership of the Security Council from eleven to fifteen, two of the four additional members shall be chosen for a term of one year. A retiring member shall not be eligible for immediate re-election.

3. Each member of the Security Council shall have one representative.

Functions and powers

Article 24. 1. In order to ensure prompt and effective action by the United Nations, its Members confer on the Security Council primary responsibility for the maintenance of international peace and security, and agree that in carrying out its duties under this responsibility the Security Council acts on their behalf.

2. In discharging these duties the Security Council shall act in accordance with the Purposes and Principles of the United Nations. The specific powers granted to the Security Council for the discharge of these duties are laid down in Chapters VI, VII, VIII, and XII.

3. The Security Council shall submit annual and, when necessary, special reports to the General Assembly for its consideration.

Article 25. The Members of the United Nations agree to accept and carry out the decisions of the Security Council in accordance with the present Charter.

Article 26. In order to promote the establishment and maintenance of international peace and security with the least diversion for armaments of the world's human and economic resources, the Security Council shall be responsible for formulating, with the assistance of the Military Staff Committee referred to in Article 47, plans to be submitted to the Members of the United Nations for the establishment of a system for the regulation of armaments.

Voting

Article 27. 1. Each member of the Security Council shall have one vote.

2. Decisions of the Security Council on procedural matters shall be made by an affirmative vote of nine members.

3. Decisions of the Security Council on all other matters shall be made by an affirmative vote of nine members including the concurring votes of the permanent members; provided that, in decisions under Chapter VI, and under paragraph 3 of Article 52, a party to a dispute shall abstain from voting.

Procedure

Article 28. 1. The Security Council shall be so organized as to be able to function continuously. Each member of the Security Council shall for this purpose be represented at all times at the seat of the Organization.

2. The Security Council shall hold periodic meetings at which each of its members may, if it so desires, be represented by a member of the government or by some other specially designated representative.

3. The Security Council may hold meetings at such places other than the seat of the Organization as in its judgment will best facilitate its work.

Article 29. The Security Council may establish such subsidiary organs as it deems necessary for the performance of its functions.

Article 30. The Security Council shall adopt its own rules of procedure, including the method of selecting its President.

Article 31. Any Member of the United Nations which is not a member of the Security Council may participate, without vote, in the discussion of any question brought before the Security Council whenever the latter considers that the interests of that Member are specially affected.

Article 32. Any Member of the United Nations which is not a member of the Security Council or any state which is not a Member of the United Nations, if it is a party to a dispute under consideration by the Security Council, shall be invited to participate, without vote, in the discussion relating to the dispute. The Security Council shall lay down such conditions as it deems just for the participation of a state which is not a Member of the United Nations.

Chapter VI

PACIFIC SETTLEMENT OF DISPUTES

Article 33. 1. The parties to any dispute, the continuance of which is likely to endanger the maintenance of international peace and security, shall, first of all seek a solution by negotiation, enquiry, mediation, conciliation, arbitration, judicial settlement, resort to regional agencies or arrangements, or other peaceful means of their own choice.

2. The Security Council shall, when it deems necessary, call upon the parties to settle their dispute by such means.

Article 34. The Security Council may investigate any dispute, or any situation which might lead to international friction or give rise to a dispute, in order to determine whether the continuance of the dispute or situation is likely to endanger the maintenance of international peace and security.

Article 35. 1. Any Member of the United Nations may bring any dispute, or any situation of the nature referred to in Article 34, to the attention of the Security Council or of the General Assembly.

2. A state which is not a Member of the United Nations may bring to the attention of the Security Council or of the General Assembly any dispute to which it is a party if it accepts in advance, for the purposes of the dispute, the obligations of pacific settlement provided in the present Charter.

3. The proceedings of the General Assembly in respect of matters brought to its attention under this Article will be subject to the provisions of Articles 11 and 12.

Article 36. 1. The Security Council may, at any stage of a dispute of the nature referred to in Article 33 or of a situation of like nature, recommend appropriate procedures or methods of adjustment.

2. The Security Council should take into consideration any procedures for the settlement of the dispute which have already been adopted by the parties.

3. In making recommendations under this Article the Security Council should also take into consideration that legal disputes should as a general rule be referred by the parties to the International Court of Justice in accordance with the provisions of the Statute of the Court.

Article 37. 1. Should the parties to a dispute of the nature referred to in Article 33 fail to settle it by the means indicated in that Article, they shall refer it to the Security Council.

2. If the Security Council deems that the continuance of the dispute is in fact likely to endanger the maintenance of international peace and security, it shall decide whether to take action under Article 36 or to recommend such terms of settlement as it may consider appropriate.

Article 38. Without prejudice to the provisions of Articles 33 to 37, the Security Council may, if all the parties to any dispute so request, make recommendations to the parties with a view to a pacific settlement of the dispute.

Chapter VII

ACTION WITH RESPECT TO THREATS TO THE PEACE, BREACHES OF THE PEACE, AND ACTS OF AGGRESSION

Article 39. The Security Council shall determine the existence of any threat to the peace, breach of the peace, or act of aggression and shall make recommendations, or decide what measures shall be taken in accordance with Articles 41 and 42, to maintain or restore international peace and security.

Article 40. In order to prevent an aggravation of the situation, the Security Council may, before making the recommendations or deciding upon the measures provided for in Article 39, call upon the parties concerned to comply with such provisional measures as it deems necessary or desirable. Such provisional measures shall be without prejudice to the rights, claims, or position of the parties concerned. The Security Council shall duly take account of failure to comply with such provisional measures.

Article 41. The Security Council may decide what measures not involving the use of armed force are to be employed to give effect to its decisions, and it may call upon the Members of the United Nations to apply such measures. These may include complete or partial interruption of economic relations and of rail, sea, air, postal, telegraphic, radio, and other means of communication, and the severance of diplomatic relations.

Article 42. Should the Security Council consider that measures provided for in Article 41 would be inadequate or have proved to be inadequate, it may take such action by air, sea, or land forces as may be necessary to maintain or restore international peace and security. Such action may include demonstrations, blockade, and other operations by air, sea, or land forces of Members of the United Nations.

Article 43. 1. All Members of the United Nations, in order to contribute to the maintenance of international peace and security, undertake to make available to the Security Council, on its call and in accordance with a special agreement or agreements, armed forces, assistance, and facilities, including rights of passage, necessary for the purpose of maintaining international peace and security.

2. Such agreement or agreements shall govern the numbers and types of forces, their degree of readiness and general location, and the nature of the facilities and assistance to be provided.

3. The agreement or agreements shall be negotiated as soon as possible on the initiative of the Security Council. They shall be concluded between the Security Council and Members or between the Security Council and groups of Members and shall be subject to ratification by the signatory

states in accordance with their respective constitutional processes.

Article 44. When the Security Council has decided to use force it shall, before calling upon a Member not represented on it to provide armed forces in fulfilment of the obligations assumed under Article 43, invite that Member, if the Member so desires, to participate in the decisions of the Security Council concerning the employment of contingents of that Member's armed forces.

Article 45. In order to enable the United Nations to take urgent military measures, Members shall hold immediately available national air-force contingents for combined international enforcement action. The strength and degree of readiness of these contingents and plans for their combined action shall be determined, within the limits laid down in the special agreement or agreements referred to in Article 43, by the Security Council with the assistance of the Military Staff Committee.

Article 46. Plans for the application of armed force shall be made by the Security Council with the assistance of the Military Staff Committee.

Article 47. 1. There shall be established a Military Staff Committee to advise and assist the Security Council on questions relating to the Security Council's military requirements for the maintenance of international peace and security, the employment and command of forces placed at its disposal, the regulation of armaments, and possible disarmament.

2. The Military Staff Committee shall consist of the Chiefs of Staff of the permanent members of the Security Council or their representatives. Any Member of the United Nations not permanently represented on the Committee shall be invited by the Committee to be associated with it when the efficient discharge of the Committee's responsibilities requires the participation of that Member in its work.

3. The Military Staff Committee shall be responsible under the Security Council for the strategic direction of any armed forces placed at the disposal of the Security Council. Questions relating to the command of such forces shall be worked out subsequently.

4. The Military Staff Committee, with the authorization of the Security Council and after consultation with appropriate regional agencies, may establish subcommittees.

Article 48. 1. The action required to carry out the decisions of the Security Council for the maintenance of international peace and security shall be taken by all the Members of the United Nations or by some of them, as the Security Council may determine.

2. Such decisions shall be carried out by the Members of the United Nations directly and through their action in the appropriate international agencies of which they are members.

Article 49. The Members of the United Nations shall join in affording mutual assistance in carrying out the measures decided upon by the Security Council.

Article 50. If preventive or enforcement measures against any state are taken by the Security Council, any other state, whether a Member of the United Nations or not, which finds itself confronted with special economic problems arising from the carrying out of those measures shall have the right to consult the Security Council with regard to a solution of those problems.

Article 51. Nothing in the present Charter shall impair the inherent right of individual or collective self-defence if an armed attack occurs against a Member of the United Nations, until the Security Council has taken measures necessary to maintain international peace and security. Measures taken by Members in the exercise of this right of self-defence shall be immediately reported to the Security Council and shall not in any way affect the authority and responsibility of the Security Council under the present Charter to take at any time such action as it deems necessary in order to maintain or restore international peace and security.

Chapter VIII

REGIONAL ARRANGEMENTS

Article 52. 1. Nothing in the present Charter precludes the existence of regional arrangements or agencies for dealing with such matters relating to the maintenance of international peace and security as are appropriate for regional action, provided that such arrangements or agencies and their activities are consistent with the Purposes and Principles of the United Nations.

2. The Members of the United Nations entering into such arrangements or constituting such agencies shall make every effort to achieve pacific settlement of local disputes through such regional arrangements or by such regional agencies before referring them to the Security Council.

3. The Security Council shall encourage the development of pacific settlement of local disputes through such regional arrangements or by such regional agencies either on the initiative of the states concerned or by reference from the Security Council.

4. This Article in no way impairs the application of Articles 34 and 35.

Article 53. 1. The Security Council shall, where appropriate, utilize such regional arrangements or agencies for enforcement action under its authority. But no enforcement action shall be taken under regional arrangements or by regional agencies without the authorization of the Security Council, with the exception of measures against any enemy state, as defined in paragraph 2 of this Article, provided for pursuant to Article 107 or in regional arrangements directed against renewal of aggressive policy on the part of any such state, until such time as the Organization may, on request of the Governments concerned, be charged with the responsibility for preventing further aggression by such a state.

2. The term enemy state as used in paragraph 1 of this Article applies to any state which during the Second World War has been an enemy of any signatory of the present Charter.

Article 54. The Security Council shall at all times be kept fully informed of activities undertaken or in contemplation under regional arrangements or by regional agencies for the maintenance of international peace and security.

Chapter IX

INTERNATIONAL ECONOMIC AND SOCIAL CO-OPERATION

Article 55. With a view to the creation of conditions of stability and well-being which are necessary for peaceful and friendly relations among nations based on respect for the principle of equal rights and self-determination of peoples, the United Nations shall promote:

a. higher standards of living, full employment, and conditions of economic and social progress and development;

b. solutions of international economic, social, health, and related problems; and international cultural and educational co-operation; and

c. universal respect for, and observance of, human rights and fundamental freedoms for all without distinction as to race, sex, language, or religion.

Article 56. All Members pledge themselves to take joint and separate action in co-operation with the Organization for the achievement of the purposes set forth in Article 55.

Article 57. 1. The various specialized agencies, established by intergovernmental agreement and having wide international responsibilities, as defined in their basic instruments, in economic, social, cultural, educational, health, and related fields, shall be brought into relationship with the United Nations in accordance with the provisions of Article 63.

2. Such agencies thus brought into relationship with the United Nations are hereinafter referred to as specialized agencies.

Article 58. The Organization shall make recommendations for the co-ordination of the policies and activities of the specialized agencies.

Article 59. The Organization shall, where appropriate, initiate negotiations among the states concerned for the creation of any new specialized agencies required for the accomplishment of the purposes set forth in Article 55.

Article 60. Responsibility for the discharge of the functions of the Organization set forth in this Chapter shall be vested in the General Assembly and, under the authority of the General Assembly, in the Economic and Social Council, which shall have for this purpose the powers set forth in Chapter X.

Chapter X

THE ECONOMIC AND SOCIAL COUNCIL

Composition

Article 61. 1. The Economic and Social Council shall consist of fifty-four Members of the United Nations elected by the General Assembly.

2. Subject to the provisions of paragraph 3, eighteen members of the Economic and Social Council shall be elected each year for a term of three years. A retiring member shall be eligible for immediate re-election.

3. At the first election after the increase in the membership of the Economic and Social Council from twenty-seven to fifty-four members, in addition to the members elected in place of the nine members whose term of office expires at the end of that year, twenty-seven additional members shall be elected. Of these twenty-seven additional members, the term of office of nine members so elected shall expire at the end of one year, and of nine other members at the end of two years, in accordance with arrangements made by the General Assembly.

4. Each member of the Economic and Social Council shall have one representative.

Functions and powers

Article 62. 1. The Economic and Social Council may make or initiate studies and reports with respect to international economic, social, cultural, educational, health, and related matters and may make recommendations with respect to any such matters to the General Assembly, to the Members of the United Nations, and to the specialized agencies concerned.

2. It may make recommendations for the purpose of promoting respect for, and observance of, human rights and fundamental freedoms for all.

3. It may prepare draft conventions for submission to the General Assembly, with respect to matters falling within its competence.

4. It may call, in accordance with the rules prescribed by the United Nations, international conferences on matters falling within its competence.

Article 63. 1. The Economic and Social Council may enter into agreements with any of the agencies referred to in Article 57, defining the terms on which the agency concerned shall be brought into relationship with the United Nations. Such agreements shall be subject to approval by the General Assembly.

2. It may co-ordinate the activities of the specialized agencies through consultation with and recommendations to such agencies and through recommendations to the General Assembly and to the Members of the United Nations.

Article 64. 1. The Economic and Social Council may take appropriate steps to obtain regular reports from the specialized agencies. It may make arrangements with the Members of the United Nations and with the specialized agencies to obtain reports on the steps taken to give effect to its own recommendations and to recommendations on matters falling within its competence made by the General Assembly.

2. It may communicate its observations on these reports to the General Assembly.

Article 65. The Economic and Social Council may furnish information to the Security Council and shall assist the Security Council upon its request.

Article 66. 1. The Economic and Social Council shall perform such functions as fall within its competence in connexion with the carrying out of the recommendations of the General Assembly.

2. It may, with the approval of the General Assembly, perform services at the

request of Members of the United Nations and at the request of specialized agencies.

3. It shall perform such other functions as are specified elsewhere in the present Charter or as may be assigned to it by the General Assembly.

Voting

Article 67. 1. Each member of the Economic and Social Council shall have one vote.

2. Decisions of the Economic and Social Council shall be made by a majority of the members present and voting.

Procedure

Article 68. The Economic and Social Council shall set up commissions in economic and social fields and for the promotion of human rights, and such other commissions as may be required for the performance of its functions.

Article 69. The Economic and Social Council shall invite any Member of the United Nations to participate, without vote, in its deliberations on any matter of particular concern to that Member.

Article 70. The Economic and Social Council may make arrangements for representatives of the specialized agencies to participate, without vote, in its deliberations and in those of the commissions established by it, and for its representatives to participate in the deliberations of the specialized agencies.

Article 71. The Economic and Social Council may make suitable arrangements for consultation with non-governmental organizations which are concerned with matters within its competence. Such arrangements may be made with international organizations and, where appropriate, with national organizations after consultation with the Member of the United Nations concerned.

Article 72. 1. The Economic and Social Council shall adopt its own rules of procedure, including the method of selecting its President.

2. The Economic and Social Council shall meet as required in accordance with its rules, which shall include provision for the convening of meetings on the request of a majority of its members.

Chapter XI

DECLARATION REGARDING NON-SELF-GOVERNING TERRITORIES

Article 73. Members of the United Nations which have or assume responsibilities for the administration of territories whose peoples have not yet attained a full measure of self-government recognize the principle that the interests of the inhabitants of these territories are paramount, and accept as a sacred trust the obligation to promote to the utmost, within the system of international peace and security established by the present Charter, the well-being of the inhabitants of these territories, and, to this end:

a. to ensure, with due respect for the culture of the peoples concerned, their political, economic, social, and educational advancement, their just treatment, and their protection against abuses;

b. to develop self-government, to take due account of the political aspirations of the peoples, and to assist them in the progressive development of their free political institutions, according to the particular circumstances of each territory and its peoples and their varying stages of advancement;

c. to further international peace and security;

d. to promote constructive measures of development, to encourage research, and to co-operate with one another and, when and where appropriate, with specialized international bodies with a view to the practical achievement of the social, economic, and scientific purposes set forth in this Article; and

e. to transmit regularly to the Secretary-General for information purposes, subject to such limitation as security and constitutional considerations may require, statistical and other information of a technical nature relating to economic, social, and educational conditions in the territories for which they are respectively responsible other than those territories to which Chapters XII and XIII apply.

Article 74. Members of the United Nations

also agree that their policy in respect of the territories to which this Chapter applies, no less than in respect of their metropolitan areas, must be based on the general principle of good-neighbourliness, due account being taken of the interests and well-being of the rest of the world, in social, economic, and commercial matters.

Chapter XII

INTERNATIONAL TRUSTEESHIP SYSTEM

Article 75. The United Nations shall establish under its authority an international trusteeship system for the administration and supervision of such territories as may be placed thereunder by subsequent individual agreements. These territories are hereinafter referred to as trust territories.

Article 76. The basic objectives of the trusteeship system, in accordance with the Purposes of the United Nations laid down in Article 1 of the present Charter, shall be:

a. to further international peace and security;

b. to promote the political, economic, social, and educational advancement of the inhabitants of the trust territories, and their progressive development towards self-government or independence as may be appropriate to the particular circumstances of each territory and its peoples and the freely expressed wishes of the peoples concerned, and as may be provided by the terms of each trusteeship agreement;

c. to encourage respect for human rights and for fundamental freedoms for all without distinction as to race, sex, language, or religion, and to encourage recognition of the interdependence of the peoples of the world; and

d. to ensure equal treatment in social, economic, and commercial matters for all Members of the United Nations and their nationals, and also equal treatment for the latter in the administration of justice, without prejudice to the attainment of the foregoing objectives and subject to the provisions of Article 80.

Article 77. 1. The trusteeship system shall apply to such territories in the following categories as may be placed thereunder by means of trusteeship agreements:

a. territories now held under mandate;

b. territories which may be detached from enemy states as a result of the Second World War; and

c. territories voluntarily placed under the system by states responsible for their administration.

2. It will be a matter for subsequent agreement as to which territories in the foregoing categories will be brought under the trusteeship system and upon what terms.

Article 78. The trusteeship system shall not apply to territories which have become Members of the United Nations, relationship among which shall be based on respect for the principle of sovereign equality.

Article 79. The terms of trusteeship for each territory to be placed under the trusteeship system, including any alteration or amendment, shall be agreed upon by the states directly concerned, including the mandatory power in the case of territories held under mandate by a Member of the United Nations, and shall be approved as provided for in Articles 83 and 85.

Article 80. 1. Except as may be agreed upon in individual trusteeship agreements, made under Articles 77, 79, and 81, placing each territory under the trusteeship system, and until such agreements have been concluded, nothing in this Chapter shall be construed in or of itself to alter in any manner the rights whatsoever of any states or any peoples or the terms of existing international instruments to which Members of the United Nations may respectively be parties.

2. Paragraph 1 of this Article shall not be interpreted as giving grounds for delay or postponement of the negotiation and conclusion of agreements for placing mandated and other territories under the trusteeship system as provided for in Article 77.

Article 81. The trusteeship agreement shall in each case include the terms under which the trust territory will be administered and designate the authority which will exercise the administration of the trust territory. Such authority, hereinafter called the administering authority, may be one or more states or the Organization itself.

Article 82. There may be designated, in any trusteeship agreement, a strategic area or areas which may include part or all of the trust territory to which the agreement applies, without prejudice to any special agreement or agreements made under Article 43.

Article 83. 1. All functions of the United Nations relating to strategic areas, including the approval of the terms of the trusteeship agreements and of their alteration or amendment, shall be exercised by the Security Council.

2. The basic objectives set forth in Article 76 shall be applicable to the people of each strategic area.

3. The Security Council shall, subject to the provisions of the trusteeship agreements and without prejudice to security considerations, avail itself of the assistance of the Trusteeship Council to perform those functions of the United Nations under the trusteeship system relating to political, economic, social, and educational matters in the strategic areas.

Article 84. It shall be the duty of the administering authority to ensure that the trust territory shall play its part in the maintenance of international peace and security. To this end the administering authority may make use of volunteer forces, facilities, and assistance from the trust territory in carrying out the obligations towards the Security Council undertaken in this regard by the administering authority, as well as for local defence and the maintenance of law and order within the trust territory.

Article 85. 1. The functions of the United Nations with regard to trusteeship agreements for all areas not designated as strategic, including the approval of the terms of the trusteeship agreements and of their alteration or amendment, shall be exercised by the General Assembly.

2. The Trusteeship Council, operating under the authority of the General Assembly, shall assist the General Assembly in carrying out these functions.

Chapter XIII

THE TRUSTEESHIP COUNCIL

Composition

Article 86. 1. The Trusteeship Council shall consist of the following Members of the United Nations:

a. those Members administering trust territories;

b. such of those Members mentioned by name in Article 23 as are not administering trust territories; and

c. as many other Members elected for three-year terms by the General Assembly as may be necessary to ensure that the total number of members of the Trusteeship Council is equally divided between those Members of the United Nations which administer trust territories and those which do not.

2. Each member of the Trusteeship Council shall designate one specially qualified person to represent it therein.

Functions and powers

Article 87. The General Assembly and, under its authority, the Trusteeship Council, in carrying out their functions, may:

a. consider reports submitted by the administering authority;

b. accept petitions and examine them in consultation with the administering authority;

c. provide for periodic visits to the respective trust territories at times agreed upon with the administering authority; and

d. take these and other actions in conformity with the terms of the trusteeship agreements.

Article 88. The Trusteeship Council shall formulate a questionnaire on the political, economic, social, and educational advancement of the inhabitants of each trust territory, and the administering authority for each trust territory within the competence of the General Assembly shall make an annual report to the General

Assembly upon the basis of such questionnaire.

Voting

Article 89. 1. Each member of the Trusteeship Council shall have one vote.

2. Decisions of the Trusteeship Council shall be made by a majority of the members present and voting.

Procedure

Article 90. 1. The Trusteeship Council shall adopt its own rules of procedure, including the method of selecting its President.

2. The Trusteeship Council shall meet as required in accordance with its rules, which shall include provision for the convening of meetings on the request of a majority of its members.

Article 91. The Trusteeship Council shall, when appropriate, avail itself of the assistance of the Economic and Social Council and of the specialized agencies in regard to matters with which they are respectively concerned.

Chapter XIV

THE INTERNATIONAL COURT OF JUSTICE

Article 92. The International Court of Justice shall be the principal judicial organ of the United Nations. It shall function in accordance with the annexed Statute, which is based upon the Statute of the Permanent Court of International Justice and forms an integral part of the present Charter.

Article 93. 1. All Members of the United Nations are ipso facto parties to the Statute of the International Court of Justice.

2. A state which is not a member of the United Nations may become a party to the Statute of the International Court of Justice on conditions to be determined in each case by the General Assembly upon the recommendation of the Security Council.

Article 94. 1. Each Member of the United Nations undertakes to comply with the decision of the International Court of Justice in any case to which it is a party.

2. If any party to a case fails to perform the obligations incumbent upon it under a judgment rendered by the Court, the other party may have recourse to the Security Council, which may, if it deems necessary, make recommendations or decide upon measures to be taken to give effect to the judgment.

Article 95. Nothing in the present Charter shall prevent Members of the United Nations from entrusting the solution of their differences to other tribunals by virtue of agreements already in existence or which may be concluded in the future.

Article 96. 1. The General Assembly or the Security Council may request the International Court of Justice to give an advisory opinion on any legal question.

2. Other organs of the United Nations and specialized agencies, which may at any time be so authorized by the General Assembly, may also request advisory opinions of the Court on legal questions arising within the scope of their activities.

Chapter XV

THE SECRETARIAT

Article 97. The Secretariat shall comprise a Secretary-General and such staff as the Organization may require. The Secretary-General shall be appointed by the General Assembly upon the recommendation of the Security Council. He shall be the chief administrative officer of the Organization.

Article 98. The Secretary-General shall act in that capacity in all meetings of the General Assembly, of the Security Council, of the Economic and Social Council, and of the Trusteeship Council, and shall perform such other functions as are entrusted to him by these organs. The Secretary-General shall make an annual report to the General Assembly on the work of the Organization.

Article 99. The Secretary-General may bring to the attention of the Security Council any matter which in his opinion may threaten the maintenance of international peace and security.

Article 100. 1. In the performance of their

duties the Secretary-General and the staff shall not seek or receive instructions from any government or from any other authority external to the Organization. They shall refrain from any action which might reflect on their position as international officials responsible only to the Organization.

2. Each Member of the United Nations undertakes to respect the exclusively international character of the responsibilities of the Secretary-General and the staff and not to seek to influence them in the discharge of their responsibilities.

Article 101. 1. The staff shall be appointed by the Secretary-General under regulations established by the General Assembly.

2. Appropriate staffs shall be permanently assigned to the Economic and Social Council, the Trusteeship Council, and, as required, to other organs of the United Nations. These staffs shall form a part of the Secretariat.

3. The paramount consideration in the employment of the staff and in the determination of the conditions of service shall be the necessity of securing the highest standards of efficiency, competence, and integrity. Due regard shall be paid to the importance of recruiting the staff on as wide a geographical basis as possible.

Chapter XVI

MISCELLANEOUS PROVISIONS

Article 102. 1. Every treaty and every international agreement entered into by any Member of the United Nations after the present Charter comes into force shall as soon as possible be registered with the Secretariat and published by it.

2. No party to any such treaty or international agreement which has not been registered in accordance with the provisions of paragraph 1 of this Article may invoke that treaty or agreement before any organ of the United Nations.

Article 103. In the event of a conflict between the obligations of the Members of the United Nations under the present Charter and their obligations under any other international agreement, their obligations under the present Charter shall prevail.

Article 104. The Organization shall enjoy in the territory of each of its Members such legal capacity as may be necessary for the exercise of its functions and the fulfilment of its purposes.

Article 105. 1. The Organization shall enjoy in the territory of each of its Members such privileges and immunities as are necessary for the fulfilment of its purposes.

2. Representatives of the Members of the United Nations and officials of the Organization shall similarly enjoy such privileges and immunities as are necessary for the independent exercise of their functions in connexion with the Organization.

3. The General Assembly may make recommendations with a view to determining the details of the application of paragraphs 1 and 2 of this Article or may propose conventions to the Members of the United Nations for this purpose.

Chapter XVII

TRANSITIONAL SECURITY ARRANGEMENTS

Article 106. Pending the coming into force of such special agreements referred to in Article 43 as in the opinion of the Security Council enable it to begin the exercise of its responsibilities under Article 42, the parties to the Four-Nation Declaration, signed at Moscow, 30 October 1943, and France, shall, in accordance with the provisions of paragraph 5 of that Declaration, consult with one another and as occasion requires with other Members of the United Nations with a view to such joint action on behalf of the Organization as may be necessary for the purpose of maintaining international peace and security.

Article 107. Nothing in the present Charter shall invalidate or preclude action, in relation to any state which during the Second World War has been an enemy of any signatory to the present Charter, taken or authorized as a result of that war by the Governments having responsibility for such action.

Chapter XVIII

AMENDMENTS

Article 108. Amendments to the present Charter shall come into force for all Members of the United Nations when they have been adopted by a vote of two thirds of the members of the General Assembly and ratified in accordance with their respective constitutional processes by two thirds of the Members of the United Nations, including all the permanent members of the Security Council.

Article 109. 1. A General Conference of the Members of the United Nations for the purpose of reviewing the present Charter may be held at a date and place to be fixed by a two-thirds vote of the members of the General Assembly and by a vote of any nine members of the Security Council. Each Member of the United Nations shall have one vote in the conference.

2. Any alteration of the present Charter recommended by a two-thirds vote of the conference shall take effect when ratified in accordance with their respective constitutional processes by two thirds of the Members of the United Nations including the permanent members of the Security Council.

3. If such a conference has not been held before the tenth annual session of the General Assembly following the coming into force of the present Charter, the proposal to call such a conference shall be placed on the agenda of that session of the General Assembly, and the conference shall be held if so decided by a majority vote of the members of the General Assembly and by a vote of any seven members of the Security Council.

Chapter XIX

RATIFICATION AND SIGNATURE

Article 110. 1. The present Charter shall be ratified by the signatory states in accordance with their respective constitutional processes.

2. The ratifications shall be deposited with the Government of the United States of America, which shall notify all the signatory states of each deposit as well as the Secretary-General of the Organization when he has been appointed.

3. The present Charter shall come into force upon the deposit of ratifications by the Republic of China, France, the Union of Soviet Socialist Republics, the United Kingdom of Great Britain and Northern Ireland, and the United States of America, and by a majority of the other signatory states. A protocol of the deposited ratifications shall thereupon be drawn up by the Government of the United States of America which shall communicate copies thereof to all the signatory states.

4. The states signatory to the present Charter which ratify it after it has come into force will become original Members of the United Nations on the date of the deposit of their respective ratifications.

Article 111. The present Charter, of which the Chinese, French, Russian, English, and Spanish texts are equally authentic, shall remain deposited in the archives of the Government of the United States of America. Duly certified copies thereof shall be transmitted by that Government to the Governments of the other signatory states.

IN FAITH WHEREOF the representatives of the Governments of the United Nations have signed the present Charter.

DONE at the city of San Francisco the twenty-sixth day of June, one thousand nine hundred and forty-five.

International Economic Organizations

The importance attached to learning the lessons of the Depression of the 1930s was reflected in the deliberations at the *United Nations Monetary Conference at Bretton Woods in New Hampshire 1–22 July 1944* at which forty-four nations were represented. Two institutions were created, the *International Bank for Reconstruction and*

Development (IBRD) which was to help to reconstruct war-devastated Europe. The resources for this could only come from the United States.

The IBRD, commonly known as the *World Bank*, started operating in December 1945. Its purpose was to promote foreign investment by guarantees and participation in loans made by private investors or its own funds. It operates on prudent financial criteria.

After 1949 the Bank's focus of lending shifted to the less developed nations. Loans are made for costly long-term essential infrastructures such as electric power, railroads, highways and ports, water supply and pipelines. As part of its provision of technical assistance, the Bank established the *Economic Development Institute* in 1955. Among organizations affiliated to the World Bank are the *International Development Association* founded in 1960 to help economic development in poorer countries granting loans on easier credit terms and no interest for the poorest countries and the *International Finance Corporation*, established in 1956 to stimulate private enterprise in less developed countries. Effective control over decisions and policies is vested in a board of executive directors, whose membership and voting system is linked to the size of the contribution made by its principal shareholders. Consequently, it is dominated by the industrialized countries, and its president is by custom always a United States citizen. The World Bank has changed its lending focus over the decades from infrastructures to projects designed to alleviate poverty, health schemes and slum clearance. Loans in the 1980s were made to overcome balance of payment problems in Africa and Latin America to prevent the collapse of their economies. In the 1990s assistance has widened to reform of political systems in sub-Saharan Africa without which other economic reforms cannot function. The Bank is also involved in assistance to post-communist Russia and eastern Europe. Its staff is recognized as highly expert. Bank membership is open only to participants in the *International Monetary Fund*. The initial prescribed capital of the Bank was $7.67 billion. By the time of the first meeting of the Board of Directors in the autumn of 1946 the Bank had thirty-eight members. Japan and West Germany joined in 1952, bringing the membership to fifty-three. By 1972 annual lending was over $3 billion. By 1979 it was over $10 billion. In 1980 communist China was permitted to occupy the Chinese seat in the Bank. In 1992 Switzerland joined, as did thirteen former republics of the USSR (which had never been a member).

The *International Monetary Fund* was established to promote international monetary co-operation; to facilitate the expansion and balanced growth of international trade; to promote exchange stability; to assist in the establishment of a multilateral system of payments; to make its general resources temporarily available to its members experiencing balance of payment difficulties under adequate safeguards; and to shorten the duration and lessen the degree of disequilibrium in the international balance of payments of members. Unlike the World Bank it was not originally intended to act as an aid agency. The IMF was formally inaugurated on *27 December 1945* when twenty-nine states signed its *Articles of Agreement* (p. 328). The USSR did not join; nor did Switzerland. Communist China, however, did. Cuba joined but later left the organization. By 1999 it had 182 members. Like the World Bank, the IMF had its headquarters in Washington DC, and its head is by custom a European. The weighted voting according to members' contributions gives control to the industrialized west.

The experts at IMF provide advice and make forecasts. Members contribute to the reserves of the IMF and receive quotas they can draw on in proportion to their contributions to meet balance of payment difficulties. Should a member wish to draw on more than a part of its quota, then the IMF experts may impose conditions. IMF support was intended to be only short term (unlike the World Bank's). With the end in 1971 of the Brettom Woods system of fixed exchange rates and the turbulence of the 1970s and 1980s, the role of the IMF became increasingly important in the Latin American and African economies and in the 1990s also in Asia. The IMF has also sought to assist economic reform in Russia by tying its loans to conditions to be met. The distinction between the IMF and the World Bank has become increasingly blurred. These two global international organizations, only loosely linked to the UN and independent in their decision making from the General Assembly, are a major force in the world economy.

The attempt to found a third 'Bretton Woods type organization', the International Trade Organization (ITO) to promote open trade, was slow to materialize. In its place, instead in 1947 a multi-lateral tariff treaty known as GATT *(General Agreement on Tariffs and Trade)* was negotiated between governments outside the UN framework at first as a 'provisional' measure; later, with the failure of the ITO it continued for the next fifty-seven years. Its purpose was to remove barriers to the growth of world trade, raise standards of living and promote the economic growth of its signatories. After 1955 it was turned into an organization by the creation of a permanent Secretariat. In 1986 there were ninety-two members, including Poland, Czechoslovakia, Romania and Switzerland, but not the USSR. One purpose of all these organizations is to ensure the liberalization of trade. This purpose has not been fulfilled completely. Between 1947 and 1979 seven lengthy 'rounds' of GATT negotiations, designed to eliminate tariff barriers, took place (Geneva 1947, Annecy 1949, Torquay 1950–51, Geneva II 1955–56, the 'Dillon round' 1961–62, 'Kennedy round' 1963–67, and 'Tokyo round' 1973–79). An eighth round of talks began at Punta del Este in Uruguay in September 1986. The Uruguay round ended in April 1994 when 109 countries signed a 'final act' embodying some sixty agreements, about 30,000 pages in total length. It created new rules for trade in services, intellectual property, and the settlement of trade disputes. The agreement also created a new organization to administer GATT rules, the *World Trade Organization* (WTO). Most countries were admitted, the major exception being China, whose membership had been blocked for several years by the United States which alleged unfair competition by Chinese manufacturers, in particular infringement of patents and copyrights; China's human rights abuses had been a further obstacle to US approval. The WTO is an intergovernmental organization independently run in a relationship with the UN.

Articles of Agreement of the International Bank for Reconstruction and Development (World Bank), 27 December 1945

The Governments on whose behalf the present Agreement is signed agree as follows:

Introductory Article. The International Bank for Reconstruction and Development is established and shall operate in accordance with the following provisions:

Article I: Purposes. The purposes of the Bank are:

(I) To assist in the reconstruction and development of territories of members by facilitating the investment of capital for productive purposes, including the restoration of economies destroyed or disrupted by war, the reconversion of productive facilities to peacetime needs and the encouragement of the development of productive facilities and resources in less developed countries.

(II) To promote private foreign investment by means of guarantees or participations in loans and other investments made by private investors; and when private capital is not available on reasonable terms, to supplement private investment by providing, on suitable conditions, finance for productive purposes out of its own capital, funds raised by it and its other resources.

(III) To promote the long-range balanced growth of international trade and the maintenance of equilibrium in balances of payments by encouraging international investment for the development of the productive resources of members, thereby assisting in raising productivity, the standard of living and conditions of labour in their territories.

(IV) To arrange the loans made or guaranteed by it in relation to international loans through other channels so that the more useful and urgent projects, large and small alike, will be dealt with first.

(V) To conduct its operations with due regard to the effect of international investment on business conditions in the territories of members and, in the immediate postwar years, to assist in bringing about a smooth transition from a war-time to a peacetime economy.

The Bank shall be guided in all its decisions by the purposes set forth above.

. . .

Articles of Agreement of the International Monetary Fund, Washington, 27 December 1945

The Governments on whose behalf the present Agreement is signed agree as follows:

Introductory Article. The International Monetary Fund is established and shall operate in accordance with the following provisions:

Article I: Purposes. The purposes of the International Monetary Fund are:

(I) To promote international monetary cooperation through a permanent institution which provides the machinery for consultation and collaboration on international monetary problems.

(II) To facilitate the expansion and balanced growth of international trade, and to contribute thereby to the promotion and maintenance of high levels of employment and real income and to the development of the productive resources of all members as primary objectives of economic policy.

(III) To promote exchange stability, to maintain orderly exchange arrangements among members, and to avoid competitive exchange depreciation.

(IV) To assist in the establishment of a multilateral system of payments in respect of current transactions between members and in the elimination of foreign exchange restriction which hamper the growth of world trade.

(V) To give confidence to members by making the Fund's resources available to them under adequate safeguards, thus providing them with opportunity to correct maladjustments in their balance of payments without resorting to measures destructive of national or international prosperity.

(VI) In accordance with the above, to shorten the duration and lessen the degree of disequilibrium in the international balances of payments of members.

The Fund shall be guided in all its decisions by the purposes set forth in this Article.

. . .

XIII · The United States treaty system

When the war came to an end the United States alone among the victorious great powers faced the future without alliance commitments to any single power or separate group of powers. Even during the course of the war Roosevelt had concluded no formal alliances but signed executive agreements not requiring a two-thirds majority of the Senate for approval. Thus the United States, for instance, was bound to its allies by only an executive agreement as one of the signatories of the *Declaration by the United Nations, 1 January 1942* (p. 297), whose obligations ceased with the end of the war. In 1945 the United States administration tried to return to its 'normal' peacetime diplomacy, rejecting exclusive alliances which, it was feared, would once again divide the world into hostile groupings. In the place of alliances, the USA had become a principal advocate and founder of the United Nations. But the objectives of American policy in 1945 remained global, based on the expectation of continued cooperation among the 'Big Three', Britain, the Soviet Union and the United States.

The United States and the Americas

At the same time as adopting the global approach to foreign policy, the United States maintained its tradition of claiming special rights and responsibilities in the western hemisphere as embodied in the Monroe Doctrine (1823). In practice this meant that the United States, whilst recognizing how varied the Latin American Republics were, and how much of the time their interests conflicted with each other, also claimed that they form part of an American system. American presidents claimed the right to intervene unilaterally, if need be, if the vital interests of the United States were held to be endangered — vital interests which were declared to be equally the interests of the American republics as a whole. This might happen if a Latin American republic developed close ties with a state potentially hostile to the United States and especially, as in Cuba, where foreign military bases or weapons were involved. Geographically, US intervention was confined in the main to the strategically vital Caribbean region; the United States possessed Guantanamo naval base in Cuba and controlled the Panama Canal. Until Franklin D. Roosevelt proclaimed the 'Good Neighbor' policy in 1933, United States armed intervention had been frequent, especially in Cuba, Panama, Nicaragua, Mexico, Haiti and the Dominican Republic, despite the attempts of inter-American conferences to prevent United States military action.

Eight international conferences of the American states met before the end of the Second World War: the first took place in Washington during 1889 and 1890, and since then numerous other special inter-American conferences have also been convened. They produced many treaties, declarations and enunciations of principles, but the gap between these aspirations and practical achievements was wide. Nor did the political, economic and international objectives of the governments of the Latin American republics always coincide with those of the much more powerful United States; the republics were also divided on many issues among each other.

The International American Conferences were concerned with four basic aspects of inter-American relations: (i) establishing the independence and sovereignty of each state, thus ensuring non-intervention by any other state especially by the United States; (ii) hemispheric security; (iii) inter-American cooperation in many fields, economic and social, which frequently entailed attempting to secure favourable trading conditions and economic aid from the United States; (iv) establishing effective machinery for settling inter-American disputes peacefully.

Inter-American solidarity was not prominently in evidence during the First World War. After the war, *the Fifth International Conference of American States, meeting in Santiago, 25 March–3 May 1923*, was notable for the conclusion of a *Treaty to Avoid or Prevent Conflicts*, generally known as the *Gondra Treaty*; this provided for a commission to investigate disputes and a six-month cooling-off period. At a special conference of American states, held in Washington, *10 December 1928–5 January 1929*, two treaties were adopted, the *General Convention of Inter-American Conciliation* and the *General Treaty of Inter-American Arbitration*; but the weakness of the latter treaty was that both parties to a dispute would have to agree to setting up arbitration machinery. A special commission of American jurists, appointed after the Sixth International Conference at Havana (1928), drew up a *Convention Defining the Rights and Duties of States* which was adopted by the *Seventh International Conference of American States at Montevideo, 3–26 December 1933*; according to Article 8 of this convention, no state had the right to intervene in the internal or external affairs of another. The United States ratified the convention in June 1934, but President Roosevelt in practice interpreted Article 8 as referring only to armed intervention.

On 29 May 1934 Roosevelt abrogated the *Platt Amendment* under which the United States enjoyed special rights in Cuba.

A large number of resolutions and conventions were agreed and signed at a special *Inter-American Conference for the Maintenance of Peace, held in Buenos Aires, December 1936* (p. 336). This conference also led to the conclusion in treaty form of acceptance of the principle of non-intervention in the *Non-Intervention Additional Protocol between the United States and Other American Republics, 23 December 1936* (p. 340). Two years later, at the *Eighth International Conference of American States at Lima, December 1938*, one of many declarations (no. 109) provided for periodic consultations of the Foreign Ministers of the American republics and affirmed the continental solidarity of the American republics in case the peace, security or territorial integrity of any one of them was threatened. But despite the many treaties and convention resolutions from 1890 to 1938 the actual degree of inter-American cooperation and solidarity remained limited, and the machinery for settling disputes in the Americas peacefully was far from effective. The twenty republics had not succeeded in achieving complete security from undue United States influence in their affairs, although Roosevelt's 'Good Neighbor' policy brought about a great improvement in their relationship. Nor had the United States secured complete security through the establishment of the kind of inter-American cooperation that would have induced all the Latin American republics to give priority to relations with America as against relations with European states.

With the outbreak of war in Europe in September 1939, inter-American cooperation was strengthened. The first meeting of the Foreign Ministers of the Republics took place in *Panama, 23 September–3 October 1939*. This conference adopted the *Act of Panama*, a multilateral executive agreement, which included a general declaration of neutrality; an agreement on the setting-up of a committee of experts for the duration of the war to study and make recommendations on problems of neutrality; a declaration that a neutral zone was established on the high seas 300 miles from the shores of the republics; and, most important of all, a resolution that if any region in the Americas belonging to a European state should change sovereignties, thereby endangering the security of the Americas, a consultative meeting should be called urgently. The German conquests of the Netherlands and of France brought about a danger of the kind contemplated at Panama, and the Foreign Ministers therefore met again in *Havana, 21–30 July 1940*, and adopted the *Act of Havana* (p. 341). It stated that should a change of sovereignty be threatened in the case of the European colonies, then the American republics would create a committee to administer them; but should the emergency arise before a committee could act, then one state could take action alone, which in practice meant the United States. Another resolution declared that aggression against one of the republics would be regarded as aggression against all, though in that event they were bound only to consult on measures of common defence. The United States concluded many bilateral agreements with individual American republics during the Second World War, providing credit, purchasing raw materials and securing bases.

When, shortly after Pearl Harbor, the *third consultative meeting of American Foreign Ministers took place in Rio de Janeiro, 15–28 January 1942*, nine Central American and Caribbean republics had declared war on the Axis and eleven Latin American republics either broke off diplomatic relations or declared non-belligerency. But inter-American military cooperation remained far from wholehearted, with the Argentine being sympathetic to the Axis, and only by the time war was drawing to a close in 1945 had all the American republics declared war on Germany and Japan. The future relations of the American republics and inter-American cooperation in the post-war world formed the principal subject of the *Inter-American Conference on Problems of War and Peace, in Mexico City, 21 February–8 March 1945*. The conference was more concerned with post-war problems, and especially with the United Nations organization, than with problems of wartime alliance. The *Dumbarton Oaks* proposals (p. 298) were generally endorsed, but resolutions were also passed urging adequate representation for Latin American states on the proposed Security Council; in general the Latin American republics wished to reduce the dominant role of the great powers. Agreement was reached on the *Act of Chapultepec* (Resolution 8) which provided for sanctions and appropriate regional action in the event of an American or non-American state committing aggression against another American state, but with the additional proviso that such action would need to be consistent with the purpose of the world international organization when established. The Act of Chapultepec remained in force only so long as the war continued; it was intended that a new treaty should replace it later in time of peace. Other resolutions called upon the next American conference to agree on measures to strengthen inter-American collaboration in the economic and other fields. At the *San Francisco Conference* establishing the United Nations (p. 298), the United States and the Latin American states secured an important modification of the Dumbarton Oaks proposals. It emerged as Article 51 of the Charter, which permitted groups of states to make treaties for collective self-defence to meet an armed attack. But this right is limited to the point of time when the Security Council takes what action it deems appropriate. It is nevertheless an important safeguard where the Security Council is dead-locked or where one of the permanent members uses its veto against any enforcement action. Article 51 is further limited by Articles 53 to 54, which state that whilst the Security Council may authorize some regional action for 'enforce-ment action', no such action may be taken without the authorization of the Security Council; the Security Council also has to be kept fully informed of any action in contemplation. Thus Article 51 confers a right only of self-defence in case of armed attack, not of enforcement against a state that is more vaguely accused of aggression or aggressive intent before an armed attack has occurred.

The Ninth Inter-American Conference for the Maintenance of Continental Peace and Security met near Rio de Janeiro, 15 August–2 September 1947, under the shadow of the 'cold war'; the deliberations concluded with the signature of the Inter-American Treaty of Reciprocal Assistance, 2 September 1947 (p. 342), also known as the Pact of Rio, which became effective after ratification by two-thirds of the signatories on 3 December 1948. It was signed by all the American states except Canada, Nicaragua and Ecuador. In March 1960 Cuba withdrew from the treaty. The Pact of Rio established an inter-American alliance of collective defence against armed attack as permitted by Article 51 of the UN Charter; it was also a regional agreement laying down the procedures to be followed in the event of any other act, or threat of aggression. Although Canada was not a party to the treaty, Article 4 defined the region covered as all of North and South America, and included Canada and Greenland and a part of Antarctica. The treaty left it to each signatory to act immediately as it considered necessary after an armed attack had taken place, until by a two-thirds majority the members of the pact decided on what future action was required. But if 'indirect aggression' was claimed to have taken place, such as the support of revolution in one state by another (many Latin American republics shared United States fears of communist subversion), then no automatic right of intervention was allowed to any one state or a group of states; in such an event members of the treaty would meet to decide on what joint measures to take. According to Article 53 of the UN Charter, any 'enforcement action' then decided on would require the Security Council's authorization. The Rio treaty made hemispheric defence the joint responsibility of the American republics, but did not supersede the Monroe Doctrine or the claim of the United States to act unilaterally in defence of its own vital interests. The Rio treaty was significant in another respect, for it provided the model for other regional treaties to which the United States was a party, especially the North Atlantic Treaty (p. 359).

The second treaty, complementing the Rio pact, which reorganized the inter-American system in the post-Second-World-War years, was the Charter of the Organization of American States, 30 April 1948 (p. 344), signed by all twenty-one American republics. Trinidad joined in February 1967, and other former colonies followed after attaining independence. Cuba was expelled in February 1962. By 1984 there were thirty-two members. This treaty emerged from the negotiations at the Ninth International Conference of American States at Bogotá, 30 March–2 May 1948. The Charter of the Organization of American States (OAS) comprised 112 articles. It placed the inter-American system on a permanent treaty basis within the UN framework. Articles 32 to 101 defined the structure and functions of the OAS The supreme organ of the OAS was the Inter-American Conference, which in ordinary session met every five years, though at the request of two-thirds of the members a special conference might be convened. The old Pan-American Union at Washington became the permanent central organ and general secretariat of the OAS Its council was composed of a representative from each member state. The council acted as a consultative body in the event of an act of aggression; it also decided by majority to call a consultative meeting of Foreign Ministers when requested by one member. The council worked through three organs: the Inter-American Economic and Social Council, the Inter-American Council of Jurists and the Inter-American Cultural Council. In addition, some twelve specialized organizations, commissions and agencies operated within the framework of the OAS The charter set out the purpose, principles, duties and rights of the OAS; the purpose of the organization was to facilitate the pacific settlements of disputes, to strengthen inter-American solidarity and to raise economic, social and cultural standards.

The third treaty on which post-war inter-American relations were to be based was the *American Treaty on Pacific Settlement, 30 April 1948*, known as the *Pact of Bogotá* (p. 346). Its purpose was to coordinate treaties signed at earlier conferences to ensure that disputes between American states would be settled by peaceful means. Although the treaty provided for compulsory arbitration (Article 46) and for the compulsory jurisdiction of the International Court (Article 32), reservations made to the pact at the time of signature by seven American republics, including the United States, made these compulsory procedures, wherein the main strength of the pact lies, inoperative in practice.

It is a characteristic of all these treaties that no state is automatically bound to offer armed assistance to any other signatory; also important is the fact that the United States is not prevented from acting in accordance with the treaty, if it decides to do so, by the possible opposition of one or more of the Latin American republics.

The United States administration endeavoured to draw the attention of the Latin American states to the dangers of international communism during the early 1950s, but without much response. The election of President Arbenz in Guatemala in 1950 alarmed the administration, which regarded him as sympathetic to communist policies. At the *Tenth International Conference of American States at Caracas, 1–28 March 1954*, Secretary of State John Foster Dulles secured the passage of a resolution directed against the control of the political institutions of any American state by the 'international communist movement'; but no resolution specifically allowed for any joint intervention in the affairs of an American state. In June 1954 Guatemala was invaded from Honduras, and Arbenz was overthrown. It was widely believed that the United States was chiefly responsible and that the Central Intelligence Agency was involved in the invasion. Latin American fears of a return by the United States to a policy of intervention, and dissatisfaction with the economic policies of the United States, made the 1950s a bleak decade in relations between the United States and its South American neighbours. The decade ended with Fidel Castro's successful Cuban revolution. The United States broke off diplomatic relations with Castro in 1961. Cuba's communist alignment represented a major challenge to United States leadership in the Americas. An attempt to bring about Castro's fall by aiding Cuban exiles to land in the Bay of Pigs and to raise a revolt ended in a fiasco in April 1961. This setback to inter-American relations was counterbalanced by President Kennedy's initiative in launching the 'Alliance for Progress'.

A special meeting of the *Inter-American Economic and Social Council held in Punta del Este, Uruguay, 5–17 August 1961, adopted the Charter of Punta del Este, establishing an Alliance for Progress* (p. 351). The United States undertook to provide 20 billion dollars, mainly from public funds, over a period of ten years. But these vast funds were not to be applied in the normal way of foreign aid. They were to be utilized to transform society in Latin America. Latin American governments pledged themselves to carry through far-reaching social reforms 'to permit a fair distribution of the fruits of economic and social progress'. These provisional reforms ranged from better use of land, housing and education, to the elimination of corruption and to economic collaboration. The results in Latin America were disappointing during the 1960s in terms of the objectives set out in the Alliance for Progress.

The United States continued to show itself ready to act unilaterally when it believed its vital interests were threatened. When Russian missiles were being erected in Cuba, Kennedy secured their removal in his confrontation with Khrushchev during the thirteen days of the *Cuban Missile Crisis of 16–28 October 1962*. But the United States also received a measure of support from the American states when the OAS adopted a resolution on 23 October which sanctioned the use of armed force if necessary against Cuba under the terms of the Rio treaty. Three years later, in April 1965, President Johnson intervened in the Dominican Republic where a revolution threatened to establish a government judged by his administration to be controlled by communists. The United States again acted unilaterally in the Caribbean since it believed its most vital interests were threatened by a hostile government which, as in Cuba, might link itself with the Soviet Union.

Similar fears by President Reagan's administration two decades later led to United States military intervention on the Caribbean island of Grenada in 1983, and to 'covert' American support for the 'contra' rebels operating from Honduras against the left-wing 'Sandinista' government of Nicaragua after 1979. 'Covert' political support was also given by the United States to the military revolt in Chile in 1973 which overthrew the leftist government of President Salvador Allende.

In spite of the defects of the Latin American treaty system established by the USA in the late 1940s (and notwithstanding the extent to which several states, most notably the USA, ignored the underlying principle of non-intervention in the internal affairs of fellow-signatories) the formal structure remained largely intact until the end of the century. The most important new security treaty affecting the region signed by the United States in the intervening period was the *Panama Canal Treaty of 7 September 1977* (see p. 777).

By contrast with the frequently troubled relations between the United States and its southern neighbours, American–Canadian relations throughout the postwar period were relatively smooth. Occasional spasms of anti-American nationalism in Canada did not seriously impair the relationship; nor did the emergence for a while in the 1970s of a movement calling for an independent Francophone Quebec. The close interlocking of the two countries' economies, and the gradual shedding by English-speaking Canadians of their residual sentimental allegiance to Great Britain, brought Canada and the United States into intimate cooperation. A Permanent Joint Board of Defense had been established between the two countries in 1940, and in 1947 they agreed to continue it indefinitely. In 1951 and 1955 agreements were signed establishing radar warning systems across Canada linking the western Alaskan islands to the eastern Canadian shore. Canada was a founding member of NATO, and after 1958 the air defences of North America were coordinated in a joint command (NORAD). In 1959 agreement was reached for establishing a ballistic missile early warning system. Numerous other agreements on questions of joint defence were reached. But Canada pursued a notably independent foreign policy, both on the world stage and in the western hemisphere. Initially because of her membership of the Commonwealth, later more because of a desire to avoid embroilment in conflicts between the USA and its southern neighbours, Canada held aloof from Pan-American organizations. (For later developments in the Americas, see Chapter XXII.)

Convention between the United States of America and other American Republics concerning the fulfillment of existing treaties between the American States, Buenos Aires, 23 December 1936

The Governments represented at the Inter-American Conference for the Maintenance of Peace,

Animated by a desire to promote the maintenance of general peace in their mutual relations;

Appreciating the advantages derived and to be derived from the various agreements already entered into condemning war and providing methods for the pacific settlement of international disputes;

Recognizing the need for placing the greatest restrictions upon resort to war; and

Believing that for this purpose it is desirable to conclude a new convention to coordinate, extend, and assure the fulfillment of existing agreements, have . . . agreed upon the following provisions:

Article 1. Taking into consideration that, by the Treaty to Avoid and Prevent Conflicts between the American States, signed at Santiago, May 3, 1923 (known as the Gondra Treaty), the High Contracting Parties agree that all controversies which it has been impossible to settle through diplomatic channels or to submit to arbitration in accordance with existing treaties shall be submitted for investigation and report to a Commission of Inquiry;

That by the Treaty for the Renunciation of War, signed at Paris on August 28, 1928 (known as the Kellogg–Briand Pact, or Pact of Paris), the High Contracting Parties solemnly declare in the names of their respective peoples that they condemn recourse to war for the solution of international controversies and renounce it as an instrument of national policy in their relations with one another;

That by the General Convention of Inter-American Conciliation, signed at Washington, January 5, 1929, the High Contracting Parties agree to submit to the procedure of conciliation all controversies between them, which it may not have been possible to settle through diplomatic channels, and to establish a 'Commission of Conciliation' to carry out the obligations assumed in the Convention;

That by the General Treaty of Inter-American Arbitration, signed at Washington, January 5, 1929, the High Contracting Parties bind themselves to submit to arbitration, subject to certain exceptions, all differences between them of an international character, which it has not been possible to adjust by diplomacy and which are juridical in their nature by reason of being susceptible of decision by the application of the principles of law, and moreover, to create a procedure of arbitration to be followed; and

That by the Treaty of Non-Aggression and Conciliation, signed at Rio de Janeiro, October 10, 1933 (known as the Saavedra Lamas Treaty), the High Contracting Parties solemnly declare that they condemn wars of aggression in their mutual relations or in those with other States and that the settlement of disputes or controversies between them shall be effected only by pacific means which have the sanction of international law, and also declare that as between them territorial questions must not be settled by violence, and that they will not recognize any territorial arrangement not obtained by pacific means, nor the validity of the occupation or acquisition of territories brought about by force of arms, and, moreover, in a case of non-compliance with these obligations, the Contracting States undertake to adopt, in their character as neutrals, a common and solidary attitude and to exercise the political, juridical, or economic means authorized by international law, and to bring the influence of public opinion to bear, without, however, resorting to intervention, either diplomatic or armed, subject nevertheless to the attitude that may be incumbent upon them by virtue of their collective treaties; and, furthermore, undertake to create a procedure of conciliation;

The High Contracting Parties reaffirm the obligations entered into to settle, by pacific means, controversies of an international character that may arise between them.

Article 2. The High Contracting Parties, convinced of the necessity for the cooperation and consultation provided for in the Convention for the Maintenance, Preservation and Re-establishment of Peace signed by them on this same day, agree that in all matters which affect peace on the continent, such consultation and co-operation shall have as their object to assist, through the tender of friendly good offices and of mediation, the fulfillment by the American Republics of existing obligations for pacific settlement, and to take counsel together, with full recognition of their juridical equality, as sovereign and independent States, and of their general right to individual liberty of action, when an emergency arises which affects their common interest in the maintenance of peace.

Article 3. In case of threat of war, the High Contracting Parties shall apply the provisions contained in Articles 1 and 2 of the

Convention for the Maintenance, Preservation, and Re-establishment of Peace, above referred to, it being understood that, while such consultation is in progress and for a period of not more than six months, the parties in dispute will not have recourse to hostilities or take any military action whatever.

Article 4. The High Contracting Parties further agree that, in the event of a dispute between two or more of them, they will seek to settle it in a spirit of mutual regard for their respective rights, having recourse for this purpose to direct diplomatic negotiations or to the alternative procedures of mediation, commissions of inquiry, commissions of conciliation, tribunals of arbitration, and courts of justice, as provided in the treaties to which they may be parties; and they also agree that, should it be impossible to settle the dispute by diplomatic negotiation and should the States in dispute have recourse to the other procedures provided in the present Article, they will report this fact and the progress of the negotiations to the other signatory States. These provisions do not affect controversies already submitted to a diplomatic or juridical procedure by virtue of special agreements.

Article 5. The High Contracting Parties agree that, in the event that the methods provided by the present Convention or by agreements previously concluded should fail to bring about a pacific settlement of differences that may arise between any two or more of them, and hostilities should break out between two or more of them, they shall be governed by the following stipulations;

(a) They shall, in accordance with the terms of the Treaty of Non-Aggression and Conciliation (Saavedra Lamas Treaty), adopt in their character as neutrals a common and solidary attitude; and shall consult immediately with one another, and take cognizance of the outbreak of hostilities in order to determine, either jointly or individually, whether such hostilities shall be regarded as constituting a state of war so as to call into effect the provisions of the present Convention.

(b) It is understood that, in regard to the question whether hostilities actually in progress constitute a state of war, each of the High Contracting Parties shall reach a prompt decision. In any event, should hostilities be actually in progress between two or more of the Contracting Parties, or between two or more signatory States not at the time parties to this Convention by reason of failure to ratify it, each Contracting Party shall take notice of the situation and shall adopt such an attitude as would be consistent with other multilateral treaties to which it is a party or in accordance with its municipal legislation. Such action shall not be deemed an unfriendly act on the part of any State affected thereby.

Article 6. Without prejudice to the universal principles of neutrality provided for in the case of an international war outside of America and without affecting the duties contracted by those American States, members of the League of Nations, the High Contracting Parties reaffirm their loyalty to the principles enunciated in the five agreements referred to in Article 1, and they agree that in the case of an outbreak of hostilities or threat of an outbreak of hostilities between two or more of them, they shall, through consultation, immediately endeavor to adopt in their character as neutrals a common and solidary attitude, in order to discourage or prevent the spread or prolongation of hostilities.

With this object, and having in mind the diversity of cases and circumstances, they may consider the imposition of prohibitions or restrictions on the sale or shipment of arms, munitions and implements of war, loans or other financial help to the States in conflict, in accordance with the municipal legislation of the High Contracting Parties, and without detriment to their obligations derived from other treaties to which they are or may become parties.

Article 7. Nothing contained in the present Convention shall be understood as affecting the rights and duties of the High Contracting Parties which are at the same time members of the League of Nations.

Article 8. The present Convention shall be

ratified by the High Contracting Parties in accordance with their constitutional procedures. The original Convention and the instruments of ratification shall be deposited with the Ministry of Foreign Affairs of the Argentina Republic, which shall communicate the ratifications to the other signatory States. It shall come into effect when ratifications have been deposited by not less than eleven signatory States.

The Convention shall remain in force indefinitely; but it may be denounced by any of the High Contracting Parties, such denunciation to be effective one year after the date upon which such notification has been given. Notices of denunciation shall be communicated to the Ministry of Foreign Affairs of the Argentine Republic which shall transmit copies thereof to the other signatory States. Denunciation shall not be regarded as valid if the party making such denunciation shall be actually in a state of war, or shall be engaged in hostilities without fulfilling the provisions established by this Convention.

In witness whereof, the plenipotentiaries above-mentioned have signed this Treaty in English, Spanish, Portuguese, and French, and have affixed thereto their respective seals, in the City of Buenos Aires, Capital of the Argentine Republic, this twenty-third day of December of the year 1936.

RESERVATIONS

Reservation of the Argentine Delegation: (1) In no case, under Article 6, can foodstuffs or raw materials destined for the civil populations of belligerent countries be considered as contraband of war, nor shall there exist any duty to prohibit credits for the acquisition of said foodstuffs or raw materials which have the destination indicated.

With reference to the embargo on arms, each nation may reserve freedom of action in the face of a war of aggression.

Reservation of the Delegation of Paraguay: (2) In no case, under Article 6, can foodstuffs or raw materials destined for the civil populations of belligerent countries be considered as contraband of war, nor shall there exist any duty to prohibit credits for the acquisition of said foodstuffs or raw materials which have the destination indicated.

With reference to the embargo on arms, each nation may reserve freedom of action in the face of a war of aggression.

Reservation of the Delegation of El Salvador: (3) With reservation with respect to the idea of continental solidarity when confronted by foreign aggression.

Reservation of the Delegation of Colombia: (4) In signing this Convention, the Delegation of Colombia understands that the phrase 'in their character as neutrals', which appears in Articles 5 and 6, implies a new concept of international law which allows a distinction to be drawn between the aggressor and the attacked, and to treat them differently. At the same time, the Delegation of Colombia considers it necessary, in order to assure the full and effective application of this Pact, to set down in writing the following definition of the aggressor:

That State shall be considered as an aggressor which becomes responsible for one or several of the following acts:

(a) That its armed forces, to whatever branch they may belong, illegally cross the land, sea, or air frontiers of other States. When the violation of the territory of a State has been effected by irresponsible bands organized within or outside of its territory and which have received direct or indirect help from another State, such violation shall be considered equivalent, for the purposes of the present Article, to that effected by the regular forces of the State responsible for the aggression;

(b) That it has intervened in a unilateral or illegal way in the internal or external affairs of another State;

(c) That it has refused to fulfill a legally given arbitral decision or sentence of international justice.

No consideration of any kind, whether political, military, economic, or of any other kind, may serve as an excuse or justification for the aggression here anticipated.

. . .

United states senate resolution when ratifying the convention, 29 June 1937

The United States of America holds that the reservations of this Convention do not constitute an amendment to the text, but that such reservations, interpretations, and definitions by separate Governments are solely for the benefit of such respective Governments and are not intended to be controlling upon the United States of America.

Additional Protocol between the United States of America and other American Republics concerning non-intervention, Buenos Aires, 23 December 1936

The Governments represented at the Inter-American Conference for the Maintenance of Peace,

Desiring to assure the benefits of peace in their mutual relations and in their relations with all the nations of the earth, and to abolish the practice of intervention; and

Taking into account that the Convention on Rights and Duties of States, signed at the Seventh International Conference of American States, December 26, 1933, solemnly affirmed the fundamental principle that 'no State has the right to intervene in the internal or external affairs of another',

Have resolved to reaffirm this principle through the negotiation of the following Additional Protocol . . .

Article 1. The High Contracting Parties declare inadmissible the intervention of any one of them, directly or indirectly, and for whatever reason, in the internal or external affairs of any other of the parties.

The violation of the provisions of this Article shall give rise to mutual consultation, with the object of exchanging views and seeking methods of peaceful adjustment.

Article 2. It is agreed that every question concerning the interpretation of the present Additional Protocol, which it has not been possible to settle through diplomatic channels, shall be submitted to the procedure of conciliation provided for in the agreements in force, or to arbitration, or to judicial settlement.

Article 3. The present Additional Protocol shall be ratified by the High Contracting Parties in conformity with their respective constitutional procedures. The original instrument and the instruments of ratification shall be deposited in the Ministry of Foreign Affairs of the Argentine Republic which shall communicate the ratifications to the other signatories. The Additional Protocol shall come into effect between the High Contracting Parties in the order in which they shall have deposited their ratifications.

Article 4. The present Additional Protocol shall remain in effect indefinitely but may be denounced by means of one year's notice after the expiration of which period the Protocol shall cease in its effects as regards the party which denounces it, but shall remain in effect for the remaining signatory States . . . .

Convention on the provisional administration of European colonies and possessions in the Americas, Havana, 30 July 1940

The Governments represented at the Second Meeting of Ministers of Foreign Affairs of the American Republics,
Considering . . .
That as a result of the events which are taking place in the European continent situations may develop in the territories of the possessions which some of the belligerent nations have in the Americas which may extinguish or materially impair the sovereignty which they exercise over them, or leave their Government without a leader, thus creating a state of danger to the peace of the continent and a state of affairs in which the rule of law, order, and respect for life, liberty and the property of inhabitants may disappear . . .
That any transfer, or attempted transfer, of the sovereignty, jurisdiction, possession of any interest in or control over any such region to another non-American State, would be regarded by the American Republics as against American sentiments and principles and the rights of American States to maintain their security and political independence . . .
That the American Republics, through their respective Government agencies, reserve the right to judge whether any transfer or attempted transfer of sovereignty, jurisdiction, cession or incorporation of geographic regions in the Americas, possessed by European countries up to September 1, 1939, has the effect of impairing their political independence even though no formal transfer or change in the status of such region or regions shall have taken place;
. . . Being desirous of protecting their peace and safety and of promoting the interests of any of the regions herein referred to which may fall within the purview of the foregoing recitations, have resolved to conclude the following convention:

Article I. If a non-American State shall directly or indirectly attempt to replace another non-American State in the sovereignty or control which it exercised over any territory located in the Americas, thus threatening the peace of the continent, such territory shall automatically come under the provisions of this Convention and shall be submitted to a provisional administrative régime.

Article II. The administration shall be exercised, as may be considered advisable in each case, by one or more American States, with their previous approval.

Article III. When the administration shall have been established for any region it shall be exercised in the interests of the security of the Americas and for the benefit of the region under administration, with a view to its welfare and progress, until such time as the region is in a position to govern itself or is restored to its former status, whenever the latter is compatible with the security of the American Republics.

. . .

Article XVI. A Commission to be known as the 'Inter-American Commission for Territorial Administration' is hereby established, to be composed of a representative from each one of the States which ratifies this Convention; it shall be the international organization to which this Convention refers. Once this Convention has become effective, any country which ratifies it may convoke the first meeting proposing the city in which it is to be held. The Commission shall elect its chairman, complete its organization and fix its definitive seat. Two-thirds of the members of the Commission shall constitute a quorum and two-thirds of the members present may adopt decisions.

Article XVII. The Commission is authorized to establish a provisional administration in the regions to which the present Convention refers; allow such administration to be exercised by the number of States which it may determine in each case, and supervise its exercise under the terms of the preceding Articles.

Inter-American Treaty of Reciprocal Assistance, Rio de Janeiro, 2 September 1947

In the name of their Peoples, the Governments represented at the Inter-American Conference for the Maintenance of Continental Peace and Security, desirous of consolidating and strengthening their relations of friendship and good neighborliness, and

Considering . . .

That the High Contracting Parties reiterate their will to remain united in an Inter-American System consistent with the purposes and principles of the United Nations, and reaffirm the existence of the agreement which they have concluded concerning those matters relating to the maintenance of international peace and security which are appropriate for regional action;

That the High Contracting Parties reaffirm their adherence to the principles of inter-American solidarity and cooperation, and especially to those set forth in the preamble and declarations of the Act of Chapultepec, all of which should be understood to be accepted as standards of their mutual relations and as the juridical basis of the Inter-American System . . .

That the obligation of mutual assistance and common defense of the American Republics is essentially related to their democratic ideals and to their will to cooperate permanently in the fulfillment of the principles and purposes of a policy of peace . . .

Have resolved, in conformity with the objectives stated above, to conclude the following Treaty, in order to assure peace, through adequate means, to provide for effective reciprocal assistance to meet armed attacks against any American State, and in order to deal with threats of aggression against any of them:

Article 1. The High Contracting Parties formally condemn war and undertake in their international relations not to resort to the threat or the use of force in any manner inconsistent with the provisions of the Charter of the United Nations or of this Treaty.

Article 2. As a consequence of the principle set forth in the preceding Article, the High Contracting Parties undertake to submit every controversy which may arise between them to methods of peaceful settlement and to endeavour to settle any such controversy among themselves by means of the procedures in force in the Inter-American System before referring it to the General Assembly or the Security Council of the United Nations.

Article 3. 1. The High Contracting Parties agree that an armed attack by any State against an American State shall be considered as an attack against all the American States and, consequently, each one of the said Contracting Parties undertakes to assist in meeting the attack in the exercise of the inherent right of individual or collective self-defense recognized by Article 51 of the Charter of the United Nations.

2. On the request of the State or States directly attacked and until the decision of the Organ of Consultation of the Inter-American System, each one of the Contracting Parties may determine the immediate measures which it may individually take in fulfillment of the obligation contained in the preceding paragraph and in accordance with the principle of continental solidarity. The Organ of Consultation shall meet without delay for the purpose of examining those measures and agreeing upon the measures of a collective character that should be taken.

3. The provisions of this Article shall be applied in case of any armed attack which takes place within the region described in Article 4 or within the territory of an American State. When the attack takes place outside of the said areas, the provisions of Article 6 shall be applied.

4. Measures of self-defense provided for under this Article may be taken until the Security Council of the United Nations has taken the measures necessary to maintain international peace and security.

Article 4. The regions to which this Treaty refers are the North and South American continents and Greenland and an area of Antarctica.

Article 5. The High Contracting Parties shall immediately send to the Security Council of the United Nations, in conformity with Articles 51 and 54 of the Charter of the United Nations, complete information concerning the activities undertaken or in contemplation in the exercise of the right of self-defense or for the purpose of maintaining inter-American peace and security.

Article 6. If the inviolability or the integrity of the territory or the sovereignty or political independence of any American State should be affected by an aggression which is not an armed attack or by an extra-continental or intracontinental conflict, or by any other fact or situation that might endanger the peace of America, the Organ of Consultation shall meet immediately in order to agree on the measures which must be taken in case of aggression to assist the victim of the aggression or, in any case, the measures which should be taken for the common defense and for the maintenance of the peace and security of the continent.

Article 7. In the case of a conflict between two or more American States, without prejudice to the right of self-defense in conformity with Article 51 of the Charter of the United Nations, the High Contracting Parties meeting in consultation shall call upon the contending States to suspend hostilities and restore matters to the *status quo ante bellum*, and shall take in addition all other necessary measures to re-establish or maintain inter-American peace and security and for the solution of the conflict by peaceful means. The rejection of the pacifying action will be considered in the determination of the aggressor and in the application of the measures which the consultative meeting may agree upon.

. . .

[*Article 8.* Sanctions ranged from breaking off diplomatic relations, to economic sanctions, to the use of armed force.]

Article 9. In addition to other acts which the Organ of Consultation may characterize as aggression, the following shall be considered as such:

(a) Unprovoked armed attack by a State against the territory, the people, or the land, sea or air forces of another State;

(b) Invasion, by the armed forces of a State, of the territory of an American State, through the trespassing of boundaries demarcated in accordance with a treaty, judicial decision, or arbitral award, or, in the absence of frontiers thus demarcated, invasion affecting a region which is under the effective jurisdiction of another State.

Article 10. None of the provisions of this Treaty shall be construed as impairing the rights and obligations of the High Contracting Parties under the Charter of the United Nations.

Article 11. The consultations to which this Treaty refers shall be carried out by means of the Meetings of Ministers of Foreign Affairs of the American Republics which have ratified the Treaty, or in the manner or by the organ which in the future may be agreed upon.

Article 12. The Governing Board of the Pan-American Union may act provisionally as an organ of consultation until the meeting of the Organ of Consultation referred to in the preceding Article takes place.

Article 13. The consultations shall be initiated at the request addressed to the Governing Board of the Pan-American Union by any of the signatory States which has ratified the Treaty.

Article 14. In the voting referred to in this Treaty only the representatives of the signatory States which have ratified the Treaty may take part.

Article 15. The Governing Board of the Pan-American Union shall act in all matters concerning this Treaty as an organ of liaison among the signatory States which have ratified this Treaty and between these States and the United Nations.

Article 16. The decisions of the Governing Board of the Pan-American Union referred to in Articles 13 and 15 above shall be taken by an absolute majority of the members entitled to vote.

Article 17. The Organ of Consultation shall take its decisions by a vote of two-thirds of the signatory States which have ratified the Treaty.

Article 18. In the case of a situation or dispute between American States, the parties directly interested shall be excluded from the voting referred to in two preceding Articles.

Article 19. To constitute a quorum in all the meetings referred to in the previous Articles, it shall be necessary that the number of States represented shall be at least equal to the number of votes necessary for the taking of the decision.

Article 20. Decisions which require the application of the measures specified in Article 8 shall be binding upon all the signatory States which have ratified this Treaty, with the sole exception that no State shall be required to use armed force without its consent.

Article 21. The measures agreed upon by the Organ of Consultation shall be executed through the procedures and agencies now existing or those which may in the future be established.

. . .

[*Articles 22–4.* Ratification and Registration. Ratification by two-thirds of signatories necessary.]

Article 25. This Treaty shall remain in force indefinitely, but may be denounced by any High Contracting Party by a notification in writing to the Pan-American Union, which shall inform all the other High Contracting Parties of each notification of denunciation received.

After the expiration of two years from the date of the receipt by the Pan-American Union of a notification of denunciation by any High Contracting Party, the present Treaty shall cease to be in force and with respect to such State, but shall remain in full force and effect with respect to all the other High Contracting Parties.

Article 26. The principles and fundamental provisions of this Treaty shall be incorporated in the Organic Pact of the Inter-American System.

RESERVATION OF HONDURAS

[Concerning Honduras–Nicaraguan boundary.]

Charter of the Organization of American States, Bogotá, 30 April 1948

IN THE NAME OF THEIR PEOPLES, THE STATES REPRESENTED AT THE NINTH INTERNATIONAL CONFERENCE OF AMERICAN STATES,

Convinced that the historic mission of America is to offer to man a land of liberty, and a favorable environment for the development of his personality and the realization of his just aspirations;

Conscious that that mission has already inspired numerous agreements, whose essential value lies in the desire of the American peoples to live together in peace, and, through their mutual understanding and respect for the sovereignty of each one, to provide for the betterment of all, in independence, in equality and under law;

Confident that the true significance of American solidarity and good neighborliness can only mean the consolidation on this continent, within the framework of democratic institutions, of a system of individual liberty and social justice based on respect for the essential rights of man;

Persuaded that their welfare and their contribution to the progress and the civilization of the world will increasingly require intensive continental cooperation;

Resolved to persevere in the noble undertaking that humanity has conferred upon the United Nations, whose principles and purposes they solemnly reaffirm;

Convinced that juridical organization is a necessary condition for security and peace founded on moral order and on justice; and

In accordance with Resolution IX of the Inter-American Conference on Problems of War and Peace, held at Mexico City,

Have agreed upon the following CHARTER OF THE ORGANIZATION OF AMERICAN STATES

Part one

Chapter 1: Nature and purposes

Article 1. The American States establish by this Charter the international organization that they have developed to achieve an order of peace and justice, to promote their solidarity, to strengthen their collaboration, and to defend their sovereignty, their territorial integrity and their independence. Within the United Nations, the Organization of American States is a regional agency.

. . .

Article 4. The Organization of American States, in order to put into practice the principles on which it is founded and to fulfill its regional obligations under the Charter of the United Nations, proclaims the following essential purposes:

(a) To strengthen the peace and security of the continent;

(b) To prevent possible causes of difficulties and to ensure the pacific settlement of disputes that may arise among the Member States;

(c) To provide for common action on the part of those States in the event of aggression;

(d) To seek the solution of political, juridical and economic problems that may arise among them; and

(e) to promote, by cooperative action, their economic, social and cultural development.

Chapter II: Principles

[*Article 5.* These affirm good faith, condemn aggression, aspire to social justice and economic cooperation.]

. . .

Chapter III: Fundamental rights and duties of states

Article 6. States are juridically equal, enjoy equal rights and equal capacity to exercise these rights, and have equal duties. The rights of each State depend not upon its power to ensure the exercise thereof, but upon the mere fact of its existence as a person under international law.

[*Articles 7–14.* Set out the rights and duties.]

. . .

Article 15. No State or group of States has the right to intervene, directly or indirectly, for any reason whatever, in the internal or external affairs of any other State. The foregoing principle prohibits not only armed force but also any other form of interference or attempted threat against the personality of the State or against its political, economic and cultural elements.

Article 16. No State may use or encourage the use of coercive measures of an economic or political character in order to force the sovereign will of another State and obtain from it advantages of any kind.

Article 17. The territory of a State is inviolable; it may not be the object, even temporarily, of military occupation or of other measures of force taken by another State, directly or indirectly, on any grounds whatever. No territorial acquisitions or special advantages obtained either by force or by other means of coercion shall be recognized.

Article 18. The American States bind themselves in their international relations not to have recourse to the use of force, except in the case of self-defense in accordance with existing treaties or in fulfillment thereof.

Article 19. Measures adopted for the maintenance of peace and security in accordance with existing treaties do not constitute a violation of the principles set forth in Articles 15 and 17.

Chapter IV: Pacific settlement of disputes

Article 20. All international disputes that may arise between American States shall be submitted to the peaceful procedures set forth in this Chapter, before being referred to the Security Council of the United Nations.

[*Articles 21–3.* Briefly set out the peaceful procedures.]

. . .

Chapter V: Collective security

Article 24. Every act of aggression by a State against the territorial integrity or the inviolability of the territory or against the sovereignty or political independence of an American State shall be considered an act of aggression against the other American States.

Article 25. If the inviolability or the integrity of the territory or the sovereignty or political independence of any American State should be affected by an armed attack or by an act of aggression that is not an armed attack, or by an extracontinental conflict, or by a conflict between two or more American States, or by any other fact or situation that might endanger the peace of America, the American States, in furtherance of the principles of continental solidarity or collective self-defense, shall apply the measures and procedures established in the special treaties on the subject.

. . .

Chapter VI: Economic standards

[*Articles 26–7.*]

Chapter VII: Social standards

[*Articles 28–9.*]

Chapter VIII: Cultural standards

[*Articles 30–1.*]

American Treaty on Pacific Settlement (Pact of Bogotá), Bogotá, 30 April 1948

In the name of their peoples, the Governments represented at the Ninth International Conference of American States have resolved, in fulfillment of Article XXIII of the Charter of the Organization of American States, to conclude the following Treaty:

Chapter One: General obligation to settle disputes by pacific means

Article I. The High Contracting Parties, solemnly reaffirming their commitments made in earlier international conventions and declarations, as well as in the Charter of the United Nations, agree to refrain from the threat or the use of force, or from any other means of coercion for the settlement of their controversies, and to have recourse at all times to pacific procedures.

Article II. The High Contracting Parties recognize the obligation to settle international controversies by regional pacific procedures before referring them to the Security Council of the United Nations.

Consequently, in the event that a controversy arises between two or more signatory

States which, in the opinion of the parties, cannot be settled by direct negotiations through the usual diplomatic channels, the parties bind themselves to use the procedures established in the present Treaty, in the manner and under the conditions provided for in the following Articles, or, alternatively, such special procedures as, in their opinion, will permit them to arrive at a solution.

Article III. The order of the pacific procedures established in the present Treaty does not signify that the parties may not have recourse to the procedure which they consider most appropriate in each case, or that they should use all these procedures, or that any of them have preference over others except as expressly provided.

Article IV. Once any pacific procedure has been initiated, whether by agreement between the parties or in fulfillment of the present Treaty or a previous pact, no other procedure may be commenced until that procedure is concluded.

Article V. The aforesaid procedures may not be applied to matters which, by their nature, are within the domestic jurisdiction of the State. If the parties are not in agreement as to whether the controversy concerns a matter of domestic jurisdiction, this preliminary question shall be submitted to decision by the International Court of Justice, at the request of any of the parties.

Article VI. The aforesaid procedures, furthermore, may not be applied to matters already settled by arrangement between the parties, or by arbitral award or by decision of an international court, or which are governed by agreements or treaties in force on the date of the conclusion of the present Treaty.

Article VII. The High Contracting Parties bind themselves not to make diplomatic representations in order to protect their nationals, or to refer a controversy to a court of international jurisdiction for that purpose, when the said nationals have had available the means to place their case before competent domestic courts of the respective State.

Article VIII. Neither recourse to pacific means for the solution of controversies, nor the recommendation of their use, shall, in the case of an armed attack, be ground for delaying the exercise of the right of individual or collective self-defense, as provided for in the Charter of the United Nations.

Chapter Two: Procedures of good offices and mediation

Article IX. The procedure of good offices consists in the attempt by one or more American Governments not parties to the controversy, or by one or more eminent citizens of any American State which is not a party to the controversy, to bring the parties together, so as to make it possible for them to reach an adequate solution between themselves. [Procedures detailed in Articles X–XIV.]

. . .

Chapter Three: Procedure of investigation and conciliation

Article XV. The procedure of investigation and conciliation consists in the submission of the controversy to a Commission of Investigation and Conciliation, which shall be established in accordance with the provisions established in subsequent Articles of the present Treaty, and which shall function within the limitations prescribed therein.

. . .

Article XVIII. Without prejudice to the provisions of the foregoing Article, the Pan-American Union shall draw up a permanent panel of American conciliators, to be made up as follows:

(a) Each of the High Contracting Parties shall appoint, for three-year periods, two of their nationals who enjoy the highest reputation for fairness, competence and integrity;

(b) The Pan-American Union shall request of the candidates notice of their formal acceptance, and it shall place on the panel of conciliators the names of the persons who so notify it;

(c) The Governments may, at any time, fill vacancies occurring among their appointees; and they may reappoint their members.

Article XIX. In the event that a controversy should arise between two or more American States that have not appointed the Commission referred to in Article XVII, the following procedure shall be observed:

(a) Each party shall designate two members from the permanent panel of American conciliators, who are not of the same nationality as the appointing party;

(b) These four members shall in turn choose a fifth member, from the permanent panel, not of the nationality of either party;

(c) If, within a period of thirty days following the notification of their selection, the four members are unable to agree upon a fifth member, they shall each separately list the conciliators composing the permanent panel, in order of their preference, and upon comparison of the lists so prepared, the one who first receives a majority of votes shall be declared elected. The person so elected shall perform the duties of chairman of the Commission.

Article XX. In convening the Commission of Investigation and Conciliation, the Council of the Organization of American States shall determine the place where the Commission shall meet . . . .

[*Articles XX–XXVI.* Procedure of Commission.]

Article XXVII. If an agreement is reached by conciliation, the final report of the Commission shall be limited to the text of the agreement and shall be published after its transmittal to the parties, unless the parties decide otherwise. If no agreement is reached, the final report shall contain a summary of the work of the Commission; it shall be delivered to the parties, and shall be published after the expiration of six months unless the parties decide otherwise. In both cases, the final report shall be adopted by a majority vote.

Article XXVIII. The reports and conclusions of the Commission of Investigation and Conciliation shall not be binding upon the parties, either with respect to the statement of facts or in regard to questions of law, and they shall have no other character than that of recommendations submitted for the consideration of the parties in order to facilitate a friendly settlement of the controversy.

. . .

Chapter Four: Judicial procedure

Article XXXI. In conformity with Article 36, paragraph 2, of the Statute of the International Court of Justice, the High Contracting Parties declare that they recognize in relation to any other American State, the jurisdiction of the Court as compulsory *ipso facto*, without the necessity of any special agreement so long as the present Treaty is in force, in all disputes of a juridical nature that arise among them concerning:

(a) The interpretation of a treaty;

(b) Any question of international law;

(c) The existence of any fact which, if established, would constitute the breach of an international obligation;

(d) The nature or extent of the reparation to be made for the breach of an international obligation.

Article XXXII. When the conciliation procedure previously established in the present Treaty or by agreement of the parties does not lead to a solution, and the said parties have not agreed upon an arbitral procedure, either of them shall be entitled to have recourse to the International Court of Justice in the manner prescribed in Article 40 of the Statute thereof. The Court shall have compulsory jurisdiction in accordance with Article 36, paragraph 1, of the said Statute.

Article XXXIII. If the parties fail to agree as to whether the Court has jurisdiction over the controversy, the Court itself shall first decide that question.

Article XXXIV. If the Court, for the reasons set forth in Articles V, VI and VII of this Treaty, declares itself to be without jurisdiction to hear the controversy, such controversy shall be declared ended.

Article XXXV. If the Court for any other reason declares itself to be without jurisdiction to hear and adjudge the controversy, the High Contracting Parties obligate themselves to submit it to arbitration, in accordance with the provisions of Chapter Five of this Treaty.

...

Chapter Five: Procedure of arbitration

Article XXXVIII. Notwithstanding the provisions of Chapter Four of this Treaty, the High Contracting Parties may, if they so agree, submit to arbitration differences of any kind, whether juridical or not, that have arisen or may arise in the future between them.

...

[*Articles XXXIX–XLV.* Details of procedure of selecting arbiters or arbiter either by the Council of the Organization from nominations of parties in dispute, or by the parties who may by mutual agreement establish the Arbitration Tribunal in the manner they deem most appropriate.]

Article XLVI. The award shall be accompanied by a supporting opinion, shall be adopted by a majority vote, and shall be published after notification thereof has been given to the parties. The dissenting arbiter or arbiters shall have the right to state the grounds for their dissent.

The award, once it is duly handed down and made known to the parties, shall settle the controversy definitively, shall not be subject to appeal, and shall be carried out immediately.

Article XLVII. Any differences that arise in regard to the interpretation or execution of the award shall be submitted to the decision of the Arbitral Tribunal that rendered the award.

...

Chapter Six: Fulfillment of decisions

Article L. If one of the High Contracting Parties should fail to carry out the obligations imposed upon it by a decision of the International Court of Justice or by an arbitral award, the other party or parties concerned shall, before resorting to the Security Council of the United Nations, propose a Meeting of Consultation of Ministers of Foreign Affairs to agree upon appropriate measures to ensure the fulfillment of the judicial decision or arbitral award.

Chapter Seven: Advisory opinions

Article LI. The parties concerned in the solution of a controversy may, by agreement, petition the General Assembly or the Security Council of the United Nations to request an advisory opinion of the International Court of Justice on any juridical question.

The petition shall be made through the Council of the Organization of American States.

...

Article LVI. The present Treaty shall remain in force indefinitely, but may be denounced upon one year's notice, at the end of which period it shall cease to be in force with respect to the State denouncing it, but shall continue in force for the remaining signatories. The denunciation shall be addressed to the Pan-American Union, which shall transmit it to the other Contracting Parties.

The denunciation shall have no effect with respect to pending procedures initiated prior to the transmission of the particular notification.

...

RESERVATIONS

Argentina. The Delegation of the Argentine Republic, on signing the American Treaty on Pacific Settlement (Pact of Bogotá), makes reservations in regard to the following Articles, to which it does not adhere:

1. VII, concerning the protection of aliens;

2. Chapter Four (Articles XXXI to XXXVII), Judicial procedure;

3. Chapter Five (Articles XXXVIII to XLIX), Procedure of arbitration;

4. Chapter Six (Article L), Fulfillment of decisions.

Arbitration and judicial procedure have, as institutions, the firm adherence of the Argentine Republic, but the Delegation cannot accept the form in which the procedures for their application have been regulated, since, in its opinion, they should have been established only for controversies arising in the future and not originating in or having any relation to causes, situations or facts existing before the signing of this instrument. The compulsory execution of arbitral or judicial decisions and the limitation which prevents the States from judging for themselves in regard to matters that pertain to their domestic jurisdiction in accordance with Article V are contrary to Argentine tradition. The protection of aliens, who in the Argentine Republic are protected by its Supreme Law to the same extent as the nationals, is also contrary to that tradition.

Bolivia. The Delegation of Bolivia makes a reservation with regard to Article VI, inasmuch as it considers that pacific procedures may also be applied to controversies arising from matters settled by arrangement between the parties, when the said arrangement affects the vital interests of a State.

Ecuador. The Delegation of Ecuador, upon signing this Pact, makes an express reservation with regard to Article VI and also every provision that contradicts or is not in harmony with the principles proclaimed by or the stipulations contained in the Charter of the United Nations, the Charter of the Organization of American States, or the Constitution of the Republic of Ecuador.

United States of America. 1. The United States does not undertake as the complainant State to submit to the International Court of Justice any controversy which is not considered to be properly within the jurisdiction of the Court.

2. The submission on the part of the United States of any controversy to arbitration, as distinguished from judicial settlement, shall be dependent upon the conclusion of a special agreement between the parties to the case.

3. The acceptance by the United States of the jurisdiction of the International Court of Justice as compulsory *ipso facto* and without special agreement, as provided in this Treaty, is limited by any jurisdictional or other limitations contained in any Declaration deposited by the United States under Article 36, paragraph 4, of the Statute of the Court, and in force at the time of the submission of any case.

4. The Government of the United States cannot accept Article VII relating to diplomatic protection and the exhaustion of remedies. For its part, the Government of the United States maintains the rules of diplomatic protection, including the rule of exhaustion of local remedies by aliens, as provided by international law.

Paraguay. The Delegation of Paraguay makes the following reservation:

Paraguay stipulates the prior agreement of the parties as a prerequisite to the arbitration procedure established in this Treaty for every question of a non-juridical nature affecting national sovereignty and not specifically agreed upon in treaties now in force.

Peru. The Delegation of Peru makes the following reservations:

1. Reservation with regard to the second part of Article V, because it considers that domestic jurisdiction should be defined by the State itself.

2. Reservation with regard to Article XXXIII and the pertinent part of Article XXXIV, inasmuch as it considers that the exceptions of *res judicata*, resolved by settlement between the parties or governed by agreements and treaties in force, determine, in virtue of their objective and peremptory nature, the exclusion of these cases from the application of every procedure.

3. Reservation with regard to Article XXXV, in the sense that, before arbitration is resorted to, there may be, at the request of one of the parties, a meeting of the Organ of Consultation, as established in the Charter of the Organization of American States.

4. Reservation with regard to Article XLV, because it believes that arbitration set up without the participation of one of the parties is in contradiction with its constitutional provisions.

Nicaragua. The Nicaraguan Delegation, on giving its approval to the American Treaty on Pacific Settlement (Pact of Bogotá) wishes to record expressly that no provisions contained in the said Treaty may prejudice any position assumed by the Government of Nicaragua with respect to arbitral decisions the validity of which it has contested on the basis of the principles of international law, which clearly permit arbitral decisions to be attacked when they are adjudged to be null or invalidated. Consequently, the signature of the Nicaraguan Delegation to the Treaty in question cannot be alleged as an acceptance of any arbitral

decisions that Nicaragua has contested and the validity of which is not certain.

Hence the Nicaraguan Delegation reiterates the statement made on the 28th of the current month on approving the text of the above-mentioned Treaty in Committee III.

The Charter of Punta Del Este establishing an Alliance for Progress, 17 August 1961

Declaration to the Peoples of America

Assembled in Punta del Este, inspired by the principles consecrated in the Charter of the Organization of American States, in Operation Pan-America and in the Act of Bogotá, the representatives of the American Republics hereby agree to establish an Alliance for Progress: a vast effort to bring a better life to all the peoples of the continent.

This Alliance is established on the basic principle that free men working through the institution of representative democracy can best satisfy man's aspirations, including those for work, home and land, health and schools. No system can guarantee true progress unless it affirms the dignity of the individual which is the foundation of our civilization.

Therefore the countries signing this Declaration in the exercise of their sovereignty have agreed to work toward the following goals during the coming years:

To improve and strengthen democratic institutions through application of the principle of self-determination by the people.

To accelerate economic and social development, thus rapidly bringing about a substantial and steady increase in the average income in order to narrow the gap between the standard of living in Latin American countries and that enjoyed in the industrialized countries.

To carry out urban and rural housing programs to provide decent homes for all our people.

To encourage, in accordance with the characteristics of each country, programs of comprehensive agrarian reform, leading to the effective transformation, where required, of unjust structures and systems of land tenure and use; with a view to replacing *latifundia* and dwarf holdings by an equitable system of property so that, supplemented by timely and adequate credit, technical assistance and improved marketing arrangements, the land will become for the man who works it the basis of his economic stability, the foundation of his increasing welfare, and the guarantee of his freedom and dignity.

To assure fair wages and satisfactory working conditions to all our workers; to establish effective systems of labor-management relations and procedures for consultation and cooperation among government authorities, employers' associations, and trade unions in the interests of social and economic development.

To wipe out illiteracy; to extend, as quickly as possible, the benefits of primary education to all Latin Americans; and to provide broader facilities, on a vast scale, for secondary and technical training and for higher education.

To press forward with programs of health and sanitation in order to prevent sickness, combat contagious disease, and strengthen our human potential.

To reform tax laws, demanding more from those who have most, to punish tax evasion severely, and to redistribute the national income in order to benefit those who are most in need, while, at the same time, promoting savings and investment and reinvestment of capital.

To maintain monetary and fiscal policies which, while avoiding the disastrous effects of inflation or deflation, will protect the purchasing power of the many, guarantee the greatest possible price stability, and form an adequate basis for economic development.

To stimulate private enterprise in order to encourage the development of Latin American countries at a rate which will help them to provide jobs for their growing populations, to eliminate unemployment, and to take their place among the modern industrialized nations of the world.

To find a quick and lasting solution to the grave problem created by excessive price fluctuations in the basic exports of Latin American countries on which their prosperity so heavily depends.

To accelerate the integration of Latin America so as to stimulate the economic and social development of the continent. This process has already begun through the General Treaty of Economic Integration of Central America and, in other countries, through the Latin American Free Trade Association.

This Declaration expresses the conviction of the nations of Latin America that these profound economic, social, and cultural changes can come about only through the self-help efforts of each country. Nonetheless, in order to achieve the goals which have been established with the necessary speed, domestic efforts must be reinforced by essential contributions of external assistance.

The United States, for its part, pledges its efforts to supply financial and technical cooperation in order to achieve the aims of the Alliance for Progress. To this end, the United States will provide a major part of the minimum of twenty billion dollars, principally in public funds, which Latin America will require over the next ten years

from all external sources in order to supplement its own efforts.

The United States will provide from public funds, as an immediate contribution to the economic and social progress of Latin America, more than one billion dollars during the twelve months which began on March 13, 1961, when the Alliance for Progress was announced.

The United States intends to furnish development loans on a long-term basis, where appropriate running up to fifty years and in general at very low or zero rates of interest.

For their part, the countries of Latin America agree to devote a steadily increasing share of their own resources to economic and social development, and to make the reforms necessary to assure that all share fully in the fruits of the Alliance for Progress.

Further, as a contribution to the Alliance for Progress, each of the countries of Latin America will formulate a comprehensive and well-conceived national program for the development of its own economy.

Independent and highly qualified experts will be made available to Latin American countries in order to assist in formulating and examining national development plans.

Conscious of the overriding importance of this Declaration, the signatory countries declare that the inter-American community is now beginning a new era when it will supplement its institutional, legal, cultural and social accomplishments with immediate and concrete actions to secure a better life, under freedom and democracy, for the present and future generations.

The Charter of Punta del Este

Establishing an Alliance for Progress within the framework of Operation Pan-America

Preamble. We, the American Republics, hereby proclaim our decision to unite in a common effort to bring our people accelerated economic progress and broader social justice within the framework of personal dignity and political liberty.

Almost two hundred years ago we began in this hemisphere the long struggle for freedom which now inspires people in all parts of the world. Today, in ancient lands, men moved to hope by the revolutions of our young nations search for liberty. Now we must give a new meaning to that revolutionary heritage. For America stands at a turning point in history. The men and women of our hemisphere are reaching for the better life which today's skills have placed within their grasp. They are determined for themselves and their children to have decent and ever more abundant lives, to gain access to knowledge and equal opportunity for all, to end those conditions which benefit the few at the expense of the needs and dignity of the many. It is our inescapable task to fulfill these just desires – to demonstrate to the poor and forsaken of our countries, and of all lands, that the creative powers of free men hold the key to their progress and to the progress of future generations. And our certainty of ultimate success rests not alone on our faith in ourselves and in our nations but on the indomitable spirit of free man which has been the heritage of American civilization.

Inspired by these principles, and by the principles of Operation Pan-America and the Act of Bogotá, the American Republics hereby resolve to adopt the following program of action to establish and carry forward an Alliance for Progress.

· · ·

[TITLE I. The Treaty sets out the objectives of the alliance in conformity with the Declaration to the Peoples of America.]
[TITLE II. Economic and social development: requirements, National Development Programs, immediate and short-term measures.]

· · ·

Chapter IV: External assistance in support of National Development Programs

1. The economic and social development of Latin America will require a large amount of additional public and private financial assistance on the part of capital-exporting countries, including the members of the Development Assistance Group and international lending agencies. The measures provided for in the Act of Bogotá and the new measures provided for in this Charter, are designed to create a framework within which such additional assistance can be provided and effectively utilized.

2. The United States will assist those participating countries whose development programs establish self-help measures and economic and social policies and programs consistent with the principles of this Charter. To supplement the domestic efforts of such countries, the United States is prepared to allocate resources which, along with those anticipated from other external sources, will be of a scope and magnitude adequate to realize the goals envisaged in this Charter. Such assistance will be allocated to both social and economic development and, where appropriate, will take the form of grants or loans on flexible terms and conditions. The participating countries will request the support of other capital-exporting countries and appropriate institutions so that they may provide assistance for the attainment of these objectives.

3. The United States will help in the financing of technical assistance projects proposed by a participating country or by the General Secretariat of the Organization of American States for the purpose of:

(a) Providing experts contracted in agreement with the Governments to work under their direction and to assist them in the preparation of specific investment projects and the strengthening of national mechanisms for preparing projects, using specialized engineering firms where appropriate;

(b) Carrying out, pursuant to existing agreements for cooperation among the General Secretariat of the Organization of American States, the Economic Commission for Latin America, and the Inter-American Development Bank, field investigations and studies, including those relating to development problems, the organization of national agencies for the preparation of development programs, agrarian reform and rural development, health, cooperatives, housing, education and professional training, and taxation and tax administration; and

(c) Convening meetings of experts and

officials on development and related problems.

The Governments or above-mentioned organizations should, when appropriate, seek the cooperation of the United Nations and its specialized agencies in the execution of these activities.

4. The participating Latin American countries recognize that each has in varying degree a capacity to assist fellow Republics by providing technical and financial assistance. They recognize that this capacity will increase as their economies grow. They therefore affirm their intention to assist fellow Republics increasingly as their individual circumstances permit.

Chapter V: Organization and procedures

1. In order to provide technical assistance for the formulation of development programs, as may be requested by participating nations, the Organization of American States, the Economic Commission for Latin America, and the Inter-American Development Bank will continue and strengthen their agreements for coordination in this field, in order to have available a group of programming experts whose service can be used to facilitate the implementation of this Charter. The participating countries will also seek an intensification of technical assistance from the specialized agencies of the United Nations for the same purpose.

2. The Inter-American Economic and Social Council, on the joint nomination of the Secretary-General of the Organization of American States, the President of the Inter-American Development Bank, and the Executive Secretary of the United Nations Economic Commission for Latin America, will appoint a panel of nine high-level experts, exclusively on the basis of their experience, technical ability, and competence in the various aspects of economic and social development. The experts may be of any nationality, though if of Latin American origin an appropriate geographical distribution will be sought. They will be attached to the Inter-American Economic and Social Council, but will nevertheless enjoy complete autonomy in the performance of their duties. They may not hold any other remunerative position. The appointment of these experts will be for a period of three years, and may be renewed.

3. Each Government, if it so wishes, may present its program for economic and social development for consideration by an *Ad hoc* Committee, composed of no more than three members drawn from the panel of experts referred to in the preceding paragraph together with an equal number of experts not on the panel. The experts who compose the *Ad hoc* Committee will be appointed by the Secretary-General of the Organization of American States at the request of the interested Government and with its consent.

4. The Committee will study the development program, exchange opinions with the interested Government as to possible modifications and, with the consent of the Government, report its conclusions to the Inter-American Development Bank and to other Governments and institutions that may be prepared to extend external financial and technical assistance in connection with the execution of the program.

. . .

[7. A Government whose program has been approved by the *Ad hoc* Committee with respect to external financial requirements may submit the program to the Inter-American Development Bank so that the Bank may negotiate the finance.

8. The Inter-American Economic and Social Council will review progress of development programs and submit recommendations to the Council of the O.A.S.]

. . .

[TITLE III. Dealt with economic integration of Latin America.]

[TITLE IV. Basic export commodities.]

The Atlantic Alliance

As has already been noted, the wartime alliance commitments of the United States ceased with the end of the war in 1945. But the American determination before 1947 to avoid new exclusive alliance commitments outside the Americans in peacetime, other than the general obligations of the United Nations Charter, was replaced after 1947 by a search for reliable allies in the new era of east–west relations that became known as the 'cold war'. It is not possible to date the origin of this cold war in the same way as the origins of a shooting war. In a sense it goes back to the Bolshevik revolution, for the mutual suspicions then aroused were never overcome, not even during the years of alliance in the Second World War. At the end of that war Soviet influence and military power had tremendously increased in Europe, and Stalin treated the region of central and eastern Europe as belonging to the Soviet sphere of influence. This attitude precluded the restoration of Poland and the Balkan states to their pre-war independence; and it also introduced to these countries, to some gradually and to others immediately, the suppression of individual political freedom, the secret police, imprisonment without trial and the 'purge'. In 1946 Churchill characterized the Soviet-imposed isolation of communist-dominated Europe as an 'iron curtain'. Genuine Allied cooperation in the government of Germany as a whole proved a pipedream. In Germany, and in the United Nations, the Soviet Union clashed with the policies of the western powers.

There was no sharing of the secrets of the atomic bomb; faced with a huge preponderance of Soviet armies in Europe, the west had retained sole possession of the atomic bomb. Many believed that this alone could restore the balance and deter Stalin from further expansion. That this appeared to be his intention Britain and the United States deduced from Soviet pressure on Turkey and from the Soviet Union's unwillingness to withdraw from northern Iran in accordance with wartime agreements; after US protests, the Soviet Union in March 1946 did announce its withdrawal from Iran. Truman saw communist revolt in Greece (which, in fact, received little help from Stalin) as part of a general Soviet strategy to spread communist power under the direction of the Soviet Union, and responded with an address to Congress, broadcast to the nation, which contained the passage that became known as the *Truman Doctrine, 12 March 1947*.

The immediate need to help Greece was placed by Truman in the wider context as he asserted of helping free peoples everywhere to maintain their institutions and their national integrity against aggressive movements that attempted to impose totalitarian government on them. He warned that such direct or indirect aggression, if successful, would undermine the foundations of international peace. American help, Truman advised, should be extended primarily through economic and financial aid. Greece and Turkey received American help. This was only a beginning. A few months later the *Marshall Plan*, originally proposed by the secretary of state on *5 June 1947*, provided massive economic support to the countries of western Europe (see p. 506).

Until the spring of 1948 the United States continued to rely mainly on granting economic support and on diplomacy to meet the threat of the extension of Soviet influence and power. But communist successes and pressures in 1948 and 1949 led to a reappraisal of American policies. In Europe the Czech communists gained complete control of Czechoslovakia in February 1948. Soon after, in April 1948, the divergence of Soviet and western policies over Germany impelled Stalin to put pressure on the western powers by impeding western land and water communications with Berlin. By 1 July 1948 the Russians had imposed a complete land and sea blockade in breach of Allied agreements, but they desisted from interfering with the air corridors.

The western powers responded to events in Czechoslovakia and to Soviet hostility in Germany with a military alliance, the *Brussels Treaty*, and later pursued a policy which would lead to the creation of a rehabilitated, sovereign and rearmed West German state (p. 511). In Washington, the *Vandenberg Resolution*, adopted by the Senate on *11 June 1948*, gave bi-partisan Congressional support for an American alliance policy within the UN framework to meet any military communist threat; the resolution did not actually use the word 'alliance', but instead referred to 'collective arrangements'. It stated that the United States government should pursue 'regional and other collective arrangements for individual and collective self-defense', and sanctioned the 'association of the United States by constitutional process' with such arrangements as affected American security. By 'constitutional process' was meant the necessary consent of the Senate to any alliance treaty as required by the constitution. The resolution also required that any treaty engagements entered into should be mutual in their application, i.e. if the United States undertook to aid another country to meet aggression, that country would be bound to aid the United States in similar conditions.

The Vandenberg Resolution made possible the association of the United States (and Canada) with the west European states in an Atlantic military alliance, the *North Atlantic Treaty, 4 April 1949* (p. 359). This treaty involved no automatic commitment on the part of the United States to go to war. The key article is no. 5; it stipulated that an armed attack against one or more signatories would be regarded as an attack on all, but only required the other signatories to assist the victim of an attack by such action as each deemed necessary. Article 6 defined the area covered by the treaty, which included the territory of the Federal Republic of Germany and West Berlin since the troops of signatories were stationed there. The practical expectation that an attack on one signatory would in fact entail war with all was brought much closer eighteen months after signature when, in accordance with Article 3 (which required the signatories to develop their collective capacity to resist), agreement was reached that NATO would establish an integrated defence force. An integrated command structure with a Supreme Commander was developed. The supreme command has always been held by an American general.

Of critical importance in the development of NATO was the question of nuclear capacity and its control. From 1957 to 1960 the United States signed agreements concerning 'cooperation' in atomic weapons with Britain, Canada, France, the Federal Republic of Germany, Greece, the Netherlands and Italy. NATO from 1957 had nuclear capacity, but its actual use was subject to the consent of the President of the United States. A Nuclear Planning Committee was intended to provide for consultation. Britain, a NATO signatory, had independent nuclear capacity and so had France, but these independent nuclear forces were small compared to the capacity of the United States. Under an agreement with the United States signed in December 1962, Britain received from the United States Polaris missiles.

A significant article of the NATO treaty from the American, or more precisely the Senate's point of view, was Article 11, which required that the treaty be ratified by each country according to its own 'constitutional processes'. This meant that ratification would be required by a two-thirds majority of the Senate. The NATO treaty was duly ratified by the Senate on 21 July 1949. There existed at that time an understanding between leaders of Congress on the one hand, and the president and his administration on the other, that treaties involving military collaboration against communism should contain a clause requiring ratification by 'constitutional process', that is by the Senate.

Supplementing the United States participation with western Europe, Congress passed the *Mutual Defense Act, 6 October 1949*, which permitted the administration to sign bilateral treaties to aid and rearm countries for broad political reasons, or for the sake of the security of the United States. Huge sums were expended in such aid. Bilateral treaties were concluded with each of the European NATO allies on 27 January 1950.

In spite of internal differences within the alliance, NATO remained the core of the American alliance system and of western security planning. Differences did sometimes develop into serious threats to alliance cohesion, as at the time of the Anglo-French invasion of Egypt in 1956, and as a result of French withdrawal from the integrated military command structure in 1966. In the early 1980s opposition, mainly from the left, in several European countries to the stationing of American missiles on their territories, and rifts, particularly after an American bombing raid on Libya in 1986, over the most effective response to international terrorism seemed to betoken increased strains within the alliance. But its inherent strength, and the centrality of the NATO connection in American strategic thinking, emerged clearly in 1982 when war broke out between two American allies,

Argentina and Great Britain (the Falklands war, see p. 797): the USA decided, with little compunction, to support its NATO ally rather than its hemispheric partner.

The original members of NATO were Belgium, Canada, Denmark, France, Iceland, Italy, Luxembourg, the Netherlands, Norway, Portugal, Britain, and the United States. These were joined by Greece (1952), Turkey (1952), and West Germany (1955).

Greece withdrew from military cooperation in NATO after the Turkish invasion of Cyprus in 1974; she resumed participation in the alliance in October 1980, but in August 1984 further disputes with Turkey led Greece to announce she would not participate in NATO joint exercises. The left-wing Greek government of Andreas Papandreou, elected in 1981, although committed to the ejection of American bases, nevertheless signed a five-year *United States–Greece agreement on defense and economic cooperation in September 1983*. This provided for the continuation of the four existing American bases in Greece and for the payment of $500 million in US military aid to Greece.

Spain, ruled by the last surviving fascist dictator, Francisco Franco, until his death in 1975, was not admitted to NATO for more than three decades. But the *United States and Spain concluded a Defense Agreement on 26 September 1953* providing for the establishment of American naval and air bases in Spain and for military and economic aid by the USA to Spain. This was not a treaty but an executive agreement, and was therefore not subject to ratification by the US Senate. Only after the death of Franco and movement towards the restoration of democracy in Spain did the two countries sign the *Treaty of Friendship and Cooperation between Spain and the United States, 24 January 1976*. A new *United States–Spain Defense Agreement was signed in 1982*. This provided for continued use by the USA of bases in Spain for a further five years. In May 1982 Spain entered NATO. Some left-wing opposition to membership of the alliance was voiced, but on 11 March 1986 a national referendum on the question approved Spanish membership by a wide margin of votes. (On NATO see also Chapter XXVIII.)

North Atlantic Treaty between Belgium, Canada, Denmark, France, Iceland, Italy, Luxembourg, the Netherlands, Norway, Portugal, Britain and the United States, Washington, 4 April 1949

The parties to this Treaty reaffirm their faith in the purposes and principles of the Charter of the United Nations and their desire to live in peace with all peoples and all Governments.

They are determined to safeguard the freedom, common heritage and civilization of their peoples, founded on the principles of democracy, individual liberty and the rule of law.

They seek to promote stability and well-being in the North Atlantic area.

They are resolved to unite their efforts for collective defence and for the preservation of peace and security.

They therefore agree to this North Atlantic Treaty:

Article 1. The parties undertake, as set forth in the Charter of the United Nations, to settle any international disputes in which they may be involved by peaceful means in such a manner that international peace and security and justice are not endangered, and to refrain in their international relations from the threat or use of force in any manner inconsistent with the purposes of the United Nations.

Article 2. The parties will contribute toward the further development of peaceful and friendly international relations by strengthening their free institutions, by bringing about a better understanding of the principles upon which these institutions are founded, and by promoting conditions of stability and well-being. They will seek to eliminate conflict in their international economic policies and will encourage economic collaboration between any or all of them.

Article 3. In order more effectively to achieve the objectives of this Treaty, the parties, separately and jointly, by means of continuous and effective self-help and mutual aid, will maintain and develop their individual and collective capacity to resist armed attack.

Article 4. The parties will consult together whenever, in the opinion of any of them, the territorial integrity, political independence or security of any of the parties is threatened.

Article 5. The parties agree that an armed attack against one or more of them in Europe or North America shall be considered an attack against them all; and consequently they agree that, if such an armed attack occurs, each of them in exercise of the right of individual or collective self-defence recognized by Article 51 of the Charter of the United Nations, will assist the party or parties so attacked by taking forthwith, individually and in concert with the other parties, such action as it deems necessary, including the use of armed force, to restore and maintain the security of the North Atlantic area.

Any such armed attack and all measures taken as a result thereof shall immediately be reported to the Security Council. Such measures shall be terminated when the Security Council has taken the measures necessary to restore and maintain international peace and security.

Article 6. For the purpose of Article 5 an armed attack on one or more of the parties is deemed to include an armed attack on the territory of any of the parties in Europe or North America, on the Algerian Departments of France, on the occupation forces of any party in Europe, on the islands under the jurisdiction of any party in the North Atlantic area north of the Tropic of Cancer, or on the vessels or aircraft in this area of any of the parties.

Article 7. This Treaty does not affect, and shall not be interpreted as affecting, in any way the rights and obligations under the Charter of the parties which are members of the United Nations, or the primary responsibility of the Security Council for the maintenance of international peace and security.

Article 8. Each party declares that none of the international engagements now in force between it and any other of the parties or any third State is in conflict with the provisions of this Treaty, and undertakes not to enter into any international engagement in conflict with this Treaty.

Article 9. The parties hereby establish a Council, on which each of them shall be represented, to consider matters concerning the implementation of this Treaty. The Council shall be so organized as to be able to meet promptly at any time. The Council shall set up such subsidiary bodies as may be necessary; in particular it shall establish immediately a Defence Committee which shall recommend measures for the implementation of Articles 3 and 5.

Article 10. The parties may, by unanimous agreement, invite any other European State in a position to further the principles of this Treaty and to contribute to the security of the North Atlantic area to accede to this Treaty. Any State so invited may become a party to the Treaty by depositing its instrument of accession with the Government of the United States of America. The Government of the United States of America will inform each of the parties of the deposit of each such instrument of accession.

Article 11. This Treaty shall be ratified and its provisions carried out by the parties in accordance with their respective constitutional processes. The instruments of ratification shall be deposited as soon as possible with the Government of the United States of America, which will notify all the other signatories of each deposit. The Treaty shall enter into force between the States which have ratified it as soon as the ratifications of the majority of the signatories, including the ratifications of Belgium, Canada, France, Luxembourg, the Netherlands, the United Kingdom and the United States, have been deposited, and shall come into effect with respect to other States on the date of the deposit of their ratifications.

Article 12. After the Treaty has been in force for ten years, or at any time thereafter, the parties shall, if any of them so requests, consult together for the purpose of reviewing the Treaty, having regard for the factors then affecting peace and security in the North Atlantic area, including the development of universal as well as regional arrangements under the Charter of the United Nations for the maintenance of international peace and security.

Article 13. After the Treaty has been in force for twenty years, any party may cease to be a party one year after its notice of denunciation has been given to the Government of the United States of America, which will inform the Governments of the other parties of the deposit of each notice of denunciation.

Article 14. This Treaty, of which the English and French texts are equally authentic, shall be deposited in the archives of the Government of the United States of America. Duly certified copies thereof will be transmitted by that Government to the Governments of the other signatories.

United States treaty relations in the Far East

On the same day the peace treaty with Japan was signed (p. 294), a *Japanese–United States Security Treaty, 8 September 1951* (p. 369) was concluded. This treaty allowed the United States to maintain armed forces 'in and about Japan', and at the request of the Japanese government to use US forces to put down large-scale internal riots in Japan caused by the instigation or intervention of an outside power. Japan undertook not to grant to any other country either bases or garrisons without the prior assent of the United States.

The 1951 treaty was replaced on *19 January 1960* by a *Treaty of Mutual Cooperation and Security between the United States and Japan.* This treaty, signed on the above date, entered into force on 23 June 1960. During the 1950s, revision of the 1951 treaty had developed into a passionate issue in Japanese internal politics. As victims of the first nuclear bombs, the Japanese evinced acute sensitivity on all nuclear-weapon-related issues. The basic Japanese desire was for security with minimal military involvement. As Japan entered a period of rapid economic growth and social transformation, the United States became more ready to acquiesce in Japanese demands. American troops stationed in Japan were greatly reduced in number. The treaty of 1960 contained important revisions: it removed all derogations of sovereignty, and acknowledged that Japanese forces could be used only in self-defence. The United States (Article 6), for the purpose of contributing to the security of Japan and the maintenance of international peace and security in the Far East, was granted the continued use of bases in Japan for its land, air and naval forces. The use of these facilities was governed by a separate exchange of notes whereby the United States agreed on prior consultation with the Japanese government before increasing US forces in Japan, making any essential change of arming its forces (nuclear weapons), or using any bases under Japanese rule outside the treaty area. On 22 June 1970 the Japanese government announced its intention to continue the Security Treaty of 1960, which would remain in force indefinitely unless either country gave one year's notice to terminate it. Negotiations for the return of the Ryukyu Islands and Okinawa were concluded by a *Japanese–United States Treaty signed on 17 June 1971*: the islands were to revert to Japan and they were returned in the spring of 1972; the Mutual Security Treaty became fully applicable to them and Japan granted continued use of bases to America on the same conditions as agreed under the Security Treaty of 1960.

The communist victory in China in 1949, the conclusion of the Sino–Soviet Treaty in February 1950 (p. 413), and American awareness that the Soviet Union also had exploded an atomic bomb in September 1949 – all these events had helped produce the end of the American occupation in Japan, and the US decision to seek to transform a defeated and occupied enemy into an ally. The United States, in pursuing this course, was following a similar policy *vis-à-vis* Japan to that adopted in Europe *vis-à-vis* Germany. Both policies were to be crowned with considerable success. Meanwhile, alarmed by the communist successes in the Chinese civil war, the United States had already begun to shore up its defences in east Asia by building a network of security treaties in the region. In the Philippines the United States had secured bases by the *Philippine–United States Treaty, 14 March 1947.*

South Korea, although ruled by a pro-American régime, was not an American ally in the formal sense prior to the outbreak of the Korean War with the North Korean invasion of the south on 25 June 1950 (see p. 647). The *Agreement between the United States and Korea to establish a Military Advisory Group, 26 January 1950* (p. 367) merely provided for the presence of 500 American military advisers in South Korea. The outbreak of the Korean War both confirmed the existing objectives of American foreign policy in the region and led to new commitments and policies.

The new elements of American policy after the outbreak of war in Korea were, firstly, the decision to commit American naval and air forces to fight on the Asian mainland in South Korea; and secondly, the decision to interpose the Seventh Fleet between the Chinese mainland and Taiwan (Formosa), thus intervening in the Chinese Civil War. This latter decision was reached by Truman on 26 June 1950, and meant that each side was forbidden to attack the other, though clearly the danger was seen to arise from a communist attack on Taiwan; Truman declared that in the new circumstances this 'would be a direct threat to the Pacific area and to the United States forces performing their lawful and necessary functions there'. (It should be noted that before the outbreak of the conflict Truman had stated in January 1950 that the United States would not 'pursue a course which will lead to involvement in the civil conflict in China'.) On 29 and 30 June 1950 Truman committed US ground forces in South Korea as well.

The Korean War, with its varying military fortunes, and especially with Communist Chinese intervention in late October 1950, changed the emphasis of America's China policy. During the months preceding the Korean War, the United States had refused to recognize Mao Zedong's proclaimed People's Republic of China (1 October 1949) as the government of China. After the outbreak of the Korean War, the United States gradually decided to give full support to Chiang Kai-shek's Republic of China established in Taiwan. The possibility of a more flexible policy towards mainland China was abandoned for some years.

During the period from 1950 to 1954 the United States administration concluded that the threat to stability and peace arising from the possibility of communist direct attack or subversion was increasing and could be met only by throwing the military weight of America behind Asian and European allies willing to resist aggression. The objective was deterrence. The cohesion of the European NATO alliance was accordingly strengthened with substantial American and German military contributions. In Asia a search for new allies was intensified in 1950. But in Asia there was no continuous ring of developed nations that could be formed among China's neighbours. Running from north to south, Japan, South Korea, Taiwan and the Philippines formed an unbroken flank, but in the South China Sea, Malaysia and Indonesia kept aloof; south of Indonesia and far removed from China were Australia and New Zealand; these two joined the United States alliance groupings. On the mainland of Asia, Thailand and South Vietnam were associated in alliances; Cambodia and Laos were never securely brought in; Burma, India and Ceylon refused to join an anti-communist alliance, but Pakistan in 1954 did so; the American arc of defensive alliances against the Soviet Union continued unbroken thereafter through Iran to Turkey and Greece.

Two further important points need to be noted: firstly, the European anti-Soviet grouping of NATO was a separate alliance system not directly linked to the alliances of Asia. The only link was provided by the United States as a member of all these alliances in both Asia and Europe; Britain and (nominally) France were also involved in one Asian alliance, SEATO, as well as in NATO. Secondly, the Asian allies did not undertake to defend each other collectively; their commitment was limited to the particular treaty which they signed. Only the United States was committed to all as the signatory of all the treaties.

The Asian alliances which the United States negotiated were of necessity a patchwork rather than a unified system, since each Asian ally was often at least as concerned with its own regional problems and conflicts as with general opposition to communist expansion. Australia and New Zealand desired assurances of American support against any renewal of a threat from a revived Japan. The Philippines were involved in disputes with Indonesia and Malaysia; Chiang Kai-shek proclaimed intentions of reconquering the Chinese mainland; Pakistan periodically remained in conflict with India especially over Kashmir; and the South Koreans refused to abandon hopes of unification. The key to American policy in the western Pacific was Japan.

To overcome the obstacles to a Japanese peace treaty and to strengthen the defences of southern Asia, *the United States concluded a Security Treaty with Australia and New Zealand, 1 September 1951 (ANZUS)* (p. 368), and also at the same time the *Philippine–American Security Treaty, 30 August 1951*. Both treaties had the same joint defence clause which bound each signatory to act against any armed attack on either signatory in the Pacific; such action would be taken in accordance with each country's 'constitutional processes'. The signatories undertook by self-help and mutual aid to develop their collective capacity to resist armed attack. In the case of the Philippine treaty no joint consultative machinery was established (until the Philippine Mutual Defense Board in 1958), but American forces continued to be stationed in the Philippines as provided for in the treaty of 1947. The ANZUS treaty established a Consultative Council of Foreign Ministers, which undertook coordinating work. Neither treaty involved any automatic commitment to go to war though their language certainly implied a moral commitment. The ANZUS treaty was significant of one great shift in the relative balance of power: Britain (which was not a party, although expressing a desire to join) was no longer seen by Australia or New Zealand as the primary guarantor of their security. Events in the Far East since 1941 dictated that the defence and foreign policies of these Dominions would henceforth be orientated primarily towards Washington rather than London.

The treaty remained in force at the close of the century, although the cohesion of the alliance was threatened after 1985 by the anti-nuclear policies of the Labour government in New Zealand headed by David Lange. The refusal of the New Zealand government to permit US ships capable of carrying nuclear weapons to visit New Zealand ports evoked a complaint by the United States that New Zealand had decided 'to renege on an essential element of its ANZUS participation'. The United States therefore declared in August 1986 that it was 'suspending its security obligations to New Zealand'. Trilateral exchange of intelligence information was halted, and New Zealand was in effect expelled from the alliance which henceforth became a bilateral one between Australia and the USA

The next United States security treaty in the region followed the signature of the *Korean Armistice, 27 July 1953* (p. 654). *The Mutual Defense Treaty between Korea and the United States, 10 October 1953* (p. 371), reassured South Korea and was the price paid by America for South Korean acceptance of the armistice, and especially for abandoning a policy of reunification by force. This treaty permitted the stationing of American troops in and about Korea; it took effect on 17 November 1954, the Senate in a reservation underscoring that the United States was committed to come to the aid of South Korea only 'in case of an external armed attack . . . against territory which has been recognized by the United States as lawfully brought under the administrative control of the Republic of Korea'.

During the year following the Korean armistice, in 1954, the Chinese communists launched a bombardment of two small islands, Quemoy and Matsu, close to the mainland of China but held by nationalist garrisons. The United States committed itself to the defence of nationalist-held Taiwan (Formosa) and the Pescadores islands, but allowed itself latitude whether or not to defend Quemoy and Matsu. *A Mutual Defense Treaty between the United States and China, 2 December 1954* (p. 374), was concluded on terms similar to the other American defence treaties in Asia. It involved a promise to act to meet armed attack in accordance with each state's constitutional processes. But in approving the treaty the United States Senate added three understandings of importance: the ultimate legal title to Formosa and the Pescadores was not affected by the treaty, thus the United States was not committed ultimately to the claims of sovereignty of either side in the Chinese civil war; secondly, the United States would act only if the nationalists were forced to fight in self-defence; finally, there was to be no extension territorially of the US commitment without the prior consent of the Senate.

Mao Zedong's victory had brought communist China to the borders of Indo-China in 1949. The opportunity for spreading communism throughout Indo-China seemed favourable. Ho Chi Minh, leader of the Vietnamese communists, and his supporters had been fighting the French army since December 1946 after abortive negotiations with the French Fourth Republic for the independence of Vietnam. Subsequently, in 1949, France recognized the independence of Vietnam,

Laos and Cambodia, but within the French Union and in practice under leadership acceptable to the French, i.e. ready to oppose Ho Chi Minh and the communists. Ho Chi Minh continued to fight. Strengthened by Chinese help, the Vietminh (communist) army began to strike at French garrisons in October 1950. The United States by then had become involved in granting aid and supplies to the French-led armies, a consequence of a decision taken by Truman the previous May. Truman acted on the conviction that there was a threat of communism spreading throughout south-east Asia and that the loss of this whole region, coming after the loss of mainland China, would undermine the global defences of the west. The outbreak of the Korean War intensified this sense of threat, and American aid to the French-led armies in Vietnam was increased. Despite this aid the French were losing the struggle, and on 6 May 1954, when the Vietminh overran the French defences at Dien Bien Phu, a conference at Geneva had already been convened to work out an armistice and a settlement of the Indo-Chinese conflicts. The French government had lost heart in the struggle and at the *Geneva Conference, 26 April–21 July 1954* (p. 610) agreed to a settlement in Indo-China which restricted their influence to South Vietnam, with the possibility of losing even that if elections to be held in 1956 should favour Ho Chi Minh.

Although the French had received massive economic support from the United States, and the Eisenhower administration in the spring of 1954 had even considered supporting the French with ground forces (provided this was a joint action with allies such as Britain, France and Australia and, if possible, Thailand and the Philippines), the French government preferred to end the first phase of the Indo-Chinese war on the terms of the Geneva settlement.

John Foster Dulles, Secretary of State in the Eisenhower administration, disapproved of the Geneva settlement; the United States would not sign it but in a declaration promised not to upset these arrangements. Dulles continued to strengthen opposition to the spread of communism in southern Asia in the face of the French military disaster. He conducted negotiations for an alliance of collective defence among the major powers interested in this region, Britain, France, Australia and New Zealand, together with such Asian states as would join in the grouping. The new treaty would thus extend and complement ANZUS.

The outcome of the negotiations was the *South-East Asia Collective Defense Treaty (SEATO), signed in Manila on 8 September 1954* (p. 371), together with a *Pacific Charter* (p. 373) of principles. The eight signatories were the United States, Britain, France, Australia, New Zealand, and three Asian states, Pakistan, Thailand and the Philippines. It followed the general structure of other United States defence treaties in that the signatories bound themselves separately and jointly by self-help and mutual aid to develop their individual and collective capacity to resist armed attack or subversion (Article 2); an armed attack on one signatory was recognized as constituting a danger to all, and each signatory agreed to 'act to

meet the common danger in accordance with its own constitutional processes';
the signatories further would consult together if the integrity or independence of
a signatory, or of any state designated in the treaty, were threatened by other than
armed attack or 'by any fact or situation which might endanger the peace of the
area'. A number of provisions, however, rendered the treaty rather vague or
flexible in its possible application. The treaty area as geographically defined in
Article 8 excluded Hong Kong and Taiwan. An additional Protocol designated
Cambodia, Laos, and the 'free territory under the jurisdiction of the State of
Vietnam' as falling within the treaty area for the purposes of Article 4. Cambodia
rejected the protection of SEATO in 1956.

From 1954 to 1961 SEATO's capacity for providing effective aid in Laos and
Vietnam was not tested; but renewal of conflict in South Vietnam by the Vietcong
and North Vietnamese in 1960, and in Laos by the Pathet Lao forces, raised the
question at SEATO's ministerial council which met in Bangkok in March 1961. In
the event neither France nor Britain would support military action in Laos. Laos
was neutralized in 1962 (p. 623). During the Laos crisis of 1962, the United States,
principally with British, New Zealand and Australian support, moved forces and
established bases in north-eastern Thailand to reassure Thailand. The United
States provided unilateral support for the neutralist régime in Laos after 1962.
SEATO was further weakened in the 1960s by Pakistan's concern over its conflict
with India. A specific American and Australian reservation had excluded the
application of the treaty to such a conflict. Pakistan drew closer to China; the
United States and Britain rushed arms to India during and after the Indian–
Chinese border conflict of 1962 (p. 596), which also strengthened India against
Pakistan and caused bitter resentment in Pakistan, a SEATO ally. France became
increasingly opposed to United States involvement in Vietnam during the 1960s
and withdrew from military cooperation in SEATO in 1967. In the Vietnamese
conflict, Britain refused active military cooperation, and after 1968 ran down its
bases east of Suez. Of the SEATO powers only Australia and the Philippines
contributed small forces to fight in South Vietnam. SEATO had been conceived
as providing United States, British and French 'big power' support to the Asian
states willing to contain the threat of communism and Chinese expansion, i.e.
Thailand, Pakistan, New Zealand, Australia, the Philippines and the three
Indo-Chinese states, by providing military and economic assistance.

The weaknesses resulting from a lack of British and French support, from
Pakistan's virtual withdrawal and the changing policies of the United States in
south-east Asia spelt the doom of the arrangement. In November 1972 Pakistan
withdrew completely from the alliance. France suspended membership payments
from January 1974. By this time SEATO had virtually ceased to exist although the
organization was not formally wound up until 1977.

The collapse of the pro-American government in South Vietnam and the communist takeovers there and in Laos and Cambodia, as well as the beginnings of the American *rapprochement* with mainland China, had by that time rendered SEATO obsolete. Thenceforth American security policy in the region was based not on a multilateral organization but on bilateral arrangements. The experience of Vietnam had rendered the United States wary of entering into far-reaching commitments which might entail military involvement. US forces, stationed in Thailand since 1962, began to be withdrawn in 1973. Between 1977 and 1979 some reductions were made in American troop strengths in South Korea. Meanwhile the United States reduced the numbers of its troops in Taiwan, and ultimately, with the abrogation of the 1954 treaty (see p. 649), withdrew its forces altogether from the island.

After the American withdrawal from Vietnam in 1973 the United States thus abandoned any significant presence on the east Asian mainland except for South Korea. The most important US military bases in the region (the largest outside the United States) were thenceforth the long-standing Subic Bay Naval Station and Clark Air Base on the Philippines. These bases, used by the United States since the turn of the century, were secured to the USA under the terms of the 1947 Philippine–United States Treaty for a period of ninety-nine years. The treaty was revised in 1965 and again in 1979. The latter revision confirmed Philippine sovereignty over the base areas and provided for five-yearly reviews. The first such review in 1983 produced a promise from the United States of $900 million in military and economic assistance to the Philippines. Following the revolution of 25 February 1986, in which President Ferdinand Marcos was replaced by Corazón Aquino, some internal pressure was manifested for the removal of US bases. But the Aquino administration, no less pro-American than its predecessor, adopted a policy of permitting the bases to remain at least until the expiration of the existing agreement in 1991. (For further discussion of treaty-making in east Asia, see Chapter XIX.)

Agreement between the United States and Korea to establish a Military Advisory Group, Seoul, 26 January 1950

Preamble. In conformity with the request of the Government of the Republic of Korea to the Government of the United States, the President of the United States has authorized the establishment of the United States Military Advisory Group to the Republic of Korea (hereinafter referred to as the Group), under the terms and conditions specified below:

Article I. The purpose of the Group will be to develop the Security Forces of the

Republic of Korea within the limitations of the Korean economy by advising and assisting the Government of the Republic of Korea in the organization, administration and training of such forces. [U.S. advisers not to exceed 500.]

Article II. This Agreement may be terminated at any time:

1. By either Government, provided that six months' written notice is given to the other Government;

2. By recall of the Group when either Government deems such recall to be in its public interest and shall have so notified the other Government without necessity of compliance with provision (1) of this Article. However, termination of this Agreement by recall does not relieve the Government of the Republic of Korea from its obligations arising under this Agreement during such time, not exceeding three months, reasonably necessary to permit the Group to terminate its functions and physically depart from Korea.

Article III. The functions of the Group shall be to provide such advice and assistance to the Government of the Republic of Korea on military and related matters as may be necessary to accomplish the purposes set forth in Article I of this Agreement . . . .

Security Treaty between Australia, New Zealand and the United States (ANZUS), San Francisco, 1 September 1951

The parties to this Treaty,

Reaffirming their faith in the purposes and principles of the Charter of the United Nations and their desire to live in peace with all peoples and all Governments, and desiring to strengthen the fabric of peace in the Pacific area,

Noting that the United States already has arrangements pursuant to which its armed forces are stationed in the Philippines, and has armed forces and administrative responsibilities in the Ryukyus, and upon the coming into force of the Japanese Peace Treaty may also station armed forces in and about Japan to assist in the preservation of peace and security in the Japan area,

Recognizing that Australia and New Zealand as members of the British Commonwealth of Nations have military obligations outside as well as within the Pacific area,

Desiring to declare publicly and formally their sense of unity, so that no potential aggressor could be under the illusion that any of them stand alone in the Pacific area, and

Desiring further to coordinate their efforts for collective defense for the preservation of peace and security pending the development of a more comprehensive system of regional security in the Pacific area,

Therefore declare and agree as follows:

Article I. The parties undertake, as set forth in the Charter of the United Nations, to settle any international disputes in which they may be involved by peaceful means in such a manner that international peace and security and justice are not endangered and to refrain in their international relations from the threat or use of force in any manner inconsistent with the purposes of the United Nations.

Article II. In order more effectively to achieve the objective of this Treaty the parties separately and jointly by means of continuous and effective self-help and mutual aid will maintain and develop their individual and collective capacity to resist armed attack.

Article III. The parties will consult together whenever in the opinion of any of them the territorial integrity, political independence or security of any of the parties is threatened in the Pacific.

Article IV. Each party recognizes that an armed attack in the Pacific area on any of the parties would be dangerous to its own peace and safety and declares that it would act to meet the common danger in accordance with its constitutional processes.

Any such armed attack and all measures taken as a result thereof shall be immediately reported to the Security Council of the United Nations. Such measures shall be terminated when the Security Council has taken the measures necessary to restore and maintain international peace and security.

Article V. For the purpose of Article IV, an armed attack on any of the parties is deemed to include an armed attack on the metropolitan territory of any of the parties, or on the island territories under its jurisdiction in the Pacific or on its armed forces, public vessels or aircraft in the Pacific.

Article VI. This Treaty does not affect and shall not be interpreted as affecting in any way the rights and obligations of the parties under the Charter of the United Nations or the responsibility of the United Nations for the maintenance of international peace and security.

Article VII. The parties hereby establish a Council, consisting of their Foreign Ministers or their Deputies, to consider matters concerning the implementation of this Treaty. The Council should be so organized as to be able to meet at any time.

Article VIII. Pending the development of a more comprehensive system of regional security in the Pacific area and the development by the United Nations of more effective means to maintain international peace and security, the Council, established by Article VII, is authorized to maintain a consultative relationship with States, Regional Organizations, Associations of States or other authorities in the Pacific area in a position to further the purpose of this Treaty and to contribute to the security of that area.

Article IX. This Treaty shall be ratified by the parties in accordance with their respective constitutional processes . . . .

Article X. This Treaty shall remain in force indefinitely. Any party may cease to be a member of the Council established by Article VII one year after notice has been given to the Government of Australia, which will inform the Governments of the other parties of the deposit of such notice.

[*Article XI.* Certified copies and deposit.]

Security Treaty between the United States and Japan, 8 September 1951

Japan has this day signed a Treaty of Peace with the Allied Powers. On the coming into force of that Treaty, Japan will not have the effective means to exercise its inherent right of self-defense because it has been disarmed.

There is danger to Japan in this situation because irresponsible militarism has not yet been driven from the world. Therefore Japan desires a Security Treaty with the United States of America to come into force simultaneously with the Treaty of Peace between the United States of America and Japan.

The Treaty of Peace recognizes that Japan as a sovereign nation has the right to enter into collective security arrangements, and further, the Charter of the United Nations recognizes that all nations possess an inherent right of individual and collective self-defense.

In exercise of these rights, Japan desires,

as a provisional arrangement for its defense, that the United States of America should maintain armed forces of its own in and about Japan so as to deter armed attack upon Japan.

The United States of America, in the interest of peace and security, is presently willing to maintain certain of its armed forces in and about Japan, in the expectation, however, that Japan will itself increasingly assume responsibility for its own defense against direct and indirect aggression, always avoiding any armament which could be an offensive threat or serve other than to promote peace and security in accordance with the purposes and principles of the United Nations Charter.

Accordingly, the two countries have agreed as follows:

Article I. Japan grants, and the United States of America accepts, the right, upon the coming into force of the Treaty of Peace and of this Treaty, to dispose United States land, air and sea forces in and about Japan. Such forces may be utilized to contribute to the maintenance of international peace and security in the Far East and to the security of Japan against armed attack from without, including assistance given at the express request of the Japanese Government to put down large-scale internal riots and disturbances in Japan, caused through instigation or intervention by an outside Power or Powers.

Article II. During the exercise of the right referred to in Article I, Japan will not grant, without the prior consent of the United States of America, any bases or any rights, powers or authority whatsoever, in or relating to bases or the right of garrison or of maneuver or transit of ground, air or naval forces to any third Power.

Article III. The conditions which shall govern the disposition of armed forces of the United States of America in and about Japan shall be determined by administrative agreements between the two Governments.

Article IV. This Treaty shall expire whenever in the opinion of the Governments of the United States of America and Japan there shall have come into force such United Nations arrangements or such alternative individual or collective security dispositions as will satisfactorily provide for the maintenance by the United Nations or otherwise of international peace and security in the Japan area.

Article V. This Treaty shall be ratified by the United States of America and Japan and will come into force when instruments of ratification thereof have been exchanged by them at Washington.

. . .

Note: The Japanese Constitution

Chapter II: Renunciation of war

Article 9. Aspiring sincerely to an international peace based on justice and order, the Japanese people forever renounce war as a sovereign right of the nation and the threat or use of force as means of settling international disputes.

In order to accomplish the aim of the preceding paragraph, land, sea, and air forces, as well as other war potential, will never be maintained. The right of belligerency of the State will not be recognized.

Mutual Defense Treaty between the United States and Korea (South), Washington, 10 October 1953

The parties to this Treaty . . . have agreed as follows:

Article I. The parties undertake to settle any international disputes in which they may be involved by peaceful means . . .

Article II. The parties will consult together whenever, in the opinion of either of them, the political independence or security of either of the parties is threatened by external armed attack. Separately and jointly, by self-help and mutual aid, the parties will maintain and develop appropriate means to deter armed attack and will take suitable measures in consultation and agreement to implement this Treaty and to further its purposes.

Article III. Each party recognizes that an armed attack in the Pacific area on either of the parties in territories now under their respective administrative control, or hereafter recognized by one of the parties as lawfully brought under the administrative control of the other, would be dangerous to its own peace and safety and declares that it would act to meet the common danger in accordance with its constitutional processes.

Article IV. The Republic of Korea grants, and the United States of America accepts, the right to dispose United States land, air and sea forces in and about the territory of the Republic of Korea as determined by mutual agreement.

Article V. This Treaty shall be ratified by the United States of America and the Republic of Korea in accordance with their respective constitutional processes . . .

Article VI. This Treaty shall remain in force indefinitely. Either party may terminate it one year after notice has been given to the other party.
[The United States ratified the Treaty on 17 November 1954 subject to the following understanding:

It is the understanding of the United States that neither party is obligated, under Article III of the above Treaty, to come to the aid of the other except in case of an external armed attack against such party; nor shall anything in the present Treaty be construed as requiring the United States to give assistance to Korea except in the event of an armed attack against territory which has been recognized by the United States as lawfully brought under the administrative control of the Republic of Korea.]

South-East Asia Collective Defense Treaty (SEATO), Manila, 8 September 1954

The parties to this Treaty,

Recognizing the sovereign equality of all the parties,

Reiterating their faith in the purposes and principle set forth in the Charter of the United Nations and their desire to live in peace with all peoples and all Governments,

Reaffirming that, in accordance with the Charter of the United Nations, they uphold the principle of equal rights and self-determination of peoples, and declaring that they will earnestly strive by every peaceful means to promote self-government and to secure the independence of all countries whose peoples desire it and are able to undertake its responsibilities,

Desiring to strengthen the fabric of peace and freedom and to uphold the principles of democracy, individual liberty and the rule of law, and to promote the economic well-being and development of all peoples in the treaty area,

Intending to declare publicly and formally their sense of unity, so that any potential aggressor will appreciate that the parties stand together in the area, and

Desiring further to coordinate their efforts for collective defense for the preservation of peace and security,

Therefore agree as follows:

Article I. The parties undertake, as set forth in the Charter of the United Nations, to settle any international disputes in which they may be involved by peaceful means in such a manner that international peace and security and justice are not endangered, and to refrain in their international relations from the threat or use of force in any manner inconsistent with the purposes of the United Nations.

Article II. In order more effectively to achieve the objectives of this Treaty, the parties, separately and jointly, by means of continuous and effective self-help and mutual aid will maintain and develop their individual and collective capacity to resist armed attack and to prevent and counter subversive activities directed from without against their territorial integrity and political stability.

Article III. The parties undertake to strengthen their free institutions and to cooperate with one another in the further development of economic measures, including technical assistance, designed both to promote economic progress and social well-being and to further the individual and collective efforts of Governments toward these ends.

Article IV. 1. Each party recognizes that aggression by means of armed attack in the treaty area against any of the parties or against any State or territory which the parties by unanimous agreement may hereafter designate, would endanger its own peace

and safety, and agrees that it will in that event act to meet the common danger in accordance with its constitutional processes. Measures taken under this paragraph shall be immediately reported to the Security Council of the United Nations.

2. If, in the opinion of any of the parties, the inviolability or the integrity of the territory or the sovereignty or political independence of any party in the treaty area or of any other State or territory to which the provisions of paragraph 1 of this Article from time to time apply is threatened in any way other than by armed attack or is affected or threatened by any fact or situation which might endanger the peace of the area, the parties shall consult immediately in order to agree on the measures which should be taken for the common defense.

3. It is understood that no action on the territory of any State designated by unanimous agreement under paragraph 1 of this Article or on any territory so designated shall be taken except at the invitation or with the consent of the Government concerned.

Article V. The parties hereby establish a Council, on which each of them shall be represented, to consider matters concerning the implementation of this Treaty. The Council shall provide for consultation with regard to military and any other planning as the situation obtaining in the treaty area may from time to time require. The Council shall be so organized as to be able to meet at any time.

Article VI. This Treaty does not affect and shall not be interpreted as affecting in any way the rights and obligations of any of the parties under the Charter of the United Nations or the responsibility of the United Nations for the maintenance of international peace and security. Each party declares that none of the international engagements now in force between it and any other of the parties or any third party is in conflict with the provisions of this Treaty, and undertakes not to enter into any international engagement in conflict with this Treaty.

Article VII. Any other State in a position to further the objectives of this Treaty and to contribute to the security of the area may, by unanimous agreement of the parties, be invited to accede to this Treaty . . . .

Article VIII. As used in this Treaty, the 'treaty area' is the general area of southeast Asia, including also the entire territories of the Asian parties, and the general area of the south-west Pacific not including the Pacific area north of 21 degrees 30 minutes north latitude. The parties may, by unanimous agreement, amend this Article to include within the treaty area the territory of any State acceding to this Treaty in accordance with Article VII or otherwise to change the treaty area.

Article IX. . . . The Treaty shall be ratified and its provisions carried out by the parties in accordance with their respective constitutional processes . . .

Article X. This Treaty shall remain in force indefinitely, but any party may cease to be a party one year after notice of denunciation has been given . . .

[*Article XI.* Languages of authentic texts.]

UNDERSTANDING OF THE UNITED STATES OF AMERICA

The United States of America in executing the present Treaty does so with the understanding that its recognition of the effect of aggression and armed attack and its agreement with reference thereto in Article IV, paragraph 1, apply only to communist aggression but affirms that in the event of other aggression or armed attack it will consult under the provisions of Article IV, paragraph 2.

Protocol to the South-East Asia Collective Defense Treaty signed at Manila on 8 September 1954

DESIGNATION OF STATES AND TERRITORY AS TO WHICH PROVISIONS OF ARTICLE IV AND ARTICLE III ARE TO BE APPLICABLE

The parties to the South-east Asia Collective Defense Treaty unanimously designate for the purposes of Article IV of the Treaty the States of Cambodia and Laos and the free territory under the jurisdiction of the State of Vietnam.

The parties further agree that the above-mentioned States and territory shall be eligible in respect of the economic measures contemplated by Article III.

This Protocol shall enter into force simultaneously with the coming into force of the Treaty.

In witness whereof, the undersigned plenipotentiaries have signed this Protocol to the South-east Asia Collective Defense Treaty.

Done at Manila, this eighth day of September, 1954.

Pacific Charter, Manila, 8 September 1954

The Delegates of Australia, France, New Zealand, Pakistan, the Republic of the Philippines, the Kingdom of Thailand, the United Kingdom of Great Britain and Northern Ireland, and the United States of America,

Desiring to establish a firm basis for common action to maintain peace and security in south-east Asia and the south-west Pacific,

Convinced that common action to this end, in order to be worthy and effective, must be inspired by the highest principles of justice and liberty,

Do hereby proclaim:

First, in accordance with the provisions of the United Nations Charter, they uphold the principle of equal rights and self-determination of peoples and they will earnestly strive by every peaceful means to promote self-government and to secure the independence of all countries whose peoples desire it and are able to undertake its responsibilities;

Second, they are each prepared to continue taking effective practical measures to ensure conditions favorable to the orderly achievement of the foregoing purposes in accordance with their constitutional processes;

Third, they will continue to cooperate in the economic, social and cultural fields in order to promote higher living standards, economic progress and social well-being in this region;

Fourth, as declared in the South-east Asia Collective Defense Treaty, they are determined to prevent or counter by appropriate means any attempt in the treaty area to subvert their freedom or to destroy their sovereignty or territorial integrity.

Mutual Defense Treaty between the United States and the Republic of China (Taiwan), Washington, 2 December 1954

The parties to this Treaty,

Reaffirming their faith in the purposes and principles of the Charter of the United Nations and their desire to live in peace with all peoples and all Governments, and desiring to strengthen the fabric of peace in the West Pacific area,

Recalling with mutual pride the relationship which brought their two peoples together in a common bond of sympathy and mutual ideals to fight side by side against imperialist aggression during the last war,

Desiring to declare publicly and formally their sense of unity and their common determination to defend themselves against external armed attack, so that no potential aggressor could be under the illusion that either of them stands alone in the West Pacific area, and

Desiring further to strengthen their present efforts for collective defense for the preservation of peace and security pending the development of a more comprehensive system of regional security in the West Pacific area,

Have agreed as follows:

Article I. The parties undertake, as set forth in the Charter of the United Nations, to settle any international dispute in which they may be involved by peaceful means in such a manner that international peace, security and justice are not endangered and to refrain in their international relations from the threat or use of force in any manner inconsistent with the purposes of the United Nations.

Article II. In order more effectively to achieve the objective of this Treaty, the parties separately and jointly by self-help and mutual aid will maintain and develop their individual and collective capacity to resist armed attack and communist subversive activities directed from without against their territorial integrity and political stability.

Article III. The parties undertake to strengthen their free institutions and to cooperate with each other in the development of economic progress and social well-being and to further their individual and collective efforts toward these ends.

Article IV. The parties, through their Foreign Ministers or their deputies, will consult together from time to time regarding the implementation of this Treaty.

Article V. Each party recognizes that an armed attack in the West Pacific area directed against the territories of either of the parties would be dangerous to its own peace and safety and declares that it would act to meet the common danger in accordance with its constitutional processes.

Any such armed attack and all measures taken as a result thereof shall be immediately reported to the Security Council of the United Nations. Such measures shall be terminated when the Security Council has taken the measures necessary to restore and maintain international peace and security.

Article VI. For the purposes of Articles II and V, the terms 'territorial' and 'territories' shall mean in respect of the Republic of China, Taiwan and the Pescadores; and in respect of the United States of America, the island territories in the West Pacific under its jurisdiction. The provisions of Articles II and V will be applicable to such other territories as may be determined by mutual agreement.

Article VII. The Government of the Republic of China grants, and the Government of the United States of America accepts, the right to dispose such United States land, air and sea forces in and about Taiwan and the Pescadores as may be required for their defense, as determined by mutual agreement.

Article VIII. This Treaty does not affect and shall not be interpreted as affecting in any way the rights and obligations of the parties under the Charter of the United Nations or the responsibility of the United Nations for the maintenance of international peace and security.

Article IX. This Treaty shall be ratified by the United States of America and the Republic of China in accordance with their respective constitutional processes . . .

Article X. This Treaty shall remain in force indefinitely. Either party may terminate it one year after notice has been given to the other party . . .

Treaty of Mutual Cooperation and Security between the United States and Japan, 19 January 1960

. . .

Article I. The parties undertake, as set forth in the Charter of the United Nations, to settle any international disputes in which they may be involved by peaceful means in such a manner that international peace and security and justice are not endangered and to refrain in their international relations from the threat or use of force against the territorial integrity or political independence of any State, or in any other manner inconsistent with the purposes of the United Nations.

The parties will endeavor in concert with other peace-loving countries to strengthen the United Nations so that its mission of maintaining international peace and security may be discharged more effectively.

Article II. The parties will contribute toward the further development of peaceful and friendly international relations by strengthening their free institutions, by bringing about a better understanding of the principles upon which these institutions are founded, and by promoting conditions of stability and well-being. They will seek to eliminate conflict in their international economic policies and will encourage economic collaboration between them.

Article III. The parties, individually and in cooperation with each other, by means of continuous and effective self-help and mutual aid, will maintain and develop, subject to their constitutional provisions, their capacities to resist armed attack.

Article IV. The parties will consult together from time to time regarding the implementation of this Treaty, and, at the request of either party, whenever the security of Japan or international peace and security in the Far East is threatened.

Article V. Each party recognizes that an armed attack against either party in the territories under the administration of Japan would be dangerous to its own peace and safety and declares that it would act to meet the common danger in accordance with its constitutional provisions and processes.

Any such armed attack and all measures taken as a result thereof shall be immediately reported to the Security Council of the United Nations in accordance with the provisions of Article 51 of the Charter. Such measures shall be terminated when the Security Council has taken the measures necessary to restore and maintain international peace and security.

Article VI. For the purpose of contributing to the security of Japan and the maintenance of international peace and security in the Far East, the United States of America is granted the use by its land, air and naval forces of facilities and areas in Japan.

The use of these facilities and areas as well as the status of United States armed forces in Japan shall be governed by a separate agreement, replacing the Administrative Agreement under Article III of the Security Treaty between the United States of America and Japan, signed at Tokyo on February 28, 1952, as amended, and by such other arrangements as may be agreed upon.

Article VII. This Treaty does not affect and shall not be interpreted as affecting in any way the rights and obligations of the parties under the Charter of the United Nations or the responsibility of the United Nations for the maintenance of international peace and security.

Article VIII. This Treaty shall be ratified by the United States of America and Japan in accordance with their respective constitutional processes . . . .

Article IX. The Security Treaty between the United States of America and Japan signed at the city of San Francisco on September 8, 1951 shall expire upon the entering into force of this Treaty.

Article X. This Treaty shall remain in force until in the opinion of the Governments of the United States of America and Japan there shall have come into force such United Nations arrangements as will satisfactorily provide for the maintenance of international peace and security in the Japan area.

However, after the Treaty has been in force for ten years, either party may give notice to the other party of its intention to terminate the Treaty, in which case the Treaty shall terminate one year after such notice has been given . . . .

Agreed Minute to the Treaty of Mutual Cooperation and Security

Japanese plenipotentiary:

While the question of the status of the islands administered by the United States under Article 3 of the Treaty of Peace with Japan has not been made a subject of discussion in the course of treaty negotiations, I would like to emphasize the strong concern of the Government and people of Japan for the safety of the people of these islands since Japan possesses residual sovereignty over these islands. If an armed attack occurs or is threatened against these islands, the two countries will of course consult together closely under Article IV of the Treaty of Mutual Cooperation and Security. In the event of an armed attack, it is the intention of the Government of Japan to explore with the United States measures which it might be able to take for the welfare of the islanders.

United states plenipotentiary:

In the event of an armed attack against these islands, the United States Government will consult at once with the Government of Japan and intends to take the necessary measures for the defense of these islands, and to do its utmost to secure the welfare of the islanders.

Exchanges of Notes between Japan and the United States

WASHINGTON, *January 19, 1960*
EXCELLENCY:

I have the honour to refer to the Treaty of Mutual Cooperation and Security between Japan and the United States of America signed today, and to inform Your Excellency that the following is the understanding of the Government of Japan concerning the implementation of Article VI thereof:

Major changes in the deployment into Japan of United States armed forces, major changes in their equipment, and the use of facilities and areas in Japan as bases for military combat operations to be undertaken from Japan other than those conducted under Article V of the said Treaty, shall be the subjects of prior consultation with the Government of Japan.

I should be appreciative if Your Excellency would confirm on behalf of your Government that this is also the understanding of the Government of the United States of America.

I avail myself of this opportunity to renew to Your Excellency the assurance of my highest consideration.

Agreement under article VI

Article 2. . . . 2. At the request of either Government, the Governments of the United States and Japan shall review such arrangements and may agree that such facilities and areas shall be returned to Japan or that additional facilities and areas may be provided.

3. The facilities and areas used by the United States armed forces shall be returned to Japan whenever they are no longer needed for purposes of this Agreement, and the United States agrees to keep the needs for facilities and areas under continual observation with a view toward such return . . . .

US treaty relations in the Middle East

Two unrelated conflicts involved the United States in the Middle East: first, the tension between the Soviet Union and its Middle Eastern neighbours, Turkey and Iran, and secondly, the foundation of Israel and the continuing conflict between Israel and the Arab states. United States policy sought both to strengthen anti-Soviet and anti-communist alignments, and to give support to the State of Israel sufficient to ensure its survival among the hostile Arab states. Beginning in about 1955 these two separate strands, the 'cold war' and 'Arab–Israeli' conflicts, began to intertwine and cause much perplexity to American policy-makers.

The first post-war involvement of the United States in the region was to provide economic, diplomatic and military aid to Iran, Turkey and Greece to withstand the Soviet Union and communist expansion (Truman Doctrine, p. 355). Aid to these three countries continued throughout the 1950s on a growing scale based on the Mutual Defense Program begun in 1949.

When Israel was proclaimed on 14 May 1948, the United States under the Truman administration expressed its moral support by recognizing the Provisional government on the same day. The armistice agreements with Egypt, Lebanon, Jordan and Syria, signed in 1949 (p. 718), established temporary boundaries for the State of Israel, which the Arabs refused to accept as permanent;

indeed, the Arab states would not accept a State of Israel itself as permanent. But the United States joined with Britain and France in the *Tripartite Declaration, 25 May 1950* (p. 725), which expressed their opposition to an arms race between Israel and the Arab states and declared that if any of the states should prepare to violate the armistice lines or the frontier, they would in these circumstances immediately take action. This declaration in effect supported Israel's right to exist within the frontiers established by force of arms pending a peace treaty. *The United States signed a Mutual Defense Assistance Agreement with Israel in July 1952* and thereafter provided growing quantities of economic aid and military equipment to Israel.

The second phase of the Middle Eastern crisis developed in 1956. Again two strands of conflict intermingled: Britain and France versus Egypt, especially over the issue of President Nasser's nationalization of the Suez Canal (July 1956); and rising tensions between Israel on the one hand and Egypt, whose leaders called for a united Arab effort to destroy Israel, on the other. The military moves of Israeli, French and British forces were secretly coordinated. On 29 October Israel launched the attack on Egypt (p. 707). On 31 October 1956 Britain and France began their attack on Egypt – first by bombing airfields and then on 5 November by landing troops on the western end of the Suez Canal. The United States, not informed in advance of the Anglo-French attack, worked for a cease-fire and for an Israeli, French and British withdrawal. The cease-fire went into force on 6 November and Britain and France withdrew in December 1956. The Soviet Union (which had supplied Egypt with arms) supported Egypt, and gained much credit in Arab eyes (see also p. 410).

The growing influence of the Soviet Union in Egypt and Syria, and a possible spread of communist influence after Suez, alarmed the American administration and led to a Joint Resolution of Congress, signed by the president, which became known as the *Eisenhower Doctrine, 5 January 1957*. It pledged American support for the independence and integrity of Middle Eastern states as a vital American interest; American armed support was promised to resist armed aggression 'from any country controlled by international communism', provided the president regarded it as necessary, and provided such armed support was requested. In accordance with this resolution the United States supported Jordan in April 1957 and sent increased arms to Lebanon, Turkey and Iraq. When in July 1958 the pro-western government of Iraq was overthrown and King Faisal was murdered, Jordan and Lebanon requested American help. American marines were landed in the Lebanon immediately (British troops went to the assistance of Jordan). *On 28 July 1958, by executive agreements with Britain, Turkey, Iran and Pakistan, the United States* (p. 715) linked herself to these states of the *Baghdad Pact*. The pact was renamed the *Central Treaty Organization* (CENTO), after the formal withdrawal of Iraq in 1959.

CENTO never established itself as a cohesive alliance on the model of NATO.

It was more or less moribund long before March 1979 when both Iran and Pakistan withdrew. CENTO was formally dissolved on 26 September 1979.

After the 'Six-Day War' of June 1967 between Israel on the one hand and Egypt, Jordan and Syria on the other, the United States found itself drawn much more deeply into involvement in the Arab–Israeli conflict. Israel henceforth came to rely ever more heavily on American arms supplies, economic aid and diplomatic support. The Israeli setbacks in the initial phases of the October 1973 war against Egypt and Syria emphasized Israel's increasing dependence on the American connection and provided the background to the imaginative diplomatic successes of the US Secretary of State, Dr Henry Kissinger, in the Middle East in the period from 1973 to 1975 (see Chapter XXI).

During this period Egypt undertook a dramatic shift in foreign policy orientation, scrapping its previous alignment with the Soviet Union in favour of a much closer relationship to the United States. The *Agreement between Egypt and the United States, 14 June 1974* (p. 381), signed on the occasion of President Nixon's visit to Cairo, heralded the new friendship. Although one of the most publicized sections of the agreement (Article III, concerning the provision to Egypt by the USA of nuclear technology) was not put into effect, the ensuing decade was marked by continuing close relations between the two countries, with the United States providing substantial economic aid to Egypt after 1979 and also instituting a large programme of military supplies and cooperation with Egypt.

At the same time the USA maintained and even extended its relations with Israel. One fruit of this triangular relationship was the signature of the *Camp David Agreements, 17 September 1978* (p. 727). The six years of negotiation after 1973 tied Israel firmly to the United States; indeed, during that period of Arab resurgence based on the power of the 'oil weapon', the United States was Israel's only important ally. Yet the two countries did not sign a formal alliance treaty. Several of the agreements between Israel and her neighbours in the 1970s did, however, include attached documents in which the United States entered into various diplomatic, economic and arms supply commitments towards Israel. The 'intelligence communities' of the USA and Israel developed close contacts at the same time. But it was only in 1981 that the two countries signed something approaching an alliance agreement: the *Israel–United States Memorandum of Understanding on Strategic Cooperation, 30 November 1981* (p. 384) marked a new stage in Israel–American relations. Although it was 'suspended' by the United States only a few weeks after its signature (because of Israel's annexation of the Golan Heights), strategic cooperation between the two countries was later quietly resumed.

By the 1980s, therefore, the USA had succeeded in forging both Egypt and Israel into linchpins of its alliance structure in the Middle East. This was all the more opportune for the United States because of complications in relations with its two other major allies in the region – Turkey and Iran.

In the case of Turkey, the United States faced the embarrassing problem of balancing the claims of two NATO allies after the Turkish attack on Cyprus in 1974 (p. 751). But the decision was never seriously in doubt: although the Greek ethnic lobby in the USA was vocal, the United States administration recognized that Turkey, militarily much stronger and strategically more important than Greece, was crucial to American interests, and the USA in effect sided with Turkey.

The problems with Iran were much more serious. As one of the 'hawks' in the oil price 'war' after 1973, the Shah of Iran, although accused of being an agent of American imperialism, in fact showed little sympathy towards western economies battered by the massive increases in oil prices after 1973. Yet the United States continued to give diplomatic support to the Shah and to help supply his grandiose projects for modernization and for the build-up of a vast arsenal of advanced weaponry. The Shah had signed several agreements with the Soviet Union, but he owed his throne to the United States (CIA agents had helped engineer his return to power in Iran in 1953) and the *Agreement of Cooperation between Iran and the United States, 5 March 1959* (see below) remained the cornerstone of his policy. The fall of the Shah in 1979 and the installation of a vehemently anti-American régime destroyed virtually all American influences in Iran, and marked a major setback for United States interests in the region. The Soviet Union was not slow to take advantage of the opportunity thus offered: in December 1979 Soviet troops occupied Afghanistan, the first significant military movement of Soviet forces outside the generally recognized Soviet sphere of influence since the Russian withdrawal from northern Iran in early 1946. (For further discussion of treaty-making in the Middle East, see Chapter XXI.)

Agreement of Cooperation between Iran and the United States, 5 March 1959

[Similar treaties were concluded between the United States and Pakistan, and Turkey.]

. . .

Article I. The Imperial Government of Iran is determined to resist aggression. In case of aggression against Iran, the Government of the United States of America, in accordance with the Constitution of the United States of America, will take such appropriate action, including the use of armed forces, as may be mutually agreed upon and as is envisaged in the Joint Resolution to Promote Peace and Stability in the Middle East, in order to assist the Government of Iran at its request.

Article II. The Government of the United

States of America, in accordance with the Mutual Security Act of 1954, as amended, and related laws of the United States of America, and with applicable agreements heretofore or hereafter entered into between the Government of the United States of America and the Government of Iran, reaffirms that it will continue to furnish the Government of Iran such military and economic assistance as may be mutually agreed upon between the Government of the United States of America and the Government of Iran, in order to assist the Government of Iran in the preservation of its national independence and integrity and in the effective promotion of its economic development.

Article III. The Imperial Government of Iran undertakes to utilize such military and economic assistance as may be provided by the Government of the United States of America in a manner consonant with the aims and purposes set forth by the Governments associated in the Declaration signed at London on July 28, 1958, and for the purpose of effectively promoting the economic development of Iran and of preserving its national independence and integrity.

Article IV. The Government of the United States of America and the Government of Iran will cooperate with the other Governments associated in the Declaration signed at London on July 28, 1958, in order to prepare and participate in such defensive arrangements as may be mutually agreed to be desirable, subject to the other applicable provisions of this Agreement.

Article V. The provisions of the present Agreement do not affect the cooperation between the two Governments as envisaged in other international agreements or arrangements.

Article VI. This Agreement shall enter into force upon the date of its signature and shall continue in force until one year after the receipt by either Government of written notice of the intention of the other Government to terminate the Agreement.

Agreement between Egypt and the United States on Principles of Relations and Cooperation, Cairo, 14 June 1974

The President of the United States of America, Richard Nixon, and the President of the Arab Republic of Egypt, Muhammed Anwar el-Sadat,

Having held wide-ranging discussions on matters of mutual interest to their two countries,

Being acutely aware of the continuing need to build a structure of peace in the world and to that end and to promote a just and durable peace in the Middle East, and,

Being guided by a desire to seize the historic opportunity before them to strengthen relations between their countries on the broadest basis in ways that will contribute to the well-being of the area as a whole and will not be directed against any of its states or peoples or against any other state,

Have agreed that the following principles should govern relations between the United States and Egypt.

I. General principles of bilateral relations

Relations between nations, whatever their economic or political systems, should be based on the purposes and principles of the United Nations Charter, including the right of each state to existence, independence and sovereignty; the right of each state freely to choose and develop its political, social, economic and cultural system; non-intervention in each other's internal affairs; and respect for territorial integrity and political independence.

Nations should approach each other in the spirit of equality respecting their national life and the pursuit of happiness.

The United States and Egypt consider that their relationship reflects these convictions.

Peace and progress in the Middle East are essential if global peace is to be assured. A just and durable peace based on full implementation of United Nations Security Council Resolution 242 of November 22, 1967, should take into due account the legitimate interests of all of the peoples in the Middle East, including the Palestinian people, and the right to existence of all states in the area. Peace can be achieved only through a process of continuing negotiations as called for by United Nations Security Council Resolution 338 of October 22, 1973, within the framework of the Geneva Middle East Peace Conference.

In recognition of these principles, the Governments of the United States of America and the Arab Republic of Egypt set themselves to these tasks:

They will intensify consultations at all levels, including further consultations between their Presidents, and they will strengthen their bilateral cooperation whenever a common or parallel effort will enhance the cause of peace in the world.

They will continue their active cooperation and their energetic pursuit of peace in the Middle East.

They will encourage increased contacts between members of all branches of their two Governments – executive, legislative and judicial – for the purpose of promoting better mutual understanding of each other's institutions, purposes and objectives.

They are determined to develop their bilateral relations in a spirit of esteem, respect and mutual advantage. In the past year, they have moved from estrangement to a constructive working relationship. This year, from that base, they are moving to a relationship of friendship and broad cooperation.

They view economic development and commercial relations as an essential element in the strengthening of their bilateral relations and will actively promote them. To this end, they will facilitate cooperative and joint ventures among appropriate governmental and private institutions and will encourage increased trade between the two countries.

They consider encouragement of exchanges and joint research in the scientific and technical field as an important mutual aim and will take appropriate concrete steps for this purpose.

They will deepen cultural ties through exchanges of scholars, students and other representatives of the cultures of both countries.

They will make special efforts to increase tourism in both directions, and to amplify person-to-person contact among their citizens.

They will take measures to improve air and maritime communications between them.

They will seek to establish a broad range of working relationships and will look particularly to their respective Foreign Ministers and Ambassadors and to the Joint Commission on Cooperation, as well as to other officials and organizations, and private individuals and groups as appropriate, to implement the various aspects of the above principles.

II. Joint Cooperation Commission

The two Governments have agreed that the intensive review of the areas of economic cooperation held by President Nixon and President Sadat on June 12 constituted the first meeting of the Joint Cooperation Commission, announced May 31, 1974. This Commission will be headed by the Secretary of State of the United States and the Minister of Foreign Affairs of Egypt. To this end, they have decided to move ahead rapidly on consultations and coordination to identify and implement programs agreed to be mutually beneficial in the economic, scientific and cultural fields.

The United States has agreed to help

strengthen the financial structure of Egypt. To initiate this process, United States Secretary of the Treasury William Simon will visit Egypt in the near future for high level discussions.

III. Nuclear energy

Since the atomic age began, nuclear energy has been viewed by all nations as a double-edged sword, offering opportunities for peaceful applications, but raising the risk of nuclear destruction. In its international programs of cooperation, the United States Government has made its nuclear technology available to other nations under safeguard conditions. In this context, the two Governments will begin negotiations of an Agreement for Cooperation in the field of nuclear energy under agreed safeguards. Upon conclusion of such an agreement, the United States is prepared to sell nuclear reactors and fuel to Egypt, which will make it possible for Egypt by the early 1980s to generate substantial additional quantities of electric power to support its rapidly growing development needs. Pending conclusion of this Agreement, the United States Atomic Energy Commission and the Egyptian Ministry of Electricity will this month conclude a provisional agreement for the sale of nuclear fuel to Egypt.

IV. Working groups

The two Governments have agreed to set up Joint Working Groups to meet in the near future to prepare concrete projects and proposals for review by the Joint Commission at a meeting to be held later this year in Washington, D.C. These Joint Working Groups will be composed of governmental representatives from each country and will include the following:

(1) A Joint Working Group on Suez Canal Reconstruction and Development to consider and review plans for reopening the Suez Canal and reconstruction of the cities along the Canal, and the United States role in this endeavor.

(2) A Joint Working Group to investigate and recommend measures designed to open the way for United States private investment in joint ventures in Egypt and to promote trade between the two countries. Investment opportunities would be guided by Egypt's need for financial, technical, and material support to increase Egypt's economic growth. The United States regards with favor and supports the ventures of American enterprises in Egypt. It is noted that such ventures, currently being negotiated, are in the field of petrochemicals, transportation, food and agricultural machinery, land development, power, tourism, banking, and a host of other economic sectors. The estimated value of projects under serious consideration exceeds two billion dollars. American technology and capital combined with Egypt's absorptive capacity, skilled manpower and productive investment opportunities can contribute effectively to the strengthening and development of the Egyptian economy. The United States and Egypt will therefore negotiate immediately a new Investment Guarantee Agreement between them.

(3) A Joint Working Group on Agriculture to study and recommend actions designed to increase Egypt's agricultural production through the use of the latest agricultural technology.

(4) A Joint Working Group on Technology, Research and Development in scientific fields, including space, with special emphasis on exchanges of scientists.

(5) A Joint Working Group on Medical Cooperation to assist the Government of Egypt to develop and strengthen its medical research, treatment and training facilities. These efforts will supplement cooperation in certain forms of medical research already conducted through the Naval Medical Research Unit (NAMRU), whose mutually beneficial work will continue.

(6) A Joint Working Group on Cultural Exchanges to encourage and facilitate exhibitions, visits, and other cultural endeavors to encourage a better understanding of both cultures on the part of the peoples of the United States and Egypt.

The two Governments have agreed to encourage the formation of a Joint Economic Council to include representatives from the private economic sector of both countries to cooperate and promote mutually beneficial cooperative economic arrangements.

In support of their economic cooperation, the United States will make the maximum feasible contribution, in accordance with Congressional authorization, to Egypt's economic development, including clearing the Suez Canal, reconstruction projects, and restoring Egyptian trade. In addition, the United States is prepared to give special priority attention to Egypt's needs for agricultural commodities.

Consistent with the spirit of cultural cooperation, the United States Government has agreed to consider how it might assist the Egyptian Government in the reconstruction of Cairo's Opera House. The Egyptian Government for its part intends to place the 'Treasures of Tutankhamen' on exhibit in the United States.

Both Governments, in conclusion, reiterate their intention to do everything possible to broaden the ties of friendship and cooperation consistent with their mutual interests in peace and security and with the principles set forth in this statement.

In thanking President el-Sadat for the hospitality shown to him and the members of his party, President Nixon extended an invitation to President el-Sadar, which President el-Sadat has accepted, to visit the United States during 1974.

Cairo, Egypt
June 14, 1974

[Signed] Richard Nixon
[Signed] Muhammed Anwar el-Sadat

Memorandum of Understanding between Israel and the United States on Strategic Cooperation, Washington, 30 November 1981

Preamble. This Memorandum of Understanding reaffirms the common bonds of friendship between the United States and Israel and builds on the mutual security relationship that exists between the two nations. The Parties recognize the need to enhance Strategic Cooperation to deter all threats from the Soviet Union to the region. Noting the long-standing and fruitful cooperation for mutual security that has developed between the two countries, the Parties have decided to establish a framework for continued consultation and cooperation to enhance their national security by deterring such threats to the whole region.

The Parties have reached the following agreements in order to achieve the above aims.

Article I. United States–Israeli Strategic Cooperation, as set forth in this Memorandum, is designed against the threat to peace and security of the region caused by the Soviet Union or Soviet-controlled forces from outside the region introduced into the region. It has the following broad purposes:

(a) To enable the Parties to act cooperatively and in a timely manner to deal with the above mentioned threat.

(b) To provide each other with military assistance for operations of their forces in the area that may be required to cope with this threat.   ·

(c) The Strategic Cooperation between the Parties is not directed at any State or group of States within the region. It is intended solely for defensive purposes against the above mentioned threat.

Article II. 1. The fields in which Strategic Cooperation will be carried out to prevent the above mentioned threat from endangering the security of the region include:

(a) Military cooperation between the Parties, as may be agreed by the Parties.

(b) Joint military exercises, including naval and air exercises in the Eastern Mediterranean Sea, as agreed upon by the Parties.

(c) Cooperation for the establishment and maintenance of joint readiness activities, as agreed upon by the Parties.

(d) Other areas within the basic scope and purpose of this agreement, as may be jointly agreed.

2. Details of activities within these fields of cooperation shall be worked out by the Parties in accordance with the provisions of Article III below. The cooperation will include, as appropriate, planning, preparations, and exercises.

Article III. 1. The Secretary of Defense and the Minister of Defense shall establish a Coordinating Council to further the purposes of this Memorandum:

(a) To coordinate and provide guidance to Joint Working Groups;

(b) To monitor the implementation of cooperation in the fields agreed upon by the Parties within the scope of this agreement;

(c) To hold periodic meetings, in Israel and the United States, for the purposes of discussing and resolving outstanding issues and to further the objectives set forth in this Memorandum. Special meetings can be held at the request of either Party. The Secretary of Defense and Minister of Defense will chair these meetings whenever possible.

2. Joint Working Groups will address the following issues:

(a) Military cooperation between the Parties, including joint US–Israeli exercises in the Eastern Mediterranean Sea.

(b) Cooperation for the establishment of joint readiness activities including access to maintenance facilities and other infrastructure, consistent with the basic purposes of this agreement.

(c) Cooperation in research and devel-

opment, building on past cooperation in this area.

(d) Cooperation in defense trade.

(e) Other fields within the basic scope and purpose of this agreement, such as questions of prepositioning, as agreed by the Coordinating Council.

3. The future agenda for the work of the Joint Working Groups, their composition, and procedures for reporting to the Coordinating Council shall be agreed upon by the Parties.

Article IV. This Memorandum shall enter into force upon exchange of notification that required procedures have been completed by each Party. If either Party considers it necessary to terminate this Memorandum of Understanding, it may do so by notifying the other Party six months in advance of the effective date of termination.

Article V. Nothing in the Memorandum shall be considered as derogating from previous agreements and understandings between the Parties.

Article VI. The Parties share the understanding that nothing in this Memorandum is intended to or shall in any way prejudice the rights and obligations which devolve or may devolve upon either government under the Charter of the United Nations or under International Law. The Parties reaffirm their faith in the purposes and principles of the Charter of the United Nations and their aspiration to live in peace with all countries in the region.

[For the Government of the United States]
Caspar W. Weinberger
Secretary of Defense

[For the Government of Israel]
Ariel Sharon
Minister of Defense

November 30, 1981

XIV · The Soviet treaty system

Soviet treaties in eastern Europe

From 1939 to 1945 Stalin sought to regain for the Soviet Union the territory that had once constituted the Tsarist Russian Empire in 1914 with two exceptions: Poland and Finland. Although accepting separate Polish and Finnish states, Stalin was not prepared to recognize as final their frontiers as established after the First World War, or to follow policies of enmity to the Soviet Union. The twin impulses of expanding Soviet power and of creating a 'buffer' of greater security against the west motivated Soviet policies from 1939 to 1945. Stalin regarded both 'fascist' and 'bourgeois–democratic' Europe as basically hostile to the Soviet Union; if the 'capitalists' were divided, the Soviet Union, still weaker than the capitalist world, should seek advantage and safety from any capitalist conflicts. Its policy towards them would be governed by the opportunism of Soviet self-interest. From 1939 to 1940 Stalin achieved his territorial objectives in alliance with Hitler.

In September 1939 the Soviet Union occupied eastern Poland and incorporated this territory some weeks later in the Soviet Union. As a result of the Winter War with Finland (November 1939–March 1940) the Soviet Union annexed Finnish territory of strategic importance, especially the Karelian isthmus and, in the extreme north of Finland, Petsamo and its district which gave the Soviet Union a common frontier with Norway in the Arctic. In June 1940, Romania under Soviet pressure and on German 'advice' returned Bessarabia to Russian rule; in August 1940 Lithuania, Latvia and Estonia were incorporated in the Soviet Union. In 1945, the Soviet Union retained all these gains of 1939–40 and added further relatively small but strategically important areas: Ruthenia, called by the Soviet leaders the Subcarpathian Ukraine, was acquired from Czechoslovakia, and thereby the Soviet Union regained a common frontier with Hungary which had been lost after the First World War. The Soviet Union also administered the northern half of German East Prussia, the southern half being administered by Poland.

A complementary aspect of Soviet policy was to ensure that those independent states on her borders still surviving should be friendly to the Soviet Union and closely linked to her politically, economically and culturally. Before 1939 only Czechoslovakia had pursued a policy of friendship and alliance with the Soviet Union. Stalin was determined that the Soviet Union's neighbours should become a source of strength and not of weakness for the Soviet Union, and that the revival of a German military threat be delayed as long as possible. Stalin's diplomatic methods were foreshadowed in the *Soviet–Czechoslovak Treaty of Friendship, 12 December 1943*. By friendly neighbours Stalin meant states which would be bound by political treaties to the Soviet alliance, whose military resources would be dominated by the Soviet Union, and which would permit the stationing or entry of Soviet troops for mutual protection. In evaluating these 'political' treaties it must be remembered that additional 'economic' agreements were just as important in the relationship. 'Friendly' also meant that the economies of Russia's allies would more or less follow the communist pattern; during the Stalinist period these economies were shaped mainly in the interests of the Soviet Union. Whilst in Poland and Czechoslovakia the political leadership at first did not have to be entirely communist in appearance and 'united front' governments were formed, the economic reorganization and the Soviet presence ensured that real political power lay in the hands of the Soviet Union and with the communist leadership of these countries, most of whom had been trained in Moscow.

The Soviet Union signed alliances with Poland on 21 April 1945 (p. 392), *and with Yugoslavia on 11 April 1945* (p. 391), in addition to the Czech alliance already cited. These followed a common pattern in that the signatories agreed to collaborate in the event of any renewed aggression on the part of Germany specifically, or in the event of any other state attacking the territorial integrity of the signatories; an agreement on the part of the signatories was included stating that they would not join in alliances directed against the other signatories. The agreement that close political, economic, social and cultural ties would be promoted meant in fact that within a few years these countries became dependent on the Soviet Union; clauses in the treaty promising non-interference in the domestic affairs of the neighbours of the Soviet Union were in practice not observed. Only Finland and Yugoslavia were allowed some genuine measure of domestic independence.

During the first six months of 1945, under the aegis of the Red Army, communist-controlled governments were set up in Romania and Bulgaria. In Poland and Hungary 'united front' governments were permitted with some non-communist participation until the summer of 1947. In 1948 Czechoslovakia came under complete communist control. In Yugoslavia Marshal Tito had established his communist government without Russian help. Denounced by Stalin in June 1948 for national deviationism, Tito successfully resisted Soviet pressure.

The Soviet Union concluded alliance treaties with Romania on 4 February 1948 (p. 394), *with Hungary on 18 February and Bulgaria on 18 March 1948.* A few months earlier in *September 1947* the *Communist Information Bureau, Cominform,* had been established with headquarters in Belgrade but with nothing really to do. Tito's successful defiance of Stalin's accusations, which Stalin had delivered through the Cominform, soon made the Cominform totally ineffective, though as an organization it remained formally in being until 1956. Tito's assertion of Yugoslav independence led to Soviet-inspired purges in Hungary, Bulgaria, Albania, Poland, Rumania and Czechoslovakia. Soviet policy was laid down by the Party and backed by Soviet Army units, which could be used as a last resort. Whilst Stalin decided not to attack Yugoslavia he was all the more determined to prevent a spread of revived Balkan nationalisms whether communist or of any other kind.

These developments in eastern and central Europe were related to the growing conflict between the western wartime allies and the Soviet Union which became known as the cold war. Western policies were viewed by Stalin as attempts under the leadership of the United States to revive in a new form a capitalist coalition of states, which would encircle the Soviet Union. Stalin saw in the same light western protests over Russian policy in the Soviet zone of Germany and in central and eastern Europe. For Stalin, 28 million Russian war casualties and the destruction of much of European Russia justified and necessitated a post-war policy that would ensure Soviet security and material reparations. Experience during the Second World War of the extent of Allied solidarity did not lessen his deep-rooted fear that in the post-war world an isolated Soviet Russia was facing a more powerful western coalition possessing the atom bomb.

Stalin interpreted the Marshall Plan (p. 506) and American economic aid as attempts to revive capitalism among Russia's neighbours to the detriment of the security of the Soviet Union. But the event which most alarmed central and eastern Europe was the creation of the Federal Republic of Germany and German rearmament. The Soviet response was to form an alliance of communist states, ostensibly among equals, with joint responsibilities and mutual decision-making organs giving the appearance of equality. *The Council for Mutual Economic Assistance (Comecon), established in January 1949* was set up as the Soviet counterpart to the *Organization for European Economic Cooperation* created by the western European states in April 1948 (see p. 507). At first Comecon was little more than a paper organization: it held only two meetings prior to the death of Stalin on 5 March 1953. The founding members were Albania (which left in 1961, but rejoined in 1971), Bulgaria, Czechoslovakia, Hungary, Poland, Romania and the Soviet Union. East Germany was admitted in 1950, Mongolia in 1962, and Cuba in 1972. After 1956 more life was breathed into the organization, which the

USSR sought to develop into a closed trading system under its control. But by the 1970s some members, notably Romania, Poland and Hungary, had succeeded in shaking loose to some extent from the restrictions of the system and built up sizeable trading relations with capitalist economies.

In June 1953 the first of a series of upheavals among Russia's satellites was crushed in East Germany. In January–February 1954 the foreign ministers of the Big Four met again in Berlin, but could not agree on a solution for a divided Germany. The post-Stalin period of flexibility over Germany drew to a close with the signature by the western allies of the *Paris Agreements, 23 October 1954*, which came into force in May 1955 and which accorded sovereignty to the Federal Republic of Germany and provided for her entry into NATO (p. 432). The Soviet response was to convene a conference in Moscow from 29 November–2 December 1954, attended by Albania, Bulgaria, Czechoslovakia, the German Democratic Republic (East Germany), Hungary, Poland, Romania and the Soviet Union. They jointly declared that if the Paris Agreements were ratified they would adopt measures to safeguard their security. On 6 May 1955, the day after the ratification of the Paris Agreements, the Soviet Union denounced the Anglo-Soviet Alliance Treaty of 1942. On *14 May 1955* the same eight communist states signed the *Treaty of Friendship, Cooperation and Mutual Assistance* known as the *Warsaw Pact* (p. 397).

The Warsaw Pact was the most important multilateral treaty between the communist States under Soviet leadership both militarily and politically. The treaty referred to a political consultative committee which had the power to set up auxiliary bodies. Militarily it formalized arrangements for Soviet control dating probably three years earlier to about August 1952, when a decision was taken to re-equip the satellite armies and place them under Soviet command. In accordance with the agreement reached in May 1955, the following January a United Military Command was established with headquarters in Moscow. A Soviet officer, Marshal Konev, became commander-in-chief, and the Defence Ministers of participating countries were to be deputy commanders-in-chief. Joint military exercises were held in member countries from the autumn of 1961.

At first the Asian communist countries – China, North Korea and North Vietnam – sent observers to the Warsaw Pact, but they withdrew by 1962. Albania was excluded and withdrew after 1961, siding with China in the Sino-Soviet conflict.

Following the momentous Twentieth Congress of the Communist Party of the Soviet Union in February 1956, when Nikita Khrushchev attacked the mistakes and cruelty of Stalin's dictatorship, Poland and Hungary sought more independence from Soviet control. Outright Soviet military intervention was only just avoided in Poland; but in November 1956 Soviet troops crushed Hungarian resistance after the Hungarian government of Imre Nagy on 1 November 1956 had seceded from the Warsaw Pact. The Soviet Union moved back into Hungary just as the Anglo-French Suez involvement was reaching its culmination (p. 708).

The limitations of independence and of the alleged equality of communist states were again exposed when on 21 August 1968 the Soviet Union and the other European Warsaw Pact countries (except Romania), acting as socialist allies, invaded Czechoslovakia, itself a member of the Warsaw Pact. The reformist communist government of Alexander Dubček was deposed, and a more pliant pro-Soviet régime installed. According to *Pravda*, the 'allied socialist' troops together with the Soviet Union, i.e. the Warsaw Pact countries, had 'a solemn commitment – to stand up in defence of the gains of socialism'. Participants of the Warsaw Treaty Organization were involved, for to tolerate a breach in this organization would contradict the vital interests of all the member countries, including the Soviet Union. Although the Czechoslovak president initially denounced the invasion as illegal and Rumania also condemned it, Czechoslovakia was occupied by the end of August 1968 and forced to submit. The Soviet justification on the basis of limited sovereignty within the socialist community became known as the Brezhnev Doctrine.

Following the invasion the Soviet Union imposed the *Soviet–Czechoslovak Treaty on the Stationing of Soviet Troops, 16 October 1968* (p. 399). This was unusual among Soviet treaties with its client states in eschewing the common courtesies of socialist fraternity and detailing the conduct to be observed by the occupied state in its relations with Soviet forces in the country. Only in 1970, when the government installed by the Soviet forces had succeeded in stamping out any tendency towards national self-assertion, did a more cordial public formulation of the relationship emerge in the *Soviet–Czechoslovak Friendship Treaty, 6 May 1970* (p. 402).

Bilateral treaties were concluded between the *Soviet Union and Poland, 17 December 1956*, the *Soviet Union and the German Democratic Republic, 12 March 1957*, the *Soviet Union and Rumania, 15 April 1957*, and the *Soviet Union and Hungary, 27 May 1957*, in the aftermath of the Polish troubles and the Hungarian uprising, to normalize and improve relations, limit Soviet supervision and direct interference, and above all to justify the stationing of Soviet troops ostensibly to fulfil the needs of the Warsaw Pact. The treaty with Poland more specifically stated that the 'temporary stay' of Soviet troops in Poland could neither affect Polish sovereignty nor lead to any interference in the domestic affairs of Poland, and that no Soviet troop movements outside specified areas of Poland would be permitted without Polish authorization. But these provisions were shown to be mere window-dressing when, following an upsurge of Polish national feeling which found expression in the late 1970s in the formation of the Solidarity trade union movement, the USSR in December 1981 brought pressure to bear, as a result of which a government headed (uniquely in the Soviet bloc) by the commander-in-chief of the armed forces took office. General Jaruzelski's régime restored order, disbanded Solidarity, curbed freedom of the press, imprisoned political opponents, and made due obeisance to its Soviet masters – very much on the model of events in Hungary after 1956 and in Czechoslovakia after 1968. On this occasion the USSR had not formally 'occupied' the country (though large Soviet forces were stationed there throughout), but as on the previous occasions the satellite state's room for independent manoeuvre had been severely limited and an example had been served to other potentially errant members of the Warsaw Pact. Although Hungary succeeded in maintaining a certain degree of economic independence and Romania remained (in its foreign but not its domestic policies) the political maverick of eastern Europe, the Warsaw Pact entered its fourth decade in 1985 in solid political and military condition.

Of all the European neighbours of the Soviet Union (apart from Norway, a member of NATO), only Finland was permitted to retain a democratic, multi-party political structure, a (limited) free press, and a liberal economy. The *Soviet–Finnish Treaty, 6 April 1948* (p. 395), extended for a further twenty years on 19 September 1955, provided the basis for relations. On 19 July 1970 the treaty was extended for another twenty years. The 1948 treaty provided that if Finland or the USSR were attacked by Germany or any state allied to Germany, Finland would repulse the aggressor, acting within her boundaries with the assistance in case of need of the Soviet Union, or jointly with the Soviet Union (Article 1). Finland was not obliged by the treaty to come to the assistance of the Soviet Union if the latter were attacked or at war in any other region. During the post-war period Finland remained neutral, leaning towards the Soviet Union in foreign policy, but towards the west economically and culturally. She became a member of the Nordic Union (p. 529), and an associate of EFTA (p. 524) and later of the EEC (p. 530). It was symbolic of Finland's delicately poised position between east and west that the Finnish capital, Helsinki, became the venue for the *European Security Conference*, of which the *Final Act, 1 August 1975* (p. 828), marked the most significant achievement of the period of east–west détente.

Treaty of Friendship, Mutual Aid and Post-War Cooperation between the Soviet Union and Yugoslavia, Moscow, 11 April 1945

The Presidium of the Supreme Soviet of the Union of Soviet Socialist Republics and the Regency Council of Yugoslavia,

Resolved to bring the war against the German aggressors to its final conclusion;

desirous still further to consolidate the friendship existing between the peoples of the Soviet Union and Yugoslavia, which together are fighting against the common enemy – Hitlerite Germany; desirous to ensure close cooperation between the peoples of the two countries and all United Nations during the war and in peacetime, and to make their contribution to the post-war organization of security and peace; convinced that the consolidation of friendship between the Soviet Union and Yugoslavia corresponds to the vital interests of the two peoples, and best serves the further economic development of the two countries, have . . . agreed on the following.

Article 1. Each of the Contracting Parties will continue the struggle in cooperation with one another and with all the United Nations against Germany until final victory. The two Contracting Parties pledge themselves to render each other military and other assistance and support of every kind.

Article 2. If one of the Contracting Parties should in the post-war period be drawn into military operations against Germany, which would have resumed her aggressive policy, or against any other State which would have joined Germany either directly or in any other form in a war of this nature, the other Contracting Party shall immediately render military or any other support with all the means available.

Article 3. The two Contracting Parties state that they will participate, in the spirit of closest cooperation, in all international activities designed to ensure peace and security of peoples, and will make their contribution for attaining these lofty purposes.

The Contracting Parties state that the application of the present Treaty will be in accordance with the international principles in the acceptance of which they have participated.

Article 4. Each of the Contracting Parties undertakes not to conclude any alliance and not to take part in any coalition directed against the other party.

Article 5. The two Contracting Parties state that after the termination of the present war they will act in a spirit of friendship and cooperation for the purpose of further developing and consolidating the economic and cultural ties between the peoples of the two countries.

Article 6. The present Treaty comes into force immediately it is signed and is subject to ratification in the shortest possible time. The exchange of ratification documents will be effected in Belgrade as early as possible.

The present Treaty will remain in force for a period of twenty years. If one of the Contracting Parties at the end of this twenty years period does not, one year before the expiration of this term, announce its desire to renounce the Treaty, it will remain in force for the following five years, and so on each time until one of the Contracting Parties gives written notice of its desire to terminate the efficacy of the Treaty one year before the termination of the current five-year period.

Agreement regarding Friendship, Mutual Assistance and Post-War Cooperation between the Soviet Union and the Polish Republic, Moscow, 21 April 1945

The President of the National Council of the Homeland and the Presidium of the Supreme Council of the Union of Socialist Soviet Republics moved by an unshaken

determination to bring, in a common effort, the war with the German aggressors to a complete and final victory;

Wishing to consolidate the fundamental

change in the history of the Polish–Soviet relations in the direction of friendly cooperation, which has taken places in the course of a common fight against German imperialism;

Trusting that a further consolidation of good neighbourly relations and friendship between Poland and her direct neighbour – the USSR – is vital to the interests of the Polish and Soviet peoples;

Confident that friendship and close co-operation between the Polish people and the Soviet people will serve the cause of successful economic development of both countries during the war as well as after the war;

Wishing to support after the war by all possible means the cause of peace and security of peoples;

Have resolved to conclude this agreement and have . . . appointed as their plenipotentiaries:

The President of the National Council of the Homeland – Edward Osóbka-Morawski, the President of the Council of Ministers and the Minister of Foreign Affairs of the Polish Republic,

The Presidium of the Supreme Council of the Union of Socialist Soviet Republics – Joseph Vissarionovitch Stalin, Chairman of the Council of People's Commissars of the USSR ;

Who, after exchange of full powers which were recognized as being in order and drawn up in due form, have agreed as follows:

Article 1. The High Contracting Parties jointly with all United Nations will continue the fight against Germany until final victory. In that fight the High Contracting Parties undertake to give one another mutual military and other assistance using all the means at their disposal.

Article 2. The High Contracting Parties, in a firm belief that in the interest of security and successful development of the Polish and Soviet peoples it is necessary to preserve and to strengthen lasting and unshaken friendship during the war as well as after the war, will strengthen the friendly cooperation between the two countries in accordance with the principles of mutual respect for their independence and sovereignty and non-interference in the internal affairs of the other Government.

Article 3. The High Contracting Parties further undertake that even after the end of the present war they will jointly use all the means at their disposal in order to eliminate every possible menace of a new aggression on the part of Germany or on the part of any other Government whatsoever which would be directly or in any other manner allied with Germany.

For this purpose the High Contracting Parties will, in a spirit of most-sincere collaboration, take part in all international activities aiming at ensuring peace and security of peoples and will contribute their full share to the cause of realization of these high ideals.

The High Contracting Parties will execute this Agreement in compliance with the international principles in the establishment of which both Contracting Parties took part.

Article 4. If one of the High Contracting Parties during the post-war period should become involved in war operations against Germany in case she should resume aggressive policy or against any other Government whatsoever which would be allied with Germany directly or in any other form in such a war the other High Contracting Party will immediately extend to the other Contracting Party which is involved in military operations military and other support with all the means at its disposal.

Article 5. The High Contracting Parties undertake not to sign without mutual consent an armistice or a peace treaty with the Hitlerite Government or any other authority in Germany which menaces or may menace the independence, territorial integrity or security of either of the two High Contracting Parties.

Article 6. Each of the High Contracting Parties undertakes not to enter into any alliance or to take part in any coalition directed against the other High Contracting Party.

Article 7. The High Contracting Parties will

cooperate in a spirit of friendship also after the end of the present war for the purpose of developing and strengthening the economic and cultural relations between the two countries and will give mutual assistance in the economic reconstruction of the two countries.

Article 8. This Agreement comes into force from the moment of signing and is liable to ratification within the shortest possible period. Exchange of ratifying documents will take place in Warsaw as soon as possible.

This Agreement will remain in force for twenty years after the moment of signing.

If one of the High Contracting Parties does not make a statement twelve months before the expiration of the twenty years period to the effect that it wishes to give notice, this Agreement will remain in force for a further period of five years and so on until one of the High Contracting Parties makes a statement in writing twelve months before the expiration of a successive five years period to the effect that it intends to give notice of the Agreement.

In witness whereof the mandatories have signed this Agreement and have apposed their seals thereto.

Drawn up in Moscow on April 21, 1945, in duplicate, each copy in Polish and in Russian, both texts being equally binding.

By authority of the President of the National Council of the Homeland
Osóbka-Morawski

By authority of the Presidium of the Supreme Council of the USSR
J. Stalin

After consideration this Agreement has been recognized equitable in its whole as well as in individual provisions contained therein; it is, therefore, announced that it has been accepted, ratified and approved and will be strictly complied with.

In witness whereof this Act has been issued with the seal of the Polish Republic duly apposed thereto.

Warsaw, September 19, 1945

President of the National Council of the Homeland
Boleslaw Bierut

President of the Council of Ministers
Edward Osóbka-Morawski

Vice-Minister of Foreign Affairs
p.p. Z. Modzelewski

Treaty of Friendship, Collaboration and Mutual Assistance between the Rumanian People's Republic and the Soviet Union, Moscow, 4 February 1948

[A treaty in similar terms was concluded between Bulgaria and the Soviet Union, 18 March 1948; and between Hungary and the Soviet Union, 18 February 1948.]

The Praesidium of the Rumanian Popular Republic and the Praesidium of the Supreme Soviet of the Union of Soviet Socialist Republics,

Desirous of consolidating friendly relations between Rumania and the Soviet Union;

Desirous of keeping up close collaboration, with a view to consolidating peace and general security, in accordance with the purposes and principles of the United Nations Organization;

Convinced that the keeping up of friendship and good neighbourliness between Rumania and the Soviet Union is in accordance with the vital interests of the peoples of both States, and will bring the best possible contribution to their economic development;

Have decided to conclude this Treaty, and have to that end full powers:

Article 1. The High Contracting Parties undertake to take jointly all measures in their power to remove any threat of repeated aggression on the part of Germany, or of any State allying itself with Germany directly or in any other way.

The High Contracting Parties state that it is their intention to participate with full sincerity in any international action aimed at ensuring the peace and security of nations, and that they will fully contribute to the carrying out of these great tasks.

Article 2. Should one of the High Contracting Parties be involved in armed conflict with Germany, attempting to renew her policy of aggression, or with any other State allying itself with Germany, directly or in any other way, in her aggressive policy, the other High Contracting Party will lose no time in giving the High Contracting Party involved in a conflict military or other aid with all the means at its disposal.

This Treaty will be applied in accordance with the principles of the United Nations Charter.

Article 3. Each of the High Contracting Par-

ties undertakes to conclude no alliance and to participate in no coalition, action or measures directed against the other High Contracting Party.

Article 4. The High Contracting Parties will consult with regard to all important international issues concerning the interests of the two countries.

Article 5. The High Contracting Parties state that they will act in a spirit of friendship and collaboration, with a view to further developing and strengthening economic and cultural relations between the two States, with due regard for the principles of mutual respect for their independence and sovereignty, and of non-interference in the internal affairs of the other State.

Article 6. This Treaty will remain in force for twenty years, as from the date of its signing. If, one year before the expiry of the twenty years, none of the High Contracting Parties expresses the wish to cancel the Treaty, it will remain in force another five years, and so on, until one of the High Contracting Parties, one year before the expiry of the current five-year period, announces in writing its intention to put an end to the validity of the Treaty . . . .

Treaty of Friendship, Cooperation and Mutual Assistance between the Soviet Union and the Finnish Republic, Moscow, 6 April 1948

The Presidium of the Supreme Soviet of the Union of Soviet Socialist Republics and the President of the Finnish Republic,

With the object of further promoting friendly relations between the USSR and Finland;

Convinced that consolidation of good-neighbourly relations and cooperation between the Union of Soviet Socialist Republics and the Finnish Republic meets the vital interests of both countries;

Considering Finland's aspiration to stand

aside from the contradictions of interests of the Great Powers, and

Expressing their unswerving aspiration to cooperate in the interests of preservation of international peace and security in conformity with the aims and principles of the United Nations Organization;

Have decided to conclude for these ends the present Treaty, and . . . have appointed as their plenipotentiaries:

for the Presidium of the Supreme Soviet of the Union of Soviet Socialist Republics –

396　THE MAJOR INTERNATIONAL TREATIES OF THE TWENTIETH CENTURY

Vyacheslav Mikhailovich Molotov, vice-chairman of the Council of Ministers and Minister of Foreign Affairs of the USSR ;

for the President of the Finnish Republic – Mauno Pekkala, Prime Minister of the Finnish Republic,

Who upon exchanging their credentials, found in due form and full order, have agreed upon the following:

Article I. In the event of Finland or the Soviet Union, across the territory of Finland, becoming the object of military aggression on the part of Germany or any State allied to the latter, Finland, loyal to her duty as an independent State, will fight to repulse the aggression. In doing so, Finland will direct all the forces at her disposal to the defence of the inviolability of her territory on land, on sea and in the air, acting within her boundaries in accordance with her obligations under the present Treaty, with the assistance, in case of need, of the Soviet Union or jointly with the latter.

In the cases indicated above, the Soviet Union will render Finland the necessary assistance, in regard to the granting of which the parties will agree between themselves.

Article II. The High Contracting Parties will consult each other in the event of a threat of military attack envisaged in Article I being ascertained.

Article III. The High Contracting Parties affirm their intention to participate most sincerely in all actions aimed at preserving international peace and security in conformity with the aims and principles of the United Nations Organization.

Article IV. The High Contracting Parties reaffirm the undertaking, contained in Article III of the Peace Treaty signed in Paris on 10 February 1947, not to conclude any alliance and not to take part in coalitions aimed against the other High Contracting Party.

Article V. The High Contracting Parties affirm their determination to act in the spirit of cooperation and friendship with the object of further promoting and consolidating the economic and cultural ties between the Soviet Union and Finland.

Article VI. The High Contracting Parties undertake to observe the principles of mutual respect for their State sovereignty and independence as well as non-interference in the domestic affairs of the other State.

Article VII. Implementations of the present Treaty will conform to the principles of the United Nations Organization.

Article VIII. The present Treaty is subject to ratification, and will be valid for ten years as from the day of its coming into force. The Treaty will come into force as from the day of the exchange of ratification instruments, which will be effected in Helsinki within the shortest possible time.

Unless either of the High Contracting Parties denounces the Treaty one year before the expiration of the above-mentioned ten-year term, it will remain in force for each of the next five-year terms until either of the High Contracting Parties gives notice in writing of its intention to terminate the operation of the Treaty.

Treaty of Friendship, Cooperation and Mutual Assistance between Albania, Bulgaria, Hungary, the German Democratic Republic, Poland, Rumania, the Soviet Union and Czechoslovakia (Warsaw Pact), Warsaw, 14 May 1955

The Contracting Parties,

Reaffirming their desire to create a system of collective security in Europe based on the participation of all European States, irrespective of their social and political structure, whereby the said States may be enabled to combine their efforts in the interests of ensuring peace in Europe;

Taking into consideration, at the same time, the situation that has come about in Europe as a result of the ratification of the Paris Agreements, which provide for the constitution of a new military group in the form of a 'West European Union', with the participation of a remilitarized West Germany and its inclusion in the North Atlantic bloc, thereby increasing the danger of a new war and creating a threat to the national security of peace-loving States;

Being convinced that in these circumstances the peace-loving States of Europe must take the necessary steps to safeguard their security and to promote the maintenance of peace in Europe;

Being guided by the purposes and principles of the Charter of the United Nations;

In the interests of the further strengthening and development of friendship, cooperation and mutual assistance in accordance with the principles of respect for the independence and sovereignty of States and of non-intervention in their domestic affairs;

Have resolved to conclude the present Treaty of Friendship, Cooperation and Mutual Assistance and have appointed as their plenipotentiaries . . . who have agreed as follows:

Article 1. The Contracting Parties undertake, in accordance with the Charter of the United Nations, to refrain in their international relations from the threat or use of force and to settle their international disputes by peaceful means in such a manner that international peace and security are not endangered.

Article 2. The Contracting Parties declare that they are prepared to participate, in a spirit of sincere cooperation, in all international action for ensuring international peace and security and will devote their full efforts to the realization of these aims.

In this connection, the Contracting Parties shall endeavour to secure, in agreement with other States desiring to cooperate in this matter, the adoption of effective measures for the general reduction of armaments and the prohibition of atomic, hydrogen and other weapons of mass destruction.

Article 3. The Contracting Parties shall consult together on all important international questions involving their common interests, with a view to strengthening international peace and security.

Whenever any one of the Contracting Parties considers that a threat of armed attack on one or more of the States parties to the Treaty has arisen, they shall consult together immediately with a view to providing for their joint defence and maintaining peace and security.

Article 4. In the event of an armed attack in Europe on one or more of the States parties to the Treaty by any State or group of States, each State party to the Treaty shall, in the exercise of the right of individual or collective self-defence, in accordance with Article 51 of the United Nations Charter, afford the State or States so attacked immediate assistance, individually and in agreement with the other States parties to the Treaty, by all the means it considers necessary, including the use of armed force. The States parties to the Treaty shall consult together immediately concerning the joint measures necessary to restore and maintain international peace and security.

Measures taken under this Article shall be reported to the Security Council in accordance with the provisions of the United Nations Charter. These measures shall be discontinued as soon as the Security Council takes the necessary action to restore and maintain international peace and security.

Article 5. The Contracting Parties have agreed to establish a Unified Command, to which certain elements of their armed forces shall be allocated by agreement between the parties, and which shall act in accordance with jointly established principles. The parties shall likewise take such other concerted action as may be necessary to reinforce their defensive strength, in order to defend the peaceful labour of their peoples, guarantee the inviolability of their frontiers and territories and afford protection against possible aggression.

Article 6. For the purpose of carrying out the consultations provided for in the present Treaty between the States parties thereto, and for the consideration of matters arising in connection with the application of the present Treaty, a Political Consultative Committee shall be established, in which each State party to the Treaty shall be represented by a member of the Government or by some other specially appointed representative.

The Committee may establish such auxiliary organs as may prove to be necessary.

Article 7. The Contracting Parties undertake not to participate in any coalitions or alliances, and not to conclude any agreements, the purposes of which are incompatible with the purposes of the present Treaty.

The Contracting Parties declare that their obligations under international treaties at present in force are not incompatible with the provisions of the present Treaty.

Article 8. The Contracting Parties declare that they will act in a spirit of friendship and cooperation to promote the further development and strengthening of the economic and cultural ties among them, in accordance with the principles of respect for each other's independence and sovereignty and of non-intervention in each other's domestic affairs.

Article 9. The present Treaty shall be open for accession by other States, irrespective of their social and political structure, which express their readiness by participating in the present Treaty, to help in combining the efforts of the peace-loving States to ensure the peace and security of the peoples. Such accessions shall come into effect with the consent of the States parties to the Treaty after the instruments of accession have been deposited with the Government of the Polish People's Republic.

Article 10. The present Treaty shall be subject to ratification, and the instruments of ratification shall be deposited with the Government of the Polish People's Republic.

The Treaty shall come into force on the date of deposit of the last instrument of ratification. The Government of the Polish People's Republic shall inform the other States parties to the Treaty of the deposit of each instrument of ratification.

Article 11. The present Treaty shall remain in force for twenty years. For Contracting Parties which do not, one year before the expiration of that term, give notice of termination of the Treaty to the Government of the Polish People's Republic, the Treaty shall remain in force for a further ten years.

In the event of the establishment of a system of collective security in Europe and the conclusion for that purpose of a General European Treaty concerning collective security, a goal which the Contracting Parties shall steadfastly strive to achieve, the present Treaty shall cease to have effect as from the date on which the General European Treaty comes into force.

Done at Warsaw, this fourteenth day of May 1955, in one copy, in the Russian, Polish, Czech and German languages, all the texts being equally authentic. Certified copies of the present Treaty shall be transmitted by the Government of the Polish People's Republic to all the other parties to the Treaty.

Soviet–Czechoslovak Treaty on Stationing of Soviet Troops, Prague, 16 October 1968

The Government of the Union of Soviet Socialist Republics and the Government of the Czechoslovak Socialist Republic,

Being firmly resolved to make every effort to strengthen friendship and cooperation between the Union of Soviet Socialist Republics and Czechoslovakia, as well as between all the countries of the socialist commonwealth, and to defend the gains of socialism, strengthen peace and security in Europe and throughout the world, in conformity with the Statement of the Bratislava Conference of August 3, 1968,

Taking into consideration the Treaty on Friendship, Mutual Assistance and Post-War Cooperation of December 12, 1943, as extended by the Protocol of November 27, 1963,

In conformity with the arrangement achieved during the Soviet–Czechoslovak negotiations held in Moscow on August 23–6 and October 3–4, 1968,

Have decided to conclude the present Treaty and have agreed upon the following:

Article 1. The Government of the Union of Soviet Socialist Republics, acting with the consent of the Governments of the People's Republic of Bulgaria, the People's Republic of Hungary, the German Democratic Republic, the People's Republic of Poland, and the Government of the Czechoslovak Socialist Republic have agreed that part of the Soviet forces situated in the Czechoslovak Socialist Republic shall remain temporarily on the territory of the Czechoslovak Socialist Republic for the purposes of ensuring the security of the countries of the socialist commonwealth against the increasing revanchist aspirations of the West German militarist forces.

The rest of the forces of the Union of Soviet Socialist Republics, as well as the forces of the People's Republic of Bulgaria, the People's Republic of Hungary, the German Democratic Republic, and the People's Republic of Poland, will be withdrawn from the territory of Czechoslovakia in accordance with the documents of the

Moscow negotiations of August 23–6 and October 3–4, 1968. The withdrawal of these forces shall begin after the ratification of the present Treaty by both Parties and shall be carried out by stages within two months.

The number and places of distribution of Soviet forces which remain temporarily on the territory of the Czechoslovak Socialist Republic shall be determined by agreement between the Governments of the Union of Soviet Socialist Republics and the Czechoslovak Socialist Republic.

The Soviet forces temporarily situated on the territory of the Czechoslovak Socialist Republic shall remain subordinated to the Soviet Military Command.

Article 2. 1. The temporary presence of Soviet forces on the territory of the Czechoslovak Socialist Republic does not violate its sovereignty. Soviet forces shall not interfere in the internal affairs of the Czechoslovak Socialist Republic.

2. Soviet forces, persons serving [with Soviet forces], and members of their families situated on the territory of the Czechoslovak Socialist Republic will observe legislation in force in the Czechoslovak Socialist Republic.

Article 3. 1. The Soviet Side shall bear the expenses for maintenance of Soviet forces on the territory of the Czechoslovak Socialist Republic.

2. The Government of the Czechoslovak Socialist Republic shall grant Soviet forces, persons serving [with Soviet forces], and members of their families, for the period of their temporary sojourn in the Czechoslovak Socialist Republic, with barrack accommodations and housing in garrison settlements, official, warehouse, and other premises, airfields with hospital structures and equipment, means of the State network of communications and transport, electric power, and other services.

Proving grounds, firing ranges, and training grounds will be used jointly with the Czechoslovak People's Army.

The procedure and conditions for use of the aforementioned facilities, as well as municipal, trade, and other services will be determined by agreement of the Contracting Parties.

Article 4. Soviet military units, persons serving with Soviet forces, and members of their families may travel to the Czechoslovak Socialist Republic to the places of distribution of Soviet forces and from the Czechoslovak Socialist Republic in through trains and railway cars belonging to the Soviet Union or transfer from the railway cars of one country to the railway cars of the other country, as well as by motor vehicle and air transport.

Persons serving with Soviet forces and members of their families shall be exempt from passport or visa control when entering, staying in, or leaving the Czechoslovak Socialist Republic.

Localities and the procedure for crossing the Soviet–Czechoslovak frontier, the methods of control, as well as types and forms of corresponding documents, shall be determined by agreement of the Contracting Parties.

Article 5. The Czechoslovak side agrees to admit across the State frontier of the Czechoslovak Socialist Republic without levying duties, and without customs and border inspection:

Soviet forces and persons serving [with Soviet forces] who are traveling with military units, contingents, and commands;

All military freight, including freight destined for trade and other services for Soviet troops;

Persons serving with the Soviet forces traveling to the Czechoslovak Socialist Republic or leaving the Czechoslovak Socialist Republic alone or together with members of their families, with their personal belongings, upon presentation to customs agencies of documents certifying their right to cross the State frontier of the Czechoslovak Socialist Republic.

Property, and military equipment and material imported into the Czechoslovak Socialist Republic by the Soviet Side may be taken back to the Union of Soviet Socialist Republics without imposition of duties and charges.

Article 6. 1. Trade and other services for the personnel of Soviet forces temporarily situated on the territory of the Czechoslovak Socialist Republic and members of the families of persons serving with Soviet forces will be provided through Soviet trade and service enterprises.

2. The Czechoslovak Side will supply Soviet trade and service enterprises goods within the limits of quantities agreed upon between competent trade organizations of the Union of Soviet Socialist Republics and the Czechoslovak Socialist Republic at State retail prices in effect in the Czechoslovak Socialist Republic and at a trade discount adopted for corresponding trade enterprises of the Czechoslovak Socialist Republic.

Payment for deliveries shall be made in the currency of the Czechoslovak Socialist Republic.

3. Under contracts concluded between appropriate Soviet and Czechoslovak foreign trade organizations and at prices in effect in trade relations between the Union of Soviet Socialist Republics and the Czechoslovak Socialist Republic, the Czechoslovak Side will deliver agreed quantities of foodstuffs and manufactured goods, including fuel (coal, coke, firewood), for the planned supply of Soviet forces.

Article 7. The Government of the Czechoslovak Socialist Republic will grant to the Government of the Union of Soviet Socialist Republics the necessary sums in Czechoslovak crowns for expenses connected with the temporary sojourn of Soviet forces on the territory of Czechoslovakia. The amount of these sums will be established by agreement between the competent agencies of the Contracting Parties.

Article 8. The procedure of payment for services provided for by Article 3, as well as the sums in Czechoslovak crowns in accordance with Article 7 of the present Treaty, will be established by an additional Agreement between the Contracting Parties within six weeks after the entry of the present Treaty into force. The said sums in

Czechoslovak crowns will be recomputed into convertible rubles on the basis of the ratio of internal prices and tariffs of the Czechoslovak Socialist Republic and of foreign trade prices.

Article 9. Questions of jurisdiction connected with the temporary sojourn of Soviet forces on the territory of the Czechoslovak Socialist Republic shall be regulated as follows:

1. In cases concerning crimes and offenses committed by persons serving with Soviet forces, or members of their families, on the territory of the Czechoslovak Socialist Republic, Czechoslovak legislation shall be applied and Czechoslovak courts, the procuracy, and other Czechoslovak agencies competent to prosecute for punishable acts shall function.

Cases concerning crimes committed by Soviet servicemen shall be investigated by the military procuracy and shall be considered by agencies of military justice of the Czechoslovak Socialist Republic.

2. The provisions of point one of the present Article shall not apply:

(a) in the event of the commission by persons serving with Soviet forces or by members of their families of crimes or offenses only against the Soviet Union, as well as against persons serving with Soviet forces or members of their families;

(b) in the event of the commission by persons serving with Soviet forces of crimes or offenses while executing official duties in areas of distribution of military units.

In cases specified in subpoints (a) and (b), the competent Soviet courts, procuracy, and other agencies shall act on the basis of Soviet legislation.

3. In the event of the commission of punishable acts against Soviet forces temporarily situated on the territory of the Czechoslovak Socialist Republic, as well as against persons serving [with Soviet forces], the persons guilty of such actions will bear the same responsibility as for punishable acts against the armed forces of the Czechoslovak Socialist Republic and persons serving [with Czechoslovak forces].

4. Competent Soviet and Czechoslovak agencies may mutually request each other

for transfer or acceptance of jurisdiction with respect to individual cases provided for in points 1 and 2 of the present Article. Such requests will be considered favorably.

5. Competent Soviet and Czechoslovak agencies will mutually render to each other legal and any kind of other assistance concerning questions of prosecuting punishable acts specified in points 1, 2, and 3 of the present Article.

Article 10. 1. The Government of the Union of Soviet Socialist Republics agrees to compensate the Government of the Czechoslovak Socialist Republic for the material damage which may be inflicted upon the Czechoslovak State by actions or omissions of Soviet military units or persons serving with them, as well as for the damage which may be inflicted by Soviet military units or persons serving with them while executing their official duties to Czechoslovak citizens, institutions, or citizens of third States situated on the territory of the Czechoslovak Socialist Republic – in both instances within amounts established (on the basis of submitted claims and with due account for provisions of Czechoslovak legislation) by Plenipotentiary representatives for the affairs of the temporary sojourn of Soviet forces in the Czechoslovak Socialist Republic, appointed in accordance with Article 13 of the present Treaty.

Disputes which might arise from the duties of Soviet military units are subject to consideration on the same grounds.

2. The Government of the Union of Soviet Socialist Republics also agrees to compensate the Government of the Czechoslovak Socialist Republic for damage which may be inflicted upon Czechoslovak institutions and citizens, as well as citizens of third States, situated on the territory of the Czechoslovak Socialist Republic, as a result of actions or omissions of persons serving with Soviet forces which were not committed while executing official duties, as well as a result of actions or omissions of members of the families of persons serving with Soviet forces – in both instances within amounts established by a competent Czechoslovak court on the basis

of claims made to persons who caused the damage.

Article 11. 1. The Government of the Czechoslovak Socialist Republic agrees to compensate the Government of the Union of Soviet Socialist Republics for damage which may be inflicted upon the property of Soviet military units temporarily situated on the territory of the Czechoslovak Socialist Republic or upon persons serving with Soviet forces by actions or omissions of Czechoslovak State institutions – in amounts established by Plenipotentiary representatives for the affairs of the temporary sojourn of Soviet forces in the Czechoslovak Socialist Republic on the basis of the submitted claims and taking into account Czechoslovak legislation.

Disputes which may arise from the duties of Czechoslovak institutions to Soviet military units are subject to consideration on the same grounds.

2. The Government of the Czechoslovak Socialist Republic also agrees to compensate the Government of the Union of Soviet Socialist Republics for damage which may be inflicted upon Soviet military units temporarily situated on the territory of the Czechoslovak Socialist Republic or persons serving with Soviet forces and members of their families by actions or omissions of Czechoslovak citizens – in amounts established by a Czechoslovak court on the basis of claims made to persons who caused the damage.

. . .

Translation by William E Butler, © American Society of International Law.

Treaty of Friendship, Cooperation and Mutual Aid between the Union of Soviet Socialist Republics and the Czechoslovak Socialist Republic, Prague, 6 May 1970

The Union of Soviet Socialist Republics and the Czechoslovak Socialist Republic,

Affirming their fidelity to the aims and principles of the Soviet–Czechoslovak Treaty of Friendship, Mutual Aid and Post-War Cooperation, concluded on December 12, 1943, and extended on November 27, 1963, a treaty that played a historic role in the development of friendly relations between the peoples of the two States and laid a solid foundation for the further strengthening of fraternal friendship and all-round cooperation between them;

Profoundly convinced that the indestructible friendship between the Union of Soviet Socialist Republics and the Czechoslovak Socialist Republic, which was cemented in the joint struggle against Fascism and has received further deepening in the years of the construction of socialism

and communism, as well as the fraternal mutual assistance and all-round cooperation between them, based on the teachings of Marxism-Leninism and the immutable principles of socialist internationalism, correspond to the fundamental interests of the peoples of both countries and of the entire socialist commonwealth;

Affirming that the support, strengthening and defence of the socialist gains achieved at the cost of the heroic efforts and selfless labour of each people are the common internationalist duty of the socialist countries;

Consistently and steadfastly favouring the strengthening of the unity and solidarity of all countries of the socialist commonwealth, based on the community of their social systems and ultimate goals;

Firmly resolved strictly to observe the

obligations stemming from the May 14, 1955, Warsaw Treaty of Friendship, Cooperation and Mutual Aid;

Stating the economic cooperation between the two States facilitates their development, as well as the further improvement of the international socialist division of labour and socialist economic integration within the framework of the Council for Mutual Economic Aid;

Expressing the firm intention to promote the cause of strengthening peace and security in Europe and throughout the world, to oppose imperialism, revanchism and militarism;

Guided by the goals and principles proclaimed in the United Nations Charter;

Taking into account the achievements of socialist and communist construction in the two countries, the present situation and the prospects for all-round cooperation, as well as the changes that have taken place in Europe and throughout the world since the conclusion of the Treaty of December 12, 1943;

Have agreed on the following:

Article 1. In accordance with the principles of socialist internationalism, the High Contracting Parties will continue to strengthen the eternal, indestructible friendship between the peoples of the Union of Soviet Socialist Republics and the Czechoslovak Socialist Republic, to develop all-round cooperation between the two countries and to give each other fraternal assistance and support, basing their actions on mutual respect for State sovereignty and independence, on equal rights and non-interference in one another's internal affairs.

Article 2. The High Contracting Parties will continue, proceeding from the principles of friendly mutual assistance and the international socialist division of labour, to develop and deepen mutually advantageous bilateral and multilateral economic, scientific and technical cooperation with the aim of developing their national economies, achieving the highest possible scientific and technical level and efficiency of social production, and increasing the material well-being of the working people of their countries.

The two sides will promote the further development of economic ties and cooperation and the socialist economic integration of the member countries of the Council for Mutual Economic Aid.

Article 3. The High Contracting Parties will continue to develop and expand cooperation between the two countries in the fields of science and culture, education, literature and the arts, the press, radio, motion pictures, television, public health, tourism and physical culture and in other fields.

Article 4. The High Contracting Parties will continue to facilitate the expansion of cooperation and direct ties between the bodies of State authority and the public organizations of the working people, with the aim of achieving a deeper mutual familiarization and a closer drawing together between the peoples of the two States.

Article 5. The High Contracting Parties, expressing their unswerving determination to proceed along the path of the construction of socialism and communism, will take the necessary steps to defend the socialist gains of the peoples and the security and independence of the two countries, will strive to develop all-round relations among the States of the socialist commonwealth, and will act in a spirit of the consolidation of the unity, friendship and fraternity of these States.

Article 6. The High Contracting Parties proceed from the assumption that the Munich Pact of September 29, 1938, was signed under the threat of aggressive war and the use of force against Czechoslovakia, that it was a component part of Hitler Germany's criminal conspiracy against peace and was a flagrant violation of the basic norms of international law, and hence was invalid from the very outset, with all the consequences stemming therefrom.

Article 7. The High Contracting Parties, consistently pursuing a policy of the peaceful coexistence of States with different social systems, will exert every effort for the defence of international peace and the security of the peoples against encroachments by the aggressive forces of imperialism and reaction, for the relaxation of international tension, the cessation of the arms race and the achievement of general and complete disarmament, the final liquidation of colonialism in all its forms and manifestations, and the giving of support to countries that have been liberated from colonial domination and are marching along the path of strengthening national independence and sovereignty.

Article 8. The High Contracting Parties will jointly strive to improve the situation and to ensure peace in Europe, to strengthen and develop cooperation among the European States, to establish good-neighbour relations among them and to create an effective system of European security on the basis of the collective efforts of all European States.

Article 9. The High Contracting Parties declare that one of the main preconditions for ensuring European security is the immutability of the State borders that were formed in Europe after the Second World War. They express their firm resolve, jointly with the other Member States of the May 14, 1955, Warsaw Treaty of Friendship, Cooperation and Mutual Aid and in accordance with this Treaty, to ensure the inviolability of the borders of the Member States of this Treaty and to take all necessary steps to prevent aggression on the part of any forces of militarism and revanchism and to rebuff the aggressor.

Article 10. In the event that one of the High Contracting Parties is subjected to an armed attack by any States or group of States, the other Contracting Party, regarding this as an attack against itself, will immediately give the first party all possible assistance, including military aid, and will also give it support with all means at its disposal, by way of implementing the right to individual or collective self-defence in accordance with Article 51 of the United Nations Charter.

The High Contracting Parties will without delay inform the United Nations Security Council of steps taken on the basis of this Article, and they will act in accordance with the provisions of the United Nations Charter.

Article 11. The High Contracting Parties will inform each other and consult on all important international questions affecting their interests and will act on the basis of common positions agreed upon in accordance with the interests of both States.

Article 12. The High Contracting Parties declare that their obligations under existing international treaties are not at variance with the provisions of this Treaty.

Article 13. This Treaty is subject to ratification and will enter into force on the day of the exchange of instruments of ratification, which will be conducted in Moscow in a very short time.

Article 14. This Treaty is concluded for a period of twenty years and will be automatically extended every five years thereafter, if neither of the High Contracting Parties gives notice that it is denouncing the Treaty twelve months before the expiration of the current period.

[Signed] L. BREZHNEV and A. KOSYGIN; G. HUSÁK and L. STROUGAL.

Soviet treaties in the Third World

Ever since the Baku Congress of Peoples of the East in September 1920, at which Zinoviev, the head of Comintern, proclaimed a 'holy people's war against the robbers and oppressors', communist Russia had posed as a champion of anti-colonial nationalism everywhere (save within its own borders). Until the end of the Second World War Soviet support for anti-colonial movements was largely confined to the realm of propaganda. In one notable instance, that of China in 1927, Comintern opposed a communist rising as 'opportunist'

With the emergence of the Soviet Union as a major actor on the international stage after 1945, rhetoric began to be translated more effectively into reality, as Stalin and his successors saw Soviet support for anti-imperialist liberation movements in Asia and Africa as a convenient weapon in the cold war. But although usually aligned with anti-colonial movements, the Soviet Union generally pursued a policy based primarily on the national interests of the Soviet state and only secondarily on consistent ideological premises. Thus in its policy towards China and Japan, the Soviet Union sought to restore or maintain Russian sovereignty over disputed border regions and initially promised support to the Chinese nationalists rather than their communist rivals. Similarly in the Middle East, the Soviet Union in the late 1940s supported Zionism (apparently in the hope of removing the British from Palestine) rather than its opponents, only later switching to support of Arab nationalist régimes. In its backing of Arab anti-western states in the Middle East, the Soviet Union often closed its eyes to the suppression by these states of their native communist parties.

THE SOVIET UNION AND CHINA

Concern for the security of the Soviet Union's frontier in Asia was a constant preoccupation of Soviet leaders. Stalin was seriously worried after 1931 by Japanese ascendancy in Manchuria, and armed conflicts occurred on the frontiers of Mongolia and Manchuria in 1939. But the growing European dangers led the Soviet Union to conciliate Japan, a new policy marked by the signature of the *Soviet–Japanese Neutrality Pact, 13 April 1941*. The Soviet Union ceased to aid nationalist China in resisting Japanese aggression. As the Germans advanced through Greece and Yugoslavia, Stalin sought security on his Asian frontiers through a policy of friendship with Japan, and signed the extensive *Soviet–Japanese Commercial Agreement, 11 June 1941*, providing for exchange of goods and reciprocal most-favoured-nation treatment. With the German attack on the Soviet Union on 22 June 1941, the Soviet Union first became Britain's ally in the war in Europe and later that of the Union States also. But Stalin did not extend the Grand Alliance to Asia where Britain and the United States were also allied with China in the war against Japan. Relations between China and the Soviet Union steadily deteriorated from June 1941 to the spring of 1945. By October 1943 nationalist China had forced Soviet influence out of the Chinese province of Sinkiang, where Stalin hoped to build up a strong economic base. The Soviet Union continued to pursue friendly relations with Japan and concluded another *Soviet–Japanese Agreement on 30 March 1944*, whereby Japan returned to Russia the oil and coal concession in northern Sakhalin which she had secured from Russia in 1925, and the Soviet Union renewed the Fisheries Convention and undertook to pay Japan an annual sum of 5 million roubles and to deliver 50,000 metric tons of oil.

At the *Yalta Conference in February 1945* (p. 267) a secret agreement was reached between Britain, the United States and the Soviet Union: the Soviet Union would enter the war against Japan two or three months after the surrender of Germany; the Soviet Union also promised to conclude an alliance with the government of China; in return the Soviet Union was to secure extensive rights in Chinese Manchuria similar to those Tsarist Russia had once enjoyed before the Russo-Japanese war of 1904–5. The agreement about Russian rights in China was made subject to Chiang Kai-shek's concurrence since he had not been consulted, but the President of the United States promised to 'take measures in order to obtain this concurrence on advice from Marshal Stalin'. The agreement was kept secret until February 1946, but Stalin's breach with Japan became public when on 5 April 1945 he unilaterally denounced the Russo–Japanese Neutrality Pact. On 8 August 1945 Russia declared war on Japan shortly after the atomic bomb had been dropped on Hiroshima.

The Soviet Union was at war only one week before the unconditional surrender of Japan on 14 August 1945. On the same day the *Soviet–Chinese Treaty of Alliance and Friendship, 14 August 1945,* was signed. The treaty had lost its purpose as a wartime alliance, but feats of a Japanese military revival remained strong in Asia for some time. For the Soviet Union the treaty gave her those rights in China promised at Yalta. The nationalist Chinese also valued the treaty, for in the summer of 1945 the government of Chiang Kai-shek was faced not only with the problem of regaining control over the Japanese-occupied regions of China, but also with the communist Chinese rival bid for power in north China; and a third difficulty was the con-tinued unrest and doubtful Chinese control of the province of Sinkiang. The treaty with the Soviet Union held out hope of support in all these problems. The Soviet Union undertook to pursue a friendly policy towards the nationalist Gov-ernment and to aid the nationalists alone (and not the communists); the treaty contained a Soviet recognition of sovereignty over all the regions of China occu-pied by Japan. Though extensive rights were granted to the Soviet Union, actual occupation of Chinese territory by Soviet troops was to last for a limited period of time and ostensibly Chinese sovereignty was not thereby diminished.

The Chinese nationalist government for their part in an exchange of notes agreed to recognize the independence of Outer Mongolia after the wishes of the Mongolian people had been tested. Formal Chinese recognition of Mongolian independence, and with it a renunciation of earlier suzerain claims, was accorded by the Chinese government on 5 January 1946; *on 27 February 1946 the Soviet Union and Outer Mongolia signed a treaty of friendship and mutual aid.* Mongolia was drawn securely into the Russian (as distinct from the Chinese) orbit by a trade treaty in 1957 and an economic assistance treaty in 1960. The *Mongolia– USSR Friendship Treaty, signed at Ulan Bator on 15 January 1966,* further consolidated Mongolia's position as a Soviet buffer state against China.

Meanwhile the Soviet relationship with China had passed through two major transformations. The first involved a Soviet switch in the late 1940s to support for the Chinese communists in their struggle against the government of Chiang Kai-shek. Despite the 1945 Sino–Soviet treaty, relations between the Soviet Union and nationalist China had soon become acrimonious. There were disputes over the delayed Soviet evacuation of northern China, over Soviet expropriation of Manchurian industry as war booty, and the nationalists charged that the Soviet Union was aiding the Chinese communists in violation of the 1945 treaty.

The victory of the Chinese communists in 1949 under Mao Zedong's leadership opened a new chapter in Sino–Soviet relations. In December 1949 Mao Zedong led a delegation to Moscow to negotiate another alliance treaty with the Soviet Union. A *Treaty of Friendship, Alliance and Mutual Assistance and a number of associated agreements were signed on 14 February 1950* (p. 413). The Sino–Soviet Alliance of 14 August 1945 was declared null and void, but Chinese recognition of the independence of Outer Mongolia was reaffirmed. The alliance was directed to resisting any renewed Japanese aggression and extended to any state collaborating with Japan. This reflected the new realities of the cold war and Soviet–American hostility. The Soviet Union also abandoned many of her rights in northern China acquired in 1945. The actual transfer of the Manchurian railway to China occurred in 1952 and of Port Arthur by 1955. The Soviet Union extended a credit to China and promised economic aid. Whilst the 1950 treaty changed the Sino–Soviet relationship, the Soviet Union continued to retain a privileged position in China and was the acknowledged leader of the communist world movement for the next decade. Until 1956 the Soviet Union and People's Republic of China acted in close collaboration internationally and domestically.

But from the late 1950s onwards a steadily widening rift became apparent between the two communist nations, with the Chinese refusing to acknowledge Soviet pre-eminence in the world communist movement and decrying the post-Stalin Soviet régime as 'revisionist'. In 1958 and 1959 the USSR would not provide nuclear assistance to China on terms acceptable to the Chinese leaders. In August 1960 Soviet technicians were withdrawn, an indication of how far Sino–Soviet relations had deteriorated. The Chinese denounced the efforts of the Soviet leader, Khrushchev, to improve relations with the United States in a new era of Soviet–United States 'peaceful co-existence'. The Chinese deeply resented Soviet military and economic aid to India which continued despite the Sino-Indian border conflict of 1962.

In March 1963 the Chinese publicly described the treaties signed by Imperial China with Tsarist Russia – the treaties of Aigun (1858), Peking (1860) and St Petersburg (1881) – as among the 'unequal treaties' imposed by imperialists on China. Mao Zedong added that they raised outstanding issues that ought to be settled by peaceful negotiation. The Soviet Union denied the Chinese claim challenging the Russian–Chinese frontiers settled by these treaties, but was ready to negotiate on specific points. These negotiations broke down in 1964.

The Sino-Soviet border can be divided into three sections: the Sinkiang sector running from the disputed frontier regions of the Pamirs where Afghanistan, Russia and Kashmir meet, northward to Mongolia; the Mongolian sector, strictly speaking not a Soviet frontier but the frontier between the Mongolian Republic (allied to the Soviet Union) and China; and thirdly, the Manchurian sector running in a great arc from the Mongolian frontier to North Korea, along the banks of the rivers Argun and Amur and down the Ussuri to Lake Khank.

Chinese efforts to place Sinkiang firmly under Chinese administration led to conflict with India in 1962. In the 1960s the Sino-Russian border on the Ili was the scene of many 'incidents'. The Chinese accused the Russians of 'unbridled subversive activities' in China's borderland among the non-Chinese minorities, about whose loyalty the Chinese were especially sensitive.

The independence of Outer Mongolia, recognized in the Sino–Soviet treaties of 1945 and 1950, continued to rankle with the Chinese. Despite these treaties Mao Zedong in July 1964 mentioned the question of Outer Mongolia as open to further discussion. On the other hand in 1962 a Sino-Mongolian boundary treaty was signed, and China made numerous territorial concessions to Mongolia.

The third section of the Sino-Russian frontier separates Manchuria from Russia. The Ussuri river and some islands in it became the scene of incidents culminating in violence in March 1969.

The Sino-Soviet frontier dispute appeared to be mainly a conflict of principle in the eyes of the Chinese, who demanded from the Soviet Union an admission that the 'unequal' treaties were not valid and that only freely negotiated treaties between the USSR and China could be made valid. The Soviet claim to these frontiers was based on orthodox international law relating to the validity of treaties (the USSR being happy, for these purposes, to claim rights of succession to the Tsarist empire), and to the Russian period of possession and effective occupation.

But in the last resort the frontier differences were more a symptom than a cause of the conflict. China's explosion of an atom bomb in 1964 and of a hydrogen bomb in 1967 intensified the Chinese determination to gain recognition as an independent communist power. Meanwhile the period of 'cultural revolution' in China in the late 1960s accentuated the radical elements in Chinese communism.

Sino-Soviet talks in the years after 1969 failed to produce a resolution of the border issue. The *rapprochement* between China and the United States in the 1970s (see p. 649) brought a new – and to the Russians, ominous – element into Sino–Soviet relations. Nevertheless, after the death of Mao Zedong in 1976, and particularly after the accession to effective power in the late 1970s of the pragmatic wing of the Chinese communist party, associated with Deng Xiao-ping, some signs of improvement in the atmosphere became evident. Although there was no sudden healing of the breach, the stridency of Chinese anti-Soviet rhetoric of the 1960s was replaced by a more cautious approach. Symptomatic of the new mood were the *Chinese–Soviet Economic Cooperation Agreement, 28 December 1984* and the *Chinese–Soviet Scientific Cooperation Agreement, 28 December 1984*. These were followed by the *Chinese–Soviet Agreement on Economic and Technical Cooperation, 10 July 1985*.

The Soviet Union and Asia

Elsewhere in Asia the Soviet Union found several opportunities after the Second World War to broaden its influence. In North Korea, occupied by Soviet forces until September 1948, a communist régime was established under the leadership of a Korean-born Soviet army officer, Kim Il-sung. After the Korean War the country remained securely in the communist orbit, without, however, taking sides in the Sino-Soviet quarrel. A *Treaty of Friendship between the Soviet Union and North Korea was signed on 6 July 1961*. This was balanced by a similar *Chinese–North Korean Treaty, 11 July 1961*. North Korea signed trade agreements with both of its communist neighbours.

In Vietnam the Soviet Union gave support to the forces under Ho Chi Minh who declared an independent republic in September 1945. A bitter war between Ho's communists and the French army ended in defeat for the French and their recognition, in the Geneva Agreements of 1954 (p. 616), that their colonial rule in the country was at an end. *The USSR signed Economic Aid Agreements with North Vietnam in 1965 and 1966*. Following the communist victory in the Vietnam war (p. 614), a *Treaty of Friendship and Cooperation between Vietnam and the Soviet Union was signed on 3 November 1978* (p. 420). The next month Vietnamese forces attacked Cambodia, occupied the country, and installed a puppet régime. In this conflict, and in associated military encounters between Vietnamese and Chinese forces, the Soviet Union gave strong diplomatic support to the Vietnamese.

India, from independence in 1947 onwards, pursued a policy of nonalignment with either bloc in the East–West conflict. But in the course of the 1960s, as a result of her wars with China and with Pakistan (see p. 596), India moved closer towards the Soviet Union. The *Soviet Union and India signed a Treaty of Peace, Friendship and Cooperation on 9 August 1971* (p. 418). This treaty strengthened India's hand in its confrontation with Pakistan. The terms of the treaty were 'negative' in character. The two signatories undertook not to join any military alliances directed against each other (Article 8), and not to provide assistance to any other state engaged in armed conflict with one of the signatories, but immediately to consult with each other if one of the signatories was attacked or under threat of attack (Article 9). The treaty thus fell short of constituting a full-fledged alliance, since neither signatory was committed to come to the aid of its treaty partner.

During much of the nineteenth and early twentieth centuries the rugged mountain country of Afghanistan had served as a buffer between the Russian empire and the British empire in India. From 1953 onwards Afghanistan received Soviet economic aid, but the country was not drawn into the Soviet political orbit. In 1979, however, the Soviet Union seized the opportunity of internal chaos in neighbouring Iran and allowed itself to be sucked into the murderous internal politics of Afghanistan. *On 5 December 1978 the Soviet Union and Afghanistan signed a Treaty of Friendship, Goodneighbourliness and Cooperation* (p. 421). Article 1 of this treaty contained a declaration of respect for each other's national sovereignty, territorial integrity and non-interference in each other's internal affairs. Nevertheless, in December 1979 the Soviet Union intervened in Afghanistan in massive military force in support of a pro-Moscow faction. A statement was issued, allegedly in the name of the Afghan government, declaring that military assistance had been requested from the USSR 'proceeding from the December 5, 1978 Treaty'. Soviet involvement in the ensuing civil war inflicted large-scale casualties, produced a horde of millions of refugees who fled to Pakistan, and gravely complicated the Soviet Union's relations with Islamic and Third World countries. But in the course of the early 1980s the Soviet forces resolutely ground down American-backed resistance and attempted to recast the institutions of the country in the familiar Soviet mould.

SOVIET TREATY RELATIONS IN THE MIDDLE East

Before 1955 most of the states of the Middle East viewed the Soviet Union with hostility, and several of them entered defensive alliances with the United States or Britain (see Chapters XIII and XXI). In 1947 and 1948 the Soviet Union gave strong support to the Zionists in Palestine, facilitating the supply of arms to the nascent Jewish state by Czechoslovakia, and racing with the USA to be the first major power to recognize Israel in May 1948. But from the early 1950s the Soviet Union pursued a policy more favourable to Israel's Arab opponents, hoping thereby to undermine the influence of western powers in the region. The Suez crisis of 1956 (p. 719) provided the USSR with its first major opportunity in the area. Egypt became the focal point of Soviet efforts. In September 1955 an agreement was concluded for Czechoslovak arms supplies to Egypt. When the USA thereupon cancelled plans for American financial assistance in the building of the Aswan High Dam, the Soviet Union stepped into the breach. Soviet experts were sent to Egypt, and the dam, built mainly with Soviet equipment and funds, was constructed in the course of the 1960s. The USSR became a major arms supplier to Egypt, particularly after the 'Six Day War' of 1967. During the years

1967–71 Soviet influence in Egypt reached its apogee, and in the 'War of Attrition' between Israel and Egypt in 1969–70, some Soviet pilots and planes took an active part in combat. The *Soviet–Egyptian Treaty of Friendship, 27 May 1971* (p. 416) marked the high point of the relationship. But thereafter relations began to cool, as the Egyptians became restive with what was seen as Soviet domination; over the next few years, under the leadership of President Sadat, the Egyptians undertook a daring switch of alliances from the Soviet Union to the USA (see p. 379).

Elsewhere in the Arab world the Soviet Union succeeded in winning friends in several countries. *A Soviet–Iraqi Treaty of Friendship was signed on 9 April 1972.* Iraq became one of the Soviet Union's closest followers in the region, and the USSR provided Iraq with considerable help in its war with Iran in the early 1980s. Although Syria was at loggerheads with Iraq during much of the 1960s and 1970s, the USSR managed to cultivate good relations with both countries. Syria too became heavily dependent on Soviet military equipment. A *Treaty of Friendship between the Soviet Union and Syria was signed on 8 October 1980.* While most of the Arabian peninsula remained strongly in the western camp (Saudi Arabia did not even have diplomatic relations with the USSR until 1991), an exception was the South Yemen which achieved independence from Britain upon the British withdrawal from Aden on 29 November 1967.

After bitter internal conflict a Marxist state was established in 1969. On *25 October 1979 the Soviet Union and South Yemen signed a Treaty of Friendship.* Meanwhile South Yemen sponsored a guerrilla war against its neighbour, North Yemen. Tension between the two countries remained high until 1989 when a draft unity constitution was agreed, although effective unity was not achieved until after a civil war in 1994.

SOVIET TREATY RELATIONS IN AFRICA

Soviet involvement in independent Africa was at first a relatively minor aspect of Soviet diplomacy, but strong Soviet support (including arms supplies, training, propaganda and diplomatic aid) for anti-colonial liberation movements in the continent eventually reaped considerable rewards. After the independence of Ghana in 1957 (see p. 669), the country established good relations with the USSR, although these deteriorated after the fall of President Kwame Nkrumah in 1966. In north Africa the USSR found its most erratic partner in President Qadhafi of Libya, who seized power in 1969. It also developed cordial relations with Algeria; a string of agreements for the expansion of trade and for Soviet military equipment failed, however, to turn Algeria into a reliable ally of the USSR.

The conflicts in the Horn of Africa afforded the Soviet Union more fruitful opportunities. A *Soviet–Somali Friendship Treaty was signed on 11 July 1974*, but when war broke out in 1977 between the Somalis and Ethiopia, the Soviet Union backed Ethiopia, whereupon the Somalis terminated the treaty. *On 20 November 1978 the Soviet Union signed a Friendship Treaty with Ethiopia.*

Elsewhere in Africa Russian courtship found many countries willing to be wooed, but few ready to tie the knot on a permanent basis. In the early stages of the Congo imbroglio (see p. 670) the Soviet Union seemed to have found a protégé in the country's first prime minister, Patrice Lumumba; but under the military government which soon took control the country (later known as Zaire) slid towards the western camp.

The USSR's most important diplomatic gains were in southern Africa, where its strong support of the liberation movements in the Portuguese colonies of Mozambique and Angola paid off after independence in the form of close relations which found formal expression in *Treaties of Friendship between the Soviet Union and Angola, 8 October 1976 and between the Soviet Union and Mozambique, 31 March 1977.*

In the struggle for power inside South Africa, the Soviet Union supported the African National Congress, originally a non-communist organization, and in the 1980s began to supply arms to guerrillas operating in South-West Africa (Namibia) and across the South African borders. But here (as in the case of the Palestine Liberation Organization to which the USSR gave similar diplomatic and other aid) the relationship remained a marriage more of convenience than of conviction, with the recipients maintaining an ideological stance distinct from that of Moscow.

Strange to relate, one of the Soviet Union's most reliable allies in Africa was not an African state at all but Cuba, communist and pro-Soviet since 1961, which in the 1970s sent military aid, including large numbers of troops, to Angola as well as other African states. These efforts in support of Soviet clients were repaid by massive economic aid by the Soviet Union to Cuba. Cuba was, in effect, transformed into a Soviet economic satellite, and indeed became a member of Comecon in 1972. Meanwhile Cuba had developed into the USSR's only long-term ally in the Americans, although after the Cuban missile crisis of October 1962 the Soviet Union moved with some circumspection. Soviet influence in Cuba remained paramount in the 1970s and early 1980s, but the details of Soviet–Cuban relations in military and security matters were not given publicity in the form of an open treaty.

Treaty of Friendship, Alliance and Mutual Assistance between the People's Republic of China and the Soviet Union, Moscow, 14 February 1950

The Central People's Government of the People's Republic of China and the Presidium of the Supreme Soviet of the Union of Soviet Socialist Republics, fully determined to prevent jointly, by strengthening friendship and cooperation between the People's Republic of China and the Union of Soviet Socialist Republics, the revival of Japanese imperialism and the resumption of aggression on the part of Japan or any other State that may collaborate in any way with Japan in acts of aggression; imbued with the desire to consolidate lasting peace and universal security in the Far East and throughout the world in conformity with the aims and principles of the United Nations; profoundly convinced that the consolidation of good neighbourly relations and friendship between the People's Republic of China and the Union of Soviet Socialist Republics meets the vital interests of the peoples of China and the Soviet Union, have towards this end decided to conclude the present Treaty and have appointed as their plenipotentiary representatives: Chou En-lai, Premier of the Government Administration Council and Minister of Foreign Affairs, acting for the Central People's Government of the People's Republic of China; and Andrei Yanuaryevich Vyshinsky, Minister of Foreign Affairs of the USSR , acting for the Presidium of the Supreme Soviet of the Union of Soviet Socialist Republics. Both plenipotentiary representatives having communicated their full powers found them in good and due form, have agreed upon the following:

Article 1. Both Contracting Parties undertake jointly to adopt all necessary measures at their disposal for the purpose of preventing the resumption of aggression and violation of peace on the part of Japan or any other State that may collaborate with Japan directly or indirectly in acts of aggression. In the event of one of the Contracting Parties being attacked by Japan or any State allied with her and thus being involved in a state of war, the other Contracting Party shall immediately render military and other assistance by all means at its disposal.

The Contracting Parties also declare their readiness to participate in a spirit of sincere cooperation in all international actions aimed at ensuring peace and security throughout the world and to contribute their full share to the earliest implementation of these tasks.

Article 2. Both Contracting Parties undertake in a spirit of mutual agreement to bring about the earliest conclusion of a peace treaty with Japan jointly with other Powers which were allies in the Second World War.

Article 3. Each Contracting Party undertakes not to conclude any alliance directed against the other Contracting Party and not to take part in any coalition or in any actions or measures directed against the other Contracting Party.

Article 4. Both Contracting Parties, in the interests of consolidating peace and universal security, will consult with each other in regard to all important international problems affecting the common interests of China and the Soviet Union.

Article 5. Each Contracting Party undertakes, in a spirit of friendship and cooperation and in conformity with the principles of equality, mutual benefit and mutual respect for the national sovereignty and territorial integrity and non-interference in the internal affairs of the other Contracting Party, to develop and consolidate economic and cultural ties between China and the Soviet Union, to render the other all possible economic assistance and to carry out necessary economic cooperation.

Article 6. The present Treaty shall come into force immediately after its ratification; the exchange of instruments of ratification shall take place in Peking.

The present Treaty shall be valid for thirty years. If neither of the Contracting Parties gives notice a year before the expiration of this term of its intention to denounce the Treaty, it shall remain in force for another five years and shall be further extended in compliance with this provision.

Done in Moscow on 14 February 1950, in two copies, each in the Chinese and Russian languages, both texts being equally valid.

On the authorization of the Central People's Government of the People's Republic of China
CHOU EN-LAI

On the authorization of the Presidium of the Supreme Soviet of the Union of Soviet Socialist Republics
A. Y. VYSHINSKY

Agreement between the People's Republic of China and the Union of Soviet Socialist Republics on the Chinese Changchun Railway, Port Arthur and Dairen

The Central People's Government of the People's Republic of China and the Presidium of the Supreme Soviet of the Union of Soviet Socialist Republics record that since 1945, fundamental changes have occurred in the situation in the Far East, namely: imperialist Japan has suffered defeat; the reactionary Kuomintang Government has been overthrown; China has become a People's Democratic Republic; a new People's Government has been established in China which has unified the whole of China, has carried out a policy of friendship and cooperation with the Soviet Union and has proved its ability to defend the national independence and territorial integrity of China and the national honour and dignity of the Chinese people.

The Central People's Government of the People's Republic of China and the Presidium of the Supreme Soviet of the Union of Soviet Socialist Republics consider that this new situation permits a new approach to the question of the Chinese Changchun Railway, Port Arthur and Dairen.

In conformity with these new circumstances the Central People's Government of the People's Republic of China and the Presidium of the Supreme Soviet of the Union of Soviet Socialist Republics have decided to conclude the present Agreement on the Chinese Changchun Railway, Port Arthur and Dairen:

Article 1. Both Contracting Parties agree that the Soviet Government transfer without compensation to the Government of the People's Republic of China all its rights to joint administration of the Chinese Changchun Railway with all the property belonging to the Railway. The transfer shall be effected immediately after the conclusion of a peace treaty with Japan, but not later than the end of 1952.

Pending the transfer, the existing Sino-Soviet joint administration of the Chinese Changchun Railway shall remain unchanged. After this Agreement becomes effective, posts (such as manager of the Railway, chairman of the Central Board, etc.) will be periodically alternated between representatives of China and the USSR

As regards concrete methods of effecting the transfer, they shall be agreed upon and determined by the Governments of both Contracting Parties.

Article 2. Both Contracting Parties agree that Soviet troops be withdrawn from the jointly utilized naval base Port Arthur, and that the installations in this area be handed over to the Government of the People's Republic of China immediately on the conclusion of a peace treaty with Japan, but not later than the end of 1952. The Government of the People's Republic of China will compensate the Soviet Union for expenses which it has incurred in restoring and constructing installations since 1945.

For the period pending the withdrawal of Soviet troops and the transfer of the above-mentioned installations the Governments of China and the Soviet Union will each appoint an equal number of military representatives to form a joint Chinese-Soviet Military Commission which will be alternately presided over by each side and which will be in charge of military affairs in the area of Port Arthur; concrete measures in this sphere will be drawn up by the joint Chinese-Soviet Military Commission within three months after the present Agreement becomes effective and shall be put into force upon approval of these measures by the Governments of both countries.

The civil administration in the aforementioned area shall be under the direct authority of the Government of the People's Republic of China. Pending the withdrawal of Soviet troops, the zone for billeting Soviet troops in the area of Port Arthur will remain unaltered in conformity with existing frontiers.

In the event of either of the Contracting Parties becoming the victim of aggression on the part of Japan or any State that may collaborate with Japan, and as a result thereof becoming involved in hostilities, China and the Soviet Union may, on the proposal of the Government of the People's Republic of China and with the agreement of the Government of the USSR, jointly use the naval base Port Arthur for the purpose of conducting joint military operations against the aggressor.

Article 3. Both Contracting Parties agree that the question of Dairen harbour be further considered on the conclusion of a peace treaty with Japan. As regards the administration of Dairen, it is in the hands of the Government of the People's Republic of China. All the property in Dairen now temporarily administered by or leased to the Soviet Union, shall be taken over by the Government of the People's Republic of China. To carry out the transfer of the aforementioned property, the Governments of China and the Soviet Union shall appoint three representatives each to form a Joint Commission which, within three months after the present Agreement comes into effect, shall draw up concrete measures for the transfer of the property; and these measures shall be fully carried out in the course of 1950 after their approval by the Governments of both countries upon the proposal of the Joint Commission.

[*Article 4.* Ratification.]

Agreement between the Central People's Government of the People's Republic of China and the Government of the Union of Soviet Socialist Republics on the granting of credit to the People's Republic of China

In connection with the consent of the Government of the Union of Soviet Socialist Republics to grant the request of the Central People's Government of the People's Republic of China for a credit to pay for the equipment and other materials which the Soviet Union has agreed to deliver to China, both Governments have agreed upon the following:

Article 1. The Government of the Union of Soviet Socialist Republics grants to the Central People's Government of the People's Republic of China a credit which in terms of American dollars, amounts to U.S.$300,000,000, taking 35 American dollars to one ounce of fine gold.

In view of the extraordinary devastation of China as a result of prolonged hostilities on its territory, the Soviet Government has agreed to grant the credit at the favourable rate of interest of 1 per cent per annum.

. . .

Article 3. The Central People's Government of the People's Republic of China shall repay the credit mentioned in Article 1, together with the interest thereon, in deliveries of raw materials, tea, gold and American dollars. Prices for raw materials and tea and their quantities and dates of delivery shall be determined by special agreement, with prices to be determined on the basis of prices on the world markets.

The credit shall be repaid in ten equal annual instalments . . .

[In the communiqué issued at the time of the signature of the treaty the following statements were made.]

. . .

In connection with the signing of the Treaty of Friendship, Alliance and Mutual Assistance, and the Agreement on the Chinese Changchun Railway, Port Arthur and Dairen, Chou En-lai, Premier and Minister of Foreign Affairs, and A.Y. Vyshinsky, Minister of Foreign Affairs, exchanged notes to the effect that the respective Treaty and Agreements concluded on August 14, 1945, between China and the Soviet Union are now null and void, and also that both Governments affirm that the independent status of the Mongolian People's Republic is fully guaranteed as a result of the plebiscite of 1945 and the establishment with it of diplomatic relations by the People's Republic of China.

At the same time, A.Y. Vyshinsky, Minister of Foreign Affairs, and Chou En-lai, Premier and Minister of Foreign Affairs, also exchanged notes on the decision of the Soviet Government to transfer without compensation to the Government of the People's Republic of China the property acquired in Manchuria from Japanese owners by Soviet economic organizations, and also on the decision of the Soviet Government to transfer without compensation to the Government of the People's Republic of China all the buildings in the former military compound in Peking . . .

Soviet–Egyptian Treaty of Friendship and Cooperation, Cairo, 27 May 1971

The Union of Soviet Socialist Republics and the United Arab Republic,

Being firmly convinced that the further development of friendship and all-round cooperation between the Union of Soviet Socialist Republics and the United Arab Republic is responsive to the interests of the peoples of both States and serves the cause of strengthening universal peace,

Being inspired by the ideals of the struggle against imperialism and colonialism, and for the freedom, independence and social progress of peoples,

Being determined to wage persistently the struggle for the consolidation of international peace and security in accordance with the invariable course of their peace-loving foreign policies,

Reaffirming their loyalty to the aims and principles of the United Nations Charter,

And being motivated by the aspiration to strengthen and consolidate the traditional relations of sincere friendship between the two States and peoples by concluding a Treaty on Friendship and Cooperation and thus creating a basis for their further development,

Have agreed on the following:

Article 1. The high contracting parties sol-

emnly declare that unbreakable friendship will always exist between the two countries and their peoples. They will continue to develop and strengthen the existing relations of friendship and all-round cooperation between them in the political, economic, scientific, technological, cultural and other fields on the basis of the principles of respect for sovereignty, territorial integrity, non-interference in one another's internal affairs, equality and mutual benefit.

Article 2. The Union of Soviet Socialist Republics, as a socialist State, and the United Arab Republic, which has set itself the aim of the socialist reconstruction of society, will cooperate closely and in all fields in ensuring conditions for preserving and further developing the social and economic gains of their peoples.

Article 3. Guided by the aspiration to promote in every way the maintenance of international peace and the security of peoples, the Union of Soviet Socialist Republics and the United Arab Republic will continue with the utmost determination to exert efforts toward achieving and ensuring a lasting and just peace in the Middle East in accordance with the aims and principles of the United Nations Charter.

In conducting a peace-loving foreign policy, the high contracting parties will come out in favor of peace, the relaxation of international tension, the achieving of general and complete disarmament and the prohibition of nuclear and other types of weapons of mass destruction.

Article 4. Guided by the ideals of the freedom and equality of all peoples, the high contracting parties condemn imperialism and colonialism in all their forms and manifestations. They will continue to come out against imperialism and for the complete and final liquidation of colonialism in pursuance of the U.N. Declaration on the Granting of Independence to All Colonial Countries and Peoples, and will wage an unswerving struggle against racism and apartheid.

Article 5. The high contracting parties also will continue to expand and deepen all-round cooperation and the exchange of experience in the economic, scientific and technological fields – in industry, agriculture, water conservation, irrigation, the development of natural resources, the development of power engineering, the training of national cadres, and other branches of the economy.

The two sides will expand trade and maritime shipping between the two States on the basis of the principles of mutual benefit and most-favored-nation treatment.

Article 6. The high contracting parties will promote further cooperation between them in the fields of science, the arts, literature, education, public health, the press, radio, television, cinema, tourism, physical education, and other fields.

The parties will promote wider cooperation and direct contacts between political and social organizations of the working people, enterprises and cultural and scientific institutions for the purpose of achieving a deeper mutual acquaintance with the life, work and achievements of the peoples of the two countries.

Article 7. Being deeply interested in ensuring peace and the security of peoples and attaching great importance to the concerted nature of their actions in the international arena in the struggle for peace, the high contracting parties will, for this purpose, regularly consult each other at various levels on all important questions affecting the interests of both States.

In the event of situations arising which, in the opinion of both sides, create a danger to peace or a breach of peace, they will contact each other without delay in order to concert their positions with a view to removing the threat that has arisen or restoring peace.

Article 8. In the interests of strengthening the defense capability of the United Arab Republic, the high contracting parties will continue to develop cooperation in the military field on the basis of appropriate agreements between them. Such cooperation will provide, in particular, for assistance in the training of U.A.R. military personnel and in mastering the armaments and equipment supplied to the United Arab Republic for the purpose of strengthening its capability in the cause of eliminating the consequences of aggression as well as increasing its ability to stand up to aggression in general.

Article 9. Proceeding from the purposes and principles of this Treaty,

Each of the high contracting parties states that it will not enter into alliances or take part in any groupings of States, or in actions or measures directed against the other high contracting party.

Article 10. Each of the high contracting parties declares that its obligations under existing international treaties are not in contradiction with the provisions of this Treaty and it undertakes not to enter into any international agreements incompatible with it.

Article 11. The present Treaty shall be valid for 15 years from the day it enters into force.

If neither of the high contracting parties announces, a year before the expiry of this term, its desire to terminate the Treaty, it shall remain in force for the next five years and so henceforward, until one of the high contracting parties, a year before the expiry of the current five-year period, gives a written warning of its intention to terminate its validity.

Article 12. The present Treaty is subject to ratification and shall enter into force on the day of the exchange of the instruments of ratification, which will take place in Moscow in the very near future.

The present Treaty is done in two copies, each in Russian and Arabic, both texts being equally authentic.

DONE in the city of Cairo on May 27, 1971, which corresponds to 3 Rabia as-Sani, 1391, Hidjra.

[For the Union of Soviet Socialist Republics]
N. Podgornyi

[For the United Arab Republic]
Anwar Sadat

Translation by William E. Butler, © American Society of International Law.

Treaty of Peace, Friendship and Cooperation between India and the Soviet Union, New Delhi, 9 August 1971

Desirous of expanding and consolidating the existing relations of sincere friendship between them,

Believing that further development of friendship and cooperation meets the basic national interests of both States as well as the interests of lasting peace in Asia and the World,

Determined to promote the consolidation of universal peace and security and to make steadfast efforts for the relaxation of international tensions and final elimination of the remnants of colonialism,

Upholding their firm faith in the principles of peaceful coexistence and cooperation between States with different political and social systems,

Convinced that in the world today international problems can only be solved by cooperation and not by conflict,

Reaffirming their determination to abide by the purposes and the principles of the United Nations Charter,

The Republic of India on one side and the Union of Soviet Socialist Republics on the other side, have decided to conclude the present Treaty, for which purpose the following plenipotentiaries have been appointed:

[On behalf of the Republic of India]
Sardar Swaran Singh, Minister of External Affairs.

[On behalf of the Union of Soviet Socialist Republics]
Mr. A. Gromyko, Minister of Foreign Affairs,

who having each presented their credentials, which are found to be in proper form and due order, have agreed as follows.

Article 1. The High Contracting Parties solemnly declare that enduring peace and friendship shall prevail between the two countries and their peoples. Each Party shall respect the independence, sovereignty and territorial integrity of the other Party and refrain from interfering in the other's internal affairs. The High Contracting Parties shall continue to develop and consolidate relations of sincere friendship, good neighbourliness and comprehensive cooperation existing between them on the basis of the aforesaid principles as well as those of equality and mutual benefit.

Article 2. Guided by a desire to contribute in every possible way to ensure an enduring peace and security of their people, the

High Contracting Parties declare their determination to continue their efforts to preserve and to strengthen peace in Asia and throughout the world, to halt the arms race and to achieve a general and complete disarmament, including both nuclear and conventional, under effective international control.

Article 3. Guided by their loyalty to the lofty ideal of equality of all peoples and nations, irrespective of race or creed, the High Contracting Parties condemn colonialism and racialism in all forms and manifestations and reaffirm their determination to strive for their final and complete elimination.

The High Contracting Parties shall cooperate with other States to achieve these aims and to support just aspirations of the peoples in their struggle against colonialism and racial domination.

Article 4. The Republic of India respects the peace-loving policy of the Union of Soviet Socialist Republics aimed at strengthening friendship and cooperation with all nations.

The Union of Soviet Socialist Republics respects India's policy of non-alignment and reaffirms that this policy constitutes an important factor in the maintenance of universal peace and international security and in lessening of tensions in the world.

Article 5. Deeply interested in ensuring universal peace and security, attaching great importance to their mutual cooperation in the international field for achieving these aims, the High Contracting Parties will maintain regular contacts with each other on major international problems affecting the interests of both States by means of meetings and exchanges of views between their leading statesmen, visits by official delegations and special envoys of the two Governments and through diplomatic channels.

. . .

[*Article 6*. Expansion of trade relations etc.

Article 7. Expansion of scientific and cultural relations etc.]

Article 8. In accordance with the traditional friendship established between the two countries, each of the High Contracting Parties solemnly declares that it shall not enter into or participate in any military alliance directed against the other Party.

Each High Contracting Party undertakes to abstain from any aggression against the other Party and to prevent the use of its territory for the commission of any act which might inflict military damage on the other High Contracting Party.

Article 9. Each High Contracting Party undertakes to abstain from providing any assistance to any third party that engages in armed conflict with the other Party. In the event of either Party being subjected to an attack or a threat thereof, the High Contracting Parties shall immediately enter into mutual consultations in order to remove such a threat and to take appropriate effective measures to ensure peace and security of their countries.

Article 10. Each High Contracting Party solemnly declares that it shall not enter into any obligation secret or public with one or more States which is incompatible with this Treaty. Each High Contracting Party further declares that no obligation exists nor shall any obligation be entered into between itself and any other State or States which might cause military damage to the other Party.

Article 11. This Treaty is concluded for a duration of twenty years and will be automatically extended for each successive period of five years unless either High Contracting Party declares its desire to terminate it by giving a notice to the other High Contracting Party twelve months prior to expiration of the Treaty. The Treaty will be subject to ratification and will come into force on the date of exchange of Instruments of Ratification which will take place in Moscow within one month of the signing of this Treaty.

. . .

Treaty of Friendship and Cooperation between the Soviet Union and Vietnam, Moscow, 3 November 1978

The Socialist Republic of Viet Nam and the Union of Soviet Socialist Republics,

Proceeding from the close cooperation in all fields in a fraternal spirit, from the unshakable friendship and solidarity between the two countries on the basis of the principles of Marxism–Leninism and socialist internationalism,

Firmly convinced that the endeavour to consolidate the solidarity and friendship between the Socialist Republic of Viet Nam and the Union of Soviet Socialist Republics is in conformity with the basic interests of the two peoples and in the interests of the consolidation of the fraternal friendship and one-mindedness among the countries in the socialist community,

In keeping with the principles and objectives of the socialist foreign policy and the desire to ensure the most favourable international conditions for the building of socialism and communism,

Confirming that the signatories to the Treaty acknowledge their international obligation to assist each other in the consolidation and preservation of the socialist achievements recorded by the two peoples through their heroic efforts and selfless labour,

Determined to work for the unity of all forces struggling for peace, national independence, democracy and social progress,

Expressing their iron-like determination to contribute to the consolidation of peace in Asia and throughout the world, and to the development of good relations and mutually beneficial cooperation among countries with different social systems,

Hoping to develop further and perfect the all-round cooperation between the two countries,

Attaching importance to the continued development and consolidation of the juridical basis of the bilateral relations,

In keeping with the objectives and principles of the United Nations Charter,

Have resolved to sign this Treaty of Friendship and Cooperation and have agreed as follows:

Article 1. In keeping with the principles of socialist internationalism, the two parties signatory to the present Treaty shall continue to consolidate the unshakable friendship and solidarity and assist each other in a fraternal spirit. The two parties shall unceasingly develop political relations and cooperation in all fields and endeavour to assist each other on the basis of respect for each other's national independence and sovereignty, equality and non-interference in each other's internal affairs.

Article 2. The two parties signatory to the present Treaty shall join efforts to consolidate and broaden the mutually beneficial cooperation in the economic and scientific–technological fields in order to push forward the building of socialism and communism and to raise constantly the material and cultural standards of the two peoples. The two parties shall continue to coordinate their long-term national economic plans, agree upon long-term measures aimed at developing the most important sectors of the economy, science and technology, and exchange knowledge and experience accumulated in the building of socialism and communism.

Article 3. The two parties signatory to the Treaty shall promote cooperation between their State bodies and mass organizations, and develop broad relations in the fields of science and culture, education, literature and art, press, broadcasting and television, health service, environmental protection, tourism, sports and physical training and others. The two parties shall encourage the development of contacts between the working people of the two countries.

Article 4. The two parties signatory to the Treaty shall consistently strive further to consolidate their fraternal relations, and to strengthen the solidarity and one-mindedness among the socialist countries on the basis of Marxism–Leninism and socialist internationalism.

The two parties shall do their utmost to consolidate the world socialist system and actively contribute to the development and defence of the socialist gains.

Article 5. The two parties signatory to the Treaty shall continue doing their utmost to contribute to defending world peace and the security of all nations. They shall actively oppose all schemes and manoeuvres of imperialism and reactionary forces, support the just struggle for the complete eradication of all forms and colours of colonialism and racism, support the struggle waged by non-aligned countries and the peoples of Asian, African and Latin American countries against imperialism, colonialism and neo-colonialism, for the consolidation of independence and the defence of sovereignty, for mastery over their natural resources, and for the establishment of a new world economic relationship with no inequity, oppression and exploitation, and support the aspirations of the Southeast Asian peoples for peace, independence and cooperation among countries in this region.

The two parties shall strive to develop the relations between countries with different social systems on the basis of the principles of peaceful coexistence, for the purpose of broadening and consolidating the process of easing tension in international relations and radically eliminating aggressions and wars of aggression from the life of all nations, for the sake of peace, national independence, democracy and socialism.

Article 6. The two parties signatory to the Treaty shall exchange views on all important international questions relating to the interests of the two countries. In case either party is attacked or threatened with attack, the two parties signatory to the Treaty shall immediately consult each other with a view to eliminating that threat, and shall take appropriate and effective measures to safeguard peace and the security of the two countries.

Article 7. The present Treaty does not concern the two parties' rights and obligations stemming from the bilateral or multilateral agreements to which they are signatories and is not intended to oppose any third country.

Article 8. The present Treaty shall be ratified and shall enter into force on the date of the exchange of instruments of ratification, which shall take place in Ha Noi as early as possible.

Article 9. The present Treaty shall remain in force for 25 years and thereafter shall be automatically extended for periods of 10 years if neither signatory party declares its desire to terminate the present Treaty by informing the other party 12 months before the Treaty expires.

Done in duplicate in the Vietnamese and Russian languages, both texts being equally authentic, in Moscow, this third day of November 1978.

FOR THE SOCIALIST REPUBLIC OF VIETNAM:
[Signed] Le Duan
      Pham Van Dong

FOR THE UNION OF SOVIET SOCIALIST REPUBLICS:
[Signed] L.I. Brezhnev
      A.N. Kosygin

Treaty of Friendship, Goodneighbourliness and Cooperation between the Soviet Union and Afghanistan, Moscow, 5 December 1978

The Union of Soviet Socialist Republics and
The Democratic Republic of Afghanistan,

Reaffirming their commitment to the aims and principles of the Soviet–Afghan Treaties of 1921 and 1931, which laid the basis for friendly and good neighbour relations between the Soviet and Afghan peoples and which meet their basic national interests,

Willing to strengthen in every way friendship and all-round cooperation between the two countries,

Being determined to develop social and economic achievements of the Soviet and Afghan peoples, to safeguard their security and independence, to come out resolutely for the cohesion of all the forces fighting for peace, national independence, democracy and social progress,

Expressing their firm determination to facilitate the strengthening of peace and security in Asia and the whole world, to make their contribution toward developing relations among states and strengthening fruitful and mutually beneficial cooperation in Asia, attaching great importance to the further consolidation of the contractual–legal basis of their relations,

Reaffirming their dedication to the aims and principles of the United Nations Charter,

Decided to conclude the present Treaty of Friendship, Goodneighbourliness and Cooperation and agreed on the following:

Article 1. The High Contracting Parties solemnly declare their determination to strengthen and deepen the inviolable friendship between the two countries and to develop all-round cooperation on the basis of equality, respect for national sovereignty, territorial integrity and non-interference in each other's internal affairs.

Article 2. The High Contracting Parties shall make efforts to strengthen and broaden mutually beneficial economic, scientific and technical cooperation between them. With these aims in view, they shall develop and deepen cooperation in the fields of industry, transport and communications, agriculture, the use of natural resources, development of the power-generating industry and other branches of economy, to give each other assistance in the training of national personnel and in planning the development of the national economy. The two sides shall expand trade on the basis of the principles of equality, mutual benefit, and most-favoured-nation treatment.

Article 3. The High Contracting Parties shall promote the development of cooperation and exchange of experience in the fields of science, culture, art, literature, education, health services, the press, radio, television, cinema, tourism, sport, and other fields.

The two sides shall facilitate the expansion of cooperation between organs of State power and public organizations, enterprises, cultural and scientific institutions with a view to making a deeper acquaintance of the life, work experience and achievements of the peoples of the two countries.

Article 4. The High Contracting Parties, acting in the spirit of the traditions of friendship and goodneighbourliness, as well as the U.N. Charter, shall consult each other and take by agreement appropriate measures to ensure the security, independence, and territorial integrity of the two countries.

In the interests of strengthening the defence capacity of the High Contracting Parties, they shall continue to develop cooperation in the military field on the basis of appropriate agreements concluded between them.

Article 5. The Union of Soviet Socialist Republics respects the policy of non-alignment which is pursued by the Democratic Republic of Afghanistan and which is an important factor for maintaining international peace and security.

The Democratic Republic of Afghanistan respects the policy of peace pursued by the Union of Soviet Socialist Republics and aimed at strengthening friendship and cooperation with all countries and peoples.

Article 6. Each of the High Contracting Parties solemnly declares that it shall not join any military or other alliances or take part in any groupings of States, as well as in actions or measures directed against the other High Contracting Party.

Article 7. The High Contracting Parties shall continue to make every effort to defend international peace and the security of the peoples, to deepen the process of relaxation of international tension, to spread it to all areas of the world, including Asia, to translate it into concrete forms of mutually beneficial cooperation among States and to settle international disputed issues by peaceful means.

The two sides shall actively contribute toward general and complete disarmament, including nuclear disarmament, under effective international control.

Article 8. The High Contracting Parties shall facilitate the development of cooperation among Asian States and the establishment of relations of peace, good-neighbourliness and mutual confidence among them and the creation of an effective security system in Asia on the basis of joint efforts by all countries of the continent.

Article 9. The High Contracting Parties shall continue their consistent struggle against machinations by the forces of aggression, for the final elimination of colonialism and racism in all their forms and manifestations.

The two sides shall cooperate with each other and with other peace-loving States in supporting the just struggle of the peoples for their freedom, independence, sovereignty and social progress.

Article 10. The High Contracting Parties shall consult each other on all major international issues affecting the interests of the two countries.

Article 11. The High Contracting Parties state that their commitments under the existing international treaties do not contradict the provisions of the present Treaty and undertake not to conclude any international agreements incompatible with it.

Article 12. Questions which may arise between the High Contracting Parties concerning the interpretation or application of any provision of the present Treaty, shall be settled bilaterally, in the spirit of friendship, mutual understanding and respect.

Article 13. The present Treaty shall remain in force within twenty years of the day it becomes effective.

Unless one of the High Contracting Parties declares six months before the expiration of this term its desire to terminate the Treaty, it shall remain in force for the next five years until one of the High Contracting Parties warns in writing the other Party, six months before the expiration of the current five-year term, about its intention to terminate the Treaty.

Article 14. If one of the High Contracting Parties expresses the wish in the course of the twenty-year term of the Treaty to terminate it before its expiration date, it shall notify in writing the other Party, six months before its suggested date of expiration of the Treaty, about its desire to terminate the Treaty before the expiration of the term and may consider the Treaty terminated as of the date thus set.

Article 15. The present Treaty shall be ratified and take effect on the day of exchange of the instruments of ratification, which is to take place in Kabul.

Done in duplicate, each in the Russian and Dari languages, both texts being equally authentic.

Done in Moscow on December 5, 1978.

[For the Union of Soviet Socialist Republics]
L. Brezhnev

[For the Democratic Republic of Afghanistan]
N. Mohammad Tarakki

XV · The German question

The German question was the most intractable issue to bedevil east–west relations during the decades after the end of the Second World War. The collapse of the Grand Alliance and its transformation into bitter enmity was symbolized by the failure of the erstwhile allies to agree on the terms of a peace treaty with their chief common enemy, Germany. Thus, in spite of the total defeat of the Third Reich in May 1945, no peace treaty was ever signed. Instead, in a succession of crises, most notably in 1948, 1958 and 1961, Berlin, the former capital of a united Germany, became a flashpoint highlighting the division of the country. Although Russian and western forces did not engage in hostilities at any stage, the Berlin crises, and the larger question of the future political shape of German repeatedly heightened east–west tension. Only in the early 1970s did the USSR and the western powers, as well as the two German states and states bordering on Germany sign a series of agreements, amounting to a pragmatic acceptance of the status quo of a Germany bifurcated into a communist east (the German Democratic Republic) and a non-communist west (the Federal Republic of Germany).

The division of Germany and the three Berlin crises

The frontiers of the Federal Republic of Germany and the German Democratic Republic had their origins in allied decisions reached in 1944 before the end of the war, and in the actions of the allies jointly and individually in 1945. The Moscow Conference in October 1943 had set up the European Advisory Commission, which prepared draft agreements delimiting the three zones of Germany respectively to be occupied by the USSR, the United States and Great Britain. The commission also proposed three zones of occupation for Greater Berlin, which was treated separately. To have allowed one power (and geography would have decreed that this must be the USSR) the sole right to occupy the capital would, in the view of the other two powers, have allowed too much weight and prestige in Germany as a whole to the USSR In these original agreements, based on the proposals of the European Advisory Commission dated 12 September 1944 and amended and made more specific in a supplementary agreement on 14 November 1944, the occupying forces of each zone were placed under the authority of a Commander-in-Chief of the country occupying the zone. Berlin was placed under the joint control of an allied governing authority composed of three Commandants appointed by their respective Commanders-in-Chief. This distinction remained an important fact relating to the status of Berlin.

The Yalta Conference in February 1945 (p. 267) confirmed and expanded the agreements reached by the European Advisory Commission. The Russian, British and American zones of Germany, and the joint control and individual zones of the three powers in Berlin, were agreed upon. Agreement was reached on inviting France to become the fourth occupying power of Germany with equal rights. The French zone was to be formed out of the British and American zones. The Russian zone extended to the eastern frontiers of Germany of 31 December 1937. The Yalta Agreement, however, envisaged that territory of eastern Germany would be transferred to Poland: 'The three Heads of Government . . . recognize that Poland must receive substantial accessions of territory in the North and West. They feel that the opinion of the new Polish Provisional Government of National Unity should be sought in due course on the extent of these accessions and that the final delimitation of the western frontier of Poland should thereafter await the peace conference.' At Yalta the establishment of an Allied Control Council for Germany was briefly referred to in connection with inviting French membership.

On 1 June 1945 the four powers were still not in occupation of the precise zones assigned to them; when hostilities ended American and British troops held portions of the zone assigned to the USSR, and the zonal division of Berlin by the four powers remained to be completed. On *5 June 1945* the four Commanders-in-Chief met in Berlin and signed a *Four-Power Declaration on the assumption of supreme authority in Germany* (p. 430), which also set out guidelines for the behaviour of the Germans. But the Soviet Marshal Zhukov rejected the setting up of the Allied Control Council until still unsettled boundaries had been determined (French zone) and the forces of each occupying power had withdrawn within their zonal boundaries. A joint statement was also issued on 5 June 1945 by the allies concerning the agreements so far reached on zones of occupation and the administration of Germany. It described the function and composition of the Allied Control Council for Germany, composed of the four Commanders-in-Chief, which was to be paramount in matters affecting Germany as a whole; but the Commanders-in-Chief were the supreme authority, each in his own sphere. Berlin would be administered by the four powers jointly, the four appointed Commandants constituting an Allied *Kommandatura* responsible to an Allied Control Council for Greater

Berlin. A timetable for effecting the military withdrawals was agreed. The American and British forces were in their zones and their garrisons in their respective Berlin sectors by 4 July 1945, and on 30 August 1945 the Allied Council proclaimed that it had begun to function. Since each Commander-in-Chief was supreme in his own zone, any disagreement at the Allied Control Council could only have the negative effect of preventing action on 'matters affecting Germany as a whole' without limiting the supreme authority of each Commander-in-Chief in his zone.

In the summer of 1945 a number of important issues remained to be settled. The question of US, British and French access to their three sectors in Berlin, embedded as they were in the Soviet zone of Germany, was first resolved in a preliminary way at a conference between the Allied Commanders in Berlin on 29 June 1945, which guaranteed the use of one main rail line, one highway and two air corridors to the three western powers. At meetings of the Allied Control Council these agreements were finalized and approved. A few months later, on 30 November, the Allied Control Council provided three air corridors (in place of two) between Berlin and the British and American zones, and it was specifically stated that 'flight over these routes (corridors) will be conducted without previous notice being given, by aircraft of the nations governing Germany'. An Allied Berlin Air Safety Centre was established to ensure the safety of all flights in the Berlin area. These rights of access derived from the military arrangement for joint occupation and joint control of 'Greater Berlin' which France, Britain and the United States continued to maintain.

The eastern frontier of Germany (western frontier of Poland) was one of the principal issues of the Potsdam Conference of July 1945 (p. 271). By the time the leaders of the Big Three, the US, USSR, and Great Britain, attended the conference, the Red Army was in occupation of the whole of its German zone of occupation, as defined in inter-allied agreements before Yalta and confirmed at the Yalta Conference; but the Soviet authorities had already handed over a part of their zone to the Poles in unilateral fulfilment of the general promise made at Yalta that Poland 'must receive substantial accessions of territory'. The *fait accompli* was partially accepted in section VIII of the Potsdam Conference Protocol. The German territories were not annexed and did not formally become a part of Poland since the Protocol stated 'that the final delimitation of the western frontier of Poland should await the peace settlement'; the extent of German territory handed over to Poland was agreed at Potsdam, and this territory was placed 'under the administration of the Polish State'; it was separated from the rest of Germany by a specific statement that it did not form part of the Soviet zone of occupation. The frontier between the German Democratic Republic and Poland corresponded to the Potsdam provisional delimitation; the relevant Potsdam section VIII did not mention the German town of Stettin which lies *west* of the Oder, but an earlier western memorandum had specifically included Stettin as falling into Polish-administered territory, and it is now Polish Szczecin.

The western frontier of the Federal Republic of Germany also corresponded to the western zonal boundaries that Britain and the United States confirmed at Yalta and Potsdam, with some minor adjustments in favour of the Netherlands and Belgium agreed as 'provisional rectifications' in March 1949. More important, the Saar region (a territory larger than the pre-war Saar) was for a time integrated economically with France but given autonomous status by the French from 1947 to 1956. With the adoption of the Schuman Plan in April 1951, which led to the setting up of the High Authority of the European Coal and Steel Community controlling the pooled Franco-German iron and steel production, including that of the Saar, the Saar problem as a cause of Franco-German contention lost some of its significance. An agreement between France and Germany, leading to a plebiscite in October 1955 and elections soon after, closed the issue, and the Saar region was reunited with the Federal Republic of Germany on 1 January 1957.

The creation of the Federal Republic of Germany as an independent sovereign state came about in a number of stages. The gradual recovery of West German sovereignty was closely bound up both with the 'cold war' situation and the movement towards western European integration. Disagreements between the four powers responsible for Germany, especially between the Soviet Union and the western allies, were reflected in the inability of the Council of Foreign Ministers during 1946 and 1947 to make any real progress towards a peace settlement for Germany as a whole. The breakdown of inter-allied control of Germany in 1948 accentuated the different interpretations and applications of allied agreements in the respective zones of the occupying powers.

On 30 March 1948 the Russians imposed restrictions on western access to Berlin by rail. In June they tightened the noose by barring road access from the west. The western powers determined to maintain their position in what was now a vulnerable island of western influence deep within Soviet-controlled territory. Rather than attempt to break the blockade on land (it was feared that such an effort might produce large-scale hostilities), the British and Americans embarked on a massive airlift of food and other essential supplies along the air corridors to Berlin. The Russians eventually gave way and lifted the blockade on 12 May 1949 after 318 days. During the blockade, however, the Soviet authorities set up a separate communist municipal government in Berlin on 30 November 1948. The unity of the city under joint allied authority was thus disrupted.

Meanwhile, in June 1948, the USA, Britain and France took the first steps towards the establishment of a unified central government for the three western zones of Germany. The Russians undertook parallel measures in the eastern zone to formalize the pro-communist government there. The inauguration of the Federal Republic of Germany on 21 September 1949, with Konrad Adenauer as its first Chancellor, was followed on 7 October by the establishment of the German Democratic Republic as its eastern neighbour.

The Soviet desire to legitimize the Oder–Neisse line as the eastern frontier of Germany was reflected in the terms of the *Agreement between Poland and the German Democratic Republic of 6 July 1950* (p. 431). This paid tribute to the 'defeat of German fascism by the USSR' (note the absence of any reference to Russia's erstwhile allies) and pronounced the Oder–Neisse line 'the inviolable frontier of peace and friendship, which does not divide but unites both nations'.

The death of Stalin in March 1953 aroused hopes in eastern Europe of relief from the grim tyranny of the Stalinist régimes. But Stalin's successors demonstrated their determination to hold on to the reins of power by sending in Russian forces to crush a rising in East Germany. A conference of the foreign ministers of the USSR, France, Britain and the United States took place in Berlin in January 1954 but without reaching any agreement on a solution of the German question. Both Russia and the western powers paid lip-service to the objective of a reunified Germany – but each side insisted on a Germany cast in its own image. The reality of a more or less permanently divided Germany now hardened into being: two German states gained formal sovereignty, mutually antagonistic and neither recognizing the other.

On 23 October 1954, Britain, the United States, France and the Federal Republic of Germany signed a Protocol on the termination of the occupation régime in western Germany (p. 432). On 5 May 1955, ten years almost to the day after the defeat of the Third Reich, the Federal Republic became an independent and sovereign state.

The Soviet Union had issued a declaration on 25 March 1954 promising that it would 'establish relations with the German Democratic Republic on the same basis as with other sovereign States'. The declaration specified, however, that the USSR would retain in the German Democratic Republic 'those functions which are related to guaranteeing security'. *On 20 September 1955 the USSR and the German Democratic Republic signed a treaty* which came into force on 6 October. This recognized the GDR as a sovereign republic – although the United States, Britain, and most other non-communist countries refused to recognize the new state. At the same time the USSR established diplomatic relations with West Germany.

A solution of one peripheral aspect of the German question, namely Austria, was found in the same year. The four-power occupation administration was ended by the *Austrian State Treaty, 15 May 1955* (p. 433). All foreign troops were to be withdrawn and Austria regained the independence she had lost at the time of the *Anschluss* in 1938. A democratic constitution was to be established and the country neutralized. As after the First World War, Austria was forbidden to rejoin a pan-German state. This treaty was, the only occasion (before German unification in 1990) when the USSR agreed to withdraw troops in Europe and permit the establishment of democratic institutions in territory thus vacated, seemed to promise further progress towards a resolution of the German problem. Any such expectations were soon dashed.

In November 1958 a renewed crisis loomed over Berlin, when the Soviet Prime Minister, Nikita Khrushchev, precipitately demanded that western occupation forces withdraw from Berlin. Western forces stayed put, however, and after a period of high tension the crisis waned.

But the anomalous situation in Berlin remained a potentially explosive powder keg, as was shown three years later in the third and last major Berlin crisis. On 13 August 1961 the East German authorities began construction of a fortified wall sealing off east from west Berlin. The purpose of this action was to prevent the massive drain of population through this chink in the iron curtain (more than three million people had left East Germany for the west prior to the erection of the wall). The flow to the west was abruptly halted. Bloody scenes at the wall, when East German border guards shot and sometimes killed would-be escapers, aroused bitter indignation in the west. But the western powers took no effective retaliatory action in response to the building of the Berlin wall. In the long run, the building of the wall ultimately stabilized the status quo in Berlin and confirmed the survival of the German Democratic Republic as a separate state for three decades, although the west withheld recognition until the 1970s.

The *Soviet–East German Treaty of 12 June 1964* (p. 435) marked a further effort by the USSR to consolidate the existing position in Germany. The treaty evoked a statement by France, Britain and the United States on 26 June 1964 commenting on the 'agreement signed by the Soviet Union and the so-called "German Democratic Republic"'. The three western powers insisted that the treaty did not affect the validity of existing agreements, particularly those under which the Soviet Union was bound regarding Berlin. The statement rejected Article 6 of the treaty in which West Berlin had been declared to be an 'independent political unit'. And the three Powers reiterated that they did not recognize the GDR, asserting that a 'final determination of the frontiers of Germany must await a peace settlement for the whole of Germany'. (The GDR–USSR Treaty of 1964 was replaced in October 1975 by a similar treaty containing a stronger mutual military assistance clause.)

After 1964 the German problem froze until the end of the 1960s. The election in West Germany in 1969 which brought to power a government headed by the Social Democrat Willy Brandt, marked a turning-point. Brandt's policy of *Ostpolitik* (cautiously introduced during his period of office as foreign minister from 1966 to 1969) represented a new departure from the sterile policies of non-recognition of existing realities pursued in Bonn for the previous two decades. In the new international atmosphere of *détente* (see Chapter **XXIII**), the readiness of the Brandt government to explore openings in the east led to accelerating progress towards a solution of the German problem.

Statement by the Governments of the United States of America, the United Kingdom, the Union of Soviet Socialist Republics, and the Provisional Government of the French Republic on zones of occupation in Germany, 5 June 1945

1. Germany, within her frontiers as they were on 31 December 1937, will, for the purposes of occupation, be divided into four zones, one to be allotted to each Power as follows:

an eastern zone to the Union of Soviet Socialist Republics;
a north-western zone to the United Kingdom;
a south-western zone to the United States of America;
a western zone to France.

The occupying forces in each zone will be under a Commander-in-Chief designated by the responsible Power. Each of the Four Powers may, at its discretion, include among the forces assigned to occupation duties under the command of its Commander-in-Chief, auxiliary contingents from the forces of any other Allied Power which has actively participated in military operations against Germany.

2. The area of 'Greater Berlin' will be occupied by forces of each of the Four Powers. An Inter-Allied Governing Authority (in Russian, *Komendatura*) consisting of four Commandants, appointed by their respective Commanders-in-Chief, will be established to direct jointly its administration.

Statement by the Governments of the United States of America, the United Kingdom, the Union of Soviet Socialist Republics, and the Provisional Government of the French Republic on control machinery in Germany, 5 June 1945

. . .

In the period when Germany is carrying out the basic requirements of unconditional surrender, supreme authority in Germany will be exercised, on instructions from their Governments, by the British, United States, Soviet and French Commanders-in-Chief, each in his own zone of occupation, and also jointly, in matters affecting Germany as a whole. The four Commanders-in-Chief will together constitute the Control Council. Each Commander-in-Chief will be assisted by a Political Adviser.

2. The Control Council, whose decisions shall be unanimous, will ensure appropriate uniformity of action by the Commanders-in-Chief in their respective zones of occupation and will reach agreed decisions on the chief questions affecting Germany as a whole.

3. Under the Control Council there will be a permanent Coordinating Committee composed of one representative of each of the four Commanders-in-Chief, and a Control Staff organized in the following Divisions (which are subject to adjustment in the light of experience): Military; Naval; Air; Transport; Political; Economic; Finance; Reparation, Deliveries and Restitution; Internal Affairs and Communications; Legal; Prisoners of War and Displaced Persons; Manpower. There will be four heads of each Division, one designated by each Power. The staffs of the Divisions may include civilian as well as military personnel, and may also in special cases include nationals of other United Nations appointed in a personal capacity.

4. The functions of the Coordinating Committee and of the Control Staff will be to advise the Control Council, to carry out the Council's decisions and to transmit them to the appropriate German organs, and to supervise and control the day-to-day activities of the latter.

5. Liaison with the other United Nations Governments chiefly interested will be established through the appointment by such Governments of military missions (which may include civilian members) to the Control Council. These missions will have access through the appropriate channels to the organs of control.

6. United Nations organizations will, if admitted by the Control Council to operate in Germany, be subordinate to the Allied control machinery and answerable to it.

7. The administration of the 'Greater Berlin' area will be directed by an Inter-Allied Governing Authority, which will operate under the general direction of the Control Council, and will consist of four Commandants, each of whom will serve in rotation as Chief Commandant. They will be assisted by a technical staff which will supervise and control the activities of the local German organs.

8. The arrangements outlined above will operate during the period of occupation following German surrender, when Germany is carrying out the basic requirements of unconditional surrender. Arrangements for the subsequent period will be the subject of a separate agreement.

Agreement between Poland and the German Democratic Republic, 6 July 1950

The President of the Republic of Poland and the President of the Democratic Republic of Germany,

Desirous of proving their will to consolidate universal peace and wishing to contribute their share to the great work of harmonious cooperation carried on by peace-loving nations,

Considering that this cooperation between the Polish people and the German people has become possible, thanks to the defeat of German fascism by the U.S.S.R. and to the progressive development of democratic forces in Germany, and

Wishing to create – after the tragic experiences of Hitlerism – unshakeable foundations for a peaceful and good-neighbour relationship between the two nations,

Wishing to stabilize and strengthen

mutual relations on the basis of the Potsdam Agreement, which established the frontiers along the Odra and Nysa Luzycka rivers,

Executing the decisions contained in the Warsaw Declaration by the Government of the Republic of Poland and the Delegation of the Provisional Government of the Democratic Republic of Germany on June 6, 1950,

Recognizing the established and existing frontier as the inviolable frontier of peace and friendship, which does not divide but unites both nations . . . .

Article 1. The High Contracting Parties jointly declare that the established and existing frontier running from the Baltic Sea along the line west of Swinoujscie and along the Odra river to the place where the Nysa Luzycka river flows into the Odra river and then along the Nysa Luzycka river to the Czechoslovak frontier, constitutes the State frontier between Poland and Germany.

[*Article 2–7.* concern Demarcation Commission, airspace and ratification.]

Protocol between Britain, the United States, France, and the Federal Republic of Germany on the termination of the occupation régime, Paris, 23 October 1954

The United States of America, the United Kingdom of Great Britain and Northern Ireland, the French Republic and the Federal Republic of Germany agree as follows:

Article 1. The Convention on Relations between the Three Powers and the Federal Republic of Germany, the Convention on the Rights and Obligations of Foreign Forces and their Members in the Federal Republic of Germany, the Finance Convention, the Convention on the Settlement of Matters arising out of the War and the Occupation, signed at Bonn on 26 May 1952, the Protocol signed at Bonn on 27 June 1952 to correct certain textual errors in the aforementioned Conventions, and the Agreement on the Tax Treatment of the Forces and their Members signed at Bonn on 26 May 1952, as amended by the Protocol signed at Bonn on 26 July 1952, shall be amended in accordance with the five Schedules to the present Protocol and as so amended shall enter into force (together with subsidiary documents agreed by the signatory States relating to any of the

aforementioned instruments) simultaneously with it.

Article 2. Pending the entry into force of the arrangements for the German Defence Contribution, the following provisions shall apply:

1. The rights heretofore held or exercised by the United States of America, the United Kingdom of Great Britain and Northern Ireland and the French Republic relating to the fields of disarmament and demilitarization shall be retained and exercised by them, and nothing in any of the instruments mentioned in Article 1 of the present Protocol shall authorize the enactment, amendment, repeal or deprivation of effect of legislation or, subject to the provisions of paragraph 2 of this Article, executive action in those fields by any other authority.

2. On the entry into force of the present Protocol, the Military Security Board shall be abolished (without prejudice to the validity of any action or decisions taken by it) and the controls in the fields of disarmament and demilitarization shall thereafter

be applied by a Joint Four-Power Commission to which each of the signatory States shall appoint one representative and which shall take its decisions by majority vote of the four members.

3. The Governments of the signatory States will conclude an administrative agreement which shall provide, in conformity with the provisions of this Article, for the establishment of the Joint Four-Power Commission and its staff and for the organization of its work.

Article 3. 1. The present Protocol shall be ratified or approved by the signatory States in accordance with their respective constitutional procedures. The Instruments of Ratification or Approval shall be deposited by the signatory States with the Government of the Federal Republic of Germany.

2. The present Protocol and subsidiary documents relating to it agreed between the signatory States shall enter into force upon the deposit by all the signatory States of the instruments of ratification or approval as provided in paragraph 1 of this Article.

3. The present Protocol shall be deposited in the Archives of the Government of the Federal Republic of Germany, which will furnish each signatory State with certified copies thereof and notify each State of the date of entry into force of the present Protocol.

[Signed] Dulles, Eden, Mendès-France, Adenauer.

Austrian State Treaty, Vienna, 15 May 1955

. . . Whereas on 13th March 1938, Hitlerite Germany annexed Austria by force and incorporated its territory in the German Reich;

Whereas in the Moscow Declaration published on 1st November 1943 the Governments of the Union of Soviet Socialist Republics, the United Kingdom and the United States of America declared that they regarded the annexation of Austria by Germany on 13th March 1938 as null and void and affirmed their wish to see Austria re-established as a free and independent State, and the French Committee of National Liberation made a similar declaration on 16th November 1943 . . .

Part I · Political and territorial clauses

Article 1. Re-establishment of Austria as a free and independent State. The Allied and Associated Powers recognize that Austria is re-established as a sovereign, independent and democratic State.

Article 2. Maintenance of Austria's independence. The Allied and Associated Powers declare that they will respect the independence and territorial integrity of Austria as established under the present Treaty.

Article 3. Recognition by Germany of Austrian independence [to be included in German peace treaty].

Article 4. Prohibition of Anschluss. 1. The Allied and Associated Powers declare that political or economic union between Austria and Germany is prohibited. Austria fully recognizes its responsibilities in this matter and shall not enter into political or economic union with Germany in any form whatsoever . . . [Austria not to promote union by any means whatever].

Article 5. Frontiers of Austria. The frontiers of Austria shall be those existing on 1st January 1938.

Article 6. Human rights [guarantee of].

Article 7. Rights of the Slovene and Croat minorities [guarantee of].

Article 8. Democratic institutions. Austria shall have a democratic Government based on elections by secret ballot and shall guarantee to all citizens free, equal and universal suffrage as well as the right to be elected to public office without discrimination as to race, sex, language, religion or political opinion.

Article 9. Dissolution of Nazi organizations [measures to be taken].

[*Article 10. Special clauses on legislation.*
1. To liquidate remnants of Nazi régime and re-establish a democratic system.
2. To maintain law of 3 April 1919, concerning the House of Hapsburg-Lorraine.]

[*Article 11.* Austria to recognize all peace treaties between other belligerents of the Second World War.]

Part II · Military and air clauses

[*Articles 12–16.* Restriction on possession of weapons including prohibition of nuclear weapons; restrictions on former Nazis serving in armed services. Austria to cooperate in preventing German rearmament.]

Articles 17. Duration of limitations. Each of the military and air clauses of the present Treaty shall remain in force until modified in whole or in part by agreement between the Allied and Associated Powers and Austria or, after Austria becomes a member of the United Nations, by agreement between the Security Council and Austria.

[*Article 18. Repatriation of prisoners of war.*]

[*Article 19. Maintenance of war graves.*]

Part III

Article 20. Withdrawal of Allied forces.
. . . The forces of the Allied and Associated Powers and members of the Allied Commission for Austria shall be withdrawn from Austria within ninety days from the coming into force of the present Treaty, and in so far as possible not later than 31st December 1955 . . . .

Part IV · Claims arising out of the war

Article 21. Reparation. No reparation shall be exacted from Austria arising out of the existence of a state of war in Europe after 1st September 1939.

Article 22. German assets in Austria. The Soviet Union, the United Kingdom, the United States of America and France have the right to dispose of all German assets in Austria in accordance with the Protocol of the Berlin Conference of 2nd August 1945.
1. The Soviet Union shall receive for a period of validity of thirty years concessions to oil-fields equivalent to 60 per cent of the extraction of oil in Austria for 1947, as well as property rights to all buildings, constructions, equipment, and other property belonging to these oil-fields, in accordance with list No. 1 and map No. 1 annexed to the Treaty . . . [details of other payments to the Soviet Union].

The United Kingdom, the United States of America and France hereby transfer to Austria all property, rights and interests held or claimed by her on behalf of any of them in Austria as former German assets or war booty.

. . .

Treaty of Friendship, Mutual Assistance and Cooperation between the Soviet Union and the German Democratic Republic (East Germany), Moscow, 12 June 1964

The Union of Soviet Socialist Republics and the German Democratic Republic, guided by the desire to continue to develop and strengthen the fraternal friendship between the Union of Soviet Socialist Republics and the German Democratic Republic, which is in line with the basic interests of the peoples of both countries and of the socialist community as a whole,

On the basis of the fraternal all-round cooperation which is the cornerstone of the policy determining the relations between both States and which has assumed a still closer and cordial nature after the conclusion of the Treaty on the Relations Between the Union of Soviet Socialist Republics and the German Democratic Republic of September 20, 1955,

Expressing firm intention to contribute to the cause of consolidating peace in Europe and throughout the world and to follow unswervingly a policy of peaceful coexistence of States with different social systems,

Fully determined to unite their efforts in order to counteract effectively – on the basis of the Warsaw Treaty of Friendship, Cooperation and Mutual Assistance of May 14, 1955 – the threat to international security and peace created by the revanchist and militarist forces which are striving for a revision of the results of World War II, and to defend the territorial integrity and sovereignty of both States from any attack,

Being of unanimous opinion that the German Democratic Republic – the first State of workers and peasants in the history of Germany – which has carried into life the principles of the Potsdam Agreement, follows the path of peace and is an important factor for ensuring security in Europe and aversion of the war danger,

Striving to facilitate the conclusion of a German peace treaty and to conduce to the realization of Germany's unity on peaceful and democratic principles,

Guided by the aims and principles of the United Nations Charter, agreed on the following:

Article 1. The High Contracting Parties, on the basis of full equality, mutual respect for the State sovereignty, non-interference in internal affairs and the lofty principles of socialist internationalism, implementing the principles of mutual advantage and mutual fraternal assistance, will continue to develop and consolidate the relations of friendship and close cooperation in all spheres.

Article 2. In the interests of peace and peaceful future of the peoples, including the German people, the High Contracting Parties will unswervingly work for the elimination of the vestiges of World War II, for conclusion of a German peace treaty and for the normalization of the situation in West Berlin on this basis.

The Sides proceed from the premise that, pending the conclusion of a German peace treaty, the United States of America, Great Britain and France continue to bear their responsibility for the realization on the territory of the Federal Republic of Germany of the demands and commitments jointly assumed by the Governments of four powers under the Potsdam and other international agreements directed towards eradication of German militarism and nazism and towards prevention of German aggression.

Article 3. The High Contracting Parties join their efforts directed towards ensuring peace and security in Europe and throughout the world in accordance with the aims and principles of the United Nations Charter. They will take all measures in their power to conduce to the settlement, on the basis of the principles of peaceful coexistence, of the cardinal international problems such as general and complete disarmament, including partial measures facilitating the discontinuation of the arms race and relaxation of international tensions, abolition of colonialism and settlement of territorial and border disputes between States by peaceful means.

Article 4. In the face of the existing danger of an aggressive war on the part of the militarist and revanchist forces the High Contracting Parties solemnly declare that the integrity of the State frontiers of the German Democratic Republic is one of the basic factors of European security. They confirm their firm determination jointly to guarantee the inviolability of these frontiers in accordance with the Warsaw Treaty of Friendship, Cooperation and Mutual Assistance.

The High Contracting Parties will also undertake all necessary measures for preventing aggression on the part of the forces of militarism and revanchism which are striving for a revision of the results of World War II.

Article 5. In case one of the High Contracting Parties becomes an object of an armed attack in Europe by some State or a group of States, the other High Contracting Party will render it immediate assistance in accordance with the provisions of the Warsaw Treaty of Friendship, Cooperation and Mutual Assistance.

The Security Council will be informed of the measures taken, in accordance with the provisions of the United Nations Charter. These measures will be discontinued as soon as the Security Council takes measures necessary for restoring and maintaining international peace and security.

Article 6. The High Contracting Parties will regard West Berlin as an independent political unit.

Article 7. The High Contracting Parties confirm their opinion that in view of the existence of the two sovereign German States – the German Democratic Republic and the Federal Republic of Germany – the creation of a peace-loving democratic united German State can be achieved only through negotiations on an equal footing and agreement between both sovereign German States.

. . .

[For the Union of Soviet Socialist Republics]
Chairman of the Council of Ministers of the Union of Soviet Socialist Republics
N. KHRUSHCHEV

[For the German Democratic Republic]
Chairman of the State
Council of the German
Democratic Republic
W. ULBRICHT

The German question stabilized

The first tangible fruit of *Ostpolitik* was *the signature in Moscow on 12 August 1970 of a treaty between the Federal Republic of Germany and the Soviet Union* (p. 438). In Article 3 of this treaty the Soviet Union gained its objective of securing acceptance of the territorial status quo, most notably in regard to the Oder–Neisse line. An accompanying letter from the West German foreign minister to his Soviet counterpart stressed that the Federal Republic still remained committed to the ultimate objective of German reunification – but this utterance was recognized by all concerned as designed primarily for internal consumption in West Germany.

The Soviet–West German treaty paved the way for the *Treaty between the Federal Republic and Poland, signed on 7 December 1970* (p. 439). The terms were similar to those of the Soviet–German treaty, including an explicit recognition by West Germany of the Oder–Neisse line as Poland's western border.

These two agreements greatly improved the atmosphere and facilitated progress in negotiations, begun by the four occupying powers in March 1970, concerning the Berlin problem. The *Four-Power Agreement on Berlin, signed on 3 September 1971* (p. 440), confirmed the status quo in the city, while humanizing some of the arrangements concerning daily life there. The USSR, France, the United States and Britain accepted their responsibilities and reaffirmed their joint rights in Berlin as unchanged. The USSR declared that transport between the western sectors of Berlin and the Federal Republic of Germany would be unimpeded. The western powers declared that the ties between West Berlin and the Federal Republic would be developed, but that their sectors did not form a constituent part of the Federal Republic and would not be governed by it. It was agreed that a Soviet Consulate-General would be established in West Berlin.

The next stage in this complex round of negotiations was direct discussion between the two German states with a view to implementing the principles laid down in the quadripartite agreement. *On 17 December 1971 the GDR and the Federal Republic signed an agreement on the transit traffic of civilian persons and goods between the Federal Republic and West Berlin. On 20 December 1971* a set of documents received signature constituting an *'Arrangement' between the Government of the GDR and the Senate of West Berlin on facilitating and improving the traffic of travellers and visitors.* A further 'arrangement' reached at this time between the GDR and the West Berlin Senate settled the question of enclaves by the exchange of small pieces of territory.

On 12 May 1972 the GDR and the Federal Republic initialled a treaty on questions relating to surface traffic. Subsequently, the Federal Republic ratified (on 17 and 19 May respectively) the treaties concluded with the USSR in August 1970 and with Poland in December 1970. Following these ratifications the treaty of 12 May 1972 was signed on 26 May; the ratification of this treaty in September 1972 marked the implicit recognition of the GDR by the Federal Republic as a sovereign state capable of signing treaties.

The Final Protocol of the Quadripartite Agreement on Berlin, signed on 3 June 1972, noted with satisfaction the conclusion of these various intra-German agreements, and declared that as a result of those agreements the four governments would immediately regard the Four-Power Berlin Agreement as having entered into force. A common declaration of the four powers on 9 November 1972 supported the applications of the two German states for membership of the United Nations. The culmination of this cascade of diplomatic documents was the *Treaty on the basis of relations between the German Democratic Republic and the Federal Republic of Germany, signed at Berlin on 21 December 1972* (p. 441). The two Germanies agreed on 14 March 1974 to exchange diplomatic missions; on 4 September 1974 the United States and the GDR agreed to establish diplomatic relations.

Meanwhile *the Federal Republic had normalized its relations with Czechoslovakia by the signature of a treaty in Prague on 11 December 1973* (p. 443). This treaty contained a declaration by the Federal Republic that the Munich Agreement of 29 September 1938 by which Czechoslovakia had been compelled to yield territory to Germany was void. Willy Brandt, the architect of all these agreements, felt obliged to resign his office as Federal German Chancellor on 6 May 1974 as the result of a spy scandal. The achievement, however, endured until the end of the cold war and it was enshrined in the *Final Act of the Helsinki Conference on European Security and Cooperation on 1 August 1975* (p. 828).

Treaty between the Federal Republic of Germany and the Soviet Union, Moscow, 12 August 1970

The High Contracting Parties

Anxious to contribute to strengthening peace and security in Europe and the world,

Convinced that peaceful cooperation among States on the basis of the purposes and principles of the Charter of the United Nations complies with the ardent desire of nations and the general interests of international peace,

Appreciating the fact that the agreed measures previously implemented by them, in particular the conclusion of the Agreement of 13 September 1955 on the Establishment of Diplomatic Relations, have created favourable conditions for new important steps destined to develop further and to strengthen their mutual relations,

Desiring to lend expression, in the form of a treaty, to their determination to improve and extend cooperation between them, including economic relations as well as scientific, technological and cultural contacts, in the interest of both States,

Have agreed as follows:

Article 1. The Federal Republic of Germany and the Union of Soviet Socialist Republics consider it an important objective of their policies to maintain international peace and achieve détente.

They affirm their endeavour to further the normalization of the situation in Europe and the development of peaceful relations among all European States, and in so doing proceed from the actual situation existing in this region.

Article 2. The Federal Republic of Germany and the Union of Soviet Socialist Republics shall in their mutual relations as well as in matters of ensuring European and international security be guided by the purposes and principles embodied in the Charter of the United Nations. Accordingly they shall settle their disputes exclusively by peaceful means and undertake to refrain from the threat or use of force, pursuant to Article 2 of the Charter of the United Nations, in any matters affecting security in Europe or international security, as well as in their mutual relations.

Article 3. In accordance with the foregoing purposes and principles the Federal Republic of Germany and the Union of Soviet Socialist Republics share the realization that peace can only be maintained in Europe if nobody disturbs the present frontiers.

- They undertake to respect without restriction the territorial integrity of all States in Europe within their present frontiers;
- they declare that they have no territorial claims against anybody nor will assert such claims in the future;
- they regard today and shall in future

regard the frontiers of all States in Europe as inviolable such as they are on the date of signature of the present Treaty, including the Oder–Neisse line which forms the western frontier of the People's Republic of Poland and the frontier between the Federal Republic of Germany and the German Democratic Republic.

Article 4. The present Treaty between the Federal Republic of Germany and the Union of Soviet Socialist Republics shall not affect any bilateral or multilateral treaties or arrangements previously concluded by them.

Article 5. [Ratification.]

Accompanying letter from the West German Foreign Minister, Walter Scheel, to the Soviet Foreign Minister

In connection with today's signature of the Treaty between the Federal Republic of Germany and the Union of Soviet Socialist Republics the Government of the Federal Republic of Germany has the honour to state that this Treaty does not conflict with the political objective of the Federal Republic of Germany to work for a state of peace in Europe in which the German nation will recover its unity in free self-determination.

Treaty between the Federal Republic of Germany and Poland concerning basis for normalizing relations, Warsaw, 7 December 1970

The Federal Republic of Germany and the People's Republic of Poland

Considering that more than 25 years have passed since the end of the Second World War of which Poland became the first victim and which inflicted great suffering on the nations of Europe,

Conscious that in both countries a new generation has meanwhile grown up to whom a peaceful future should be secured,

Desiring to establish durable foundations for peaceful coexistence and the development of normal and good relations between them,

Anxious to strengthen peace and security in Europe,

Aware that the inviolability of frontiers and respect for the territorial integrity and sovereignty of all States in Europe within their present frontiers are a basic condition for peace,

Have agreed as follows:

Article I. 1. The Federal Republic of Germany and the People's Republic of Poland state in mutual agreement that the existing boundary line the course of which is laid down in Chapter IX of the Decisions of the Potsdam Conference of 2 August 1945 as running from the Baltic Sea immediately west of Swinemunde, and thence along the Oder River to the confluence of the western Neisse River and along the western Neisse to the Czechoslovak frontier, shall constitute the western State frontier of the People's Republic of Poland.

2. They reaffirm the inviolability of their existing frontiers now and in the future and undertake to respect each other's territorial integrity without restriction.

3. They declare that they have no territorial claims whatsoever against each other and that they will not assert such claims in the future.

Article II. 1. The Federal Republic of Germany and the People's Republic of Poland shall in their mutual relations as well as in matters of ensuring European and international security be guided by the purposes and principles embodied in the Charter of the United Nations.

2. Accordingly they shall, pursuant to Articles 1 and 2 of the Charter of the United Nations, settle all their disputes exclusively by peaceful means and refrain from any threat or use of force in matters affecting European and international security and in their mutual relations.

Article III. 1. The Federal Republic of Germany and the People's Republic of Poland

shall take further steps towards full normalization and a comprehensive development of their mutual relations of which the present Treaty shall form the solid foundation.

2. They agree that a broadening of their cooperation in the sphere of economic, scientific, technological, cultural and other relations is in their mutual interest.

Article IV. The present Treaty shall not affect any bilateral or multilateral international arrangements previously concluded by either Contracting Party or concerning them.

Article V. [Ratification.]

Four-Power Agreement on Berlin, Berlin (American Sector), 3 September 1971

The Governments of the United States of America, the French Republic, the Union of Soviet Socialist Republics, and the United Kingdom of Great Britain and Northern Ireland, represented by their Ambassadors, who held a series of meetings in the building formerly occupied by the Allied Control Council in the American Sector of Berlin,

Acting on the basis of their quadripartite rights and responsibilities, and of the corresponding wartime and post-war agreements and decisions of the Four Powers, which are not affected,

Taking into account the existing situation in the relevant area,

Guided by the desire to contribute to practical improvements of the situation,

Without prejudice to their legal positions,

Have agreed on the following:

Part I

GENERAL PROVISIONS

1. The four Governments will strive to promote the elimination of tension and the

prevention of complications in the relevant area.

2. The four Governments, taking into account their obligations under the Charter of the United Nations, agree that there shall be no use or threat of force in the area and that disputes shall be settled solely by peaceful means.

3. The four Governments will mutually respect their individual and joint rights and responsibilities, which remain unchanged.

4. The four Governments agree that, irrespective of the differences in legal views, the situation which has developed in the area, and as it is defined in this Agreement as well as in the other agreements referred to in this Agreement, shall not be changed unilaterally.

Part II

PROVISIONS RELATING TO THE WESTERN SECTORS OF BERLIN

(a) The Government of the Union of Soviet Socialist Republics declares that transit traffic by road, rail and waterways through the territory of the German Democratic

Republic of civilian persons and goods between the Western Sectors of Berlin and the Federal Republic of Germany will be unimpeded; that such traffic will be facilitated so as to take place in the most simple and expeditious manner; and that it will receive preferential treatment.

Detailed arrangements concerning this civilian traffic, as set forth in Annex I, will be agreed by the competent German authorities.

(b) The Governments of the French Republic, the United Kingdom and the United States of America declare that the ties between the Western Sectors of Berlin and the Federal Republic of Germany will be maintained and developed, taking into account that these Sectors continue not to be a constituent part of the Federal Republic of Germany and not to be governed by it.

Detailed arrangements concerning the relationship between the Western Sectors of Berlin and the Federal Republic of Germany are set forth in Annex II.

(c) The Government of the Union of Soviet Socialist Republics declares that communications between the Western Sectors of Berlin and areas bordering on these Sectors and those areas of the German Democratic Republic which do not border on these Sectors will be improved. Permanent residents of the Western Sectors of Berlin will be able to travel to and visit such areas for compassionate, family, religious, cultural or commercial reasons, or as tourists, under conditions comparable to those applying to other persons entering these areas.

The problems of the small enclaves, including Steinstücken, and of other small areas may be solved by exchange of territory.

Detailed arrangements concerning travel, communications and the exchange of territory, as set forth in Annex III, will be agreed by the competent German authorities.

(d) Representation abroad of the interests of the Western Sectors of Berlin and consular activities of the Union of Soviet Socialist Republics in the Western Sectors of Berlin can be exercised as set forth in Annex IV.

Part III

FINAL PROVISIONS

This Quadripartite Agreement will enter into force on the date specified in a Final Quadripartite Protocol to be concluded when the measures envisaged in Part II of this Quadripartite Agreement and in its Annexes have been agreed.

Done at the building formerly occupied by the Allied Control Council in the American Sector of Berlin, this 3rd day of September, 1971, in four originals, each in the English, French and Russian languages, all texts being equally authentic.

[Four annexes, two agreed minutes, and one final quadripartite protocol were attached to the agreement: these set out the detailed provisions for giving effect to the general principles outlined in the agreement.]

Treaty on the basis of relations between the Federal Republic of Germany and the German Democratic Republic, East Berlin, 21 December 1972

The High Contracting Parties,

Conscious of their responsibility for the preservation of peace,

Anxious to render a contribution to détente and security in Europe,

Aware that the inviolability of frontiers

and respect for the territorial integrity and sovereignty of all States in Europe within their present frontiers are a basic condition for peace,

Recognizing that therefore the two German States have to refrain from the threat or use of force in their relations,

Proceeding from the historical facts and without prejudice to the different views of the Federal Republic of Germany and the German Democratic Republic on fundamental questions, including the national question,

Desirous to create the conditions for cooperation between the Federal Republic of Germany and the German Democratic Republic for the benefit of the people in the two German States,

Have agreed as follows:

Article 1. The Federal Republic of Germany and the German Democratic Republic shall develop normal, good-neighbourly relations with each other on the basis of equal rights.

Article 2. The Federal Republic of Germany and the German Democratic Republic will be guided by the aims and principles laid down in the United Nations Charter, especially those of the sovereign equality of all States, respect for their independence, autonomy and territorial integrity, the right of self-determination, the protection of human rights, and non-discrimination.

Article 3. In conformity with the United Nations Charter the Federal Republic of Germany and the German Democratic Republic shall settle any disputes between them exclusively by peaceful means and refrain from the threat or use of force.

They reaffirm the inviolability now and in the future of the frontier existing between them and undertake fully to respect each other's territorial integrity.

Article 4. The Federal Republic of Germany and the German Democratic Republic proceed on the assumption that neither of the two States can represent the other in the international sphere or act on its behalf.

Article 5. The Federal Republic of Germany and the German Democratic Republic

shall promote peaceful relations between the European States and contribute to security and cooperation in Europe.

They shall support efforts to reduce forces and arms in Europe without allowing disadvantages to arise for the security of those concerned.

The Federal Republic of Germany and the German Democratic Republic shall support, with the aim of general and complete disarmament under effective international control, efforts serving international security to achieve armaments limitation and disarmament, especially with regard to nuclear weapons and other weapons of mass destruction.

Article 6. The Federal Republic of Germany and the German Democratic Republic proceed on the principle that the sovereign jurisdiction of each of the two States is confined to its own territory. They respect each other's independence and autonomy in their internal and external affairs.

Article 7. The Federal Republic of Germany and the German Democratic Republic declare their readiness to regulate practical and humanitarian questions in the process of the normalization of their relations. They shall conclude agreements with a view to developing and promoting on the basis of the present Treaty and for their mutual benefit cooperation in the fields of economics, science and technology, transport, judicial relations, posts and telecommunications, health, culture, sport, environmental protection, and in other fields. The details have been agreed in the Supplementary Protocol.

Article 8. The Federal Republic of Germany and the German Democratic Republic shall exchange Permanent Missions. They shall be established at the respective Government's seat.

Practical questions relating to the establishment of the Missions shall be dealt with separately.

[A number of documents were exchanged at the same time as the treaty. These included the supplementary protocol which dealt with the detailed application of Articles 3 and 7 of the treaty. The other documents included correspondence concerning the applications by the two states for membership of the United Nations, correspondence on the reunification of families, and exchanges concerning the improvement of travel and communications facilities between East and West Germany.]

Treaty establishing normal relations between the Federal Republic of Germany and Czechoslovakia, Prague, 11 December 1973

Preamble. The Federal of Republic of Germany and the Czechoslovak Socialist Republic,

In the historic awareness that the harmonious coexistence of the nations in Europe is a necessity for peace,

Determined to put an end once and for all to the disastrous past in their relations, especially in connection with the Second World War which has inflicted immeasurable suffering on the peoples of Europe,

Recognizing that the Munich Agreement of 29 September 1938 was imposed on the Czechoslovak Republic by the National Socialist régime under the threat of force,

Considering the fact that a new generation has grown up in both countries which has a right to a secure and peaceful future,

Intending to create lasting foundations for the development of good-neighbourly relations,

Anxious to strengthen peace and security in Europe,

Convinced that peaceful cooperation on the basis of the purposes and principles of the United Nations Charter complies with the wishes of nations and the interests of peace in the world,

Have agreed as follows:

Article I. The Federal Republic of Germany and the Czechoslovak Socialist Republic, under the present Treaty, deem the Munich Agreement of 29 September 1938 void with regard to their mutual relations.

Article II. 1. The present Treaty shall not affect the legal effects on natural or legal persons of the law as applied in the period between 30 September 1938 and 9 May 1945.

This provision shall exclude the effects of measures which both Contracting Parties deem to be void owing to their incompatibility with the fundamental principles of justice.

2. The present Treaty shall not affect the nationality of living or deceased persons ensuing from the legal system of either of the two Contracting Parties.

3. The present Treaty, together with its declarations on the Munich Agreement, shall not constitute any legal basis for material claims by the Czechoslovak Socialist Republic and its natural and legal persons.

Article III. 1. The Federal Republic of Germany and the Czechoslovak Socialist Republic shall in their mutual relations as well as in matters of ensuring European and international security be guided by the purposes and principles embodied in the United Nations Charter.

2. Accordingly they shall, pursuant to Articles 1 and 2 of the United Nations Charter, settle all their disputes exclusively by peaceful means and shall refrain from any threat or use of force in matters affecting European and international security, and in their mutual relations.

Article IV. 1. In conformity with the said purposes and principles, the Federal Republic of Germany and the Czechoslovak Socialist Republic reaffirm the inviolability of their common frontier now and in the future and undertake to respect each other's territorial integrity without restriction.

2. They declare that they have no territorial claims whatsoever against each other and that they will not assert any such claims in the future.

Article V. 1. The Federal Republic of Germany and the Czechoslovak Socialist Republic will undertake further steps for the comprehensive development of their mutual relations.

2. They agree that an extension of their neighbourly cooperation in the economic and scientific fields, in their scientific and technological relations, and in the fields of culture, environmental protection, sport, transport and in other sectors of their relations, is in their mutual interest.

. . .

The Reunification of Germany, 1989–90

The speed of the process of German reunification took all the parties, the two German states, the three western powers and the Soviet Union by surprise. The pace of events from the autumn of 1989, when refugees from the German Democratic Republic began to flood to the west, accelerated. The opening of the Berlin wall on 9 November 1989 and the rapid disintegration of the German Democratic Republic occurred with unexpected rapidity. West German Chancellor Helmut Kohl recognized early on the opportunity of achieving complete German unity in one stage, but British Prime Minister Margaret Thatcher and French President Mitterrand felt misgivings. They feared a reunified Germany might prove too powerful for the balance of Europe. Kohl was able to reassure Mitterrand. What proved decisive was the backing he received from US President Bush. Time was of the essence. The Soviet leader Gorbachev's hold on power could, and actually soon did, weaken. It was to take just nine months, in a flurry of negotiation, to overcome all the obstacles to unity.

Before unification could occur a whole complex of relationships settled by previous treaties had to be replaced and modified. Simultaneous negotiations had to be conducted both bilaterally between the two Germanies, between the Federal Republic of Germany and the Soviet Union, and multilaterally among the four wartime allies, the United States, Britain, France and the Soviet Union, to end their treaty rights in regard to Germany and Berlin.

Crucial in the settlement were overriding considerations of security and disarmament and assurances to the Soviet Union involving NATO and the Conference on Security Co-operation in Europe. The diplomatic efforts, agreements and treaties which in the end brought all these strands together are best followed chronologically.

On the 28 November 1989, Kohl put forward a ten-point plan envisaging an eventual 'confederation' of the two German states. He quickly realized that it was out of date almost as soon as proposed; the separate East German state would not survive for much longer. The crucial issue to be resolved in December 1989 was the diplomatic sequence of dealing with the German question. A meeting of the

Allied Control Commission of the United States, Britain, France and the Soviet Union at ambassadorial level on 11 December 1989 indicated that the four powers expected to lead and reach agreement to open the way for later negotiation between the two German states, the so-called 4 + 2 formula. Kohl, however, wanted the initiative to lie with the two German states; they would first reach agreement which would then be followed by agreements with the four wartime allies, the 2 + 4 formula. In February 1990 at the Ottawa summit, with the backing of President Bush, the 2 + 4 formula was adopted by the four powers. In practice multilateral and bilateral negotiations and agreements interlocked.

On 18 March 1990 the newly freely elected parliament of the German Democratic Republic (*Volkskammer*) had to make the choice between paths to unification: they could either negotiate a new constitution for Germany, or simply accept the existing constitution of the Federal German Republic, the Basic Law. They chose to accept the Basic Law; from this followed that the five East German Länder and east Berlin had to accept all the treaties and international obligations of the Federal Republic. The groundwork of solving the complex problems arising from the unification of two states whose currencies, laws and economic systems were different was laid in negotiations culminating in the conclusion of the *Treaty Between the Federal Republic of Germany and the German Democratic Republic Establishing a Monetary Economic and Social Union concluded 18 May 1990 and ratified 25 June 1990* (p. 448). This treaty was supplemented by the *Treaty on the Establishment of German Unity signed in Berlin on 31 August 1990* (p. 456). The German Democratic Republic was required to adjust its laws, economic system and international obligations in accordance with those of West Germany and the European Economic Community. Provision was made for substantial financial assistance from West Germany to do so. The treaty of 18 May stated that starting on 1 July 1990 the two states were to form a monetary union with the Federal Republic's *Deutschmark* as the currency. Annex 1 was of particular importance setting out in part 2 the provisions for converting the East German Mark into the Federal Republic's *Deutschmark*.

A particularly grave issue was the question whether unified Germany could remain a member of NATO. The Soviet Union was at first opposed. The principle on which this turned was whether Germany was fully sovereign to choose her international obligations. To overcome Soviet opposition, Bush secured Kohl's agreement to a number of specific commitments. These included a promise to start negotiations over short-range nuclear weapons, a revision of NATO strategy emphasizing its defensive purpose, agreement that for a transitional period NATO troops would not be stationed in the territory of the former German Democratic Republic and that no nuclear, biological or chemical weapons would be developed by Germany in the future. It was also agreed that transitional arrangements would be made for the Soviet troops and dependants stationed in

East Germany and that the Soviet Union would receive substantial German financial and economic assistance. Bush then communicated these undertakings to Gorbachev during their summit in Washington 31 May to 1 June 1990. NATO on 8 June 1990 welcomed a declaration of the previous day by the Warsaw Pact that the ideological confrontation of the two alliances no longer conformed to the spirit of the times; NATO now stated it looked forward to increasing constructive co-operation within the framework of the Conference on Security and Co-operation in Europe. The Warsaw Pact in its declaration emphasized the need to consider the security interests of Germany's neighbours requiring a guarantee of the inviolability of the existing European frontiers. On 21 June 1990 the *Bundestag* (lower house of parliament of the Federal German Republic) also made a declaration which, however, linked admission of the crimes committed in Poland during the Second World War to the post-war expulsion of millions of Germans from the country. But the *Bundestag* statement went on to stress the need for reconciliation and declared that the Polish-German frontier of a unified Germany was inviolable and would follow the frontier delimited between the German Democratic Republic and Poland in 1950. The parliament of the German Democratic Republic passed a similar declaration.

Kohl and Gorbachev met in mid-July in the Caucasus and on 17 July 1990 Kohl announced that a comprehensive agreement had been reached on all aspects including Soviet acceptance that as a sovereign state Germany could choose to remain in the NATO alliance. This removed the last remaining obstacle.

On 23 August 1990 the *Volkskammer* formally decided that the five Länder and east Berlin would join the Federal German Republic according to Article 23 of the Basic Law with effect from 3 October 1990. A week later the *Unification Treaty between the German Federal Republic and the German Democratic Republic was concluded on 31 August 1990* (p. 456). *The Six Power Treaty covering final agreements with Germany followed and was signed on 12 September 1990* (p. 453). It included in Article 3 the declaration that Germany would not develop or exercise control over nuclear, biological or chemical weapons; that the military forces of unified Germany would be reduced to 370,000 men; that by an agreement to be concluded the later departure of the Soviet troops from the former German Democratic Republic and east Berlin would be completed by the end of 1994; until that time no NATO troops, only German military forces not in the NATO command structure, would be stationed in the territory of the former German Democratic Republic and Berlin. It was also agreed that until the withdrawal of the Soviet troops, France, Britain and the United States, if requested by Germany, would continue to station military units in Berlin; once the withdrawal of Soviet troops had been completed only German troops in the command structure of NATO would be permitted in the territory of the former German Democratic Republic and Berlin, and no nuclear weapons would be based in this part of Germany; Germany had the right to belong to alliances (Article 6); finally, the agreement stated that the four powers, France, Britain, the Soviet Union and United States, would end their rights and responsibility for Germany as a whole and for Berlin in particular. On 1 October 1990, by a *Four Power Declaration*, Britain, the US, France and the Soviet Union suspended their rights in Germany and Berlin during the months that would elapse before the ratification of the Six Power Treaty of 12 September 1990. This treaty came into force after ratification on 15 March 1991. A formal peace treaty with Germany was still not concluded, but the groups of treaties with the wartime allies effectively fulfilled the same function.

On 3 October 1990 the unification of Germany was completed. Germany subsequently concluded a number of treaties with the Soviet Union. *On 9 October 1990 an agreement about the withdrawal of Soviet troops by the end of 1994*, which provided for the payment of 3 billion DM to the Soviet Union in the interim for the maintenance of the Soviet military, 1 billion DM to cover costs of transport of the troops, withdrawal, 7 billion DM for the construction of civilian housing in the European Soviet Union, and 2 billion DM for the education of the military personnel and dependants to assist their reintegration into the Soviet economy; the total cost of payments to the Soviet Union thus amounted to 12 billion DM. *On 12 October 1990 a treaty regulating relations between the German authorities and the Soviet military during the interim period was signed. On 9 November 1990 a Treaty on Good Neighbourly Relations, Partnership and Co-operation* was concluded between Germany and the USSR. Article 3 of this treaty at first aroused some consternation in the west when it stated that should one of the two parties to the treaty be attacked, the other would provide no assistance to the aggressor. The question was whether this provision was in conflict with Germany's NATO obligations. Since NATO, however, is a defensive alliance it was agreed this could not apply to NATO members and so did not contradict Germany's NATO obligations. It does apply to non-NATO countries. *Also on 9 November 1990 a German–Soviet Treaty of Co-operation in the areas of the Economy, Industry, Science and Technology* was concluded.

The *Treaty between Germany and Poland of 14 November 1990* stated in articles 1 and 2 that the frontier as demarcated between Poland and the former German Democratic Republic was inviolate and that Poland and Germany would respect the territorial integrity and sovereignty resulting therefrom. This treaty thus abandoned with finality any claim of Germany for the restoration of the territories lost in the east as a result of the Second World War. A treaty with the Czech Republic, concluded on 21 January 1997 after a long delay, in part caused by the peaceful separation of the Czech Republic and Slovakia, settled all remaining outstanding issues between the two countries. Thus Germany was finally at peace and in friendly relations with all her neighbours.

Treaty between the Federal Republic of Germany and the German Democratic Republic establishing a monetary, economic and social union, 18 May 1990

The High Contracting Parties,

Owing to the fact that a peaceful and democratic revolution took place in the German Democratic Republic in the autumn of 1989,

Resolved to achieve in freedom as soon as possible the unity of Germany within a European peace order,

Intending to introduce the social market economy in the German Democratic Republic as the basis for further economic and social development, with social compensation and social safeguards and responsibility towards the environment, and thereby constantly to improve the living and working conditions of its population,

Proceeding from the mutual desire to take an initial significant step through the establishment of a monetary, economic and social union towards national unity in accordance with Article 23 of the Basic Law of the Federal Republic of Germany as a contribution to European unification, taking into account that the external aspects of establishing unity are the subject of negotiations with the Governments of the French Republic, the Union of Soviet Socialist Republics, the United Kingdom of Great Britain and Northern Ireland and the United States of America,

Recognizing that the establishment of national unity is accompanied by the development of federal structures in the German Democratic Republic,

Realizing that the provisions of this Treaty are intended to safeguard the application of European Community law following the establishment of national unity,

Have agreed to conclude a Treaty establishing a Monetary, Economic and Social Union, containing the following provisions.

Chapter 1

BASIC PRINCIPLES

Article 1. Subject of the Treaty. (1) The Con-tracting Parties shall establish a monetary, economic and social union.

(2) Starting on 1 July 1990 the Contracting Parties shall constitute a monetary union comprising a unified currency area and with the Deutsche Mark as the common currency. The Deutsche Bundesbank shall be the central bank in this currency area. The liabilities and claims expressed in Mark of the German Democratic Republic shall be converted into Deutsche Mark in accordance with this Treaty.

(3) The basis of the economic union shall be the social market economy as the common economic system of the two Contracting Parties. It shall be determined particularly by private ownership, competition, free pricing and, as a basic principle, complete freedom of movement of labour, capital, goods and services; this shall not preclude the legal admission of special forms of ownership providing for the participation of public authorities or other legal entities in trade and commerce as long as private legal entities are not subject to discrimination. It shall take into account requirements of environmental protection.

(4) The social union together with the monetary and economic union shall form one entity. It shall be characterized in particular by a system of labour law that corresponds to the social market economy and a comprehensive system of social security based on merit and social justice.

Article 2. Principles. (1) The Contracting Parties are committed to a free, democratic, federal and social basic order governed by the rule of law. To ensure the rights laid down in or following from this Treaty, they shall especially guarantee freedom of contract, freedom to exercise a trade, freedom of establishment and occupation, and freedom of movement of Germans in the entire currency area, freedom to form associations to safeguard and enhance working and economic conditions and, in accordance with Annex IX, ownership of land and means of production by private investors.

(2) Contrary provisions of the Constitution of the German Democratic Republic relating to its former socialist social and political system shall no longer be applied.

Article 3. Legal Basis. The establishment of a monetary union and the currency conversion shall be governed by the agreed provisions listed in Annex 1 . . .

Article 4. Legal Adjustments. (1) Legal adjustments in the German Democratic Republic necessitated by the establishment of the monetary, economic and social union shall be governed by the principles laid down in Article 2 (1) and the guidelines agreed in the Protocol; legislation remaining in force shall be interpreted and applied in accordance with said principles and guidelines. . . .

(2) The proposed amendments to legislation in the Federal Republic of Germany are listed in Annex V. The proposed legislative adjustments in the German Democratic Republic are listed in Annex VI.

(3) In the transmission of personal information, the principles contained in Annex VII shall apply.

Article 5. Administrative Assistance. The authorities of the Contracting Parties shall, subject to the provisions of domestic law, assist each other in the implementation of this Treaty. Article 32 of the Treaty shall remain unaffected.

Article 6. Recourse to the Courts. (1) Should any person's rights guaranteed by or following from this Treaty be violated by public authority he shall have recourse to the courts. In so far as no other jurisdiction has been established, recourse shall be to the ordinary courts . . .

Article 7. Arbitral Tribunal. (1) Disputes concerning the interpretation or application of this Treaty, including the Protocol and the Annexes, shall be settled by the Governments of the two Contracting Parties through negotiation.

(2) If a dispute cannot thus be settled, either Contracting Party may submit the dispute to an arbitral tribunal. Such submission shall be admissible irrespective of whether a court has jurisdiction in accordance with Article 6 of this Treaty.

. . .

Article 8. Intergovernmental Committee. The Contracting Parties shall appoint an Intergovernmental Committee. The Committee shall discuss – and where necessary reach agreement on – questions relating to the implementation of the Treaty. The tasks of the Committee shall include the settlement of disputes under Article 7 (1) of the Treaty.

Article 9. Amendments to the Treaty. Should amendments or additions to this Treaty appear necessary in order to achieve any of its aims, such amendments or additions shall be agreed between the Contracting Parties.

Chapter II

PROVISIONS CONCERNING MONETARY UNION

Article 10. Prerequisites and Principles. (1) Through the establishment of a monetary union between the Contracting Parties, the Deutsche Mark shall be the means of payment, unit of account and means of deposit in the entire currency area. To this end, the monetary responsibility of the Deutsche Bundesbank as the sole issuing bank for this currency shall be extended to the entire currency area. The issuance of coin shall be the exclusive right of the Federal Republic of Germany.

(2) Enjoyment of the advantages of monetary union presupposes a stable monetary value for the economy of the German Democratic Republic, while currency stability must be maintained in the Federal Republic of Germany. The Contracting Parties shall therefore choose conversion modalities which do not cause any inflationary tendencies in the entire area of the monetary union and which at the same time increase the competitiveness of enterprises in the German Democratic Republic.

(3) The Deutsche Bundesbank, by deploying its instruments on its own responsibility and, pursuant to Section 12

of the Bundesbank Law, independent of instructions from the Governments of the Contracting Parties, shall regulate the circulation of money and credit supply in the entire currency area with the aim of safeguarding the currency.

(4) Monetary control presupposes that the German Democratic Republic establishes a free-market credit system. This shall include a system of commercial banks operating according to private-sector principles, with competing private, cooperative and public-law banks, as well as a free money and a free capital market and non-regulated interest-rate fixing on financial markets.

(5) To achieve the aims described in paragraphs 1 to 4 above, the Contracting Parties shall, in accordance with the provisions laid down in Annex 1, agree on the following principles for monetary union:

With effect from 1 July 1990 the Deutsche Mark shall be introduced as currency in the German Democratic Republic. The bank notes issued by the Deutsche Bundesbank and denominated in Deutsche Mark, and the federal coins issued by the Federal Republic of Germany and denominated in Deutsche Mark or Pfennig, shall be sole legal tender from 1 July 1990.

Wages, salaries, grants, pensions, rents and leases as well as other recurring payments shall be converted at a rate of one to one.

All other claims and liabilities denominated in Mark of the German Democratic Republic shall be converted to Deutsche Mark at the rate of two to one.

The conversion of bank notes and coin denominated in Mark of the German Democratic Republic shall only be possible for persons or agencies domiciled in the German Democratic Republic via accounts with financial institutions in the German Democratic Republic into which the cash amounts to be converted may be paid.

Deposits with financial institutions held by individuals domiciled in the German Democratic Republic shall be converted upon application at a rate of one to one up to certain limits, there being a differentiation according to the age of the beneficiaries.

Special regulations shall apply to deposits of persons domiciled outside the German Democratic Republic . . .

(6) Following an inventory of publicly owned assets and their earning power and following their primary use for the structural adaptation of the economy and for the recapitalization of the budget, the German Democratic Republic shall ensure where possible that a vested right to a share in publicly owned assets can be granted to savers at a later date for the amount reduced following conversion at a rate of two to one.

(7) The Deutsche Bundesbank shall exercise the powers accorded it by this Treaty and by the Law concerning the Deutsche Bundesbank in the entire currency area . . .

Chapter III

PROVISIONS CONCERNING ECONOMIC UNION

Article 11. Economic Policy Foundations. (1) The German Democratic Republic shall ensure that its economic and financial policy measures are in harmony with the social market system. Such measures shall be introduced in such a way that, within the framework of the market economy system, they are at the same time conducive to price stability, a high level of employment and foreign trade equilibrium, and thus steady and adequate economic growth.

. . .

(3) The German Democratic Republic, taking into consideration the foreign trade relations that have evolved with the member countries of the Council for Mutual Economic Assistance, shall progressively bring its policy into line with the law and the economic policy goals of the European Communities.

Article 13. Foreign Trade and Payments. (1) In its foreign trade, the German Democratic Republic shall take into account the principles of free world trade, as expressed in particular in the General Agreement on Tariffs and Trade. The Federal Republic of

Germany shall make its experience fully available for the further integration of the economy of the German Democratic Republic into the world economy.

(2) The existing foreign trade relations of the German Democratic Republic, in particular its contractual obligations towards the countries of the Council for Mutual Economic Assistance, shall be respected. They shall be further developed and extended in accordance with free-market principles, taking account of the facts established by monetary and economic union and the interests of all involved. Where necessary, the German Democratic Republic shall adjust existing contractual obligations in the light of those facts, in agreement with its partners.

(3) The Contracting Parties shall cooperate closely in advancing their foreign trade interests, with due regard for the jurisdiction of the European Communities.

Article 14. Structural Adjustment of Enterprises. In order to promote the necessary structural adjustment of enterprises in the German Democratic Republic, the Government of the German Democratic Republic shall, for a transitional period and subject to its budgetary means, take measures to facilitate a swift structural adjustment of enterprises to the new market conditions. The Governments of the Contracting Parties shall agree on the specific nature of these measures. The objective shall be to strengthen the competitiveness of enterprises on the basis of the social market economy and to build up, through the development of private initiative, a diversified, modern economic structure in the German Democratic Republic, with as many small and medium-sized enterprises as possible, and thereby to create the basis for increased growth and secure jobs.

Article 15. Agriculture and Food Industry. (1) Because of the crucial importance of the European Community rules for the agriculture and food industries, the German Democratic Republic shall introduce a price support and external protection scheme in line with the EC market regime so that agricultural producer prices in the German Democratic Republic become

adjusted to those in the Federal Republic of Germany. The German Democratic Republic shall not introduce levies or refunds vis-à-vis the European Community, subject to reciprocity . . .

Chapter IV

PROVISIONS CONCERNING THE SOCIAL UNION

[*Articles 17–25.* required the German Democratic Republic to adapt their laws in conformity to the laws of the Federal Republic in the area of labour law permitting freedom of association, autonomy of collective bargaining and protection against dismissal (17); social insurance (18); unemployment insurance and employment promotion (19); pension insurance law (20); health insurance (21); medical care and health protection were declared of particular concern to the two parties, the GDR was to gradually provide the same services (22); accident insurance law (23); social assistance to correspond to Federal Republic (24); Federal Republic's subsidy to cover shortfalls in the GDR pension funds (25).]

Section 1.
The Budget

[*Article 26.* declares as the aim for the establishment of a system of budgeting adapted to the market economy. The budgets are to be balanced as regards revenue and expenditure.

Article 27. set the borrowing limits of the GDR at 10 billion Deutsche Mark for 1990 and 14 billion Deutsche Mark for 1991.]

Article 28. Financial Allocations granted by the Federal Republic of Germany. (1) The Federal Republic of Germany shall grant the German Democratic Republic financial allocations amounting to 22 billion Deutsche Mark for the second half of 1990 and 35 billion Deutsche Mark for 1991 for the specific purpose of balancing its budget. Furthermore, initial financing shall be made available from the federal budget, in accordance with Article 25, amounting to 750 million Deutsche Mark for the second half of 1990 for pension insurance as well as 2 billion Deutsche Mark for the second half of 1990 and 3 billion Deutsche Mark for 1991 for unemployment insurance. Payments shall be made as required.

(2) The Contracting Parties agree that the transit sum payable under Article 18 of the Agreement of 17 December 1971 on the Transit of Civilian Persons and Goods between the Federal Republic of Germany and Berlin (West) shall lapse upon the entry into force of this Treaty. The German Democratic Republic shall cancel with effect for the two Contracting Parties the regulations on fees laid down in that Agreement and in the Agreement of 31 October 1979 on the Exemption of Road Vehicles from Taxes and Fees. In amendment of the Agreement of 5 December 1989, the Contracting Parties agree that from 1 July 1990 no more payments shall be made into the hardcurrency fund (for citizens of the German Democratic Republic travelling to the Federal Republic of Germany). A supplementary agreement shall be concluded between the Finance Ministers of the Contracting Parties on the use of any amounts remaining in the fund upon the establishment of monetary union.

[*Article 29*. Transitional regulations in the public service.]

Article 30. Customs and Special Excise Taxes. (1) In accordance with the principle set out in Article 11 (3) of this Treaty, the German Democratic Republic shall adopt step by step the customs law of the European Communities, including the Common Customs Tariff, and the special excise taxes stipulated in Annex IV to this Treaty.

. . .

Part 2

CURRENCY CONVERSION IN THE GERMAN DEMOCRATIC REPUBLIC

Article 5. Day of Conversion; Bank Account Arrangements. (1) Banknotes denominated in Mark of the German Democratic Republic and coin denominated in Mark and Pfennig of the German Democratic Republic belonging to the persons or agencies referred to in paragraph 3 below on the

day of entry into force of these provisions may be paid into bank accounts in the German Democratic Republic up to and including 6 July 1990 for conversion.

(2) The persons or agencies referred to in paragraph 3 below may apply up to and including 6 July 1990, at a bank where they keep an account, for conversion of their deposits in Mark of the German Democratic Republic in bank accounts in the German Democratic Republic.

(3) With the exception of banks, all natural or legal persons or other agencies whose domicile, seat, or place of establishment is in the German Democratic Republic shall be entitled to pay their money into an account and file an application. When handing in their applications for currency conversion these persons or agencies must confirm that the deposits to be converted were not obtained directly or indirectly from banknotes or coin denominated in Mark of the German Democratic Republic which were brought to or acquired in the German Democratic Republic in violation of its foreign exchange regulations. . . .

(6) Upon expiry of the periods specified in paragraphs 1, 2, 4 shown above, claims in respect of banknotes and coins which have not been deposited at a bank in the German Democratic Republic, or of deposits with banks in the German Democratic Republic which have not been included in an application for conversion, shall cease to be valid.

. . .

Article 6. Conversion of Bank Deposits. (1) Natural persons domiciled in the German Democratic Republic may bank at a bank where they keep an account to have up to the following balances in Mark of the German Democratic Republic credited to their account an exchange rate of 1 Mark of the German Democratic Republic to 1 Deutsche Mark:

Natural persons born after 1 July 1976: up to 2,000 Mark,
Natural persons born between 2 July 1931 and 1 July 1976: up to 4,000 Mark,
Natural persons born before 2 July 1931: up to 6,000 Mark.

An application may be made only once at a bank.

(2) Deposits of natural persons which exceed the amounts in Mark of the German Democratic Republic specified in paragraph 1, and deposits of legal persons or other agencies, shall be converted in such a way that for 2 Mark of the German Democratic Republic 1 Deutsche Mark shall be credited.

(3) Deposits existing on 31 December 1989 of natural or legal persons or agencies with domicile or seat outside the German Democratic Republic shall be converted in such a way that for 2 Mark of the German Democratic Republic 1 Deutsche Mark shall be credited. Deposits of the persons or agencies mentioned in the first sentence of this paragraph which have been accumulated after 31 December 1989 shall be converted in such a way that for 3 Mark of the German Democratic Republic 1 Deutsche Mark shall be credited.

(4) Transactions designed to circumvent these provisions shall be void.

Article 7. Conversion of Liabilities and Claims denominated in Mark of the German Democratic Republic to Deutsche Mark; Opening Balances in Deutsche Mark.

Section 1.

(1) Subject to the provisions of paragraphs 2 and 3 below, all liabilities and claims denominated in Mark of the German Democratic Republic which were incurred before 1 July 1990 or would have to be met in Mark of the German Democratic Republic in line with the regulations applicable before the entry into force of these provisions shall be converted into Deutsche Mark with the effect that the debtor has to pay the creditor 1 Deutsche Mark for 2 Mark of the German Democratic Republic.

(2) Notwithstanding paragraph 1 above, the following liabilities and claims denominated in Mark of the German Democratic Republic shall be converted into Deutsche Mark with the effect that the debtor has to pay the creditor 1 Deutsche Mark for 1 Mark of the German Democratic Republic:

1. Salaries and wages at the levels provided for in the collective agreements on salaries and wages applicable on 1 May 1990, as well as grants payable after 30 June 1990.
2. Pensions payable after 30 June 1990. The provisions of Article 20 of the Treaty shall remain unaffected.
3. Rents and leases as well as other regular periodical payments which are due after 30 June 1990, with the exception of recurring payments from or to life insurance and private pension insurance policies. . . .

Treaty on the final settlement with respect to Germany, 12 September 1990

The Federal Republic of Germany, the German Democratic Republic, the French Republic, the Union of Soviet Socialist Republics, the United Kingdom of Great Britain and Northern Ireland and the United States of America,

Conscious of the fact that their peoples have been living together in peace since 1945;

Mindful of the recent historic changes in Europe which make it possible to overcome the division of the continent;

Having regard to the rights and responsibilities of the Four Powers relating to Berlin and to Germany as a whole, and the corresponding wartime and post-war agreements and decisions of the Four Powers;

Resolved in accordance with their

obligations under the Charter of the United Nations to develop friendly relations among nations based on respect for the principle of equal rights and self-determination of peoples, and to take other appropriate measures to strengthen universal peace;

Recalling the principles of the Final Act of the Conference on Security and Cooperation in Europe, signed in Helsinki;

Recognizing that those principles have laid firm foundations for the establishment of a just and lasting peaceful order in Europe;

(3) The united Germany has no territorial claims whatsoever against other states and shall not assert any in the future.

(4) The Governments of the Federal Republic of Germany and the German Democratic Republic shall ensure that the constitution of the united Germany does not contain any provision incompatible with these principles. This applies accordingly to the provisions laid down in the preamble, the second sentence of Article 23, and Article 146 of the Basic Law for the Federal Republic of Germany.

(5) The Governments of the French Republic, the Union of Soviet Socialist Republics, the United Kingdom of Great Britain and Northern Ireland and the United States of America take formal note of the corresponding commitments and declarations by the Governments of the Federal Republic of Germany and the German Democratic Republic and declare that their implementation will confirm the definitive nature of the united Germany's borders.

Article 2. The Governments of the Federal Republic of Germany and the German Democratic Republic reaffirm their declarations that only peace will emanate from German soil. According to the constitution of the united Germany, acts tending to and undertaken with the intent to disturb the peaceful relations between nations, especially to prepare for aggressive war, are unconstitutional and a punishable offence. The Governments of the Federal Republic of Germany and the German Democratic Republic declare that the united Germany will never employ any of its weapons except

in accordance with its constitution and the Charter of the United Nations.

Article 3. (1) The Governments of the Federal Republic of Germany and the German Democratic Republic reaffirm their renunciation of the manufacture and possession of and control over nuclear, biological and chemical weapons. They declare that the united Germany, too, will abide by these commitments. In particular, rights and obligations arising from the Treaty on the Non-Proliferation of Nuclear Weapons of 1 July 1968 will continue to apply to the united Germany.

(2) The Government of the Federal Republic of Germany, acting in full agreement with the Government of the German Democratic Republic, made the following statement on 30 August 1990 in Vienna at the Negotiations on Conventional Armed Forces in Europe:

"The Government of the Federal Republic of Germany undertakes to reduce the personnel strength of the armed forces of the united Germany to 370,000 (ground, air and naval forces) within three to four years. This reduction will commence on the entry into force of the first CFE agreement. Within the scope of this overall ceiling no more than 345,000 will belong to the ground and air forces which, pursuant to the agreed mandate, alone are the subject of the Negotiations on Conventional Armed Forces in Europe. The Federal Government regards its commitment to reduce ground and air forces as a significant German contribution to the reduction of conventional armed forces in Europe. It assumes that in follow-on negotiations the other participants in the negotiations, too, will render their contribution to enhancing security and stability in Europe, including measures to limit personnel strengths."

The Government of the German Democratic Republic has expressly associated itself with this statement.

(3) The Governments of the French Republic, the Union of Soviet Socialist Republics, the United Kingdom of Great

Britain and Northern Ireland and the United States of America take note of these statements by the Governments of the Federal Republic of Germany and the German Democratic Republic.

Article 4. (1) The Governments of the Federal Republic of Germany, the German Democratic Republic and the Union of Soviet Socialist Republics state that the united Germany and the Union of Soviet Socialist Republics will settle by treaty the conditions for and the duration of the presence of Soviet armed forces on the territory of the present German Democratic Republic and of Berlin as well as the conduct of the withdrawal of these armed forces which will be completed by the end of 1994, in connection with the implementation of the undertaking of the Federal Republic of Germany and the German Democratic Republic referred to in paragraph 2 of Article 3 of the present Treaty.

(2) The Governments of the French Republic, the United Kingdom of Great Britain and Northern Ireland and the United States of America take note of this statement.

Article 5. (1) Until the completion of the withdrawal of the Soviet armed forces from the territory of the present German Democratic Republic and of Berlin in accordance with Article 4 of the present Treaty, only German territorial defence units which are not integrated into the alliance structures to which German armed forces in the rest of German territory are assigned will be stationed in that territory as armed forces of the united Germany. During that period and subject to the provisions of paragraph 2 of this Article, armed forces of other states will not be stationed in that territory or carry out any other military activity there.

(2) For the duration of the presence of Soviet armed forces in the territory of the present German Democratic Republic and of Berlin, armed forces of the French Republic, the United Kingdom of Great Britain and Northern Ireland and the United States of America will, upon German request, remain stationed in Berlin by agreement to this effect between the Government of the united Germany and the Governments of the states concerned. The number of troops and the amount of equipment of all non-German armed forces stationed in Berlin will not be greater than at the time of signature of the present Treaty. New categories of weapons will not be introduced there by non-German armed forces. The Government of the united Germany will conclude with the Governments of those states which have armed forces stationed in Berlin treaties with conditions which are fair taking account of the relations existing with the states concerned.

(3) Following the completion of the withdrawal of the Soviet armed forces from the territory of the present German Democratic Republic and of Berlin, units of German armed forces assigned to military alliance structures in the same way as those in the rest of German territory may also be stationed in that part of Germany, but without nuclear weapon carriers. This does not apply to conventional weapon systems which may have other capabilities in addition to conventional ones but which in that part of Germany are equipped for a conventional role and designated only for such. Foreign armed forces and nuclear weapons or their carriers will not be stationed in that part of Germany or deployed there.

Article 6. The right of the united Germany to belong to alliances, with all the rights and responsibilities arising therefrom, shall not be affected by the present Treaty.

Article 7. (1) The French Republic, the Union of Soviet Socialist Republics, the United Kingdom of Great Britain and Northern Ireland and the United States of America hereby terminate their rights and responsibilities relating to Berlin and to Germany as a whole. As a result, the corresponding, related quadripartite agreements, decisions and practices are terminated and all related Four Power institutions are dissolved.

(2) The united Germany shall have accordingly full sovereignty over its internal and external affairs.

Article 8. (1) The present Treaty is subject to ratification or acceptance as soon as possible. On the German side it will be ratified by the united Germany. The Treaty will therefore apply to the united Germany.

(2) The instruments of ratification or acceptance shall be deposited with the Government of the united Germany. That Government shall inform the Governments of the other Contracting Parties of the deposit of each instrument of ratification or acceptance.

Article 9. The present Treaty shall enter into force for the united Germany, the French Republic, the Union of Soviet Socialist Republics, the United Kingdom of Great Britain and Northern Ireland and the United States of America on the date of deposit of the last instrument of ratification or acceptance by these states.

Article 10. The original of the present Treaty, of which the English, French, German and Russian texts are equally authentic, shall be deposited with the Government of the Federal Republic of Germany, which shall transmit certified true copies to the Governments of the other Contracting Parties.
IN WITNESS WHEREOF, the undersigned plenipotentiaries, duly authorized thereto, have signed this Treaty.

DONE at Moscow this twelfth day of September 1990.

Agreed minute to the treaty on the final settlement with respect to Germany of 12 September 1990

Any questions with respect to the application of the word "deployed" as used in the last sentence of paragraph 3 of Article 5 will be decided by the Government of the united Germany in a reasonable and responsible way taking into account the security interests of each Contracting Party as set forth in the preamble.

Treaty between the Federal Republic of Germany and the German Democratic Republic on the Establishment of German Unity, 31 August 1990

The Federal Republic of Germany and the German Democratic Republic,

Resolved to achieve in free self-determination the unity of Germany in peace and freedom as an equal partner in the community of nations,

Mindful of the desire of the people in both parts of Germany to live together in peace and freedom in a democratic and social federal state governed by the rule of law,

In grateful respect to those who peacefully helped freedom prevail and who have unswervingly adhered to the task of establishing German unity and are achieving it,

Aware of the continuity of German history and bearing in mind the special responsibility arising from our past for a democratic development in Germany committed to respect for human rights and to peace,

Seeking through German unity to contribute to the unification of Europe and to the building of a peaceful European order in which borders no longer divide and which ensures that all European nations can live together in a spirit of mutual trust,

Aware that the inviolability of frontiers and of the territorial integrity and sovereignty of all states in Europe within their frontiers constitutes a fundamental condition for peace,

Have agreed to conclude a Treaty on the Establishment of German Unity, containing the following provisions:

Chapter 1

EFFECT OF ACCESSION

Article 1. Länder. (1) Upon the accession of the German Democratic Republic to the Federal Republic of Germany in accordance with Article 23 of the Basic Law taking effect on 3 October 1990 the Länder of Brandenburg, Mecklenburg-Western Pomerania, Saxony, Saxony-Anhalt and Thuringia shall become Länder of the Federal Republic of Germany. The establishment of these Länder and their boundaries shall be governed by the provisions of the Constitutional Act of 22 July 1990 on the Establishment of Länder in the German Democratic Republic (Länder Establishment Act) (Law Gazette 1, No. 51, p. 955) in accordance with Annex II.

(2) The 23 boroughs of Berlin shall form Land Berlin.

Article 2. Capital City, Day of German Unity. (1) The capital of Germany shall be Berlin. The seat of the parliament and government shall be decided after the establishment of German unity.

(2) 3 October shall be a public holiday known as the Day of German Unity.

Chapter II

BASIC LAW

Article 3. Entry into Force of the Basic Law. Upon the accession taking effect, the Basic Law of the Federal Republic of Germany, as published in the Federal Law Gazette

Part III, No. 100–1, and last amended by the Act of 21 December 1983 (Federal Law Gazette 1, p. 1481), shall enter into force in the Länder of Brandenburg, Mecklenburg-Western Pomerania, Saxony, Saxony-Anhalt and Thuringia and in that part of Land Berlin where it has not been valid to date, subject to the amendments arising from Article 4, unless otherwise provided in this Treaty.

Article 4. Amendments to the Basic Law Resulting from Accession. The Basic Law of the Federal Republic of Germany shall be amended as follows:

1. The preamble shall read as follows:

"Conscious of their responsibility before God and men,

Animated by the resolve to serve world peace as an equal partner in a united Europe, the German people have adopted, by virtue of their constituent power, this Basic Law.

The Germans in the Länder of Baden-Württemberg, Bavaria, Berlin, Brandenburg, Bremen, Hamburg, Hesse, Lower Saxony, Mecklenburg-Western Pomerania, North-Rhine/Westphalia, Rhineland-Palatinate, Saarland, Saxony, Saxony-Anhalt, Schleswig-Holstein and Thuringia have achieved the unity and freedom of Germany in free self-determination. This Basic Law is thus valid for the entire German people."

2. Article 23 shall be repealed.

3. Article 51 (2) shall read as follows:

"(2) Each Land shall have at least three votes; Länder with more than two million inhabitants shall have four, Länder with more than six million inhabitants five, and Länder with more than seven million inhabitants six votes."

. . .

Chapter I

EFFECT OF ACCESSION

Article 1. Länder. (1) Upon the accession of the German Democratic Republic to the Federal Republic of Germany in accordance with Article 23 of the Basic Law taking effect on 3 October 1990 the Länder of Brandenburg, Mecklenburg-Western Pomerania, Saxony, Saxony-Anhalt and Thuringia shall become Länder of the Federal Republic of Germany. The establishment of these Länder and their boundaries shall be governed by the provisions of the Constitutional Act of 22 July 1990 on the Establishment of Länder in the German Democratic Republic (Länder Establishment Act) (Law Gazette 1, No. 51, p. 955) in accordance with Annex II.

(2) The 23 boroughs of Berlin shall form Land Berlin.

Article 2. Capital City, Day of German Unity. (1) The capital of Germany shall be Berlin. The seat of the parliament and government shall be decided after the establishment of German unity.

(2) 3 October shall be a public holiday known as the Day of German Unity.

Chapter II

BASIC LAW

Article 3. Entry into Force of the Basic Law. Upon the accession taking effect, the Basic Law of the Federal Republic of Germany, as published in the Federal Law Gazette Part III, No. 100–1, and last amended by the Act of 21 December 1983 (Federal Law Gazette 1, p. 1481), shall enter into force in the Länder of Brandenburg, Mecklenburg-Western Pomerania, Saxony, Saxony-Anhalt and Thuringia and in that part of Land Berlin where it has not been valid to date, subject to the amendments arising from Article 4, unless otherwise provided in this Treaty.

Article 4. Amendments to the Basic Law Resulting from Accession. The Basic Law of the Federal Republic of Germany shall be amended as follows:

1. The preamble shall read as follows:

"Conscious of their responsibility before God and men,

Animated by the resolve to serve world peace as an equal partner in a united

Europe, the German people have adopted, by virtue of their constituent power, this Basic Law.

The Germans in the Länder of Baden-Württemberg, Bavaria, Berlin, Brandenburg, Bremen, Hamburg, Hesse, Lower Saxony, Mecklenburg-Western Pomerania, North-Rhine/Westphalia, Rhineland-Palatinate, Saarland, Saxony, Saxony-Anhalt, Schleswig-Holstein and Thuringia have achieved the unity and freedom of Germany in free self-determination. This Basic Law is thus valid for the entire German people."

2. Article 23 shall be repealed.
3. Article 51 (2) shall read as follows:

"(2) Each Land shall have at least three votes; Länder with more than two million inhabitants shall have four, Länder with more than six million inhabitants five, and Länder with more than seven million inhabitants six votes."

4. The existing text of Article 135a shall become paragraph 1. The following paragraph shall be inserted after paragraph 1:
5. The following new Article 143 shall be inserted in the Basic Law:

(1) Law in the territory specified in Article 3 of the Unification Treaty may deviate from provisions of this Basic Law for a period not extending beyond 31 December 1992 in so far as and as long as no complete adjustment to the order of the Basic Law can be achieved as a consequence of the different conditions. Deviations must not violate Article 19 (2) and must be compatible with the principles set out in Article 79 (3).

(2) Deviations from sections II, VIII, VIIIa, IX, X and XI are permissible for a period not extending beyond 31 December 1995.

(3) Notwithstanding paragraphs 1 and 2 above, Article 41 of the Unification Treaty and the rules for its implementation shall remain valid in so far as they provide for the irreversibility of interferences with property in the territory specified in Article 3 of the said Treaty.

6. Article 146 shall read as follows:

"Article 146

This Basic Law, which is valid for the entire German people following the achievement of the unity and freedom of Germany, shall cease to be in force on the day on which a constitution adopted by a free decision of the German people comes into force."

Article 5. Future Amendments to the Constitution. The Governments of the two Contracting Parties recommend to the legislative bodies of the united Germany that within two years they should deal with the questions regarding amendments or additions to the Basic Law as raised in connection with German unification . . .

Article 6. Exception. For the time being, Article 131 of the Basic Law shall not be applied in the territory specified in Article 3 of this Treaty.

Article 7. Financial System. (1) The financial system of the Federal Republic of Germany shall be extended to the territory specified in Article 3 unless otherwise provided in this Treaty . . .
[(2–6) The apportionment of the tax revenue, the share the Länder receive from turnover tax and the annual allocations from the German Unity Fund.]

Chapter III

HARMONIZATION OF LAW

Article 8. Extension of Federal Law. Upon the accession taking effect, federal law shall enter into force in the territory specified in Article 3 of this Treaty unless its area of application is restricted to certain Länder or parts of Länder of the Federal Republic of Germany and unless otherwise provided in this Treaty, notably Annex I.

Article 9. Continued Validity of Law of the German Democratic Republic. (1) Law of the German Democratic Republic valid at the time of signing of this Treaty which is Land law according to the distribution of competence under the Basic Law shall remain in force in so far as it is compatible with the Basic Law, notwithstanding Article

143, with the federal law put into force in the territory specified in Article 3 of this Treaty and with the directly applicable law of the European Communities, and unless otherwise provided in this Treaty. Law of the German Democratic Republic which is federal law according to the distribution of competence under the Basic Law and which refers to matters not regulated uniformly at the federal level shall continue to be valid as Land law under the conditions set out in the first sentence pending a settlement by the federal legislator.

. . .

Article 10. Law of the European Communities. (1) Upon the accession taking effect, the Treaties on the European Communities together with their amendments and supplements as well as the international agreements, treaties and resolutions which have come into force in connection with those Treaties shall apply in the territory specified in Article 3 of this Treaty.
(2) . . . unless the competent institutions of the European Communities enact exemptions. These exemptions are intended to take account of administrative requirements and help avoid economic difficulties.

. . .

Chapter IV

INTERNATIONAL TREATIES AND AGREEMENTS

Article 11. Treaties of the Federal Republic of Germany. The Contracting Parties proceed on the understanding that international treaties and agreements to which the Federal Republic of Germany is a contracting party, including treaties establishing membership of international organizations or institutions, shall retain their validity and that the rights and obligations arising therefrom, with the exception of the treaties named in Annex I, shall also relate to the territory specified in Article 3 of this Treaty. Where adjustments become necessary in individual cases, the all-German Government shall consult with the respective contracting parties.

Article 12. Treaties of the German Democratic Republic. (1) The Contracting Parties are agreed that, in connection with the establishment of German unity, international treaties of the German Democratic Republic shall be discussed with the contracting parties concerned with a view to regulating or confirming their continued application, adjustment or expiry, taking into account protection of confidence, the interests of the states concerned, the treaty obligations of the Federal Republic of Germany as well as the principles of a free, democratic basic order governed by the rule of law, and respecting the competence of the European Communities.

(2) The united Germany shall determine its position with regard to the adoption of international treaties of the German Democratic Republic following consultations with the respective contracting parties and with the European Communities where the latter's competence is affected.

(3) Should the united Germany intend to accede to international organizations or other multilateral treaties of which the German Democratic Republic but not the Federal Republic of Germany is a member, agreement shall be reached with the respective contracting parties and with the European Communities where the latter's competence is affected.

Chapter V

PUBLIC ADMINISTRATION AND THE ADMINISTRATION OF JUSTICE

Article 13. Future Status of Institutions. (1) Administrative bodies and other institutions serving the purposes of public administration or the administration of justice in the territory specified in Article 3 of this Treaty shall pass under the authority of the government of the Land in which they are located. Institutions whose sphere of activities transcends the boundaries of a Land shall come under the joint responsibility of the Länder concerned. Where institutions consist of several branches each of which is in a position to carry out its activities independently, the branches shall come under the responsibility of the government of the respective Land in which they are

located. The Land government shall be responsible for the transfer or winding-up. Section 22 of the Länder Establishment Act of 22 July 1990 shall remain unaffected.

(2) To the extent that before the accession took effect the institutions or branches mentioned in paragraph 1, first sentence, performed tasks that are incumbent upon the Federation according to the distribution of competence under the Basic Law, they shall be subject to the competent supreme federal authorities. The latter shall be responsible for the transfer or winding-up.

(3) Institutions under paragraphs 1 and 2 above shall also include such
1. cultural, educational, scientific and sports institutions,
2. radio and television establishments as come under the responsibility of public administrative bodies.

Article 14. Joint Institutions of the Länder. (1) Institutions or branches of institutions which, before the accession took effect, performed tasks that are incumbent upon the Länder according to the distribution of competence under the Basic Law shall continue to operate as joint institutions of the Länder pending a final settlement by the Länder named in Article 1 (1) of this Treaty. This shall apply only to the extent that it is necessary for them to remain in place under this transitional arrangement so as to allow the Länder to carry out their responsibilities.

(2) The joint institutions of the Länder shall be under the authority of the Land plenipotentiaries pending the election of minister-presidents in the Länder. Subsequently they shall be under the authority of the minister-presidents. The latter may charge the responsible Land minister with their supervision.

Article 15. Transitional Arrangements for Land Administration. (1) The Land spokesmen in the Länder named in Article 1 (1) of this Treaty and the government plenipotentiaries in the districts shall continue to discharge their present responsibilities on behalf of the Federal government and subject to instructions from the date when the accession takes effect until election of minister-presidents.

Article 16. Transitional Provision Pending the Constitution of a Single Land Government for Berlin. Until the constitution of a single Land government for Berlin its responsibilities shall be discharged by the Berlin Senat jointly with the Magistrat.

Article 17. Rehabilitation. The Contracting Parties reaffirm their intention to create without delay a legal foundation permitting the rehabilitation of all persons who have been victims of a politically motivated punitive measure or any court decision contrary to the rule of law or constitutional principles. The rehabilitation of these victims of the iniquitous SED regime shall be accompanied by appropriate arrangements for compensation.

Article 18. Continued Validity of Court Decisions. (1) Decisions handed down by the courts of the German Democratic Republic before the accession took effect shall retain their validity and may be executed in conformity with the law put into force according to Article 8 of this Treaty or remaining in force according to Article 9. This law shall be taken as the yardstick when checking the compatibility of decisions and their execution with the principles of the rule of law. Article 17 of this Treaty shall remain unaffected.

(2) Subject to Annex 1, persons sentenced by criminal courts of the German Democratic Republic are granted by this Treaty a right of their own to seek the quashing of final decisions through the courts.

Article 19. Continued Validity of Decisions Taken by Public Administrative Bodies. Administrative acts of the German Democratic Republic performed before the accession took effect shall remain valid. They may be revoked if they are incompatible with the principles of the rule of law or with the provisions of this Treaty. In all other respects the rules on the validity of administrative acts shall remain unaffected.

Article 20. Legal Status of Persons in the Public Service. (1) The agreed transitional arrangements set out in Annex I shall apply to the legal status of persons in the public service at the time of accession.

Chapter VI

PUBLIC ASSETS AND DEBTS

Article 21. Administrative Assets. (1) The assets of the German Democratic Republic which are used directly for specific administrative purposes (administrative assets) shall become federal assets unless their designated purpose as of 1 October 1989 was primarily to meet administrative responsibilities which, under the Basic Law, are to be exercised by Länder, communes (associations of communes) or other agencies of public administration . . .

Article 22. Financial Assets. (1) Public assets of legal entities in the territory specified in Article 3 of this Treaty, including landed property and assets in agriculture and forestry, which do not directly serve specific administrative purposes (financial assets), with the exception of social insurance assets, shall, unless they have been handed over to the Trust Agency or will be handed over by law according to Section 1 (1), second and third sentences, of the Trusteeship Act, to communes, towns and cities or rural districts, come under federal trusteeship upon the accession taking effect. Where financial assets were primarily used for the purposes of the former Ministry of State Security/National Security Office, they shall accrue to the Trust Agency unless they have already been given over to new social or public purposes since 1 October 1989. Financial assets shall be divided by federal law between the Federation and the Länder named in Article 1 of this Treaty in such a way that the Federation and the Länder named in Article 1 each receive one half of the total value of the assets. The communes (associations of communes) shall receive an appropriate share of the Länder portion. Assets accruing to the Federation under this provision shall be used for public purposes in the territory specified in Article 3 of this Treaty . . .

Article 23. Debt Arrangements. (1) Upon the accession taking effect, the total debts of the central budget of the German Democratic Republic which have accumulated up to this date shall be taken over by a federal Special Fund without legal capacity, which shall meet the obligations arising from debt servicing. The Special Fund shall be empowered to raise loans:

1. to pay off debts of the Special Fund,
2. to cover due interest and loan procurement costs,
3. to purchase debt titles of the Special Fund for the purposes of market cultivation.

(2) The Federal Minister of Finance shall administer the Special Fund. The Special Fund may, in his name, conduct legal transactions, sue and be sued. The general legal domicile of the Special Fund shall be at the seat of the Federal Government. The Federation shall act as guarantor for the liabilities of the Special Fund.

. . .

(5) The Special Fund shall be abolished at the end of 1993.

. . .

[*Article 24:* Settlement of claims in regard to foreign governments and the Federal Republic.]

[*Article 25:* Assets held in trust.]

[*Article 26:* Special fund for G.D.R. railways.]

[*Article 27:* G.D.R. postal service to become F.R.G. postal service, special fund.]

Article 28. Economic Assistance. (1) Upon the accession taking effect, the territory specified in Article 3 of this Treaty shall be incorporated into the arrangements of the Federation existing in the territory of the Federal Republic for economic assistance, taking into consideration the competence of the European Communities. The specific requirements of structural adjustment shall be taken into account during a transitional period. This will make a major contribution to the speediest possible development of a balanced economic structure with particular regard for small and medium-sized businesses.

(2) The relevant ministries shall prepare concrete programmes to speed up economic growth and structural adjustment in the territory specified in Article 3 of this Treaty. The programmes shall cover the following fields:

measures of regional economic assistance accompanied by a special programme for the benefit of the territory specified in Article 3 of this Treaty; preferential arrangements shall be ensured for this territory;
measures to improve the general economic conditions in the communes, with particular emphasis being given to infrastructure geared to the needs of the economy;
measures to foster the rapid development of small and medium-sized businesses;
measures to promote the modernization and restructuring of the economy, relying on restructuring schemes drawn up by industry of its own accord (e.g. rehabilitation programmes, including ones for exports to COMECON countries);
debt relief for enterprises following the examination of each case individually.

Article 29. Foreign Trade Relations. (1) The established foreign trade relations of the German Democratic Republic, in particular the existing contractual obligations vis-à-vis the countries of the Council for Mutual Economic Assistance, shall enjoy protection of confidence. They shall be developed further and expanded, taking into consideration the interests of all parties concerned and having regard for the principles of a market economy as well as the competence of the European Communities. The all-German Government shall ensure that appropriate organizational arrangements are made for these foreign trade relations within the framework of departmental responsibility.

(2) The Federal Government, or the all-German Government, shall hold consultations with the competent institutions of the European Communities on which exemptions are required for a transitional period in the field of foreign trade, having regard to paragraph 1 above.

Treaty; preferential arrangements shall be ensured for this territory;
measures to improve the general economic conditions in the communes, with particular emphasis being given to

infrastructure geared to the needs of the economy;

measures to foster the rapid development of small and medium-sized businesses;

measures to promote the modernization and restructuring of the economy, relying on restructuring schemes drawn up by industry of its own accord (e.g. rehabilitation programmes, including ones for exports to COMECON countries);

debt relief for enterprises following the examination of each case individually.

Article 29. Foreign Trade Relations. (1) The established foreign trade relations of the German Democratic Republic, in particular the existing contractual obligations vis-à-vis the countries of the Council for Mutual Economic Assistance, shall enjoy protection of confidence. They shall be developed further and expanded, taking into consideration the interests of all parties concerned and having regard for the principles of a market economy as well as the competence of the European Communities. The all-German Government shall ensure that appropriate organizational arrangements are made for these foreign trade relations within the framework of departmental responsibility.

(2) The Federal Government, or the all-German Government, shall hold consultations with the competent institutions of the European Communities on which exemptions are required for a transitional period in the field of foreign trade, having regard to paragraph 1 above.

Chapter VII

LABOUR, SOCIAL WELFARE, FAMILY, WOMEN, PUBLIC HEALTH AND ENVIRONMENTAL PROTECTION

Article 30. Labour and Social Welfare. (1) It shall be the task of the all-German legislator

1. to recodify in a uniform manner and as soon as possible the law on employment contracts and the provisions on working hours under public law, including the admissibility of work on Sundays and public holidays, and the specific industrial safety regulations for women;

2. to bring public law on industrial safety into line with present-day requirements in accordance with the law of the European Communities and the concurrent part of the industrial safety law of the German Democratic Republic.

[*Article 31*. Legislation for family, equal rights for men and women.]

Article 32. Voluntary Organizations. Voluntary welfare and youth welfare organizations play an indispensable part through their institutions and services in fashioning the socially oriented state described in the Basic Law. The establishment and expansion of voluntary welfare and youth welfare organizations shall be promoted in the territory specified in Article 3 of this Treaty in line with the distribution of competence under the Basic Law.

Article 33. Public health. (1) It shall be the task of the legislators to create the conditions for effecting a rapid and lasting improvement in in-patient care in the territory specified in Article 3 of this Treaty and for bringing it into line with the situation in the remainder of the federal territory.

Article 34. Protection of the Environment. (1) On the basis of the German environmental union established under Article 16 of the Treaty of 18 May 1990 in conjunction with the Skeleton Environment Act of the German Democratic Republic of 29 June 1990 (Law Gazette 1, No. 42, p. 649), It shall be the task of the legislators to protect the natural basis of man's existence, with due regard for prevention, the polluter-pays principle, and co-operation, and to promote uniform ecological conditions of a high standard at least equivalent to that reached in the Federal Republic of Germany.

Chapter VIII

CULTURE, EDUCATION AND SCIENCE, SPORT

Article 35. Culture. (1) In the years of division, culture and the arts – despite different paths of development taken by the two states in Germany – formed one of the foundations for the continuing unity of the German nation. They have an indispensable contribution to make in their own right as the Germans cement their unity in a single state on the road to European unification. The position and prestige of a united Germany in the world depend not only on its political weight and its economic strength, but also on its role in the cultural domain. The overriding objective of external cultural policy shall be cultural exchange based on partnership and cooperation.

(2) The cultural substance in the territory specified in Article 3 of this Treaty shall not suffer any damage.

. . .

[*Article 36*. Transitional arrangements for broadcasting organizations.]

[*Article 37*. Education, continued validation of G.D.R. qualifications; reorganizations of G.D.R. schools.]

[*Article 38*. Transitional provisions for G.D.R. scientific and architectural academies.]

[*Article 39*. Reorganization of sporting organizations.]

Chapter IX

TRANSITIONAL AND FINAL PROVISIONS

Article 40. Treaties and Agreements. (1) The obligations under the Treaty of 18 May 1990 between the Federal Republic of Germany and the German Democratic Republic on the Establishment of a Monetary, Economic and Social Union shall continue to be valid unless otherwise provided

in this Treaty and unless they become irrelevant in the process of establishing German unity.

(2) Where rights and duties arising from other treaties and agreements between the Federal Republic of Germany or its Länder and the German Democratic Republic have not become irrelevant in the process of establishing German unity, they shall be assumed, adjusted or settled by the competent national entities.

[*Article 41*. Settlement of Property Issues.]

Article 42. Delegation of Parliamentary Representatives. (1) Before the accession of the German Democratic Republic takes effect, the Volkskammer shall, on the basis of its composition, elect 144 Members of Parliament to be delegated to the 11th German Bundestag together with a sufficient number of reserve members. Relevant proposals shall be made by the parties and groups represented in the Volkskammer.

. . .

Article 43. Transitional Rule for the Bundesrat Pending the Formation of Länder Governments. From the formation of the Länder named in Article 1 (1) of this Treaty until the election of minister-presidents, the Land plenipotentiaries may take part in the meetings of the Bundesrat in a consultative capacity.

Article 44. Preservation of Rights. Rights arising from this Treaty in favour of the German Democratic Republic or the Länder named in Article 1 of this Treaty may be asserted by each of these Länder after the accession has taken effect.

[*Article 45*. Entry into force of Treaty.]

[NOTE: The Treaty entered into force on 29 September 1991.]